Litigation Under the Federal Open Government Laws 2002

Covering the Freedom of Information Act, the Privacy Act, the Government in the Sunshine Act, and the Federal Advisory Committee Act

Harry A. Hammitt, David L. Sobel, and Mark S. Zaid, Editors

Published Jointly By:

EPIC Publications
1718 Connecticut Ave. N.W.
Suite 200
Washington, DC 20009

Visit the EPIC Bookstore
epic.org/bookstore

Access Reports
1624 Dogwood Lane
Lynchburg, VA 24503

accessreports.com

The James Madison Project
1275 K Street, N.W.
Suite 770
Washington, DC 20005

jamesmadisonproject.org

Price: $40

Twenty-first Edition 2002
Printed in the United States of America

ISBN: 1-893044-17-3

Harry A. Hammitt, David L. Sobel, and Mark S. Zaid, Editors

Contributors

Allan Robert Adler. Vice President for Legal and Governmental Affairs, Association of American Publishers. Formerly an attorney with Cohn and Marks in Washington, D.C. and Legislative Counsel to the ACLU. He has appeared before congressional committees and lectured frequently on legislative matters affecting the FOIA.

Amy Atwood. Associate Attorney, Meyer & Glitzenstein in Washington, D.C. Ms. Atwood has litigated many public interest FOIA cases.

Patrick J. Carome. Partner in the Washington, D.C. law firm of Wilmer, Cutler & Pickering. Formerly Staff Attorney for *The Washington Post* and Staff Counsel to the House Iran-Contra Select Committee. He has litigated many FOIA and privacy cases on behalf of journalists, news organizations and other media companies. He also has served as a chairperson of the Administrative Law Section of the D.C. Bar and the Government Information and Right to Privacy Committee of the ABA's section on Administrative Law.

Elaine English. Partner, Graybill & English. Attorney in private practice in Washington, D.C. where she specializes in media and publishing law, including Freedom of Information matters. Formerly Director of the FOI Service Center, a special project of the Reporters Committee for Freedom of the Press.

Eric R. Glitzenstein. Partner, Meyer & Glitzenstein in Washington, D.C. Formerly an attorney with the Public Citizen Litigation Group in Washington, D.C. He also served as Director of the Freedom of Information Clearinghouse, and was a law clerk for Judge Thomas A. Flannery of the U.S. District Court for the District of Columbia.

Harry A. Hammitt. Editor, *Access Reports*, a biweekly newsletter about the Freedom of Information Act, open government laws, information policy, and informational privacy. He is a contributing editor for *Government Technology* and has published articles on FOIA in a variety of periodicals and lectured on the subject before government and private groups.

Chris Jay Hoofnagle. Legislative Counsel with the Electronic Privacy Information Center. He is a frequent user of the FOIA and concentrates on the privacy impacts of commercial and government-sector profiling.

Katherine A. Meyer. Partner, Meyer & Glitzenstein in Washington, D.C. Formerly an attorney with the Public Citizen Litigation Group in Washington, D.C. and the Freedom of Information Clearinghouse. She has litigated numerous FOIA cases, testified before Congress, and lectured frequently on open government issues.

Eleanor H. Smith. Partner, Zuckerman Spaeder, L.L.P., in Washington, D.C. She has litigated numerous open government cases, dealt with many agencies and advisory committees regarding access to information, and counseled clients and trained other lawyers on information access and protection. Prior to joining Zuckerman Spaeder, she was an attorney with the Public Citizen Litigation Group, Director of the Freedom of Information Clearinghouse, and law clerk to Judge Harold H. Greene of the U.S. District Court for the District of Columbia.

David L. Sobel. General Counsel of the Electronic Privacy Information Center. He has a longstanding interest in national security and information access issues and has litigated FOIA cases for more than 20 years. He was formerly counsel to the National Security Archive, and his FOIA clients have included Coretta Scott King, the *Nation* magazine and ABC News.

David C. Vladeck. Associate professor of law and co-director of the Institute for Public Representation at Georgetown University Law Center and of counsel to Public Citizen Litigation Group. He has extensive experience litigating open government cases and writing and lecturing on open government matters.

Mark S. Zaid. Of Counsel to Lobel, Novins & Lamont. He is also Executive Director of the James Madison Project, a Washington, D.C.-based non-profit, with the primary purpose of educating the public on issues relating to intelligence gathering and operations, secrecy policies, national security and government wrongdoing. He has testified numerous times before Congress on international and national security matters.

Acknowledgments

This manual was first published more than 20 years ago by the Washington Legislative Office of the American Civil Liberties Union (ACLU). After producing 20 editions, the last published in 1997, the ACLU office ceased publication of the book.

Those in the FOIA litigation community who had relied upon the handbook often inquired when the next edition would appear. In 2001, the ACLU Foundation transferred its copyright to the James Madison Project, which, in partnership with the Electronic Privacy Information Center (EPIC), undertook the task of reissuing an updated version of the manual. The book was updated and revised by Harry Hammitt, editor/publisher of *Access Reports*, along with contributions on specific chapters by many of the authors from earlier editions of the book. In this regard, the editors are indebted to David Vladeck of Public Citizen Litigation Group; Eric Glitzenstein, Kathy Meyer and Amy Atwood of the law firm of Meyer & Glitzenstein; Pat Carome of the law firm of Wilmer, Cutler & Pickering; Elaine English of the law firm of Graybill & English; and Eleanor Smith of the law firm of Zuckerman Spaeder.

This updated version of the litigation manual would not exist without the contributions of many public interest attorneys and knowledgeable experts who wrote and revised the chapters in previous years. Chief among these is Allan Adler, formerly legislative counsel for the ACLU, who edited the book for many years up through the 1997 edition. Besides Allan, who, as editor-in-chief kept this project on track and assured the completion of each edition, the long list includes David Vladeck, Eric Glitzenstein, Kathy Meyer, Pat Carome, Elaine English, and Eleanor Smith, who have continued their contributions in this edition. However, the contributions of many others also should be recognized: Morton Halperin (who was the first editor when he headed the ACLU's Washington Office), Ron Plesser, Con Hitchcock, Patti Goldman, Gary Stern, Tom Blanton, Sheryl Walter, and Marc Rotenberg.

At EPIC, Chris Hoofnagle and Kate Rears provided invaluable assistance in the final production phase of the project, ensuring a consistent format and comprehensive index of case citations.

This new edition of the manual adheres to the same high standards as previous editions and, while written as a guide for plaintiffs, attempts to present the relevant caselaw in an objective manner. For those who litigate open government cases (or need to learn how to litigate them), this new, fully updated edition of the manual is good news indeed. We hope it will help ensure continued public access to critical information concerning government activities.

Harry A. Hammitt
David L. Sobel
Mark S. Zaid

Editors

Table of Contents

Contributors i

Acknowledgments iii

Chapter 1. Overview of the Freedom of Information Act 1

1. *The Basic Concepts* *1*
2. *Publication and Availability Requirements* *1*
3. *FOIA Invalidation of Agency Action* *4*
4. *Requests for Access* *5*
5. *Judicial Review* *7*
6. *Legislative History* *7*

Chapter 2. Administrative Process 19

1. *Procedures for Processing Requests* *19*
2. *Who May Make a FOIA Request* *19*
3. *Choosing the Correct Agency* *19*
4. *Contents of Initial Request Letter* *20*
5. *Expedited Processing* *25*
6. *Agency Determinations* *26*
7. *Transfer of Requests* *28*
8. *Administrative Appeals* *29*
9. *Alternatives to Litigation* *33*

Chapter 3. Exemption 1—National Security Information 35

1. *Text* *35*
2. *"Criteria Established By An Executive Order"* *35*
3. *Judicial Review of Substantive Criteria.* *41*
4. *Special Issues.* *42*
5. *Judicial Review Of Procedural Criteria* *49*
6. *CIA Operational Files.* *50*
7. *Legislative History* *51*

Chapter 4. Exemption 2—Internal Agency Rules 55
1. *Text* 55
2. *Legislative History* 55
3. *Supreme Court Interpretation: Rose* 56
4. *Matters Lacking Public Interest ("Low 2")* 57
5. *Matters Which Risk Circumvention of the Law ("High 2")*. 58
6. *Law Enforcement Manuals* 63
7. *Names and Addresses of Military Personnel*...................................... 64

Chapter 5. Exemption 3—Information Exempted by Other Statutes 67
1. *Text* 67
2. *1976 Amendment* 67
3. *Purpose of the 1976 Amendment*. 67
4. *Criteria for Withholding*. 68
5. *Statute Authorizes or Requires Withholding* 68
6. *Qualifying the Statute* 69
7. *Qualifying the Requested Records*.. 79
8. *Procedural Considerations*. 82
9. *Annual Reports* 83

Chapter 6. Exemption 4—Business Information 85
1. *Text* 85
2. *Legislative History*. 85
3. *Trade Secrets* 85

Chapter 7. Reverse FOIA Litigation 99
1. *Definition of Reverse FOIA* 99
2. *Two Supreme Court Cases on Reverse FOIA* 99
3. *Do the Records Fall within FOIA's Nine Exemptions?*.................... 100
4. *Records Falling within an Exemption and the Trade Secrets Act*.... 100
5. *§ 1095 and Exemption 3* 101
6. *Authorization by Law Under § 1905* 101
7. *Critical Mass (II) and Voluntary Submissions* 101
8. *Scope of Review* 102
9. *Judicial Review on the "Whole Record"* 103
10. *Burden of Proof* 103
11. *Predisclosure Notification to Submitters* 103

Chapter 8. Exemption 5—Inter- and Intra-Agency Memoranda 105
1. *Text* 105
2. *Clarity of Language* 105
3. *Basis in Discovery Privileges* 105
4. *Deliberative Process Privilege* 106
5. *Attorney Work-Product Privilege* 115
6. *Attorney-Client Privilege* 116
7. *Confidential Commercial Information Privilege* 117
8. *Weber: Air Crash Investigation* 118
9. *Presentence Reports* 118
10. *Expert Witness Privilege* 119
11. *Settlement Negotiations* 119
12. *Definition of "Inter-Agency" and "Intra-Agency"* 120
13. *Waiver by Disclosure to Third Parties* 122

Chapter 9. Exemption 6—Personal Privacy 125
1. *Text* 125
2. *Legislative History.* 125
3. *Personnel and Medical Files and Similar Files* 125
4. *"Clearly Unwarranted Invasion Of Personal Privacy"* 129
5. *Lists of Names and Addresses* 155
6. *Segregability* 158
7. *Reverse FOIA Litigation Under Exemption 6* 160
8. *Relationship Between Exemptions 6 and 7(C)* 160

Chapter 10. Exemption 7—Law Enforcement Records 163
1. *Text* 163
2. *Legislative History.* 163
3. *Threshold Tests for Protection* 167
4. *Protected Interests* 173

Chapter 11. Exemption 8—Records of Financial Institutions 193
1. *Text.* 193
2. *Legislative History.* 193
3. *Definition of "Financial Institutions"* 193
4. *Examination, Operating, or Condition reports* 195
5. *Regulation Financial Institutions* 195

Chapter 12. Exemption 9—Oil Well Data 197
1. *Text 197*
2. *Legislative History. 197*
3. *Litigation. 197*

Chapter 13. Agency 199
1. *Text 199*
2. *Legislative History 199*
3. *Litigation 200*
4. *Independent Agencies 201*
5. *Sub-units of Agencies 202*
6. *Advisory Groups. 202*
7. *Congressional Savings Clause 203*

Chapter 14. Agency Records 205
1. *Lack of Statutory Definition of Records 205*
2. *Supreme Court: Tax Analysts 205*
3. *"Possession" and "Control" Tests. 205*
4. *Government Burden of Obtaining "Control" 208*
5. *Authority to Obtain the Record 210*
6. *Distinguishing "Agency Records" from Personal Materials 211*
7. *Special Materials 213*
8. *Computer Records 214*
9. *Handwritten Notes 217*
10. *Request to Agency in Possession 218*

Chapter 15. Segregable Portions 219
1. *Text 219*
2. *Legislative History 219*
3. *Attorney General's Memorandum 220*
4. *Claims of Non-Segregability 220*
5. *EFOIA Amendments Effect on Segregability 221*
6. *In Camera Inspection 221*
7. *The "Compilation" or "Mosaic" Theory 222*
8. *Results of Adverse FOIA Appeals 222*

Chapter 16. Fees and Fee Waivers **223**
1. *Text* 223
2. *Legislative History* 223
3. *Agency Regulations and OMB Guidelines* 224
4. *General Limitations* 224
5. *Categories of Requesters.* 225
6. *DOJ Guidelines for Public Interest Fee Waivers* 230
7. *Applying Public Interest Fee Waiver Criteria* 233
8. *Judicial Review* 235
9. *Requester Guidance for Obtaining Fee Waivers* 236

Chapter 17. Attorney Fees and Litigation Costs **239**
1. *Text* 239
2. *Legislative History* 239
3. *Award Criteria* 240
4. *Miscellaneous Issues* 246

Chapter 18. Records Exclusions **253**
1. *The General Effect of "Exclusion" Authority* 253
2. *Interference with Criminal Proceedings* 254
3. *Informant Records Requested by Third Parties* 255
4. *Classified FBI Records Relating to Intelligence or Terrorism.* 255

Chapter 19. The Electronic Freedom of Information Act (EFOIA) Amendments of 1996 .... **257**
1. *Purpose of Amendments* 257
2. *Legislative History* 257
3. *Definition of "Record"* 257
4. *Information Availability in Electronic Format* 257
5. *Honoring Form or Format Requests* 259
6. *Time Limits for Response to Requests* 259
7. *Expedited Processing* 261
8. *Computer Redaction* 264
9. *Reporting Requirements* 264
10. *EFOIA and Exemption 7* 265

Chapter 20. Using the FOIA as an Alternative or Adjunct to Civil or Criminal Discovery **267**
1. *Introduction* *267*
2. *Differences Between the FOIA and the Rules of Civil Discovery* *268*
3. *Tactical Considerations for Civil Discovery* *269*
4. *Examples of FOIA Use as an Adjunct to Civil Discovery* *269*
5. *Differences Between Civil and Criminal Discovery* *270*
6. *Tactical Considerations for Criminal Discovery* *270*

Chapter 21. Litigation Strategy in FOIA Cases **273**
1. *Exhaustion of Administrative Remedies* *273*
2. *Jurisdiction* *276*
3. *Choice of Forum* *279*
4. *The Complaint* *279*
5. *The Answer* *282*
6. *Motion for Summary Judgment* *282*
7. *Discovery* *284*
8. *In Camera Inspection.* *291*
9. *Segregability* *295*
10. *Trials* *295*
11. *Motion for Reconsideration or Clarification* *295*
12. *Attorney Fees* *296*
13. *Sanctions* *296*
14. *Appeals* *298*
15. *Remands* *301*

Chapter 22. The Privacy Act **303**
1. *Introduction* *303*
2. *Legislative History* *304*
3. *Privacy Act Definitions* *305*
4. *The Restriction on Disclosures* *310*
5. *Accounting of Disclosures* *318*
6. *Agency Recordkeeping Requirements* *318*
7. *Access to Records under the Privacy Act* *323*
8. *Amendment and Correction* *325*
9. *Privacy Act Exemptions* *327*
10. *Judicial Review of Privacy Act Violations* *332*
11. *Social Security Numbers* *340*
12. *Miscellaneous Provisions* *341*
13. *The Computer Matching and Privacy Protection Act of 1988* *342*

Chapter 23. Government in the Sunshine Act **345**
1. *Introduction* *345*
2. *Legislative History* *345*
3. *Definition of "Agency"* *345*
4. *Definition of "Member"* *347*
5. *Definition of "Meeting"* *348*
6. *Public Access to Agency Meetings* *349*
7. *Business Outside the Act's Provisions* *352*
8. *Closing a Meeting* *353*
9. *Notice of Meetings* *354*
10. *Transcripts or Minutes* *355*
11. *Challenging Agency Regulations.* *355*
12. *Enforcing Subsections (b)-(f).* *356*
13. *Attorney Fees and Costs.* *358*
14. *Miscellaneous* *358*

Chapter 24. Federal Advisory Committee Act **361**
1. *Introduction* *361*
2. *Legislative History* *361*
3. *Definition of "Advisory Committee"* *362*
4. *What May an Advisory Committee Do?* *368*
5. *Who May Advisory Committees Advise?* *368*
6. *Membership Must be "Fairly Balanced"* *369*
7. *Undue Influence over Advisory Committee's Activities* *370*
8. *Chartering a Committee* *371*
9. *Public Access* *372*
10. *Government Supervision of Advisory Committees* *375*
11. *Termination of Advisory Committees* *375*
12. *Filing a Complaint.* *376*
13. *Discovery* *377*
14. *Mootness* *378*
15. *Miscellaneous.* *378*

Appendix A. The Freedom of Information Act.
Text of the Freedom of Information Act 379
Legislative History of the FOIA 389
Conference Report on the 1974 Amendments 393
1996 EFOIA Amendments House Report (Excerpts) 405
Statement of Attorney General Ashcroft 415

Appendix B. The Privacy Act.
Text of the Privacy Act of 1974 417
Legislative History of The Privacy Act of 1974 435

Appendix C. The Government in the Sunshine Act.
Text of the Government in the Sunshine Act 439
Legislative History—The Government in the Sunshine Act 445

Appendix D. The Federal Advisory Committee Act.
Text of the Federal Advisory Committee Act 447
Legislative History—The Federal Advisory Committee Act 455

Appendix E. Executive Orders and Regulations.
Executive Order 12958 Classified National Security Information 457
Executive Order 13142 Amendment to Executive Order 12958 479
Executive Order 12600 Predisclosure Notification Procedures for Confidential Commercial Information 481

Appendix F. Sample Legal Documents.
Sample Freedom of Information Act Request 485
Sample Request for Expedited Processing 487
Sample Freedom of Information Act Complaint 489
Sample Privacy Act Complaint 493
Sample Government in the Sunshine Act Complaint 497
Sample Federal Advisory Committee Act Complaint 503

Table of Cases 511

CHAPTER 1

Overview of the Freedom of Information Act

Harry A. Hammitt

1. The basic concept of the Freedom of Information Act (FOIA) is that all records of agencies of the federal government must be accessible to the public unless specifically exempt from this requirement. The FOIA is codified at 5 U.S.C. § 552.

1.1. Although FOIA discussion inevitably focuses on what may be withheld, "[d]isclosure, not secrecy, is the dominant objective of the Act." *Department of the Air Force v. Rose*, 425 U.S. 352 (1976).

1.2. The FOIA controls executive secrecy:

1.2.1. by substituting legislative judgment for administrative discretion as to what may be kept secret. *American Jewish Congress v. Kreps*, 574 F.2d 624, 628, n.34 (D.C. Cir. 1978), citing *Department of the Air Force v. Rose*, 425 U.S. 352, 361-362 (1976) and *EPA v. Mink*, 410 U.S. 73, 79, 80 (1973);

1.2.2. in order to prevent the development of "secret law." (See Chapter 4 on Internal Agency Rules and Chapter 8 on Inter- or Intra-Agency Memoranda.)

1.3. The FOIA establishes requirements for disclosure by:

1.3.1. publication in the *Federal Register*;

1.3.2. availability for public inspection and copying; or

1.3.3. release pursuant to a request for access from "any person."

2. Material which agencies are required to make available on their own initiative. §§ 552(a)(1) and (a)(2).

2.1. Requirement to publish materials in the *Federal Register*, § 552(a)(1).

2.1.1. Sections 552(a)(1)(A) through (C) require agencies to publish in the *Federal Register* descriptions of agency organization; procedures for the public to obtain information, make submittals or requests, or obtain agency decisions; statements of agency functions; rules of procedure; and descriptions of forms to be used by agency.

2.1.2. Section 552(a)(1)(D) requires agencies to publish in the *Federal Register*: "substantive rules of general applicability adopted as authorized by law, and statements of general policy or interpretations of general applicability formulated and adopted by the agency."

2.1.3. Agencies must also publish any changes in the material that is required to be published. § 552(a)(1)(E).

2.1.4. The publication requirement is additionally important because "[e]xcept to the extent that a person has actual and timely notice of the terms thereof, a person may not in any manner be required to resort to, or be adversely affected by, a matter required to be published in the Federal Register and not so published." § 552(a)(1). This means, in effect, that failure to comply with the publication requirements of (a)(1) can, under certain circumstances, result in invalidation of related agency actions. *See* Section 3 of this chapter, *infra*.

2.1.5. Pursuant to the Government Printing Office Electronic Information Access Enhancement Act of 1993, P.L. 103-40, the GPO is required to make the *Federal Register* available to the public by computer telecommunications. Thus, the material required to be published in the *Federal Register* under § 552(a)(2)(i) is, in effect, required to be available online.

2.2. Requirement to make material publicly available, § 552(a)(2).

2.2.1. Section 552(a)(2) requires that agencies make available for public inspection or copying: (A) final opinions made in the adjudication of cases; (B) statements of policy and adopted interpretations not published in the *Federal Register*; (C) "administrative manuals and staff manuals that affect a member of the public, unless the materials are promptly published and copies offered for sale; (D) copies of all records, regardless of form or format, which have been released to any person under paragraph (3) and which, because of the nature of their subject matter, the agency determines have become or are likely to become the subject of subsequent requests for substantially the same records; and (E) a general index of the records referred to under subparagraph (D)." *See* Section 6.6 of this chapter, *infra*, regarding the 1996 amendments that added subparagraphs (D) and (E) to the statute.

2.2.2. Section (a)(2) requires that agencies maintain current indices of such material. *See NLRB v. Sears, Roebuck & Co.*, 421 U.S. 132, 153-54 (1975), and *Skelton v. U.S. Postal Service*, 678 F.2d 35, 40-41 (5th Cir. 1982), for discussion of "final opinions" under (a)(2)(A), and Chapter 8 on Exemption 5, *infra*.

2.2.3. Final orders, opinions, statements of policy, interpretations, or staff manuals or instructions which affect a member of the public may be used only if they have been indexed, made available or published, or the party affected otherwise has timely notice of them. §§ 552(a)(2)(i) and (ii).

2.2.4. *See, e.g.*, *Lonsdale v. United States*, 919 F.2d 1440, 1446 (10th Cir. 1990), and *Capuano v. National Transportation Safety Board*, 843 F.2d 56, 58 (1st Cir. 1988), and outline on "Internal Agency Rules," *infra*, for detailed discussion of caselaw interpreting and applying (a)(2)(C) with respect to law enforcement manuals.

2.2.5. Pursuant to the Electronic Freedom of Information Act Amendments of 1996, *see* Section 6.6. of this chapter, *infra*, all materials subject to the requirements of § 552(a)(2) which are created on or after November 1, 1996 must be made available to the public by computer telecommunications as well as in hard copy, within a year after enactment. If an agency lacks the means for online availability, such materials must be made available in some other electronic form.

2.3. Distinguishing materials under §§ 552(a)(1) and (a)(2).

2.3.1. Read together, (a)(1)(D) and (a)(2)(B) "can only mean that interpretations of general applicability are to be published in the *Federal Register* while all other interpretations adopted by an agency, i.e., those not *of general applicability*, are to be made available to the public, albeit they need not be published." *Anderson v. Butz*, 550 F.2d 459, 463 (9th Cir. 1977) (citation omitted) (emphasis supplied).

2.3.2. In determining what is meant by interpretations "of general applicability," the court in *Anderson* found it necessary to "inquire into the substance and effect of the policy pronouncement." *Id.* An administrative interpretation is not "of general applicability" if (1) only a clarification or explanation of existing laws or regulations is expressed, and (2) no significant impact upon any segment of the public results. *Id.* (citation omitted).

2.4. Availability of materials covered by §§ 552(a)(1) and (a)(2)

2.4.1. Judicial review of the adequacy of adherence to these provisions is available. *See, e.g., Vietnam Veterans of America v. Department of the Navy*, 875 F.2d 350 (D.C. Cir. 1989) (holding that Judge Advocate's legal opinions do not contain statements of policy or interpretations adopted by the Navy, and do not have the effect of law). *See also Green v. FBI*, No. 89-699-CIV-5-RB (E.D.N.C. Jan. 6, 1992) (court ordered FBI to make materials concerning public reading room policies publicly available, and rejected argument that (a)(2) applies only to "regulatory or licensing governmental agencies").

2.4.2. Most agencies (generally the larger ones) have established public reading rooms for access to material covered by (a)(1) and (a)(2). (Check agency regulations or call the FOIA or public affairs office for information.)

2.4.2.1. Availability in a public reading room may reduce access under (a)(3): if requested material is already available in a public documents room, no records have been withheld. *See Oglesby v. Department of the Army*, 920 F.2d 57, 70 (D.C. Cir. 1990) and cases cited therein. *But see Fitzgibbon v. AID*, 724 F. Supp. 1048 (D.D.C. 1989), *vacated* 1992 U.S. Dist. LEXIS 999 (D.D.C. Jan. 28, 1992) (availability of FOIA materials in an agency's public reading room "does not thrust the material into the public domain" and does not undercut a fee waiver claim that release to the plaintiff-author would further public understanding of the information at issue).

2.4.2.2. Where access to (a)(3) request material is provided through a reading room, even as a matter of agency discretion, regulations must be published describing the availability of documents. *Sims v. CIA (II)*, 479 F. Supp. 84 (D.D.C. 1979).

2.4.3. As with publication requirements under (a)(1), an agency's failure to comply with requirements under (a)(2) to make certain materials available for public inspection and copying may lead to invalidation of related agency actions.

3. FOIA Invalidation of Agency Action Under (a)(1) and (a)(2).

3.1. Although there is obviously some overlap between arguments that can be made for invalidating agency action based on an agency's failure to follow the rulemaking requirements of the Administrative Procedure Act, 5 U.S.C. § 551, reliance on failure to comply with the FOIA's publication requirements will in some instances furnish a basis for invalidating agency action that would not be subject to attack on rulemaking grounds. Compare *Anderson v. Butz*, 550 F.2d 459, 462-63 (9th Cir. 1977), with *Allen v. Bergland*, 661 F.2d 1001, 1006-07 (4th Cir. 1981).

3.2. Examples of agency actions invalidated because of violation of the FOIA's publication requirements: *Morton v. Ruiz*, 415 U.S. 199, 232-235 (1974); *Smith v. National Transportation Safety Board*, 981 F.2d 1326 (D.C. Cir. 1993); *D&W Food Center, Inc. v. Block*, 786 F.2d 751, 757 (6th Cir. 1986); *Vigil v. Andrus*, 667 F.2d 931, 938-939 (10th Cir. 1982); *Anderson v. Butz*, 550 F.2d 459, 463 (9th Cir. 1977); *City of Santa Clara v. Kleppe*, 418 F. Supp. 1243, 1258 (N.D. Cal. 1976), *aff'd in part, vacated in part sub nom. City of Santa Clara v. Andrus*, 572 F.2d 660 (9th Cir. 1978), *cert. denied sub nom.*, 439 U.S. 859 (1978); *W.G. Cosby Transfer & Storage Corp. v. Froehlke*, 480 F.2d 498, 503 (4th Cir. 1973); *Onweiler v. United States*, 432 F. Supp. 1226, 1230, 1231 (D. Idaho 1977); *Berends v. Butz*, 357 F. Supp. 143, 155, 156 (D. Minn. 1973).

3.3. Examples of agency actions not invalidated because of violation of the FOIA's publication requirements:

3.3.1. The FOIA's publication requirements do not apply to substantive rules, or statements of interpretation or general policy that are not of "general applicability." *See Tearney v. National Transportation Safety Board*, 868 F.2d 1451, 1454 (5th Cir. 1989), *reh'g en banc denied*, 875 F.2d 858 (5th Cir.), *cert. denied*, 493 U.S. 937 (1989); *McKenzie v. Bowen*, 787 F.2d 1216, 1222 (8th Cir. 1986); *American Broadcasting Companies, Inc. v. FCC*, 682 F.2d 25, 31-32 (2d Cir. 1982).

3.3.2. The FOIA's publication requirements do not apply to opinions announced in agency adjudicatory proceedings, even when those opinions announce and apply new interpretations or rules. *See City of Gillette, Wyo. v. FERC*, 737 F.2d 883 (10th Cir. 1984); *Cheshire Hospital v. N.H.-Vt. Hospitalization Service*, 689 F.2d 1112, 1123 (1st Cir. 1982); *Nicholson v. Brown*, 599 F.2d 639, 642, 648-49 (5th Cir. 1979), *modified*, 605 F.2d 209 (5th Cir. 1979); *Mehta v. INS*, 574 F.2d 701, 705 (2d Cir. 1978).

3.3.3. With respect to those agency records subject to the publication requirements of the FOIA, not every failure to publish such records in the *Federal Register* requires invalidation of agency action. Section 552(a)(1) recognizes that a person with "actual and timely notice" may not be legally adversely affected by unpublished matter required to be published by the FOIA. *See United States v. Bowers*, 920 F.2d 220, 222 (4th Cir. 1990); *Hudson v. United States*, 766 F.2d 1288 (9th Cir. 1985); *Kahn v. United States*, 753 F.2d 1208 (3d Cir. 1985); *Welch v. United States*, 750 F.2d 1101, 1110 (1st Cir. 1985); *Nason v. Kennebec County CETA*, 646 F.2d 10, 19 (1st Cir. 1981); *Perri v. Department of the Treasury*, 637 F.2d 1332, 1337 (9th Cir. 1981); *Yassini v. Crosland*, 618

F.2d 1356, 1361-62 (9th Cir. 1980); *United States v. Mowat*, 582 F.2d 1194, 1202 (9th Cir.), *cert. denied*, 439 U.S. 967 (1978); *Giles Lowery Stockyards, Inc. v. Department of Agriculture*, 565 F.2d 321, 326 (5th Cir. 1977), *cert. denied*, 436 U.S. 957 (1978); *Whelan v. Brinegar*, 538 F.2d 924, 927 (2d Cir. 1976).

3.3.4. The language of § 552(a)(1) also contemplates invalidation of agency action violative of publication requirements of the FOIA only at the behest of one who has been "adversely affected" by non-publication or, as some courts have held, "would have been able to pursue an alternative course of conduct." *See Alliance for Cannabis Therapeutics v. DEA*, 15 F.3d 1131, 1136 (D.C. Cir. 1994); *Mada-Luna v. Fitzpatrick*, 813 F.2d 1006 (9th Cir. 1987), *appeal after remand*, 874 F.2d 816 (9th Cir. 1989); *Zaharakis v. Heckler*, 744 F.2d 711 (9th Cir. 1984); *Donovan v. Wollaston Alloys, Inc.*, 695 F.2d 1, 9 (1st Cir. 1982); *TRW, Inc. v. FTC*, 647 F.2d 942, 951-952 (9th Cir. 1981); *Chevron Oil Co. v. Andrus*, 588 F.2d 1383, 1388 n.8 (5th Cir. 1979), *cert. denied*, 444 U.S. 879 (1979); *United States v. Goodman*, 605 F.2d 870, 887-88 (5th Cir. 1979).

3.3.5. However, the publication requirement protects only against enforcement of unpublished regulations, not delay in publication. *Alcaraz v. Block*, 746 F.2d 593 (9th Cir. 1984).

3.3.6. On the other hand, "FOIA cannot be used to force an agency to adopt a new regulation that it withdrew from publication for the specific purpose of determining whether or not it should be adopted." *Si v. Slattery*, 864 F. Supp. 397, 404 (S.D.N.Y. 1994).

4. Requests for Access.

4.1. Pursuant to § 552(a)(3), all records not covered by (a)(1) and (a)(2) or exempted from mandatory disclosure by § 552(b) are to be made public on proper identification and request according to rules established by the agency.

4.2. Procedures for requesting access under § 552(a)(3) are discussed in Chapter 2 on Administrative Process.

4.3. There are nine exemptions [§§ 552(b)(1)-(9)] which permit an agency to withhold access to records requested under § 552(a)(3). "These exemptions are specifically made exclusive...and must be narrowly construed." *Department of the Air Force v. Rose*, 425 U.S. 352 at 361 (1976). Consult individual chapters, *infra*, for an explanation of each. The exemptions are for matters that are:

4.3.1. national defense or foreign policy information properly classified pursuant to an Executive order. § 552(b)(1).

4.3.2. "related solely to the internal personnel rules and practices of an agency." § 552(b)(2).

4.3.3. "specifically exempted from disclosure by statute" other than the FOIA, but only if such statute absolutely requires that the matters be withheld, or establishes particular criteria for withholding or refers to particular types of information to be withheld. § 552(b)(3).

4.3.4. "[t]rade secrets and commercial or financial information obtained from a person and privileged or confidential." §552(b)(4).

4.3.5. "inter-agency or intra-agency memorandums or letters" which would be privileged in civil litigation. §552(b)(5).

4.3.6. "personnel and medical and similar files the disclosure of which would constitute a clearly unwarranted invasion of personal privacy." § 552(b)(6).

4.3.7. "records or information compiled for law enforcement purposes," but only to the extent that one or more of six specified forms of harm would or could reasonably be expected to result from disclosure. § 552(b)(7).

4.3.8. in or related to certain reports prepared by, on behalf of, or for the use of agencies which regulate or supervise financial institutions. § 552(b)(8).

4.3.9. oil well data. § 552(b)(9).

4.4. The exemptions under § 552(b) are discretionary, not mandatory. *Chrysler Corp. v. Brown*, 441 U.S. 281, 293 (1979).

4.4.1. Discretionary releases may be restricted by other statutes. Exemption 3 statutes may eliminate agency discretion to release information. *See* Chapter 5 on Information Exempted by Other Statutes.

4.4.2. *Chrysler Corp. v. Brown*, 441 U.S. 281 (1979), *supra*, establishes that release of material may be reviewed under the Administrative Procedure Act, 5 U.S.C. 551 § 706, to determine whether release is an abuse of discretion. *See* Chapter 7 on Reverse FOIA Litigation.

4.4.3. Agencies have no discretion to release material if a court, in a "Reverse FOIA" suit, has ordered withholding. *GTE Sylvania, Inc. v. Consumers Union of the United States, Inc.*, 445 U.S. 375 (1980). *See* Chapter 7 on Reverse FOIA Litigation.

4.5. In certain circumstances, an agency may refuse to confirm or deny the existence or nonexistence of records responsive to the request.

4.5.1. The current Executive Order on Classified National Security information allows an agency to refuse to confirm or deny the existence or nonexistence of requested information "whenever the fact of its existence or nonexistence is itself classified under this Order." *See* Chapter 3 on National Security Information.

4.5.2. Even prior to the Executive Order, courts recognized the propriety of this response, popularly known as "Glomarization," from the factual setting of the national security case in which it first received judicial approval. *See Phillippi v. CIA*, 655 F.2d 1325 (D.C. Cir. 1981) (whether agency could refuse to confirm or deny use of exploratory vessel, the Glomar Explorer) and subsequent cases discussed in Chapter 3.

4.5.3. More recently, courts have upheld agency "Glomarization" where to confirm that an individual is the subject of, or even mentioned in, a law enforcement record entails the unwarranted invasion of personal privacy that would justify the agency's withholding of the record under subsection (b)(7)(C). *See* Chapter 10 on Law Enforcement Records.

4.5.4. FOIA amendments enacted in the Anti-Drug Abuse Act of 1986 provide specific statutory authority for "Glomarization" responses by certain agencies in certain circumstances in connection with (1) records concerning an ongoing and undisclosed criminal investigation; (2) informant records maintained under an informant's name or personal identifier; (3) classified records of the FBI pertaining to foreign intelligence, counterintelligence, or international terrorism investigations. *See* Chapter 18 on Record Exclusions.

5. Judicial Review.

5.1. The FOIA provides that a federal district court "has jurisdiction to enjoin the agency from withholding agency records and to order the production of any agency records improperly withheld from the complainant." § 552(a)(4)(B).

5.2. Cases construing the FOIA have not fully resolved the issue of whether the court must exercise its statutory jurisdiction, or may utilize "equitable discretion" to balance the competing interests of the parties and decline to order nonexempt records released. However, the leading judicial opinions have generally come to the conclusion that such equitable discretion cannot be exercised except in the "extraordinary," "extreme," or "special" case where the government would be entitled to an injunction against publication. *See, e.g.*, *Halperin v. Department of State*, 565 F.2d 699, 706-7 (D.C. Cir. 1977).

5.3. *See generally* discussion of "Jurisdiction" in Chapter 21 on Litigation Strategy in FOIA Cases.

6. Legislative History of the FOIA.

6.1. The original FOIA was enacted in 1966 and went into effect in 1967.

6.1.1. It established, for the first time, a statutory right of access by any person to federal agency records.

6.1.2. After the Senate passed the bill, President Johnson threatened a veto. The House committee wrote a report, in negotiation with the Department of Justice (DOJ), which gave a broader interpretation to the exemptions. The House then passed the text exactly as approved by the Senate.

6.1.3. There is thus an important distinction between the Senate Report (S. Rep. No. 813, 89th Cong., 1st Sess. (1965)) and the House Report (H.R. Rep. No. 1497, 89th Cong. 2d Sess. (1966)), U.S. Code Cong. and Admin. News, p. 2418. "Almost all courts that have considered the difference between the Reports have concluded that the Senate Report more accurately reflects the congressional purpose," *Department of the Air Force v. Rose*, 425 U.S. 352 at 363 (1976). *See* citations for this sentence and *Vaughn v. Rosen (II)*, 523 F.2d 1136 (D.C. Cir. 1975), cited with approval in *Rose, supra*.

6.1.4. The legislative history of the 1966 Act is reprinted in *Freedom of Information Act Source Book*, Subcommittee on Administrative Practice and Procedure,

Senate Judiciary Committee, 93rd Cong., 2d Sess., 1974, Sen. Doc. No. 93-82. *See* Appendix A for the legislative history.

6.2. Operation of the original (1966) Act.

6.2.1. Agencies interpreted the exemptions broadly and employed a variety of means to discourage use of the Act, including high fees, long delays, and claims that they could not find the requested materials.

6.2.2. Courts interpreted most exemptions narrowly and fashioned procedural remedies against agency intransigence—most notably in the requirement for a *Vaughn* showing, i.e., a detailed indexing of requested documents explaining the rationale for applying exemptions, *Vaughn v. Rosen (I)*, 484 F.2d 820 (D.C. Cir. 1973), *cert. denied*, 415 U.S. 977 (1974), and in requiring the release of segregable portions of a file which was partially exempt, *EPA v. Mink*, 410 U.S. 73 at 91 (1973).

6.2.3. However, courts interpreted two exemptions—Exemption 1, relating to national defense, *EPA v. Mink*, 410 U.S. 73 at 81-84 (1973), and Exemption 7, relating to law enforcement records, *see, e.g.*, *Frankel v. SEC*, 460 F.2d 813 (2d Cir. 1972) *cert. denied*, 409 U.S. 889 (1972)—very broadly so as to permit agencies to withhold all investigatory files and all classified documents for all time.

6.3. The 1974 Amendments.

6.3.1. Legislative Action.

6.3.1.1. Following extensive hearings and a comprehensive Report [H.R. Rep. No. 92-1419 (1972)], the House Government Operations Committee unanimously reported a series of amendments [H.R. Rep. No. 93-876 (1974)] which the House approved by a vote of 383-8 on March 14, 1974. The bill made a number of procedural changes and amended Exemption 1.

6.3.1.2. On May 16, 1972, the Senate Judiciary Committee reported its own set of amendments [Senate Report No. 93-854] which included procedural revisions and a change in Exemption 1 but with limited judicial review.

6.3.1.3. On the Senate floor, the limitations on judicial review of Exemption 1 claims were removed from the bill and the Senate added an amendment revising Exemption 7 relating to law enforcement records (May 30, 1974).

6.3.1.4. The House and Senate conferees met over an extended period and received a communication from Gerald Ford, who became President in the midst of their deliberations. They accepted most of the liberalizing provisions from each chamber and reported the bill (Senate Report No. 93-1200) (Text reprinted at Appendix A). The Senate and the House quickly approved by overwhelming votes.

6.3.1.5. On October 17, 1974, President Ford vetoed the bill, objecting to the changes in Exemptions 1 and 7 and to the timetable set for agency response to requesters. He called the bill "unconstitutional and unworkable."

6.3.1.6. Both Houses overrode the President's veto (House 371-31, Nov. 20; Senate 65-27, Nov. 21) and the amendments came into effect on February 19, 1975.

6.3.2. Content of Amendments.

6.3.2.1. The amendments were designed to deal primarily with administrative issues and the national defense and law enforcement exemptions. Other exemptions were left untouched.

6.3.2.2. Procedural changes related to:

6.3.2.2.1. Indexing of documents not published in the *Federal Register*. § 552(a)(2), *supra*.

6.3.2.2.2. Identification of records for purposes of FOIA requests. *See* Chapter 2 on Administrative Process.

6.3.2.2.3. Fees—agencies could only charge actual costs for search and copying, and were required to waive fees in certain cases. *See* Chapter 2 on Administrative Process.

6.3.2.2.4. Administrative deadlines by which FOIA requests must be processed or requester has standing to sue. *See* Chapter 21 on Litigation Strategy in FOIA Cases.

6.3.2.2.5. Segregable portions—even where some portion of material is exempt, the remainder must be released. *See* Chapter 15 on Segregable Portions.

6.3.2.2.6. In camera review by courts—authority made explicit. *See* Chapter 21 on Litigation Strategy in FOIA Cases.

6.3.2.2.7. *De novo* review by the courts. *See* Chapter 21 on Litigation Strategy in FOIA Cases.

6.3.2.2.8. Expedited cases—FOIA suits were to be given precedence on court dockets. *See* Chapter 21 on Litigation Strategy in FOIA Cases.

6.3.2.2.9 Attorney fees and costs—may be awarded if plaintiff substantially prevails. *See* Chapter 17 on Attorney Fees and Litigation Costs.

6.3.2.2.10. Sanctions established against the officials responsible for arbitrary and capricious withholding of material. *See* Chapter 21 on Litigation Strategy in FOIA Cases.

6.3.2.3. Two exemptions were narrowed in scope to require review of each document and release of segregable, non-exempt portions:

6.3.2.3.1. Exemption 1—national security information.

6.3.2.3.2. Exemption 7—law enforcement investigatory records.

6.3.2.4. An authoritative legislative history is reprinted in *Freedom of Information Act and Amendments of 1974, Source Book*, Joint Committee Print, 94th Cong., 1st Sess. (March, 1975). *See* Appendix A, Legislative History of the FOIA, for citations.

6.4. The 1976 Amendments. Only Exemption 3 was amended, providing standards to determine more precisely which "other statutes" may be used as grounds for withholding. *See* discussion in Chapter 5 on Information Exempted By Other Statutes. *See* Appendix A, Legislative History of the FOIA, for citations.

6.5. The 1986 Amendments. As part of the Anti-Drug Abuse Act of 1986, Congress enacted the FOIA amendments affecting fee policies and access to certain law enforcement and national security records. *See* Appendix A, Legislative History of the FOIA.

6.5.1. Background.

6.5.1.1. For five years, bills to comprehensively rewrite the FOIA were bottled up in Congress as press and public interest groups fought with the Reagan Administration and Senator Orrin Hatch (R-UT) Chairman of the Senate Subcommittee with jurisdiction for FOIA, over a range of substantive and procedural FOIA issues. *See, e.g., Freedom of Information Act: Hearings on S. 587, S. 1235, S. 1247, S. 1730, and S. 1751 Before the Subcomm. on the Constitution of the Senate Comm. on the Judiciary, 97th Cong., 1st Sess. Vol. 1 & 2 (1981); Freedom of Information Reform Act: Hearings on S. 774 Before a Subcomm. of the House Comm. on Government Operations, 98th Cong., 2nd Sess. (1984).*

6.5.1.2. One driving force behind the Government's desire to amend the FOIA was the argument by law enforcement officials that confidential sources, ongoing investigations, and certain kinds of manuals and other sensitive non-investigative law enforcement materials were not adequately protected from disclosure by the Act's exemptions. *See* Hearings, *supra* (statements by representatives of the FBI and the DOJ).

6.5.1.3. An opportunity to "break-out" the FOIA amendments addressing law enforcement concerns and attach them to legislation with a significant likelihood of enactment came in September 1986 as Congress worked frantically to enact comprehensive anti-drug abuse legislation before adjournment and the November elections.

6.5.2. Legislative Action.

6.5.2.1. Senator Hatch, participating in the development of a Senate Republican drug bill, added three provisions from a so-called "compromise" package of FOIA amendments that had been passed by the Senate in the 98th Congress (S. 774) and reintroduced by Hatch in the 99th Congress (S. 150). The three provisions (1) modified the language and scope of Exemption 7 for law enforcement records; (2) excluded informant records requested by a third-party according to the name or personal identifier under which they are maintained; and, (3) excluded records of an organized crime investigation which were generated or acquired by a criminal law enforcement agency within five years of the date of request.

6.5.2.2. When the FOIA provisions were included in the "compromise" drug bill (S. 2878) that Senate Democrats and Republicans introduced as the vehicle for Senate consideration, Senator Patrick Leahy (D-VT) negotiated a floor amendment with Senator Hatch that (1) deleted the "organized crime records" provision; (2) added exclusions for records concerning certain classified investigations and other criminal law enforcement proceedings; and, (3) added provisions revising fee policies and the statutory fee waiver standard.

6.5.2.3. Rep. Glenn English (D-OK), chairman of the House subcommittee with jurisdiction over the FOIA, and Rep. Tom Kindness (R-OH), the subcommittee's ranking minority member, made several minor changes to the Senate-passed FOIA provisions on behalf of the House, including a transition provision clarifying the bill's effect on pending FOIA requests and litigation. The Senate accepted these changes with minor revisions.

6.5.2.4. In the absence of hearings and committee reports, floor statements by the key players provided the only detailed explanations of the intended purpose and effect of the FOIA amendments enacted as part of the Anti-Drug Abuse Act of 1986, P.L. 99-570, Title I, Subtitle N, Sec. 1801-1804. *See* Appendix A, Legislative History of the FOIA.

6.5.2.4.1. The only relevant committee report is that of the Senate Judiciary Committee three years earlier on S. 774, the FOIA bill from which the Exemption 7 amendments and the informant record exclusion were derived. *See* S. Rep. No. 221, 98th Cong., 1st Sess. 22-25 (1983). Each of the key players makes explicit reference to S. 774; in addition, Senator Leahy and Reps. English and Kindness explicitly rely on the committee report, excerpted in the Kindness statement, for their understanding of those provisions. *See also King v. DOJ*, 830 F.2d 210, 229 n.141 (D.C. Cir. 1987) (explaining reliance on Senate Judiciary Committee report.).

6.5.2.4.2. Each of the key players also makes explicit reference to an earlier bill sponsored by Reps. English and Kindness as the source for the amendments regarding fee policies and the statutory fee waiver standard, *see* H.R. 6414, 98th Cong., 2d Sess. (1984), and to a draft bill that was the subject of extensive discussions between the House subcommittee staff and the Justice Department earlier in 1986, from which the exclusions for records concerning certain classified investigations and other criminal proceedings were derived.

6.5.2.4.3. The acknowledged derivation of all but the Exemption 7 amendments from proposals that originated with Reps. English and Kindness and the House subcommittee staff is significant because, despite their status as cosponsors in the Senate, the statements of Senator Leahy and Senator Hatch generally present conflicting interpretations of the FOIA amendments. Insofar as the jointly-written explanatory materials provided for the benefit of the House by Reps. English and Kindness clearly concur with the statements of Senator Leahy, the contradictory statements of Senator Hatch take on the character of minority views. *See McClellan Ecological Seepage Situation v. Carlucci*, 835 F.2d 1282, 1284-1287 (9th Cir. 1987) (relies on Leahy-English-Kindness explanations in construing revised fee waiver standard).

6.5.3. Content of the Amendments.

6.5.3.1. Law Enforcement Records (Exemption 7).

6.5.3.1.1. Substituting "records or information" for "investigatory records" as the threshold qualification for exemption from disclosure.

6.5.3.1.2. Substituting "could reasonably be expected to" for "would" as a standard for the risk of harm with respect to subparagraphs (A) interference with enforcement proceedings, (C) unwarranted invasion of personal privacy, (D) disclosure of the identity of a confidential source, and (F) endangering the life or physical safety of any individual.

6.5.3.1.3. Including state, local, and foreign agencies or authorities and private institutions within the meaning of "confidential source" in subparagraph (D), and deleting "only" from the subparagraph's second clause.

6.5.3.1.4. Deleting "investigative" and adding "guidelines for law enforcement and prosecutions" in subparagraph (E).

6.5.3.1.5. Substituting "any individual" for "law enforcement personnel" in subparagraph (F).

6.5.3.2. Exclusions—New FOIA Subsection 552(c).

6.5.3.2.1. Records whose disclosure would interfere with criminal proceedings of which the subject is not aware.

6.5.3.2.2. Informant record requested by a third-party according to the name or personal identifier by which it is maintained.

6.5.3.2.3. Classified records of the FBI pertaining to foreign intelligence, counterintelligence or international terrorism.

6.5.3.3. Fees and Fee Waivers.

6.5.3.3.1 OMB Guidelines and Agency Regulations—The amendments require each agency to promulgate, pursuant to notice-and-comment procedures, regulations specifying a schedule of fees and establishing procedures and guidelines for determining when such fees should be waived or reduced. Such agency fee schedules must "conform" to guidelines promulgated, pursuant to notice-and-comment procedures, by the Office of Management and Budget. § 552(a)(4)(A)(i).

6.5.3.3.2. Categories of requesters—distinguishing appropriate fees when records are (1) "requested for commercial use;" (2) not sought for a commercial use and are requested by (a) an educational or noncommercial scientific institution whose purpose is scholarly or scientific research, or (b) a representative of the news media; and, (3) sought by any other requesters. § 552(a)(4)(ii).

6.5.3.3.3. Statutory fee waiver standard—The amended standard provides for waiver or reduction of fees "if disclosure of the information is in the public interest because it is likely to contribute significantly to public understanding of the operations or activities of the government and is not primarily in the commercial interest of the requester." *Id.* at (iii).

6.5.3.3.4. General limitations on fees—§ 552(a)(4)(A)(iv)-(v).

6.5.3.3.5. Other fee statutes—relation to FOIA fee provisions. *Id.* at (vi).

6.5.3.3.6. Judicial review of waiver determinations—The amendments establish that in an action regarding the waiver of fees, the court shall determine the matter de novo except that its review of the matter shall be limited to the administrative record. *Id.* at (vii).

6.6. The 1996 Amendments. After several years of legislative hearings and government-wide surveys conducted by the DOJ regarding agency practices in applying the FOIA to records in electronic formats, Congress enacted the Electronic Freedom of Information Act Amendments of 1996 to clarify the treatment of such records under the FOIA. In addition, the legislation revised the FOIA to address delays in the processing of FOIA requests, provide for expedited processing in certain circumstances, and promote the maintenance and availability of agency records in electronic formats. *See* Appendix A for citations to legislative history.

Overview of the Freedom of Information Act

6.6.1. Background.

6.6.1.1. Although federal courts have long-recognized the application of the FOIA to agency records in electronic formats, *see, e.g., Yeager v. Drug Enforcement Administration*, 678 F.2d 315, 321 (D.C. Cir. 1982), they have had virtually no guidance from Congress regarding the manner in which certain FOIA concepts, such as record searches and redaction, should be applied in processing requests for such records.

6.6.1.2. In the late 1980s, House and Senate oversight hearings on the FOIA began to explore federal agency practices in applying the FOIA to electronic records. *See, e.g. Federal Information Dissemination Policies & Practices: Hearings Before the Government Information, Justice & Agriculture Subcommittee of the House Committee on Government Operations, 101st Cong. 1st Sess. (1989); The Freedom of Information Act: Hearing Before the Subcommittee on Technology & the Law of the Senate Committee on the Judiciary Committee, 100th Cong., 2d Sess. (1988).*

6.6.1.3. After conducting a survey of federal agency positions and practices in 1989, the Office of Information and Privacy in the DOJ issued a "Report on 'Electronic Record' Issues Under the Freedom of Information Act" (October 1990), which indicated that conflict, uncertainty and reluctance on the part of many agencies in applying the FOIA to electronic records warranted the development and application of uniform administrative policies and practices in this area on a government-wide basis.

6.6.2. Legislative Action.

6.6.2.1. Senator Patrick Leahy (D-VT), one of the chief sponsors of the 1986 FOIA amendments, and Senator Hank Brown (R-CO) introduced and proposed Electronic Freedom of Information Improvement Act of 1991 (S. 1940) during the 102nd Congress. Although hearings were held, no further action was taken on the bill.

6.6.2.2. In 1993, Senators Leahy and Brown introduced a slightly modified version of their earlier bill. This bill (S. 1782) was approved by the Senate Judiciary Committee and passed by the Senate in August 1994, but made no further progress toward enactment during the 103rd Congress.

6.6.2.3. In 1995, following lengthy discussions with an OMB-led interagency working group that had produced a draft set of "Consensus Electronic Record Principles" in November 1994, Senators Leahy and Brown, joined by Senator John Kerry (D-MA) introduced S. 1090, a slightly modified version of the bill passed by the Senate the previous year.

6.6.2.4. After S. 1090 was approved by the Senate Judiciary Committee in April 1996, action shifted to the House, where a similar bill (H.R. 3802) was introduced in July and reported by the House Committee on

Government Reform in September. Following a flurry of negotiations between OMB officials of the Clinton Administration and House and Senate sponsors, a revised version of H.R. 3802 was passed by the House and Senate in September, and signed into law (P.L. 104-231) by the President on October 2, 1996.

6.6.3. Content of the Amendments

6.6.3.1. Definition of "Record"—§ 552(f)(2)—to clarify that any information which would otherwise be an agency record for FOIA purposes is subject to the requirements of the Act "when maintained by an agency in any format, including an electronic format."

6.6.3.2. Information Availability in Electronic Format—§ 552(a)(2)

6.6.3.2.1. Requiring that materials subject to paragraph (a)(2) which are created on or after November 1, 1996 must be made available to the public by computer telecommunications, as well as in hard copy, within a year after enactment; if an agency lacks the means for online availability, such materials must be made available in some other electronic form.

6.6.3.2.2. Requiring agencies to make available under paragraph (a)(2) copies of records that were previously released in response to FOIA requests, to the extent that the agency determines such records, because of their subject matter, have become or are likely to become the subject of subsequent requests for substantially the same records.

6.6.3.2.3. Requiring agencies to make available to the public a general index of such prior-released records, with such index to be available by computer telecommunications by December 31, 1999.

6.6.3.2.4. Requiring agencies to indicate the extent of any redaction of the prior-released records, including, where technically feasible, the place on the record where any deletion was made.

6.6.3.3. Honoring Form or Format Requests—§ 552(a)(3)

6.6.3.3.1. Requiring agencies to provide information to requesters in the form requested, including electronic forms, thus overruling *Dismukes v. Department of the Interior*, 603 F. Supp. 760, 763 (D.D.C. 1984).

6.6.3.3.2. Requiring agencies to make "reasonable efforts" to search for records maintained in electronic forms or formats, unless such efforts "would significantly interfere with the operation of the agency's automated information systems."

6.6.3.3.3. Defining "search" to clarify that the result produced by searching computerized records in response to a FOIA request does not constitute the creation of a record, something an agency is not obliged to do in order to respond to a FOIA request.

6.6.3.4. Standard for Judicial Review—§ 552(a)(4)(B)—to require courts to "accord substantial weight" to agency determinations as to both the technical feasibility of indicating the redaction of nonreleasable material at the place on the record where the deletion was made under subparagraph (2)(C) and subsection (b) as amended, and the reproducibility of the requested form or format of records under subparagraph (3)(B) as amended.

6.6.3.5. Ensuring Timely Response to Requests—§ 552(a)(6)

6.6.3.5.1. Permitting agencies to utilize multitrack, rather than just "first-in, first-out" processing of FOIA requests.

6.6.3.5.2. Permitting an agency to negotiate with a requester to limit the scope of a request or arrange an agreed-upon timeframe for processing the request, when the request cannot be processed in timely fashion under the "unusual circumstances" extension provision.

6.6.3.5.3. Clarifying that routine, predictable agency backlogs for FOIA request processing do not constitute "exceptional circumstances," unless the agency can demonstrate reasonable progress in efforts to reduce its backlog.

6.6.3.6. Time Limits for Consideration of Requests—§ 552(a)(6)

6.6.3.6.1. Requiring agencies to issue regulations authorizing "expedited access" for requesters who demonstrate a "compelling need" for a speedy response, with limited judicial review of an agency's denial of such treatment.

6.6.3.6.2. Doubling the time limit for agency response from ten to twenty working days.

6.6.3.6.3. Requiring agencies, in denying FOIA requests, to make reasonable efforts to estimate the volume of any denied material and provide such estimates to the requester, unless doing so would harm an interest protected by the exemption on which the denial is based.

6.6.3.7. Computer Redaction—§ 552(b)—requiring agencies to indicate deletions from the released portion of a record and, where technically feasible, to indicate the deletion at the place on the record where it was made, unless such place indication would harm an interest protected by the exemption on which the deletion is based.

6.6.3.8. Other Provisions.

6.6.3.8.1. Requiring additional information in the agencies' reports to Congress regarding their implementation of FOIA, and requiring availability of such reports to the public by computer telecommunications or other electronic means.

6.6.3.8.2. Requiring agencies to make publicly available, upon request, any reference materials or guides concerning requesting information from such agencies.

6.6.3.8.3. Providing that new statutory requirements regarding agency response to FOIA requests will become effective 180 days after enactment, while the remainder of the new provisions will become effective the year after enactment.

CHAPTER 2

Administrative Process

Harry A. Hammitt

1. The FOIA specifies certain administrative procedures for processing requests, as well as options for enforcing the rights of access.

2. "[A]ny person" may make a FOIA request: § 552(a)(3). The term "person" is defined at § 551(2).

2.1. Foreign citizens, corporations, and governments are included within the meaning of "any person." *Stone v. Export-Import Bank of the United States*, 552 F.2d 132 (5th Cir. 1977), *reh'g denied*, 555 F.2d 1391 (5th Cir. 1977), *cert. denied*, 434 U.S. 1012 (1978).

2.2. The statute nowhere differentiates between the "person" entitled to receive disclosable information under (a)(3) and the "complainant" entitled to sue for judicial enforcement of that right under (a)(4)(B). *Doherty v. DOJ*, 596 F. Supp. 423 (S.D.N.Y. 1984) (plaintiff was "illegal alien"). *See also DeLaurentiis v. Haig*, 528 F. Supp. 601 (E.D. Pa. 1981), *aff'd*, 686 F.2d 192 (3d Cir. 1982) (plaintiff was non-resident alien); *Cox v. DOJ*, 576 F.2d 1302, 1305 n.5 (8th Cir. 1978) (plaintiff was federal prison inmate). However, it has also been held that fugitives from justice cannot obtain court enforcement of FOIA provisions. Having removed themselves from the jurisdiction of the courts, they cannot expect judicial aid in compelling the release of government records. *Doyle v. DOJ*, 494 F. Supp. 842 (D.D.C. 1980), *aff'd*, 668 F.2d 1365 (D.C. Cir. 1981), *cert. denied*, 455 U.S. 1002 (1982).

2.3. Neither a court nor an agency may require one person's requests to be in a form different from that of any other person requesting information under FOIA. *Zemansky v. EPA*, 767 F.2d 569, 574 (9th Cir. 1985).

3. Choosing the Correct Agency and Addressing Initial Requests.

3.1. If it is not obvious which agency has the record sought, check the *United States Government Manual* (updated yearly and available from libraries or the Government Printing Office and at http://www.access.gpo.gov/nara/nara001.html), which describes agency functions. However, there are many agencies which are not identified completely in that directory. A more comprehensive listing is contained in the Federal Yellow Book and the Federal Regional Yellow Book, published quarterly by Leadership Directories, Inc., http://www.leadershipdirectories.com.

3.2. If in doubt about which agency has the record, make a reasonable guess or call the public affairs or FOIA offices of likely agencies in order to get informed opinions as to which agency might have the record. If you are still uncertain which agency may have custody of the records after doing some preparatory research, you may send your request to more than one agency.

3.3. A requester should check current regulations concerning FOIA/PA requests. Agency contact information and copies of FOIA regulations are also available online. The homepage of the DOJ (www.usdoj.gov) includes a "FOIA" link that will take the visitor to a list of contacts at principal agencies and will allow a visitor to link to the FOIA pages of various agencies for more specific information.

3.4. Decide whether to write a local or regional office instead of (or in addition to) the agency headquarters. HQs usually have more policy-related and general materials; field offices typically have the working files.

3.4.1. Some agencies will automatically forward requests to the appropriate field offices; some (such as the FBI) will not forward requests to field offices unless specifically asked to do so.

3.4.2. However, one court has held that where a check of FBI central files indicates a likelihood of field office files, or where the requester asks for a check of field office files, such searches should be made. *Peck v. FBI*, No. C79-486 (N.D. Ohio, Aug. 31, 1979). However, in *Kowalczyk v. DOJ*, 73 F.3d 386 (D.C. Cir. 1996), the court ruled that headquarters had no obligation to search field offices absent some indication by the requester that responsive records would be found there.

3.5. To avoid mail room delays, envelopes should be clearly marked, "Attention: Freedom of Information/Privacy Act Unit." If the agency regulations give more precise instructions on addressing, those should be followed. If time is crucial, you may wish to arrange for hand delivery to the FOIA office. Sending a request by FAX (followed by a confirmatory phone call) usually helps to avoid postal handling delays. Most agencies accept FOIA requests by FAX; some accept requests by email.

3.6. Requesters should consider the age of the documents. Older records may be stored at Federal Records Centers or at the National Archives. (If an agency says it doesn't have the documents, find out if it knows who does.)

3.7. Requests should be filed as soon as possible if there is any danger that material may be removed from an agency and no longer subject to the FOIA; the courts retain jurisdiction, under the FOIA, of a request made before such removal has taken place, but not afterwards. *See Kissinger v. Reporters Committee for Freedom of the Press*, 445 U.S. 136 (1980). It sometimes helps to remind agencies in the request letter that the existence of the request should preclude the destruction of relevant documents.

3.8. In some instances, there may be strategic reasons for making the request to one agency rather than another. One agency may have an Exemption 3 statute exempting the records, but comparable material from another agency may not be exempt. *Legal Aid Soc'y of Alameda County v. Shultz*, 349 F. Supp. 771 (N.D. Cal. 1972) (certain Equal Employment Opportunity Commission records are exempt where similar Treasury records are not).

4. Contents of Initial Request Letter.

4.1. The FOIA requires that a request "reasonably describe" the records sought. § 552(a)(3)(A).

4.1.1. Legislative history, in H.R. Rep. No. 93-876 (1974) at 6, defines "reasonably describe" as a description that "would be sufficient if it enabled a professional employee of the agency who was familiar with the subject area of the request to locate the record with a reasonable amount of effort."

4.1.2. Courts recognize that "broad, sweeping requests lacking specificity are not permissible" under the FOIA. *Marks v. DOJ*, 578 F.2d 261, 263 (9th Cir. 1978). *See also Mason v. Callaway*, 554 F.2d 129 (4th Cir. 1977), *cert. denied*, 434 U.S. 877, *reh'g denied*, 434 U.S. 935 (1977) (request for all correspondence, documents, memoranda, tape recordings, notes, and any other material pertaining to the atrocities committed against plaintiffs, including, but not limited to, the files of various government offices, is not reasonably descriptive) and *Keese v. United States*, 632 F. Supp. 85, 91 (S.D. Tex. 1985) (requests for all documents containing a requester's name are not "reasonably specific").

4.1.3. The more precise and limited the request, the more likely you are to get a prompt response. It is the duty of the requester to frame the request with sufficient specificity so that it is not excessively broad. *Hunt v. Commodity Futures Trading Commission*, 484 F. Supp. 47, 51 (D.D.C. 1979). *See Meeropol v. Meese*, 790 F.2d 942, 950-951 (D.C. Cir. 1986) (upheld lower court order defining search, although records "arguably within the category originally requested...might now be outside the boundaries of the required search") and *Ferri v. Bell*, 645 F.2d 1213, 1220 (3d Cir. 1981), *modified*, 671 F.2d 769 (1982) ("[I]f the administrative burden imposed upon an agency by a request is 'unreasonable,'...courts may in their discretion decline to order disclosure.") *See also AFGE, Local 2782 v. Department of Commerce*, 907 F.2d 203, 208-209 (D.C. Cir. 1990) (Request for "every chronological office file and correspondence file, internal and external, for every branch office, staff office [etc.]" was found to identify the records requested "with sufficient precision to enable the agency to identify them," but was held to impose "an unreasonable burden upon the agency...for...a vast quantity of material.") However, "the agency must be careful not to read the request so strictly that the requester is denied information the agency well knows exists in its files, albeit in a different form from that anticipated by the requester. To conclude otherwise would frustrate the central purpose of the Act." *Hemenway v. Hughes*, 601 F. Supp. 1002, 1005 (D.D.C. 1985). However, the purpose of some requests may be frustrated by specificity—in such cases it may be best to ask for an entire record set or database from the agency.

4.1.4. Regardless of the identity or expertise of the requester, the governing principle is "reasonableness" in describing the requested materials. "A FOIA request should not require the specificity and cunning of a carefully drawn set of discovery requests, so as to outwit narrowing legalistic interpretations by the government." *Providence Journal Co. v. FBI*, 460 F. Supp. 762, 792 (D.R.I. 1978), *rev'd on other grounds*, 602 F.2d 1010 (1st Cir. 1979), *cert. denied*, 444 U.S.1071 (1980). In practice, however, agencies will often rely on hypertechnical interpretation of the words of a request. Therefore, the requester should be very careful in stating the records sought, and should not inadvertently limit the scope of the request to exclude useful records.

4.2. Be certain that your request is made "in accordance with published rules stating the time, place, fees (if any), and procedures to be followed." § 552(a)(3)(B).

Administrative Process

4.3. Does the FOIA require an explanation of need in a request letter?

4.3.1. In general, the Act requires release of all material not exempted by provisions in section (b); it does not permit the agency to consider the requester's need or intended use in determining whether to disclose. *See DOJ v. Reporters Comm. for Freedom of the Press*, 489 U.S. 749 (1989). Therefore, in most cases, there is no need to describe the reason for the request, or the circumstances which led to the filing of the request, except as identified below.

4.3.2. Nor does the importance of the material to public debate originally affect the right of access. "The Freedom of Information Act certainly does not permit a court to balance the public good or harm involved in a disclosure or confidential retention of any individual document. The balancing of the public interest in disclosure or nondisclosure has been done by Congress by categories." *Jordan v. DOJ*, 591 F.2d 753 (D.C. Cir. 1978) (*en banc*).

4.3.3. A statement of need is relevant, however, in certain specific circumstances:

4.3.3.1. Policy arguments may convince agency officials to make a discretionary release of material which may arguably be exempt from mandatory disclosure. *See* Chapter 1, Overview of the FOIA, at 4.4.

4.3.3.2. To justify a fee waiver. *See* Chapter 16 on Fee and Fee Waivers.

4.3.3.3. To justify requiring an overburdened agency to answer an FOIA request out of turn. *Open America v. Watergate Special Prosecution Force*, 547 F.2d 605 (D.C. Cir. 1976), or for the agency to grant expedited processing status.

4.3.3.4. To maintain that Exemption 2 is inapplicable because public interest in the material demonstrates that it is not *solely* an internal agency matter. *Department of the Air Force v. Rose*, 425 U.S. 352, 369-70 (1976). *See* Chapter 4 on Internal Agency Rules.

4.3.3.5. Exemption 6 permits withholding only where there is a "clearly unwarranted invasion of personal privacy"; Exemption 7 permits withholding only where there is an "unwarranted invasion of personal privacy." Therefore, arguments for release against these exemption claims will require a showing of public interest in disclosure that outweighs the asserted privacy interests. *See* Chapter 9 on Personal Privacy and Chapter 10 on Law Enforcement Records.

4.3.3.6. Judicial interpretations of Exemption 9 require a showing of the public interest in disclosure. *See* Chapter 12 on Oil Well Data.

4.3.3.7. Where deemed necessary, an explanation of need should ordinarily relate to the general public value of the information, rather than the particular need of the requester. *But see* discussion of the Supreme Court's *Reporters Committee* decision in Chapter 10 on Law Enforcement Records, for a narrow interpretation of "public interest in disclosure."

4.3.4. Agencies may try to deny requests on grounds that the information is sought in connection with an ongoing administrative action or litigation to which the requester is a party. However, the FOIA does not permit withholding on these grounds. Such status does not confer a greater or lesser right of access on the requester, nor is it a bar to using the Act to secure information not otherwise available. *See NLRB v. Sears, Roebuck & Co.*, 421 U.S. 132, 143 n.10 (1975). *See* Chapter 20 on FOIA and Civil or Criminal Discovery.

4.3.5. As a general rule, you need not explain in your request why you want the material unless you think it will encourage the agency to release the data, or to waive or reduce fees.

4.4. Initial request should make arrangements for agency fees.

4.4.1. The 1974 FOIA amendments limited fees to those covering the direct costs of searching and copying. However, the 1986 FOIA amendments authorize agencies to also assess "review costs" when records are "requested for commercial use." *See* Chapter 16 on Fees and Fee Waivers.

4.4.2. The 1974 Conference Report notes that "fees should not be used for the purpose of discouraging requests for information or as obstacles to disclosure of requested information." S. Rep. No. 93-1200, *supra*, at 8. *See* Appendix A, *infra*. *See also Rizzo v. Tyler*, 438 F. Supp. 895, 898 (S.D.N.Y. 1977) ("An attempt to condition disclosure upon the payment of fees improperly imposed is the sort of improper withholding that this court may enjoin.") In practice, agencies often invoke sizable search and review fees to discourage users who are obliged to pay such fees for the particular fee category.

4.4.3. Agencies are required to publish fee schedules which, under the 1986 FOIA amendments, must conform to the uniform schedule of fees provided in guidelines promulgated by the Director of the Office of Management and Budget. *See* Chapter 16 on Fees and Fee Waivers. It is wise to check an agency's regulations regarding fees, especially in light of requirements to agree in advance to pay anticipated fees, or, in some cases, to actually make advance payment of a portion of such fees. *See, e.g., Ehm v. Amtrak Board of Directors*, 780 F.2d 516 (5th Cir. 1986) (court required requester to post a costs bond before the agency began to process the request, where requester had previously failed to pay assessed fees); *Irons v. FBI*, 571 F. Supp. 1241 (D. Mass. 1983) (upholding validity of agency regulation providing that FOIA request "will not be deemed to have been received until the requester is notified of the anticipated cost and agrees to bear it").

4.4.4. Under the OMB uniform fee guidance, most requesters receive two hours of free search time, but requesters may be charged for unsuccessful searches. However, the fact that little or no non-exempt material is likely to be found in response to a request of admitted public interest is not grounds for denying a waiver of search fees "Of course, where the search is small its unproductiveness is persuasive ground for waiver." *See* Attorney General's Memorandum on the 1974 Amendments to The Freedom of Information Act, U.S. Department of Justice (February 1975) (hereafter "AG's Memorandum"), reprinted in *1975 Source Book* at 507-571, 549.

4.4.5. Most requesters are eligible for 100 pages of free photocopying, but to reduce potential copying fees, requesters may be able to arrange to inspect some or all of the non-exempt material responsive to the request and then select specific documents for copying. Agency reading rooms are typically available for this, but the requester must be prepared to travel to them.

4.4.6. Fees should, if possible, be arranged in advance. The initial request letter should state a willingness to pay all fees or all fees up to a particular amount. Some agencies will respond to an initial request letter by giving an estimate of the costs. If fees seem excessive, ask for an itemization of chargeable fees. Agencies often err in their fee calculations, and in many cases do not automatically provide a detailed accounting of fees. It is possible to bargain at this stage—to narrow the request, limit the number of file systems and offices to be searched, shape the request to the organization of the file system, and so on. For example, one can request the first several pages of a number of reports, rather than the complete text of the reports.

4.4.7. Search fees—as opposed to copying fees—are generally charged only to the first requester of the materials. If materials have been released earlier to another requester, the initial request letter should point this out and suggest that the prior disclosure may well obviate the need for a new search.

4.4.8. Search fees can sometimes be avoided by making a more inclusive request, so that an entire file does not have to be reviewed in order to separate out only that material which responds to the request. This will increase copying fees, but may prove cheaper than paying for professional rather than clerical search time.

4.4.9. Fee waivers or reductions may be requested. Agencies have discretion to grant full or even partial fee waivers under applicable circumstances. However, any court review will be based on the administrative record, so your request letter and subsequent appeal must explain in reasonable detail why you are entitled to a fee waiver or reduction. *See* Chapter 16 on Fees and Fee Waivers.

4.4.10. Fee categorization is not the same as a fee waiver, and the discussion of which fee category a requester is to be placed is a completely different issue than that of whether a full or partial fee waiver will be granted.

4.5. Initial request should mention that a reply is expected within the statutory time limits.

4.5.1. An agency is required to make a "determination" on any FOIA request within 20 working days of receipt. § 552(a)(6)(A)(i).

4.5.2. An agency is required to make a "determination" on any appeal within 20 working days of receipt. § 552(a)(6)(A)(ii). *See* Section 8 of this chapter.

4.5.3. Agencies can take another ten working days in "unusual circumstances." § 552(a)(6)(B). Anticipate in your request the need to contact outside offices, to handle a voluminous request, or to consult with other agencies or components.

4.5.4. If an agency has an Exemption 3 statute providing submitters of information an extended notice period, the time provisions of the Exemption 3 statute will govern. *GTE Sylvania v. Consumers Union of the United States, Inc.*, 445 U.S. 375 (1980).

4.5.5. Many agencies meet FOIA time limits, but some, particularly the FBI, CIA, IRS, State Department, National Security Agency, and Immigration & Naturalization Service can take up to several years to respond.

4.5.6. It is a good idea to phone the FOIA office of the agency to try to get them committed to a release date, and to clear up any confusion about the request.

4.5.7. The only sanction for the violation of statutory time limits is to construe it as a denial, and to write an appeal letter or sue. *See, e.g.*, *Daniels v. St. Louis VA Regional Office*, 561 F. Supp. 250 (E.D. Mo. 1983) (no private right of action for monetary damages under FOIA for delay in producing requested documents).

4.5.7.1. An appeal will speed up the process in some agencies (but not, for example, in the FBI).

4.5.7.2. Although the EFOIA amendments provide that routine backlogs do not justify a court stay, courts still look at such factors in determining whether or not to stay proceedings and grant the agency additional time in which to respond. *See* Chapter 21 on Litigation Strategy.

4.6. Initial request letters should remind agencies that the Act requires release of all *reasonably segregable portions* which are not themselves exempt. § 552(b). *See* Chapter 15 on Segregable Portions.

4.7. The initial request letter should state that you are aware of your administrative appeal rights, even though the agency is required to inform you of these rights upon denying your request. § 552(a)(6)(A)(i).

5. Expedited processing under § 552(a)(6)(E).

5.1. The 1996 EFOIA amendments added procedures for expedited processing of a request where the requester "demonstrates a compelling need" for the information, § 552(a)(6)(E)(i)(I), or "in other cases determined by the agency." § 552(a)(6)(E)(i)(II). Agencies in practice have granted expedited processing status very infrequently.

5.1.1. "Compelling need" is defined as: (I) "a failure to obtain requested records on an expedited basis under this paragraph could reasonably be expected to pose an imminent threat to the life or physical safety of an individual" or (II) "with respect to a request made by a person primarily engaged in disseminating information, urgency to inform the public concerning actual or alleged Federal Government activity." § 552(a)(6)(v)(I) and(II).

5.1.2. A request for expedited processing must be accompanied by a statement certifying that the basis for the compelling need is "true and correct to the best of such person's knowledge and belief." § 552(a)(6)(E)(vi).

5.2. An agency must determine whether to provide expedited processing, and provide notice of the determination to the requester, within 10 working days of the date of the request. § 552(a)(6)(E)(ii)(I).

5.2.1. An agency must also provide "expeditious consideration" of an administrative appeal of such a determination. § 552(a)(6)(E)(ii)(II).

5.3. An agency must process a request for which expedited processing has been granted "as soon as practicable." § 552(a)(6)(E)(iii).

5.4. Agency action to deny or affirm the denial of a request for expedited processing, and failure of an agency to respond to such a request in a timely manner, is subject to the standard for judicial review in § 552(a)(4).

5.4.1. However, the court's review is limited to the administrative record. § 552(a)(6)(E)(iii).

5.4.2. A court will not have jurisdiction to review the denial of an expedited processing request once the agency has provided a complete response to the request. § 552(a)(6)(E)(iv).

5.5. For analysis of court interpretation of the expedited processing provisions, see Chapter 19 on the EFOIA amendments.

6. Agency determinations under § 552(a)(6).

6.1. A "determination" response sent to a person requesting information under the FOIA must include at least four elements: (1) a statement of what the agency will release and will not release; (2) a statement of the reasons for not releasing the withheld records; (3) a statement notifying the requesting person of his right to appeal to the head of the agency or seek judicial review of any adverse determination; and (4) if a fee is charged for releasing documents, a statement for the charges for document search and duplication of the releasable documents, and, if a fee waiver was requested, a statement of why the agency believes that waiver or reduction of the fee is not in the public interest and does not benefit the general public. Explaining the need for an agency to provide such information, the court in *Shermco Industries, Inc. v. Secretary of the Air Force*, 452 F. Supp. 306, 317 (N.D. Tex. 1978), *rev'd on other grounds*, 613 F.2d 1314 (5th Cir. 1980) noted: "A person cannot effectively appeal a decision about the releasability of documents or the charging of fees if he is not informed of at least a list of the documents to which he was denied access, what fees he will be charged for releasable documents, and why those decisions were made. Denial of this information would in all likelihood be a violation of due process as well as effectively gutting the reasons for applying the exhaustion doctrine in FOIA cases." 452 F. Supp. at 317 n.7. *See Oglesby v. Department of the Army*, 920 F.2d 57, 65 (D.C. Cir. 1990) (citing *Shermco*).

6.2. One court has held that an agency's "acknowledgement" of a request within the statutory time limits "cannot be construed as a 'determination' sufficient to satisfy the requirements of 5 U.S.C. § 552(a)(6)(A)" if it does not grant or deny the right to appeal. *Martinez v. FBI*, No. 82-1547 (D.D.C. Oct. 11, 1983), citing *Shermco Industries, Inc., v. Secretary of the Air Force*, 452 F. Supp. 306 (N.D. Tex. 1978), *supra*, and *Marschner v. Department of State*, 470 F. Supp. 196, 199 (D. Conn. 1979). *See also Morrow v. FBI*, 2 F.3d 642, 644 n.5 (5th Cir. 1993) (notice to death-row inmate that his request would involve a "delay of many months" does not qualify as an agency determination).

6.3. Sometimes agency responses are misleading, e.g. that records are "unavailable," rather than that they don't exist or are being denied. Ambiguous responses should always be pursued.

6.3.1. Were the records once in the agency's possession?

6.3.2. Where are they now? At a Federal Record Center? National Archives? Another agency? Contractor? If so, when were they moved? *See* Chapter 14 on Agency Records.

6.4. If an agency says the records do not exist, the requester has several options before (or in addition to) writing an administrative appeal letter.

6.4.1. First, determine whether the agency's denial that the records exist is really a denial of their existence or actually a refusal to acknowledge their existence, sometimes called a "Glomar response." *See* Chapter 1, Overview of the FOIA, at 4.5 and materials cited therein.

6.4.2. If an agency is in fact denying the existence of the records, write or call the agency and find out how such records, if they exist, might be indexed. Although the FOIA does not require requesters to specify a particular record system, problems may be avoided by learning more about agency record-keeping practices.

6.4.3. Rewrite your request, so that the description is more explicit; explain why you believe the records do in fact exist.

6.4.4. Informal avenues can be useful. Are there any present or former agency employees who might be able to shed light on where the material might be and what it might be called? A search of the Internet for the phrases describing the records may uncover clues as to their present location or status. Websites such as google.com, alltheweb.com, dejanews.com, searchgov.com and searchmil.com are helpful in this regard. A news database search using Nexis/Lexis or Westlaw is also helpful in identifying the location of records.

6.4.5. Try to find out which files were searched, by whom the search was done, what systematic search procedures were tried, and why further searches would be unreasonable. The adequacy of search procedures can be reviewed in court. *Weisberg v. DOJ*, 627 F.2d 365 (D.C. Cir. 1980), *appeal on remand*, 705 F.2d 1344 (D.C. Cir. 1983). *See* Chapter 21 on Litigation Strategy for detailed discussion of caselaw regarding the adequacy of an agency's search. Agencies typically keep a "boilerplate" standard affidavit describing the adequacy of their searches for FOIA lawsuits; such affidavits can be helpful in identifying agency databases for search. In some agencies, a search defaults to the simplest search of only the most basic indices unless the requester specifies otherwise in his/her request.

6.4.6. A lawsuit sometimes motivates an agency to find the requested material.

6.5. If an agency says that records have been destroyed, the requester will want to verify that the material has in fact been destroyed and look for indications of improper destruction of records.

Administrative Process

6.5.1. Filing a FOIA request is one procedure for stopping the proposed destruction of the material.

6.5.2. Once material has been destroyed, agencies cannot be ordered to reconstruct it. *Nolen v. Rumsfeld*, 535 F.2d 890 (5th Cir. 1976); however, one court required reconstruction of records where destruction occurred after suit was filed. *Levine v. United States*, No. 73-1215-Civ-CA (S.D. Fla., Order of Mar. 22, 1974). *But see Jefferson v. Reno*, 123 F. Supp. 2d 1 (D.D.C. 2000), where the court ordered the agency to reconstruct a file that had been improperly destroyed.

6.5.3. The FOIA provides standing to sue to enjoin programmatic destruction of documents. *American Friends Service Committee v. Webster*, 485 F. Supp. 222 (D.D.C. 1980), *aff'd*, 720 F.2d 29 (D.C. Cir. 1983). Records are required to be properly managed under the Archival Administration Act (44 U.S.C. § 2101, *et seq.*); the Records Management by Federal Agencies Act (44 U.S.C. § 3101, *et seq.*); and the Disposal of Records Act (44 U.S.C. § 3301, *et seq.*). Destruction is required to be duly documented. If material of historical interest, which is required to be preserved, is said to be destroyed, you should ask for an explanation. (Sometimes a search for such internal documentation will turn up the missing records.)

6.6. If the requested records are located and determined to be releasable, the agency "shall make the records promptly available." § 552(a)(3).

6.6.1. While there is a substantial body of caselaw holding that an agency "need not respond to a FOIA request for copies of documents where the agency itself has provided an alternative form of access," for example, making records available in a reading room, a panel of the D.C. Circuit appears to have gone beyond the pale in holding that an agency is not required by the FOIA to mail copies of records to requesters if it would rather make "all responsive records available in one central location for [the requester's] perusal." *Oglesby v. Department of the Army*, 920 F.2d 57, 70 (D.C. Cir. 1990).

6.6.2. In response to *Oglesby*, 920 F.2d 57, 70 (D.C. Cir. 1990), the Justice Department's Office of Information and Privacy has urged that, "[a]s a matter of sound policy and administrative practice," agencies "should decline to follow such a practice except where it is the requester's preference as well." *See Freedom of Information Act Case Guide & Privacy Act Overview*, Office of Information and Privacy, Office of Policy Development, U.S. Department of Justice (September 1994 edition) pp. 25-26 and note 76.

6.7. An agency may deny some or all of the requested material under the FOIA's exemptions to mandatory disclosure. §§ 552(b)(1)-(9). The denial is required to note which exemptions are being claimed.

7. Transfer of requests.

7.1. Section 552(a)(6)(B)(iii)(III) provides for an extension of time if there is a need "for consultation, which shall be conducted with all practicable speed, with another agency having a substantial interest in the determination of the request or among two or more components of the agency having substantial subject-matter interest therein."

7.1.1. This is the only statutory provision concerning the possible transfer of a request, but administrative practice has evolved over time to include several possible situations in which a request may be transferred to another office or an entirely different agency.

7.1.1.1. An agency may find that responsive records reside with another component or another agency. Typically, the agency will refer the request to other pertinent offices, inform the requester that other components or agencies are responding to all or part of the request, and inform the requester that he or she will hear independently from the component or agency to which the request was transferred.

7.1.1.2. The agency may also decide to treat the request as a "no records" request and provide the requester with no further information. The agency may also decline to refer the request to another agency, but inform the requester in its response letter that another named agency may have responsive records.

7.1.2. Once an agency has referred a request, the agency to which it was referred in all likelihood will treat it for purposes of the statutory time limits as a new request. In an agency like the FBI, this can well mean that the request will be sent to the end of the line to await processing.

7.1.3. Some agencies may do a good job tracking the various agencies or components to which a request has been referred and keeping the requester apprised of the existence of these referrals. Other agencies may shift the burden of keeping track of such administrative matters to the requester. Regardless, administrative appeals must be filed with the agency which made the determination on the records, whether or not it is the agency to which the request was originally sent. This can necessitate a variety of appeals to various agencies or components depending on how many offices are ultimately involved.

7.1.4. If the agency to which the request was originally submitted is sued, it has no legal obligation to justify the withholdings or lack of response by another agency to which the request was referred.

8. Administrative Appeals under § 552(a)(6).

8.1. The FOIA includes several requirements about agency denials which are intended to facilitate appeals.

8.1.1. Section 552(a)(6)(A)(i) provides that the agency is to notify the requester of the right to appeal adverse determinations to the head of the agency. As a matter of policy, the denial letter is to include the name and address of the official to whom appeals are to be directed. Agency denials are sometimes incomplete or misleading but this does not affect the availability or requirements of the appeal process.

8.1.1.1. Some agencies, if they cannot find records, do not consider a "no records" response to be a denial, and do not inform the requester of appeal rights. But in *Oglesby v. Department of the Army*, 920 F.2d 57,

70 (D.C. Cir. 1990), *supra*, the D.C. Circuit ruled that "no records" responses were appealable and that agencies were required to provide appeals rights under such circumstances.

8.1.1.2. Some agencies will decide, incorrectly, that an FOIA request for personal files is to be processed under the Privacy Act, and will not inform a requester of FOIA appeals procedures. *See* Chapter 22 on Privacy Act.

8.1.2. Section 552(a)(6)(C) provides that denials of requests for records (including denials of appeals) "shall set forth the names and titles or positions of each person responsible for the denial."

8.1.3. Even without a formal denial (i.e., when the agency does not comply with the statutory time limits for responding to initial requests), requesters may exercise appeal rights. See 4.5., *supra*.

8.2. The administrative appeal must be handled within twenty 20 working days. See 4.5.2., *supra*.

8.3. Exhaustion of Administrative Remedies.

8.3.1. Although some legal scholars have noted the 1974 Amendments' "failure to make appeals mandatory," *see, e.g.*, J. O'Reilly, *Federal Information Disclosure*, Section 7.04 (1979), the weight of authority, in reading the language and legislative history of § 552(a)(6), has concluded that those amendments "presuppose that agencies will have a basically two-step, rather than a single-step, procedure in their regulations, i.e., that they will provide for an initial determination whether to grant or deny access, followed by an administrative appeal." AG's Memorandum, *1975 Source Book* at 544.

8.3.2. As a practical matter, exhaustion of the administrative appellate process before filing suit generally results in voluntary release of at least some of the material withheld in the initial review; creates a complete record of the agency's actions for purposes of judicial review (e.g., claims of bad faith); and, avoids later delays that occur when a court feels further agency consideration might eliminate prolonged judicial proceedings.

8.3.3. The Act expressly provides that a requester "shall be deemed to have exhausted his administrative remedies…if the agency fails to comply with the applicable time limit provisions" for initial and appellate determinations. § 552(a)(6)(C). *See Spannaus v. DOJ*, 824 F.2d 52, 57-59 (D.C. Cir. 1987); *Grove v. CIA*, 752 F. Supp. 28, 31 (D.D.C. 1990).

8.3.4. However, the court in such cases may retain jurisdiction and allow the agency "additional time to complete its review of the records" if the Government can show that "exceptional circumstances exist" and that the agency is exercising due diligence in responding to the request. § 552(a)(6)(C).

8.3.5. An administrative appeal is mandatory if the agency cures its failure to respond within the statutory period by responding to the FOIA request before suit is filed. *Oglesby v. Department of the Army*, 920 F.2d 57, 63-65 (D.C. Cir. 1990).

8.3.6. Failure to file a "proper" FOIA request according to agency regulations may also result in a failure to exhaust administrative remedies. *Lilienthal v. Parks*, 574 F. Supp. 14 (E.D. Ark. 1983).

8.3.7. "The burden of producing evidence of a proper appeal is on the person requesting documents under the FOIA. If the person requesting documents satisfies this burden, the agency has the burden of proof to establish that the appeal was not valid." *Shermco Industries, Inc. v. Secretary of the Air Force*, 452 F. Supp. 306, 318 (N.D. Tex. 1978). A proper appeal should be directed to the correct official, identifying the decision being appealed and the grounds upon which the appeal is based.

8.3.8. The FOIA does not specify how many days a requester is allowed in which to write an appeal letter. Most agency regulations provide for a 30-day limit, suggested in the AG's Memorandum, 1975 *Source Book* at 544. Some agencies provide a shorter time period, as little as 10 days. However, many agencies will seldom strictly enforce such limitations because they know such action would typically result in the filing of a new request for the same materials. The Department of Justice issued a memorandum in December 2001 advising agencies not to deny administrative appeals received after the deadline if the delay was due to mail processing delays.

8.4. What can be appealed?

8.4.1. Denial of a request, in full or in part. If requested records are released in part, clues as to what may be missing (gaps in number sequences, context of deletions, etc.) may be useful in drafting a highly specific appeal letter.

8.4.2. Adequacy of an agency's search for records responsive to the request. *See* discussion of "reasonableness" standard in Chapter 21 on Litigation Strategy.

8.4.3. Failure to respond within time limits.

8.4.4. Excessive fees.

8.4.5. Denial of a request for waiver or reduction of fees.

8.4.6. Denial of a request for expedited processing.

8.5. What should be in an appeal letter?

8.5.1. State that it is an appeal under the FOIA, § 552(a)(6).

8.5.2. Identify the initial request by the date of that letter and provide any number or other means of identifying your request that the agency is using; describe requested and withheld material; give names and positions of officials processing the initial request.

8.5.3. State that a reply is expected within the 20 working-day time limit.

8.5.4. Give your name, address and phone number and offer to discuss your request and appeal.

8.5.5. Appeals are often (but not always) considered by senior personnel who may be moved by:

8.5.5.1. Policy arguments: i.e., discretionary release, value to public debate, balancing tests, release would be harmless.

8.5.5.2. Legal arguments suggesting that the Government would lose its case in court on the grounds that:

8.5.5.2.1. exemptions are improperly claimed;

8.5.5.2.2. segregable portions (§ 552(b)) have not been released (*see* Chapter 15 on Segregable Portions);

8.5.5.2.3. age of documents renders them harmless;

8.5.5.2.4. material, or a substantial portion of it, has already been released or otherwise made public. *See* Chapter 1 on Overview.

8.5.5.3. An indication that refusal will lead to a lawsuit. Thus it makes sense to have appeal letters signed by an attorney. (But this sometimes has the opposite effect—some agencies seem happy to get the request out of their office and over to the U.S. Attorney who is responsible for FOIA litigation.)

8.5.6. Appeal letters should demand a complete list of documents covered by the request and a specific indication of what material is being withheld and what exemptions are claimed.

8.5.6.1. Some agencies routinely provide this; others refuse. "[T]he objective of the *Vaughn* requirements, to permit the requesting party to present its case effectively, is equally applicable to proceedings within the agency." *Mead Data Central, Inc. v. Department of the Air Force*, 402 F. Supp. 460 (D.D.C. 1974), *remanded*, 566 F.2d 242 (D.C. Cir. 1977).

8.5.6.2. There is no explicit requirement in the FOIA for such itemization at the administrative level, but, since courts now uniformly require such a showing under *Vaughn*, it is possible to argue that it must be provided in administrative appeals or should be provided to avoid needless litigation. *See, e.g.*, Department of Justice regulations requiring that a component denying a FOIA request in whole or in part must give the requester "[a] brief statement of the reason or reasons for the denial, including the FOIA exemption or exemptions which the component has relied upon in denying the request *and a brief explanation of the manner in which the exemption or exemptions apply to each record withheld...*" 28 CFR § 16.5(b)(2) (1994 edition) (emphasis added).

9. Alternatives to Litigation if Appeal Process Fails.

9.1. Appeal to Congressional representatives. Unless working with the subpoena power or other specific authority of a Congressional committee, members of Congress generally have no stronger right of access to government records than other persons, but they do sometimes have influence with particular agencies, and may be willing to try to help a constituent.

9.2. Office of the Special Counsel of the Merit Systems Protection Board. The Civil Service Reform Act of 1978 (P.L. 95-454) amended Title 5, United States Code and established a Special Counsel having authority to conduct investigations related to the FOIA. This Act, as amended by the Whistleblower Protection Act of 1989 (P.L. 101-12), authorizes the Special Counsel to conduct an investigation of any allegation concerning "arbitrary or capricious withholding of information prohibited under Section 552 of this title [the FOIA], except that the Special Counsel shall make no investigation under this subsection of any withholding of foreign intelligence or counter-intelligence information the disclosure of which is specifically prohibited by law or Executive Order." 5 U.S.C. § 1216(a)(3).

9.2.1. The legislative history of the Civil Service Reform Act (S. Rep. No. 95-969 also explicitly instructs the Special Counsel to assume mandatory duties formerly held by the Civil Service Commission to investigate and make binding recommendations for discipline of officials after a court orders the production of agency records improperly withheld, assesses attorney fees and other litigation costs against the United States, and, issues a written finding that the circumstances surrounding the withholding raise questions whether agency personnel acted arbitrarily or capriciously. *See* § 552(a)(4)(F).

9.2.2 However, subsection (a)(4)(F) is rarely invoked because courts generally will not enter such a finding where the agency disclosure is not pursuant to a court order. *See, e.g.*, *Wilder v. Commissioner of Internal Revenue Service*, 601 F. Supp. 241 (M.D. Ala. 1984).

CHAPTER 3

Exemption 1—National Security Information

Harry A. Hammitt and Mark S. Zaid

1. Exemption 1 provides that the FOIA does not apply to matters that are: specifically authorized under criteria established by an Executive order to be kept secret in the interest of national defense or foreign policy and are in fact properly classified pursuant to such Executive order.

2. "Criteria Established By An Executive Order."

2.1. On April 17, 1995 President Clinton issued the current Executive Order on Classified National Security Information, No. 12958, 3 C.F.R. 166 (1982 Comp.) which became effective on October 17, 1995. *Id.* at 178. *See* Appendix E.

2.1.1. This order revoked the previous Executive Order, No. 12356, 3 C.F.R. 66 (1982), which was issued by President Reagan on April 2, 1982.

2.1.2. The Executive Order sets out both substantive and procedural criteria for withholding national security information. In order to withhold information under Exemption 1 of the FOIA, the government must demonstrate that the information "is 'in fact, properly classified pursuant to' both procedural and substantive criteria contained in the Executive Order." Conference Report, No. 93-1200, 93d Cong, 2d Sess., in Appendix A. *See also Goldberg v. Department of State*, 818 F.2d 71, 77 (D.C. Cir. 1987), *cert. denied*, 485 U.S. 904 (1988); *Lesar v. DOJ*, 636 F.2d 472, 483 (D.C. Cir. 1980); *Allen v. CIA*, 636 F.2d 1287 (D.C. Cir. 1980).

2.1.3. In rejecting a constitutional challenge to CIA prepublication censorship of "secret" information contained in former agents' writings and obtained by former agents during the course of CIA employment, the D.C. Circuit held that the classification criteria for "secret" information under the earlier Executive Order issued by President Carter were not excessively vague or otherwise impermissible under the First Amendment. *McGehee v. Casey*, 718 F.2d 1137 (D.C. Cir. 1983). The court declined to express a view on the constitutionality of the Reagan Executive Order, *id.* at 1139, n.4, but noted that the definition of "secret" information had not been altered. *Id.*

2.1.4. As a general matter, Executive Orders on Classification issued by Republican Presidents have tended to be more concerned about classifying information and protecting classified information. By contrast, Democratic Executive Orders on Classification have emphasized that declassification of records is just as important as classification. While President George W. Bush has not yet issued his own executive order on classification, most observers believe it will stress preserving the confidentiality of classified documents to a greater extent than did the Clinton executive order. However, it has been pointed out that the automatic declassification program instituted by the Clinton E.O. has become so institutionalized at this point that it is unlikely the program will be significantly rolled back by any EO issued during the Bush presidency.

Exemption 1

2.2. Substantive Criteria.

2.2.1. Categories of information. Executive Order No. 12958, §§ 1.5(a) to (g), states that information may not be considered for classification unless it concerns one of the following categories:

2.2.1.1. military plans, weapons systems, or operations;

2.2.1.2. foreign government information;

2.2.1.3. intelligence activities (including special activities), intelligence sources or methods, or cryptology;

2.2.1.4. foreign relations or foreign activities of the United States, including confidential sources;

2.2.1.5. scientific, technological, or economic matters relating to the national security;

2.2.1.6. United States Government programs for safeguarding nuclear materials or facilities; or

2.2.1.7. the vulnerabilities or capabilities of systems, installations, projects, or plans relating to the national security.

2.2.2. Minimum standard. Information in one of the categories listed above may be classified only if "the unauthorized disclosure of the information reasonably could be expected to cause damage to the national security and the original classification authority is able to identify or describe the damage." § 1.2.

2.2.2.1. "'Top Secret' shall be applied to information, the unauthorized disclosure of which reasonably could be expected to cause exceptionally grave damage to the national security that the original classification authority is able to identify or describe." § 1.3(a)(1).

2.2.2.2. "'Secret' shall be applied to information, the unauthorized disclosure of which reasonably could be expected to cause serious damage to the national security that the original classification authority is able to identify or describe." § 1.3(a)(2).

2.2.2.3. "'Confidential' shall be applied to information, the unauthorized disclosure of which reasonably could be expected to cause damage to the national security that the original classification authority is able to identify or describe." § 1.1(a)(3).

2.2.2.4. "'National security' means the national defense or foreign relations of the United States." § 1.1(a).

2.2.3. The difference between the language of EO 12356 (the Reagan/Bush administrations' classification order) and EO 12958 (the Clinton administration's order) was highlighted when the Ninth Circuit ruled that a letter from the British Home Office concerning the extradition of two British citizens for conspiracy charges in a plot to murder a U.S. Attorney in Oregon could not be withheld because the State Department had made only generalized claims of harm to foreign relations and had not shown how the disclosure of this *specific* document would harm foreign relations as required under the Clinton EO. *Weatherhead v. USA*, 157 F.3d 735 (9th Cir. 1998). The Supreme Court granted cert for the case, but days before oral argument was scheduled, the government withdrew the case, contending that it was moot because Weatherhead had previously received the disputed document directly from the British consulate. Pursuant to the government's request, the Court vacated the Ninth Circuit's opinion. *United States v. Weatherhead*, 528 U.S. 1042 (1999).

2.2.4. Duration of classification.

2.2.4.1. The original classification authority, at the time of original classification, must attempt to establish a specific date or event for declassification based on the duration of the "national security sensitivity" of the information. § 1.6(a).

2.2.4.2. Absent an earlier specific date or event for declassification, information shall be marked for declassification 10 years from the date of the original decision, unless the original classification authority determines that the information requires classification for a longer period because its release could reasonably be expected to result in one of eight specified harms. §§ 1.6(b) and (d).

2.2.4.3. An original classification authority may extend the duration of classification or reclassify specific information for successive periods not to exceed 10 years at a time "if such action is consistent with the standards and procedures established" under the Order. However, this provision does not apply to information contained in records that are more than 25 years old and have been determined to have permanent historical value under title 44 of the U.S. Code. In *Oglesby v. Department of the Army*, 79 F.3d 1172 (D.C. Cir. 1996), the court ruled that, while the age of records was one consideration to be taken into account in a decision to declassify, the age of documents themselves was not adequate standing alone to suggest current classification was improper.

2.2.4.4. State Department Records. In 1991, a new law was enacted requiring that all State Department records be automatically declassified after 30 years, except where specifically determined that continued classification is necessary under certain narrow conditions. Foreign Relations Authorization Act, P.L. 102-138, Sec. 198, 105 Stat. 685-91.

2.2.4.5. John F. Kennedy Assassination Records. In 1992, Congress passed the JFK Assassination Records Collection Act of 1992. P.L. No. 102-526, 106 Stat. 3443, codified at 44 U.S.C. § 2107. This law requires the government to release all records concerning the assassination of President Kennedy. It allows the government to postpone the release of information for national security reasons, but under much more stringent standards than those in Executive Order 12356. *See Assassination Archives & Research Center v. DOJ*, 43 F.3d 1542 (D.C. Cir. 1995) (holding that Congress did not create an implied private right of action in the JFK Act, and did not intend that the Act's standards be applied in FOIA cases involving assassination records). The Ninth Circuit found, in *Minier v. CIA*, 88 F.3d 796 (9th Cir. 1996), that the JFK Act did not enhance a requester's FOIA rights of access.

2.2.5. Compilations. A collection of pre-existing items of information which are individually unclassified may be classified if, in aggregation, the compiled information "reveals an additional association or relationship" that meets the standards for classification and is not otherwise revealed in the individual items of information. § 1.8(e). *See* Sec. 4.1.2., *infra.*

2.2.6. Prohibitions and Limitations. Documents may not be classified in order to "conceal violations of law, inefficiency, or administrative error, prevent embarrassment to a person, organization or agency; restrain competition; or prevent or delay the release of information that does not require protection in the interest of national security." § 1.8(a). In addition, basic scientific research information not clearly related to the national security may not be classified. § 1.8(b).

2.2.7. Declassification and Downgrading.

2.2.7.1. In general, information shall be declassified "as soon as it no longer meets the standards for classification." § 3.2(a). Although it is "presumed" that information which continues to meet the classification standards requires continued protection, an agency head or senior agency official, as an exercise of discretion, shall determine whether, in exceptional cases, "the need to protect such information may be outweighed by the public interest in disclosure of the information," and the information should be declassified. § 3.2(b). *See Oglesby v. Department of the Army*, 79 F.3d 1172 (D.C. Cir. 1996) (mere passage of time is not in itself a bar to the government's continued reliance on Exemption 1).

2.2.7.2. If the Director of the Information Security Oversight Office determines that information is classified in violation of the Order, the Director may require the information to be declassified by the agency that originated the classification, subject to an appeal to the President through the Assistant to the President for National Security Affairs. § 3.2(c). *See* Sec. 5.3. of the Order regarding the establishment and responsibilities of the Information Security Oversight Office.

2.2.7.3. Automatic Declassification. Within five years of the date of the Order, all classified information contained in records that are more than 25 years old and have been determined to have permanent historical value under title 44 of the U.S. Code shall be automatically declassified, whether or not the records have been reviewed. § 3.4(a). Subsequently, all classified information in such records shall be automatically declassified no longer than 25 years from the date of its original classification, unless it is exempted from automatic declassification by an agency head because its release would be expected to result in one of nine specified harms. § 3.4(b).

2.2.7.4. Systematic Declassification Review. Each agency that has originated classified information must conduct a program of prioritized systematic review of historically valuable records that are exempted from automatic declassification under the Order. § 3.5(a). The Archivist shall conduct such a review program for classified information in the possession of the National Archives and Records Administration. § 3.5(b).

2.2.7.5. Mandatory Review for Declassification. Executive Order 12958 has an FOIA-like provision which requires that classified information "shall be subject to a review for declassification by the originating agency" if: (1) the request for review describes the document or material containing the information with sufficient specificity to enable the agency to locate it with a reasonable amount of effort, (2) the information is not exempted from search and review under the CIA Information Act, and (3) the information has not been reviewed for declassification within the past 2 years. § 3.6(a). This requirement is subject to restrictions regarding information originated by the President or certain related persons and entities. § 3.4(b). Requests for mandatory review for declassification under this provision can serve as an alternative or additional means for seeking the release of classified information; mandatory declassification is also used for presidential records, which are not subject to the FOIA. However, unlike the FOIA, the Executive Order procedure does not provide for administrative or judicial remedies when a request is denied.

2.2.7.6. Classified information "shall not be declassified automatically as a result of any unauthorized disclosure of identical or similar information." § 1.2(c). The argument that a similar provision in a predecessor Executive Order required re-evaluation of the status of disclosed documents was rejected. *Simmons v. DOJ*, 796 F.2d 709, 712 n.2 (4th Cir. 1986). *But see* 4.6.1., *infra* ("Publicly Known Information").

2.2.8. Reclassification. Information may not be reclassified after it has been declassified and released to the public under proper authority. § 1.8(c). *See, e.g., American Library Association v. Faurer*, 631 F. Supp. 416 (D.D.C. 1986) (National Security Agency classified materials previously disclosed in public library), *aff'd for lack of standing, sub nom., American Library Association v. Odom*, 818 F.2d 81 (D.C. Cir. 1987).

2.3. Procedural Criteria.

2.3.1. Classification Authority. Only certain designated officials may classify information. § 1.4. The court in *Council for a Livable World v. Dept. of State*, No. 96-1807 (D.D.C. Nov. 23, 1998), indicated that records requested under FOIA could not be classified by the agency's FOIA Officer because the classification authority must be an agency head, deputy head or senior officials authorized under Section 5.6 of EO 12958.

2.3.2. Identification and Markings.

2.3.2.1. Basic Markings—At the time of original classification the document must be marked to show the identity of the classification authority, the classification level, declassification instructions, the agency and office of origin, and "a concise reason for classification" which, at a minimum, cites the applicable classification categories. § 1.7(a).

2.3.2.2. Unclassified portions—Unless a special waiver is obtained, documents must be marked to clearly indicate which portions are classified, which portions are exempt from declassification, and which portions are unclassified (and hence subject to release under the segregable portions provision of the FOIA). § 1.7(b).

2.3.3. Classification after an FOIA request. Information not previously disclosed to the public under proper authority may be classified or reclassified after an agency has received a request for it under the Freedom of Information Act or the Privacy Act, or the mandatory review provisions of the Executive Order (§ 3.6) "if such classification meets the requirements of this Order and is accomplished on a document-by-document basis with the personal participation or under the direction of" particular designated officials. § 1.7(d). *See Miller v. Department of State*, 779 F.2d 1378, 1388 (8th Cir. 1985), citing *Baez v. DOJ*, 647 F.2d 1328, 1332-33 (D.C. Cir. 1980). *See also Goldberg v. Department of State*, 818 F.2d 71, 80-81 (D.C. Cir. 1987), ("Neither FOIA nor Executive Order 12356 impose any additional requirements on agencies when they reclassify documents than when they initially classify them pursuant to a FOIA request. In order to controvert a reclassification decision, a FOIA petitioner must do more than point to evidence that the information sought was at some previous time classified differently. His contrary evidence must somehow undermine or call into question the correctness of the classification status of the withheld information or the agency's explanation for the classification.").

2.3.4. Refusal to confirm or deny. Section 3.7(a) of the Executive Order provides that "[a]n agency may refuse to confirm or deny the existence or nonexistence of requested information whenever the fact of its existence or nonexistence is itself classified under this Order." *See* § 4.5., *infra*.

2.3.5. Executive Order Restrictions on Access to Classified Information.

2.3.5.1. Access to classified information may be given only to persons with a "need-to-know" the information in order to perform or assist in a lawful and authorized governmental function, provided that such persons have also received a favorable determination of eligibility for such access and have signed an approved nondisclosure agreement. § 4.2(a).

2.3.5.2. The "need-to-know" requirement may be waived for persons engaged in historical research projects or who previously occupied policy-making positions to which they were appointed by the President. § 4.5(a).

3. **Judicial Review of Substantive Criteria. The FOIA allows the courts to make an independent determination regarding the withholding of records: "[T]he court shall determine the matter *de novo*, and may examine the contents of such agency records in camera to determine whether such records or any part thereof shall be withheld under any of the exemptions set forth in subsection (b) of this section, and the burden is on the agency to sustain its action." § 552(a)(4)(B).**

3.1. A panel of the D.C. Circuit, in *Ray v. Turner*, 587 F.2d 1187 (D.C. Cir. 1978), explained the standard for such judicial review in national security cases: The salient characteristics of *de novo* review in the national security context can be summarized as follows: (1) the government has the burden of establishing an exemption. (2) The court must make a *de novo* determination. (3) In doing this, it must first "accord substantial weight to an agency's affidavit concerning the details of the classified status of the disputed record." (4) Whether and how to conduct an *in camera* examination of the documents rests in the sound discretion of the court, in national security cases as in all other cases. To these observations should be added an excerpt from our opinion in *Weissman* (as revised): "If exemption is claimed on the basis of national security the District Court must, of course, be satisfied that proper procedures have been followed, and that by its sufficient description the contested document logically falls into the category of the exemption indicated." *Ray v. Turner*, 587 F.2d 1187, 1194-95 (D.C. Cir. 1978), *quoting Weissman v. CIA*, 565 F.2d 692, 687 (1977). *See also Hayden v. NSA*, 608 F.2d 1381, 1384 (D.C. Cir. 1979), *cert. denied*, 446 U.S. 937 (1980).

3.2. In the original unreported version of an opinion later amended *sua sponte*, a panel of the U.S. Court of Appeals for the D.C. Circuit mistakenly held that a court could not "substitute its judgment for that of the agency." *Weissman v. CIA*, No. 76-1566 (D.C. Cir., Jan. 6, 1977) slip op. at 10-12 n.10. The amended opinion, corrected by Order of April 4, 1977, is reported at 565 F.2d 692 (D.C. Cir. 1977).

3.3. "Unfortunately, some courts…relied on the version of *Weissman* before the amendments were published." *Ray v. Turner*, 587 F.2d 1187, 1192 n. 14 (D.C. Cir. 1978). *See, e.g., Bell v. United States*, 563 F.2d 484, 487 (1st Cir. 1977). *Ray* suggested that, in making its *de novo* determination, the court must decide that the information is properly classified.

3.4. Most post-*Ray* panel decisions have held, however, that the court need not do so if there is a "reasonable" basis for finding potential harm, the information logically falls within the claimed exemption, and there is no evidence to controvert the government's claim or to suggest bad faith. *See, e.g., Abbotts v. NRC*, 766 F.2d 604, 606 (D.C. Cir. 1985); *Miller v. Casey*, 730 F.2d 773, 776 (D.C. Cir. 1984); *Salisbury v. United States*, 690 F.2d 966, 970 (D.C. Cir. 1982); *Gardels v. CIA*, 689 F.2d 1100, 1104-05 (D.C. Cir. 1982); *Military Audit Project v. Casey*, 656 F.2d 724, 738 (D.C. Cir. 1981); *Lesar v. DOJ*, 636 F.2d 472, 481 (D.C. Cir. 1980); *Baez v. DOJ*, 647 F.2d 1328, 1335 (D.C. Cir. 1980); *Halperin v. CIA*, 629 F.2d 144, 147-48 (D.C. Cir. 1980); *Hayden v. NSA*, 608 F.2d 1381, 1387 (D.C. Cir. 1979). *But see Goldberg v. Department of State*, 818 F.2d 71, 77 (D.C. Cir. 1987), stating that courts should accord "substantial weight" to an agency's affidavit "without relinquishing their independent responsibility" to determine the propriety of a classification decision; and *Allen v. CIA*, 636 F.2d 1287,

1294 (D.C. Cir. 1980), applying the *Ray* standard and emphasizing that the 1974 FOIA amendments established a *de novo*, rather than a "reasonable basis," review standard. *See also Fitzgibbon v. CIA*, 578 F. Supp. 704 (D.D.C. 1983), *rev'd in part and remanded*, 911 F.2d 755 (D.C. Cir. 1990), where the district court applied the *de novo* review standard and ordered the release of documents which the CIA asserted were exempt from disclosure on national security grounds. However, the effect of this decision was reversed by the Supreme Court in *CIA v. Sims*, 471 U.S. 159 (1985), resulting in the subsequent withholding of most of the information previously ordered to be released. *See Fitzgibbon v. CIA*, 911 F.2d 755 (D.C. Cir. 1990).

3.5. Another panel opinion of the U.S. Court of Appeals for the D.C. Circuit stopped short even of the "reasonable basis" standard of review in a FOIA case regarding U.S. Army classified documents. Citing a "state secrets" case in support of the "utmost deference" standard of review, the court stated, "[i]n view of the knowledge, experience and positions held by the three affiants regarding military secrets, military planning and national security, their affidavits were entitled to the 'utmost deference.'" *Taylor v. Department of the Army*, 684 F.2d 99, 109 (D.C. Cir. 1982), citing *Halkin v. Helms*, 598 F.2d 1, 9 (1978).

3.6. Failure to show a legitimate national security reason for conducting an investigation into an individual's activities does not invalidate the agency's Exemption 1 claim for denying the individual's FOIA request, since "the focus in Exemption 1 cases is the withheld information itself, not the reason for the underlying investigation." *Lieverman v. DOJ*, 597 F. Supp. 84, 87 (E.D. Pa. 1984), *citing Lesar v. DOJ*, 636 F.2d 472, 483 (D.C. Cir. 1980), and *LaRouche v. Kelley*, 522 F. Supp. 425, 435 (S.D.N.Y. 1981).

4. Special Issues.

4.1. Segregability.

4.1.1. The segregability provision of the FOIA, § 552(b), ("Any reasonably segregable portion of a record shall be provided ...") applies to documents even where Exemption 1 is claimed. *Paisley v. CIA*, 712 F.2d 686, 700 (D.C. Cir. 1983), *vacated in part, mot. to intervene granted, reh'g granted*, 724 F.2d 201 (D.C. Cir. 1984); *Founding Church of Scientology v. Bell*, 603 F.2d 945, 950-51 (D.C. Cir. 1979); *Church of Scientology v. Department of the Army*, 611 F.2d 738, 743-44 (9th Cir. 1979); *Ray v. Turner*, 587 F.2d 1187, 1197 (D.C. Cir. 1978); *Branch v. FBI*, 658 F. Supp. 204, 210-11 (D.D.C. 1987). *Accord Allen v. CIA*, 636 F.2d 1287, 1293 (D.C. Cir. 1980). *See also Hoch v. CIA*, 593 F. Supp. 675 (D.D.C. 1984).

4.1.2. The segregability provision does not mean, however, that unclassified items or portions of a document must be released if a compilation of the individual unclassified items of information viewed together warrants classification of the whole document. *See American Friends Service Committee v. Department of Defense*, 831 F.2d 441, 444-45 (3d Cir. 1987); *Taylor v. Department of the Army*, 684 F.2d 99, 109 (D.C. Cir. 1982); *Halperin v. NSC*, 452 F. Supp. 47 (D.D.C. 1978), *aff'd without opinion*, 612 F.2d 586 (D.C. Cir. 1980).

4.1.3. *See* Chapter 15 on Segregable Portions.

4.2. Affidavits.

4.2.1. For Exemption 1 claims, as elsewhere, "the significance of agency affidavits in a FOIA case cannot be underestimated." *King v. DOJ*, 830 F.2d 210, 218 (D.C. Cir. 1987).

4.2.2. In *King*, the court refused to accept the FBI's *Vaughn* affidavit in the form of copies of the released documents with deletions annotated by a code that referred to explanations for withholding in an accompanying code-catalogue. Although the FBI asserted this would "provide a more workable *Vaughn* index format and thus reduce the burden of analyzing Exemption 1 claims," the court found that the system "neither adequately describes redacted material nor explains, with sufficient specificity to enable meaningful review, how its disclosure would likely impair national security." *King v. DOJ*, 830 F.2d 210, 220 (D.C. Cir. 1987).

4.2.3. However, in *Keys v. DOJ*, 830 F.2d 337 (D.C. Cir. 1987), a different panel of the same court accepted the same system that was rejected in *King* for an exemption 7 claim. The *King* case was distinguished on the grounds that the similar system used there for Exemption 1 claims left the court "no contextual description for documents or substantial portions of documents withheld in their entirety," and it was noted that the same coding system used in *Keys* for Exemption 7 claims was upheld as adequate in *King*. *See King v. DOJ*, 830 F.2d 210, 350 (D.C. Cir. 1987), comparing system in *Keys* with other cases where "functional categories" were used.

4.2.4. In *Wiener v. FBI*, 943 F.2d 972 (9th Cir. 1991), *cert. denied*, 505 U.S. 1212 (1992), the Ninth Circuit concurred with *King* in finding FBI affidavits inadequate in support of exemptions 1, 3 (CIA information), and 7. The court termed the affidavits "boilerplate," and noted that "[n]o effort is made to tailor the explanation to the specific document withheld." 943 F.2d at 978-79. The Supreme Court refused the government's request for review. *See also Canning v. DOJ*, 848 F. Supp. 1037, 1042-5 (D.D.C. 1994) (citing *King* on standards for use of coded affidavits).

4.3. *In Camera* Inspection of Records.

4.3.1. Before undertaking *in camera* inspection of the withheld records, the court must give the government an opportunity to demonstrate by affidavits that the documents are exempt; but in many situations, *in camera* inspection will "plainly be necessary and appropriate." Conference Report on 1974 amendments at 8-9 (reprinted at Appendix at A). *See Allen v. CIA*, 636 F.2d 1287, 1298-1300 (D.C. Cir. 1980), for a description of when *in camera* inspection is especially appropriate. *See also Patterson v. FBI*, 893 F.2d 595, 598-601 (3d Cir), *cert. denied*, 498 U.S. 812 (1990); *Pollard v. FBI*, 705 F.2d 1151, 1154 (9th Cir. 1983); *Salisbury v. United States*, 690 F.2d 966, 973 n.3 (D.C. Cir. 1982) (resort to *in camera* proceedings was not strictly necessary but was within the discretion of the district court); *Hrones v. CIA*, 685 F.2d 13, 18 (1st Cir. 1982) ("It is well within the discretion of a district judge to [not conduct] an *in camera* inspection if the agency submits [adequate] affidavits"); *Hayden v. NSA*, 608 F.2d 1381, 1386-87 (D.C. Cir. 1979) (the court is to afford the agency the opportunity to meet its burden by submitting affidavits and other evidence to the court before ordering an *in camera* inspection of documents); *Church of Scientology v. Department of the Army*, 611 F.2d 738, 743-44 (9th Cir. 1979) ("the burden of proof in FOIA cases remains squarely on the government, and...*in camera* inspection is a procedure which the trial court need invoke only where it finds inspection appropriate, in its discretion"); *Ray v. Turner*, 587 F.2d 1187, 1195 (D.C. Cir. 1978) (*in camera* inspection may be undertaken "without anxiety that the law interposes an extraordinary hurdle to such inspection"). *But see Hoch v. CIA*, 593 F. Supp. 675, 680-84 (D.D.C. 1984) (court refused to conduct *in camera* review, despite allegations of agency's "bad faith" and "conclusory" affidavits).

4.3.2 However, courts have also refused to conduct *in camera* inspections where the government failed to provide an adequate public *Vaughn* index. *See Wiener v. FBI*, 943 F.2d 972, 979 (9th Cir. 1991) ("*In camera* review of the withheld documents by the court is not an acceptable substitute for an adequate *Vaughn* index. *In camera* review does not permit effective advocacy").

4.3.3. Bad faith. "Where the record contains a showing of bad faith, the district court would likely require *in camera* inspection." *Ray v. Turner*, 587 F.2d 1187, 1195 (D.C. Cir. 1978). *See also Allen v. CIA*, 636 F.2d 1287, 1298 (D.C. Cir. 1980). However, "*[i]n camera* inspection does not depend on a finding or even tentative finding of bad faith. A judge has discretion to order *in camera* inspection on the basis of an uneasiness, or a doubt he wants satisfied before he takes responsibility for a *de novo* determination. Government officials who would not stoop to misrepresentation may reflect an inherent tendency to resist disclosure, and judges may take this natural inclination into account." *Ray*, 587 F.2d at 1195.

4.3.3.1. The courts have rejected arguments that a subsequent release of information that had initially been withheld in the course of FOIA litigation proves that the agency was acting in "bad faith" by submitting a false affidavit. See *Military Audit Project v. Casey*, 656 F.2d 724, 738 (D.C. Cir. 1981); *Ground Saucer Watch v. CIA*, 692 F.2d 770, 772 (D.C. Cir. 1981). In *Military Audit Project*, the court noted that the contrary position "would work mischief in the future by creating a disincentive for an agency to reappraise its position, and when appropriate, release documents previously withheld." 656 F.2d at 754.

4.3.3.2. For further discussions of "bad faith" and *in camera* inspection, *see Meeropol v. Meese*, 790 F.2d 942, 958 (D.C. Cir. 1986); *McGehee v. CIA*, 697 F.2d 1095 (D.C. Cir. 1983), *vacated in part and aff'd in part*, 711 F.2d 1076 (D.C. Cir. 1983); and *Hoch v. CIA*, 593 F. Supp. 675, 680-81 (D.D.C. 1984).

4.3.4. Public Interest in Disclosure. "In cases that involve a strong public interest in disclosure there is...a greater call for *in camera* inspection." *Allen v. CIA*, 636 F.2d 1287, 1294 (D.C. Cir. 1980).

4.4. *Ex Parte* Submissions of Government Affidavits.

4.4.1. Where the government seeks to present *ex parte, in camera* affidavits, the court should attempt to establish as detailed a public record as possible, first by requiring the submission of detailed public affidavits and then by allowing plaintiffs to test them through appropriate discovery. Only when this process is complete should the court "if necessary, consider arguments or information which the Agency is unable to make public." *Phillippi v. CIA*, 546 F.2d 1009, 1013 (D.C. Cir. 1976). *Accord Hayden v. NSA*, 608 F.2d 1381, 1384 (D.C. Cir. 1979).

4.4.2. Although in some cases *in camera* affidavits have been found to be appropriate, courts have held that such affidavits do not permit plaintiffs to respond, and thus should be employed "only where absolutely necessary." *Allen v. CIA*, 636 F.2d 1287, 1294 (D.C. Cir. 1980). *See also Doyle v. FBI*, 722 F.2d 554, 556-57 (9th Cir. 1983); *Ray v. Turner*, 587 F.2d 1187, 1212 (Wright, J., concurring) (D.C. Cir. 1978). *But see Hayden v. NSA*, 608 F.2d 1381, 1385 (D.C. Cir. 1979) (*in camera* affidavit accepted without *in camera* review of documents themselves).

4.4.3. The district court, in permitting the government to submit an *ex parte, in camera* affidavit, may subsequently order that a portion of the affidavit be made public. *Hayden v. NSA*, 608 F.2d 1381, 1388 (footnote omitted) (D.C. Cir. 1979). ("This court has held that when materials exempt under the FOIA contain reasonably segregable parts that are not exempt, those parts should be disclosed; the same policy applies to segregable, nonsensitive portions of a classified affidavit").

4.4.4. Any *ex parte* oral communications made to the district court should be recorded and made available for appellate review. *Pollard v. FBI*, 705 F.2d 1151, 1154 (9th Cir. 1983).

4.4.5. The district court may permit counsel for plaintiff to participate in an *in camera* review. *See* general discussion of this issue in Chapter 21 on Litigation Strategy.

4.4.6. No court has authorized counsel for the plaintiff to participate in an *in camera* proceeding in an Exemption 1 case; but Judge Wright, in his concurring opinion in *Ray v. Turner*, 587 F.2d 1187, 1212 and n.50 (D.C. Cir. 1978), pointed out that the Congress which passed the 1974 amendments to the FOIA encouraged such participation by counsel "whenever possible." *See also Founding Church of Scientology of Washington v. NSA*, 610 F.2d 824, 833 n.74 (D.C. Cir. 1979); *but see Hayden v. NSA*, 608 F.2d 1381, 1385-86 (D.C. Cir. 1979), holding that such a procedure is most likely inappropriate in national security cases ("We agree that a court has inherent discretionary power to allow such access where appropriate; but it is not appropriate, and not possible without grave risk, to allow access to classified defense-related material to counsel who lack security clearance..." *Id.* at 1386.). *See also Arieff v. Department of the Navy*, 712 F.2d 1462, 1470 (D.C. Cir. 1983) (as a general matter, access to *in camera* submissions by counsel is not appropriate in FOIA cases); *Salisbury v. United States*, 690 F.2d 966, 973 n.3 (D.C. Cir. 1982) ("In any FOIA case in which considerations of national security mandate *in camera* proceedings, the District Court may act to exclude outside counsel when necessary for secrecy or other reasons"); *Weberman v. NSA*, 668 F.2d 676, 678 (2d Cir. 1982) ("The risk presented by participation of counsel... outweighs the utility of counsel, or adversary process, in construing a [classified affidavit]").

4.4.7. Adversary *in camera* proceedings have been approved in non-FOIA cases involving national security materials. *See, e.g., United States v. AT&T*, 567 F.2d 121, 133-34 (D.C. Cir. 1977). *But see Ellsberg v. Mitchell*, 709 F.2d 51, 61 (D.C. Cir. 1983), *cert. denied sub nom., Russo v. Mitchell*, 465 U.S. 1038 (1984).

4.5. Existence of Documents.

4.5.1. In some situations the government argues that it cannot confirm or deny the existence of documents responsive to a request. *See* Chapter 1, Overview, and section 2.3.4. of this chapter.

4.5.2. In such cases, known as "Glomarization," the court must first treat the fact of the existence of the documents as the request and proceed with the procedures fashioned by the courts. *Phillippi v. CIA*, 546 F.2d 1009, 1012-13 (D.C. Cir. 1976) ("The Agency [must] provide a public affidavit explaining in as much detail as is possible the basis for its claim that it can be required neither to confirm nor to deny the existence of the requested records." This case concerned a request for records about the Glomar Explorer, a ship designed to retrieve a sunken Soviet submarine). *See also Miller v. Casey*, 730 F.2d 773 (D.C. Cir. 1984); *Gardels v. CIA*, 689 F.2d 1100 (D.C. Cir. 1982); *Nuclear Control Institute v. Nuclear Regulatory Commission*, 563 F. Supp. 768 (D.D.C. 1983) (document "unquestionably exists" where court received sworn affidavit of authorship; it was a major topic of discussion at three Congressional hearings; and, "even more importantly," defendant itself did not refuse to confirm or deny its existence).

4.5.3. Examples of courts upholding the "neither confirm nor deny" response include *Hudson River Sloop Clearwater v. Department of the Navy*, 891 F.2d 414 (2d Cir. 1989) (whether certain navy ships carried nuclear weapons); and *Marrera v. DOJ*, 622 F. Supp. 51 (D.D.C. 1985) (records pertaining to targets of surveillance under the Foreign Intelligence Surveillance Act).

4.5.4. In the Anti-Drug Abuse Act of 1986, Congress enacted amendments to the FOIA which, *inter alia*, authorize the FBI to refuse to acknowledge the existence of records pertaining to foreign intelligence, counterintelligence, or international terrorism, for "as long as the existence of the records remains classified information." § 552(c)(3). *See* Chapter 18 on Records Exclusions.

4.6. Publicly Known Information.

4.6.1. A number of courts have shown a willingness to accept the argument that publicly known information cannot be withheld under Exemption 1. *See, e.g., Founding Church of Scientology of Washington v. NSA*, 610 F.2d 824, 831-32 (D.C. Cir. 1979) (suppression of "well publicized" information would frustrate policies of Act without advancing countervailing considerations); *Lamont v.*

DOJ, 475 F. Supp. 761, 772 (S.D.N.Y. 1979) (the "sunshine" purposes of FOIA would be thwarted if information remained classified after it became part of the public domain); *see also Military Audit Project v. Casey*, 656 F.2d 724, 741-45 (D.C. Cir. 1981) (concluding that precise information withheld had not been previously revealed); *Washington Post Co. v. Department of Defense*, 766 F. Supp. 1, 9-14 (D.D.C. 1991) ("It is a matter of common sense that the presence of information in the public domain makes the disclosure of that information less likely to 'cause damage to the national security'" *Id.* at 8).

4.6.2. However, even if a fact is the subject of widespread media and public speculation, "its official acknowledgment by an authoritative source might well be new information that could cause damage to the national security. Unofficial leaks and public surmise can often be ignored by foreign governments...but official acknowledgement may force a government to retaliate." *Afshar v. Department of State*, 702 F.2d 1125, 1130-31 (D.C. Cir. 1983). *See also Abbotts v. NRC*, 766 F.2d 604, 606 (D.C. Cir. 1985).

4.6.3. The D.C. Circuit has established three criteria for showing that information has been "officially acknowledged": "First, the information requested must be as specific as the information previously released. Second, the information requested must match the information previously disclosed;... Third,... the information requested must already have been made public through an official and documented disclosure." *Fitzgibbon v. CIA*, 911 F.2d 755, 765 (D.C. Cir. 1990), *citing Afshar v. Department of State*, 702 F.2d 1125, 1133 (D.C. Cir. 1983). *See also Public Citizen v. Department of State*, 11 F.3d 198, 201-204 (D.C. Cir. 1993) (reaffirming *Afshar* and *Fitzgibbon* in holding that information in transcript of U.S. Ambassador's conversation with Saddam Hussein was not officially released even though the Ambassador testified before Congress on the substance of the conversation).

4.6.4. Congressional publications, media reports, and "generalized statements" by the President and other Executive Branch officials do not constitute "official acknowledgment." *Peterzell v. CIA*, No. 85-2685 (D.D.C. July 11, 1986), slip op. at 4. *See also Hudson River Sloop Clearwater v. Department of the Navy*, 891 F.2d 414, 421-22 (2d Cir. 1989).

4.6.5. However, information disclosed by the government in an "off-the-record" press briefing is considered previously released, publicly known information. "[The] State [Department] would not logically have discussed such information with the press unless it was sure that a 'leak' would not breach national security." *Lawyers Committee for Human Rights v. INS*, 721 F. Supp. 552, 569 (S.D.N.Y. 1989), *reh'g denied*, 1990 U.S. Dist. LEXIS 6191 (S.D.N.Y. May 23, 1990).

4.6.6. The D.C. Circuit ruled that a letter from OPM telling a plaintiff that his retirement records were in the custody of the CIA did not constitute an official disclosure. Such a disclosure can only come from the agency with custody and control of the records. *Frugone v. CIA*, 169 F.3d 772 (D.C. Cir. 1999).

4.6.7. In *Students Against Genocide v. Department of State*, 257 F.3d 828 (D.C. Cir. 2001), the D.C. Circuit held that disclosure of satellite photos by UN Ambassador Madeleine Albright at a session of the UN Security Council did not constitute an official public disclosure. The court noted the disclosure was limited and controlled and that there was no indication Albright intended the use of the photos during her presentation to constitute a public disclosure.

4.6.8. A district court denied access to the CIA's FY 1999 budget even though the budget figures had been disclosed the two previous years and President Clinton had publicly indicated he believed the figures should normally be disclosed. The court ruled that it would not second-guess the affidavit of the Director of the CIA explaining why disclosure could be harmful. *Aftergood v. CIA*, 1999 U.S. Dist 18135 (D.D.C. Nov. 12, 1999).

4.6.9. A district court ruled that the CIA could not refuse to confirm the existence of biographies of Eastern bloc leaders because the agency had admitted in an officially-sanctioned journal article that it maintained biographies on the leaders of those countries. *National Security Archive v. CIA*, No. 99-1160 (D.D.C. July 31, 2000).

4.7. Constitutional Issue Concerning Court Ordered Release of Classified Information.

4.7.1. In 1974, President Ford vetoed the amendments to the FOIA that give the courts the power to release information that is classified by executive officials, on the grounds that it was an "unconstitutional" infringement of executive power. Congress overrode the veto, enacting the amendments into law. *See* section 7.3.6 *infra*.

4.7.2. In its briefs, the government has occasionally suggested that the courts do not have such power. *See, e.g.*, Petition for A Writ of Certiorari at 23, *Holy Spirit Association v. CIA*, 455 U.S. 997 (1982), *vacating in part as moot*, 636 F.2d 838 (D.C. Cir. 1980) ("[T]he Court should adopt a construction of the FOIA that avoids the grave constitutional question that would be presented if that Act were construed to permit the courts, in a case such as this, to substitute their judgment for that of the Executive regarding the need to maintain the confidentiality of information that could disclose intelligence sources or secret foreign government information.").

4.7.3. Because courts have so rarely ordered the release of materials that the government claims should remain classified, the constitutional issue has not been considered by any court thus far. In one case in which a court of appeals rejected an agency challenge to a district court's order to release assertedly classified information, *Holy Spirit Association v. CIA*, 455 U.S. 997 (1982), *supra*, possible consideration of this issue was eliminated when the requesters gave up their pursuit of the disputed materials and the Supreme Court ordered the judgment of the appellate court to be vacated "insofar as it affirms the decision of the United States District Court for the District of Columbia requiring the disclosure of the six documents in question" and remanded the case to the appellate court with directions to instruct the district court "to dismiss this aspect of the case as moot." 455 U.S. 997 (1982). *See Donovan v. FBI*, 806 F.2d 55, 60 (2d Cir. 1986) (appellate court affirmed lower court order to disclose classified documents based on finding that FBI "did not establish the logical basis for classifying the material"); *Bowers v. DOJ*, 930 F.2d 350 (4th Cir. 1991), *cert denied*, 502 U.S. 911 (1991).

4.8. Which Executive Order to Apply. Questions sometimes arise regarding which Executive Order to apply. The rule appears to be that the court, since it is reviewing an agency decision, will apply whatever order was in effect at the time of the last administrative review. *Lesar v. DOJ*, 636 F.2d 472, 480 (D.C. Cir. 1980) ("The general principle espoused here, then, is that a reviewing court should assess classification under the Executive Order in force at the time the responsible official finally acts"). *See also King v. DOJ*, 830 F.2d 210, 216-17 (D.C. Cir. 1987); *Meeropol v. Meese*, 790 F.2d 942, 959 (D.C. Cir. 1986); *Military Audit Project v. Casey*, 656 F.2d 724, 737 n.41 (D.C. Cir. 1981); *Baez v. DOJ*, 647 F.2d 1328, 1333-34 (D.C. Cir. 1980) (where "the governing Executive Order changes while the case is still under consideration in the trial court, the agency should be permitted to reassess its classification determination under the standards of the new Executive Order"). Similarly, if an Executive Order changes while a case is on appeal, the agency can apply the new Executive Order on remand if the original classification decision is found to be faulty. *Afshar v. Department of State*, 702 F.2d 1125, 1135-37 (D.C. Cir. 1983).

4.9. Exemption 3 Statutes.

4.9.1. Information may be withheld on national security grounds pursuant to Exemption 3, notwithstanding the fact that it is not classified. § 552(b)(3). *See* Chapter 5 on Information Exempted By Other Statutes, Sec. 6.4.1. Examples of such statutes include 50 U.S.C. § 403(d)(3) (protecting CIA intelligence sources and methods); 50 U.S.C. § 402 (protecting the activities of the National Security Agency); 10 U.S.C. § 2796 (Supp. 1991) (protecting certain information produced by the Defense Mapping Agency).

4.9.2. The CIA asserts that virtually all classified information exempt under Exemption 1 is also exempt under Exemption 3 as an intelligence source or method. The Supreme Court has interpreted Exemption 3 as allowing the CIA to withhold virtually all of its records from release under the FOIA. *CIA v. Sims*, 471 U.S. 159 (1985); *see also Knight v. CIA*, 872 F.2d 660, 664 (5th Cir. 1989), *cert denied*, 494 U.S. 1004 (1990); *Hunt v. CIA*, 981 F.2d 1116, 1120 (9th Cir. 1992) ("we are now 'only a short step [from] exempting all CIA records' from FOIA"); *Maynard v. CIA*, 986 F.2d 547 (1st Cir. 1993), (reversing a district court ruling that had found that the CIA's claim that disclosure would reveal sources and methods "is without substance and is, indeed, the height of bureaucratic disingenuousness"; the court of appeals found that "it is at very least 'arguable' that the requested" information falls within the CIA's exemption (b)(3) statute"). See also *Arabian Shield Development Co. v. CIA*, No. 3-98-0624 (N.D. Tex., Feb. 26, 1999) (agency need not confirm or deny existence of agency interest in award of oil producing sharing agreement with former Yemen Arab Republic in early 1980s) and *Frugone v. CIA*, 169 F.3d 772 (D.C. Cir. 1999) (agency need not confirm or deny that plaintiff was covert agent in Chile). See *generally* Chapter 5, Information Exempted by Other Statutes, Sec. 6.4.1.3.

5. Judicial Review Of Procedural Criteria.

5.1. "Exemption 1 requires that the most recent classification of a requested document be in conformity with both the procedural and substantive criteria of the then applicable

Executive Order." *See Lesar v. DOJ*, 636 F.2d 472, 480 (D.C. Cir. 1980); *Allen v. CIA*, 636 F.2d 1287, 1294-97 (D.C. Cir. 1980). *See* Conference Report at 12, in Appendix A.

5.2. Plaintiffs are entitled to discovery to determine if proper procedures were followed. *Schaffer v. Kissinger*, 505 F.2d 389, 390-91 (D.C. Cir. 1974); *Halperin v. NSC*, 452 F. Supp. 47 (D.D.C. 1978), *aff'd without opinion*, 612 F.2d 586 (D.C. Cir. 1980).

5.3. The consequences of failure to follow procedural requirements will vary depending on the degree to which the procedural error may have affected the classification decision. *Lesar v. DOJ*, 636 F.2d 472, 485 (D.C. Cir. 1980) (some procedural violations "may be of such importance to reflect adversely on the agency's overall classification decision, requiring a remand to the district court for *in camera* inspection; while others may be insignificant, undermining not at all the agency's classification decision"); *Baez v. DOJ*, 647 F.2d 1328, 1332-33 (D.C. Cir. 1980) (failure to classify at time of origin is insignificant error); *See also Taylor v. Department of the Army*, 684 F.2d 99, 105-6 (D.C. Cir. 1982) (purported failure of the Army to comply with its regulations regarding classification of documents was not a violation of sufficient significance to affect the result in the case); *Halperin v. Department of State*, 565 F.2d 699, 703-07 (D.C. Cir. 1977) (failure to apply the correct substantive standard and other procedural errors is sufficient to require disclosure unless the government can meet the standard for prior restraint; on remand, documents were released pursuant to a stipulation between the parties).

6. CIA Operational Files.

6.1. In 1984, Congress amended the National Security Act of 1947 to authorize the Director of Central Intelligence to exempt certain "operational" files of the CIA from the search and review requirements of the FOIA. CIA Information Act, P.L. 98-477, 50 U.S.C. § 431.

6.2. Through this statute, Congress hoped to relieve the agency of its frustrating administrative burden in having to search and review certain files that "almost invariably prove not to be releasable under the FOIA," thereby reducing the processing backlog and delays in responding to FOIA requests, "while preserving undiminished the amount of meaningful information releasable to the public," and providing additional assurance of confidentiality to CIA sources. H.R. Rep. No. 726, Part 1, 98th Cong., 2d Sess. 4 (1984) (House Permanent Select Committee on Intelligence).

6.3. The term "operational files" is defined in the statute (50 U.S.C. § 431(b)) to mean: (1) files of the Directorate of Operations which document the conduct of foreign intelligence or counterintelligence operations or intelligence or security liaison arrangements or information exchanges with foreign governments or their intelligence or security services; (2) files of the Directorate for Science and Technology which document the means by which foreign intelligence or counterintelligence is collected through scientific and technical systems; and (3) files of the Office of Security which document investigations conducted to determine the suitability of potential foreign intelligence or counterintelligence sources.

6.3.1. The House Intelligence Committee's exhaustively detailed report explains that the exemptions only apply to "the intelligence process as distinguished from the intelligence product." H.R. Rep. No. 726, *supra*, at p. 20-22. The statutory definition of "operational files" specifically excludes files "which are the sole repository of disseminated intelligence." 50 U.S.C. § 431(b).

6.4. The statute does not broaden the CIA's authority to withhold information, but it narrows the CIA's obligation to search and review files which, by definition, consist almost entirely of information the CIA already has authority to withhold as properly classified or subject to an Exemption 3 statute. *See* discussion at 6.4.1.3. in Chapter 5 on Information Exempted By Other Statutes.

6.5. CIA testimony before Congress indicated that the legislation would leave all intelligence disseminations including raw intelligence reports direct from the field, and all matters of policy formulated at Agency executive levels, including operational policy, subject to search and review requirements. House Report, *supra* at 8-9. The statute specifically provides that search and review requirements shall apply to:

6.5.1. exempted operational files for information concerning (1) U.S. citizens or permanent resident aliens who have requested information on themselves under FOIA or the Privacy Act; (2) any special activity, or covert action, the existence of which is no longer classified; or (3) the specific subject matter of an investigation for any impropriety or illegality in the conduct of an intelligence activity, 50 U.S.C. § 431(c); *see Sullivan v. CIA*, 992 F.2d 1249 (1st Cir. 1993) (construing these search and review exceptions);

6.5.2. files that are not exempted which contain information derived or disseminated from exempted operational files, 50 U.S.C. § 431(d)(1); and,

6.5.3. records from exempted operational files which have been disseminated to and referenced in files that are not exempted and which have been returned to exempted operational files for sole retention, 50 U.S.C. § 431(d)(3).

6.6. Subject to certain procedural limitations, the statute provides for *de novo* judicial review of a requester's claim that the CIA has improperly withheld records because of any violation of its provisions, including improper exemption of operational files and improper placement solely in exempted operational files. 50 U.S.C. § 431(f).

7. Legislative History of Exemption 1.

7.1. When Congress enacted the original version of the FOIA in 1966, it gave scant attention to national security information. The original FOIA exempted material "specifically required by Executive order to be kept secret in the interest of national defense or foreign policy."

7.2. In *EPA v. Mink*, 410 U.S. 73 (1973) the Supreme Court provided a definitive interpretation of the original FOIA exemption for national security information.

7.2.1. The Court held that Congress did not build into Exemption 1 any authority for judicial inspection of purportedly exempt records—the mere fact of classification was sufficient for withholding. Justice Stewart, concurring, characterized the FOIA as providing "no means to question any Executive decision to stamp a document 'secret', however cynical, myopic, or even corrupt that decision might have been." *Id.* at 95.

7.2.2. The Court also held that federal judges could not examine a classified document *in camera* to determine if there were segregable portions which were not classified and could be released. If any part of a document or even a file was classified, all of it was exempt. *Id.* at 84.

7.2.3. The Court noted, however, that "Congress could certainly have provided that the Executive Branch adopt new procedures or it could have established its own procedures—subject only to whatever limitation the Executive privilege may be held to impose upon such congressional ordering. *Cf. United States v. Reynolds*, 345 U.S. 1 (1953)." *Id.* at 83.

7.3. Through enactment of the 1974 amendments to the FOIA, Congress accepted part of the invitation of the *Mink* court by specifically authorizing *in camera* review and release of segregable portions even of classified documents. It also instructed courts to determine *de novo* whether information was properly classified according to the procedures and criteria of the Executive Order on national security information. § 552(a)(4)(B). Congress declined the invitation to establish its own standards and procedures for classification.

7.3.1. Even before the decision in *EPA v. Mink*, 410 U.S. 73 (1973), Congress had shown increasing concern with overclassification of national security information. Comprehensive hearings on government secrecy were held by the subcommittees of the House Government Operations Committee and the Senate Judiciary Committee which were responsible for the FOIA. *See* generally Executive Privilege, Secrecy in Government, Freedom of Information: Hearings on S.1142, S.858, S.Con.Res.30, S.J.Res. 72, S.1106, S.1520, S.1923, and S.2073 Before the Subcommittees on Administrative Practice and Procedure and Separation of Powers of the Senate Committee on the Judiciary and the Subcommittee on Intergovernmental Relations of the Senate Committee on Government Operations, 93d Cong., 2d Sess., Volumes I-III (1973); and U.S. Government Information Policies and Practices: Hearings Before A Subcommittee of the House Committee on Government Operations, 92nd Cong., 1st and 2d Sess. (9 parts) (1971 and 1972).

7.3.2. In considering what were to become the 1974 amendments, the House Government Operations Committee unanimously reported amendments to the FOIA, including a revision of Exemption 1.

7.3.2.1. The revised exemption would apply to matters which were "authorized under criteria established by an Executive order to be kept secret in the interest of the national defense or foreign policy." Another amendment specifically authorized *in camera* judicial inspection of classified documents. H.R. 12471, reprinted in House Committee on Government Operations and Senate Committee on Judiciary, *Freedom of Information Act and Amendments of 1974* (P.L. 93-502), 94th Cong., 1st Sess., March 1975, (cited as *Source Book*) at 147, 148.

7.3.2.2. The committee report stated that both changes were "aimed at increasing the authority of the courts to engage in a full review of agency action," thus reversing the decision, and to permit the court to look at the "reasonableness or propriety" of a classification. House Report No. 93-875 in *Source Book* at 127.

7.3.3. After extended discussion, the Senate Judiciary Committee proposed a revised Exemption 1 applying to matters which are "specifically required by an Executive order or statute to be kept secret in the interest of national defense or foreign policy and are in fact covered by such order or statute." *Source Book* at 192. Another amendment proposed by the Senate Judiciary Committee permitted *in camera* judicial inspection of classified materials but limited the scope of judicial review to determining if the classification decision had a "reasonable basis." S. 2543, *Source Book* at 189.

7.3.4. On the Senate floor, there was vigorous objection to the proposed "reasonable basis" scope of judicial review. On a motion by Senator Edmund Muskie, all of the proposed language relating to the scope of judicial review (proposed section (4)(B)(ii)) was stricken from the bill by a 56-29 vote. This left intact the authority for *in camera* inspection and the changed criteria for Exemption 1. *Source Book* at 302-328.

7.3.5. Following passage of proposed amendments in both Houses of Congress, the Conference Committee combined elements of both bills and reported Exemption 1 as it now appears in the statute.

7.3.5.1. The Conference report mandated *de novo* judicial review and authorized *in camera* inspection, and made clear that these provisions apply to Exemption 1.

7.3.5.2. "While *in camera* examination need not be automatic, in many situations it will plainly be necessary and appropriate. Before the court orders *in camera* inspection, the Government should be given the opportunity to establish by means of testimony or detailed affidavits that the documents are clearly exempt from disclosure. The burden remains on the Government under this law." Senate Report No. 93-1200 (Conference Report), 93d Cong., 2d Sess. at 9. (See the full text, at Appendix A).

7.3.5.3. In discussing the revised language of Exemption 1, the conferees noted that they "recognize that the Executive departments responsible for national defense and foreign policy matters have unique insights into what adverse affects might occur as a result of public disclosure of a particular classified record. Accordingly the conferees expect that Federal courts, in making *de novo* determinations in § 552(b)(1) cases under the Freedom of Information law will accord substantial weight to an agency's affidavit concerning the details of the classified status of the disputed record." *Report* at 12; Appendix A. The "substantial weight" language has been interpreted by many courts as giving the government exceedingly broad authority to withhold "national security" information.

7.3.6. After both houses approved the amendments, President Ford vetoed the bill, citing, *inter alia*, the provisions relating to national security. The President proposed that: where classified documents are requested the courts could review the classification, but would have to uphold the classification if there is a reasonable basis to support it. He called the bill "unconstitutional." *Source Book* at 484-85. Congress overrode the veto.

7.3.7. The legislative history is reviewed in *Ray v. Turner*, 587 F.2d 1187, 1192-94 (D.C. Cir. 1978). *See also* the opinion of Judge Wright, concurring in the interpretation of the legislative history, *Id.* at 1206-09, and *Allen v. CIA*, 636 F.2d 1287, 1294-97 (D.C. Cir. 1980).

CHAPTER 4

Exemption 2—Internal Agency Rules

Elaine English

1. **Exemption 2 provides that the FOIA does not apply to matters that are: "related solely to the internal personnel rules and practices of an agency."**

2. **Legislative History. It is clear that Congress intended Exemption 2 to significantly narrow the earlier Administrative Procedures Act exemption for "any matter relating solely to the internal management of an agency."** H.R. Rep. No. 1497, 89th Cong., 2d Sess. 5 (1966); S. Rep. No. 1219, 88th Cong. 2d Sess. 12 (1964); *Vaughn v. Rosen* (II), 523 F.2d 1136, 1141 (D.C. Cir. 1975). However, exactly what Congress meant this exemption to cover is less than certain. Exemption 2 is one of the best examples of the conflicts between the House and Senate Reports to the 1966 Act.

2.1. The Senate Report takes a narrow view of the exemption: "Exemption No. 2 relates only to the internal personnel rules and practices of an agency. Examples of these may be rules as to personnel's use of parking facilities or regulations of lunch hours, statements of policy as to sick leave, and the like." S. Rep. No. 813, 89th Cong., 1st Sess. 8 (1965), reprinted in *Freedom of Information Source Book: Materials, Cases, Articles Subcommittee on Administrative Practice and Procedures of the Committee on the Judiciary, U.S. Senate*, 93d Cong., 2d Sess. 43 (1974) (hereinafter cited as 1966 *Source Book*).

2.2. The House Report not only describes the exemption in much broader terms, as covering "[o]perating rules, guidelines, and manuals of procedure for Government investigators or examiners," but also contradicts the Senate Report by stating that the exemption "would not cover all matters of internal management such as employees relations and working conditions and routine administrative procedures... ." H.R. Rep. No. 1497, 89th Cong., 2d Sess. 10 (1966). (Reprinted in 1966 *Source Book* at 31).

2.3. The Senate Report has been favored and the House Report discredited by an overwhelming number of courts, including the Supreme Court. *See Department of the Air Force v. Rose*, 425 U.S. 352, 362-366 (1976); *Jordan v. DOJ*, 591 F.2d 753, 763-771 (D.C. Cir. 1978) (en banc); *Vaughn v. Rosen* (II), 523 F.2d 1136, 1140-1143 (D.C. Cir. 1975); *Stokes v. Brennan*, 476 F.2d 699, 703 (5th Cir. 1973); *Hawkes v. IRS*, 467 F.2d 787, 789 (6th Cir. 1972) *appeal after remand*, 507 F.2d 481 (6th Cir. 1974).

2.3.1. The Senate Report is consistent with the actual language of the exemption.

2.3.2. The Senate Report comports with the expressed congressional intention to narrow the scope of the previous exemption under the Administrative Procedure Act.

2.3.3. The Senate Report is more consonant with the FOIA's overall policy favoring broad disclosure and narrowly construed exemptions.

2.3.4. The Senate Report was the only committee report before both Houses when the Act was passed, and as one noted legal scholar has reasoned, "the basic principle is quite elementary: the context of the law must depend upon the intent of both Houses, not of just one." K. C. Davis, *Administrative Law Treatise* Sec. 5.3 (1978) at 313.

2.3.5. There is evidence that Executive pressure was responsible for the House language and that the managers of the House bill agreed to the broad report language in order to stave off a threatened veto. 1973 Senate Hearings, Vol. II at 122-26. *See Jordan v. DOJ*, 591 F.2d 753, 768-769 (D.C. Cir. 1978) (House report characterized as "last minute chicanery"); *Cox v. DOJ*, 576 F.2d 1302, 1309 (8th Cir. 1978).

3. **Exemption 2 has been construed by the Supreme Court in *Department of the Air Force v. Rose, supra.***

3.1. The Supreme Court held Exemption 2 inapplicable to case summaries of hearings concerning violations of the Air Force Academy's Honor and Ethics Code. Although the summaries clearly related to internal personnel matters—the discipline of Air Force cadets—the Court found that the public's interest in the integrity of its armed services removed this information from the category of matters of internal significance. "[This factor] differentiate[s] the summaries from matters of daily routine like working hours, which in the words of Exemption 2 do relate *solely* to the internal personnel rules and practices of an agency." *Department of the Air Force v. Rose*, 425 U.S. 352, 369 (1976), *quoting* from the court of appeals decision, 495 F.2d 261, 265 (2d Cir. 1974) (emphasis in original).

3.2. In reaching its conclusion in *Rose*, the Court relied heavily upon Judge Wilkey's opinion in *Vaughn v. Rosen* (II), 523 F.2d 1136, 1141 (D.C. Cir. 1975), *supra.*

3.2.1. The Court affirmed the distinction "between minor or trivial matters and those more substantial matters which might be the subject of legitimate public interest." *Id.* at 1142.

3.2.2. The Court affirmed Judge Wilkey's reasons for favoring the Senate Report over the House Report.

3.3. The Court's opinion in *Rose* identified the two divergent themes of Exemption 2 which have been developed by subsequent case law.

3.3.1. The Supreme Court stated that the "general thrust of the exemption is simply to relieve agencies of the burden of assembling and maintaining for public inspection matter in which the public could not reasonably be expected to have an interest." *Id. at* 369-70.

3.3.2. Because it was not at stake in the case before it, the Supreme Court left open the issue of whether Exemption 2 might permit "withholding of matters of some public interest… where necessary to prevent the circumvention of agency regulations that might result from disclosure to the subjects of regulation of the procedural manuals and guidelines used by the agency in discharging its regulatory function." *Id.* at 364.

4. Internal agency matters in which the public could not reasonably be expected to have an interest. ("Low 2" Exemption.)

4.1. The D.C. Circuit has held that Exemption 2 protects from disclosure symbols used to refer to FBI informants on the grounds that these are routine matters of merely *internal* significance in which the public lacks any legitimate interest. *Lesar v. DOJ*, 636 F.2d 472, 485 (D.C. Cir. 1980); *see also Branch v. FBI*, 658 F. Supp. 204, 208 (D.D.C. 1987); and *Albuquerque Publ'g Co. v. DOJ*, 726 F. Supp. 851 (D.D.C. 1989) (Ex. 2 protects both informant and violator identifier codes). The Fourth, Sixth and Seventh Circuits similarly have held that the FBI file numbers fall within the exemption); *Kiraly v. FBI*, 728 F.2d 273, 276 n.6 (6th Cir. 1984); *Scherer v. Kelley*, 584 F.2d 170, 175-76 (7th Cir. 1978), *cert. denied sub nom. Scherer v. Webster*, 440 U.S. 964 (1979); *Nix v. United States*, 572 F.2d 998, 1005 (4th Cir. 1978); *Maroscia v. Levi*, 569 F.2d 1000 (7th Cir. 1977). *See also Lieverman v. DOJ*, 597 F. Supp. 84 (E.D.Pa. 1984); *Malizia v. DOJ*, 519 F. Supp. 338 (S.D.N.Y. 1981).

4.2. Administrative file markings have been held exempt in *Meeropol v. Smith*, No. 75-1121 (D.D.C. Feb. 29, 1984) (handling and dissemination instructions of the FBI and internal markings of the Bureau of Prisons are "routine, housekeeping matters," "not substantively related to the Rosenberg investigation," and therefore neither the plaintiffs nor the public can "demonstrate a substantial interest in obtaining these instructions and markings"); *Nunez v. DEA*, 497 F. Supp. 209 (S.D.N.Y. 1980) (in the absence of any perceptible public interest in disclosure, internal markings used for storing, locating, retrieving or transmitting DEA documents are exempt); *Texas Instruments, Inc. v. U.S. Customs Service*, 479 F. Supp. 404 (D.D.C. 1979) (internal report numbers or access numbers relating solely to practices of Customs Service and of use only by agency personnel are exempt). *See also McCoy v. Moschella*, No. 89-2155, 1991 U.S. Dist. LEXIS 13618 (D.D.C. Sept. 30, 1991) (FBI file numbers classifying for internal purposes certain bank robbery investigation files are exempt). Similarly, computer codes have been held to be exempt in *Wightman v. BATF*, 755 F.2d 979, 982 (1st Cir. 1985). *But see, Thompson v. DOJ*, No. 96-1118 (D. Kan. July 14, 1998) (internal routing codes must be disclosed because they do not quality for 10th Circuit's limitation of Exemption 2 to only personnel matters)

4.3. Under the terms of a 1993 Attorney General memorandum, "Low 2" had virtually ceased to be a viable exemption to protect administrative markings. That memorandum had urged agencies to make discretionary releases in all cases except where the agency could reasonably foresee that disclosure would be harmful to an interest protected by the FOIA; since no foreseeable harm is associated with "Low 2," the DOJ had advised agencies to consider discretionary releases of administrative markings. On October 12, 2001 Attorney General Ashcroft issued a memorandum that expressly reverses the 1993 guidance and, therefore, is likely to reinvigorate agency use of "Low 2." *Ashcroft Memo, Appendix A. Also see Exemption 2 discussion in Applying the "Foreseeable Harm" Standard Under Exemption 5, FOIA Update, Spring 1994 (www.usdoj.gov/oip/foia_updates/Vol_XV_2/page3.htm) and Exemption 2 discussion in New Attorney General FOIA Memorandum, FOIA Post, Oct. 15, 2001 (www.usdoj.gov/oip/foiapost/mainpage.htm).*

4.4. The exemption was held inapplicable to instructions concerning the FBI's domestic surveillance program—COINTELPRO—on the ground that such communications have nothing to do with the internal personnel rules and practices of the agency. *Stern v. Richardson*, 367 F. Supp. 1316 (D.D.C. 1973). More recently, a federal court in Illinois found that materials dealing with how an agency responds to customer surveys and correspondence does not "bring the (b)(2) exemption into play." *Berg v. Commodity Futures Trading Commission*, No. 93C6741 (N.D. Ill. June 23, 1994).

4.5. The District of Columbia Circuit had earlier held CIA filing and routing instructions for information concerning the assassination of President Kennedy were not covered by Exemption 2 because such matters were not included in the narrow category of administrative personnel rules discussed in the Senate Report. *Allen v. CIA*, 636 F.2d 1287, 1290 (D.C. Cir. 1980). *See also Fonda v. CIA*, 434 F. Supp. 498, 503 (D.D.C. 1977) (filing instructions are not personnel matters). However, in *Founding Church of Scientology of Washington v. Smith*, 721 F.2d 828, 830 (D.C. Cir. 1983), the Court repudiated this narrow interpretation of Exemption 2 and overruled *Allen* at least to the extent it conflicts with the *(en banc) Crooker* decision. *See* Section 6, *infra*. *See also Hoch v. CIA*, 593 F. Supp. 675, 688 (D.D.C. 1984) (information processing and filing instructions of CIA are intelligence methods protected under 50 U.S.C. § 403(d)(3) and Exemption 3). *But see Fitzgibbon v. U.S. Secret Service*, 747 F. Supp. 51 (D.D.C. 1990) (rejecting use of Exemption 2 to protect administrative file markings because such markings are not related to an agency rule or practice, as required by *Schwaner v. Department of the Air Force*, 898 F.2d 793 (D.C. Cir. 1990)). *See* Section 7.3, *infra*.

4.6 More recently courts in the 6th, 9th, and 10th Circuits have rejected agencies' efforts to use Exemption 2 broadly to protect a variety of databases of information on the theory that each was designed solely for internal agency use. "We reject the claim that materials manifesting only an agency's 'practice of collecting information' are sufficiently related to an internal personnel rule or practice to be covered by the statutory language of Exemption 2." *Abraham & Rose, P.L.C. v. United States*, 138 F.3d 1075, 1081 (6th Cir. 1998) (IRS database of federal tax liens). *See also Maricopa Audubon Society v. U.S. Forest Service*, 108 F.3d 1082 (9th Cir. 1997) (nesting site maps of northern goshawks); *Audubon Society v. U.S. Forest Service*, 107 F.3d 1201 (10th Cir. 1997) (nesting site maps of Mexican spotted owl). *See also Schwaner v. Department of the Air Force*, 898 F.2d 793 (D.C. Cir. 1990) (for exemption 2 to apply, information must relate to the internal rules and practices of an agency). *See* section 7.3, *infra*.

5. Internal agency matters of some public interest where disclosure would risk circumvention of the law (i.e., law enforcement manuals) ("High 2" Exemption).

5.1. A split in authority exists over whether Exemption 2 authorizes the withholding of portions of agency manuals where disclosure would risk circumvention of agency regulation.

5.1.1. The Fifth, Sixth, and Eighth Circuits, relying on the Senate Report, have held that the exemption does not apply to such matters since they are not of merely internal personnel significance. *Stokes v. Brennan*, 476 F.2d 699, 703 (5th Cir. 1973) (training manuals for Occupational Safety and Health Administration); *Hawkes v. IRS*, 467 F.2d 787, 789 (6th Cir. 1972), *appeal after remand*, 507 F.2d 481 (6th Cir. 1974) (IRS auditing manual); *Cox v. DOJ*, 576 F.2d 1302, 1309 (8th Cir. 1978) (DEA enforcement manual). *But see Hobart Corp. v. EEOC*, 603 F. Supp. 1431 (S.D. Ohio 1984), *vacated*, 716 F. Supp. 307 (S.D. Ohio 1985) (applying *Crooker* test for Exemption 2). *See also* Section 7, *infra*.

5.1.2. The Second and Ninth Circuits, relying on the House Report, have held that the exemption applies to a manual of the Bureau of Alcohol, Tobacco and Firearms concerning how agents conduct raids and searches. *Caplan v. BATF*, 587 F.2d 544 (2d Cir. 1978); *Hardy v. BATF*, 631 F.2d 653 (9th Cir. 1980).

5.2. The District of Columbia Circuit has evolved its position more slowly, distinguishing between those aspects of agency manuals which set out "secret law" that must be disclosed and those portions which provide enforcement procedures where disclosure could risk circumvention of the law.

5.2.1. In an *en banc* decision in *Jordan v. DOJ*, 591 F.2d 753 (1978), the D.C. Circuit held that Exemption 2 "was not designed to protect documents where disclosure might risk circumvention of agency regulation" because such documents were not solely related to internal personnel rules and practices. *Id.* at 763-771. *See also Ginsberg, Feldman & Bress v. FEA*, 591 F.2d 717, 723-725 (D.C. Cir. 1978), *vacated and opinion of the district court affirmed by an equally divided court*, 591 F.2d 752 (D.C. Cir. 1978) (*en banc*), *cert. denied* 441 U.S. 906 (1979). *Accord Playboy Enterprises, Inc. v. DOJ*, 516 F. Supp. 233 (D.D.C. 1981) (rules, regulations and procedures relating to FBI's handling of informants are not protected by Exemption 2 because they have an impact on the public).

5.2.2. Subsequent to *Jordan*, a panel of the D.C. Circuit in *Cox v. DOJ*, 601 F.2d 1, 4 (D.C. Cir. 1979) (*per curiam*) held that portions of a manual specifying equipment to be used by U.S. marshals fell within Exemption 2 because such matters were of "merely internal interest" and were "unlikely to engage legitimate public interest."

5.2.3. The D.C. Circuit squarely faced the issue in *Crooker v. BATF*, No. 80-1278 (D.C. Cir. Nov. 12, 1980), *panel opinion vacated* (June 30, 1981), *reheard en banc,* 670 F.2d 1051 (D.C. Cir. 1981).

5.2.3.1. The full circuit overturned a panel decision written by Judge Wilkey which held that portions of a training manual concerning surveillance techniques were not exempt under Exemption 2. Deeming *Jordan* controlling, the panel held that "there could be little doubt that citizens have an interest in the manner in which they may be observed by federal agents" and that the portions of the manual could not possibly be assimilated to mere "internal housekeeping" concerns.

5.2.3.2. This position was rejected by the *en banc* court (with a vigorous dissent by Judge Wilkey), which held that the deleted portions of the training manual were exempt under Exemption 2. In reaching its conclusion, the court conducted a thorough analysis of both the legislative history and case law. Stating that the FOIA reflects an accommodation among goals of eliminating government secrecy, protecting individual rights and permitting the effective operation of the government, the Court carved out a narrow standard under the exemption for law enforcement materials.

5.2.3.3. It held that such material is exempt if (1) it is "predominantly internal" in nature, meaning it is designed to establish rules and practices of internal interest to agency personnel, and is not applicable to matters where there is a substantial public interest in disclosure; and (2) disclosure "significantly risks circumvention of agency regulations or statutes." *Id.* at 1056-57, 1073-74.

5.2.3.4. The court went to great lengths to explain that it was rejecting the rationale of *Jordan*, but concurring with its result. It recognized a distinction between information designed to regulate members of the public (the prosecutorial guidelines in *Jordan*), and those designed solely to regulate agency personnel (the manual instructing agents on how to observe, rather than regulate, the public conduct at issue in *Crooker*). The court also reiterated that the exemption could not be used to withhold material which amounted to "secret law." *See Fund for a Conservative Majority v. Federal Election Commission*, No. 84-1342 (D.D.C. Feb. 26, 1985) ("The critical test of predominantly internal is not whether the public is affected by the rules, but whether those rules constitute 'secret law.'"). *See also Windels, Marx, Davies & Ives v. Department of Commerce*, 576 F. Supp. 405, 411-413 (D.D.C. 1983) (computer program used to detect violations of U.S. anti-dumping laws may be withheld under Exemption 2 because the information instructs an internal agency computer, does not regulate public behavior, and disclosure would significantly risk circumvention of the law); *Wilder v. Commissioner*, 601 F. Supp. 241 (M.D. Ala. 1984) (part of agreement between state and federal revenue agencies that concerns exchange of information on potential tax law violations is exempt because it involves internal procedures which do not interpret substantive law applicable to the public, and disclosure could reveal "when violators will not be pursued."); *PHE, Inc. v. DOJ*, 983 F.2d 248 (D.C. Cir. 1993) (documents detailing records and sources of information utilized by agents in investigating obscenity cases may be withheld under Exemption 2 as disclosure would provide "violators with opportunity to impede lawful investigations by destroying or altering evidence"). *Cf. Don Ray Drive-a-way Co. v. Skinner*, 785 F. Supp. 198 (D.D.C. 1992) where the court found an algorithm used to determine safety ratings of motor carriers was not "purely internal" because of its legal effect on the carriers.

5.2.4. The 1986 FOIA amendments codified *Crooker*, as it applies to law enforcement agencies, into Exemption 7. *See Kaganove v. EPA*, 856 F.2d 884 (7th Cir. 1988), *cert. denied*, 488 U.S. 1011 (1989); *O'Connor v. IRS*, 698 F. Supp. 204 (D. Nev. 1988), *aff'd sub nom. O'Connor v. United States*, 1991 U.S. App. LEXIS 11989 (9th Cir. June 4, 1991); Chapter 10 on Law Enforcement Records.

5.2.5. After *Crooker*, however, the D.C. Circuit still faced an apparent conflict in its precedents. In *Founding Church of Scientology of Washington v. Smith*, 721 F.2d 828 (D.C. Cir. 1983), the court explained further how Exemption 2 should be construed in light of its *en banc* repudiation of the *Jordan* rationale.

5.2.5.1. Administrative filing and routing instructions, like those at issue in *Founding Church*, had been held to be unprotected by Exemption 2 in *Allen v. CIA*, 636 F.2d 1287, 1289-91 (D.C. Cir. 1980), despite an earlier ruling by the D.C. Circuit which approvingly cited contradictory holdings from other circuits with respect to identical materials. *See Lesar v. DOJ*, 636 F.2d 472, 486 n.77 (D.C. Cir. 1980), *citing Nix v. United States*, 572 F.2d 998, 1005 (4th Cir. 1978), and *Maroscia v. Levi*, 569 F.2d 1000 (7th Cir. 1977).

5.2.5.2. The court in *Founding Church* concluded that "to the extent *Allen* conflicts with our subsequent *en banc* decision in *Crooker*, it no longer represents the law of this circuit." *Founding Church*, 721 F.2d 828.

5.2.5.3. The court in *Founding Church* noted the "implication" in *Crooker* that materials such as routing and filing instructions, although within "the broader reading" of Exemption 2, "must be shown to threaten circumvention of agency regulation upon disclosure before withholding can be approved under the exemption." *Founding Church*, 721 F.2d 830 , *citing Crooker v. BATF*, 670 F.2d 1051, 1068 n. 48 (D.C. Cir. 1981). However, the court did not have to address this issue because the district court had found that disclosure of the information at issue "would risk circumvention of federal statutes," and thereby "satisfie[d] even the more rigorous standard applied in *Crooker*." *Founding Church*, 721 F.2d at 831.

5.2.5.4. In a lengthy footnote, the court in *Founding Church* set forth a suggested analysis for all Exemption 2 cases. *Founding Church*, 721 F.2d at 830-831 n.4. "First, the material withheld should fall within the terms of the statutory language as a personnel rule or internal practice of an agency...Then, if the material relates to trivial administrative matters of no genuine public interest, exemption would be automatic under the statute...If withholding frustrates legitimate public interest, however, the material should be released unless the government can show that disclosure would risk circumvention of lawful agency regulation." In order to comport with the FOIA's presumption favoring disclosure, the court stated that "a reasonably low threshold should be maintained for determining when withheld administrative material relates to significant public interests." *Id.*

5.3. Application of the *Crooker* and *Founding Church* analysis is not limited to situations where circumvention of "law" is at risk.

5.3.1. In *National Treasury Employees Union (NTEU) v. U.S. Customs Service*, 802 F.2d 525 (D.C. Cir. 1986), "crediting plans" used in selecting agency personnel for promotion were withheld on "circumvention" grounds and because disclosure "might provide unfair advantage to some candidates," thereby hampering the agency's ability to fairly evaluate all candidates.

5.3.1.1. The D.C. Circuit applied the "circumvention" standard of *Crooker*, "though this case does not snugly fit that decision's reference to agency regulations and statutes." *Id.* at 528.

5.3.1.2. The court noted that "an agency cannot be regarded as having satisfied the second prong of the *Crooker* test simply by promulgating a regulation designating certain material as confidential.... What a court obviously must do in this context is to determine whether the release of purportedly confidential material risks circumvention of some statute or regulation other than the one designating the material as confidential. Normally, an agency will be unable to satisfy the *Crooker* test unless it identifies such a statute or regulation and persuades the reviewing court that disclosure of the disputed documents will facilitate conduct that the statute or regulation proscribes." *Id.* at 530.

5.3.1.3. Although the Customs Service did not cite such a statute or regulation, the court viewed the case as "factually very similar" to *Crooker* and held that, "[w]here disclosure of a particular set of documents would render those documents operationally useless, the *Crooker* analysis is satisfied whether or not the agency identifies a specific statute or regulation threatened by disclosure." *Id.* at 530-531.

5.3.1.4. "Whatever else may be included within exemption (b)(2)," the court concluded, "we are of the view that Congress meant to include materials traditionally used by personnel officials to evaluate candidates for job promotion." *Id.* at 531.

5.3.2. The *NTEU* rationale was approved by the Seventh Circuit in *Kaganove v. EPA*, 856 F.2d 884 (7th Cir. 1988), *cert. denied*, 488 U.S. 1011 (1989), but only upon reversal of a district court decision which had distinguished the *NTEU* case while expressly declining to state whether it agreed with that decision.

5.3.2.1. The district court in *Kaganove* asserted that the appellate court in *NTEU* could not find a specific statute or regulation upon which the Customs Service could rely to withhold its crediting plan, so it "proceeded to judicially legislate a new exemption into the FOIA" to apply whenever "disclosure would quickly render those documents obsolete for the purpose for which they were designed." *Kaganove v. EPA*, 664 F. Supp. 352, 359 (N.D. Ill. 1987).

5.3.2.2. The district court found the *NTEU* rationale to be inapplicable to the EPA merit promotion rating plan because the plan did not contain exam questions and other detail which if disclosed would make it "obsolete" as in the case of the crediting plan at issue in *NTEU*. *Id.* at 361.

5.3.2.3. However, the appellate court in *Kaganove* found the construction of Exemption 2 in *NTEU* to be "consistent with the purposes of the FOIA," *Kaganove v. EPA*, 856 F.2d 884, 889 (7th Cir. 1988), and saw "no significant difference" between *NTEU* and the case before it. *Id.* at 890.

5.3.2.4. The appellate court noted that the question left open by the Supreme Court in *Rose* was whether Exemption 2 applied when "regulations or *standards*" might be circumvented, 425 U.S. at 364 (emphasis supplied), *Kaganove*, 856 F.2d at 889). "The word 'standards,'" the appellate court reasoned, "suggests that the Court envisioned that internal personnel documents might be exempt under Exemption 2 even if disclosure would not necessarily risk circumvention of 'law.'" *Id.*

5.3.2.5. Thus, the *Kaganove* court agreed with the court in *NTEU* "that *Crooker* was apposite whenever a document related to predominantly internal personnel matters and if disclosure of the document would render it 'obsolete for the purpose for which [it was] designed.'" *Id.* citing *NTEU*, 802 F.2d at 530.

5.3.3. In *Dirksen v. HHS*, 803 F.2d 1456 (9th Cir. 1986), the Ninth Circuit upheld Exemption 2 protection for Medicare claims processing guidelines on "circumvention" grounds. A vigorous dissent argued that, if disclosure of such a "claims processing blueprint" would in fact make it easier for claimants to conform their conduct more closely to the agency's rules, "the risk of circumvention is indistinguishable from the prospect of enhanced compliance." *But see Archer v. HHS*, 710 F. Supp. 909 (S.D.N.Y. 1989) (analysis of *Dirksen* used to allow withholding of only specific, segregable information which could lead to circumvention of Medicare claims system, but not the bulk of information necessary to permit a claimant to know the actual basis on which a claim was denied).

5.3.4. In *Institute for Policy Studies v. Department of the Air Force*, 676 F. Supp. 3 (D.D.C. 1987), a Security Classification Guide for a program designed to facilitate official radio communications in the event of a nuclear attack, though itself unclassified, was held exempt under the *Crooker* test for national security reasons. The court found that the use of Exemption 2 to withhold internal agency information on national security grounds "is not inconsistent with Exemption 1 [because]...[t]here is considerable overlap among the FOIA exemptions." *Id. See also* DOJ Guidance issued October 15, 2001 suggesting agencies should use Exemption 2 to protect vulnerability assessments and critical infrastructure information in light of terrorist events of September 11, 2001. *See New Attorney General Memorandum, FOIA Post, Oct. 15, 2001, infra.* and *Protecting Vulnerability Assessments Through Application of Exemption Two, FOIA Update, Spring 1989 (www.usdoj.gov/oip/foia_updates/Vol_X_3/page3.htm).*

5.3.5. In *Schiller v. NLRB*, 964 F.2d 1205 (D.C. Cir. 1992), agency guidelines on implementing the Equal Access to Justice Act were found withholdable under Exemption 2 because their disclosure "would quickly render the documents obsolete for the purpose for which they were designed," thereby compromising the Board's ability to defend itself in EAJA actions.

6. **The application of Exemption 2 to law enforcement manuals should also be considered in conjunction with § 552(a)(2)(C) which requires that "administrative staff manuals and instructions to staff that affect a member of the public" must be made available for public inspection and copying.**

Exemption 2

6.1. The government has argued that this section of the Act provides an independent exemption, in addition to the exemptions in § 552(b), for law enforcement manuals which are requested under § 552(a)(3). This argument is based on the legislative history, which indicates that the use of the word "administrative" was intended to exclude law enforcement manuals from the operation of § 552(a)(2)(C). S. Rep. No. 813, 89th Cong., 1st Sess. 2 (1965), reprinted in 1966 *Source Book* at 37; H.R. Rep. No. 1497, 89th Cong. 2d Sess. 7-8 (1965), reprinted in 1966 *Source Book* at 28-29.

6.2. This argument has been rejected by the D.C. Circuit, *en banc*, in both *Jordan*, 591 F.2d at 759-63, and *Crooker*, 670 F.2d at 1070-71, on the ground that § 552(b) provides the exclusive grounds for exemption in response to requests under § 552(a)(3). *See also Windels, Marx, Davies & Ives v. Department of Commerce*, 576 F. Supp. at 410 (because material falls within Exemption 2, it cannot be within § 552(a)(2)(C)). However, this argument has been accepted by the Eighth Circuit in *Cox v. DOJ*, 576 F.2d 1302 at 1306-09 (8th Cir. 1978). *See also Sladek v. Bensinger*, 605 F.2d 899 at 900-901 (5th Cir. 1979), *reh'g denied*, 618 F.2d 781 (5th Cir. 1980) (the court recognized an implicit exemption in § 552(a) (2)(C) but held it was not applicable to matters whose disclosure "would not obstruct DEA's law enforcement efforts").

6.3. The Sixth Circuit has held that whether § 552(a)(2)(c) is an additional exemption to requests under § 552(a)(3), or exempts only law enforcement matters from the affirmative publication requirement, it is "a very narrow one and is to be applied only where the sole effect of disclosure would be to enable law violators to escape detection." *Hawkes v. IRS*, 467 F.2d at 795.

6.3.1. This is because "secret law is an abomination," and one of the principal purposes of the FOIA is to eliminate secret law. *See NLRB v. Sears, Roebuck & Co.*, 421 U.S. 132, 153 (1975); *Ash Grove Cement Co. v. FTC*, 511 F.2d 815, 817-18 (D.C. Cir. 1975), *reh'g denied*, 519 F.2d 934 (D.C. Cir. 1975); *Hawkes v. IRS*, 467 F.2d at 795 n.10; *Sterling Drug, Inc. v. FTC*, 450 F.2d 698, 708 (D.C. Cir. 1971). "Information which merely enables an individual to conform his actions to an agency's understanding of the law applied by that agency does not impede law enforcement and is not excluded from compulsory disclosure under (a)(2)(C)." *Hawkes v. IRS*, 467 F.2d at 795.

6.3.2. Following the *Hawkes* rationale, the district court in *Roberts v. IRS*, 584 F. Supp. 1241 (E.D. Mich. 1984), held that the Law Enforcement Manual of the Internal Revenue Service is not subject to disclosure under § 552(a)(2)(c) because it contains "the kind of sensitive law enforcement information, disclosure of which will only serve to undermine law enforcement." *See also Hobart Corp. v. EEOC*, 603 F. Supp. at 1451, where the court found Title VII target criteria to be subject to § 552(a)(2)(c) mandatory disclosure because they encourage compliance, but ruled other criteria detailing enforcement guidelines to be exempt on "circumvention" grounds.

7. The application of Exemption 2 to lists of names and addresses of military personnel became a controversial issue when the Defense Department realized that, after *Hopkins v. Department of the Navy*, No. 84-1868 (D.D.C. Feb. 5, 1985), it could not rely on Exemption 6 to withhold the names and duty addresses of service members. *See* Chapter 9 on Personal Privacy.

7.1. In *Army Times Publ'g Co. v. Department of the Army*, 684 F. Supp. 720 (D.D.C. 1988), the court rejected the application of Exemption 2 and granted an Army-oriented newspaper's request for the names, addresses, grade levels, and installation locations of all active-duty Army personnel in the U.S.

7.1.1. The Army did not invoke the "circumvention" prong of the *Founding Church* analysis, but asserted that the databases of personnel names and stations have the exclusive purpose of "supporting and facilitating internal personnel activities." The court, however, rejected this "struggle to squeeze this case into the Exemption 2 mold" as "not pervasive." 684 F. Supp. at 723.

7.1.2. Although the plaintiff conceded that the requested lists would be used for direct solicitation efforts to find new subscribers, the court found that the record supported a substantial public interest in the broad circulation of the publication, and concluded that requester's commercial motive "does not detract significantly from the service that release of the requested records would provide to the public...." *Id.* at 723-724.

7.2. In *Retired Officers Ass'n v. Department of the Navy*, 716 F. Supp. 662 (D.D.C. 1989), *aff'd in part, rev'd in part*, 744 F. Supp. 1 (D.D.C. 1990), the court rejected an Exemption 2 claim for a list of the names and addresses of retired and retiring personnel when sought by a non-profit organization.

7.2.1. Citing *Army Times*, the court said it is not enough that the information was generated for facilitating matters of internal management; it must be disclosed if there is a "significant public interest," which is judged by "a reasonably low threshold." *Retired Officers Association*, 716 F. Supp. at 665. The court concluded that this non-profit organization, which benefited not only its members, but also the military and the general public, had stated a "significant public purpose."

7.2.2. The court, relying on *Schwaner*, *infra*, later affirmed its ruling in response to the government's request for reconsideration, *Retired Officers Association*, 744 F. Supp. 1 (D.D.C. 1990).

7.3. In *Schwaner v. Department of the Air Force*, 898 F.2d 793 (D.C. Cir. 1990), a panel of the D.C. Circuit rejected an Exemption 2 claim and granted an insurance seller's request for a list of enlisted personnel stationed at a particular base.

7.3.1. The district court had upheld the exemption claim, finding that the requester's "vague assertions of a theoretical public interest" in release of the records did not meet the "low threshold" of *Founding Church* in "this routine commercial context." *Schwaner v. Department of the Air Force*, 698 F. Supp. 4, 6 (D.D.C. 1988).

7.3.2. The court of appeals reversed, finding that the requested information did not meet the threshold of Exemption 2.

7.3.2.1. The court of appeals focused on the language limiting the exemption to the "rules and practices of an agency."

7.3.2.2. The Air Force had argued that the names and addresses were related to two agency practices—the practice of extracting and compiling data into its computerized personnel data system and the practice of assigning personnel. The court rejected both arguments as too "all-encompassing." The agency's first argument was rejected because its reasoning would literally protect all information maintained by the agency. The second was rejected because the court concluded that the list of names and addresses would shed only "insignificant light" on the agency's assignment practices.

7.3.3. Citing the Supreme Court's holding in *DOJ v. Reporters Comm. for Freedom of the Press*, 489 U.S. 749 (1989), that the identity of the requester must be disregarded, the court concluded that the commercial purposes of the requester could not be considered, no matter how "repugnant...it may seem to order disclosure to an insurance agency."

7.3.4. Judge Revercomb, in his dissent, argued that the court's emphasis on limiting the exemption to the "rules and practices" of an agency had turned the fundamental policy of FOIA on its head. He concluded not only that the list of names and addresses met the exemption's threshold but, because its disclosure would not serve any "core purpose" of the Act as required by the *Reporters Committee* case in the balancing of interests in Exemption 7(C) cases, there was no countervailing public interest to justify the disclosure of this list. See Chapter 9 on Personal Privacy.

CHAPTER 5

Exemption 3—Information Exempted by Other Statutes

Harry A. Hammitt

1. **Exemption 3 provides that the FOIA does not apply to matters that are: "specifically exempted from disclosure by statute (other than § 552b of this title), provided that such statute (A) requires that the matters be withheld from the public in such a manner as to leave no discretion on the issue, or (B) establishes particular criteria for withholding or refers to particular types of matters to be withheld."**

2. **The original language of Exemption 3, which Congress amended in 1976, provided simply that the FOIA did not apply to matters that are: "specifically exempted from disclosure by statute."**

2.1. The original purpose of Exemption 3 was to provide for the continued use of non-disclosure or confidentiality provisions already included in other statutes. Rather than require that each statute be cited as a separate exemption, Congress decided to allow agencies to cite Exemption 3 and then reference the other statute. *See* "Clarifying and Protecting the Right of the Public to Information," House Committee on Government Operations, Report No. 1497, 89th Cong., 2d Sess., May 9, 1966, p. 10.

2.2. Exemption 3 statutes are typically created as the result of parochial concerns at agencies or political pressure exerted on Congress by constituency groups. While arguably much of the information protected by Exemption 3 statutes could be protected by another of the broader based exemptions, an Exemption 3 statute is often seen as preferable to the interested segment of government or the private sector because it provides specific protection to a category of records and is more difficult to challenge in court.

3. **Purpose of the 1976 Amendment.**

3.1. Congress adopted the new language in 1976 to overcome the Supreme Court's ruling in *Administrator, FAA v. Robertson*, 422 U.S. 255 (1975).

3.2. In *Robertson*, plaintiffs sought disclosure of Systems Worthiness Analysis Reports (SWAP). The Federal Aviation Administration claimed Exemption 3 on the basis of § 1104 of the FAA Act of 1958, which allowed the Administrator to withhold data when, in his judgment, disclosure would adversely affect the submitter and is not required in the public interest.

3.3. The Supreme Court upheld the broad grant of discretion to the Administrator on the ground that a statute need not precisely name or list specific categories of data which may be withheld in order to fall within the exemption. Thus "when an agency asserts a right to withhold information based on a specific statute of the kind described in Exemption 3," the only question "to be determined in a district court's *de novo* inquiry is the factual existence of such a statute, regardless of how unwise, self-protective, or inadvertent the enactment might be." *Robertson*, 422 U.S. at 269-70 (concurring opinion of Stewart, J.).

3.4. Congress believed this interpretation was overly broad, gave too much discretion to agency officials to withhold data, and was therefore against the overall policy of the FOIA in favor of disclosure. H.R. Rep. No. 880, 94th Cong., 1st Sess. 23 (1976). It thus amended Exemption 3 in the process of enacting the Government in the Sunshine Act, P.L. 94-409, 90 Stat. 1241, codified at 5 U.S.C. § 552b. *See* Chapter 23 on Government in the Sunshine Act.

3.5. For further general discussion, see, e.g., *Association of Retired R.R. Workers v. U.S. R.R. Retirement Board.*, 830 F.2d 331, 333 (D.C. Cir. 1987); *Lessner v. Department of Commerce*, 827 F.2d 1333, 1336 (9th Cir. 1987).

4. Criteria for Withholding under Revised Exemption.

4.1. In order to support an Exemption 3 claim, (1) the statute must authorize or require withholding; (2) the language of the statute must meet the criteria of amended Exemption 3; and (3) the information requested must fit within a category of information that the statute authorizes to be withheld.

4.2. As with all FOIA exemptions, the government bears the burden of proving that requested records are properly withheld. Accordingly, the obligation to prepare a detailed *Vaughn* index applies fully in Exemption 3 cases, and the agency must "show specifically and clearly that the requested materials fall into the category of documents" that Congress has exempted from mandatory disclosure. *Hayden v. NSA*, 608 F.2d 1381, 1390 (D.C. Cir. 1979), *cert. denied*, 446 U.S. 937 (1980); *see also Founding Church of Scientology of Washington v. NSA*, 610 F.2d 824, 830 (D.C. Cir. 1979). Moreover the requirement regarding segregability applies in Exemption 3 cases so that agencies must divulge all portions of documents which are not specifically exempted from disclosure by statute. *See Irons v. Gottschalk*, 548 F.2d 992 (D.C. Cir. 1976), *cert. denied sub nom. Irons v. Parker*, 434 U.S. 965 (1977). Finally, since the applicability of Exemption 3 often turns on the factual content of specific documents, the criteria for determining the appropriateness of an *in camera* inspection is the same for Exemption 3 as for other exemptions. *See Ray v. Turner*, 587 F.2d 1187 (D.C. Cir. 1978) (specifically rejecting a lower court's conclusion that, with respect to documents withheld under Exemption 3, *in camera* inspection is seldom, if ever, appropriate or necessary).

5. The Statute Must Authorize or Require Withholding.

5.1. Is the authority cited for withholding under Exemption 3 a "statute?"

5.1.1. In *Founding Church of Scientology v. Bell*, 603 F.2d 945, 952 (D.C. Cir. 1979), the court held that Fed. R. Civ. P. 26(c) was not a "statute" within the meaning of Exemption 3 because the Federal Rules, which are issued by the Supreme Court under rulemaking powers delegated by Congress, "are not affirmatively adopted by the legislature, as all statutes must be."

5.1.2. In *Fund for Constitutional Gov't v. National Archives,* 656 F.2d 856 (D.C. Cir. 1981), however, the court upheld an Exemption 3 claim based upon Fed. R. Crim. P. 6(e). Distinguishing its ruling in *Bell*, the court found that Rule 6(e), unlike Rule 26(c), was "positively enacted by Congress." *Id.* at 867. See also *McDonnell v. U.S.*, 4 F.3d 1227, 1246-1249 (3d Cir. 1993) (construing exceptions to general rule of grand jury secrecy).

5.1.3. In *Berry v. DOJ*, 612 F. Supp. 45 (D. Ariz. 1985), the court concluded that Fed. R. Crim. P. 32, which requires a sentencing court to allow a defendant to read a presentence report excluding information that might result in harm to the defendant or others, was "affirmatively enacted" by Congress and is therefore a "withholding statute," but only to the extent that the court has properly ordered material withheld. *But see Fendler v. U.S. Parole Comm'n*, 774 F.2d 975, 978 (9th Cir. 1985) (court rules permitting viewing, but not copying, of documents are "irrelevant" in a FOIA action).

5.2. Did Congress intend the statute cited as authority for withholding to be a "delegation of authority to withhold information?" *See FAA Robertson*, 422 U.S. at 265.

5.2.1. This will sometimes be obvious on the face of the statute; however, where it is not obvious, the government has an obligation to meet its normal burden of proof under the FOIA by reference to the legislative history of the statute relied on for withholding.

5.2.2. Ordinarily, the authority to disclose particular types of information does not imply the converse authority to keep other types of information secret. For example, in *Mobil Oil Corp. v. FTC*, 406 F. Supp. 305 (S.D.N.Y. 1976), the court held that § 6(f) of the Federal Trade Commission Act (15 U.S.C. § 46(f)), which authorizes publication of information "except trade secrets and names of customers" when in the public interest, was not to be construed as authority to withhold information even if the Commission felt disclosure was not in the public interest. Similarly, in *Public Citizen Health Research Group v. FDA*, 704 F.2d 1280, 1284-85 (D.C. Cir. 1983), the court held that a statute which compels the FDA to divulge *summaries* of safety and effectiveness data regarding medical devices, 21 U.S.C. § 360j(h), does not reflect a congressional authorization for the FDA to withhold raw data submitted by manufacturers.

5.2.3. Responsibility to prevent unauthorized disclosure is authority to withhold in certain circumstances.

5.2.3.1. The National Security Act of 1947, as amended, provides, in pertinent part, "that the Director of Central Intelligence shall be responsible for protecting intelligence sources and methods from unauthorized disclosure." 50 U.S.C. § 403-3(c)(5) (1992).

5.2.3.2. The legislative history of the 1974 and 1976 amendments to the FOIA both contain references to 403(d)(3) as an Exemption 3 statute. *See CIA v. Sims*, 471 U.S. 159 (1985). In 1992, Congress reauthorized this provision. In its legislative history, Congress refused to endorse *CIA v. Sims*, and suggested that the provision be amended because of the *Sims* court's overbroad interpretation. Conf. Rep. No. 102-963, at 88, 1992 U.S. Code Cong. & Admin. News 2614.

6. The Language of the Statute Must Meet the Criteria of Exemption 3.

6.1. By the terms of Exemption 3, a statute must:

6.1.1. require withholding without permitting any discretion (Subpart (A)); or,

6.1.2. establish particular criteria for withholding or refer to particular types of matter to be withheld (Subpart (B)). *See Seymour v. Barabba*, 559 F.2d 806 (D.C. Cir. 1977).

6.1.2.1. There is no inconsistency between FOIA's *de novo* judicial review standard and Subpart B's inclusion of statutes authorizing agency discretion; Exemption 3 claims, like those of other exemptions, were expressly made subject to *de novo* review to "better serve the congressional purpose of assuring that any particular nondisclosure decision was the product of legislative rather than executive judgment." *Long v. IRS*, 742 F.2d 1173, 1182 (9th Cir. 1984).

6.1.2.2. A statute can qualify as withholding authority under the "particular types of matters" prong of Subpart (B) even if it identifies matters to be withheld by reference to the process by which they are collected, rather than their content. *Chong v. Drug Enforcement Administration*, 929 F.2d 729, 733-34 (D.C. Cir. 1991) (upholding Exemption 3 status of federal wiretap statute).

6.2. In essence, the statute must incorporate a Congressional mandate of confidentiality that is:

6.2.1. "absolute and without exception," *American Jewish Congress v. Kreps*, 574 F.2d 624, 628 (D.C. Cir. 1978); or,

6.2.2. the product of an appreciation of the dangers inherent in airing particular data, prescribing "a formula whereby the administrator may determine precisely whether disclosure in any instance would pose the hazard that Congress foresaw." *Id.* at 628-29.

6.3. The legislative history of the 1976 amendment included examples of what would and would not qualify under these criteria.

6.3.1. Exemption 3 statutes include:

6.3.1.1. 50 U.S.C. § 403g [122 Cong. Rec. H9260 (daily ed.) Aug. 31, 1976]. However, the scope of 403g extends only to information about the internal structure of the CIA and not to the Agency's functions in general. *Phillippi*, 546 F.2d 1009 (D.C. Cir. 1976).

6.3.1.2. 42 U.S.C. § 2000e-5(b) and 8(e), directing the EEOC to keep information based on charges of employment discrimination secret prior to the initiation of formal proceedings. (H.R. Rep. No. 880, 94th Cong., 2d Sess., Part I, p.23).

6.3.1.3. 42 U.S.C. § 2161-66, relating to atomic energy information. *Id.*

6.3.2. Statutes not included under Exemption 3:

6.3.2.1. 49 U.S.C. § 1504 (*Robertson statute*), S. Rep. No.1178, 94th Cong., 2d Sess. 25 (1976); H.R. Rep. No. 1441, 94th Cong., 2d Sess. 25 (1976).

6.3.2.2. 42 U.S.C. § 1306, prohibits disclosure of certain information except as prescribed by regulations. *Florida Medical Ass'n v. HEW*, 479 F. Supp. 1291 (M.D. Fla. 1979).

6.3.2.3. 18 U.S.C. § 1905, regarding trade secrets, although there has continued to be some confusion on this point. See discussion under 6.5, *infra*, and in Chapter 6 on Business Information and Chapter 7 on Reverse FOIA.

6.4. Since the 1976 amendment, courts have ruled on the Exemption 3 status of a number of statutes.

6.4.1. Statutes held qualified under Exemption 3:

6.4.1.1. 13 U.S.C. §§ 8(b) and 9(a), prohibiting use of information furnished under the Census Act for any purpose other than the statistical purposes for which it is supplied. *Baldridge v. Shapiro*, 455 U.S. 345 (1982); *Seymour v. Barabba, supra.*

6.4.1.2. Fed. R. Crim. P. 6(e), requiring that secrecy prevail regarding matters occurring before a grand jury. The scope of the secrecy encompasses not only the direct revelation of grand jury transcripts but also the disclosure of information which would reveal "the identities of witnesses or jurors, the substance of testimony, the strategy or direction of the investigation, the deliberations or questions of the jurors and the like." *Fund for Constitutional Gov't v. National Archives,* 656 F.2d at 869), quoting *SEC v. Dresser Industries, Inc.*, 628 F.2d 1368, 1382 (D.C. Cir.) (*en banc*), *cert. denied*, 449 U.S. 993 (1980). *But see Senate of the Commonwealth of Puerto Rico v. DOJ*, 823 F.2d 574, 581-584 (D.C. Cir. 1987), discussing the kinds of information that would or would not be exempt, and stating that presentation of materials to a grand jury does not automatically exempt them from disclosure; rather, there must be "some affirmative demonstration of a nexus between disclosure and revelation of protected aspect of the grand jury's investigation." *See also Church of Scientology Int'l v. DOJ*, 30 F.3d 224, 235 (1st Cir. 1994), distinguishing between "grand jury exhibits...whose contents are testimonial in nature or otherwise directly associated with the grand jury process" and business records or similar documents "created for purposes independent of grand jury investigations, which have legitimate uses unrelated to the substance of the grand jury proceedings."

6.4.1.3. 50 U.S.C. § 403-3(1)(5) (1992) (formerly codified at § 403(d)(3)), directing the CIA to protect "intelligence sources and methods from unauthorized disclosure," and § 403g, exempting the CIA from any law requiring "disclosure of the organization, functions, names, official titles, salaries, or numbers of personnel employed by the Agency." *CIA v. Sims*, 471 U.S. 159 (1985). It is now settled that these provisions may be invoked by the CIA regardless of whether the information is properly classified within the meaning of Exemption 1.

See Afshar v. Department of State, 702 F.2d 1125, 1138 (D.C. Cir. 1983), *citing Gardels v. CIA*, 689 F.2d 1100, 1107 (D.C. Cir. 1982). *See also Knight v. CIA*, 872 F.2d 660 (5th Cir. 1989); *Fitzgibbon v. CIA*, 911 F.2d 755, 762-763 (D.C. Cir. 1990) (application of Exemption 1 analysis to Exemption 3 matter is improper, at least if read to require consideration of the effect of passage of time on the sensitivity of withheld materials); *Hunt v. CIA*, 981 F.2d 1116 (9th Cir. 1992) ; *Maynard v. CIA*, 986 F.2d 547 (1st Cir. 1993) .

6.4.1.3.1. The CIA can more easily assert § 403g than § 403-3(c)(5) (1992), since the former requires no actual nexus between an intelligence function and the information withheld while the latter requires some showing that the release of data may lead to the unauthorized disclosure of intelligence sources and methods. *See Baker v. CIA*, 580 F.2d 664, 669 (D.C. Cir. 1978); *Times Newspapers of Great Britain, Inc. v. CIA*, 539 F. Supp. 678, 684 (S.D.N.Y. 1982).

6.4.1.3.2. For example, CIA could not use "intelligence sources and methods" language to protect authors, publishers and books involved in clandestine propaganda activities from disclosure. However, withholding would be proper if release of such material could reasonably be expected to lead to disclosure of intelligence sources and methods. *Navasky v. CIA*, 499 F. Supp. 269 (S.D.N.Y. 1980).

6.4.1.3.3. An "intelligence source" is any person or entity, whether confidential or not, that provides, has provided, or has been engaged to provide the CIA with information the Agency needs to fulfill its statutory obligations with respect to foreign intelligence. *CIA v. Sims*, 471 U.S. 159 (1985).

6.4.1.3.4. 403-3(c)(5) (1992) and 403g can encompass the names of writers or publishers employed by the CIA, the costs or the expenses or salaries paid by the CIA to those persons or groups, and the involvement of the CIA with the publication of the book. *Edwards v. CIA*, 512 F. Supp. 689 (D.D.C. 1981).

6.4.1.3.5. 403-3(c)(5) (1992) is a proper basis upon which the CIA may refuse to confirm or deny the existence of records where either answer to the FOIA inquiry "can reasonably be expected to lead to unauthorized disclosure of intelligence sources and methods." *Miller v. Casey*, 730 F.2d 773 (D.C. Cir. 1984), *Gardels v. CIA*, 689 F.2d at 1105.

6.4.1.3.6. 403-3(c)(5) (1992) permits the CIA to withhold disclosure of documents containing accounts and transcripts of conversations between CIA officials and members of the press regarding purposes and results of an intelligence operation. *Phillippi v. CIA*, 655 F.2d 1325 (D.C. Cir. 1981).

6.4.1.3.7. 403-3(c)(5) (1992) permits the CIA to withhold materials in personnel file of rejected applicant for CIA employment, including all records concerning his polygraph examination. *Villanueva v. DOJ*, 782 F.2d 528 (5th Cir. 1986).

6.4.1.3.8. Since *Sims*, the courts have tended to give a very broad reading to 403-3(c)(5) (1992) as a withholding statute. *See, e.g.*, *Knight v. CIA, supra*, in which the court ruled that "the FOIA simply does not apply to material the DCI specifically has exempted on the grounds that it pertains to or could give use to inferences about intelligence sources and methods.... Once the DCI makes that determination, the Supreme Court effectively held, the matter is beyond the provision of the courts." *Id.* at 664. *See also Fitzgibbon v. CIA, supra* ; *Hunt v. CIA, supra*; *Maynard v. CIA, supra* .

6.4.1.3.9. In 1992, the conference report to the Intelligence Authorization bill stated: "Whether there is justification to permit the DCI to withhold information concerning intelligence sources and methods which is not classified in response to requests made under the FOIA is a matter which deserves closer, more systematic review by the committees of jurisdiction prior to taking further legislative action." Conf. Rep. No. 102-963, at 88, 1992 U.S. Code Cong. & Admin. News 2614.

6.4.1.4. 26 U.S.C. § 6103, as amended, which controls the dissemination of income tax "return information" by the IRS.

6.4.1.4.1. Although they have agreed that § 6103 qualifies as an Exemption 3 statute, courts have differed in their response to the IRS's contention that § 6103 is a self-contained statutory scheme regulating the disclosure of tax return information and judicial review of disclosure determinations should, therefore, be under the limited "abuse of discretion" standard of the Administrative Procedure Act, 5 U.S.C. § 706, rather than the FOIA *de novo* standard. The IRS view prevailed in *Zale Corp. v. IRS*, 481 F. Supp. 486, 489 (D.D.C. 1979), where the court concluded that "to decide that the generalized strictures of FOIA take precedence over this subsequently enacted, particularized disclosure scheme would in effect render the tax reform provision an exercise in legislative futility." *Zale* was rejected by the Ninth Circuit, which found the legislative history of the 1976 Tax Reform Act "highly persuasive of an intent not to preempt the procedural provisions of FOIA as to requests under section 6103." *Long v. IRS*, 742 F.2d at 1178. After ignoring the issue in several cases decided solely by reference to the FOIA, the D.C. Circuit, in *Church of Scientology of California v. IRS*, 792 F.2d 146, 150 (D.C. Cir. 1986), expressly rejected *Zale* and held that "Section 6103 does not supersede FOIA but rather gives rise to an exemption under Exemption 3." The decision, written by now-Supreme Court Justice Antonin Scalia, has generally precluded further debate on the issue.

6.4.1.4.2. Under § 6103, persons are entitled to their own return information, as long as such disclosure "would not seriously impair Federal tax administration." 26 U.S.C. § 6103(e)(6). Thus internal IRS memoranda which reveal the scope and direction of a criminal or civil investigation do not have to be divulged to the subject of the investigation. *See Currie v. IRS*, 704 F.2d 523 (11th Cir. 1983); *Hulsey v. IRS*, 497 F. Supp. 617 (N.D. Tex. 1980).

6.4.1.4.3. Although some tax return information filed by tax-exempt organizations is publicly available, the D.C. Circuit has indicated that the existence of audits or investigations of tax-exempt organizations would be protected information under § 6103. The court pointed out that "the statutory phrase—'the existence, or possible existence, of liability'—naturally encompasses the issue of tax exemption *vel non*." *Landmark Legal Found. v. IRS*, 267 F.3d 1132 (D.C. Cir. 2001).

6.4.1.4.4. Under subsection 6103(b)(2), popularly known as the Haskell amendment, "return information" includes a taxpayer's identity, the nature, source, or amount of his income, payments, receipts, deductions, exemptions, credits, assets, liabilities, other listed specific data, but does not include "data in a form which cannot be associated with, or otherwise identify, directly or indirectly, a particular taxpayer." But in *Church of Scientology v. IRS*, 484 U.S. 9 (1987), the Supreme Court ruled that "as with a return itself, removal of identification from return information would not deprive it of protection under Section 6103(b)," and the agency therefore "has no duty under the FOIA to undertake such redaction." The Court affirmed the *en banc* decision of the D.C. Circuit, holding that the phrase "in a form" suggests more than the mere absence of identifying information and "envisions...agency *reformulation* of the return information into a statistical study or some other composite product—presumably on the theory that such reformulation gives added assurance that a taxpayer's identity will not be disclosed." *Church of Scientology*, 792 F.2d 153, 160 (D.C. Cir. 1986) (*en banc*) (emphasis in original).

6.4.1.5. 35 U.S.C. § 122, prohibiting disclosure of patent applications and information concerning them. *Irons & Sears v. Dann*, 606 F.2d 1215 (D.C. Cir. 1979), *cert. denied*, 444 U.S. 1075 (1980); *Lee*

Pharmaceuticals v. Kreps, 577 F.2d 610 (9th Cir. 1978), *cert. denied*, 439 U.S. 1073 (1979).

6.4.1.6. Section 6 of P.L. 86-36, 50 U.S.C. § 402, exempting from disclosure the organization or function of the National Security Agency, or "any information with respect to the activities thereof, or of names, titles, salaries, or number of persons employed by such agency." *Founding Church of Scientology of Washington v. NSA*, 610 F.2d 824 *supra*. Concluding that "Congress certainly had rational grounds to enact for the NSA a protective statute broader than the CIA's," the court found "the plain wording of the statute conclusive" in authorizing withholding of NSA materials "integrally related" to any NSA function or activity that is "authorized by statute and not otherwise unlawful." *Hayden v. NSA*, 608 F.2d at 1389-90.

6.4.1.7. 15 U.S.C. § 2055(b)(1) of the Consumer Product Safety Act, which governs public disclosure of information submitted to the Consumer Product Safety Commission. *Consumer Product Safety Commission v. GTE Sylvania*, 447 U.S. 102 (1980). *See also Honeywell, Inc. v. Consumer Product Safety Commission*, 582 F. Supp. 1072 (D.D.C. 1984).

6.4.1.8. 42 U.S.C. § 2000e-8(e) of the Civil Rights Act of 1964, which prohibits employees of the Equal Employment Opportunity Commission from disclosing information made available to them pursuant to the reporting provisions of the equal employment provision. This statute, however, does not prohibit disclosure by another government agency, e.g., the Office of Federal Contract Compliance, of an annual report containing statistics on the number of women and minorities employed by a government contractor. *United Technologies Corp. v. Marshall*, 464 F. Supp. 845 (D. Conn. 1979).

6.4.1.9. 18 U.S.C. § 2510-20 of the Omnibus Crime Control & Safe Streets Act of 1968, as amended, which exempts from disclosure the contents of electronic surveillance conducted in violation of the Act. *See Chong v. Drug Enforcement Administration*, 929 F.2d 729 (D.C. Cir. 1991); *Providence Journal Co. v. FBI*, 460 F. Supp. 762 (D.R.I. 1978), *rev'd.*, 602 F.2d 1010 (1st Cir. 1979), *cert. denied*, 444 U.S. 1071 (1980).

6.4.1.10. Section 8 of the Commodity Exchange Act, 7 U.S.C. § 12, providing that the Commission may publish information gathered in the course of its investigations "except data and information which would separately disclose the business transactions of any person and trade secrets or names of customers." *Hunt v. Commodity Futures Trading Commission*, 484 F. Supp. 47, 49 (D.D.C. 1979).

6.4.1.11. Section 222(f) of the Immigration and Naturalization Act, 8 U.S.C. § 1202(f) which authorizes the withholding of information pertaining to visa applications, falls within both prongs of Exemption 3. *Medina-*

Hincapie v. Department of State, 700 F.2d 737 (D.C. Cir. 1983); *DeLaurentiis v. Haig*, 686 F.2d 192 (3d Cir. 1982).

6.4.1.12. 49 U.S.C. § 1504, the Federal Aviation Act of 1958, which requires nondisclosure of information that would prejudice formulation and presentation of positions of United States in international negotiations or adversely affect the competitive position of any air carrier in foreign air transportation, is a qualified exempting statute under Exemption 3. *British Airports Authority v. Department of State*, 530 F. Supp. 46 (D.D.C. 1981).

6.4.1.13. Section 12(d) of the Railroad Unemployment Insurance Act, 45 U.S.C. § 362(d), which bars disclosure of information obtained by the U.S. Railroad Retirement Board, in connection with its duties, "in any manner revealing an employee's identity," qualified under the second prong but not under the first prong, since the Board has discretion to release where "disclosure is clearly in the interest of the employer or his estate." *DiPersia v. Railroad Retirement Bd.*, 638 F. Supp. 485 (D. Conn. 1986). *See also Association of Retired R.R. Workers v. U.S. R.R. Retirement Board.*, 830 F.2d 331, 334 (D.C. Cir. 1987).

6.4.1.14. 42 U.S.C. § 2167(a) and (d) of the Atomic Energy Act of 1954 (Section 147 of the Act, as enacted in 1980), exempting (1) summary descriptions of the capabilities of law enforcement authorities to respond to emergency calls from a transporter of spent nuclear fuel and (2) information concerning segments of the routes where mobile telephone coverage between the carrier and receiving station is either erratic or nonexistent, as "safeguards information" disclosure. *Virginia Sunshine Alliance v. NRC*, 509 F. Supp. 863 (D.D.C. 1981), *aff'd*, 669 F.2d 788 (D.C. Cir. 1981).

6.4.1.15. The Parole Commission and Reorganization Act, 18 U.S.C. § 4208(b), constitutes an Exemption 3 statute for specific categories of information sometimes contained in presentence reports. *Berry v. DOJ*, 733 F.2d 1343 (9th Cir. 1984). The Parole Act, however, does not constitute on Exemption 3 statute for the purpose of withholding any material in presentence reports which does not fall within the specific categories of information enumerated in the statute. *DOJ v. Julian*, 486 U.S. 1 (1988); *Crooker v. U.S. Parole Comm'n*, 760 F.2d 1 (1st Cir. 1985); *White v. DOJ*, 606 F. Supp. 880 (D.D.C. 1985).

6.4.1.16. Section 12(c)(1) of the Export Administration Act, 50 U.S.C. § 2411(c)(1), exempting "information obtained for the purpose of consideration of, or concerning, license application," was held to include the names of exporters granted licenses to export to a particular country. *Lessner v. Department of Commerce*, 827 F.2d 1333 (9th Cir. 1987); *Durnan v. Department of Commerce*, 777 F. Supp. 965 (D.D.C. 1991). Because an Exemption 3 claim must be based on a statute, not a regulation, there has been some controversy over whether 12(c)(1) was a legitimate (b)(3) provision because the Export Administration Act expired and was never directly reauthorized by Congress. However, several courts have found that the executive authority to enforce the provision was delegated by Congress through the International Emergency Economic Powers Act. For a thorough analysis of the controversy, *see Times Publ'g Co. v. Dept of Commerce*, 236 F.3d 1286 (11th Cir. 2001).

6.4.1.17. Section 777 of the Tariff Act of 1930, as amended, 19 U.S.C. § 1671 *et. seq.*, 1677f, providing that information submitted in connection with an antidumping or countervailing duty investigation shall not be disclosed if designated as proprietary by the submitter. *Mudge Rose Guthrie Alexander & Ferdon v. International Trade Commission*, 846 F.2d 1527 (D.C. Cir. 1988).

6.4.1.18. The Ethics in Government Act, 5 U.S.C. Supp. 4, § 207(a), which requires special government employees to submit "confidential" financial disclosure reports. *Meyerhoff v. EPA*, 958 F.2d 1498 (9th Cir. 1992).

6.4.1.19. Section 21(f) of the Federal Trade Commission Act, 15 U.S.C. § 57b-2(f), for investigatory materials that were (1) submitted in response to FTC requests, (2) relevant to an ongoing investigation within the agency's jurisdiction, and (3) could have been subpoenaed had the party refused to comply with the requests. *A. Michael's Piano, Inc. v. Federal Trade Commission*, 18 F.3d 138, 146 (2d Cir. 1994).

6.4.1.20. Section 3710a(c)(7) of the Federal Technology Transfer Act, 15 U.S.C. § 3710a, which limits disclosure in certain instances of information that is "privileged and confidential," was treated as an Exemption 3 statute when the plaintiff failed to contest the agency's assertion of its FOIA relevance. *DeLorme Publ. Co. v. NOAA*, 917 F. Supp. 867, 870-872 (D. Me. 1996). *See also Public Citizen Health Research Group v. NIH*, 2002 U.S. Dist. LEXIS 7457, No. 00-1847 (CKK) (D.D.C. Mar. 12, 2002).

6.4.1.21. 38 U.S.C. 5706(a), which prohibits disclosure of morbidity and mortality statistics for single physician specialty programs that could implicitly identify a physician. *Schulte and Sun-Sentinel Co. v. Veterans Administration*, No. 86-6251 (S.D. Fla, Feb. 2, 1996).

6.4.1.22. The Smith-Mundt Act, 22 U.S.C. §§ 1461, 1461-a, which limits the dissemination of USIA materials domestically. *Essential Information, Inc. v. U.S. Information Agency*, No. 134 F.3d 1165 (D.C. Cir. 1998).

6.4.1.23. 10 U.S.C. 1102(a), which protects military medical quality assurance programs. In *Dayton Newspapers v. Department of the Air Force*, 107 F. Supp. 2d 912 (S.D. Ohio 1999), the court found this provision protected a medical malpractice database from disclosure.

6.4.2. Statutes failing to qualify under Exemption 3:

6.4.2.1. 50 U.S.C. § 2406(c) of the Export Administration Act of 1969, providing that certain information obtained under the Act shall not be disclosed unless the agency determines that withholding the information is "contrary to the national interest." *American Jewish Congress v. Kreps*, 574 F.2d 624 *supra; Green v. Department of Commerce*, 618 F.2d 836 (D.C. Cir. 1980).

6.4.2.2. 42 U.S.C. § 1320c-15 of Professional Standards Review Organization legislation is not a "statute" for (b)(3) purposes because it gives the administrator too much discretion to choose between secrecy and disclosure of health care service records. *Public Citizen Health Research Group v. HEW*, 477 F. Supp. 595 (D.D.C. 1979), *rev'd on other grounds with directions to dismiss the complaint*, 668 F.2d 537 (D.C. Cir. 1981).

6.4.2.3. 39 U.S.C. § 410(c)(6), the Postal Reorganization Act's investigatory files exemption, allows the Postal Service "total discretion" regarding disclosure of its files. *Church of Scientology of California v. U.S. Postal Service*, 633 F.2d 1327 (9th Cir. 1980).

6.4.2.4. 22 U.S.C. § 2671, authorizing the Secretary of State to make expenditures for "unforeseen emergencies arising in the diplomatic and consular service," and 31 U.S.C. § 107, authorizing the President or the Secretary of State to account secretly for foreign affairs expenditures, are not Exemption 3 statutes because they are too broad to meet the requirement for identifying particular matters to be withheld. *Washington Post Co. v. Department of State*, 632 F. Supp. 607 (D.D.C. 1986).

6.4.2.5. 21 U.S.C. § 360j(h), which authorizes the disclosure of summaries of safety and effectiveness data pertaining to medical devices is not an Exemption 3 statute. *Public Citizen Health Research Group v. FDA*, 704 F.2d 1280 *supra.*

6.4.2.6. 28 U.S.C. § 534, which authorizes the Attorney General to collect certain criminal information and to exchange such information with other federal and state officials, is not an Exemption 3 withholding statute because it does not address authority to disclose or refuse to disclose such information to the public. *Reporters Committee v. DOJ*, 816 F.2d 730, 735-36 (D.C. Cir. 1987), *modified on other grounds*, 831 F.2d 1124 (D.C. Cir. 1987), *reversed on other grounds*, 489 U.S. 749 (1989).

6.5. The Trade Secrets Act, 18 U.S.C. § 1905, is often asserted to be an Exemption 3 withholding statute, despite legislative history and court holdings to the contrary.

6.5.1. When Congress revised Exemption 3 to its current form, it indicated that it did not consider the Trade Acts Secret to be withholding authority within the exemption's scope. *See* H.R. Rep. No. 880, 99th Cong., 1st Sess., 23 U.S. Code Cong. & Admin. News, 2183, 2205 (1976).

6.5.2. The Supreme Court, however, at least partially reopened the issue in *Chrysler Corp. v. Brown*, 441 U.S. 281, 319 n.49 (1979), by suggesting that the Trade

Secrets Act may indeed be an independent basis to force the withholding of access to agency records.

6.5.3. Nevertheless, more recent court decisions have thoroughly considered and rejected the contention that the Trade Secrets Act is an Exemption 3 statute. *See generally CNA Fin. Corp. v. Donovan*, 830 F.2d 1132, 1137-41 (D.C. Cir. 1987), *cert. denied*, 485 U.S. 977 (1988). *See also General Electric Co. v. NRC*, 740 F.2d 1394, 1401-02 (7th Cir. 1984).

6.6. A split of authority formerly existed regarding whether 5 U.S.C. § 552a, the Privacy Act, is an Exemption 3 statute.

6.6.1. *Compare Painter v. FBI*, 615 F.2d 689 (5th Cir. 1980); *Terkel v. Kelly*, 599 F.2d 214, 216 (7th Cir. 1979), *cert. denied*, 444 U.S. 1013 (1980); and *Shapiro v. Drug Enforcement Administration*, 721 F.2d 215 (7th Cir. 1983) *vacated and remanded*, 469 U.S. 14 (1985) (holding that the Privacy Act is an Exemption 3 statute) *with Greentree v. U.S. Customs Service*, 674 F.2d 74 (D.C. Cir. 1982); *Porter v. DOJ*, 717 F.2d 787 (3d Cir. 1983); and *Provenzano v. DOJ*, 717 F.2d 799 (3d Cir. 1983) (holding that the Privacy Act is not a barrier to FOIA access).

6.6.2. The Supreme Court ruled the issue moot after Congress, in enacting the CIA Information Act, P.L. 98-477, 98 Stat. 2209, amended subsection (q) of the Privacy Act and endorsed the *Greentree* view. *See* section 2(C) of P.L. 98-477; H. Rep. No. 726 Part 2, 98th Cong., 2d Sess. 17 (1984); *Provenzano v. DOJ*), *supra; Shapiro v. Drug Enforcement Administration, supra; Wightman v. BATF*, 755 F.2d 979 (1st Cir. 1985). *See also* Chapter 21 on the Privacy Act.

6.6.3. However, although the Privacy Act is not an Exemption 3 statute, it often serves the same purpose. Because agencies are allowed only to disclosure information *required* to be released under FOIA, information that could be disclosed as a matter of discretion but is not legally required to be released is subject to the Privacy Act's statutory prohibition on non-consensual disclosures of personal information.

7. As a Matter of Statutory Construction—Does the Requested Information Fit Within the Category of Information Authorized to be Withheld?

7.1. This is obvious where the statute refers to particular documents and one such document is requested—e.g., request for a tax return where a statute prohibits release of such returns. *See Mason v. Callaway*, 554 F.2d 129 (4th Cir. 1977), *cert. denied*, 434 U.S. 877, *reh. denied.*, 434 U.S. 935 (1977).

7.2. Where it is not obvious, the government has the burden of proof and courts will examine the legislative history of the statutes at issue. Mere labeling by the government is not sufficient. *Tax Analysts & Advocates v. IRS*, 505 F.2d 350 (D.C. Cir. 1974); *Tax Reform Research Group v. IRS*, 419 F. Supp. 415 (D.D.C. 1976). *See also Mudge Rose*, 846 F.2d at 1531-32 (agency failed to provide "coherent explanation" why aggregate data requested was within nondisclosure mandate of the statute).

Exemption 3

7.3. There are two lines of authority concerning the standard of review for the application of an Exemption 3 statute. In *Association of Retired R.R. Workers v. U.S. R.R. Retirement Board*, 830 F.2d 331 (D.C. Cir. 1987), the court indicated that once an Exemption 3 claim was upheld the court's review came to an end and it would not explore whether the agency had properly invoked the exemption. But in *Long v. IRS*, 742 F.2d 1173 (9th Cir. 1984)., the court adopted the opposite view, indicating that the appropriateness of a statute's invocation must be assessed even after it was found that the statute qualified under Exemption 3.

7.4. Cases holding that requested information is within the scope of what Congress authorized to be withheld:

7.4.1. *Sears v. Gottschalk*, 502 F.2d 122 (4th Cir. 1974), *cert. denied sub nom. Sears v. Dann*, 425 U.S. 904 (1976). Congress, by requiring in 35 U.S.C. § 122 that applications for patents be kept secret, intended to include abandoned applications. The court's holding was based on a full review of the legislative history. *See also Lee Pharmaceuticals v. Kreps*, 577 F.2d 610 (9th Cir. 1978), holding that abandoned patent applications are within the protection of section 122 even when sought as evidence of prior art; and *Irons and Sears v. Dann*, 606 F.2d 1215, *supra*, holding that Patent Office early filing date decisions that relate to pending or abandoned patent applications fall within section 122, a decision reaffirmed by *Irons v. Diamond*, 670 F.2d 265 (D.C. Cir. 1981), in which the court stressed that no information concerning patent applications that have not been granted can be disclosed under section 122.

7.4.2. *Parker v. EEOC*, 534 F.2d 977 (D.C. Cir. 1976). Congress, by mandating in 42 U.S.C. § 2000e-5(b) that discrimination charges not be made public and informal efforts to adjudicate disputes be kept confidential, meant to exclude agreements to settle disputes from disclosure. Legislative history of the 1976 amendments cites this statute as still a valid Exemption 3 statute.

7.4.3. *Hayden v. NSA*, 608 F.2d 1381, *supra*. Congress intended in P.L. 86-36 to authorize the NSA to withhold information on its functions and activities. *See also Kruh v. GSA*, 421 F. Supp. 965 (E.D.N.Y. 1976).

7.4.4. *Consumer Product Safety Commission v. GTE Sylvania, Inc.*, 447 U.S. 102 *supra*. The requirements of Section 6(b)(1) of the Consumer Product Safety Act (providing manufacturers with a 30-day notice and comment period before the release of information concerning them) apply not only to "affirmative disclosures" of information by the Commission (press releases, etc.), but also to the Commission's "passive release" of information pursuant to an FOIA request. *Pierce & Stevens Chemical Corp. v. Consumer Product Safety Commission*, 585 F.2d 1382 (2d Cir. 1978).

7.4.5. *Fruehauf Corp. v. IRS*, 566 F.2d 574 (6th Cir. 1977). The 26 U.S.C. § 6103 definition of "return information" incorporates those portions of written determinations exempted from disclosure under 26 U.S.C. § 6110(c). In *Moody v. IRS*, 527 F. Supp. 535 (D.D.C. 1981), portions of IRS documents were properly withheld under 26 U.S.C. § 6103, including taxpayer's identity, descriptive material which would create a risk of identifying taxpayer, and "other information of a trivial nature, which is meaningless when the taxpayer's name is deleted." *Id.* at 536. The *Moody* decision was affirmed as to its rejection of any further need for a more detailed justification for its withheld return information, and remanded for further consideration of the attorney work-product privilege. *Moody v. IRS*, 682 F.2d 266 (D.C. Cir. 1982).

7.4.6. *Fund for Constitutional Government v. National Archives & Records Service*, 656 F.2d 856, supra. Federal R. Crim. P. 6(e) acts as a basis for withholding such information "as the identity of witnesses, the identification of documents, descriptions, evaluations and summaries of testimony, materials revealing the scope and extent of grand jury investigation, etc."

7.4.6.1. An unauthorized leak of grand jury materials fails to waive Exemption 3 when the release of videotapes would undermine the inner workings of the grand jury. *Murphy v. FBI*, 490 F. Supp. 1138 (D.D.C. 1980).

7.4.6.2. Documents already in the agency's possession and turned over to the grand jury, containing summaries of testimony before a grand jury and names of witnesses, are protected from disclosure by Fed. R. Crim. P. 6(e). *Kanter v. IRS*, 496 F. Supp. 1004, 1006 (N.D. Ill. 1980).

7.4.7. *Halperin v. CIA*, 629 F.2d 144 (D.C. Cir. 1980). The names of CIA attorneys and the amount of their legal fees are protected from disclosure under 50 U.S.C. § 403(d)(3) and § 403(g) respectively.

7.4.8. *Agee v. CIA*, 517 F. Supp. 1335 (D.D.C. 1981). 50 U.S.C. § 403(d)(3) and 50 U.S.C. § 403g qualify as Exemption 3 statutes. In ruling that a *Vaughn* index must be crafted so as to maintain the confidentiality that the exemptions were designed to protect, the court held that since the former CIA officer-plaintiff could use his own knowledge in combination with a more detailed index to create a threat to national security, a more detailed index was not required by FOIA. *See* subsequent memorandum opinion, *Agee v. CIA*, 524 F. Supp. 1290 (D.D.C. 1981), detailing the court's disposition of remaining FOIA issues.

7.5. Cases holding that requested information is *not* within the scope of what Congress authorized to be withheld:

7.5.1. While 26 U.S.C. § 6103(a) is an exempting statute for the purposes of 5 U.S.C. § 552(b)(3), a court may examine each document to determine that the documents are in fact tax return information. *Stauss v. IRS*, 516 F. Supp. 1218 (D.D.C. 1981). Thus, the exemption does not include letter rulings, *Tax Analysts & Advocates v. IRS*, 505 F.2d 350, *supra*; letter ruling indices and background files of published rulings, *Fruehauf Corp. v. IRS*, 566 F.2d 574 *supra*; technical advice memoranda from the national service office of the IRS, *Arthur Andersen, Inc. v. IRS*, 514 F. Supp. 1173 (D.D.C. 1981); copies of checks and deposit slips, *Stephenson v. IRS*, 629 F.2d 1140 (5th Cir. 1980), and computer tapes prepared by the IRS in connection with its tax compliance measurement activities. *Long v. Bureau of Economic Analysis*, 646 F.2d 1310 (9th Cir. 1981), *vacated and remanded*, 454 U.S. 934 (1981), *vacated and remanded*, 671 F.2d 1229 (9th Cir. 1982) (for further consideration in light of Economic Recovery Tax Act of 1981). *See also Kamman v. IRS*, 56 F.3d 46 (9th Cir. 1995) (affidavits failed to show that appraisals of property seized from a third-party taxpayer were furnished to the IRS in connection with a tax return or to a determination of the existence of a tax liability or the amount thereof). The D.C. Circuit has also found that § 6103 does not protect Field Service Memoranda prepared by the IRS because the memoranda essentially create agency law. *See Tax Analysts v. IRS*, 117 F.3d 607 (D.C. Cir. 1997).

7.5.2. *Aviation Consumer Action Project v. CAB*, 412 F. Supp. 1028 (D.D.C. 1976). 49 U.S.C. § 1461, section 801 of the Federal Aviation Act of 1958, which prohibits the FAA from disclosing certain information relating to a foreign air route application prior to its submission to the President for his decision on the route award, does not permit the FAA to withhold information after submission but before decision by the President.

7.5.3. *Stretch v. Weinberger*, 495 F.2d 639 (3d Cir. 1974). Congress, in authorizing Secretary to keep certain Social Security reports secret, except under regulations, 42 U.S.C. § 1306(a), did not consider types of reports requested here, i.e. concerning performance of nursing and old age homes which receive Medicare funds, and cannot be said to have authorized their withholding.

7.5.4. *Phillippi v. CIA*, 546 F.2d 1009, *supra.* 50 U.S.C. § 403g is limited to exempting the CIA from statutes that would otherwise require it to divulge its structure or information relating to personnel.

7.5.5. *Irons & Sears v. Dann*, 606 F.2d 1215, *supra.* Patent Office early filing date decisions relating to patent applications which have issued as patents do not fall within 35 U.S.C. § 122.

7.5.6. *Charlotte-Mecklenburg Hospital Authority v. Perry*, 571 F.2d 195 (4th Cir. 1978). 42 U.S.C. § 2000e-5(b), 8(e) do not prohibit disclosure of allegations of unlawful employment practice to the party charged, as opposed to the public generally, and will not defeat the charged party's "*prima facie right*" to disclosure, even though disclosure to some other party is prohibited.

7.5.7. State juvenile records are not within the scope of 18 U.S.C. § 5038, which requires that records related to *federal* juvenile delinquency proceedings must be safeguarded from disclosure to unauthorized persons. *McDonnell v. U.S.*, 4 F.3d at 1249-1250.

8. Procedural Considerations.

8.1. One court has suggested that where documents are claimed exempt under both Exemptions 3 and 7, as a matter of the sound administration of justice and because of the delicacy and difficulty of the legal issues involved in Exemption 7 (e.g., determining the lawfulness of a national security investigation), the Exemption 3 claim should be determined first. *See Marks v. CIA*, 590 F.2d 997 (D.C. Cir. 1978).

8.2. Another appellate court, in a case where the documents were also held exempt under (b)(1), ruled that the lower court decision "to keep the statute supporting the (b)(3) exemption secret for security reasons...was consonant with the FOIA's exemptions and was a correct decision even though [the plaintiff] could hardly respond to this claimed exemption." *Simmons v. DOJ*, 796 F.2d 709, 711 (4th Cir. 1986).

8.3. In *Parkridge Hospital, Inc. v. Califano*, 625 F.2d 719 (6th Cir. 1980), plaintiffs sought to enjoin public disclosure of financial reports they were required to file under the

Medicare program. The Sixth Circuit held that FOIA Exemption 3 does not provide a cause of action for such an injunction.

8.4. In *British Airports Authority v. Department of State*, 530 F. Supp. 46, *supra*, where the defendant failed to invoke Exemption 3 prior to entry of judgment, the court permitted the defendant to invoke the exemption in a motion to alter or amend the judgment because there was a clear statutory basis for claiming the exemption, e.g., 49 U.S.C. § 1504, and there was no display of bad faith.

8.5. The Supreme Court has suggested that other statutory schemes may preempt FOIA's procedures. Thus, the court has held that the special procedures applicable to CPSC consumer complaints preclude application of FOIA's strict time deadlines for responding to requests for information. *Consumer Product Safety Commission v. GTE Sylvania*, 447 U.S. 102, *supra*.

9. Annual Reports

9.1. The reporting provisions of FOIA require agencies to list the Exemption 3 statutes claimed during the period covered by the report. § 552(e)(1)(B)(ii).

9.2. The EFOIA Amendments of 1996 added the following clause: "a description of whether a court has upheld the decision of the agency to withhold information under each such statute, and a concise description of the scope of information withheld." § 552(e)(1)(B)(ii). This provision was added to ensure that agencies had a reasonable legal basis for invoking Exemption 3.

CHAPTER 6

Exemption 4—Business Information

David C. Vladeck

1. **Exemption 4 provides that the FOIA does not apply to matters that are: "trade secrets and commercial or financial information obtained from a person and privileged or confidential."**

2. **Legislative History. The language of the provision has frequently been criticized as providing little guidance for determining its scope. *9 to 5 Organization for Women Office Workers v. Board of Governors of the Federal Reserve System,* 721 F.2d 1, 6 (1st Cir. 1983) (criticizing "the tortured, not to say obfuscating legislative history"). Although the legislative history is sparse, it can be read to suggest that the exemption should be broadly applied. S. Rep. No. 89-813, 89th Cong., 1st Sess. 9 (1965); H.R. Rep. No. 89-1497, 89th Cong., 2d Sess. 10 (1966). The courts, however, have generally found the legislative history unhelpful and have construed the exemption narrowly according to its terms and the general intent of Congress regarding application of the FOIA exemptions. *See, e.g., Brockway v. Department of the Air Force,* 518 F.2d 1184, 1189 (8th Cir. 1975); *Soucie v. David,* 448 F.2d 1067, 1078 (D.C. Cir. 1971). Other courts have concluded that the legislative history "firmly supports the inference that [Exemption 4] is intended for the benefit of persons who supply information," *Public Citizen Health Research Group v. FDA,* 185 F.3d 898, 904 (D.C. Cir. 1999) (quoting *National Parks and Conservation Ass'n v. Morton (I),* 498 F.2d 765, 770 (D.C. Cir. 1974)).**

3. **In order to bring a record within Exemption 4, it must be shown that the information is (A) a trade secret, or (B) information which is (1) commercial or financial, (2) obtained from a person, and (3) privileged or confidential.** *Public Citizen Health Research Group v. FDA,* 185 F.3d at 903; *National Parks & Conservation Ass'n v. Morton (I)*, 498 F.2d at 766; *Getman v. NLRB*, 450 F.2d 670, 673 (D.C. Cir. 1971), *stay denied*, 404 U.S. 1204 (1971), *quoting Consumers Union v. Veterans Administration*, 301 F. Supp. 796, 802 (S.D.N.Y. 1969), *appeal dismissed as moot*, 436 F.2d 1363 (2d Cir. 1971). *Accord Board of Trade v. Commodity Futures Trading Comm'n*, 627 F.2d 392, 403 (D.C. Cir. 1980); *Sharyland Water Supply Corp. v. Block*, 755 F.2d 397 (5th Cir. 1985), *cert. denied*, 471 U.S. 1137 (1985); *Washington Research Project, Inc. v. HEW*, 504 F.2d 238, 244-45 (D.C. Cir. 1974), *cert. denied*, 421 U.S. 963 (1975); *Brockway v. Department of the Air Force*, 518 F.2d at 1188.

3.1. Is the Information a Trade Secret?

3.1.1. During the early years of FOIA litigation, there was no clear-cut view of the appropriate definition of "trade secret" to be applied in FOIA litigation. Parties opposing disclosure uniformly relied on the definition set forth in the Restatement of Torts, Sec. 757, comment b (1939), which broadly defines a trade secret as: Any formula, pattern, device, or compilation of information which is used in one's business, and which gives him an advantage over competitors who do not know it or use it.

3.1.1.1. The Supreme Court has cited this definition in a case arising under the Federal Insecticide, Fungicide and Rodenticide Act, *see Ruckelshaus v. Monsanto Co.,* 467 U.S. 986 (1984), and in a case holding that federal patent law does not preempt state trade secrets law. *Kewanee Oil Co. v. Bicron Corp.*, 416 U.S. 470, 474-475 (1974). This definition has also been referred to in several FOIA cases. *See, e.g., Washington Research Project, Inc. v. HEW*, 504 F.2d at 245 n.8; *Union Oil Co. of California v. Federal Power Commission*, 542 F.2d 1036, 1044 (9th Cir. 1976); *Chevron Chemical Co. v. Costle*, 443 F. Supp. 1024, 1032 n.4 (N.D. Cal. 1978).

3.1.1.2. *Pressure Science, Inc. v. Kramer*, 413 F. Supp. 618 (D. Conn. 1976), contains a useful discussion on proving the elements of a trade secret under the Restatement definition.

3.1.2. However, the D.C. Circuit has expressly rejected "the broad Restatement approach... as inconsistent with the language of the FOIA and its underlying policies." *Public Citizen Health Research Group v. FDA*, 704 F.2d 1280, 1288 (D.C. Cir. 1983). The court instead held that, for FOIA purposes, the term "trade secret" should be limited in meaning to: "a secret, commercially valuable plan, formula, process, or device that is used for the making, preparing, compounding, or processing of trade commodities and that can be said to be the end product of either innovation or substantial effort." In fashioning this definition, the court relied on a similar definition set forth in a pre-FOIA case defining the term under the federal Trade Secrets Act, *United States ex. rel. Norwegian Nitrogen Products Co. v. United States Tariff Comm'n.*, 6 F.2d 491, 495 (D.C. Cir. 1925), *vacated as moot*, 274 U.S. 106 (1927), a case which had been cited with approval in FOIA litigation. *Consumers Union v. Veterans Administration*, 301 F. Supp. at 801. The Tenth Circuit has expressly adopted the *Public Citizen* test. *Anderson v. HHS*, 907 F.2d 936, 944 (10th Cir. 1990). The D.C. Circuit has since reaffirmed the *Public Citizen* approach. *See Center for Auto Safety v. NHTSA*, 244 F.3d 144 (D.C. Cir. 2001) (concluding that information relating to the characteristics of airbags do not qualify for protection as trade secrets). Applying this definition, the court in *Northwest Coalition for Alternatives to Pesticides v. Browner*, 941 F. Supp. 197 (D.D.C. 1996) rejected the argument that information relating to the common names and inert ingredients in certain widely used pesticides were trade secrets.

3.1.3. It is important to understand the marked difference between the Restatement definition and the definition adopted in *Public Citizen*. Under the Restatement definition, virtually any compilation of business information which provides a competitive advantage constitutes a trade secret and would be entitled to *per se* protection in FOIA cases. In sharp contrast, the definition formulated in *Public Citizen* is limited to information which relates directly to the production process. *See, e.g., AT&T Information Systems v. GSA*, 627 F. Supp. 1396, 1401 n.9 (D.D.C. 1986), *reversed and remanded on other grounds,* 810 F.2d 1233 (D.C. Cir. 1987) (parties in a reverse FOIA action agreed that "this narrow definition excluded pricing information submitted by plaintiff in successful bid for government contract"). *But see Canal Refining Co. v. Corrallo*, 616 F. Supp. 1035, 1042 (D.D.C. 1985) (post-*Public Citizen* case which does not mention that decision and concludes that the Restatement test "appears merely to parallel the 'substantial competitive harm' prong of the standard Exemption 4 analysis").

3.1.4. While the Restatement definition is thus plainly more encompassing, it should be noted that under either definition the information must be (1) commercially valuable; (2) used in one's business; and (3) maintained in secrecy.

3.1.5. The *Public Citizen* decision is only binding in the D.C. and Tenth Circuits. Given the importance of the issue, however, other courts may well be induced to reexamine the definitional question. *See, e.g., Burnside-Ott Aviation Training v. United States*, 617 F. Supp. 279 (S.D. Fla. 1985) (adopting *Public Citizen* definition). When arguing in favor of the narrower *Public Citizen* definition, plaintiffs should stress the factors relied on by the D.C. Circuit in rejecting the Restatement definition: (1) that engrafting the broader Restatement definition onto Exemption 4 would be contrary to the FOIA's express mandate that the exemptions be narrowly construed, *Department of the Air Force v. Rose*, 425 U.S. 352, 360-62 (1976); (2) that the Restatement definition, which represents a refinement of common law tort doctrine stemming principally from cases concerning breaches of trust by former employees and competing rights of ownership under state tort law, has little bearing on the markedly different issues raised in Exemption 4 litigation, *see Public Citizen*, 704 F.2d at 1286-90; and (3) that adopting the Restatement definition would render the remaining portions of Exemption 4 "superfluous." *Anderson v. HHS*, 907 F.2d at 944.

3.1.6. For detailed discussions of the relationship between the FOIA and the Trade Secrets Act, 18 U.S.C. § 1905, see Chapter 5 on Information Exempted By Other Statutes, and Chapter 7 on Reverse FOIA.

3.2. Is the Information Actually Commercial or Financial Information?

3.2.1. Courts have consistently held that the terms "commercial" and "financial" in Exemption 4 should be given their "ordinary" meaning. *See, e.g., Public Citizen*, 704 F.2d at 1290; *Board of Trade*, 627 F.2d at 403.

3.2.2. "Thus, information is commercial if it relates to commerce, *American Airlines, Inc. v. National Mediation Board*, 588 F.2d 863, 870 (2d. Cir. 1978), or it has been compiled in pursuit of profit." *Public Citizen*, 704 F.2d at 1290.

3.2.3. Examples of items generally regarded as commercial or financial information include: business sales statistics, research data, technical designs, overhead and operating costs, and information on financial condition. *See Washington Post Co. v. HHS,* 690 F.2d 252, 266 (D.C. Cir. 1982).

3.2.4. However, claims of confidentiality are frequently made for information which does not literally fall within the terms of the exemption. *See Washington Research Project, Inc. v. HEW*, 504 F.2d at 244 (research designs in grant applications); *Public Citizen Health Research Group v. FDA,* 185 F.3d 898 (research on experimental drugs that are no longer being developed); *Public Citizen Health Research Group v. FDA*, 539 F. Supp. 1320, 1327 (D.D.C. 1982), *aff'd in part, rev'd in part*, 704 F.2d 1280 (D.C. Cir. 1983) (aggregate manufacturers summary reports of adverse reactions in medical device testing); *Bowen v. FDA,* 925 F.2d 1225 (9th Cir. 1991) (information concerning poison tamperings with drug products); *Teich v. FDA*, 751 F. Supp. 243 (D.D.C. 1990) (animal tests on the safety of silicone gel breast implants); *Wiley Rein & Fielding v. Department of Commerce,* No. 91-890 (SS) (D.D.C., Order of Jan. 31, 1992) (government official's notes regarding efforts to sell aerospace equipment); *American Airlines, Inc. v. National Mediation Board*, 588 F.2d at 870 (number of union authorization cards supporting certification); *Getman v. NLRB*, 450 F.2d at 673 ("bare list of names"); *Brockway v. Department of the Air Force*, 518 F.2d at 1188-1189 (witness statements).

3.2.5. The non-profit status of the entity from which the information was obtained is a factor to be considered, but "is not determinative of the character of the information." *Critical Mass Energy Project v. NRC,* 830 F.2d 278, 281 (D.C. Cir. 1987) (nuclear industry trade association's reports held "commercial" because information could affect profitability of constituent commercial utility companies). *See also American Airlines, Inc.*, 588 F.2d at 870.

3.3. Is the Information Obtained from a Person?

3.3.1. If the information was generated by the government, it cannot fall within Exemption 4. *Consumers Union*, 301 F. Supp. at 803; *Grumman Aircraft Engineering Corp. v. Renegotiation Board*, 425 F.2d 578, 582 (D.C. Cir. 1970).

3.3.2. The term "person," however, refers to a wide range of entities. *See* 5 U.S.C. § 551(2); *Judicial Watch v. Export-Import Bank,* 108 F. Supp. 2d 19, 28 (D.D.C. 2000) (noting that anyone other than the government is a "person" under the Act); *Stone v. Export-Import Bank of the United States*, 552 F.2d 132 (5th Cir. 1977), *cert. denied*, 434 U.S. 1012 (1978) (foreign government as "person" under FOIA); *Comstock International v. Export-Import Bank of the United States*, 464 F. Supp. 804 (D.D.C. 1979) (corporation as "person" under FOIA).

3.3.3. While Exemption 4 cannot be invoked to protect government-generated information, the Supreme Court, citing Rule 26(c)(7), Fed. R. Civ. P., has held that Exemption 5 incorporates a qualified privilege for sensitive government commercial or financial information. *Federal Open Market Committee of the Federal Reserve Bank v. Merrill*, 443 U.S. 340 (1979). *See* Chapter 8 on Exemption 5, Inter- and Intra-Agency Memoranda.

3.4. Is the Information Privileged or Confidential?

3.4.1. The D.C. Circuit has ruled that, in light of the explicit reference in the legislative history to particular privileges, the terms "privileged" and "confidential" should not be treated as "synonymous." *Washington Post Co. v. HHS*, 690 F.2d 252, 268 n. 50 (D.C. Cir. 1982).

3.4.1.1. As the first circuit court to consider the meaning of "privileged" under Exemption 4, the majority in *Washington Post* noted that, as under Exemption 5, "discovery rules will provide only rough analogies, and...a particular privilege should be incorporated only after careful consideration of the language and legislative history of Exemption 4, its relationship to other exemptions, and the general disclosure mandate of FOIA." *Id.* at 268.

3.4.1.2. On remand, the district court, after reviewing the legislative history of Exemption 4, together with the Supreme Court's discussion of the relationship between discovery rules and FOIA exemptions, *United States v. Weber Aircraft Corp.*, 465 U.S. 792 (1984), held that forms protected by the "confidential report privilege" under Rule 26(b)(1) of the Federal Rules of Civil Procedure are thereby "privileged" from disclosure under Exemption 4. *Washington Post Co. v. HHS*, 603 F. Supp. 235, 237-238 (D.D.C. 1985). However, this decision was reversed by the court of appeals on grounds that the privilege argument was not raised in a timely fashion. *See Washington Post Co. v. HHS*, 795 F.2d 205 (D.C. Cir. 1986) and discussion in Chapter 20 on Litigation Strategy.

3.4.1.3. In *Sharyland Water Supply Corp. v. Block*, 755 F.2d 397, 399-400 (5th Cir. 1985), *cert. denied.*, 471 U.S. 1137 (1985), the court refused to recognize an implied "lender-borrower" privilege under this exemption on the ground that the term "privileged" in this context refers only to privileges created by the Constitution, statute, or common law.

3.4.1.4. Other published decisions dealing with a claim of privilege under this exemption concern the assertion of the "attorney-client" privilege that is explicitly referenced in the legislative history. *See Artesian Industries, Inc. v. HHS*, 646 F. Supp. 1004, 1008 (D.D.C. 1986) and cases cited therein.

3.4.1.5. In *Anderson v. HHS, supra,* the court held that the fact that the requested records were subject to a state court protective order that shielded "trade secrets" and other commercial information from disclosure did not render them "privileged" under Exemption 4. The court reasoned that the determination whether such documents contain protectable information, such as trade secrets, must be made solely with reference to Exemption 4 standards, not those that govern state court protective orders. 907 F.2d at 945.

3.4.2. "Confidential" is the key term in Exemption 4 caselaw, but it means more than that the information would not customarily be available for public perusal.

3.4.3. The test for "confidential" is an objective one requiring a showing of likely specific harm. Commercial or financial information is confidential "if disclosure of the information is likely to have either of the following effects: (1) to impair the government's ability to obtain the necessary information in the future; or (2) to cause substantial harm to the competitive position of the person from whom the information was obtained." *National Parks and Conservation Association v. Morton (I)*, 498 F.2d at 770 (D.C. Cir. 1974). *See also Worthington Compressors, Inc. v. Costle*, 662 F.2d 45, 51 (D.C. Cir. 1981), *request for modification denied sub nom. Worthington Compressors, Inc. v. Gorsuch*, 668 F.2d 1371 (D.C. Cir. 1981); *Board of Trade v. Commodity*

Futures Trading Comm'n, 627 F.2d at 401 (D.C. Cir. 1980); *Gulf & Western Industries v. United States*, 615 F.2d 527 (D.C. Cir. 1979); *Continental Oil Co. v. FPC*, 519 F.2d 31, 35 (5th Cir. 1975), *cert. denied*, 425 U.S. 971 (1976); *Continental Stock Transfer & Trust Co. v. SEC*, 566 F.2d 373, 375 (2d Cir. 1977); *American Airlines, Inc. v. National Mediation Bd.*, 588 F.2d at 871; *Westinghouse Electric Corp. v. Schlesinger*, 542 F.2d 1190 (4th Cir. 1976), *cert. denied*, 431 U.S. 924 (1977). In *McDonnell Douglas Corp. v. NASA*, 180 F.3d 303, 306-07 (D.C. Cir. 1999), the Court construed the term "confidential" in quite broad terms, suggesting that any information that, if disclosed to a competitor, might give the competitor insight into the submitters' business, then the information should be deemed confidential for Exemption 4 purposes.

3.4.4. In *9 to 5 Organization for Women Office Workers v. Board of Governors of the Federal Reserve System*, 721 F.2d 1 (1st Cir. 1983), the First Circuit adopted the National Parks test for determining what constitutes "confidential" information, and answered a question expressly left open in *National Parks*: namely, what governmental interests are protected by Exemption 4 in addition to ensuring the voluntary submission of commercial information the government could not otherwise obtain? In *9 to 5*, the court recognized that "program effectiveness" was a governmental interest protected by the exemption. Thus, the First Circuit held that, if the government can establish that disclosure of commercial records would interfere with an important governmental program, Exemption 4 would provide protection, regardless of whether the submitter would be harmed by disclosure. Subsequently, in *Critical Mass Energy Project v. NRC*, the D.C. Circuit adopted the *9 to 5* court's view that the government could sustain its Exemption 4 burden "where disclosure would harm the agency in ways unrelated to its ability to gather information," and instructed the district court on remand to afford the agency the opportunity to show that reliance on compulsory process to obtain information presently submitted on a voluntary basis "would damage some identifiable agency interest relating to program effectiveness or efficiency." 830 F.2d 278, 287 (D.C. Cir. 1987) ("*Critical Mass I*"). The Second Circuit appears to have adopted this approach as well. *Nadler v. FDIC*, 92 F.3d 93, 96 (2d Cir. 1996).

3.5. What impairs the government's ability to obtain necessary information in the future?

3.5.1. In *Critical Mass Energy Project v. NRC (II)*, 975 F.2d 871 (D.C. Cir. 1992) (*en banc*) ("*Critical Mass II*"), *cert. denied*, 507 U.S. 984 (1993), the D.C. Circuit fundamentally altered the analysis that had previously been employed to assess the possibility of "impairment." Drawing a bright-line between those instances in which submission of information is *compelled* by the government and those where submission is *voluntary*, the Court reaffirmed the application of the *National Parks* test where submission is mandatory, but held that where information is submitted voluntarily, it is exempt if the submitter can show that the information is not customarily released to the public. 975 F.2d at 879-80. *See also Center for Auto Safety v. NHTSA*, 244 F.3d 144, 148 (D.C. Cir. 2001); *Nadler v. FDIC*, *supra*.

3.5.2. The consequences of this decision are far-reaching. To begin with, it is not always clear whether information obtained by the government from private parties is submitted voluntarily or under compulsion. The D.C. Circuit in *Critical Mass II* suggests that, even where the government could use compulsory process to obtain information, it is nonetheless exempt if submitted "voluntarily." 975 F.2d at 880. In *Center for Auto Safety*, that Court held that "actual legal authority [invoked to obtain the records], rather than the parties' beliefs or intentions, governs judicial assessments of the character of submissions." 244 F.3d at 149. *Center for Auto Safety* involved a demand by the National Highway Traffic Safety Administration ("NHTSA") that a number of auto manufacturers furnish information about airbag design to the agency. Ordinarily, NHTSA "Information Requests" are compulsory and must be followed. But here, the court held that because the Information Requests demanded responses from more than ten companies, the procedures of the Paperwork Reduction Act had to be followed by the agency, but were not, rendering the information collection unlawful. Thus, the Court held that "because NHTSA lacked legal authority to enforce its request for information, the submissions cannot be considered mandatory, even if the parties reasonably believed the Information Requests were mandatory at the time. When an agency obtains information from private entities by asserting legal authority which it cannot enforce, private-party submissions are entitled to the same protection from disclosure as voluntary submissions." *Id.* At 146. This reading opens the way to agencies evading public disclosure of information *agencies* want to keep secret; the agency can always agree to accept information on a voluntary basis even if it could, and would, compel submission of the same information if necessary. The decision also creates incentives for commercial submitters to bring reverse-FOIA cases—a topic discussed in the next chapter of this book.

3.5.3. *Critical Mass II* also cast doubt on prior Exemption 4 jurisprudence. Prior to *Critical Mass II*, the fact that the government had promised confidentiality was not sufficient to bring information within Exemption 4: "It will obviously not be enough for the agency to assert simply that it received the file under a pledge of confidentiality to the one who supplied it. Undertakings of this nature cannot, in and of themselves, override the Act." *Ackerly v. Ley*, 420 F.2d 1336, 1339-40 n.3 (D.C. Cir. 1969). *See also Robles v. EPA*, 484 F.2d 843, 846 (4th Cir. 1973). Although these two cases involved Exemption 6, this principle has also been applied to Exemption 4. *Public Citizen*, 704 F.2d 1280, 1287 (D.C. Cir. 1983) ; *Teich v. FDA*, 751 F. Supp. at 249 (collecting cases); *Petkas v. Staats*, 501 F.2d 887, 889 (D.C. Cir. 1974); *9 to 5 Organization for Women Office Workers*, 721 F.2d at 10; *Legal Aid Soc'y of Alameda County v. Shultz*, 349 F. Supp. 771, 776 (N.D. Cal. 1972); *Getman v. NLRB*, 450 F.2d at 673; K. Davis, *Administrative Law Treatise*, Sec. 3A.22 (Supp. 1970). It is unclear whether this is still prevailing law in the D.C. Circuit.

3.5.4. Similarly, prior to *Critical Mass II*, if information was required to be submitted pursuant to a statute, regulation, some less formal mandate, or as a condition for a valuable benefit, it was unlikely that a court would hold that the government's ability to obtain such information would be impaired by disclosure. *General Electric Co. v. NRC*, 750 F.2d 1394 (7th Cir. 1984); *Van Bourg, Allen, Weinberg & Roger v. NLRB*, 728 F.2d 1270 (9th Cir. 1984); *Worthington Compressor, Inc.*, 662 F.2d at 51; *National Parks*, 498 F.2d at

770; *Buffalo Evening News v. SBA*, 666 F. Supp. 467, 471 (W.D.N.Y. 1987); *Neal-Cooper Grain Co. v. Kissinger*, 385 F. Supp. 769, 776-77 (D.D.C. 1974). *But see Green v. Department of Commerce*, 468 F. Supp. 691, 693 (D.D.C. 1979), *app. dismissed*, 618 F.2d 836 (D.C. Cir. 1980) (promise of confidentiality is a factor to be considered); *Lee Pharmaceuticals v. Kreps*, 577 F.2d 610, 616 n.7 (9th Cir. 1978), *cert. denied*, 439 U.S. 1073 (1979) (same). The D.C. Circuit appears to have reaffirmed this approach in *Niagara Mohawk Power Corp. v. DOE*, 169 F.3d 16, 18 (D.C. Cir. 1999), where the court emphasized that a claim that disclosure of information submitted under statutory compulsion would impair the government's ability to obtain similar information in the future is "inherently weak."

3.5.5. Following *Critical Mass II*, it no longer appears that the "impairment" prong of the *National Parks* analysis is "not at issue" where submission of the information is "compulsory." *CNA Fin. Corp. v. Donovan*, 830 F.2d 1132, 1152 n.143 (D.C. Cir. 1987). *See also Canal Refining Co.*, 616 F. Supp. at 1042, *citing Worthington Compressors*, 662 F.2d at 51 and *NOW v. SSA*, 736 F.2d 727, 737 n. 97 (D.C. Cir. 1984). *But see Critical Mass I*, 830 F.2d at 284-286 (court acknowledged that compelled production of reports now voluntarily submitted could entail qualitative impairment of the information they contain, and ordered district court on remand to permit agency "to document its necessarily uncertain prediction that disclosure would impair either the factual basis, or analytical quality" of the reports; to pass muster, the agency must "spell out comprehensibly" both the nature of the information it fears will not be obtained, and the nexus between the disclosure and the anticipated impairment).

3.5.6. Although the D.C. Circuit's *en banc* decision in *Critical Mass II* may eventually influence the Exemption 4 jurisprudence in the other circuits that have endorsed the *National Parks* test, only the Second in *Nadler* has adopted it explicitly. 92 F.3d at 96. Two other circuits have noted the modification brought about in *Critical Mass II.* In *Frazee v. U.S. Forest Service,* 97 F.3d 367 (9th Cir. 1996) the Ninth Circuit declined to reach the question of whether the *Critical Mass* test should be adopted; in *State of Utah v. Dep't of the Interior*, 256 F.3d 967 (10th Cir. 2001) the Tenth Circuit referred in passing to *Critical Mass II,* but did not expressly adopt it.

3.5.6.1. The only two reported district court decisions that considered the issue reached opposite results with respect to the *National Parks* precedent in the Fourth Circuit. *Compare Environmental Technology, Inc. v. EPA*, 822 F. Supp. 1226 (E.D. Va. 1993) with *Comdisco, Inc. v. GSA*, 864 F. Supp. 510 (E.D. Va. 1994).

3.5.6.2. In *Comdisco,* a "reverse FOIA" case, the court criticized the earlier opinion in *Environmental Technology* as providing "little justification for its conclusion that *Critical Mass* would be persuasive to the Fourth Circuit." 864 F. Supp. at 517. The court also concluded that the *Critical Mass* modification was unnecessary because the first prong of the *National Parks* test "already largely incorporates the voluntary/mandatory distinction urged in *Critical Mass*, and in so doing, properly accommodates the governmental interest in ensuring continued access to desired information." *Id.* at 518.

3.5.6.3. In ruling that unit price information in a public contract bid was not exempt from disclosure, the court in *Comdisco* asserted that the voluntary/mandatory distinction, though generally consistent with the results of the "impairment" prong analysis, is "certainly not dispositive" of the inquiry in a given case. *Id.* at 518 n.9. Moreover, the court concluded, the distinction is relevant only to the initial "impairment" inquiry, and applying it to the second prong of the *National Parks* test converts the objective "competitive harm" test into a "purely subjective one over which the submitter has exclusive or substantial control." *Id.* There have been a number of decisions post-dating *Critical Mass II* regarding disclosure of government contract information, generally requiring the disclosure of unit pricing information because it is required to be submitted, but generally upholding decisions to shield other bid information which is not required to be submitted. *See, e.g., McDonnell Douglas Corp. v. NASA,* 180 F.3d 303 (D.C. Cir. 1999) (line item pricing—which is different than unit pricing—need not be disclosed because competitors would "ratchet down" bids to NASA if information were released); *MCI Worldcom v. GSA,* 2001 U.S. DIST. LEXIS 20292 (D.D.C. 2001) (detailed pricing information does not constitute unit prices and must be withheld under Exemption 4 and the Trade Secrets Act); *Mallinckrodt Inc. v. West*, 140 F. Supp. 2d 1 (D.D.C. 2000) (unit prices must be disclosed, but other information in bid was submitted voluntarily and need not be disclosed); *Cortez III Service Corp. v. NASA,* 921 F. Supp. 8 (D.D.C. 1996) (reverse-FOIA case holding that "rate ceiling" information was voluntarily submitted and customarily kept confidential and hence could not be disclosed).

3.5.7. One court has ruled that records generated during unsuccessful settlement negotiations concerning a debarment action brought by an agency against a government contractor were properly denied to a competing contractor under Exemption 4. *M/A-COM Information Systems, Inc. v. HHS*, 656 F. Supp. 691 (D.D.C. 1986). Although the court characterized the corporation-contractor's commercial interest in the information as "slight," the court upheld the exemption claim on grounds that "it is in the public interest to encourage settlement negotiations in matters of this kind and it would impair the ability of HHS to carry out its governmental duties if disclosure of this kind of material under FOIA were required." *Id.* at 692.

3.5.8. The D.C. Circuit has held that an agency must demonstrate that the impairment will be "significant," and that a "minor impairment" cannot overcome the disclosure mandate of the FOIA. *Critical Mass I,* 830 F.2d at 283; *Washington Post Co. v. HHS,* 690 F.2d at 269. The agency's claim of impairment must be supported by a "detailed factual justification," not just generalized or conclusory affidavits. *Critical Mass I,* 830 F.2d at 283. Determining the degree of impairment "necessarily involves a rough balancing of the extent of impairment and the importance of the information against the public interest in disclosure." *Washington Post Co. v. HHS,* 690 F.2d at 269. In a later decision in the *Washington Post* case, the D.C. Circuit elaborated on the "balancing" test, holding that "information will be withheld only when the affirmative interests in disclosure on the one side are outweighed by the factors identified in *National Parks I* (and its progeny) militating against disclosure on the other side." *Washington Post Co. v. HHS,* 865 F.2d 320, 326-27 (D.C. Cir. 1989).

3.5.9. "The agency is in the best position to determine the effect of disclosure on its ability to obtain necessary technical information." *Orion Research Inc. v. EPA,* 615 F.2d 551, 554 (1st Cir. 1980), *cert. denied,* 449 U.S. 833 (1980); *see also Durnan v. Department of Commerce,* 777 F. Supp. 965 (D.D.C. 1991). This view has led at least one court to hold that the "impairment" test does not apply in a submitter's reverse FOIA suit because the agency, "by deciding to release the information, necessarily made the determination that disclosure will not impair its ability to obtain information in the future." *AT&T Information Systems,* 627 F. Supp. at 1401. *See also Hercules, Inc. v. Marsh,* 839 F.2d 1027, 1030 (4th Cir. 1988) (contractor precluded from raising impairment claim on agency's behalf).

3.6. Will Disclosure Cause Substantial Harm to the Submitter's Competitive Position?

3.6.1. Some cases for disclosure can be won if it can be shown that the information relates to matters as to which there is no competition. *Niagara Mohawk Power,* 169 F.3d at 18-19 (reaffirming that burden of showing actual and substantial competition must be borne by party resisting disclosure); *Hughes Aircraft Co. v. Schlesinger,* 384 F. Supp. 292, 297 (C.D. Cal. 1974) (no competitive harm where labor cost information which might be derived from requested material is already shared with competitors in industry-wide wage-and-salary surveys). *But see National Parks and Conservation Ass'n v. Morton (II),* 351 F. Supp. 404 (D.D.C. 1975), *aff'd sub nom. National Parks and Conservation Ass'n v. Kleppe (II),* 547 F.2d 673, 681-684 (D.C. Cir. 1976) ("meaningful day-to-day competition with businesses offering similar goods and services" met the harm test where "contract renewal" competition did not). On the other hand, the D.C. Circuit has stated that "[i]n order to show the likelihood of substantial competitive harm, it is not necessary to show actual competitive harm. Actual competition and the likelihood of substantial competitive injury is all that need be shown." *Gulf & Western Industries, Inc. v. United States,* 615 F.2d at 530; *accord CNA Fin. Corp. v. Donovan,* 830 F.2d at 1152.

3.6.2. One court has held that patent protection does not necessarily preclude application of Exemption 4. *Johnson v. HEW,* 462 F. Supp. 336, 337-38 (D.D.C. 1978).

3.6.3. Most cases will turn on the question of whether disclosure would be likely to cause substantial competitive harm to the submitter. *See, e.g., Niagara Mohawk Power, supra; Orion Research Inc. v. EPA, supra; Shermco Industries, Inc. v. Secretary of the Air Force,* 613 F.2d 1314 (5th Cir. 1980).

3.6.4. Courts have traditionally protected several categories of records: data revealing assets, profits, losses and market shares [*see, e.g., National Parks and Conservation Ass'n v. Morton (I),* 498 F.2d 765 (D.C. Cir. 1974), *subsequent opinion*, 547 F.2d 673 (D.C. Cir. 1976); *Sterling Drug, Inc. v. FTC*, 450 F.2d 698 (D.C. Cir. 1971); *McCoy v. Weinberger*, 386 F. Supp. 504 (W.D. Ky. 1974); *Benson v. GSA*, 289 F. Supp. 590 (W.D. Wash. 1968), *aff'd*, 415 F.2d 878 (9th Cir. 1969)]; detailed reports concerning natural gas reserve data and intrastate sales information, including name of purchaser, dates and locations of sales, sales volume and price terms [*see, e.g., Continental Oil Co. v. FPC, supra; Union Oil Co. of California v. Federal Power Commission*, 542 F.2d 1036 (9th Cir. 1976)]; data describing a company's workforce from which competitors could deduce labor costs, profit margins, competitive vulnerability and predict product and process changes [*see, e.g., Westinghouse Electric Corp. v. Schlesinger*, 392 F. Supp. 1246 (E.D. Va. 1974), *aff'd*, 542 F.2d 1190 (4th Cir. 1976), *cert. denied*, 431 U.S. 924 (1977)]; information concerning the development of drugs and medical devices [*Public Citizen Health Research Group v. FDA,* 185 F.3d 898 (D.C. Cir. 1999); *Public Citizen Health Research Group v. FDA*, 704 F.2d 1280 (D.C. Cir. 1983)]; reports which include information given by and concerning borrowers and applicants for loans [*see, e.g., Nadler v. FDIC,* 92 F.3d 93 (2d Cir. 1996); *Rural Housing Alliance v. USDA*, 498 F.2d 73 (D.C. Cir. 1974)]; and information relating to government contracts [*see, e.g., McDonnell Douglas Corp. v. NASA, supra; Gulf & Western Industries, Inc. v. United States, supra; Orion Research Inc. v. EPA, supra; Shermco Industries v. Secretary of the Air Force, supra*].

3.6.5. Information which has been publicly disseminated or is available from other sources falls outside of the exemption. *Niagara Mohawk Power Corp.,* 169 F.3d at 19; *Frazee v. U.S. Forest Service*, 97 F.3d 367 (9th Cir. 1996); *Anderson v. HHS*, 907 F.2d at 952; *CNA Fin. Corp. v. Donovan,* 830 F.2d at 1154; *Sharyland Water Supply Corp. v. Block,* 755 F.2d at 399-400; *Continental Oil Co. v. FPC*, 519 F.2d at 35. However, government disclosure to a state attorney general of material relating to an antitrust investigation is not considered a public release, *Interco, Inc. v. FTC*, 478 F. Supp. 103 (D.D.C. 1979); nor is limited disclosure to opposing counsel pursuant to an understanding of confidentiality. *Gulf & Western Industries, Inc. v. United States*, 615 F.2d at 533.

3.6.6. In *Worthington Compressors, Inc. v. Costle, supra*, the court rejected the notion that Exemption 4 was inapplicable simply because the requested information (air compressor manufacturer's noise test results and design specifications) might also be available to the requester through private testing and "reverse engineering." The court remanded the case to determine, among other things, whether the information has "commercial value" to competitors, and, if so, to evaluate the "commercial practicability of private acquisition of the commercially valuable information." The court indicated that the "substantial competitive harm" test would be met "[i]f private reproduction of the information would be so expensive or arcane as to be impracticable." 662 F.2d at 50-54. *See also Northwest Coalition for Alternatives to Pesticides v. Browner*, 941 F. Supp. 197 (D.D.C. 1996).

3.6.7. There is some dispute within the D.C. Circuit over the application of its *Worthington Compressors* decision to summary judgment motions in cases where the cost and availability of the requested information from alternative sources is contested. Citing that decision, the majority in *Greenberg v. FDA*, 803 F.2d 1213 (D.C. Cir. 1986), denied summary judgment to the agency as inappropriate in light of the requester's affidavits suggesting that "a close facsimile of the disputed customer list" could be constructed from publicly available information. But the dissent, noting the submitter's contention that lists compiled as the requester suggested would require the searcher to expend substantial amounts of time and money, and would only be partial lists at best, argued that *Worthington Compressors* "does not stand for the proposition that summary judgment barring disclosure of information is never warranted when some of the requested information may be available from additional sources. Where it is clear...that the information requested can be obtained from additional sources only partially, and only by expending tremendous amounts of time, money, and effort, the use of summary judgment to bar disclosure is appropriate." 803 F.2d at 1222-23 n.2 (Bork, J., dissenting).

3.6.8. Several courts, including the D.C. Circuit, have held that the harms flowing from "embarrassing" disclosures, or disclosures that could cause customer or employee disgruntlement, are not cognizable under Exemption 4. *Public Citizen Health Research Group v. FDA,* 704 F.2d at 1291 n.30; *CNA Fin. Corp. v. Donovan,* 830 F.2d at 1154; *General Electric Co. v. NRC,* 750 F.2d at 1402-3; *Center to Prevent Handgun Violence v. Dep't of Treasury,* 981 F. Supp. 20 (D.D.C. 1997). *But see Occidental Petroleum Corp. v. SEC,* 873 F.2d 325, 341 (D.C. Cir. 1989) (reverse FOIA case, avoiding question of what harms could flow from disclosure of allegedly commercial records).

3.6.9. In order to demonstrate the likelihood of substantial competitive harm to the submitter, the agency must (1) show that the submitter faces actual competition, *Niagara Mohawk Power Corp., supra, Worthington Compressors, Inc. v. Costle, supra; Gulf & Western Industries v. U.S. , supra; National Parks and Conservation Ass'n v. Kleppe (II),* 547 F.2d 673 (D.C. Cir. 1976) and (2) demonstrate, with specific and direct evidence, the likely consequences of disclosure. *Id.* While the agency "need not conduct a sophisticated economic analysis of the likely effects of disclosure," *Public Citizen Health Research Group v. FDA*, 704 F.2d at 1291, it cannot rest on "conclusory and generalized allegations of substantial competitive harm." *Id. See also Niagara Mohawk Power Corp.,* 169 F.3d at 18-19 (same); *GC Micro Corp v. Defense Logistics Agency,* 33 F.3d 1109, 1115 (9th Cir. 1994) (reports of government contractors' compliance with Small Disadvantaged Business program's subcontracting goals held not exempt as "confidential" because data on the percentage and dollar amount of work subcontracted to SDBs on each defense contract "is made up of too many fluctuating variables" and would provide "little if any help to competitors attempting to estimate and undercut the contractors bids"); *Hercules, Inc. v. Marsh,* 839 F.2d at 1030 (contractor's claims regarding competitive injury were "entirely conclusive or speculative").

3.6.10. The existence of such adverse consequences is a factual question. *Niagara Mohawk Power Corp.,* 169 F.3d at 18; *Worthington Compressors, Inc. v. Costle,* 662 F.2d at 54; *Sears, Roebuck & Co. v. GSA,* 553 F.2d 1378, 1382 (D.C. Cir. 1977); *National Ass'n of Government Employees v. Campbell,* 593 F.2d 1023, 1028 (D.C. Cir. 1978); *Pacific Architects &Engineers, Inc. v.*

Renegotiation Bd., 505 F.2d 383, 385 (D.C. Cir. 1974). When affidavits are in dispute, the trial court must resolve the issue through an adversarial procedure. An evidentiary hearing in court, however, is not necessarily required, and discovery techniques may provide a sufficient degree of adversarial testing. *Compare Sears*, 553 F.2d at 1382-83 (remanded for discovery by interrogatories, oral depositions, requests for admissions, or an open hearing in court with or without the preceding discovery procedure) *with National Ass'n of Government Employees v. Campbell*, 593 F.2d at 1028 (remanded for full evidentiary trial); *see also Black Hills Alliance v. U.S. Forest Service,* 603 F. Supp. 117 (D.S.D. 1984); and *Professional Review Org. of Florida, Inc. v. HHS*, 607 F. Supp. 423 (D.D.C. 1985). Many lower courts, however, require an evidentiary hearing to resolve issues of likeliness of competitive harm. *Public Citizen Health Research Group v. FDA*, 953 F. Supp. 400 (D.D.C. 1996). *Braintree Electric Light Department v. DOE*, 494 F. Supp. 287 (D.D.C. 1980); *Green v. Department of Commerce*, 468 F. Supp. at 692; *Johnson v. HEW*, 462 F. Supp. at 338; *but see Burke Energy Corp. v. DOE*, 583 F. Supp. 507 (D. Kan. 1984) (decided Exemption 4 issue on the basis of agency affidavits and *Vaughn* index).

3.6.11. In *Save the Dolphins v. Department of Commerce,* 404 F. Supp. 407 (N.D. Cal. 1975), the court conducted *in camera* proceedings in which all parties participated under a protective order. 404 F. Supp. at 409. Although this procedure has been approved by the Fifth Circuit in *Seafarers International Union AFL-CIO v. Baldovin*, 508 F.2d 125, 129 (5th Cir. 1975), joint party participation in *in camera* proceedings is likely to be the exception rather than the rule. *See Arieff v. Department of the Navy*, 712 F.2d 1462 (D.C. Cir. 1983).

3.6.12. Submitters of information that might arguably fall within Exemption 4 are entitled to notification by the agency prior to the agency disclosing the information to a third party under FOIA. Since 1987, Executive Order 12600 has required each agency to establish procedures to notify submitters of records of a pending request and to give submitters an opportunity to demonstrate to the agency that the documents are subject to withholding under Exemption 4. *See infra*,, Chapter 7, Reverse FOIA Litigation, ¶ 11. In practice, agencies generally work closely with submitters to ensure that the submitter's position is fully considered before the agency decides whether to disclose the submitter's information.

CHAPTER 7

Reverse FOIA Litigation

David C. Vladeck

1. **"Reverse" FOIA cases are those in which a private party—usually a corporation—which has submitted information to the government sues in federal court to prevent the disclosure of that information in response to a FOIA request.** Although these cases were once somewhat unusual, they are now common, and many of the key questions about the procedures to be used and the substantive standards to be applied have been answered.

2. **There are two lead Supreme Court decisions in reverse-FOIA cases:**

2. 1. The first was *Chrysler Corp. v. Brown,* 441 U.S. 281 (1979), which involved Chrysler's effort to bar the release of certain affirmative action data by the Department of Defense. When the Department informed Chrysler that it would release the company's data, Chrysler brought suit for an injunction, contending that disclosure was barred by both Exemption 4 and the Trade Secrets Act, 18 U.S.C. § 1905, a criminal law forbidding the disclosure of trade secret and confidential business information unless disclosure is "authorized by law." After a trial, the district court enjoined disclosure of the data on the grounds that it fell within both Exemption 4 and the Trade Secrets Act. The Third Circuit reversed. *Chrysler Corp. v. Schlesinger*, 565 F.2d 1172 (3d Cir. 1977). The Supreme Court unanimously reversed, holding that: (1) the FOIA is exclusively a disclosure statute and that the Act provides no right of action to enjoin the disclosure of records; (2) submitters of information have a legally cognizable interest in information provided to the government; (3) review is available to challenge agency decisions to disclose materials under FOIA through the Administrative Procedure Act (APA), with subject-matter jurisdiction properly invoked under 28 U.S.C. § 1331; and (4) agency decisions to disclose materials that fall within the Trade Secrets Act are not "authorized by law" unless the disclosures are made pursuant to a statute or substantive regulation promulgated in accordance with the notice and comment procedures of the APA, 5 § 553.

2.2. The second key decision came in *GTE Sylvania, Inc. v. Consumers Union of the United States, Inc.*, 445 U.S. 375 (1980). In *GTE*, requesters who had filed an FOIA suit in one jurisdiction after the submitters obtained an order restraining disclosure in another jurisdiction were effectively barred from litigating their FOIA action in the jurisdiction of their choice because the Court ruled that the agency's nondisclosure pursuant to the submitter's court order was not an "improper withholding" of information under the FOIA. The resolution of the case has resulted not only in a race to the courthouse but also a race to obtain the first order. After *GTE*, therefore, sophisticated requesters have sought to devise more ingenious ways to initiate FOIA actions before submitters initiate reverse FOIA actions.

2.2.1. Regardless of the wishes of the parties, the failure of a district court to bring in a corporation whose interest in the records at issue would be affected by the litigation was found to be the basis for a remand with directions to the lower court to follow Rule 19(a), F.R.C.P. *See Weisberg v. DOJ*, 631 F.2d 824 (D.C. Cir. 1980), *see also subsequent opinion at*, 745 F.2d 1476, 1481-82 n. 7 (D.C. Cir. 1984). The court relied, in part, on its conclusion that, in the context of the issues involved in the case, *GTE* might not bar a subsequent suit by the corporation, and therefore the possibility of duplicative litigation should have prompted the district court to obtain the corporation's participation. *See id.* at 830 n.39. *But see LaRouche v. Kelley*, No. 75 Civ. 6010 (S.D.N.Y. 1979), *reversed and remanded sub nom. LaRouche v. FBI*, 677 F.2d 256 (2d Cir. 1982), in which the district court refused to permit a requester to intervene in a suit brought by another requester who, having obtained some of the documents, was seeking to prevent their disclosure to others.

3. The first question in resolving a reverse FOIA claim is whether the requested records fall within any of the FOIA's nine exemptions. Most reverse FOIA cases involve Exemption 4.

3.1. If the records are not exempt, the mandatory disclosure provisions of the FOIA apply and the material must be disclosed. The courts have no equitable discretion to refuse to disclose non-exempt information. *See Department of the Air Force v. Rose*, 425 U.S. 352, 371-75 (1976). *See also* Chapter 1, Overview, at 5.2.

3.2. If the records fall within any FOIA exemption, they may nonetheless be disclosed at the agency's discretion. The FOIA's exemptions are permissive, not mandatory. *Chrysler Corp. v. Brown*, 441 U.S. at 293.

3.3. If an agency decides to disclose information that falls within an FOIA exemption, the submitter may challenge the agency's exercise of discretion, under the APA on the grounds that it is arbitrary and capricious, an abuse of discretion, or otherwise not in accordance with law. *Id.* at 317-18. *See* 5 U.S.C. § 706.

4. The Supreme Court in *Chrysler Corp. v. Brown*, 441 U.S. at 318, made clear that a disclosure of information which falls within both an FOIA exemption (usually Exemption 4) and the Trade Secrets Act, 18 U.S.C. § 1905, would be "not in accordance with law" under the APA.

4.1. The Court explicitly did not determine the scope of either Exemption 4 or § 1905, except to imply in a cryptic footnote that the two provisions would in most cases be co-extensive. *See id.*, at 319 n. 49. In those few "theoretical[ly] possib[le]" cases in which material might be outside Exemption 4 yet within the substantive provisions of § 1905, the Court indicated that the FOIA "might provide the necessary authoriz[ation] by law" under § 1905 to release § 1905 material. *Id.*

4.2. Post-*Chrysler* decisions by circuit courts on the scope of both Exemption 4 and § 1905 have essentially resolved the question left open by the *Chrysler* Court. With respect to the respective ambits of the Trade Secrets Act and Exemption 4, the D.C. Circuit has ruled that the Act's scope is "at least co-extensive with that of Exemption 4." *McDonnell Douglas Corp. v. NASA*, 180 F.3d 303, 305 (D.C. Cir. 1999); *Bartholdi Cable Co. v. FCC*, 114 F.3d 274, 279 (D.C. Cir. 1997); *CNA Fin. Corp. v. Donovan*, 830 F.2d 1132, 1151 (D.C. Cir. 1987). Other Circuits have expressed a similar view. *See, e.g., Pacific Architects & Engineers, Inc. v. Department of State*, 906 F.2d 1345, 1347 (9th Cir. 1990) (information falling within Trade Secrets Act may not be disclosed); *Dowty Decoto, Inc. v. Department of the Navy*, 883 F.2d 774 (9th Cir. 1989) (same); *General Electric Co. v. NRC*, 750 F.2d 1394, 1401-1402 (7th Cir. 1984) (where the document is not protected by Exemption 4, "even more clearly it is not protected by Section 1905 either"); *9 to 5 Organization for Women Office Workers v.*

Board of Governors of the Federal Reserve System, 721 F.2d 1, 12 (1st Cir. 1983) ("If the government cannot prove that the requested documents are within FOIA Exemption 4, their disclosure will not violate section 1905."); *General Motors Corp. v. Marshall*, 654 F.2d 294, 297 (4th Cir. 1981) (Section 1905 is no broader than Exemption 4, and if material is exempt under Exemption 4 it is prohibited from disclosure under § 1905). Thus, when information falls within Exemption 4, the government generally is precluded from releasing it due to the constraints of the Trade Secrets Act. *McDonnell Douglas Corp*., 180 F.3d at 305, *Bartholdi*, 114 F.3d at 281; *Pacific Architects & Eng'rs*, 906 F.2d at 1347. On the other hand, where information falls outside the scope of Exemption 4, it is not protected from disclosure by the Trade Secrets Act. *Frazee v. U.S. Forest Service*, 79 F.3d 367, 373 (9th Cir. 1996); *CNA*, 830 F.2d at 1152 n.139.

5. **Whether § 1905 is a statute within Exemption 3 was also explicitly *not* decided by the Supreme Court in *Chrysler Corp. v. Brown. See* 441 U.S. at 319 n. 49. For discussion of the lower court case law on this issue, see Chapter 5 on Information Exempted By Other Statutes.**

6. **Valid agency regulations, as well as statutes, may provide the "authoriz[ation] by law" necessary under § 1905 to disclose § 1905 material. *Chrysler Corp. v. Brown*, 441 U.S. at 295.**

6.1. The Office of Federal Contract Compliance Programs (OFCCP) regulations relied upon respectively by the Third, Seventh and Eighth Circuits in *Chrysler*, in *Sears, Roebuck & Co. v. Eckerd*, 575 F.2d 1197 (7th Cir. 1978), *vacated and remanded sub nom. Sears, Roebuck & Co. v. Dahm*, 441 U.S. 918 (1979), and in *General Dynamics Corp. v. Marshall*, 572 F.2d 1211 (8th Cir. 1978), *vacated and remanded*, 441 U.S. 919 (1979), *remanded*, 607 F.2d 234 (8th Cir. 1979), as "authoriz[ation] by law" under § 1905 do not, however, provide such authority. *Chrysler Corp. v. Brown*, 441 U.S. at 295-316.

6.2. The impact on other cases of the analysis employed by the *Chrysler* Court to reach its conclusion on the OFCCP regulations is unclear. For cases since *Chrysler* in which courts have found other disclosure regulations, or statutes, to provide the "authoriz[ation] by law" to disclose § 1905 material, *see, e.g., Parkridge Hospital, Inc. v. Califano*, 625 F.2d 719 (6th Cir. 1980); *Humana of Virginia, Inc. v. Blue Cross of Virginia*, 622 F.2d 76 (4th Cir. 1980); *St. Joseph's Hospital Health Center v. Blue Cross of Central New York*, 614 F.2d 1290 (2d Cir. 1979); *St. Mary's Hospital v. Harris*, 604 F.2d 407 (5th Cir. 1979); *Interco, Inc. v. FTC*, 490 F. Supp. 39 (D.D.C. 1979); *Cedars Nursing & Convalescent Center, Inc. v. Aetna Life & Casualty Insurance Co.*, 472 F. Supp. 296 (E.D. Pa. 1979); *Brookwood Medical Center, Inc. v. Califano*, 470 F. Supp. 1247 (N.D. Ga. 1979), *aff'd sub nom. Brookwood Medical Center, Inc. v. Harris*, 614 F.2d 1295 (5th Cir. 1980); *RBR Corp. v. Browner*, 924 F. Supp. 504 (S.D.N.Y. 1996).

7. **The D.C. Circuit's *en banc* decision in *Critical Mass Energy Project v. NRC (II)*, 975 F.2d 871 (D.C. Cir. 1992), has reinvigorated reverse-FOIA litigation.** Many of the cases involve bid submitters who have brought reverse actions to enjoin the disclosure of commercial information contained in their bids on the theory that the submissions were "voluntary" within the meaning of *Critical Mass*. Under this theory, voluntary submissions fall within Exemption 4, and hence disclosure would violate the

Trade Secrets Act, 18 U.S.C. § 1905. The courts have divided on whether information submitted in the bidding process is, in fact, submitted voluntarily. *Compare Environmental Technology, Inc. V. EPA*, 822 F. Supp. 1226 (E.D. Va. 1993) (enjoining disclosure of bid information) *with Frazee v. U.S. Forest Service*, 97 F.3d 367 (9th Cir. 1996) (refusing to enjoin bid information); *Comdisco, Inc. v. GSA*, 864 F. Supp. 510 (E.D. Va. 1994) (same). In *Comdisco,* the court criticized the earlier opinion in *Environmental Technology* as providing "little justification for its conclusion that *Critical Mass* would be persuasive to the Fourth Circuit." 864 F. Supp. at 517. The court also concluded that the *Critical Mass* modification was unnecessary because the first prong of the *National Parks* test "already largely incorporates the voluntary/mandatory distinction urged in *Critical Mass*, and in so doing, properly accommodates the governmental interest in ensuring continued access to desired information." *Id.* at 518.

7.1. There have been a number of decisions post-dating *Critical Mass II* regarding disclosure of government contract information, generally requiring the disclosure of unit pricing information because it is required to be submitted, but generally upholding decisions to shield other bid information which is not required to be submitted. *See, e.g., McDonnell Douglas Corp. v. NASA,* 180 F.3d 303 (D.C. Cir. 1999) (line item pricing "which is different than unit pricing" need not be disclosed because competitors would "ratchet down" bids to NASA if information were released); *MCI Worldcom v. GSA,* 2001 U.S. DIST. LEXIS 20292 (D.D.C. 2001) (detailing pricing information does not constitute unit prices and must be withheld under Exemption 4 and the Trade Secrets Act); *Mallinckrodt Inc. v. West*, 140 F. Supp. 2d 1 (D.D.C. 2000) (unit prices must be disclosed, but other information in bid was submitted voluntarily and need not be disclosed); *Cortez III Service Corp. v. NASA,* 921 F. Supp. 8 (D.D.C. 1996) (reverse-FOIA case holding that "rate ceiling" information was voluntarily submitted and customarily kept confidential and hence could not be disclosed). The question of the voluntariness of the submission has been addressed in other contexts as well. *See, e.g., McDonnell Douglas Corp. v. EEOC*, 922 F. Supp. 235 (E.D. Mo. 1996) (employee data obtained from company by subpoena was not voluntarily submitted; injunction entered barring disclosure); *RSR Corp. v. Browner*, 924 F. Supp. 504 (S.D.N.Y. 1996) (refusing to enjoin disclosure of information submitted pursuant to regulatory requirement).

8. **The Supreme Court in *Chrysler Corp. v. Brown* did not squarely address the question of the proper scope of review in reverse FOIA cases.** Insofar as the Court held that such cases are properly based on the APA and not on the FOIA or § 1905, the scope of review provided in the APA, 5 U.S.C. § 706, would seem to govern. In most circumstances, this should be review based on the agency's own record, not *de novo* review. *See Camp. v. Pitts*, 411 U.S. 138 (1973); *Citizens to Preserve Overton Park, Inc. v. Volpe*, 401 U.S. 402 (1971). The *Chrysler* Court seemed to approve this approach in its statement that a determination of whether a disclosure is "not in accordance with law" under the APA because it is contrary to § 1905 would "ordinarily" not necessitate *de novo* review. 441 U.S. at 318.

8.1. Post-*Chrysler* courts have uniformly held that judicial review in reverse-FOIA cases should be APA—arbitrary and capricious review, based on the administrative record. *See, e.g., Campaign for Family Farms v. Glickman,* 200 F.3d 1180, 1184 (8th Cir. 2000); *Reliance Elec. Co. v. CPSC,* 924 F.2d 274, 277 (D.C. Cir. 1991); *Pacific*

Architects & Engineers, Inc. v. Department of State, 906 F.2d 1345, 1348 (9th Cir. 1990); *Accumenics Research & Tech. v. DOJ*, 843 F.2d 800, 804-805 (4th Cir. 1988); *CNA Fin. Corp. v. Donovan*, 830 F.2d 1132, 1162 (D.C. Cir. 1987). Under this approach, *de novo* review is limited to cases where the agency's administrative procedures are severely defective. *McDonnell Douglas Corp. v. Widnall*, 57 F.3d 1162, 1167 (D.C. Cir. 1995).

9. **Judicial review on the "whole record," 5 U.S.C. § 706(2), means the administrative record compiled by the agency in advance of litigation, not any record thereafter constructed in the reviewing court. *Camp v. Pitts*, 411 U.S. at 142; *Citizens to Preserve Overton Park*, 401 U.S. at 419-20.** Where the agency provided no justification at the administrative level for its refusal to withhold submitted data, it is precluded from initially offering one on judicial review. *AT&T Information Systems v. GSA*, 810 F.2d 1233, 1236 (D.C. Cir. 1987). Faced with an inadequate record, the court must remand to the agency for development of its reasons for deciding not to withhold. *Id. See generally General Electric Co. v. NRC,* 750 F.2d 1394, 1403 (7th Cir. 1984); *Occidental Petroleum Corp. v. SEC*, 873 F.2d 325, 342 (D.C. Cir. 1989).

9.1. However, it has been held permissible for the court to consider an agency affidavit while reviewing the administrative record, where the submission "did no more than summarize" that record. *Hercules, Inc. v. Marsh,* 839 F.2d 1027, 1030 (4th Cir. 1988). *See also Acumenics Research & Technology,* 843 F.2d at 806 n.7 (court found affidavit "does no more than explain and elaborate on the administrative record"). Both decisions cite *Camp v. Pitts, supra,* as precedential authority.

10. **The *Chrysler* Court did not resolve the question of burden of proof. The law is now clear that in a reverse-FOIA case, the party seeking to prevent the disclosure of information that the government is willing to make public bears the burden of justifying non-disclosure.** *Frazee v. U.S. Forest Service*, 97 F.3d 367, 371 (9th Cir. 1996); *Occidental Petroleum Corp. v. SEC*, 873 F.2d 325, 342 (D.C. Cir. 1989); *TRIFID Corp. v. National Imagery & Mapping Agency,* 10 F. Supp. 2d 1087, 1097 (E.D. Mo. 1998).

11. **FOIA contains no requirement governing predisclosure notification to submitters.** Executive Order 12600, issued by President Reagan on June 23, 1987 and entitled "Predisclosure Notification Procedures for Confidential Commercial Information," required each agency to establish procedures to notify submitters of records "that arguably contain material exempt from release under Exemption 4" when those records are requested under the FOIA "if after reviewing the request, the responsive records, and any appeal by the requester," the agency determines that it may be required to disclose the records. *See* Executive Order, No. 12600, 3 C.F.R. 235 (1988), *reprinted in* 5 U.S.C. § 552 note*; see also* 52 Fed. Reg. 23781 (June 25, 1987).

11.1. Individual agency regulations govern the precise notification procedures. Agencies must give submitters reasonable time to object to disclosure of any of the requested material. E.O. 12600 § 4. *McDonnell Douglas Corp. v. NASA*, 895 F. Supp. 319, 323 (D.D.C. 1995). Nothing in the Executive Order requires agencies to give submitters a hearing prior to the release of information. *CNA Fin. Corp. v. Donovan*, 830 F.2d at 1159; *TRIFID Corp.*, 10 F. Supp. 2d at 1093-94.

CHAPTER 8

Exemption 5—Inter- and Intra-Agency Memoranda

Harry A. Hammitt

1. **Exemption 5 provides that the FOIA does not apply to matters that are: "inter-agency or intra-agency memorandums or letters which would not be available by law to a party other than an agency in litigation with the agency."**

2. **Of all the exemptions, the plain language of Exemption 5 is the least clear. One court has noted that the language provides only a "rough guide" to what the exemption protects.** *Coastal States Gas Corp. v. DOE*, 617 F.2d 854, 858 n.2 (D.C. Cir. 1980). Consequently, a high judicial gloss has been placed on the statutory language.

3. **Exemption 5 was intended to incorporate the government's common law privilege from discovery in litigation.** H.R. Rep. No. 1497, 89th Cong., 2d Sess. 10 (1966); S. Rep. No. 813, 89th Cong., 1st Sess. 29 (1965); S. Rep. No. 1219, 88th Cong., 2d Sess. 6-7, 13-14 (1964).

3.1. Therefore, pre-FOIA cases dealing with the privilege are important for Exemption 5 analysis. *See Carl Zeiss Stiftung v. V. E. B. Carl Zeiss, Jena*, 40 F.R.D. 318 (D.D.C. 1966), *aff'd sub nom. V.E.B. Carl Zeiss, Jena v. Clark*, 384 F.2d 979 (D.C. Cir. 1967), *cert. denied,* 389 U.S. 952 (1967) (citing numerous cases).

3.2. However, the Supreme Court has cautioned that discovery rules should be applied to FOIA cases only "by way of rough analogies." *EPA v. Mink*, 410 U.S. 73, 86 (1973).

3.3. Since the exemption is intended to permit disclosure of documents that would "routinely be disclosed" in private litigation, H.R. Rep. No. 1497, *supra* at 10, it does not permit a showing of compelling need which might overcome a claim of privilege in litigation. *FTC v. Grolier, Inc.*, 462 U.S. 19, 25-28 (1983); *Federal Open Market Committee of the Federal Reserve Bank v. Merrill*, 443 U.S. 340, 361-62 (1979); *NLRB v. Sears, Roebuck & Co.*, 421 U.S. 132, 149 n.16 (1975); *AFGE, Local 2782 v. Department of Commerce,* 907 F.2d 203, 207 (D.C. Cir. 1990); *Skelton v. U.S. Postal Service*, 678 F.2d 35, 38 n.2 (5th Cir. 1982); *Swisher v. Department of the Air Force*, 660 F.2d 369, 371 (8th Cir. 1981); *Hoover v. Department of the Interior*, 611 F.2d 1132, 1138-39 (5th Cir. 1980); *Bristol-Myers Co. v. FTC*, 598 F.2d 18, 29 (D.C. Cir. 1978) (as amended on denial of reh'g); *Sterling Drug, Inc. v. FTC*, 450 F.2d 698, 704-705 (D.C. Cir. 1971).

3.4. The Supreme Court has also noted that "it is not clear that Exemption 5 was intended to incorporate every privilege known to civil discovery," and that it would "hesitate to construe Exemption 5 to incorporate a civil discovery privilege that would substantially duplicate another [FOIA] exemption." *Federal Open Market Committee of the Federal Reserve System v. Merrill*, 443 U.S. at 354-55.

3.5. The Supreme Court later refined that statement to indicate that privileges which are "well-settled" in the case law, even if they are not expressly referenced in the legislative history of Exemption 5, may be included within the ambit of the exemption far more readily than privileges which are "novel" or have "found less than universal acceptance." *United States v. Weber Aircraft Corp.*, 465 U.S. 792, 801 (1984). The

Court reasoned that "the history of Exemption 5 can be understood by means of 'rough analogies' to privileges recognized by Congress." *Id.* at 802. *See Van Bourg, Allen, Weinberg & Roger v. NLRB*, 751 F.2d 982 (9th Cir. 1985) ("If an internal document would be immune from civil discovery, it is similarly protected from mandatory disclosure under FOIA.").

3.6. Thus far, the Supreme Court has held five privileges to be incorporated in Exemption 5. *See* Sections 4-8, *infra*. Additionally, the Fifth Circuit has recognized a sixth, *see* Section 10., *infra*.

4. **The first discovery privilege incorporated into Exemption 5 is the deliberative process privilege which protects advice, recommendations, and opinions which are part of the deliberative, consultative, decision-making processes of government.** *NLRB v. Sears, Roebuck & Co.*, 421 U.S. at 150-54; *EPA v. Mink*, 410 U.S. at 85-91.

4.1. The ultimate purpose of this privilege is to prevent injury to the quality of agency decisions. *NLRB v. Sears, Roebuck & Co.*, 421 U.S. at 151. Its particular purposes are (1) to encourage open, frank discussions on policy matters between subordinate and chief; (2) to protect against premature disclosure of proposed policies before they are finally adopted; and (3) to protect against public confusion by disclosure of reasons and rationales that were not in fact the actual reasons for the agency's actions. *Coastal States Gas Corp. v. DOE*, 617 F.2d at 866; *Jordan v. DOJ*, 591 F.2d 753, 772-73 (D.C. Cir. 1978) (en banc); *Fisher v. DOJ*, 772 F. Supp. 7, 10-11 (D.D.C. 1991).

4.2. In construing this deliberative process privilege, the Supreme Court has recognized a distinction between predecisional documents, which are protected, and post-decisional documents, which are not protected by Exemption 5. *NLRB v. Sears, Roebuck & Co.*, 421 U.S at 151-53.

4.2.1. In *Sears*, the Court held that memoranda which explain the NLRB General Counsel's decisions not to file complaints are final administrative decisions and must be disclosed, because Exemption 5 can never apply to final opinions or dispositions. 421 U.S. at 155-59.

4.2.2. However, memoranda which explain the General Counsel's decisions to direct regional directors to file a complaint are not final dispositions of the matter but instead commence litigation. Although the Court was reluctant to extend Exemption 5 to documents which explain a decision that has real operative effect, these memoranda were ruled exempt because they fall squarely within Exemption 5's protection of an attorney's work product. *NLRB v. Sears, Roebuck & Co.*, 421 U.S. at 159-60. *See Iglesias v. CIA*, 525 F. Supp. 547, 559 (D.D.C. 1981). *But cf. Bristol-Myers Co. v. FTC*, 598 F.2d at 24 n.10 (suggesting disclosure of reasons to initiate proceedings might be required if decision-maker is agency itself rather than General Counsel and therefore would not be covered by work product rule).

4.2.3. The Supreme Court in *Sears* stated that its emphasis on *predecisional* documents "does not mean that the existence of the privilege turns on the ability of an agency to identify a specific decision in connection with which a memorandum is prepared." 421 U.S. at 151 n.18.

4.2.3.1. Nevertheless, some courts have appeared to take the position that a document is predecisional only if a specific decision to which it relates can be identified. *See, e.g., Senate of the Commonwealth of Puerto Rico v. DOJ*, 823 F.2d 574, 585 (D.C. Cir. 1987); *see also Paisley v. CIA*, 712 F.2d 686, 698 (D.C. Cir. 1983), *vacated in part on other grounds*, 724 F.2d 201 (D.C. Cir. 1984) ("Accordingly, to approve exemption of a document as predecisional, a court must be able 'to pinpoint an agency decision or policy to which the document contributed.'").

4.2.3.2. *See also City of Virginia Beach, VA v. Dept. of Commerce*, 995 F.2d 1247 (4th Cir. 1993) (National Marine Fisheries Service (NMFS) documents that looked back to completed environmental permit proceedings before Army Corps of Engineers were predecisional regarding a pending FERC hearing, because documents were sought to undermine NMFS's position while FERC decision was pending and it was thus reasonable to infer that NMFS would use them with eye toward these proceedings as well.)

4.2.3.3. In *Access Reports v. DOJ,* 926 F.2d 1192 (D.C. Cir. 1991), *reversing* No. 88-1443 (HHG) (D.D.C. Mar. 8, 1989), the D.C. Circuit attempted to explain the "predecisional" and "deliberative" requirements as focusing on two different functions: "While the 'predecisional' label clearly focuses attention on the role of the entire document in the decision-making process, the 'deliberative' criterion may be useful in distinguishing between privileged and non-privileged material within a single 'predecisional document.'" 926 F.2d at 1195.

4.3. In reaching its conclusions in *Sears*, the Court considered not only the nature of the deliberative process and traditional discovery privileges, but also the interplay of Exemption 5 with the FOIA's affirmative disclosure requirements, § 552(a)(2). *NLRB v. Sears, Roebuck & Co.*, 421 U.S. at 153-54.

4.3.1. In addition to holding that Exemption 5 can never apply to final opinions (§ 552(a)(2)(A)), the Court also noted that it would be reluctant to construe Exemption 5 to apply to "statements of policy and interpretations which have been adopted by the agency" and "instructions to staff that affect a member of the public" (§ 552(a)(2)(B) and (C)). 421 U.S. at 153-54. *See Federal Open Market Comm. of the Reserve Bank v. Merrill*, 443 U.S. at 360 n.23.

4.3.2. This approach is consistent with the principle that Exemption 5 does not protect "secret law" or an agency's "working law," i.e., orders, decisions, interpretations, instructions, and guidelines which have precedential weight and affect the public. *See e.g., Schlefer v. United States*, 702 F.2d 233 (D.C. Cir. 1983) (opinion of agency's chief counsel interpreting statutes which agency administers); *Taxation With Representation Fund v. IRS*, 646 F.2d 666, 682-84 (D.C. Cir. 1981) (memoranda explaining agency rulings and decisions); *Coastal States Gas Corp. v. DOE*, 617 F.2d at 867-68 (interpretations of agency regulations); *Jordan v. DOJ*, 591 F.2d at 774 (prosecutorial guidelines).

4.3.3. When those who consult opinions have the discretion to follow or not to follow them because of their persuasive value rather than their character as working law, the opinions are exempt. *Pies v. IRS*, 668 F.2d 1350, 1353 (D.C. Cir. 1981); *Brinton v. Department of State*, 636 F.2d 600, 605 (D.C. Cir. 1980), *cert. denied*, 452 U.S. 905 (1981). Conversely, when subordinates are obliged to follow opinions, such opinions will not be exempt. *Schlefer v. United States*, 702 F.2d at 237-38.

4.4. *Sears* also held that if an agency, in making a final decision, "chooses *expressly* to adopt or incorporate by reference" a predecisional recommendation, that document loses its protection under Exemption 5. 421 U.S. at 161 (emphasis in original). *See, e.g., American Mail Line, Ltd. v. Gulick*, 411 F.2d 696 (D.C. Cir. 1969).

4.4.1. This principle applies to recommendations on a wide range of agency operations. *Afshar v. Department of State*, 702 F.2d 1125, 1141-43 (D.C. Cir. 1983) (investigative decision).

4.4.2. *Niemeier v. Watergate Special Prosecution Force*, 565 F.2d 967, 973 (7th Cir. 1977), holds that, where an underlying memorandum is expressly relied on in a final dispositional document, the entire underlying memoranda will be disclosed unless the agency shows that exemptions other than Exemption 5 apply.

4.4.3. If it is not clear that a recommendation provided the basis for a decision, the recommendation is exempt. *Renegotiation Board v. Grumman Aircraft Eng. Corp.*, 421 U.S. 168, 184-85 (1975); *King v. IRS*, 684 F.2d 517, 520-21 (7th Cir. 1982); *Swisher v. Department of the Air Force*, 660 F.2d at 371; *Common Cause v. IRS*, 646 F.2d 656 (D.C. Cir. 1981); *Brinton v. Department of State*, 636 F.2d at 605. *See also Providence Journal Co. v. Department of the Army*, 981 F.2d 552 (1st Cir. 1992), where the court held that an IG report containing a "subjective" evaluation of evidence against the two senior officers, as well as the IG's recommendations, was predecisional, and that the Army's failure to take any action within a reasonable time after the report issued did not mean that the court would infer "implied adoption" by the agency. Moreover, the documents at issue were held to be deliberative.

4.5. The Act "imposes no independent obligation on agencies to write opinions. It simply requires them to disclose the opinions which they do write." *Renegotiation Board v. Grumman Aircraft Eng. Corp.*, 421 U.S. at 192. *Grumman* rejected the notion that documents in the deliberative process lose their exemption because they may be the "nearest thing" to a final opinion. *Id.* at 191. *See Sterling Drug, Inc. v. FTC*, 450 F.2d at 706-08.

4.6. *Vaughn v. Rosen (II)*, 523 F.2d 1136, 1144 (D.C. Cir. 1975), held that, to come within Exemption 5, a document must be a direct part of the predecisional process in that it makes recommendations or expresses opinions on legal or policy matters to be decided by the agency, and the government must carry its burden of establishing the existence of a genuine predecisional process. *See ITT World Communications, Inc. v. FCC*, 699 F.2d 1219, 1239 (D.C. Cir. 1983), *rev'd and remanded on other grounds,* 466 U.S. 463 (1984); *Arthur Andersen Inc. v. IRS*, 679 F.2d 254, 258 (D.C. Cir. 1982); *Taxation With Representation Fund v. IRS*, 646 F.2d at 678; *Coastal States Gas Corp. v. DOE*,

617 F.2d at 868; *Mead Data Central, Inc. v. Department of the Air Force*, 566 F.2d 242, 256 n.40 (D.C. Cir. 1977). *But see Conoco, Inc. v. DOJ*, 687 F.2d 724, 726-27 (3d Cir. 1982) (notes to the file which are never circulated are part of the deliberative process).

4.7. In determining whether a document is predecisional, it is essential to examine the agency's administrative process and the role of the document in that process. *Renegotiation Board v. Grumman Aircraft Eng. Corp.*, 421 U.S. at 172-79; *NLRB v. Sears, Roebuck & Co.*, 421 U.S. at 138-44; *Schlefer v. United States*, 702 F.2d at 237-43; *Playboy Enterprises, Inc. v. DOJ*, 677 F.2d 931, 935 (D.C. Cir. 1982); *Coastal States Gas Corp. v. DOE*, 617 F.2d at 866-67. The agency must explain how the decisions at issue are reached, providing the necessary information to establish the applicability of the deliberative process exemption. *SafeCard Services, Inc. v. SEC*, 926 F.2d 1197, 1204-05 (D.C. Cir. 1991).

4.8. In summary, factors to consider in determining whether a document falls within the predecisional deliberative privilege include whether the document (1) is "so candid or personal in nature that public disclosure is likely in the future to stifle honest and frank communication within the agency"; (2) "is recommendatory in nature or is a draft"; (3) "weigh[s] the pros and cons of agency adoption of one view-point or another"; and (4) even if predecisional at the time it was prepared, has been "adopted, formally or informally, as the agency position on an issue or is used by the agency in its dealings with the public." *Coastal States Gas Corp. v. DOE*, 617 F.2d at 866. *See ITT World Communications, Inc. v. FCC*, 699 F.2d 1219, 1235-37 (D.C. Cir. 1983), *rev'd and remanded on other grounds*, 466 U.S. 463 (1984). *See also Chemical Mfrs. Ass'n v. Consumer Product Safety Commission*, 600 F. Supp. 114, 118 (D.D.C. 1984) (courts should show "considerable deference" to an agency's judgment as to what constitutes part of its deliberative process).

4.9. In construing the deliberative process privilege, the Supreme Court has also recognized a distinction between "materials reflecting deliberative or policy-making processes on the one hand, and purely factual, investigative matters on the other." *EPA v. Mink*, 410 U.S. at 89. Thus, even if a document is predecisional, "the privilege applies only to the 'opinion' or 'recommendatory' portion of [a document], not to factual information which is contained in the document." *Coastal States Gas Corp. v. DOE*, 617 F.2d at 867. *See also ITT World Communications, Inc. v. FCC*, 699 F.2d at 1236; *Playboy Enterprises, Inc. v. DOJ*, 677 F.2d at 935.

4.10. Generally, facts in a predecisional document must be segregated and disclosed unless they are "inextricably intertwined" with exempt portions. *Ryan v. DOJ*, 617 F.2d 781, 790-91 (D.C. Cir. 1980); *Mead Data Central, Inc. v. Department of the Air Force*, 566 F.2d at 260. *See also Professional Review Org. of Florida, Inc. v. HHS*, 607 F. Supp. 423, 427 (D.D.C. 1985). *But see Tabcor Sales Clearing, Inc. v. Department of the Treasury*, 471 F. Supp. 436 (N.D. Ill. 1979), suggesting that the Supreme Court in *NLRB v. Sears, Roebuck & Co., supra*, "modified" the fact/opinion test so that "even factual communications, so long as they are predecisional, are exempt." 471 F. Supp. at 438.

4.10.1. This procedure was adopted by the courts as early as 1971, *Sterling Drug, Inc. v. FTC*, 450 F.2d at 704), approved by the Supreme Court in *EPA v. Mink*, *supra*, and codified by Congress when it added the final sentence regarding segregation to § 552(b) of the FOIA in 1974.

4.10.2. *Army Times Publ'g Co. v. Department of the Air Force*, 998 F.2d 1067, 1071-2 (D.C. Cir. 1993) (remanded with instructions to enter a finding of segregability; Air Force must demonstrate that withheld poll results, unlike poll results voluntarily released, would actually inhibit candor in the decision-making process if made available to the public.) The district court found that an agency's claim that it would discontinue collecting such information if required to disclose it carried no weight. "Information that must be disclosed pursuant to FOIA becomes no less subject to disclosure simply because an obstinate agency claims that it will no longer do its job if required to make that information public." *Army Times Publ'g Co. v. Department of the Air Force*, No. 90-1383 (D.D.C. Feb. 28, 1995).

4.10.3. The D.C. Circuit has held that claims of non-segregability must be made with the same degree of detail as required for claims of exemption by *Vaughn v. Rosen (I)*, 484 F.2d 820 (D.C. Cir. 1973), *cert. denied*, 415 U.S. 977 (1974). *Mead Data Central, Inc. v. Department of the Air Force*, 566 F.2d at 260- 62.

4.10.4. In *Krikorian v. Department of State,* 984 F.2d 461 (D.C. Cir. 1993), the D.C. Circuit remanded the case because the district court erred by failing to enter a finding on segregability or the lack thereof. The court suggested that the lower court might find that, in the context of foreign relations information, *in camera* review would be preferable to more detailed affidavits.

4.10.5. The D.C. Circuit has refused to adopt a *per se* rule that trial courts must conduct an *in camera* inspection of documents where the agency claims that it is withholding factual material because such material is inextricably intertwined with exempt deliberative material under Exemption 5. *Center for Auto Safety v. EPA*, 731 F.2d 16 (D.C. Cir. 1984). It did agree, however, to determine whether denial of such a request for *in camera* inspection was an abuse of discretion by the district court judge. *Id.*

4.10.7. The Fourth Circuit found that the EPA had not adequately explained why summaries and charts were part of the deliberative process. In remanding the case, the court noted that where the agency's affidavits failed "to identify either the author or its recipient, those persons' relationship to the decision making process cannot be identified and becomes difficult, if not impossible, to perceive how the disclosure of such documents would result in a chilling effect upon the open and frank exchange of opinions within the agency." *Ethyl Corporation v. EPA*, 25 F.3d 1241 (4th Cir. 1994).

4.11. There are three exceptions to the general rule that facts in deliberative documents must be disclosed.

4.11.1. *Nevas v. DOJ,* 789 F. Supp. 445 (D.D.C. 1992) was vacated and remanded by *Mapother v. DOJ*, 3 F.3d 1533 (D.C. Cir. 1993). In *Mapother*, the D.C. Circuit limited the application of the fact/opinion distinction, saying that it must not be applied mechanically because "the privilege serves to protect the deliberative process itself, not merely the documents containing deliberative material." *Id.* at 1537. In this case, protected material included factual information about

Kurt Waldheim (the "Waldheim Report") compiled by DOJ in advising the Attorney General to list Waldheim as an excludable alien. The court held that factual material assembled through discretionary selection from a large number of primary documents was exempt from FOIA under Exemption 5 *Id.* at 1539. Conversely, a purely chronological document about Waldheim's military service was not excludable. It was held to be purely factual and did not possess a significant relationship to the Justice Department deliberations. *Id.* at 1540.

4.11.2. In certain limited circumstances, facts can be withheld if their disclosure would impair the agency's ability to obtain or deter the agency from seeking information which is essential to the agency's decision-making process. *See* Section 8, *infra*; *Quarles v. Department of the Navy,* 893 F.2d 390, 393 (D.C. Cir. 1990).

4.11.3. Factual reports of the recommendations are protected just like the recommendations themselves. *National Security Archive v. FBI,* 799 F. Supp. 872 (D.D.C. 1991).

4.12. "In some circumstances,... the disclosure of even purely factual material may so expose the deliberative process within an agency that it must be deemed exempted by [Exemption 5]." *Mead Data Central*, 566 F.2d at 256. The significance of the fact/opinion distinction is eclipsed in such cases, and "the key question... [is] whether disclosure of materials would expose an agency's decision making process in such a way as to discourage discussion within the agency and thereby undermine the agency's ability to perform its functions." *Dudman Communications Corp. v. Department of the Air Force*, 815 F.2d 1565 (D.C. Cir. 1987). *See also Schell v. HHS*, 843 F.2d 933, 940 (6th Cir. 1988).

4.12.1. Disclosure of the deliberative process itself was viewed as tantamount to disclosure of deliberations on specific matters under agency consideration when the D.C. Circuit, in a 7-5 split *en banc* decision in *Wolfe v. HHS*, 839 F.2d 768 (D.C. Cir. 1988), held that factual information from the agency's "Regulations Log" was privileged because its release would disclose that "preliminary recommendations have been accepted or rejected, at various levels of review," and would "reveal the timing of the deliberative process." *Id.* at 774-75.

4.12.1.1. While the majority in *Wolfe*, per Bork, J., noted the utility of the fact/opinion distinction in resolving most disputes regarding this privilege, it found "no case in which a court has used the fact/opinion distinction to support disclosure of facts about the inner workings of the deliberative process itself." *Id.* at 774.

4.12.1.2. In considering plaintiffs' request for the dates on which regulatory proposals, identified by subject matter title, were transmitted from one agency to another, the majority viewed the "fact of forwarding" to be "the functional equivalent" of an intra-agency or inter-agency memorandum stating, in each instance, whether the sender approves or disapproves of the regulation proposed. *Id.* Although the information sought "does not fully reveal the reasoning of the recommendation but merely memorializes it," the majority concluded that release "will generally disclose the recommended outcome of the consultative process at each stage of that process," and thus result in the premature revelation of policies and "fishbowl" decision making environment that Congress sought to prevent through Exemption 5. *Id.* at 775-76.

4.12.1.3. In one of three dissents joined by five members of the court, Chief Judge Wald argued that the majority "vastly overstates how definitive a message is actually communicated by the mere knowledge of the fact of such a transmittal or nontransmittal," and "assumes a rigidified, and therefore predictable deliberation process that the record and the realities of government decision making do not support." 839 F.2d at 776-77.

4.12.1.4. The dissenters in *Wolfe* asserted that Exemption 5 protects "only the substantive content of the decision making process," not its "procedural workings." *Id.* at 779 n.5. "[T]here is no independent basis under Exemption 5 for protecting facts about the 'deliberative process itself' unless such information discloses an agency's substantive views in a way that may chill candid deliberations." *Id.*

4.12.1.5. Finally, the dissenters noted that the majority's conclusion that Exemption 5 will bar disclosure of "the mere existence of communications between agencies prior to a formal rulemaking proposal" regardless of whether the fact of their existence reveals anything about their content, "creates an inherent conflict with our traditional requirement of a *Vaughn* index, as a prerequisite to exemption." *Id.*

4.12.2. In *National Wildlife Federation v. U.S. Forest Service*, 861 F.2d 1114 (9th Cir. 1988), the court similarly eschewed the fact/opinion distinction in ruling that "opinions or recommendations regarding facts or consequences of fact" are not automatically ineligible for protection under the deliberative process privilege.

4.12.2.1. The court rejected the plaintiff's argument that *Ryan v. DOJ, supra*, allows factual matters to be withheld only when their disclosure would reveal the substance of predecisional policy discussions. 861 F.2d at 1117-18. It also refused to hold that a document must contain "non-binding and advisory recommendations regarding law or policy" in order to qualify as "deliberative." *Id.* at 1118.

4.12.2.2. Instead, the court adopted a "process-oriented" or "functional" test wherein factual materials would be exempt "to the extent that they reveal the mental process of decision makers." *Id.* at 1119, citing *Wolfe* and *Dudman Communications*, both *supra*.

4.12.2.3. The court in *National Wildlife Federation* upheld the withholding of portions of the agency's draft Forest Plans containing projected levels of implementation activities, estimated costs and benefits of such activities, and estimates of the Service's maximum capacity for sustaining such activities. "While these opinions might be characterized as opinions on facts or the consequences of facts," the court concluded, "[a]s long as these opinions reveal the issues that the Forest Service considers important and provide telling clues as to [its] proposed course of action in addressing conflicting demands on the Forest's resources, they are as much a part of the deliberative process as opinions on pure matters of law or policy." *Id.* at 1121.

4.12.3. The extent to which processed data may be withheld is disputed.

4.12.3.1. *Florida House of Representatives v. Department of Commerce*, 961 F.2d 941 (11th Cir. 1992), held that the privilege applies to adjusted block level census data when the information was a subordinate's opinion, in the form of numbers, not facts, thus reflecting deliberative process. *See also Times Journal Company v. Department of the Air Force*, 793 F. Supp. 1 (D.D.C. 1991) (survey results containing the opinions and recommendations of Air Force personnel, used to make briefings and recommendations to the Director of Personnel, were properly withheld under Exemption 5 because they were deliberative, even though plaintiff sought aggregate, not individual, responses, and the survey participants were not acting as policy advisors but only as survey subjects).

4.12.3.2. *Assembly of State of California v. Department of Commerce,* 968 F.2d 916 (9th Cir. 1992), held that computer tapes containing adjusted block counts from census figures were neither predecisional nor deliberative even though they were prepared prior to the Secretary's decision not to adjust the census. The court found that they were prepared solely for the purpose of post-decision dissemination, and not to contribute to the decisionmaking, and the adjusted data did not reveal anything about the formulas used, the process which created the formulas, or the decision to adopt the set of figures as the official United States census.

4.12.3.3. The Florida and California census cases are in direct conflict. In the Florida case, the state did not challenge the predecisional aspect of the numbers. Therefore, the court focused on the deliberative process issue and relied on *Quarles v. Department of the Navy,* 893 F.2d 390 (D.C. Cir. 1990), and *Federal Open Market Committee of the Federal Reserve System,* 443 U.S. at 359-60, to conclude that these numbers reflect a "complex set of judgments" that remain privileged even though the decision to which they relate had already been made. *Florida House of Representatives*, 961 F.2d at 947-50. The California court distinguished *Quarles* since that case does not "say that numbers never represent facts." *Assembly of State of California*, 968 F.2d at 922, *citing Quarles,* 893 F.2d at 392-93.

4.12.3.4. In *Petroleum Information Corp. v. Department of the Interior,* 976 F.2d 1429 (D.C. Cir. 1992), the D.C. Circuit held that a computer data base containing information available on paper documents had to be released, despite the government's invocation of Exemption 5. The Court explained that "[t]o fall within the deliberative process privilege, materials must bear on the formulation or exercise of agency policy-oriented *judgment.*" *Id.* at 1435 (emphasis in original). "The deliberative process privilege, we underscore, is centrally concerned with protecting the process by which *policy* is formulated." *Id.* (emphasis in original). "To the extent that predecisional materials, even if 'factual' in form, reflect an agency's preliminary positions or ruminations about how to exercise discretion on some policy matter, they are protected under Exemption 5. Conversely, when material could not reasonably be said to reveal an agency's or official's mode of formulating or exercising policy-implicating judgment, the deliberative process privilege is inapplicable." *Id.*

4.12.3.5. The Court noted two determinative aspects. First, public availability of paper documents that were used to prepare the data base diminished the agency's contention that release of the file would confuse the public with erroneous information because the not yet official file contained errors. If the agency's description of its difficulties with its current record-keeping systems was correct, availability in another form, notwithstanding *Dismukes v. Department of the Interior,* 603 F. Supp. 760 (D.D.C. 1984), would not provide the requester with information in "reasonably accessible form." *Petroleum Information Corp.,* 976 F.2d at 1437 & n.

4.12.3.6. Second, the information that the agency sought to withhold was not associated with any significant policy decision. Thus, unlike those cases where factual material was winnowed, the agency's repackaging of dispersed public information into a database did not involve deliberative behavior. 976 F.2d at 1438, distinguishing *Quarles,* 893 F.2d at 393.

4.12.3.7. The Court in Petroleum Information noted that neither *Assembly of State of California v. Department of Commerce*, 968 F.2d at 922, nor *Florida House of Representative v. Department of Commerce*, 961 F.2d at 950, detracted from its ruling and distinguished the 11th Circuit's decision as involving broader, more politically-charged choices than those involved here.

4.13. There is also a gray area between facts and opinions consisting of investigations, evaluations, and analyses.

4.13.1. Several courts have required disclosure of such material. *Vaughn v. Rosen (II)*, 383 F. Supp. 1049 (D.D.C. 1974), *aff'd*, 523 F.2d 1136 (D.C. Cir. 1975) ("factual, investigative, and evaluative portions" of documents which "reflect final objective analyses of agency performance under existing policy" and "reveal whether the agencies' policies are being carried out"); *Sterling Drug, Inc. v. Harris*, 488 F. Supp. 1019, 1028-29 (S.D.N.Y. 1980) (objective medical analyses of drug tests); *Union of Concerned Scientists v. NRC*, 2 Med. L. Rpt. 1458 (D.D.C. 1977) (expert scientific opinion). *See Soucie v. David*, 448 F.2d at 1067, 1078 (D.C. Cir. 1971).

4.13.2. However, the results have been different in cases that involve evaluations which are prospective in nature and relate to a single decision, rather than retrospective evaluations of agency performance. For example, in *Quarles v. Department of the Navy,* 893 F.2d at 392-93, cost estimates prepared in the course of selecting homeports for a battleship group were found to "derive from a complex set of judgments...[which] partake of just that elasticity that has persuaded courts to provide shelter for opinions generally." *See also Skelton v. U.S. Postal Service*, 678 F.2d at 38-39 (evaluation of alleged misconduct exempt); *Mead Data Central, Inc. v. Department of the Air Force (II)*, 575 F.2d 932, 934-35 (D.C. Cir. 1978) (cost comparisons and feasibility opinions used in contract award decision exempt); *Washington Research Project, Inc. v. HEW*, 504 F.2d 238, 249-50 (D.C. Cir. 1974), *cert. denied*, 421 U.S. 963 (1975) (evaluations used in awarding grants exempt); *Texas Instruments, Inc. v. U.S. Customs Service*, 479 F. Supp. 404, 406 (D.D.C. 1979) (evaluations of investigative material exempt); *American Federation of Government Employees (AFGE) v. Department of the Army*, 441 F. Supp. 1308, 1312-13 (D.D.C. 1977) (evaluations of alleged improprieties exempt).

5. **The second discovery privilege incorporated into Exemption 5 is the attorney work-product privilege which protects documents prepared by an attorney which reveal the theory of his case or litigation strategy.** *FTC v. Grolier, Inc., supra; NLRB v. Sears, Roebuck & Co.*, 421 U.S. at 154-55. *See Hickman v. Taylor*, 329 U.S. 495 (1947).

5.1 The work product privilege applies even if some of the withheld documents may have been prepared in anticipation of *closing* the investigation. "Reports and recommended action with respect to the status of an investigation submitted prior to issuance of a final decision qualify as materials prepared in anticipation of investigation." *A. Michael's Piano, Inc. v. Federal Trade Commission*, 18 F.3d 138, 146-47 (2d Cir. 1994).

5.2. Attorney work-product is protected by Exemption 5 "without regard to the status of the litigation for which it was prepared." *FTC v. Grolier*, 462 U.S. at 28, *reversing*, 671 F.2d 553 (D.C. Cir. 1982). The Supreme Court rejected the holding of the court of appeals in *Grolier* that the privilege expires when the litigation for which the documents were prepared is terminated, all related litigation is terminated, and the potential for related litigation no longer exists. However, the fact that the work product privilege survives the end of litigation does not excuse an asserting agency from having to show that the document at issue was prepared in contemplation of litigation, *Dow Jones & Co. v. DOJ*, 724 F. Supp. 985 (D.D.C. 1989), *aff'd in part, rev'd in part*, 917 F.2d 571 (D.C. Cir. 1990); *Watson v. DOJ*, 799 F. Supp. 193 (D.D.C. 1992) (89 documents properly withheld under attorney work product privilege because privilege does not end at close of litigation for which material prepared and documents, which are attorney work product, were prepared in anticipation of specific litigation against plaintiff).

5.2.1. The First Circuit has ruled that a standard protecting records prepared because of existing or expected litigation is too broad for FOIA purposes. The court noted that "agency decision making on controversial regulations, as this case highlights, usually involves the prospect of litigation and in many cases does lead to litigation. [This broad] standard would hinder the openness that Congress envisioned in enacting FOIA and shield from disclosure documents that would aid in understanding the decision making process of an agency." *State of Maine v. United States Department of Interior*, 2002 WL 499331 (1st Cir. 2002).

5.3. The D.C. Circuit has ruled that there is no difference between factual and opinion material for purposes of application of the attorney work product privilege. In *Martin v. Office of Special Counsel*, 819 F.2d 1181 (D.C. Cir. 1987), the court indicated that "the work-product privilege simply does not distinguish between factual and deliberative material...[W]e find that if the work-product privilege protects the documents at issue here, Exemption (b)(5) protects them as well regardless of their status as 'factual' or 'deliberative.'" Some courts in other circuits still recognize a fact/opinion dichotomy and require facts be disclosed while opinion can be protected. *See, e.g., Fine v. DOE*, No. 88-1033, No. 89-0031 (D.N.M. June 23, 1991).

5.3.1. *See also A. Michael's Piano, Inc. v. Federal Trade Commission,* 18 F.3d 138, 147 (2d Cir. 1994) ("The work-product privilege draws no distinction between materials that are factual in nature and those that are deliberative."); *Norwood v. FAA*, 993 F.2d 570 (6th Cir. 1993) (no deliberative-factual distinction for documents exempt as attorney work product).

5.4. Documents that reveal an attorney's appraisal of factual evidence fall within the work-product privilege. *Bristol-Myers Co. v. FTC*, 598 F.2d at 28-29; *Mervin v. FTC*, 591 F.2d 821, 826 (D.C. Cir. 1978). The time at which a factual document is prepared in the course of an investigation, relative to actual litigation, is a highly relevant factor in determining the availability of this privilege in FOIA cases. *Coastal States Gas Corp. v. DOE*, 617 F.2d at 865.

5.5. In any event, since courts are less rigorous in requiring disclosure of segregable factual portions with respect to attorney work-product documents than with respect to general deliberative documents, *in camera* review is less frequently required. *Bristol-Myers Co. v. FTC*, 598 F.2d at 29-30 n.23; *Mervin v. FTC*, 591 F.2d at 826-27. *But see Radowich v. U.S. Attorney, District of Maryland*, 501 F. Supp. 284, 286 (D. Md. 1980), *rev'd on other grounds*, 658 F.2d 957 (4th Cir. 1981). Nonetheless, the agency should still be required to demonstrate through detailed affidavits that disclosure of factual material is not possible. *Mervin v. FTC*, 591 F.2d at 831-32 (distinguishing *Bristol-Myers and Mervin*) (Bazelon, J. dissenting).

5.6. Even though a document may be a final opinion, an instruction to staff, or a recommendation which has been adopted as the basis of an agency decision and subject to the affirmative disclosure requirements of § 552(a)(2), it may be exempt if it falls within the work-product privilege. *NLRB v. Sears, Roebuck & Co.*, 421 U.S. at 159-61; *Federal Open Market Committee of the Federal Reserve Bank v. Merrill*, 443 U.S. at 360 n.23; *Exxon Corp. v. FTC (II)*, 476 F. Supp. 713, 724-26 (D.D.C. 1979).

5.7. The release of a document prepared specifically for settlement negotiations to the opposing party does not require waiver of the attorney work-product privilege for identical information in another document prepared for the agency's internal use. *Mobil Oil Corp. v. EPA,* 879 F.2d 698 (9th Cir. 1989).

6. The third discovery privilege incorporated into Exemption 5 is the attorney-client privilege which protects confidential communications, including facts, (a) from a client to an attorney, and (b) from an attorney to a client, if the communication is based on confidential information provided by the client. *NLRB v. Sears, Roebuck & Co.*, 421 U.S. at 154; *Schlefer v. United States*, 702 F.2d at 245. In the FOIA context, this privilege protects an agency's communications with its attorneys, provided that the communications are necessary to obtain informed legal advice and their disclosure is limited to those who are authorized to speak or act for the agency. *Coastal States Gas Corp. v. DOE*, 617 F.2d at 862-64.

7. **The fourth discovery privilege incorporated into Exemption 5 is a qualified privilege based on Fed. R. Civ. P. 26(c)(7) for confidential commercial information, at least to the extent that the information is generated by the government itself in the process leading up to awarding a contract.** *Federal Open Market Committee v. Merrill*, 443 U.S. at 360. *See Morrison-Knudson Co. v. Department of the Army*, 595 F. Supp. 352, 354 (D.D.C. 1984), *aff'd,* 762 F.2d 138 (D.C. Cir. 1985); *Hack v. DOE*, 538 F. Supp. 1098, 1100 (D.D.C. 1982).

7.1. Since this discovery privilege is qualified rather than absolute, a court must determine the sensitivity of the information and the harm that would be inflicted on the government by disclosure. In making this determination, the court may not take into account the individual's need for the information. *Federal Open Market Committee v. Merrill*, 443 U.S. at 362-63.

7.2. Moreover, since the policy behind this privilege is "not that the flow of advice may be hampered but rather that the government will be placed at a competitive disadvantage or that the consummation of the contract may be endangered...the rationale for protecting such information expires as soon as the contract is awarded or the offer withdrawn." *Id.* at 360.

7.3. This privilege has been construed as strictly limited to confidential commercial information and does not extend to legal memoranda prepared to aid in deliberations on awarding the contract. *Shermco Industries, Inc. v. Secretary of the Air Force*, 613 F.2d 1314, 1319-20 n.11 (5th Cir. 1980).

7.4. In *Taylor Woodrow International v. Department of the Navy,* No. C88-424R (W.D. Wash. March 31, 1989), the court upheld a claim based on Rule 26(c)(7) in connection with a request for contract cost estimates *after* the contract was awarded, based on the fact that the requester-contractor was seeking cost increases above its winning bid, and thus could gain an unfair commercial advantage if it had access to the Navy's pre-bid cost estimate.

7.5. In *Burka v. Dept. of Health and Human Services*, 87 F.3d 508 (D.C. Cir. 1996), the D.C. Circuit reversed Judge Louis Oberdorfer's earlier finding in the same case. The D.C. Circuit ruled that a data tape in the custody of a contractor, which was part of a study of youth attitudes towards smoking, was not protected under the confidential research privilege of Rule 26(c)(7). The court observed that "if Exemption 5 is triggered every time an agency can point to [cases extending a protective order to a certain category of information], the exception carved out of FOIA's overarching policy of disclosure will quickly swallow up the rule." The court noted that "at this juncture in the development of the law, we cannot say that there is an established or well-settled practice of protecting research data in the realm of civil discovery on the grounds that disclosure would harm a researcher's publication prospects." The court added that "this is not to say that there never will be such a well-established practice; we would not presume to say how many cases are sufficient to transform an occasional grant into a generally recognized protection. But as of now, however, the precedent does not rise to the level of a routinely accepted dispensation shielding data from discovery in order to preserve a researcher's opportunities for publication."

8. **In *United States v. Weber Aircraft Corp., supra*, the Supreme Court recognized the discovery privilege established for factual statements made to air crash safety investigators with an assurance of confidentiality. That privilege, as it was articulated in *Machin v. Zuckert*, 316 F.2d 336 (D.C. Cir. 1963), *cert. denied*, 375 U.S. 896 (1963), is intended to encourage witnesses and crash participants to speak freely about the facts of the incident. The *Machin* privilege was previously recognized in *Cooper v. Department of the Navy*, 558 F.2d 274, 278 (5th Cir. 1977), and *Brockway v. Department of the Air Force*, 518 F.2d 1184 (8th Cir. 1975). *See also AFGE v. Department of the Army*, 441 F. Supp. at 1313-14 (assurance of confidentiality not necessary to invoke privilege). *Cf. Deering Milliken, Inc. v. Irving*, 548 F.2d at 1138 n.9 (4th Cir. 1977). In *Badhwar v. Department of the Air Force*, 829 F.2d 182 (D.C. Cir. 1987), the court refused to consider arguments that *Machin* had been discredited and should be abandoned, stating that the appropriate context for revisiting *Machin* would be a case involving the discovery process, and not an FOIA case, because Exemption 5 "requires the application of existing rules regarding discovery, not their reformulation." *Id.* at 184.**

9. **The Supreme Court has also addressed whether presentence reports are privileged under Exemption 5.**

9.1. In *Durns v. Bureau of Prisons*, 804 F.2d 701 (D.C. Cir. 1986), *vacated*, 486 U.S. 1029 (1988), a divided panel of the D.C. Circuit held that presentence reports are privileged and within the scope of Exemption 5.

9.1.1. The majority in *Durns* utilized the analysis supporting the Supreme Court's recognition of a "judicially-fashioned privilege" in *Weber Aircraft* and concluded that "relevant case law establishes that presentence reports are not routinely available in discovery."

9.1.2. In further reliance on *Weber Aircraft*, the majority reasoned that the privilege against disclosure of presentence reports is "roughly analogous" to those Congress meant to codify in Exemption 5, since "the reports are protected primarily to maintain the government's ability to gather information from confidential sources." *Id.*

9.2. However, in *Julian v. DOJ*, 806 F.2d 1411 (9th Cir. 1986), *aff'd*, 486 U.S. 1 (1988), *on remand*, 859 F.2d 124 (9th Cir. 1988), the Ninth Circuit drew "an opposite conclusion" from that of the *Durns* court, holding that Exemption 5 does not create a *per se* exemption for presentence reports because the government "has failed to identify an existing statutory or common law privilege that exempts presentence reports from discovery." *Id.* at 1418. In addition, the *Julian* court noted that presentence reports primarily contain "factual data about the prisoner," rather than the advice, opinions, recommendations, and subjective analysis that Exemption 5 was intended to protect. *Id.* at 1419-420.

9.3. The Supreme Court resolved the issue by holding in *Julian* that Exemption 5 does not support withholding a presentence report from a requester who is the subject of the report. *Julian v. DOJ*, 486 U.S. 1 (1988).

9.3.1. Chief Justice Rehnquist, writing for the majority in a 5-3 decision, noted that courts in both civil and criminal cases have been reluctant to give third parties access to presentence reports absent a showing of special need, but have not invoked similar restrictions when the individual seeking discovery is the subject of the report. Moreover, the majority concluded that "the thrust of the disclosure portions of Rule 32(c) and the Parole Act speak so strongly against the existence of a privilege on the part of the government when the request is from the subject of the report that we think it accurate to say that Congress has strongly intimated, if it has not actually provided, that no privilege should exist." 486 U.S. at 13.

10. **A divided panel of the Fifth Circuit has held that Exemption 5 incorporates a privilege corresponding to Fed. R. Civ. P. 26(b)(4) for reports of an expert witness.** Therefore an appraiser's report prepared for an unsuccessful negotiation over a piece of property that led to a condemnation proceeding is exempt. *Hoover v. Department of the Interior*, 611 F.2d at 1138-42. *Accord Martin Marietta Aluminum, Inc. v. Administrator, GSA*, 444 F. Supp. 945 (C.D. Cal. 1977). *See Deering Milliken Corp. v. Irving*, 548 F.2d at 1138.

10.1. *Hoover* emphasizes, as did *Federal Open Market*, that premature disclosure would put the government at a competitive disadvantage. *Hoover* distinguishes other cases which have required release of appraisals on the ground that those appraisals "were no longer being actively used." 611 F.2d at 1140 n.10.

10.2. Consequently, as with the privilege recognized in *Federal Open Market*, the rationale for the privilege recognized in *Hoover* should expire when a condemnation or negotiation is completed.

10.3. The dissent in *Hoover* argued that, since the appraisal had been prepared for the negotiation without anticipating the necessity of a condemnation proceeding, it does not fall within Rule 26(b)(4) because it was not prepared in anticipation of litigation. The dissent would rule that the appraisal is exempt under the reasoning of *Federal Open Market* as long as the negotiation was pending, but not after it broke down. 611 F.2d at 1143-48).

10.4. The First Circuit, relying on *Federal Open Market* rather than *Hoover*, has held that a property appraisal is exempt until the property is sold or withdrawn from the market. *Government Land Bank v. GSA*, 671 F.2d 663 (1st Cir. 1982).

11. **One unresolved issue regarding Exemption 5 is whether it incorporates a privilege covering materials generated in the course of settlement negotiations.**

11.1. The *Weber Aircraft* incorporation rationale was found to be "inapplicable," since there is no "long-standing or universally recognized privilege" for such materials. *NAACP Legal Defense and Education Fund, Inc. v. DOJ*, 612 F. Supp. 1143, 1146 (D.D.C. 1985).

11.2. Rule 408 of the Federal Rules of Evidence, which limits the admissibility of settlement offers and acceptances for certain purposes in litigation, does not establish a settlement negotiations privilege cognizable under the FOIA. *See Center for Auto Safety v. DOJ*, 576 F. Supp. 739 (D.D.C. 1983) ("FRE 408 limits a document's relevance at trial, not its disclosure for other purposes"); *NAACP Legal Defense and Education Fund, supra*

("Although the intent of FRE 408 is to foster settlement negotiations, the sole means used to effectuate that end is a limitation on the admission of evidence...for the purpose of proving liability at trial.").

11.3. Notwithstanding the strong public policy of favoring settlements, and the related public interest in insulating negotiations from inhibiting publicity, courts do not have equitable discretion to create a "settlement exemption" under the FOIA. *County of Madison, N.Y. v. DOJ*, 641 F.2d 1036, 1040-41 (1st Cir. 1981). *See* Chapter 1, Overview.

11.4. Even if a cognizable privilege existed for materials generated in settlement negotiations, its assertion under Exemption 5 would be limited to "inter-agency or intra-agency" documents. *See County of Madison, N.Y.* and *NAACP Legal Defense and Education Fund*, both *supra*.

11.5. In *Brownstein Zeidman and Schomer v. Department of the Air Force,* 781 F. Supp. 31 (D.D.C. 1991), the court held that although Exemption 5 does not cover negotiations between the government and outside parties, summaries of negotiations, reflecting the thoughts and impressions of government personnel who drafted them may be withheld because disclosure "would inhibit the free flow of information within an agency if staff had to worry that the choices they make about the significance of particular information, as reflected in the substance of negotiation summaries they write, were to be disclosed and scrutinized." 781 F. Supp. at 36.

12. Exemption 5 by its terms applies only to "inter-agency and intra-agency" documents. *Federal Open Market Comm. of the Reserve Bank v. Merrill*, 443 U.S. at 352; *ITT World Communications, Inc. v. FCC*, 699 F.2d at 1238; *County of Madison, N.Y. v. DOJ*, 641 F.2d at 1039-1040; *Conoco, Inc. v. DOJ*, 521 F. Supp. 1301, 1305-06 (D. Del. 1981), *aff'd in part, rev'd and remanded in part*, 687 F.2d 724 (3d Cir. 1982).

12.1. Although the Supreme Court has expressly declined to determine what constitutes "inter-agency or intra-agency" documents, *Weber Aircraft*, 465 U.S. at 798 n. 13, the D.C. Circuit and other courts have employed "a functional rather than a literal test in assessing" whether memoranda are "inter-agency or intra-agency" and have held that the exemption also authorizes withholding of documents generated at the government's request by outside parties. *Ryan v. DOJ*, 617 F.2d at 789-90 (Senators' responses to agency's questionnaire); *Hoover v. Department of Interior*, 611 F.2d at 1138 (report of private appraiser); *Lead Industries Association, Inc. v. OSHA*, 610 F.2d 70 at 83 (2d Cir. 1979) (analyses of scientific testimony prepared by consultants); *Brockway v. Department of the Air Force*, 518 F.2d at 1191 (witness statements solicited by agency); *Washington Research Project, Inc. v. HEW*, 504 F.2d at 249 (reports submitted by an advisory committee to an agency); *Wu v. National Endowment for the Humanities*, 460 F.2d 1030, 1032 (5th Cir. 1972), *cert. denied*, 410 U.S. 926 (1973) (work product of unpaid consultants); *Soucie v. David*, 448 F.2d at 1078 n.44 (report of outside experts).

12.2 In each of these cases, however, the outsiders had a formalized, non-adversarial consulting relationship with the agency, and the information was prepared at the agency's request for the benefit of its internal decision-making. Where the outside party is not acting on behalf of the agency, the exemption does not apply. *See County of Madison, N.Y. v. DOJ*, 641 F.2d at 1040-42 (correspondence between agency attorneys and "past and potential adversaries," "self-seeking petitioners...with their own interest in mind," not exempt); *NAACP Legal Defense and Education Fund, Inc. v. DOJ*, 612 F. Supp. at 1146 (letters from adversaries in past litigation not exempt); *M/A-COM Information Systems, Inc. v. HHS*, 656 F. Supp. 691 (D.D.C. 1986); *Kilroy v. NLRB*, 633 F. Supp. 136 (S.D. Ohio 1985); *Canadian Javelin, Ltd. v. SEC*, 501 F. Supp. 898, 903 (D.D.C. 1980) (information prepared by consultants prior to agency request not exempt).

12.3. The Supreme Court found that correspondence to the Interior Department from Indian tribes did not meet the "inter-agency" threshold because the tribes and the agency had adverse interests. *Department of Interior v. Klamath Water Users Protective Association*, 531 US 425 (2001).

12.4. In *CNA Fin. Corp. v. Donovan,* 830 F.2d 1132 (D.C. Cir. 1987), *cert. denied,* 485 U.S. 977 (1988), the court stated that the deliberative process privilege may broadly embrace "reports of outsiders commissioned by an agency to perform agency work, when such reports would be protected if compiled within the agency itself." "Whether the author is a regular agency employee or a temporary consultant is irrelevant; the pertinent element is the role, if any, that the document plays in the process of agency deliberations." 830 F.2d at 1161 (footnote omitted). Subsequently, in *Formaldehyde Institute v. HHS,* 889 F.2d 1118 (D.C. Cir. 1989), another panel of the D.C. Circuit relied on *Donovan* in extending Exemption 5 protection to prepublication reviews of a report submitted by an agency employee when there was no "formal relationship" between the outside reviewers and the agency, and the reviews were not "solicited" by the agency. The court found that, while the agency does not "solicit" reviews "in the sense that it contracts to receive them," the agency does "actively seek to do business with journals from which reviews are both expected and then used by" the agency to determine what should be published in its name. *Id.* at 1124. Concluding that this "reflects a mutual understanding" between the agency and journals regarding how the agency will use such reviews, the court held that the "existence of such an arrangement is more than enough" to make the review at issue "a part of the deliberative process of the agency." *Id.*

12.5. A statutory limitation on the "functional" analysis spawned by *Ryan* and applied in *Donovan* and *Formaldehyde Institute* was explicated in *Dow Jones & Co. v. DOJ,* 724 F. Supp. 985 (D.D.C. 1989), *aff'd in part, rev'd in part*, 917 F.2d 571 (D.C. Cir. 1990), where the district court found Exemption 5 inapplicable to a letter sent from the Justice Department to the House Ethics Committee summarizing an investigation of a House member. Finding that DOJ had completed its own probe before summarizing the results in the letter sent to the House, the court concluded that the only deliberative process to which the letter might relate was that of the House committee. The court then ruled that members of Congress are not within the FOIA's definition of "agency," and the protections of Exemption 5 cannot be extended to deliberations of a "non-agency." *Id.*

12.6. In *Thurner Heat Treating Corp. v. NLRB,* 839 F.2d 1256 (7th Cir. 1988), a panel of the Seventh Circuit determined the "precise question" left open by the Supreme Court in *Weber*—whether statements made by non-agency employees to agency employees are "intra-agency memorandums."

12.6.1. The court in *Thurner* agreed with the NLRB that "intra-agency" means "within an agency," but rejected the Board's contention that this denotes location or possession, rather than origin. "Congress intended within an agency to refer to 'internal' documents, not to documents that happen to be in the possession of the agency." 839 F.2d at 1259-60.

12.6.2. The court held that witness statements taken from employees of a company under investigation for labor law violations are not "intra-agency" memoranda because such affidavits are the product of the Thurner employees who made the statements rather than of the NLRB agents who recorded them." *Id.* at 1258.

12.7. The D.C. Circuit found correspondence between the National Archives and the Department of Justice on the one hand, and attorneys for former Presidents Reagan and Bush on the other, could be considered "intra-agency" if they were "created for the purpose of aiding the agency's deliberative process." *Public Citizen v. DOJ*, 111 F.3d 168 (D.C. Cir. 1997).

13. **Claims of Exemption 5 generally are waived if the agency has disclosed the documents to third parties or non-federal agencies.** *Chilivis v. SEC*, 673 F.2d 1205, 1212 (11th Cir. 1982); *Cooper v. Department of the Navy*, 594 F.2d at 486; *Shell Oil Co. v. IRS*, 772 F. Supp. 202 (D. Del. 1991). However, there are a number of circumstances where this principle does not apply. *See Mobil Oil Corp. v. EPA,* 879 F.2d at 702-02 (disclosure of information in one document released in settlement agreement did not waive agency's claim for identical information in another document). *Chilivis v. SEC*, 673 F.2d at 1211 (disclosure to another federal agency); *Murphy v. Department of the Army*, 613 F.2d 1151 (D.C. Cir. 1979) (disclosure to Member of Congress). *See also Public Citizen v. Department of State,* 782 F. Supp. 144 (D.D.C. 1992), *judgment amended on reconsideration,* 787 F. Supp. 12 (D.D.C. 1992), *aff'd*, 11 F.3d 198 (D.C. Cir. 1993) (documents concerning Ambassador to Iraq's meeting with Saddam Hussein are predecisional and deliberative, even where facts contained in memoranda were revealed in ambassador's extensive congressional testimony); *Florida House of Representatives v. Department of Commerce,* 961 F.2d 941, 946 (11th Cir. 1992) (agency did not waive deliberative process privilege by releasing information pursuant to court order in prior action, which agency protested on ground that information was protected by privilege, or by releasing it to Congress under threat of Congress' power of subpoena); *Mehl v. United States Environmental Protection Agency,* 797 F. Supp. 43 (D.D.C. 1992) (release of report, describing in general terms and quoting several passages of withheld documents, does not waive exemption for documents where report merely reveals the subject of the withheld documents and the information specifically disclosed is not segregable from the exempt information). *See also Rockwell International v. DOJ*, 235 F.3d 598 (D.C. Cir. 2001), where the court found the agency had not waived privilege when Congress quoted extensively from internal memos in a published report.

13.1. In *Sharyland Water Supply Corp. v. Block*, 755 F.2d 397 (5th Cir. 1985), *cert. denied,* 471 U.S. 1137 (1985), the court suggested that FOIA exemptions for privileged materials would be irrelevant under an "absolutely literal interpretation" of the common rule that a privilege is waived by disclosure to a third-party, since some party must have disclosed the disputed information to the government in the first place. "To have any content," it reasoned, "the statute must be read as referring to information that would have been privileged but for the requirement that it be revealed to the government." *Id.* at 399-400. *But see Artesian Industries, Inc. v. HHS*, 646 F. Supp. 1004, 1008 (D.D.C. 1986), where the court held the attorney-client privilege waived by disclosure to the government, but criticized *Sharyland* as incorrect in light of cases where disclosure in response to a government request did not automatically terminate a privilege. *See also United States v. Metropolitan St. Louis Sewer Dist.*, 952 F.2d 1040 (8th Cir. 1992) (remand to district court to determine whether attorney work-product privilege was waived by alleged disclosures to 16 outside consulting firms and media of draft consent decrees prepared by federal agency involved in litigation).

13.2. The waiver question occasioned by disclosure of privileged materials to a third-party generally must be distinguished from the situation in which the materials have been disclosed in the discovery context because the privilege has been defeated or waived. The Supreme Court has ruled that Exemption 5 continues to apply to such materials because the ability to obtain them in discovery based on a particularized showing of need does not show that the materials are "routinely" or "normally" available in the civil discovery context. *Grolier*, 462 U.S. at 27-28. *See also Julian, supra.*

Attorney General Janet Reno's October 1993 memorandum instructing agencies to employ a presumption of disclosure and to apply the exemptions only in instances where there is a reasonable expectation of harm flowing from disclosure has had some impact on the release of Exemption 5 documents. The Justice Department stated that such elements as the passage of time and the breadth of information encompassed by the privilege should be taken into account when deciding whether or not to release the records and encouraged agencies to segregate out as much material as possible for release. However, the "foreseeable harm" test contained in the Reno memo was superseded by the "sound legal basis" standard contained in the subsequent Ashcroft memo of Oct. 12, 2001. *See* Appendix A.

CHAPTER 9

Exemption 6—Personal Privacy

Patrick J. Carome

1. **Exemption 6 provides that the FOIA does not apply to matters that are: "personnel and medical files and similar files the disclosure of which would constitute a clearly unwarranted invasion of personal privacy."**

2. **The Legislative History.**

2.1. Exemption 6 language has not changed since enactment in 1966.

2.2. Senate and House Committee reports do not seriously differ on the purpose of the subsection: It requires a "balancing of interests" (by agencies and courts) between individual privacy and the public's right to information: The phrase "clearly unwarranted invasion of personal privacy" enunciates a policy that will involve a balancing of interests between the protection of an individual's private affairs from unnecessary public scrutiny, and the preservation of the public's right to government information. S. Rep. No. 813, 89th Cong., 1st Sess. at 9 (1965). *See also* H.R. Rep. No. 1497, 89th Cong., 2d Sess. at 11 (1966).

2.3. Both reports say that the exemption is to protect "intimate" or "personal" details in files such as (but not limited to) those maintained by the Veterans Administration, Department of Health Education and Welfare (now Health and Human Services), Selective Service System, and the like. *Id.*

2.4. Although Exemption 6 was unchanged by the 1974 and 1986 amendments, a related provision was enacted under Exemption 7 in 1974 and amended in 1986 exempting "records or information compiled for law enforcement purposes" to the extent that production of such material "could reasonably be expected to constitute an unwarranted invasion of personal privacy." The relationship between Exemptions 6 and 7(C) is discussed *infra.*

2.5. The Electronic Freedom of Information Act Amendments of 1996 did not alter FOIA's privacy exclusions or the private-public interest balancing test. *O'Kane v. Customs Serv.*, 169 F.3d 1308, 1310 (11th Cir. 1999) (per curiam) (Exemption 7(C) case).

3. **The Meaning of "Personnel and Medical Files and Similar Files."**

3.1. Personnel and medical files.

3.1.1. In *Department of the Air Force v. Rose*, 425 U.S. 352 (1976), the Supreme Court held that the phrase "the disclosure of which would constitute a clearly unwarranted invasion of personal privacy" modifies "personnel and medical files" as well as "similar files." The statute's reference to personnel and medical files is merely illustrative. Congress did not intend any *per se* exemption for these types of files, but intended that their contents, like the contents of "similar files," be subject to the balancing process. *Id.* at 370; *see also Arieff v. Department of the Navy*, 712 F.2d 1462 (D.C. Cir. 1983) (medical files not *per se* exempt); *Schonberger v. National Transp. Safety Bd.*, 508 F.

Supp. 941 (D.D.C. 1981) (exemption for material in personnel files depends on outcome of balancing).

3.2. "...similar files..."

3.2.1. In *Rose*, the Supreme Court held that case summaries of Air Force disciplinary actions were "similar files." The primary reason was that disclosure of the summaries "implicates similar privacy values" as disclosure of personnel and medical files. 425 U.S. at 376-77. *See also Harbolt v. Department of State*, 616 F.2d 772, 774 (5th Cir. 1980), *cert. denied*, 449 U.S. 856 (1980).

3.2.2. The leading case on the scope of "similar files" is *Department of State v. Washington Post Co.*, 456 U.S. 595 (1982), which held that records reflecting the citizenship of individuals meet the threshold.

3.2.2.1. The decision rejected a test employed in the early 1980s by the D.C. Circuit, which had held in several cases that the "similar files" requirement encompasses only files containing information "of the same magnitude—as highly personal or intimate in nature—as that at stake in personnel and medical records." *Washington Post Co. v. Department of State*, 647 F.2d 197, 198-99 (D.C. Cir. 1981), *rev'd*, 456 U.S. 595 (1982), quoting from *Simpson v. Vance*, 648 F.2d 10, 13 (D.C. Cir. 1980), in turn quoting from *Board of Trade v. Commodity Futures Trading Comm'n*, 627 F.2d 392, 398 (D.C. Cir. 1980).

3.2.2.2. The Supreme Court firmly announced that the phrase "similar files" is to have "a broad, rather than narrow, meaning" and that it is "the balancing of private against public interests, not the nature of the files," that governs the applicability of Exemption 6. 456 U.S. at 599-600.

3.2.2.3. The Court concluded that Congress intended Exemption 6 to cover "detailed government records on an individual which can be identified as applying to that individual," rather than just "a narrow class of files containing only a discrete kind of personal information." *Id.* at 602 (quoting from H.R. Rep. No. 1497, 89th Cong., 2d Sess. at 11 (1966)).

3.2.2.4. "When disclosure of information which applies to a particular individual is sought from government records, courts must determine whether release of the information would constitute a clearly unwarranted invasion of that person's privacy." *Id.* The Court concluded that "[t]his construction of Exemption 6 will not render meaningless the threshold requirement that information be contained in personnel, medical, and similar files" because "[i]nformation unrelated to any particular person presumably would not satisfy the threshold test." *Id.* at n.4.

3.2.3. Very few decisions have ruled that records sought to be withheld under Exemption 6 are not "similar files."

3.2.3.1. The D.C. Circuit has stated that the "similar files" requirement "is fairly minimal and is easily satisfied." *Washington Post Co. v. HHS*, 690 F.2d 252, 260 (D.C. Cir. 1982).

3.2.3.2. In *New York Times Co. v. NASA*, 920 F.2d 1002 (D.C. Cir. 1990) (*en banc*), the Court of Appeals held, by a vote of 6 to 5, that a voice recording of the Challenger shuttle crew constituted a "similar file," even though the words spoken on the tape pertained solely to the shuttle launch. The majority reasoned that because the tape "applies to particular individuals" in the sense that it portrays their voices, it met the "similar files" threshold. *See also Lepelletier v. FDIC*, 164 F.3d 37, 46 (D.C. Cir. 1999) ("The Supreme Court has interpreted the phrase 'similar files' to include all information that applies to a particular individual."); *Hemenway v. Hughes*, 601 F. Supp. 1002, 1005 (D.D.C. 1985) ("to survive the initial inquiry the agency need only establish that the records in question apply to 'a particular individual'").

3.2.3.3. The following are additional examples of records that have been held to be "similar files:"

3.2.3.3.1. Reports of interviews of persons who unsuccessfully sought to immigrate to the United States. *Department of State v. Ray*, 502 U.S. 164 (1991).

3.2.3.3.2. Lists of names and home addresses of present government employees. *Local 3, I.B.E.W. v. NLRB*, 845 F.2d 1177, 1181 (2d Cir. 1988); *Department of the Navy v. FLRA*, 840 F.2d 1131, 1135 (3d Cir. 1988), *cert. dismissed*, 488 U.S. 881 (1988).

3.2.3.3.3. Lists of names and home addresses of private citizens. *Minnis v. Department of Agriculture*, 737 F.2d 784, 786 (9th Cir. 1984) (applicants for permits to travel on a river), *cert. denied*, 471 U.S. 1053 (1985); *Van Bourg, Allen, Weinberg & Roger v. NLRB*, 728 F.2d 1270 (9th Cir. 1984) (employees eligible to vote in union election); *Wine Hobby USA, Inc. v. IRS*, 502 F.2d 133, 135 (3d Cir. 1974) (taxpayers claiming exemption for home winemaking).

3.2.3.3.4. Financial disclosure forms submitted to an agency by its outside consultants. *Washington Post Co. v. HHS*, 690 F.2d 252 (D.C. Cir. 1982).

3.2.3.3.5. Union authorization cards. *Howard Johnson Co. v. NLRB*, 618 F.2d 1 (6th Cir. 1980); *Madeira Nursing Ctr., Inc. v. NLRB*, 615 F.2d 728 (6th Cir. 1980); *Pacific Molasses Co. v. NLRB*, 577 F.2d 1172 (5th Cir. 1978); *Committee on Masonic Homes v. NLRB*, 556 F.2d 214 (3d Cir. 1977).

3.2.3.3.6. Inmate presentence report. *Berry v. DOJ*, 733 F.2d 1343, 1353 (9th Cir. 1984).

3.2.3.3.7. Records reflecting information regarding individual Veterans Administration mortgage loans. *Heights Cmty. Cong. v. Veterans Admin.*, 732 F.2d 526, 529 (6th Cir. 1984), *cert. denied*, 469 U.S. 1034 (1984).

3.2.3.3.8. Suggestions made by agency employees under an "Employee Suggestion Program" and a list of employees who submitted suggestions. *Matthews v. U.S. Postal Serv.*, No. 92-1208-CV-W-8, slip op. at 5 (W.D. Mo. Apr. 15, 1994).

3.2.3.3.9. Portions of racial harassment investigation records containing the name of a person who hung a noose in an army hospital break room and reports of coworkers' perceptions regarding the complainant's work habits. *Ford v. West*, 149 F.3d 1190 (unpublished table decision) 1998 WL 317561 (10th Cir. June 12, 1998).

3.2.4. Recent decisions finding records not to be "similar files" are extremely rare and tend to be based upon an absence of "personal information" in the records.

3.2.4.1. In *Viacom Int'l, Inc. v. EPA*, No. 95-2243, 1995 WL 695098 (E.D. Pa. Nov. 17, 1995), the court held that records of EPA soil testing, including names and addresses of persons residing where samples were collected, were not "similar files" because they were not detailed records about individuals. *See also Viacom Int'l, Inc. v. EPA*, No. 95-2243, 1996 WL 46419 (E.D. Pa. Jan. 29, 1996) (rejecting EPA's motion to reconsider).

3.2.4.2. In *Commodity News Serv., Inc. v. Farm Credit Admin.*, No. 88-3146 (HHG), 1989 U.S. Dist. LEXIS 8848 (D.D.C. July 31, 1989), the court held that proposals prepared by an individual for his previous employers are not "similar files" because the information they contain is not "personal data." *See also Greenpeace U.S.A., Inc. v. EPA*, 735 F. Supp. 13, 14 (D.D.C. 1990) (records relating to agency employee's participation at privately sponsored meeting are not subject to withholding under Exemption 6 because they "do[] not go to personal information about" the employee).

3.2.4.3. In *National Ass'n of Criminal Def. Lawyers v. DOJ*, No. 97-CV-372 (GK) (D.D.C. Oct. 1, 1999) (vacated after settlement), the court held that an e-mail referring to allegations of misconduct by FBI employees was not a "personnel file" and Exemption 6 therefore did not apply.

3.2.4.4. One court of appeals has, *in dicta*, expressly cast doubt on a claim by the government that a memorandum is a similar file simply because it bears the signature of the government official who authored it. *Schell v. HHS*, 843 F.2d 933 (6th Cir. 1988). *But see Steyermark v. von Raab*, 682 F. Supp. 788 (D. Del. 1988) (customs agent's name deemed a "similar file").

4. The Meaning of "A Clearly Unwarranted Invasion Of Personal Privacy."

4.1. The Need to Balance Interest in Personal Privacy Against Public Interest in Disclosure.

4.1.1. The substantive test for Exemption 6—that is, whether disclosure "would constitute a clearly unwarranted invasion of personal privacy"—requires "a balancing of the individual's right of privacy against the preservation of the basic purpose of the Freedom of Information Act 'to open agency action to the light of public scrutiny.'" *Department of the Air Force v. Rose*, 425 U.S. 352, 372 (1976); *accord Department of State v. Ray*, 502 U.S. 164 (1991).

4.1.2. The cases are uniform in holding that, in the phrase "clearly unwarranted," the statute "instructs the court to tilt the balance in favor of disclosure." *Getman v. NLRB*, 450 F.2d 670, 674 (D.C. Cir. 1971), *stay denied*, 404 U.S. 1204 (1971). *See also Rose*, 425 U.S. at 378 n.16 (phrase is the major restraining feature of Exemption 6 which controls the ability of the agency to withhold information); *United Association of Journeymen and Apprentices of the Plumbing and Pipefitting Industry, Local 598 v. Department of the Army, Corps of Engineers*, 841 F.2d 1459, 1463 (9th Cir. 1988) ("particularly under Exemption (6), there is a strong presumption in favor of disclosure"); *Department of the Air Force v. FLRA*, 838 F.2d 229 (7th Cir. 1988) ("The FOIA's status as a disclosure law has led the Supreme Court to read [Exemption 6] with strong emphasis on 'clearly unwarranted.'"), *cert. dismissed*, 488 U.S. 880 (1988), *overruled on other grounds, Department of the Navy v. FLRA*, 975 F.2d 348 (7th Cir. 1992); *see also, e.g., Avondale Indus., Inc. v. NLRB*, 90 F.3d 955, 960 (5th Cir. 1996) ("[T]he burden is on the government to establish that the invasion of privacy is clearly unwarranted."); *Kurzon v. HHS*, No. Civ. 00-395-JD, 2001 WL 821531, at *11 (D.N.H. July 17, 2001) (ordering disclosure where the privacy and public interests were "at near equipoise").

4.1.3. For Exemption 6 to support withholding, the privacy invasion must be tangible and substantial; that is, "Exemption 6 was directed at threats to privacy interests more palpable than mere possibilities." *Rose*, 425 U.S. at 380 n.19; *see also National Ass'n of Retired Fed. Employees v. Horner*, 879 F.2d 873, 874 (D.C. Cir. 1989) (privacy interest at stake must be significant or substantial), *cert. denied*, 494 U.S. 1078 (1990). *But see FLRA v. Department of Veterans Affairs*, 958 F.2d 503, 510 (2d Cir. 1992) (FOIA requires only greater than *de minimus* privacy interest to trigger balancing).

4.1.3.1. The First Circuit has said that the case in which "the calculus unequivocally supports withholding [is] a rare case because Congress has weighted the balance so heavily in favor of disclosure..." *Kurzon v. HHS*, 649 F.2d 65, 67 (1st Cir. 1981). *See also Washington Post Co. v. HHS*, 690 F.2d 252, 261 (D.C. Cir. 1982) ("under Exemption 6, the presumption in favor of disclosure is as strong as can be found anywhere in the Act"); *Arieff v. Department of the Navy*, 712 F.2d 1462, 1467 (D.C. Cir. 1983) (request for the names, unit prices, quantities and dates of shipments of prescription drugs to the Attending Physician to Congress for prescription for congressional members, families and staff held to pose only the "mere possibility" that particular diseases could be linked to particular patients); *see also*

Chicago Tribune Co. v. HHS, No. 95 C 3917, 1997 WL 1137641, at *18 (N.D. Ill. Mar. 28, 1997) (releasing breast cancer study information that identified patients by coded "study numbers"; "a 'mere possibility' of identification will not suffice to invoke the application of Exemption 6") (adopting magistrate report).

4.1.3.2. *Arieff* also held that it is the "production" of the records, not the resultant speculation to which they may give rise, by which the invasion of privacy must be measured. 712 F.2d at 1469.

4.1.4. As is true elsewhere for FOIA, the fact that something might not be discoverable in federal civil litigation because of privacy concerns does not mean that the same records are unavailable under Exemption 6. "In short, privilege against discovery and exemption under Exemption 6 are separate issues and require separate analysis." *Washington Post Co. v. HHS*, 690 F.2d at 259.

4.2. The existence and degree of invasion of privacy.

4.2.1. For there to be a cognizable privacy interest, the material must usually be "personal" or "intimate details" of one's life, illustrated in the committee reports by Veterans Administration, HEW, and the Selective Service files. S. Rep. No. 813, at 9; H.R. Rep. No. 1497, at 11. Much case law supports this view. *See, e.g., Rose*, 425 U.S. at 375-76; *Rural Housing Alliance v. USDA*, 498 F.2d 73 (D.C. Cir. 1974).

4.2.2. Those cases protecting records that are not obviously "intimate" personal details usually involve little or no public interest in disclosure, *see, e.g., Wine Hobby USA, Inc. v. IRS*, 502 F.2d 133, 135 (3d Cir. 1974) (protecting names and addresses of amateur wine makers from a commercial mailing); *Professional Programs Group v. Department of Commerce*, 29 F.3d 1349, 1354 (9th Cir. 1994) (protecting names of patent bar applicants from probable commercial mailing), or reflect a fear of retaliation or harassment (frequently in a labor-management context). See cases cited *supra* protecting union authorization cards and cases discussed *infra* involving lists of names and addresses. *See also AFGE, Local 1923 v. HHS*, 712 F.2d 931 (4th Cir. 1983) (protecting home addresses of non-union employees from union request).

4.2.3. The language of the Supreme Court in *Department of State v. Washington Post Co.*, 456 U.S. 595 (1982), emphasizes "personal" over "intimate" and suggests that information is "personal" when it may cause some harm to an individual. *Id.* at 600. A footnote suggests, however, that there is some information "not personal" to anyone which may embarrass certain individuals, and that such information would not be covered by Exemption 6. *Id.* at 602 n.4; *see also Brown v. FBI*, 658 F.2d 71 (2d Cir. 1981); *cf. Schell v. HHS*, 843 F.2d 933, 939 (6th Cir. 1988) ("Without more, the disclosure of a document will not constitute a clearly unwarranted invasion of personal privacy simply because it would invite a negative reaction or cause embarrassment in the sense that a position is thought by others to be wrong or inadequate.").

4.2.4. In *Department of State v. Ray*, 502 U.S. 164 (1991), a majority of the Supreme Court stated that the weight on the privacy side of the scale is greater when there is reason to believe that disclosure of personal information would put the individuals identified in the records (in that case, Haitians who had unsuccessfully sought to immigrate to the U.S.) in danger of retaliation and mistreatment at the hands of third persons. Justice Scalia, in a concurrence joined by Justice Kennedy, stated that this was merely *dicta*, and that a literal and narrow reading of Exemption 6 requires a court to focus "solely upon what the requested information *reveals*, not upon what it might lead to." *Id.* at 180 (Scalia, J., concurring) (emphasis in original).

4.2.5. The Supreme Court has held that there can be a cognizable invasion of privacy—even if the disclosure, by itself, would not cause embarrassment—if the disclosure would invite unwarranted intrusions upon the person who is the subject of the disclosure. *Department of Defense v. FLRA*, 510 U.S. 487, 500-01 (1994); *see also National Ass'n of Retired Fed. Employees v. Horner*, 879 F.2d 873, 878 (D.C. Cir. 1989), *cert. denied*, 494 U.S. 1078 (1990). *But see Arieff*, 712 F.2d at 1468 (Scalia, J.) (Exemption 6 "does not apply to an invasion of privacy produced *as a secondary effect* of the release" (emphasis in original)); *National Ass'n of Atomic Veterans, Inc. v. Director, Def. Nuclear Agency*, 583 F. Supp. 1483, 1487 (D.D.C. 1984) (news media inquiries likely to flow from disclosure are "not the sort of invasion of privacy envisioned by Exemption 6"); *Washington Post Co. v. Department of Agric.*, 943 F. Supp. 31, 36 (D.D.C. 1996) (same).

4.2.6. On the other hand, the D.C. Circuit has held that an invasion of privacy should not justify withholding information where disclosure would result in a net benefit to the individuals whose privacy interest the government seeks to protect. *Lepelletier v. FDIC*, 164 F.3d 37, 47 (D.C. Cir. 1999) (ordering release of names of depositors with unclaimed funds at banks under FDIC receivership because "it is overly paternalistic to insist on protecting an individual's privacy interest when there is good reason to believe that he or she would rather have both the publicity and the money than have neither").

4.2.7. Public officials' privacy interests are not as strong as those of private citizens. *See Lissner v. U.S. Customs Service*, 241 F.3d 1220, 1223 (9th Cir. 2001) ("It is true that individuals do not waive all privacy interests in information relating to them simply by taking an oath of public office, ...but by becoming public officials, their privacy interests are somewhat reduced.") (Exemption 7(C) case); *Kimberlin v. DOJ*, 139 F.3d 944 (D.C. Cir. 1998) (government officials may have "somewhat diminished" privacy interest but "they do not surrender all rights to personal privacy when they accept a public appointment") (Exemption 7(C)), *cert. denied*, 525 U.S. 891 (1998); *Hardy v. Department of Defense*, No. CV-99-523-TUC-FRZ (D. Ariz. Aug. 27, 2001) ("federal employees have a diminished privacy interest" which is further diminished when the employee "holds a high-level position").

4.2.8. Only individuals have cognizable privacy interests. "[C]orporations, businesses and partnerships have no privacy interest whatsoever under Exemption 6." *Washington Post Co. v. Department of Agric.*, 943 F. Supp. at 37 n.6; *see also Sims v. CIA (I)*, 642 F.2d 562, 572 n.47 (D.C. Cir. 1980); *National Parks &*

Conservation Ass'n v. Kleppe (National Parks II), 547 F.2d 673, 685 n.44 (D.C. Cir. 1976); *Hill v. Department of Agric.*, 77 F. Supp. 2d 6, 8 (D.D.C. 1999) (suggesting that records of government loans to family-owned company may be subject to Exemption 6, but only if the family owners are "identical" with the company), *aff'd*, 2000 WL 520724 (D.C. Cir. Mar. 7, 2000); *Ivanhoe Citrus Ass'n v. Handley*, 612 F. Supp. 1560, 1567 (D.D.C. 1985). *But cf. Beard v. Espy*, 76 F.3d 384 (unpublished table decision) 1995 WL 792071 (9th Cir. Dec. 11, 1995) (Exemption 6 applicable to documents concerning FMHA loans made to closely held companies with only two or three stockholders).

4.2.9. Courts have frequently held that disclosure of information about an individual's business or professional activities does not impinge significantly on cognizable interests in personal privacy. *See Washington Post Co. v. HHS*, 690 F.2d 252, 261-62 (D.C. Cir. 1982); *Washington Post Co. v. DOJ*, 863 F.2d 96, 100 (D.C. Cir. 1988) (Exemption 7(C)); *Sims v. CIA (I)*, 642 F.2d 562, 575 (D.C. Cir. 1980) ("Exemption 6 was developed to protect intimate details of personal and family life, not business judgments and relationships."); *Board of Trade v. Commodity Futures Trading Comm'n*, 627 F.2d 392, 399-400 (D.C. Cir. 1980); *Kurzon v. HHS*, 649 F.2d 65, 69 (1st Cir. 1981); *Washington Post Co. v. Department of Agric.*, 943 F. Supp. at 35-36; *Cohen v. EPA*, 575 F. Supp. 425, 429 (D.D.C. 1983) ("The privacy exemption does not apply to information regarding professional or business activities.") (Exemption 7(C)); *Commodity News Serv., Inc. v. Farm Credit Admin.*, No. 88-3146 (HHG), 1989 U.S. Dist. LEXIS 8848, at *5 (D.D.C. July 31, 1989); *see also Oregon Natural Desert Ass'n v. Department of the Interior*, 24 F. Supp. 2d 1088, 1093-94 (D. Or. 1998) (fact that cattle operators' relationship with the government was "at least quasi-business related" weighed in favor of disclosure) (decided on Exemption 7(C) grounds). *But see Campaign for Family Farms v. Glickman*, 200 F.3d 1180, 1188-89 (8th Cir. 2000) ("An overly technical distinction between individuals acting in a purely private capacity and those acting in an entrepreneurial capacity fails to serve the exemption's purpose of protecting the privacy of individuals.").

4.2.10. The weight of the authorities is that the personal privacy interests protected by Exemptions 6 and 7(C) lapse upon the death of the individual. *See McDonnell v. U.S.*, 4 F.3d 1227, 1257 (3d Cir. 1993) ("[p]ersons who are deceased have no privacy interest in nondisclosure of their identities"); *Davin v. DOJ*, 60 F.3d 1043, 1058-59 (3d Cir. 1995) (government may properly be required to prove subject of record is still alive before being permitted to withhold it) (Exemption 7(C)); *Diamond v. FBI*, 532 F. Supp. 216 (S.D.N.Y. 1981), *aff'd*, 707 F.2d 75 (2d Cir. 1983) ("[D]eath or voluntary disclosure so diminished any privacy interest as to amount to a waiver") (Exemption 7(C)), *cert. denied*, 465 U.S. 1004 (1984); *Samuel Gruber Educ. Project v. DOJ*, 24 F. Supp. 2d 1, 13 (D.D.C. 1998) ("Though not universally settled, it is generally accepted that, when the subject is deceased, the subject's privacy interest no longer exists."); *Journal-Gazette Publ'g Co. v. Department of the Army*, No. F-89-147 (N.D. Ind. Jan. 8, 1990) ("courts have seldom found that the disclosure of medical records of a deceased person" would invade personal privacy) (Exemption 6); *Silets v. FBI*, 591 F. Supp. 490, 498 (N.D. Ill. 1984); *Providence Journal Co. v. FBI*, 460 F. Supp. 762, 778, 793 (D.R.I. 1978), *rev'd on other grounds*, 602

F.2d 1010 (1st Cir. 1979), *cert. denied*, 444 U.S. 1071 (1980); *United States v. Amalgamated Life Ins. Co.*, 534 F. Supp. 676, 679 (S.D.N.Y. 1982); *Na Iwi O Na Kupuna O Mokapu v. Dalton*, 894 F. Supp. 1397, 1413 (D. Haw. 1995); Restatement (Second) of Torts § 652I. *But see Kiraly v. FBI*, 728 F.2d 273, 277-78 (6th Cir. 1984) (court distinguished tort recovery right for invasion of privacy from FOIA disclosure exemption, holding latter does not lapse upon death) (Exemption 7(C)).

4.2.10.1. The Supreme Court's recent holding in *Swidler & Berlin v. U.S.*, 524 U.S. 399, 406 (1998), that the attorney-client privilege survives a client's death has prompted the D.C. Circuit to begin treating death as only a "relevant factor" that "diminishes" but does not "extinguish" privacy interests. *Schrecker v. DOJ*, 254 F.3d 162, 166 (D.C. Cir. 2001) (Exemption 7(C) case); *see also Campbell v. DOJ*, 164 F.3d 20, 33-34 (D.C. Cir. 1998) ("death clearly matters," but the *Swidler & Berlin* decision would appear to undercut the Third Circuit's categorical rule stated in *Davin* and *McDonnell*, *supra*) (Exemption 7(C)). *Cf. Accuracy in Media, Inc. v. National Park Serv.*, 194 F.3d 120, 123 (D.C. Cir. 1999) (noting that some privacy interest may survive death, but declining to "explore whether the interest belongs to living close survivors (in which case it might end at their deaths), or alternatively may inhere posthumously in the subject himself (in which case it would seem to be of indefinite duration), or both") (Exemption 7(C)), *cert. denied*, 529 U.S. 1111 (2000).

4.2.10.2. The federal district court for the District of Columbia has upheld claims of Exemption 6 on a theory that surviving family members may have cognizable privacy interests in government records relating to the death of a loved one. *Katz v. National Archives & Records Admin.*, 862 F. Supp. 476, 485-86 (D.D.C. 1994) (x-rays and photographs from President Kennedy's autopsy are exempt under Exemption 6 because public display of the records would cause extreme anguish to the Kennedy family), *aff'd*, 68 F.3d 1438 (D.C. Cir. 1995); *New York Times Co. v. NASA*, 782 F. Supp. 628 (D.D.C. 1991) (permitting NASA to withhold tape recording of voices of astronauts aboard final flight of Challenger space shuttle). *See also Accuracy in Media, Inc. v. National Park Serv.*, 194 F.3d 120, 123 (D.C. Cir. 1999) (noting without deciding that "living close survivors" may retain some privacy interest) (Exemption 7(C)); *Coleman v. FBI*, 13 F. Supp. 2d 75, 80 (D.D.C. 1998) (photographs or records of murder victim withheld due to privacy interests of the victim's family) (Exemption 7(C)); *Badhwar v. Department of the Air Force*, 829 F.2d 182, 185-86 (D.C. Cir. 1987) (noting, in *dicta*, that some parts of autopsy report might "shock the sensibilities of surviving kin" and therefore be exempt under Exemption 6); *Outlaw v. Department of the Army*, 815 F. Supp. 505 (D.D.C. 1993) (no substantial privacy interest in 25 year old photographs of a murder victim, absent a showing that there were surviving relatives who would be offended); *Dow Jones & Co. v. DOJ*, No. 94-0527, 1995 WL 6155, at *8 (S.D.N.Y. Jan. 9, 1995) (holding that torn-up suicide note of former deputy White House counsel

Vincent Foster falls outside Exemption 7(C) "because the Foster family's privacy interest in the Note is weaker than the deceased Challenger astronauts families' interest in the audiotape" and because of a stronger public interest in disclosure of the note); *Epps v. DOJ*, 801 F. Supp. 787, 793 (D.D.C. 1992) (individual's interest in not having his or her autopsy photographs released is substantial, as is interest of family), *aff'd without opinion*, 995 F.2d 305 (D.C. Cir. 1993); *Isley v. Executive Office for U.S. Attorneys*, No. 96-0123 (JR) (D.D.C. Feb. 15, 1998) (withholding victim's medical records, autopsy reports, and inmate injury reports to protect surviving family members' privacy interests), *aff'd on other grounds*, 203 F.3d 52 (D.C. Cir. 1999).

4.2.11. It is difficult to generalize about whether certain kinds of files are or are not exempt. As the D.C. Circuit said of similar balancing of "the myriad of considerations involved" in Exemption 7(C) cases, "*per se* rules of nondisclosure based upon the type of document requested, the type of individual involved, or the type of activity inquired into, are generally disfavored." *Stern v. FBI*, 737 F.2d 84, 91 (D.C. Cir. 1984); *Summers v. DOJ*, 140 F.3d 1077, 1083 (D.C. Cir. 1998) (characterizing Exemption 6 balancing inquiries as "fact-intensive" and "delicate"). *But see* discussion in Chapter 10 on Law Enforcement Records, regarding *DOJ v. Reporters Comm. for Freedom of the Press*, 489 U.S. 749 (1989) (approving "categorical balancing" in holding "rap sheets" exempt from disclosure under 7(C)). One must usually proceed by example.

4.2.12. The following are examples of records eligible for protection under Exemption 6, subject to removal of identifying details or a stronger interest in disclosure:

4.2.12.1. Property addresses, identities of lenders and loan amounts of VA-insured home loans. *Heights Cmty. Cong. v. Veterans Admin.*, 732 F.2d 526 (6th Cir.) (held exempt), *cert. denied*, 469 U.S. 1034 (1984) .

4.2.12.2. Records relating to government loans to individuals. *Hill v. Department of Agric.*, 77 F. Supp. 2d 6, 9 (D.D.C. 1999), *aff'd*, 2000 WL 520724 (D.C. Cir. Mar. 7, 2000); *Green v. United States*, 8 F. Supp. 2d 983, 998 (W.D. Mich. 1998) (withholding names and loan amounts of borrowers from the Farm Services Agency; privacy interest heightened by the fact that agency was a lender of last resort, which may connote a tenuous financial position).

4.2.12.3. Records indicating citizenship. *Department of State v. Washington Post Co.*, 456 U.S. 595 (1982) (remanded for balancing). It should be noted that such records would only be eligible for protection when harm might result from their release. In *Washington Post*, the request was for records indicating U.S. citizenship, if any, of two employees of the Revolutionary Government of Iran. The evidence was that the release of such information might harm the two men concerned. A request for, say, the citizenship of employees of the British government would presumably not implicate similar privacy values.

See, e.g., Simpson v. Vance, 648 F.2d 10 (D.C. Cir. 1980). See also *Hemenway v. Hughes*, 601 F. Supp. at 1006-1008, for detailed discussion of rationale in considering application of Exemption 6 to "citizenship information."

4.2.12.4. Interviews of persons who unsuccessfully sought to immigrate to the U.S. and were returned to their home country. *Department of State v. Ray*, 502 U.S. 164 (1991) (redaction of names permitted).

4.2.12.5. Identities of alien investors who participated in the INS's "Alien Entrepreneur" preferred visa and residency program. *Perlman v. DOJ*, No. 00 CIV 5842 (JGK), 2001 WL 910406 (S.D.N.Y. Aug. 13, 2001) (redaction of identifying information permitted under Exemptions 6 and 7(C), but release of exhibits to an Inspector General report required after redaction).

4.2.12.6. Information in passport files. *Schwarz v. Department of State*, 172 F.3d 921 (unpublished table decision) 1998 WL 700164 (D.C. Cir. July 29, 1998).

4.2.12.7. Names and official positions of individuals who provided information for Inspector General's investigation. *Walsh v. Department of the Navy*, No. 91-C-7410, 1992 WL 67845 (N.D. Ill. Mar 23, 1992); *see also Ford v. West*, 149 F.3d 1190 (unpublished table decision) 1998 WL 317561 (10th Cir. June 12, 1998) (allowing redaction of names from racial harassment investigation records); *Cotton v. Adams*, 798 F. Supp. 22, 26 (D.D.C. 1992) (identified Smithsonian Museum Shop employees had significant privacy interest in records of investigation, even if it focused on seemingly innocuous internal agency matter).

4.2.12.8. Letter to an Assistant United States Attorney, characterized simply as a "private document." *In re Wade*, 969 F.2d 241 (7th Cir. 1992) (exempt; no reason for dissemination).

4.2.12.9. Case summaries of honor and ethics hearings maintained by Air Force Academy. *Department of the Air Force v. Rose*, 425 U.S. 352 (1976) (release ordered due to public interest after removal of identifying details).

4.2.12.10. Arrest record of prosecution witness. *Ferri v. Bell*, 645 F.2d 1213 (3d Cir. 1981) (released due to public interest).

4.2.12.11. Marital status of State Department employees. *Simpson v. Vance*, 648 F.2d 10 (held exempt). *But see Department of State v. Washington Post Co.*, 456 U.S. at 602 n.5.

4.2.12.12. Names and addresses of Americans incarcerated in foreign prisons on drug charges. *Harbolt v. Department of State*, 616 F.2d 772, 774 (5th Cir.) (held exempt), *cert. denied*, 449 U.S. 856 (1980).

4.2.12.13. Names, work locations, and social security numbers of FAA air traffic controllers who were reinstated after having been fired for participating in an illegal strike. *Norwood v. FAA*, 993 F.2d 570, 574

(6th Cir. 1993). In the same decision, however, the court of appeals rejected the FAA's contention that Exemption 6 also permitted much broader withholding of all other information that might be used to piece together the identity of a reinstated controller. *Id.* at 574-76. *Cf. Manna v. DOJ*, 832 F. Supp. 866 (D.N.J. 1993), (cannot withhold "personal information" under Exemption 7(C) absent a showing that deletion of identifying information is inadequate to protect privacy interest), *aff'd*, 51 F.3d 1158 (3d Cir.), *cert. denied*, 516 U.S. 975 (1995).

4.2.12.14. FBI logs of illegal wiretaps. *Providence Journal Co. v. FBI*, 602 F.2d 1010, 1013-14 (1st Cir. 1979) (held exempt under Exemption 7(C) in reliance upon Omnibus Crime Control and Safe Streets Act), *cert. denied*, 444 U.S. 1071 (1980).

4.2.12.15. Employment records, including evaluations. *FLRA v. Department of Commerce*, 962 F.2d 1055, 1059 (D.C. Cir. 1992) (employee's outstanding or commendable ratings withheld; recognizing favorable information may be embarrassing and is therefore protected); *Stern v. FBI*, 737 F.2d 84 (D.C. Cir. 1984) (two censure letters withheld; one released); *Chamberlain v. Kurtz*, 589 F.2d 827, 841-42 (5th Cir. 1979) (records of disciplinary proceedings; identifiers excised), *cert. denied* 444 U.S. 842 (1979); *Campbell v. U.S. Civil Serv. Comm'n*, 539 F.2d 58 (10th Cir. 1976) (held exempt); *Peralta v. U.S. Attorney's Office*, 69 F. Supp. 2d 21, 33 (D.D.C. 1999) (letters of commendation withheld), *vacated on reconsideration*, (May 17, 1999); *Warren v. SSA*, No. 98-CV-0116E (SC), 2000 WL 1209383 (W.D.N.Y. Aug. 22, 2000) (nomination forms for awards and bonuses withheld), *aff'd in part and remanded*, 2001 WL 514312 (2d Cir. May 15, 2001); *Claudio v. Social Sec. Admin.*, No. Civ. A. H-98-1911, 2000 WL 33379041 (S.D. Tex. May 24, 2000) (correspondence indicating employee complaints and agency investigation into Administrative Law Judge's conduct held exempt); *Gilbey v. Department of Interior*, No. 89-0801 (RCL), 1990 U.S. Dist. LEXIS 14021 (D.D.C. Oct. 22, 1990) (police officer's job performance evaluation held exempt). *But see Hardy v. Department of Defense*, No. CV-99-523-TUC-FRZ (D. Ariz. Aug. 27, 2001) (privacy interest in favorable performance ratings and evaluations was minimal after employee had retired).

4.2.12.16. Department of Agriculture study of housing containing information regarding marital status, legitimacy of children, medical condition, welfare payments, family fights, alcoholic consumption, reputation, etc. *Rural Housing Alliance v. USDA*, 498 F.2d 73 (D.C. Cir. 1974) (remanded for balancing process).

4.2.12.17. Social Security numbers of individuals in Air Force investigative file. *Swisher v. Department of the Air Force*, 495 F. Supp. 337 (W.D. Mo. 1980) (held exempt), *aff'd*, 660 F.2d 369 (8th Cir. 1981); *see also Sherman v. Department of the Army*, 244 F.3d 357 (5th Cir. 2001) (Social Security numbers of recipients of army award orders held exempt); *Philadelphia Newspapers, Inc. v. HHS*, 69 F. Supp. 2d 63,

68-69 (D.D.C. 1999) (Medicare beneficiaries' identification numbers exempt because they are "typically a person's social security number"); *Oliva v. United States*, 756 F. Supp. 105 (E.D.N.Y. 1991) (Social Security numbers and birth dates held exempt); *Aronson v. IRS*, 767 F. Supp. 378, 388 (D. Mass. 1991) (Social Security numbers held exempt), *aff'd in part, rev'd in part*, 973 F.2d 962 (1st Cir. 1992).

4.2.12.18. Information concerning personal and family life of organized crime figure; names of FBI agents and informants. *Providence Journal Co. v. FBI*, 460 F. Supp. 762 (D.R.I. 1978) (held exempt), *rev'd on other grounds*, 602 F.2d 1010 (1st Cir. 1979), *cert. denied*, 444 U.S. 1071 (1980).

4.2.12.19. Records of past criminal activity or investigation of it. *Congressional News Syndicate v. DOJ*, 438 F. Supp. 538 (D.D.C. 1977) (held exempt) (7(C) case); see Chapter 10 on Law Enforcement Records.

4.2.12.20. Prison records. *National Prison Project of ACLU Found. v. Sigler*, 390 F. Supp. 789 (D.D.C. 1975) (released, deletion of identifying details held sufficient).

4.2.12.21. Records relating to applications for employment. *Core v. U.S. Postal Serv.*, 730 F.2d 946 (4th Cir. 1984) (employment records of successful applicants released; those of unsuccessful applicants withheld); *Barvick v. Cisneros*, 941 F. Supp. 1015 (D. Kan. 1996) (records on successful applicants withheld in part; records on unsuccessful applicants withheld in full); *Warren v. SSA*, No. 98-CV-0116E (SC), 2000 WL 1209383 (W.D.N.Y. Aug. 22, 2000) (identities of unsuccessful applicants and scoring of all applicants withheld); *Heckman v. Olive*, No. CV-88-2981, 1992 WL 390249 (E.D.N.Y. Dec. 9, 1992) (personnel files of selected candidates withheld), *aff'd without opinion*, 9 F.3d 1537 (2d Cir. 1993); *Holland v. CIA*, No. 91-1233 (D.D.C. Aug. 31, 1992) (identity and resume of applicant for CIA General Counsel position held exempt); *Samble v. Department of Commerce*, No. CV192-225, slip op. at 9-10 (S.D. Ga. Sept. 23, 1994) (information about unsuccessful applicants withheld).

4.2.12.22. Identities of applicants for Air Force post-graduate study program. *Manos v. Department of the Air Force*, No. C-92-3986 MHP, 1993 U.S. Dist. LEXIS 1501 (N.D. Cal. Feb. 10, 1993) (*in camera* submission to determine whether any privacy concerns remained after redaction of name, social security number, and address; applications not exempt because of "mere possibility" of deducing identity after redaction).

4.2.12.23. Name of Customs Service agent who was subject of a citizen's complaint. *Steyermark v. von Raab*, 682 F. Supp. 788 (D. Del. 1988) (held exempt); *see also Ligorner v. Reno*, 2 F. Supp. 2d 400 (S.D.N.Y. 1998) (withholding complaint letter accusing Justice Department lawyer of misconduct; redaction would not protect the identities of the accuser or accused) (Exemptions 6 and 7(C)).

4.2.12.24. Names of physicians investigated for but not charged with Medicare fraud. *Philadelphia Newspapers, Inc. v. HHS*, 69 F. Supp. 2d 63, 68 (D.D.C. 1999) (held exempt under Exemptions 6 and 7(C)).

4.2.12.25. Status and termination information contained in the Coast Guard's Register of Officers. *Fidell v. Commandant of the US. Coast Guard*, No. 88-2922 (LFO) (D.D.C. May 31, 1989) (held exempt).

4.2.12.26. Current whereabouts and employer of former federal prisoner. *Andrews v. DOJ*, 769 F. Supp. 314 (E.D. Mo. 1991).

4.2.12.27. Information identifying persons who have defaulted on student loans. *Gannett Satellite Information Network, Inc. v. Department of Education*, No. 90-1392, 1990 WL 251480 (D.D.C. Dec. 21, 1990) (held exempt).

4.2.12.28. "Excelsior Lists"—lists of names and addresses of union members eligible to vote in representation elections. *Reed v. NLRB*, 927 F.2d 1249 (D.C. Cir. 1991) (ruling such lists are categorically exempt, and effectively overruling the contrary result in *Getman v. NLRB, infra*), *cert. denied*, 502 U.S. 1047 (1992); *see also FLRA v. Department of the Navy*, 941 F.2d 49 (1st Cir. 1991).

4.2.12.29. Names and addresses of individuals who submitted consumer complaints to federal agency. *Center for Auto Safety v. NHTSA*, 809 F. Supp. 148 (D.D.C. 1993).

4.2.12.30. Names, addresses, and phone numbers of pork producers who petitioned the Department of Agriculture seeking a referendum to terminate mandatory assessments for pork promotion. *Campaign for Family Farms v. Glickman*, 200 F.3d 1180 (8th Cir. 2000) (reverse FOIA) (withheld; petition included a clear indication of how petitioners intended to vote in the referendum, and release would therefore invade petitioners' privacy interest in a secret ballot).

4.2.12.31. Payroll information, including job titles, hourly wages and salary of agency employees. *News Group Boston, Inc. v. National R.R. Passenger Corp.*, 799 F. Supp. 1264 (D. Mass. 1992) (released due to public interest after removal of names and addresses). *But cf.* 5 C.F.R. § 293.311(a) (stating that the Office of Personnel Management will release the name, title and position description, grade, annual salary rate including bonuses, and duty stations of most present and former federal employees).

4.2.12.32. Names of agency employees who received disaster assistance payments from agency. *Stabasefski v. United States*, 919 F. Supp. 1570 (M.D. Ga. 1996) (permitting redaction of names from payment vouchers).

4.2.12.33. Payroll records of government contractors. *Sheet Metal Workers Int'l Ass'n, Local Union #19 v. Department of Veterans Affairs*, 135 F.3d 891, 904-05 (3d Cir. 1998) (permitting agency to delete names, addresses and Social Security numbers of employees of a government contractor from payroll records); *Sheet Metal Workers Int'l Ass'n v. Air Force*, 63 F.3d 994 (10th Cir. 1995) (same); *Painting Indus. of Hawaii Market Recovery Fund v. Department of the Air Force*, 26 F.3d 1479, 1485 (9th Cir. 1994) (same); *Painting & Drywall Work Preservation Fund v. HUD*, 936 F.2d 1300 (D.C. Cir. 1991); *Hopkins v. HUD*, 929 F.2d 81, 86-87 (2d Cir. 1991).

4.2.12.34. Names of patent bar applicants. *Professional Programs Group v. Department of Commerce*, 29 F.3d 1349, 1354 (9th Cir. 1994) (held exempt; no public interest in disclosure).

4.2.12.35. Names and addresses of persons who wrote letters to Parole Commission opposing plaintiff's parole. *Strout v. U.S. Parole Comm'n*, 40 F.3d 136, 139 (6th Cir. 1994) (held exempt). *See also Ortiz v. HHS*, 874 F. Supp. 570, 575 (S.D.N.Y. 1995), *aff'd*, 70 F.3d 729 (2d Cir. 1995) (identity of person who wrote anonymous letter to Social Security Administration concerning plaintiff's social security fraud which prompted criminal investigation held exempt), *cert. denied*, 517 U.S. 1136 (1996); *cf. Judicial Watch of Florida, Inc. v. DOJ*, 102 F. Supp. 2d 6, 18 (D.D.C. 2000) ("A person who has written a letter to a federal official may have a great privacy interest in the nondisclosure of his name. On the other hand, the court can imagine scenarios in which disclosing the identity of those who wrote letters to the AG regarding campaign finance issues or Independent Counsel Act matters might not 'constitute a clearly unwarranted invasion of personal privacy' ...").

4.2.12.36. IRS agent's time records, including names of third parties and amount of time spent investigating such parties. *Vosburgh v. IRS*, No. 93-1493, 1994 WL 564699, at *3 (D. Or. July 5, 1994) (held exempt), *aff'd*, 106 F.3d 411 (unpublished table decision), 1997 WL 30257 (9th Cir. Jan. 6, 1997).

4.2.12.37. Personal data and fingerprints of foreign soldiers under investigation by foreign government. *Joya-Martinez v. FBI*, No. 91-1433, 1994 WL 118206, at *2 (D.D.C. Mar. 31, 1994) (held exempt).

4.2.12.38. Records concerning Senate candidate's military service, including information about assignments, pay and medical treatment. *Hunt v. U.S. Marine Corps*, 935 F. Supp. 46 (D.D.C. 1996) (held exempt).

4.2.13. The following are examples of records which courts have found to implicate privacy values not at all, or only minimally:

4.2.13.1. Names and addresses of unsuccessful applicants for research grants from the National Cancer Institute. *Kurzon v. HHS*, 649 F.2d 65 (1st Cir. 1981) (released due to public interest); *see also Kurzon v. HHS*, No. Civ. 00-395-JD, 2001 WL 821531 (D.N.H. July 17, 2001) (released because privacy interest was more than *de minimis* but less than significant).

4.2.13.2. Resumes of unsuccessful nominees for a federal advisory committee. *Physicians Comm. for Responsible Med. v. Glickman*, 117 F. Supp. 2d 1, 6 (D.D.C. 2000) (released after redaction of addresses, telephone numbers, e-mail addresses, and social security numbers; privacy interest "minimal").

4.2.13.3. Most data in Biographic Register of State Department employees (date and place of birth, date of naturalization (if any), educational background work experience, military service, initial appointment, promotion history, post assignments, awards received, foreign languages). *Simpson v. Vance*, 648 F.2d 10 (D.C. Cir. 1980) (released; not "similar file"). *But see Department of State v. Washington Post Co.*, 456 U.S. 595 (1982).

4.2.13.4. Names of agency officers and staff members. *Lawyers Committee for Human Rights v. INS*, 721 F. Supp. 552 (S.D.N.Y. 1989) (released; no substantial evidence of privacy interest); *see also LaRouche v. DOJ*, No. 90-2753 (HHG), 1993 WL 388601 (D.D.C. June 25, 1993) (no demonstrated privacy interest in names of employees in Tax Division of DOJ).

4.2.13.5. Institutional and personal names of researchers contracting with the CIA for drug research in MK-ULTRA program. *Sims v. CIA (I)*, 642 F.2d 562 (D.C. Cir. 1980) (released; not "similar file"). *But see Department of State v. Washington Post Co.*, 456 U.S. 595.

4.2.13.6. Data regarding non-federal employment and financial interests of agency consultants. *Washington Post Co. v. HHS*, 690 F.2d 252, 261-64 (D.C. Cir. 1982) (privacy interest "minimal"); *see also Physicians Comm. for Responsible Med. v. Glickman*, 117 F. Supp. 2d 1 (requiring disclosure of identity of corporation paying a government advisory committee member to serve on its editorial board; privacy interest "minimal"). *But cf. Meyerhoff v. EPA*, 958 F.2d 1498 (9th Cir. 1992) (agency advisors' conflict of interest forms withheld under Exemption 3; applying Ethics in Government Act); *id.* at 1504 (Kozinski, C.J., concurring) (applying Exemption 6).

4.2.13.7. Employment history and personal qualifications of person selected to be receiver in liquidation of a federal bank. *Commodity News Serv., Inc. v. Farm Credit Admin.*, No. 88-3146 (HHG), 1989 U.S. Dist. LEXIS 8848 (D.D.C. July 31, 1989) (released; no serious privacy interest).

4.2.13.8. Identities of "trade sources" who had complained to the Commodity Futures Trading Commission about the business practices of the Chicago Board of Trade. *Board of Trade v. Commodity Futures Trading Comm'n*, 627 F.2d 392 (D.C. Cir. 1980) (released; business rather than personal). *But see Department of State v. Washington Post Co.*, 456 U.S. 595.

4.2.13.9. Identities of members of the public associated with requests for IRS audits or inquiries into the tax status of 501(c)(3) tax-exempt organizations. *Landmark Legal Found. v. IRS*, 87 F. Supp. 2d 21, 27-28 (D.D.C. 2000) (released; no more than *de minimis* privacy interest found).

4.2.13.10. Names and addresses of members of the public who submitted written comments on an agency's proposed rulemaking regarding reintroduction of the grizzly bear in portions of Idaho and Montana. *Alliance for the Wild Rockies v. Department of Interior*, 53 F. Supp. 2d 32 (D.D.C. 1999) (released; court found it remarkable that agency objected).

4.2.13.11. Statements of fellow employees to NLRB investigators. *Poss v. NLRB*, 565 F.2d 654, 658 (10th Cir. 1977) (7(C)) case; "[t]he subject matter itself looks away from...privacy"). *But see Alirez v. NLRB*, 676 F.2d 423 (10th Cir. 1982) (similar records held exempt on stronger showing of potential harm).

4.2.13.12. Data supporting NLRB back pay specification. *Deering Milliken, Inc. v. Irving*, 548 F.2d 1131 (4th Cir. 1977) (released; privacy interest "minimal").

4.2.13.13. Attendance records of government official indicating leaves and vacations. *Dobronski v. FCC*, 17 F.3d 275, 280 (9th Cir. 1994) (released; privacy interest "minimal at best").

4.2.13.14. Names and addresses of amateur wine makers. *Wine Hobby USA, Inc. v. IRS*, 502 F.2d 133 (3d Cir. 1974) (held exempt because no public interest; privacy interest not serious).

4.2.13.15. Names of mushroom producers conducting business in their personal names. *Ackerson & Bishop Chartered v. Department of Agriculture*, No. 92-1068 (D.D.C. July 15, 1992) (released; no expectation of privacy).

4.2.13.16. Names and addresses of purchasers of property seized by the U.S. Marshals Service. *Baltimore Sun v. Marshals Serv.*, 131 F. Supp. 2d 725, 729 (D. Md. 2001) (released; "[a]lthough the receivers of the seized property may prefer not to have their identities disclosed, that preference alone is not a persuasive privacy interest").

4.2.13.17. Names and addresses of, and amounts paid to, persons receiving federal agricultural subsidies. *Washington Post Co. v. Department of Agric.*, 943 F. Supp. 31 (D.D.C. 1996) (released; privacy interest "small").

4.2.13.18. Names and addresses of employees who voted in NLRB-sponsored union representative election. *Avondale Indus., Inc. v. NLRB*, 90 F.3d 955 (5th Cir. 1996) (released; privacy interest only minimal because content of votes not sought).

4.2.13.19. Mug shots of indicted individuals whom the government identified and who made a court appearance in an ongoing criminal prosecution. *Detroit Free Press, Inc. v. DOJ*, 73 F.3d 93, 96-97 (6th Cir. 1996) (released; "no privacy rights implicated") (Exemptions 6 and 7(C)). *But see Times Picayune Publ'g Co. v. DOJ*, 37 F. Supp. 2d 472 (E.D. La. 1999) (disagreeing with *Detroit Free Press* and withholding mug shots of an individual who pled guilty and was convicted prior to the FOIA request) (Exemption 7(C)).

4.2.13.20. Names, addresses and phone numbers of persons who had voluntarily reported wolf sightings in Wyoming. *Urbigkit v. Department of Interior*, No. 93-CV-0232-J, *slip op.* at 12-13 (D. Wyo. Jun. 1, 1994) (released; only *de minimus* privacy interest). *See also Thott v. Department of Interior*, No. 93-0177-B, *slip. op.* (D. Me. Apr. 14, 1994).

4.2.13.21. Handgun serial numbers reflected on gun purchase reports from which names of purchasers was deleted. *Center to Prevent Handgun Violence v. Dep't of Treasury*, 981 F. Supp. 20, 23-24 (D.D.C. 1997) (released; privacy interest "vanishingly small") (Exemption 7(C)).

4.3. The public interest in disclosure.

4.3.1. According to the Supreme Court in *Rose*, the weight in the scale opposite privacy is "the preservation of the basic purpose of the Freedom of Information Act 'to open agency action to the light of public scrutiny.'" *Department of the Air Force v. Rose*, 425 U.S. 352, 372 (1976). More specifically, "the purpose of FOIA is to permit the public to decide for itself whether government action is proper..." *I.B.E.W. Local No. 41 v. HUD*, 763 F.2d 435, 436 (D.C. Cir. 1985) (citing *Washington Post Co. v. HHS*, 690 F.2d at 264); see also *National Ass'n of Atomic Veterans, Inc. v. Director, Def. Nuclear Agency*, 583 F. Supp. 1483, 1487 (D.D.C. 1984) (public oversight of government operations provides a public benefit even if the requesters' efforts overlap the government's in full or in part); *Citizens for Environ. Quality, Inc. v. Department of Agric.*, 602 F. Supp. 534 (D.D.C. 1984).

4.3.2. The leading case governing the public interest analysis in the closely related context of Exemption 7(C) is *DOJ v. Reporters Comm. for Freedom of the Press*, 489 U.S. 749 (1989), which is discussed in Chapter 10 on Law Enforcement Records. Extending the holding of that case to the Exemption 6 context, the Supreme Court has stated that the only public interest weighed in the balance against privacy concerns is FOIA's "core purpose" of contributing to public understanding of government operations or activities. *Department of Defense v. FLRA*, 510 U.S. 487, 497 (1994); *Bibles v. Oregon Natural Desert Ass'n*, 519 U.S. 355 (1997) (per curiam) (same); *National Ass'n of Retired Fed. Employees v. Horner*, 879 F.2d 873, 879 (D.C. Cir. 1989) ("unless the public would learn something directly about the workings of the *Government* [from the information in the requested records], ...disclosure is not affected with the public interest") (emphasis in original), *cert. denied*, 494 U.S. 1078 (1990).

4.3.3. In *Department of State v. Ray*, 502 U.S. 164 (1991), the Supreme Court, applying the public interest standard set out in the Reporters Committee case, found a "cognizable" public interest "in knowing whether the State Department has adequately monitored Haiti's compliance with its promise not to prosecute"

Haitian nationals who had unsuccessfully sought to immigrate to the United States. *Id.* at 178. The Court concluded, however, that this interest had been satisfied by disclosure of redacted documents from which the names of Haitian returnees who had been interviewed by U.S. officials had been deleted. *Id.*

4.3.3.1. The Court reasoned that "[t]he addition of the redacted identifying information would not shed any additional light on the Government's conduct of its obligation." 502 U.S. at 178.

4.3.3.2. The plaintiffs had argued that there was a public interest in disclosure of the names of the interviewees so that the plaintiffs could communicate directly with the interviewees to ascertain, among other things, the veracity of the government's interview reports. 502 U.S. at 178. The government had argued for a categorical rule that such "derivative use" of government information to gain additional information not contained in government records should never be considered in assessing whether there is a public interest in disclosure. *Id.*

4.3.3.3. The Court declined to adopt any "rigid rule" against considering "derivative uses" of information for purposes of measuring the public interest in disclosure. 502 U.S. at 178-79. It said, however, that there was nothing more than "mere speculation" to suggest that plaintiffs' proposed use of the information "would produce any relevant information that is not set forth in the documents that have already been produced." *Id.* In these circumstances, the Court said, "we need not address the question whether a 'derivative use' theory would ever justify release of information about private individuals." *Id.*

4.3.3.4. Since the decision in *Department of State v. Ray*, several courts have recognized that potential "derivative uses" of the requested information may be weighed on the public interest side of the balance. *See Painting Indus. of Hawaii Market Recovery Fund v. Department of the Air Force*, 26 F.3d 1479, 1482 (9th Cir. 1994) (court urges evaluation of "both the public benefit and the potential invasion of privacy by looking at the nature of the information requested and the uses to which it could be put if released to any member of the public"); *Painting & Drywall Work Pres. Fund v. HUD*, 936 F.2d 1300, 1303 (D.C. Cir. 1991) (derivative use is a public interest cognizable under FOIA); *Ray v. DOJ*, 852 F. Supp. 1558 (S.D. Fla. 1994) (court ruled that logs identifying interdicted Haitian nationals could not be withheld under Exemption 6 because of the public interest in follow-up interviews that were only possible with the release of the unredacted logs) (relying on *Department of State v. Ray*, 908 F.2d 1549 (11th Cir. 1990), *rev'd on other grounds*, 502 U.S. 164 (1991)); *Sheet Metal Workers' Int'l Ass'n, Local Union #19 v. Department of Veteran Affairs*, 940 F. Supp. 712 (E.D. Pa. 1995) (finding strong public interest in disclosure based in part on union's ability to monitor compliance with Davis-Bacon Act by interviewing workers identified in payroll records). *But see Hopkins v. HUD*, 929 F.2d 81, 88 (2d Cir. 1991) ("Disclosure of information affecting privacy interests is permissible only if the information reveals something directly about the character of a government agency or official"). *Cf. Sheet Metal Workers Int'l Ass'n, Local Union #19 v. Department of Veterans Affairs*, 135 F.3d 891, 903-04 (3d Cir. 1998) (even assuming a public interest in monitoring, in this case disclosure of worker information in contractor payroll records "will not contribute significantly to the public's understanding of government activities").

4.3.4. Thus, the weightiest cases for the public interest are those in which the information will serve to inform the public about agency or official [mis]behavior. For example:

4.3.4.1. In *Rose*, case summaries of honors and ethics disciplinary proceedings were sought by a law review to assess the workings of a part of the military justice system—a goal the Supreme Court thought important. 425 U.S. at 367.

4.3.4.2. In *Arieff v. Department of the Navy, 712 F.2d 1462* (D.C. Cir. 1983), the District of Columbia Circuit found a strong public interest in the names, unit prices, quantities, and dates of shipments of prescription drugs to the Attending Physician to Congress for prescriptions for congressional members, families, and staff. 712 F.2d at 1468-69.

4.3.4.3. In *Washington Post Co. v. HHS*, 690 F.2d 252, 264-65 (D.C. Cir. 1982), the D.C. Circuit found that the "public has a singularly strong interest in disclosure of" records showing employment histories and private financial holdings of federal consultants.

4.3.4.4. In cases decided both before and after the Supreme Court's decision in *Reporters Committee*, courts in the First Circuit have held that there is a cognizable public interest in the release of information identifying individuals to whom the government has failed to pay tax refunds or other money that is lawfully owed to them. *See Aronson v. HUD*, 822 F.2d 182, 187-88 (1st Cir. 1987); *Aronson v. IRS*, 767 F. Supp. 378 (D. Mass. 1991), *aff'd in part, rev'd in part*, 973 F.2d 962 (1st Cir. 1992) (applying Exemption 3). The theory of these decisions is that "there is a significant public interest in disclosure concerning those individuals whose tax refunds remain undelivered: these materials would be useful, if not essential, to someone evaluating the efforts of the IRS to locate those owed the refunds. Such monitoring of an agency's practices 'is exactly the kind of public interest Congress intended FOIA to facilitate.'" *Aronson v. IRS*, 767 F. Supp. at 392 (quoting *I.B.E.W. Local Union No. 5 v. HUD*, 852 F.2d 87, 91 (3d Cir. 1988)); *accord Aronson v. HUD*, No. 88-1188-S (Apr. 29, 1991). *Cf. Lepelletier v. FDIC*, 164 F.3d 37, 47 (D.C. Cir. 1999) (ordering release of names of depositors with unclaimed funds at banks under FDIC receivership, based on those individuals' interests rather than public's); *But see Pennies From Heaven, Inc. v. Dep't of Treasury*, No. 88-1808, *slip op*. at 8-9 (D.D.C. Aug. 14, 1992) ("release of name and address data will not shed light on the agency's performance any more than mere statistics").

4.3.4.5. In *Ferri v. Bell*, 645 F.2d 1213, 1218 (3d Cir. 1981), the Third Circuit held that exposure by an inmate of a deal between a prosecutor and a witness could serve an "indirect public purpose" that overcame the privacy interest in the witness's arrest record. *But see Johnson v. DOJ*, No. 85-714-SSH, 1991 WL 251940 (D.D.C. Nov. 13, 1991) (upholding claim of Exemption 7(C) in similar circumstances).

4.3.4.6. In *Outlaw v. Department of the Army*, 815 F. Supp. 505, 506 (D.D.C. 1993), the court ruled that neither Exemption 6 nor 7(C) permitted withholding allegedly exculpatory photographs of a murder victim from a requester who was convicted by court-martial 25 years earlier, since there was "an obvious public interest in the disclosure as a check on the administration of justice by the United States Army." Similarly, a district judge prohibited redaction of the names of FBI supervisors from records alleged to establish that the plaintiff was convicted for drug activity that was within the scope of his work as an FBI informant, because the "public interest in seeing that Mr. Butler's due process rights are protected in this criminal case" was significant and outweighed unsupported claims regarding privacy interest. *Butler v. DOJ*, No. 86-2255 (D.D.C. Feb. 3, 1994) (Exemption 7(C) case).

4.3.4.7. In *Steinberg v. DOJ*, 179 F.R.D. 366 (D.D.C. 1998), *aff'd*, 1999 WL 1215779 (D.C. Cir. Nov. 5, 1999) (per curiam), the court found a "significant" public interest in disclosure of documents that relate to "criminal investigation of alleged counter-terrorist activities." 179 F.R.D. at 370-71 (Exemption 7(C) case) (ordering release of documents describing FBI interviews after redaction of names and identifying information of undisclosed agents and sources); *see also Goldstein v. Office of Indep. Counsel*, No. Civ. A. 87-2028TPJJM, 1999 WL 570862 at *9 (D.D.C. July 29, 1999) (public interest in documents relating to "criminal investigations by the FBI of terrorism, counter-terrorism, domestic subversion, counterintelligence, and electronic surveillance" was "significant" and "substantial") (Exemption 7(C) case).

4.3.4.8. In *Detroit Free Press, Inc. v. DOJ*, 73 F.3d 93 (6th Cir. 1996), the court stated that public disclosure of individuals' mug shots could "serve to subject the government to public oversight" by, for example, more clearly revealing the government's error in detaining the wrong person, or revealing the circumstances surrounding an arrest and initial incarceration of an individual in a way that written information cannot." *Id.* at 97-98 (Exemption 6 and 7(C) case); *cf. Times Picayune Publ'g Co. v. DOJ*, 37 F. Supp. 2d 472, 480 (E.D. La. 1999) (acknowledging that disclosure of mug shots in some circumstances could subject the government to public oversight, but finding no such circumstances existed in that case) (Exemption 7(C) case).

4.3.4.9. In *Rosenfeld v. DOJ*, 57 F.3d 803 (9th Cir. 1995), *cert. dismissed*, 516 U.S. 1103 (1996), the Ninth Circuit held that disclosing names of FBI investigation subjects would promote the public interest in "knowing whether and to what extent the FBI investigated individuals for participating in political protests, not federal criminal activity." *Id.* at 812 (Exemption 7(C) case); *see also National Ass'n of Criminal Def. Lawyers v. DOJ*, No. 97-CV-372 (GK) (D.D.C. Oct. 1, 1999) (vacated after settlement) (Exemption 7(C) case) (finding an "extraordinarily significant" public interest, "far outweighing" substantial privacy interests, in release of names of FBI agents in order to confirm or deny allegations that the agents and internal investigators may have engaged in misconduct).

4.3.4.10. In *Columbia Packing Co. v. Department of Agric.*, 563 F.2d 495 (1st Cir. 1977), the First Circuit found a substantial public interest in the personnel records of two former meat inspectors because they had been convicted of taking bribes, and there was some suspicion that the practice was widespread. *See also McLaughlin v. Sessions*, No. 92-0454 (JHG), 1993 U.S. Dist. LEXIS 13817 (D.D.C. Sept. 22, 1993) (Exemption 7(C) case) (where records sought related to specific investigation, "Plaintiff's interest in the scope and course of the investigation constitutes a recognized public interest"). Courts in the District of Columbia Circuit have concluded, however, that there is no great public interest in the alleged malfeasance or negligence of low-ranking agency employees. *Beck v. DOJ*, 997 F.2d 1489, 1493 (D.C. Cir. 1993) ("the identity of one or two individual relatively low-level government wrongdoers, released in isolation, does not provide information about the agency's own conduct"); *Cotton v. Adams*, 798 F. Supp. 22, 27 (D.D.C. 1992) (generalized public interest in management of agency did not override privacy interests of low-level employees names as witnesses or subjects of internal investigation); *cf. Hardy v. Department of Defense*, No. CV-99-523-TUC-FRZ, slip op. at 15 (D. Ariz. Aug. 27, 2001) (a federal employee's position and level of responsibility are relevant in determining the extent of the public's interest; requiring disclosure of agency director and associate director evaluations and performance ratings).

4.3.4.11. A district court ordered release of the unredacted medical records of a deceased veteran to his ex-wife, after he had shot and killed her new husband and two children. Discerning a strong public interest in whether the V.A.'s treatment and discharge of the man had been appropriate, the court ruled that the V.A. could not withhold the names of the employees and medical personnel involved. *Palmer v. Derwinski*, No. 91-197, slip op. at 6-7 (E.D. Ky. June 10, 1992).

4.3.4.12. In *Congressional News Syndicate v. DOJ*, 438 F. Supp. 538 (D.D.C. 1977), the district court found a compelling public interest in the names of contributors to the Watergate-related "Townhouse" operation. *But see Fund for Constitutional Gov't v. National Archives*, 656 F.2d 856, 865-66 (D.C. Cir. 1981), in which a panel of the D.C. Circuit found the privacy of individuals mentioned in Watergate-related investigative files more important than the exposure of governmental wrongdoing, as the latter had been the subject of exhaustive study by all three branches of government (7(C) cases).

4.3.4.13. Disclosure of the names and addresses of servicemen who participated in an atmospheric nuclear weapons testing program was held to be in the public interest where the requester was a non-profit veterans association seeking to conduct scientific and medical studies of adverse health effects of such testing, as well as to inform atomic veterans about VA benefits. *National Ass'n of Atomic Veterans, Inc. v. Director, Def. Nuclear Agency*, 583 F. Supp. 1483, 1487 (D.D.C. 1984).

4.3.4.14. In *Alliance for the Wild Rockies v. Department of Interior*, 53 F. Supp. 2d 32, 37 (D.D.C. 1999), the court held that agency formulations of final rules, which rely in part on written comments submitted by the public, "clearly warrant[] full disclosure of those comments, including the names and addresses of the contributors."

4.3.4.15. The very similarly worded Exemption 6 in the Government in the Sunshine Act, 5 U.S.C. § 552b(c)(6), has been held to afford more protection to private individuals than to government officials with executive responsibilities, since it was "not intended to shelter substandard performance" by the latter. *Common Cause v. Nuclear Regulatory Comm'n*, 674 F.2d 921, 938 (D.C. Cir. 1982).

4.3.4.16. In *Cochran v. United States*, 770 F.2d 949, 956 (11th Cir. 1985), the court ruled that "the balance struck under FOIA exemption 6 overwhelmingly favors the disclosure of information relating to a violation of the public trust by a government official, which certainly includes the situation of a misuse of public funds or facilities by a Major General of the United States Army."

4.3.4.17. Where a former government employee sought documents relating to an allegedly improper contract procurement, a district court found that the public interest in oversight of agency activities outweighed unfounded claims of possible harassment to individuals mentioned in the documents. As to the identities of employees who "processed" documents or were interviewed during an investigation, the court ruled that any privacy interest fell short of "Exemption 6's rigorous standard," although the court allowed the application of Exemption 7(C) in similar circumstances. *Fine v. DOE*, 823 F. Supp. 888 (D.N.M. 1993), *motion to modify denied*, 830 F. Supp. 570 (D.N.M. 1993).

4.3.4.18. In *Southern Utah Wilderness Alliance, Inc. v. Hodel*, 680 F. Supp. 37 (D.D.C. 1988), the court ruled that the Exemption 6 balance would not bar disclosure of Interior Department lists of names and addresses of persons who visited seven national parks where requester was non-profit environmental group seeking to warn park users of environmental threats from nuclear waste dumps, coal strip-mining, and commercial development on public lands.

4.3.4.19. In *Thott v. Department of Interior,* No. 93-0177-B, slip op. at 6-7 (D. Me. Apr. 14, 1994), the court ruled that there was a strong public interest in disclosure of names and addresses of persons who had sold their homes to the Fish and Wildlife Service because the information was the only way in which the public may be informed about that agency's methods in acquiring property.

4.3.4.20. In *The Nation Magazine v. U.S. Customs Serv.*, 71 F.3d 885 (D.C. Cir. 1995) (Exemption 7(C)), the court found there would be a cognizable public interest in disclosure of records pertaining to former presidential candidate Ross Perot's alleged offers to assist Customs Service in interdicting illegal drugs. "[T]he mere fact that records pertain to an individual's activities does not necessarily qualify them for exemption. Such records may still be cloaked with the public interest if the information would shed light on agency action." *Id.* at 895.

4.3.4.21. In *Avondale Indus., Inc. v. NLRB*, 90 F.3d 955, 961 (5th Cir. 1996), the court found a strong public interest in marked voting lists that could be used to determine whether the NLRB conducted its elections in accordance with federal law.

4.3.4.22. In *Washington Post Co. v. Department of Agriculture*, 943 F. Supp. 31 (D.D.C. 1996) , the court found a strong public interest in disclosure of the names and addresses of persons receiving agricultural subsidies, because it would shed light on agency's operation of subsidy program, which had been the subject of allegations of fraud and conflict of interest.

4.3.4.23. In *Baltimore Sun v. Marshals Serv.*, 131 F. Supp. 2d 725, 729-30 (D. Md. 2001), the court found a cognizable public interest in disclosure of the names and addresses of persons who purchased seized property from the U.S. Marshals Service, because it would allow the public to scrutinize the agency's exercise of its powers to seize property and its performance in disposal of that property.

4.3.4.24. In *Bartholdi Cable Co. v. FCC*, 114 F.3d 274 (D.C. Cir. 1997), the court agreed that the FCC's decision to release a licensee's internal investigation report was supported by a cognizable public interest because the information was "clearly relevant to the public's understanding of the type of entities to which the government is distributing a valuable public asset, FCC licenses." *Id.* at 282 (reverse FOIA case).

4.3.5. Conversely, the less disclosure has to do with informing the public about governmental activity, the less courts are impressed with the public purpose of disclosure.

4.3.5.1. Commercial interests of the requester generally do not qualify for consideration on the "public interest" side of the balance. *See Wine Hobby USA, Inc. v. IRS*, 502 F.2d 133, 137 (3d Cir. 1974) (nondisclosure upheld because requester's purpose was purely commercial and "wholly unrelated to the purposes behind" the FOIA); *Multnomah County Med. Soc. v. Scott*, 825 F.2d 1410, 1414 (9th Cir. 1987); *Minnis v. Department of Agriculture*, 737 F.2d 784 (9th Cir. 1984), *cert. denied*, 471 U.S. 1053 (1985); *Professional Review Org. of Florida, Inc. v. HHS*, 607 F. Supp. 423 (D.D.C. 1985). But just as the presence of a commercial interest does not help demonstrate a cognizable public interest, the fact that one effect of disclosure may be to advance the requester's commercial interest should not weaken a claim for disclosure. *Aronson v. HUD*, 822 F.2d 182, 185-86 (1st Cir. 1987).

4.3.5.2. Other interests not found weighty range from the self-defensive inquiry into the state of government files, *see, e.g.*, *Church of Scientology v. Department of the Army*, 611 F.2d 738, 747 (9th Cir. 1979), to the interests of jailhouse writ writers. *See, e.g.*, *Harbolt v. Department of State*, 616 F.2d 772 (5th Cir.), *cert. denied*, 449 U.S. 856 (1980); *Wagner v. FBI*, No. 90-1314-LFO (D.D.C. June 4, 1991), *aff'd*, 976 F.2d 47 (unpublished table decision) 1992 WL 198096 (D.C. Cir. Aug. 3, 1992) (per curiam).

4.3.5.3. In *Roberts v. HHS*, No. 88-2041, 1988 U.S. Dist LEXIS 10162 (E.D. Pa. Sept. 9, 1988), the court found no public interest in disclosure where the requester's motive was to identify witnesses for a lawsuit being litigated by the requester.

4.3.5.4. See also the cases cited, *supra*, at section 3.2.3.3.5. holding exempt union authorization cards, in part on the theory that only the employer stands to benefit from disclosure. *See also AFGE, Local 1923 v. HHS*, 712 F.2d 931 (4th Cir. 1983) (union would be primary beneficiary); *Deering Milliken, Inc. v. Irving*, 548 F.2d 1131 (4th Cir. 1977).

4.3.5.5. Some courts have suggested that disclosures in response to requests focused on specific individuals or cases are less likely to serve a FOIA-recognized public interest than disclosures in response to "more generic" search requests. *See Grove v. DOJ*, 802 F. Supp. 506, 513 (D.D.C. 1992) (release of individual criminal files would not further purposes of FOIA); *Cappabianca v. U.S. Customs Service*, 847 F. Supp. 1558, 1564 (M.D. Fla. 1994) (no public interest in names and identifying information about witnesses, investigators, and other subjects of investigation in which plaintiff was a subject; plaintiff only seeking documents to help him pursue job-related causes of action); *see also Triestman v. DOJ*, 878 F. Supp. 667, 670 (S.D.N.Y. 1995) (only interest served by disclosure of information on certain DEA agents is plaintiff's personal interest of mounting collateral challenge to his conviction) (Exemption 7(C)); *Wickline v. FBI*, No. 92-1189, 1994 WL 549756, at *3 (D.D.C. Sept. 30, 1994) (same); *Bongiorno v. Reno*, No. 95-72143, 1996 WL 426451 (E.D. Mich. Mar. 19, 1996) (no public interest in individual's request for INS records of daughter's naturalization).

4.3.5.6. One court of appeals has concluded that there is no cognizable public interest in disclosure of records depicting misconduct of state, as opposed to federal, officials. *Landano v. DOJ*, 956 F.2d 422, 430 (3d Cir. 1992) (Exemption 7(C)), *vacated on other grounds and remanded*, 508 U.S. 165 (1993); *see also Thomas v. U.S. Attorney*, 928 F. Supp. 245, 251 (E.D.N.Y. 1996) (same).

4.3.6. A public interest argument which rests upon the value of disclosure for oversight of government activity must be convincingly made, because "assertions of a public interest in merely 'monitoring' the operation of a federal program, without more, have not been viewed favorably by the courts." *Heights Cmty. Cong. v. Veterans Admin.*, 732 F.2d 526, 530 (6th Cir.), *cert. denied*, 469 U.S. 1034 (1984) (citing *Miller v. Bell*, 661 F.2d 623, 630 (7th Cir. 1981), *cert. denied*, 456 U.S. 960 (1982)); *Brown v. FBI*, 658 F.2d 71, 76 (2d Cir. 1981); *see also Sheet Metal Workers Int'l Ass'n, Local Union #19 v. Department of Veterans Affairs*, 135 F.3d 891, 903 (3d Cir. 1998) ("After the decisions in *Reporters Committee* and *Department of Defense*, no court of appeals has given much weight to the monitoring function."); *Hopkins v. HUD*, 929 F.2d 81, 88 (2d Cir. 1991) (proposed union use of information to verify violations of wage laws that HUD should have detected was too "attenuated a relationship to governmental activity" to outweigh privacy interests); *Painting Indus. of Hawaii Market Recovery Fund v. Department of the Air Force*, 26 F.3d 1479 (9th Cir. 1994) (labor organizations' efforts to monitor government's diligence in enforcing wage standards for employees of government contractors was insufficient to outweigh the workers' privacy interests in their payroll records). *But see Oregon Natural Desert Ass'n v. Department of the Interior*, 24 F. Supp. 2d 1088, 1093-94 (D. Or. 1998) (releasing names of violators of federal cattle trespass laws, "for the purpose of monitoring the [agency's] treatment and enforcement of federal grazing laws").

4.3.7. The public interest in disclosure is strengthened when the requester presents evidence of governmental wrongdoing to which the records may relate. *Washington Post Co. v. HHS*, 690 F.2d 252, 264 (D.C. Cir. 1982) (recent allegations and investigations on same subject as FOIA request magnify public interest in disclosure); *Washington Post Co. v. Department of Agric.*, 943 F. Supp. at 36 (plaintiff "identified allegations of fraud and conflict of interest, supported by government reports and investigations, ...sufficient to raise nonspeculative questions about the workings of the USDA"). On the other hand, claims of a public interest in disclosure premised on unsubstantiated allegations of governmental misconduct are often given little weight. *See, e.g., Computer Prof'ls for Soc. Responsibility v. Secret Serv.*, 72 F.3d 897, 905 (D.C. Cir. 1996) (Exemption 7(C)) ("[W]hen governmental misconduct is alleged as the justification for disclosure, the public interest is insubstantial unless the requester puts forward compelling evidence that the agency denying the FOIA request is engaged in illegal activity and shows that the information sought is necessary in order to confirm or refute that evidence.").

4.3.8. It is particularly unhelpful to the requester's side of the balancing if the court finds either that the requested material is not needed to inform the interested public, or would not further that objective even if released. *See, e.g., Minnis v.*

Department of Agriculture., 737 F.2d at 787). *See also Marzen v. HHS*, 825 F.2d 1148, 1153-54 (7th Cir. 1987) (Despite existence of substantial public interest and extensive public record in "Infant Doe" discrimination case, medical records held exempt because "intimate details" of infant's deteriorating condition and conversations between his parents and doctors "would not appreciably serve the ethical debate" but would certainly cause anguish to parents.); *New York Times Co. v. NASA*, 782 F. Supp. 628 (D.D.C. 1991) (minimal public interest in disclosure of voice tape from Challenger shuttle because sounds on tape would "shed[] absolutely no light on the conduct of any Government agency or official" and because transcript of tape had already been released).

4.4. The requester's interest.

4.4.1. The relevance of the requester's interest to the Exemption 6 balancing analysis was the subject of some confusion and disagreement in early FOIA cases.

4.4.1.1. In an early and influential D.C. Circuit case, the court focused nearly exclusively on the interest of the requesters themselves (two law professors seeking data for a study of NLRB voting regulations) and even hinted that a restriction on any use other than that proposed might be proper. *Getman v. NLRB*, 450 F.2d 670, 677 n.24 (D.C. Cir. 1971).

4.4.1.2. Other early cases declared that the requester's motive for making the request was absolutely irrelevant. *Robles v. EPA*, 484 F.2d 843, 847 (4th Cir. 1973); *Kurzon v. HHS*, 649 F.2d at 68 & n.2.

4.4.2. Later cases frequently held that the Exemption 6 balancing approach is an exception to the Act's general "any person" rule, and that while the public interest is predominant on the disclosure side of the scale, the requester is certainly part of the public, and his interest can be considered for that reason alone. *See, e.g., Ditlow v. Shultz*, 517 F.2d 166, 170-71 & n.21 (D.C. Cir. 1975).

4.4.3. Some courts, particularly in the Ninth Circuit, identified four factors appropriate to the Exemption 6 balancing process: (1) the requester's interest; (2) the public interest; (3) the degree of invasion of personal privacy; and (4) the availability of alternative means of obtaining the information. *See, e.g., Minnis v. Department of Agriculture.*, 737 F.2d at 786; *Van Bourg, Allen, Weinberg & Roger v. NLRB*, 728 F.2d 1270, 1273 (9th Cir. 1984); *Church of Scientology v. Department of the Army*, 611 F.2d at 746.

4.4.4. Courts have also given weight to a requester's interests where it is demonstrated that they relate to the requester's "own legal obligations to the government agency involved." *Jafari v. Department of the Navy*, 728 F.2d 247, 250 (4th Cir. 1984) (information on individual's non-attendance at Marine Corps Reserve drills released to civilian employer who is required by statute to grant leave of absence to the employee for such duty).

4.4.5. Prior case law giving special weight to the particularized interests and proposed uses of the requester has now been substantially undermined. In *DOJ v. Reporters Comm. for Freedom of the Press*, 489 U.S. 749 (1989), the Supreme

Court declared, in the closely analogous Exemption 7(C) context, that the privacy versus public interest balance "cannot turn on the purposes for which the request for information is made ...[T]he identity of the requesting party has no bearing on the merits of his or her FOIA request." *Id.* at 771; *see also Reed v. NLRB*, 927 F.2d 1249, 1252 (D.C. Cir. 1991) (identity of requester and its purposes are not to be weighed in the balancing process), *cert. denied*, 502 U.S. 1047 (1992); *Commodity News Serv., Inc. v. Farm Credit Admin.*, No. 88-3146 (HHG), 1989 U.S. Dist. LEXIS 8848 at *2 (D.D.C. July 31, 1989) ("it is the public's right to government information, and not the specific interest of a person seeking disclosure in the particular case, which must be weighed against the individual's privacy rights").

4.4.6. The Supreme Court has affirmed, in the context of Exemption 6, that all FOIA requesters have an equal, and equally qualified, right to information, and except in certain cases involving claims of privilege, the identity of the requester is irrelevant to the outcome of the request. *Department of Defense v. FLRA*, 510 U.S. 487 (1994); *Bibles v. Oregon Natural Desert Ass'n*, 519 U.S. 355 (1997) (purposes for which request is made "have no bearing on whether information must be disclosed under FOIA").

4.5. Special factors affecting the balance.

4.5.1. Statutory policies on disclosure or confidentiality will occasionally affect a particular case because courts usually give them great weight. *See, e.g., Washington Post Co. v. HHS*, 690 F.2d at 263, 265 (Ethics in Government Act argues for disclosure of private employment and holdings of federal consultants); *Common Cause v. National Archives and Records Serv.*, 628 F.2d 179, 184-85 (D.C. Cir. 1980) (Federal Corrupt Practices Act policy of disclosure of campaign contributions); *Providence Journal Co. v. FBI*, 602 F.2d 1010, 1012-14 (1st Cir. 1979) (wiretap statutory policy of non-disclosure of illegally obtained conversations held determinative), *cert. denied*, 444 U.S. 1071 (1980). *Pennies From Heaven, Inc. v. Dep't of Treasury*, No. 88-1808, *slip op.* at 4-5 (D.D.C. Aug. 14, 1992) (privacy interest greater given Treasury regulation assuring confidentiality). *FLRA v. Department of the Navy*, 941 F.2d 49, 54 (1st Cir. 1991) (collective bargaining values reflected in labor laws have no bearing on FOIA).

4.5.2. Common law concepts of privacy, while not binding, are sometimes appropriate and sometimes useful to consider.

4.5.2.1. "The question of the statutory meaning of privacy under FOIA is, of course, not the same as the question whether a tort action might lie for invasion of privacy or the question whether an individual's interest in privacy is protected by the Constitution." *Reporters Comm.*, 489 U.S. at 762 n.13; *see also Times Picayune Publ'g Co. v. DOJ*, 37 F. Supp. 2d 472, 476 (E.D. La. 1999) ("The right of privacy formulated under the Constitution and the common law are different from the privacy interests protected under the FOIA.") (Exemption 7(C)).

4.5.2.2. "Although the common law doctrine of privacy may assist analysis, the privacy exemption under FOIA is not designed to prevent what would be tortious at common law. Congress intended that the privacy interest protected under FOIA extend beyond the common law...[and] a separate body of privacy law has developed under FOIA in which courts seldom look to the common law for more than an analytical framework." *Marzen v. HHS*, 825 F.2d at 1152-53. *See generally Tennessean Newspaper, Inc. v. Levi*, 403 F. Supp. 1318, 1321 n.1 (M.D. Tenn. 1975).

4.5.2.3. In particular, the concept of the "public figure" in the law of defamation—of which tort privacy is a close relative—has been employed to support disclosure arguments in Exemption 6 cases. *See, e.g., Fund for Constitutional Gov't v. National Archives*, 656 F.2d 856, 864-65 (D.C. Cir. 1981); *Common Cause*, 628 F.2d at 184; *Congressional News Syndicate v. DOJ*, 438 F. Supp. 538, 543 (D.D.C. 1977). *But see Times Picayune Publ'g Co. v. DOJ*, 37 F. Supp. 2d at 478-79 (the fact that a person is well-known "may well exacerbate the privacy intrusions" that could result from disclosure) (Exemption 7(C)).

4.5.3. Promises and expectations of confidentiality.

4.5.3.1. A prior promise of confidentiality, while sometimes relevant to the degree of invasion of personal privacy, is not determinative and cannot be used to frustrate the policy of the Act. *Washington Post Co. v. HHS*, 690 F.2d at 263. "It will obviously not be enough for the agency to assert simply that it received the file under a pledge of confidentiality to the one who supplied it. Undertakings of that nature cannot, in and of themselves, override the Act." *Ackerly v. Ley*, 420 F.2d 1336, 1339-40 n.3 (D.C. Cir. 1969). Exemption 6 cases in accord include *Kurzon*, 649 F.2d at 69-70 (names of unsuccessful grant applicants not exempt notwithstanding regulation to contrary); *Robles v. EPA*, 484 F.2d at 846; *Citizens for Environ. Quality, Inc. v. Department of Agric.*, 602 F. Supp. 534, 538 (D.D.C. 1984); *Providence Journal Co. v. FBI*, 460 F. Supp. 778, 786 (D.R.I. 1978), *rev'd on other grounds*, 602 F.2d 1010 (1st Cir. 1979), *cert. denied*, 444 U.S. 1071 (1980); *Legal Aid Soc'y v. Schultz*, 349 F. Supp. 771, 776 (N.D. Cal. 1972).

4.5.3.2. A promise of confidentiality has "special significance" where it helped elicit "private matters" that the individual would not otherwise have exposed to the public and where the individual would be in danger of mistreatment absent anonymity. *Department of State v. Ray*, 502 U.S. 164 (1991).

4.5.3.3. In the related context of FOIA Exemption 7(D), which pertains to confidential law enforcement sources, the Supreme Court has held that while some circumstances may provide a basis for inferring confidentiality in individual cases, a presumption of confidentiality for all criminal investigative sources is unwarranted. *DOJ v. Landano*, 508 U.S. 165 (1993).

4.5.3.4. Knowledge of the proposed disclosure plus lack of objection may weaken confidentiality, *Robles v. EPA*, 484 F.2d at 847; as may partial disclosure, *Simpson v. Vance*, 648 F.2d 10, 16 (D.C. Cir. 1980).

4.5.3.5. An insufficiently complete promise of confidentiality may be ineffective. *Poss v. NLRB*, 565 F.2d 654, 658 (10th Cir. 1977) (7(C) case).

4.5.3.6. Knowledge by those complained against will defeat the effect of an expectation of confidentiality. *See Wellford v. Hardin*, 444 F.2d 21, 23-24 (4th Cir. 1971) (7(C) case).

4.5.3.7. An expectation of disclosure in litigation can defeat the exemption. *See Miami Herald Publ'g Co. v. Small Bus. Admin.*, 670 F.2d 610, 615-16 (5th Cir. 1982) (defaulting SBA borrower can expect exposure in litigation to collect and therefore cannot expect privacy).

4.5.3.8. Signing an acknowledgement that information provided to an agency could be subject to release does not operate to waive privacy interests. *Hill v. Department of Agric.*, 77 F. Supp. 2d 6, 8 (D.D.C. 1999), *aff'd*, 2000 WL 520724 (D.C. Cir. Mar. 7, 2000) (per curiam).

4.5.4. Prior disclosure and alternative sources.

4.5.4.1 Prior public disclosure can defeat the exemption. *The Nation Magazine v. U.S. Customs Serv.*, 71 F.3d 885, 896 (D.C. Cir. 1995) (Ross Perot's prior public statements about his dealings with agency "effectively waive[d]" his privacy interests in records relating to those dealings) (Exemption 7(C)); *see also Detroit Free Press, Inc. v. DOJ*, 73 F.3d 93, 96-97 (6th Cir. 1996) (release of mug shots implicated no privacy rights where defendants' names had already been released and defendants had made a court appearance) (Exemptions 6 and 7(C)); *Steinberg v. DOJ*, 179 F.R.D. 366, 371 (D.D.C. 1998) (after the government disclosed the names of FBI sources, it could not argue that the contents of their FBI interviews should be withheld to protect their identities), *aff'd*, 1999 WL 1215779 (D.C. Cir. Nov. 5, 1999); *Palmer v. Derwinski*, No. 91-197, slip op. at 8 (E.D. Ky. June 10, 1992) (prior press reports concerning gunman's relatives and listings in telephone book tipped balance in favor of release of medical records disclosing relatives' names and addresses); *Gannett River States Publ. Corp. v. Bureau of Nat'l Guard*, No. J91-0455(L), 1992 U.S. Dist. LEXIS 11287, 20 Media L. Rep. 1183 (S.D. Miss. Mar. 2, 1992) (privacy interest in disciplinary records *de minimis* in view of information already disclosed). *Aronson v. IRS*, 767 F. Supp. 378, 389 (D. Mass. 1991), *aff'd in part, rev'd in part*, 973 F.2d 962 (1st Cir. 1992).

4.5.4.2. However, speculative publicity in the media, as opposed to accurate disclosure of the contents of documents, does not defeat the privacy right since the latter would be more damaging. *Bast v. DOJ*, 665 F.2d 1251, 1255 (D.C. Cir. 1981) (7(C) case).

4.5.4.3. Nor is testimony as to some personal facts a waiver of privacy for others. *Kiraly v. FBI*, 728 F.2d 273, 279-80 (6th Cir. 1984); *Brown v. FBI*, 658 F.2d 71, 75 (2d Cir. 1981).

4.5.4.4. The fact that something is on the public record somewhere in the country may affect the expectation of privacy, but it does not necessarily defeat a claim of Exemption 6. *See DOJ v. Reporters Comm. for Freedom of the Press*, 489 U.S. 749 (1989) (permitting withholding of FBI rap sheets even though some information contained therein might be available, in dispersed and fragmented form, from state or local governments' public records); *Department of State v. Washington Post Co.*, 456 U.S. 595, 603 n.5 (1982) ("public nature of information may be a reason to conclude" that release would not constitute a "clearly unwarranted invasion of personal privacy"); *Linn v. DOJ*, No. 92-1406, 1995 WL 631847 at *21 (D.D.C. Aug. 22, 1995) (same); *see also Fiduccia v. DOJ*, 185 F.3d 1035, 1047 (9th Cir. 1999) (withholding documents regarding ten-year-old searches of two individuals' homes despite media publicity at the time of the searches; individuals had an interest in not having the publicity repeated years later) (decided under Exemption 7(C)); *Abraham & Rose, P.L.C. v. United States*, 138 F.3d 1075, 1083 (6th Cir. 1998) ("[A] clear privacy interest exists with respect to such information as names, addresses, and other identifying information, even if such information is already available on publicly recorded filings."); *Katz v. National Archives & Records Admin.*, 862 F. Supp. 476, 485-86 (D.D.C. 1994), *aff'd*, 68 F.3d 1438 (D.C. Cir. 1995) (although x-rays and photographs from President Kennedy's autopsy had been previously published without authorization, their further release would cause additional anguish to the Kennedy family, and thus they are exempt under Exemption 6).

4.5.4.5. The Fifth Circuit has held that an agency's prior disclosure of the same type of information that is at issue in a particular case does not waive an individual's privacy interest; "only the individual whose informational privacy interests are protected by exemption 6 can effect a waiver of those privacy interests." *Sherman v. Department of the Army*, 244 F.3d 357, 364 (5th Cir. 2001); *see also Ford v. West*, 149 F.3d 1190 (unpublished table decision) 1998 WL 317561 at *3 (10th Cir. June 12, 1998) (inadequate redaction or fact that information was obtained from other sources does not waive privacy interests).

4.5.4.6. One opinion of the D.C. Circuit concluded that the availability of the same information (or related information which could serve the same purpose) from non-FOIA sources can weigh against disclosure by diminishing the public interest. *Department of Defense v. FLRA*, 964 F.2d 26, 29-30 (D.C. Cir. 1992).

5. Lists of Names and Addresses.

5.1. A great many Exemption 6 cases have involved requests for names and addresses of individuals. Over the years, courts have ascribed "wildly different" weights to the strength of privacy interests in one's home address. *FLRA v. Department of the Navy*,

941 F.2d 49, 55-56 (1st Cir. 1991) (collecting cases); *FLRA v. Department of Treasury*, 884 F.2d 1446, 1459 (D.C. Cir. 1989) (R. B. Ginsburg, J., concurring) (same). During the 1980s and early 1990s, a number of courts held that requests for lists of names and home addresses raised "substantial privacy interests." *See, e.g., Reed v. NLRB*, 927 F.2d 1249, 1252 (D.C. Cir. 1991), *cert. denied*, 502 U.S. 1047 (1992); *DiPersia v. Railroad Retirement Bd.*, 638 F. Supp. 485, 489 (D. Conn. 1986); *Falzone v. Department of the Navy*, No. 85-3862 (D.D.C. Oct. 16, 1986), *motion to reconsider denied*, 1988 WL 128474 (D.D.C. Nov. 21, 1988).

5.2. In *AFGE, Local 1760 v. FLRA*, 786 F.2d 554, 556 (2d Cir. 1986), the court of appeals held that the privacy interest of the average employee in his address "is not particularly compelling" since such information is often available through other public records. The court stated that *Getman* and the court's own holding in *Brown v. FBI*, 658 F.2d 71, limited the application of Exemption 6 to facts which, if public, "could subject the person to harassment, disgrace, loss of employment, or friends." The court rejected the argument that *Getman* and its progeny had been overturned by the Supreme Court in the *Washington Post* case, concluding that "the Supreme Court ruled solely on whether certain files fell within the ambit of exemption (b)(6) and expressly declined to apply the balancing test [cite omitted]." *AFGE, Local 1760*, 786 F.2d at 557. *See also I.B.E.W. Local Union No. 5 v. HUD*, 852 F.2d 87 (3d Cir. 1988) (names and addresses of employees of federal contractor not exempt).

5.3. In *National Ass'n of Retired Fed. Employees v. Horner*, 879 F.2d 873 (D.C. Cir. 1989), *cert. denied*, 494 U.S. 1078 (1990), a panel of the D.C. Circuit unanimously adopted an approach that turns on the specific nature of the list. "[W]hether it is a significant or a *de minimis* threat depends upon the characteristic(s) revealed by virtue of being on the particular list, and the consequences likely to ensue." 879 F.2d at 877. The court concluded that the particular list at issue—which consisted of the names and addresses of recently retired and disabled federal employees—implicated substantial privacy concerns because it reflected that the listed individuals receive monthly annuity checks from the federal government. The court reasoned that disclosure of such information would "subject the listed annuitants 'to an unwanted barrage of mailings and personal solicitations,'" and held that "such a fusillade cannot readily be deemed a de minimis assault on...privacy..." *Id.* at 876. *See also Painting Indus. of Hawaii Market Recovery Fund v. Department of the Air Force*, 26 F.3d 1479, 1483-84 (9th Cir. 1994) (substantial privacy interest in avoiding disclosure of name and address, particularly where coupled with personal financial information); *Hopkins v. HUD*, 929 F.2d at 87 (same); *Aronson v. HUD*, 822 F.2d 182, 186 (1st Cir. 1987) (privacy interest "becomes more significant...when names and addresses are combined with financial information"); *Schoettle v. Kemp*, 733 F. Supp. 1395 (D. Haw. 1990). *But see Retired Officers Ass'n v. Department of the Navy*, 744 F. Supp. 1 (D.D.C. 1990).

5.4. In *Department of State v. Ray*, 502 U.S. 164, 176 n.12 (1991), the Supreme Court endorsed the approach of *Horner*, emphasizing that disclosure of a list of names and other identifying information is not "inherently and always a significant threat to the privacy" of the named individuals.

5.5. Since *Horner* and *Ray*, a number of decisions have found particular lists of names and addresses of private citizens not to be covered by Exemption 6 because disclosure would cause only a minimal invasion of privacy while shedding significant light on agency operations. *See Avondale Indus., Inc. v. NLRB*, 90 F.3d 955 (5th Cir. 1996) (request for names and addresses of employees who voted in NLRB-sponsored election; no privacy interest in mere fact of having voted in election; strong public interest in determining whether NLRB is properly conducting elections); *Washington Post Co. v. Department of Agric.*, 943 F. Supp. 31 (D.D.C. 1996) (request for names and addresses of, and amounts paid to, recipients of federal agricultural subsidies; privacy interest minimal due to generic, business-oriented, non-stigmatizing nature of information; public interest significant due to usefulness of information in probing allegations of fraud and conflict of interest); *Alliance for the Wild Rockies v. Department of Interior*, 53 F. Supp. 2d 32 (D.D.C. 1999) (ordering disclosure of the names and addresses of persons submitting written comments on the Department's proposed rulemaking to reintroduce grizzly bears); *Kurzon v. HHS*, No. Civ. 00-395-JD, 2001 WL 821531 (D.N.H. July 17, 2001) (request for names and business addresses of unsuccessful applicants for grants from the National Institute of Mental Health; privacy interest insignificant because rejection is not sufficiently stigmatizing); *Urbigkit v. Department of Interior*, No. 93-CV-0232-J (D. Wyo. May 31, 1994) (request for names and addresses of persons reporting wolf sightings; privacy interests *de minimis* because individuals will not be exposed to any retaliatory action or embarrassment, public interest will be served increasing public scrutiny of agency efforts to comply with Endangered Species Act); *Thott v. Department of Interior*, No. 93-0177-B (D. Me. Apr. 14, 1994) (ordering disclosure of list of names and addresses of persons who sold land to the Fish and Wildlife Service, which could be used to contact individuals to discover methods used by the agency to acquire property).

5.6. In *Bibles v. Oregon Natural Desert Ass'n*, 519 U.S. 355 (1997) (per curiam), the Supreme Court reversed a decision by the Ninth Circuit that had held Exemption 6 inapplicable to a list of the names and addresses of persons to whom the Bureau of Land Management had distributed information. The court of appeals had recognized a public interest in disclosure based on the prospect that it would have enabled the requester and others to send "additional information" to the people on BLM's mailing list. The Supreme Court held that this was not a cognizable public interest.

5.7. In *Armstrong v. Executive Office of the President*, 97 F.3d 575, 581 (D.C. Cir. 1996), the D.C. Circuit rejected the claim that names of all FBI agents below a certain grade are categorically exempt from disclosure. Stating that "[t]he scope of a privacy interest under Exemption 6 will always be dependent on the context in which it has been asserted," the court overturned a lower court ruling that had permitted the government to withhold the names of all lower-ranking FBI agents who had participated in meeting at the White House. The court said that while disclosure could sometimes implicate important privacy interests (e.g., if the context linked the names to discussion of counter-intelligence operations), in other instances (e.g., if the context involved recreational activities) the privacy interests would be minimal and a weaker public interest would warrant disclosure.

5.8. In *Lepelletier v. FDIC*, 164 F.3d 37, 47 (D.C. Cir. 1999), the D.C. Circuit held that courts must consider whether release of a particular list may result in a benefit to those on the list. The court therefore ordered the release of a list of those with unclaimed deposits at banks under FDIC receivership.

5.9. There has been much litigation involving either requests for names and addresses of personnel in the Armed Forces, or requests from unions seeking names and addresses of employees presently represented by the requester.

Exemption 6

5.9.1. A number of important issues have arisen from consideration of whether Exemption 6 permits withholding names and addresses of federal employees sought by unions in the context of a federal labor relations law requiring the disclosure of information that facilitates the collective bargaining process.

5.9.1.1. Initially, numerous courts viewed the minimal privacy interest involved as outweighed by the substantial public interest in encouraging collective bargaining. *See FLRA v. Department of the Navy*, 966 F.2d 747, 754 & n.7 (3d Cir. 1992) (citing cases).

5.9.1.2. After *Reporters Committee,* almost every circuit reconsidered the issue of whether Exemption 6 shields from disclosure the names and addresses of federal employees sought by their representative labor union. A split emerged. The majority of circuits held that Exemption 6 permits withholding in this context on the theory that the employees have a significant privacy interest in their names and addresses and that there is no FOIA recognized public interest favoring disclosure. *See, e.g., FLRA v. Department of Defense*, 984 F.2d 370 (10th Cir. 1993); *FLRA v. Department of Treasury*, 884 F.2d 1446 (D.C. Cir. 1989), *cert. denied*, 493 U.S. 1055 (1990). The minority view was that disclosure of employees' addresses to a union that is their exclusive bargaining agent is required under the FOIA (and therefore permitted under the Privacy Act, § 552a), at least where the request is made within the context of the federal labor relations statute. *See e.g., FLRA v. Department of Defense*, 975 F.2d 1105 (5th Cir. 1992), *rev'd*, 510 U.S. 487 (1994).

5.9.1.3. The Supreme Court has resolved the split between the circuits in favor of the majority view. Furthering understanding of the Government and its activities is the only public interest that weighs in the balance against privacy concerns under Exemption 6 as well as 7(C). The Court explicitly overruled the contention that objectives identified in other statutes could be considered for purposes of Exemption 6 balancing. *Department of Defense v. FLRA*, 510 U.S. 487 (1994) (reversing *FLRA v. Department of Defense*, 975 F.2d 1105 (5th Cir. 1992)).

5.9.2. An Exemption 6 claim was upheld to deny an insurance company's request for information on overseas military personnel who had registered a motor vehicle, *Hudson v. Department of the Army*, No. 86-1114, 1987 WL 46755 (D.D.C. Jan. 29, 1987), *aff'd without opinion*, 926 F.2d 1215 (D.C. Cir. 1991), as well as a realtor's request for the names and addresses of overseas naval personnel, *Falzone v. Department of the Navy*, No. 85-3862 (D.D.C. Oct. 16, 1986), *motion to reconsider denied*, 1988 WL 128474 (D.D.C. Nov. 21, 1988).

6. The Importance of Segregability.

6.1. Where the disclosure of an entire record would result in a clearly unwarranted invasion of privacy, the statute requires that the agency must provide "[a]ny reasonably segregable portion...after deletion of the portions which are exempt." § 552(b).

6.2. That provision complements subsection (a)(2) of the statute which provides, as to records required to be published by agencies, that "[t]o the extent required to prevent a clearly unwarranted invasion of personal privacy, an agency may delete identifying details when it makes available or publishes an opinion, statement of policy, interpretation or staff manual or instruction."

6.3. Accordingly, an agency (or a District Court) must apply the Exemption 6 calculus separately with respect to each disputed portion of each document, as its outcome differs from portion to portion. *See Arieff v. Department of the Navy, 712 F.2d 1462,* 1466 (D.C. Cir. 1983) ("[T]he exemptions of the FOIA do not apply wholesale. An item of exempt information does not insulate from disclosure the entire file in which it is contained, or even the entire page on which it appears."); *see also Lame v. DOJ*, 654 F.2d 917, 923 (3d Cir. 1981).

6.4. Wherever a requester's interest can be served by obtaining data that is not personally identifiable, pursuit of a request which excludes the identifiers helps substantially in overcoming an Exemption 6 claim. For example, the segregability issue was a major one for the Supreme Court in *Rose*; it was resolved by the majority in favor of segregation and release. *See Department of the Air Force v. Rose*, 425 U.S. 352, 375, 378-82 (1976). *See also Department of State v. Ray*, 502 U.S. 164 (1991) (disclosure of personal information without identifying details "constitutes only a de minimis invasion of privacy"); *Carter v. Department of Commerce*, 830 F.2d 388 (D.C. Cir. 1987) (upholding release of records concerning dismissed disciplinary investigations after deletion of information which would identify the subject of the investigation); *Norwood v. FAA*, 993 F.2d 570, 575 (6th Cir. 1993) (upholding release of information regarding reinstatement of air traffic controllers involved in illegal strike after redaction of identifying information). *Dayton Newspapers v. Department of the Air Force*, 107 F. Supp. 2d 912, 919-20 (S.D. Ohio 1999) (ordering release of medical malpractice settlement amounts after redaction of identifying information). *Cf. Manna v. DOJ,* 832 F. Supp. 866 (D.N.J. 1993) (cannot withhold "personal information" under Exemption 7(C) absent a showing that deletion of identifying information is inadequate to protect privacy interest), *aff'd*, 51 F.3d 1158 (3d Cir. 1995), *cert. denied*, 516 U.S. 975 (1995).

6.5. Related to the issue of segregability is the question of whether information in a record that is exempt under a privacy exemption must nonetheless be disclosed in a different format. This question has been addressed in cases involving audiotapes of voices and handwritten documents. *See New York Times Co. v. NASA*, 782 F. Supp. 628 (D.D.C. 1991) (audiotapes withheld but redacted transcript released); *Dow Jones & Co. v. DOJ,* No. 94-0527, 1995 WL 6155 (S.D.N.Y. Jan. 9, 1995) (typed document containing text of torn-up handwritten suicide note not an adequate substitute for original note, particularly in light of public interest in disclosure and negligible incremental privacy invasion); *Church of Scientology v. IRS*, 816 F. Supp. 1138 (W.D. Tex. 1993) (holding that documents should be typed, at the requester's expense, since Exemption 7(C) did not permit nondisclosure solely because of privacy concerns based on handwriting). *But cf. Church of Scientology Int'l v. IRS*, 995 F.2d 916 (9th Cir. 1993) (remanding for determination whether public interest outweighs privacy concerns based on handwriting) (7(C) case). Non-FOIA cases have recognized that transcripts derived from audiotapes fail to convey important information contained in the original. *See, e.g.*, *Nixon v. Freeman*, 670 F.2d 346, 357 (D.C. Cir. 1982) ("To name but a few of the differences between the spoken and written word, phrases may be inaudible or indiscernible, inflections may vary the meaning of a particular word or phrase, and silences or pauses may form part of conversation's content."), *cert. denied,* 459 U.S. 1035 (1982).

7. Reverse FOIA Litigation Under Exemption 6.

7.1. Cases in which data subjects seek to enjoin its release under FOIA Exemption 6 are quite rare, but they do exist and there is no reason in theory why they should not. *See, e.g., Campaign for Family Farms v. Glickman*, 200 F.3d 1180 (8th Cir. 2000); *NOW v. SSA*, 736 F.2d 727 (D.C. Cir. 1984); *Ivanhoe Citrus Ass'n v. Handley*, 612 F. Supp. 1560, 1567 (D.D.C. 1985); *Sonderegger v. Department of Interior*, 424 F. Supp. 847 (D. Idaho 1976); *Sears, Roebuck & Co. v. GSA*, 402 F. Supp. 378 (D.D.C. 1975), *remanded on other grounds*, 553 F.2d 1378 (D.C. Cir. 1977), *cert. denied,* 434 U.S. 826 (1977); *Alexander & Alexander Servs. v. SEC*, No. 92-112 (JHG), 1993 U.S. Dist. LEXIS 14945 (D.D.C. Oct. 18, 1993); *Church Universal & Triumphant, Inc. v. United States*, No. 95-0163, 1995 WL 271578 (D.D.C. 1995). *Cf. United States v. Westinghouse Elec. Corp.*, 638 F.2d 570 (3d Cir. 1980) (employees can intervene in employer's resistance to subpoena to assert privacy interests).

7.2. Paucity of cases is explained in part by lack of financial incentive, in part by lack of notice prior to release, and, in part, by the novelty of such litigation.

7.3. *Chrysler Corp. v. Brown*, 441 U.S. 281 (1979), now the leading case on reverse FOIA litigation in the trade secrets area, should govern these cases, too, in many respects. (See Chapter 7 on Reverse FOIA Litigation).

7.4. In *Crumpton v. Stone*, 59 F.3d 1400, 1404 (D.C. Cir. 1995), *cert. denied,* 516 U.S. 1147 (1996), plaintiff unsuccessfully brought Federal Tort Claims Act action for Army's release of information related to her husband's suicide. Court held that even when FOIA exemption applies, it is not mandatory; FOIA does not limit an agency's discretion to disclose information. *See also Bartholdi Cable Co. v. FCC*, 114 F.3d 274, 282-83 (D.C. Cir. 1997) (FCC not required to withhold information if it was covered by Exemption 6; "[u]nlike information falling within Exemption 4, information falling within Exemption 6 is not necessarily protected from disclosure by the Trade Secrets Act").

8. Relationship Between Exemptions 6 and 7(C).

8.1. Until amended in 1986, § 552(b)(7)(C) provided: "(b) This section does not apply to matters that are…(7) [investigatory records] compiled for law enforcement purposes, but only to the extent that the production of such records would…(C) constitute an unwarranted invasion of personal privacy."

8.2. There was little substantive difference between Exemptions 6 and 7(C), except for the different thresholds and the absence of "clearly" in 7(C).

8.2.1. The legislative history of the original version of 7(C) indicates that the exemption intended to "make clear that the protections in [Exemption] 6 for personal privacy also apply to disclosure under [Exemption] 7." 1975 FOIA Source Book at 333 (remarks of Senator Hart).

8.2.2. The Attorney General's Memorandum states that "in determining the meaning of [Exemption 7(C)], it is appropriate to consider the body of court decisions regarding [Exemption] 6." Attorney General's Memorandum on the 1974 Amendments to the FOIA at 9 (February 1975).

8.2.3. There is, however, a great deal of authority suggesting that the absence of the word "clearly" makes the test for exemption under 7(C) less stringent. *See, e.g., Department of State v. Ray*, 502 U.S. 164 (1991); *FBI v. Abramson*, 456 U.S. 615, 629 n.13 (1982); *Department of the Air Force v. Rose*, 425 U.S. at 379 n.16; *Stern v. FBI*, 737 F.2d 84, 91 (D.C. Cir. 1984); *Alirez v. NLRB*, 676 F.2d 423, 426-27 n.3 (10th Cir. 1982); *Bast v. DOJ*, 665 F.2d 1251, 1256 (D.C. Cir. 1981); *Fund for Constitutional Gov't v. National Archives*, 656 F.2d 856, 862 (D.C. Cir. 1981); *Ferri v. Bell*, 645 F.2d 1213, 1217 n.5 (3d Cir. 1981); *Deering Milliken, Inc. v. Irving*, 548 F.2d 1131, 1136 n.7 (4th Cir. 1977).

8.3. The 1986 amendment to Exemption 7(C), which substituted "could reasonably be expected to" for "would," further augmented the distinction between the two exemptions. *See DOJ v. Reporters Comm. for Freedom of the Press*, 489 U.S. 749, 756 n.9 (1989). The difference is now considerable. *See Providence Journal Co. v. Department of the Army*, 981 F.2d 552 (1st Cir. 1992) (Exemption 6 affords agency far less protection against compelled disclosure than does Exemption 7(C)); *see also FLRA v. Department of Veterans Affairs*, 958 F.2d 503, 509 (2d Cir. 1992) (differences result from an explicit compromise making disclosure under 7(C) more difficult to obtain). Exemption 6 requires proof that the requested documents qualify as "similar files," that the invasion of privacy would be "clearly unwarranted" and that disclosure would in fact constitute an invasion of privacy. Since it was amended, Exemption 7(C) requires merely a showing of a reasonable expectation of such an invasion. *See Hunt v. FBI*, 972 F.2d 286, 288 (9th Cir. 1992); *see also Painting Indus. of Hawaii Market Recovery Fund v. Department of the Air Force*, 26 F.3d 1479, 1481 (9th Cir. 1994) (Exemption 7(C) imposes "a slightly lighter burden of proof" upon agencies than Exemption 6); *Nadler v. DOJ*, 955 F.2d 1479, 1488 (11th Cir. 1992) (amended language represents relaxation of standard); *Dobronski v. FCC*, 17 F.3d 275, 278 (9th Cir. 1994) ("threat to privacy interests that may justify nondisclosure in an Exemption 7(C) case may warrant disclosure in an Exemption 6 case"); *LaRouche v. DOJ*, No. 90-2753 (HHG), 1993 WL 388601 (D.D.C. June 25, 1993) (bald claims that privacy interests of employees were "obvious and substantial" did not meet "heightened" burden for nondisclosure under Exemption 6, although same information exempt from disclosure under 7(C) due to negligible public interest).

8.4. See the much more detailed discussion of Exemption 7(C) cases in Chapter 10 on Law Enforcement Records.

CHAPTER 10

Exemption 7—Law Enforcement Records

Harry A. Hammitt

1. **Exemption 7 provides that the FOIA does not apply to matters that are: "records or information compiled for law enforcement purposes, but only to the extent that the production of such law enforcement records or information (A) could reasonably be expected to interfere with enforcement proceedings, (B) would deprive a person of a right to a fair trial or an impartial adjudication, (C) could reasonably be expected to constitute an unwarranted invasion of personal privacy, (D) could reasonably be expected to disclose the identity of a confidential source, including a state, local, or foreign agency or authority or any private institution which furnished information on a confidential basis, and, in the case of a record or information compiled by a criminal law enforcement authority in the course of a criminal investigation or by an agency conducting a lawful national security intelligence investigation, information furnished by a confidential source, (E) would disclose techniques and procedures for law enforcement investigations or prosecutions, or would disclose guidelines for law enforcement investigations or prosecutions if such disclosure could reasonably be expected to risk circumvention of the law, or (F) could reasonably be expected to endanger the life or physical safety of any individual."**

2. **Legislative History.**

2.1. As originally enacted in 1966, Exemption 7 was interpreted to provide broad protection to an "investigatory file."

2.1.1. Exemption 7 as originally enacted permitted agencies to withhold "investigatory files compiled for law enforcement purposes except to the extent available by law to a party other than an agency."

2.1.2. After first giving the exemption a narrow interpretation, the D.C. Circuit issued a series of decisions which afforded a *per se* exemption to all files which were found to be "investigatory" in nature. *Compare Bristol-Myers Co. v. FTC*, 424 F.2d 935 (D.C. Cir. 1970), *cert. denied*, 400 U.S. 824 (1970), with the later decisions in *Weisberg v. DOJ*, 489 F.2d 1195 (D.C. Cir. 1973) (en banc), *cert. denied*, 416 U.S. 993 (1974); *Center for National Policy Review on Race and Urban Issues v. Weinberger*, 502 F.2d 370 (D.C. Cir. 1974); *Ditlow v. Brinegar*, 494 F.2d 1073 (D.C. Cir.), *cert. denied*, 419 U.S. 974 (1974); *Aspin v. Department of Defense*, 491 F.2d 24 (D.C. Cir. 1973).

2.1.3. In these cases, judicial inquiry became limited to an examination of how and under what circumstances the requested files were compiled, regardless of whether any further enforcement proceeding was likely or would be harmed by disclosure. *See, e.g., Weisberg v. DOJ*, 489 F.2d at 1197, where the court held that the spectrographic analysis of the bullet that killed President Kennedy was "part of the investigatory files compiled by the FBI for law enforcement purposes" and was therefore exempt *per se* despite the fact that no related law enforcement proceedings were contemplated.

Exemption 7

2.2. The 1974 amendments to Exemption 7 were enacted specifically to reverse these broad judicial interpretations of the law enforcement exemption.

2.2.1. Exemption 7, in essentially the language Congress ultimately adopted, was introduced by Senator Philip Hart on the Senate floor and was intended to override *Weisberg, Aspin, Ditlow*, and *Center for National Policy Review*. 120 Cong. Rec. S9336 (daily ed., May 30, 1974).

2.2.2. Exemption 7, as amended, provided that the FOIA did not apply to matters that were: "investigatory records compiled for law enforcement purposes, but only to the extent that the production of such records would (A) interfere with enforcement proceedings, (B) deprive a person of a right to a fair trial or an impartial adjudication, (C) constitute an unwarranted invasion of personal privacy, (D) disclose the identity of a confidential source and, in the case of a record compiled by a criminal law enforcement authority in the course of a criminal investigation, or by an agency conducting a lawful national security intelligence investigation, confidential information furnished only by the confidential source, (E) disclose investigative techniques and procedures, or (F) endanger the life or physical safety of law enforcement personnel."

2.2.3. Amended Exemption 7 allowed—but did not require—withholding of investigatory records—not whole files—"compiled for law enforcement purposes, but only to the extent that the production of such records would" cause one of six specifically enumerated harms.

2.3 The 1986 amendments to Exemption 7 were enacted as part of the Anti-Drug Abuse Act of 1986 after several years of political dispute over whether the withholding language adopted in 1974, as applied by both agencies and courts, provided adequate protection for confidential sources, ongoing investigations, and certain manuals and other sensitive non-investigatory law enforcement materials. *See* general discussion of 1986 FOIA amendments in Chapter 1, Overview.

2.3.1. Substituting "records or information" for "investigatory records" as the threshold qualification for exemption from disclosure.

2.3.1.1. The Senate Judiciary Committee's report on S. 774, S. Rep. No. 221, 98th Cong., 1st Sess. (1983) [*reprinted in relevant part* at 132 Cong. Rec. H9466 (daily ed., Oct. 8, 1986)] (hereafter "the Report"), states that this change was "intended to insure that sensitive law enforcement information is protected under Exemption 7 regardless of the particular format or record in which the record [sic] is maintained. *Cf. FBI v. Abramson*, 456 U.S. 615 (1982)." S. Rep. No. 221 at 23. It seems likely that the Committee meant to say "regardless of the particular format or record in which the *information* is maintained." (emphasis supplied). *See* discussion of the importance of the Senate Judiciary Committee report as legislative history for the 1986 amendments to Exemption 7 in Chapter 1.

2.3.1.2. The change was also intended to "resolve any doubt that law enforcement manuals and other non-investigatory materials can be withheld...if they were compiled for law enforcement purposes and their disclosure would result in one of the six recognized harms to law enforcement interests set forth in the subparagraphs of the exemption." *Id.*

2.3.1.3. Several subsequent decisions have noted the change, but primarily to acknowledge that the requirement for materials to be "compiled for law enforcement purposes," as interpreted in *Pratt v. Webster*, 673 F.2d 408 (D.C. Cir. 1982), "clearly survives the 1986 amendments." *Keys v. DOJ*, 830 F.2d 337, 340 (D.C. Cir. 1987); *King v. DOJ*, 830 F.2d at 229 n.141; *Reporters Committee v. DOJ*, 816 F.2d 730, 737 n.10 (D.C. Cir. 1987) *modified on other grounds,* 831 F.2d 1124 (D.C. Cir.) *rev'd on other grounds,* 489 U.S. 749 (1989).

2.3.2. Substituting "could reasonably be expected to" for "would" as a standard for the risk of harm with respect to subparagraphs (A) interference with enforcement proceedings, (C) unwarranted invasion of personal privacy, (D) disclosure of the identity of a confidential source, and (F) endanger the life or physical safety of any individual.

2.3.2.1. The Report states that this change was "intended to clarify the degree of risk of harm from disclosure which must be shown to justify withholding under any of these subparagraphs" and that it "recognizes the lack of certainty in attempting to predict harm, but requires a standard of reasonableness in that process, based on an objective test." *Id.* at 23.

2.3.2.2. Senator Leahy and Reps. English and Kindness each cited with approval a study by the Congressional Research Service of the Library of Congress which reviewed extant caselaw on Exemption 7 and concluded that this change "would not seem to materially alter the construction that the courts have already given to the provision." *See* Memorandum from American Law Division, Congressional Research Service, to House Government Operations Committee, Subcommittee on Government Information, Justice and Agriculture (February 28, 1986), *reprinted* at 132 Cong. Rec. S14299 (daily ed. September 30, 1986).

2.3.2.3. The House amendment to the Senate-passed provisions would have deleted this change as applied to subparagraph (C), unwarranted invasion of personal privacy, based upon the sponsors' reasoning that the existing unamended exemption standard was "nearly identical" to the privacy standard in Exemption 6 and it was "unnecessary" and "inappropriate to make any changes that increase the difference between these two privacy standards." *See* 132 CONG. REC. H9466 (daily ed. October 8, 1986) (statement of Rep. Kindness). However, Senator Leahy joined Senator Hatch in restoring the Senate amendment to subparagraph (C), expressing confidence that "the courts will recognize this change as simply codifying their present objective approach to assessing the degree of risk, rather than calling for a departure to a less rigorous standard." 132 Cong. Rec. S16496 (daily ed. October 15, 1986).

2.3.2.4. Senator Leahy's confidence in the courts appears to have been justified. *See Reporters Committee,* 489 U.S. at 756 n.9 (although change "represents a considered congressional effort" to move to a "more flexible standard," Court found "no indication that the shift was intended to eliminate *de novo* review in favor of agency deference in Exemption 7(C) cases"); *Curran v. DOJ*, 813 F.2d 473, 474 n.1 (1st Cir. 1987) (court found the "drift" of the "relatively minor" change was to ease, rather than increase, the government's burden through "the new (slightly more relaxed) phraseology"); *Spannaus v. DOJ*, 813 F.2d 1285, 1288 (4th Cir. 1987) (agency's showing now "is to be measured by a standard of reasonableness, which takes into account the lack of certainty in attempting to predict harm while providing an objective test").

2.3.3. Including state, local, and foreign agencies or authorities and private institutions within the meaning of "confidential source" in subparagraph (D), and deleting the words "confidential" and "only" from the subparagraph's second clause.

2.3.3.1. The addition of the specific references to agencies, authorities and institutions was "intended to codify the caselaw in which the weight of judicial interpretation has held that 'confidential source' protection...is applicable to entities, as well as natural persons, that furnished information to an agency on a confidential basis." Report at 24.

2.3.3.2. The deletion of "only" was intended "to make clear that, in the case of a record compiled by a criminal law enforcement authority in the course of a criminal investigation, or by an agency conducting a lawful national security intelligence investigation, confidential information furnished by a confidential source is exempt, regardless of whether it might also have been obtained from another source." *Id.* However, the deletion of "confidential"— which was *not* part of the amendments originally proposed as part of S. 774—went further to codify caselaw establishing that *all* information furnished by a confidential source is exempt, so long as it was furnished in connection with a criminal or lawful national security investigation. *See, e.g., Shaw v. FBI*, 749 F.2d 58, 61 (D.C. Cir. 1984).

2.3.4. Deleting "investigative" and adding "guidelines for law enforcement and prosecutions" in subparagraph (E).

2.3.4.1. The deletion of "investigative" was intended to make clear that law enforcement techniques and procedures which are not routine or already well known to the public can be protected from disclosure, regardless of whether they are "investigative" or not. Report at 24-25.

2.3.4.2. The amendment also expanded subparagraph (E) to codify the D.C. Circuit's *en banc* decision in *Crooker v. BATF*, 670 F.2d 1051 (D.C. Cir. 1981), permitting the withholding of "guidelines for law enforcement investigations or prosecutions if such disclosure could reasonably be expected to risk circumvention of the law." In applying this standard, agencies and courts are instructed to "consider the danger of creating 'secret law' together with the potential for aiding lawbreakers to avoid detection or prosecution." *Id.* *See also* discussion of *Crooker* in Chapter 4 on Internal Agency Rules.

2.3.4.3. Reps. English and Kindness argued that the authority to withhold prosecutorial guidelines should be narrowly construed, based on a realization that the government cannot prevent former prosecutors who were privy to them from using the otherwise non-public guidelines to further a private practice. The two House members reasoned that, notwithstanding a "circumvention of law" determination, withholding should be limited to situations where "prosecutorial guidelines are changed temporarily or there are other circumstances where there is no risk of public disclosure from other sources...." 132 Cong. Rec. H9467 (daily ed. October 8, 1986).

2.3.4.4. However, Senator Hatch argued that the amended subparagraph (E) permits withholding of such guidelines "without question," and "should be applied where necessary to protect critical law enforcement interests, regardless of the extent of their availability within the law enforcement community." 132 Cong. Rec. S16505 (daily ed. October 15, 1986).

2.3.5. Substituting "any individual" for "law enforcement personnel" in subparagraph (F).

2.3.5.1. Although S. 774 proposed a similar change, substituting "any natural person" for "law enforcement personnel," the committee report on that bill failed to provide an explanation of the provision's intended purpose and effect.

2.3.5.2. However, there was no controversy among the key players over changing what Senator Hatch characterized as "an obvious and absurd limitation" which made records exempt under subparagraph (F) if their disclosure endangered the life and physical safety of a police officer, but not when disclosure endangered any other individual. *Id.*

2.3.6. The amendments also added a new subsection (c) to the FOIA establishing that, in certain circumstances, a criminal law enforcement agency which receives a request for (1) records concerning an ongoing and undisclosed criminal investigation; (2) informant records maintained under an informant's name or personal identifier; or, (3) classified FBI records pertaining to foreign intelligence, counterintelligence, or international terrorism investigations, "may treat the records as not subject to the requirements of this section." *See* Chapter 18 on Record Exclusions.

3. Threshold Tests: The first question is whether the requested "records or information" are "compiled for law enforcement purposes."

3.1. Both civil and criminal judicial and administrative enforcement proceedings qualify for protection. H. Rep. No. 1497, 89th Cong., 2d Sess. 11 (1966); *see also* S. Rep. No.

1200, 93d Cong., 2d Sess. 13 (1974) (Conference Report); *Stern v. FBI*, 737 F.2d 84 (D.C. Cir. 1984).

3.2. Agency manuals which contain instructions to law enforcement personnel formerly were not considered "investigatory" records compiled in the course of a specific law enforcement proceeding, and therefore were not covered by Exemption 7 as amended in 1974. *Caplan v. BATF*, 445 F. Supp. 699 (S.D.N.Y. 1978), *aff'd on other grounds*, 587 F.2d 544 (2d Cir. 1978); *Sladek v. Bensinger*, 605 F.2d 899 (5th Cir. 1979).

3.3. The agency manual decisions, however, would likely have different results under the exemption as amended in 1986 because records no longer need to be "investigatory" to qualify for withholding, and "guidelines for law enforcement investigations or prosecutions"—which are clearly not "investigative" in nature—may nonetheless now be protected if their disclosure "could reasonably be expected to risk circumvention of the law." *See* discussion of 1986 amendments in this chapter, *supra*. Other pre-1986 Exemption 7 cases which turned on the characterization of records as "investigatory" or "investigative" should be closely read to determine whether they have any precedential value under current law.

3.4. Exemption 7 does not apply to information compiled in an agency's general internal monitoring of its own employees to insure compliance with the agency's statutory mandate and regulations. Thus, it is important "to distinguish between internal investigations conducted for law enforcement purposes and general agency internal monitoring that might reveal evidence that later could give rise to a law enforcement investigation: an agency's investigation of its own employees is for 'law enforcement purposes' only if it focuses directly on specifically alleged illegal acts, illegal acts of particular identified officials, acts which could, if proved, result in civil or criminal sanctions.'" *Stern v. FBI,* 737 F.2d at 89, *citing Rural Housing Alliance v. USDA*, 498 F.2d 73, 81-82 (D.C. Cir. 1974); *Church of Scientology v. Department of the Army*, 611 F.2d 738, 748 (9th Cir. 1979); *See also Hatcher v. U.S. Postal Service*, 556 F. Supp. 331 (D.D.C. 1982) (documents acquired in course of routine contract negotiations and oversight developed well before investigation into alleged criminal violations are not "compiled for law enforcement purposes"). *But see Fedders Corp. v. FTC*, 494 F. Supp. 325, 328 (S.D.N.Y. 1980) *aff'd*, 646 F.2d 560 (2d Cir. 1980) (unsolicited complaint letters received by FTC prior to the institution of an enforcement proceeding which had become, at the time requested, an integral part of the record relating to a pending investigation, were deemed to be compiled for law enforcement purposes). *See also Church of Scientology Int'l v. IRS*, 995 F.2d 916 (9th Cir. 1993) (Exempt Organizations division of IRS has law enforcement function and qualifies as a law enforcement agency).

3.5. A separate issue concerns the question of whether Exemption 7 can be invoked by criminal law enforcement agencies for records which relate to non-law enforcement or allegedly unlawful agency activities—e.g., FBI programs of surveillance and harassment of political activist groups. Although the courts have generally shown deference to agency claims in such cases, they have applied different tests in determining the threshold question of whether such records are "compiled for law enforcement purposes."

3.5.1. The D.C. Circuit has established a two-prong test, under which a criminal law enforcement agency must show that:

3.5.1.1. the investigatory activities giving rise to the documents sought were related to the enforcement of federal laws or to the maintenance of national security, and

3.5.1.2. the nexus between the investigation and one of the agency's law enforcement duties is based on information sufficient to support at least "a colorable claim" of its rationality. *See Pratt v. Webster*, 673 F.2d 408, 420-21 (D.C. Cir. 1982). *See also King v. DOJ*, 830 F.2d 210, 229-31 (D.C. Cir. 1987) ("*Pratt* counsels against 'second-guessing' a law enforcement agency's showing of investigatory purpose if there is a plausible basis for the undertaking."); *Keys v. DOJ*, 830 F.2d 337, 340-42 (D.C. Cir. 1987) ("An objective finding of such a nexus is refutable only by 'persuasive evidence that in fact another, nonqualifying reason prompted the investigation,'" citing *Shaw v. FBI*, 749 F.2d at 63). Both *King* and *Keys* note that the "compiled for law enforcement purposes" language and its interpretation in the courts were in no way changed by the 1986 amendments. *Id.*

3.5.2. Similar standards have been adopted by different courts. *See Davin v. DOJ*, 60 F.3d 1043 (3d Cir. 1995) ("the simple recitation of statutes, orders and public laws is an insufficient showing of a rational nexus to a legitimate law enforcement concern...[T]he paucity of information about these lengthy investigations casts doubt on the government's assertion that withheld documents pertain to law enforcement investigations."); *see Binion v. DOJ,* 695 F.2d 1189 (9th Cir. 1983); *Church of Scientology v. Department of the Army*, 611 F.2d at 748 ("An agency which has a clear law enforcement mandate, such as the FBI, need only establish a 'rational nexus' between enforcement of federal law and the document for which an exemption is claimed."); *Dunway v. Webster*, 519 F. Supp. 1059, 1076 (N.D. Cal. 1981) ("An agency with a clear law enforcement purpose... need only be held to a minimal showing that the activity which generated the documents was related to the agency's function."). *Rosenfeld v. DOJ,* 761 F. Supp. 1440 (N.D. Cal. 1991) (investigation of the Berkeley Free Speech Movement ceased being a legitimate law enforcement investigation when the FBI had reason to believe no laws were being violated). In *Summers v. DOJ,* 140 F.3d 1077 (D.C. Cir. 1998), the court questioned whether J. Edgar Hoover's confidential files could be considered to have been compiled for law enforcement purposes because they were kept in his office and were not available for agency use. *See also Campbell v. DOJ*, 164 F.3d 20 (D.C. Cir. 1998), where the court ruled the FBI had not provided adequate proof that records on author James Baldwin were compiled for law enforcement purposes.

3.5.2.1. In a thorough examination of the issue, the Sixth Circuit concluded, in *Jones v. FBI*, 41 F.3d 238 (6th Cir. 1994), that "even where there is no evidence that the agency acted in bad faith with regard to the FOIA action itself there may be evidence of bad faith or illegality with regard to the underlying activities which generated the documents at issue. Where such evidence is strong, it would be an abdication of the court's responsibility to treat the case in the standard way and grant summary judgment on the basis of *Vaughn* affidavits alone." The court further concluded that the threshold language of Exemption 7—that records be compiled for law enforcement purposes—was not meant to be the initial determinant as to whether records were truly protected by the exemption. Rather, the court pointed out that "Congress considered the enumeration of the specific bases for withholding material to be the principal means for narrowing the law enforcement exemption." The concern about overbroad withholding should therefore be addressed by proper scrutiny of the claimed exemptions themselves and not by use of a blunt instrument at the threshold which would harm the other policies Congress deemed important.

3.5.3. Other courts have ruled that FBI records are *per se* "compiled for enforcement purposes" within the meaning of Exemption 7, and thus proceeded to address the additional question of whether one or more of the exemption's subsections were properly invoked. *See Williams v. FBI,* 730 F.2d 882, 883 (2d Cir. 1984) ("Congress intended that subcategories (A)-(F) protect from disclosure the described information whether or not the reviewing judicial tribunal believes there was a sound law enforcement basis for the particular investigation."); *Ferguson v. FBI,* 957 F.2d 1059 (2d Cir. 1992) (district court should not engage in a factual inquiry as to the legitimacy of the FBI's asserted law enforcement purpose); *See also Kuehnert v. FBI*, 620 F.2d 662 (8th Cir. 1980); *Irons v. Bell*, 596 F.2d 468, 474 (1st Cir. 1979) (interpreting "law enforcement purposes" as defining the type of agency at which the exemption is aimed); *see also Arenberg v. DEA,* 849 F.2d 579 (11th Cir. 1988) (discussion of conflict between *Pratt* test and *per se* approach to "compiled for law enforcement purpose" requirement).

3.5.4. Although it is generally assumed that Exemption 7 addresses records compiled for *federal* law enforcement purposes, no such qualification appears in the language of the statute or in its legislative history.

3.5.4.1. In *Wojtczak v. DOJ*, 548 F. Supp. 143, 148 (E.D. Pa. 1982), apparently the first case which directly confronted the issue, the court held that Exemption 7 "applies to all law enforcement records, federal, state, or local, that lie within the possession of the federal government." Finding no "on-point precedent," the court applied a "plain meaning" construction to the statutory language, reasoning that "[i]f Congress had intended to exempt only federal law enforcement records from disclosure, it could easily have drafted the statute to include the word 'federal.'" *Id.*

3.5.4.2. The court in *Donovan v. FBI*, 579 F. Supp. 1111 (S.D.N.Y. 1983), similarly faced with what it viewed as a "novel issue of law," found the *Wojtczak* court's analysis "useful" in concluding that Exemption 7 was applicable to FBI records concerning FBI aid in a foreign law enforcement proceeding. *Accord Peterzell v. DOJ*, 576 F. Supp. 1492 (D.D.C. 1983), *aff'd in part and remanded in part sub nom. Bevis v. Department of State*, 801 F.2d 1386 (D.C. Cir. 1986).

3.5.4.3. Both the *Wojtczak* and *Donovan* courts rejected the argument that language in cases like *Pratt v. Webster, supra* ("documents sought must be related to the enforcement of federal laws or the maintenance of national security") limited the scope of Exemption 7 to *federal* law enforcement, asserting rather that the precise question of the exemption's applicability to federal records concerning non-federal law enforcement proceedings was not considered in such cases.

3.5.5. Union authorization cards submitted to the NLRB to support a petition for election have been found not to be protected by Exemption 7 because they are not "compiled for law enforcement purposes," *Committee on Masonic Homes v. NLRB,* 556 F.2d 214 (3d Cir. 1977).

3.6. Information contained in records originally compiled for law enforcement purposes does not lose Exemption 7 protection when it is summarized or reproduced in a new document which is compiled for other than law enforcement purposes. *FBI v. Abramson*, 456 U.S. 615 (1982).

3.6.1. In *Abramson*, the Supreme Court held that summaries of information supplied in response to White House "name check" requests on prominent liberal public personalities were "compiled for law enforcement purposes" and thus could be withheld under Exemption 7. Although the documents at issue were actually compiled for political and not law enforcement purposes, it was not disputed that the summaries were derived from information in FBI files which did qualify under the threshold test. The Court held that such information does not lose its exempt status when it is reproduced or summarized in a new document which is compiled for other than law enforcement purposes.

3.6.2. In the converse situation—where requested summaries were plainly compiled for law enforcement purposes but the underlying records were not—the D.C. Circuit has held that the documents meet the threshold test and therefore may qualify for protection under Exemption 7. *See Lesar v. DOJ*, 636 F.2d 472 (D.C. Cir. 1980) (summaries of Task Force Investigation of Dr. Martin Luther King were compiled for law enforcement purposes, regardless of Court's "serious doubts" whether the original surveillance records—which were not at issue in that case—were compiled in connection with a lawful investigation).

3.7. In *John Doe Agency v. John Doe Corp.*, 493 U.S. 146 (1989), the Supreme Court resolved a split among the circuits on the application of Exemption 7 to information which is originally compiled as part of a routine contractor audit but subsequently becomes part of an investigatory file compiled for a law enforcement purpose.

3.7.1. Justice Harry Blackmun, writing for the majority stated: "We thus do not accept the distinction the Court of Appeals drew between documents that originally were assembled for law enforcement purposes and those that were not so originally assembled but were gathered later for such purposes. The plain language of Exemption 7 does not permit such a distinction. Under the statute, documents need only to have been compiled when the response to the FOIA request must be made." 493 U.S. at 155.

3.7.2. Justice Antonin Scalia dissented, noting that the term "compiled for law enforcement purposes" "is readily evaded (or illusory) if it requires nothing more than gathering up documents the government does not wish to disclose, with a plausible law-enforcement purpose in mind. That is a hole one can drive a truck through." 493 U.S. at 163-64.

3.7.3. The Supreme Court's decision reversed the ruling of the Second Circuit in *John Doe Corp. v. John Doe Agency*, 850 F.2d 105 (2d Cir. 1988). There, the court had rejected Exemption 7 protection for such documents because of their failure to meet the threshold test, concluding that substituting the word "records" for "files" in the 1974 FOIA amendments was intended to prevent agencies from withholding records "produced in the routine course of government operations...merely because they had been commingled with investigative materials generated later in the course of a law enforcement proceeding." *Id.* at 109.

3.7.4. However, in *Gould, Inc. v. GSA,* 688 F. Supp. 689, 697 (D.D.C. 1988), a different court had interpreted the same legislative history that was cited in *John Doe Corp.* as simply prohibiting agencies from commingling "otherwise benign materials" with sensitive law enforcement records in order to withhold them under Exemption 7. The court concluded that "at no time has the plain meaning of the statute required an exclusive focus on whether records or information were *originally* compiled for law enforcement purposes." *Id.* at 691 (emphasis in original). *See also Crowell & Moring v. Department of Defense,* 703 F. Supp. 1004 (D.D.C. 1989).

3.8. Where it is clear that an agency does not have law enforcement power to conduct the investigation, Exemption 7 cannot be invoked. *Weissman v. CIA*, 565 F.2d 692, 696 (D.C. Cir. 1977) (exemption does not apply to records of extensive CIA investigation of American citizens living in the U.S., since CIA is statutorily prohibited from conducting domestic law enforcement activities). *See also Church of Scientology v. Department of the Army*, 611 F.2d at 749 (since Office of Naval Intelligence is not an agency with a clear law enforcement mandate, court must question whether investigation involved the enforcement of any statute or regulation within its authority).

3.9. Likewise, agencies must do more than just name one or a series of broad-based laws as the basis for their law enforcement purpose. The Seventh Circuit, in *Patterson v. IRS*, 56 F.3d 832 (7th Cir. 1995), pointed out that citing a series of equal employment opportunity statutes did not provide an adequate justification for claiming a law enforcement purpose. "The IRS could hardly have hoped to satisfy its burden of demonstrating a law enforcement purpose by naming such a huge set of laws. Nor could the reference to possible violation of the Rules of Conduct satisfy the IRS' burden since such violations could not constitute a law enforcement purpose unless the activity which allegedly violate the rules independently violated the law." The D.C. Circuit noted, in *Quinon v. FBI*, 86 F.3d 1222 (D.C. Cir. 1996), that "the affidavits filed by the FBI fail to supply facts that would justify an obstruction of justice investigation; rather, they allude to 'certain facts,' which they fail to describe or characterize, that allegedly supplied the basis for one…To allow the FBI to satisfy the [rational nexus] requirement with a vague reference to another 'event' would render that requirement a virtual nullity."

4. **Even if the requested material "constitutes records or information compiled for law enforcement purposes," it is not exempt unless disclosure would or could reasonably be expected to cause the harm embodied in one or more of Exemption 7's six subsections regarding protected law enforcement interests.**

4.1. Records or information may be withheld if disclosure could reasonably be expected to "(A) interfere with enforcement proceedings."

4.1.1. Senator Hart explained that, when there is a concrete prospect of enforcement proceedings, documents or portions of documents may be withheld if disclosure of information unknown to defendants would impede the investigation or harm the government's case "in the particular proceeding." 120 Cong. Rec. S9330 (daily ed., May 30, 1974) (remarks of Senator Hart).

4.1.2. Thus, because the exemption affords protection to records or information in order to prevent "harm to the government's case in court," the government must demonstrate that the information relates to a pending or prospective law enforcement proceeding. *NLRB v. Robbins Tire & Rubber Co.*, 437 U.S. 214 (1978). Some courts have ruled that the exemption is applicable to investigations which, although concededly dormant, could be revived. *See, e.g., Erb v. DOJ*, 572 F. Supp. 954 (W.D. Mich. 1983) (Exemption 7(A) applies even after investigation announced as "concluded 'for the time being'"); *ABC Home Health Services v. HHS*, 548 F. Supp. 555 (N.D. Ga. 1982) (Exemption 7(A) deemed applicable after settlement so long as "further proceedings are not foreclosed"). *But see Senate of the Commonwealth of Puerto Rico v. DOJ,* 823 F.2d 574 (D.C. Cir. 1987) (records compiled after investigation was closed are not covered, even though investigation was subsequently reopened). After examining a sample of documents chosen by the agency, the Sixth Circuit found the FBI's investigation into the disappearance and supposed death of Jimmy Hoffa still open. *Dickerson v. DOJ*, 992 F.2d 1426 (6th Cir. 1993). *See also City of Chicago v. Dept. of Treasury*, No. 00-3417 (D.N.D. Ill., Mar. 6, 2001), *aff'd* No. 01-2167, 2002 WL 724621 (7th Cir., Apr. 25, 2002), in which the court found the Bureau of Alcohol, Tobacco and Firearms had failed to show the existence of any ongoing investigations involving its multiple gun sales database.

4.1.3. The 1974 amendment was particularly aimed at eliminating Exemption 7 claims for matters relating to closed files. *NLRB v. Robbins Tire, supra; Coastal States Gas Corp. v. DOE,* 617 F.2d 854 (D.C. Cir. 1980). *But see New England Medical Center Hospital v. NLRB*, 548 F.2d 377 (1st Cir. 1976), *reh'g denied,* 548 F.2d 387 (1977) (NLRB witness statements in closed file are exempt under 7(A) where disclosure would interfere with pending related case). *Compare Nemacolin Mines Corp. v. NLRB*, 467 F. Supp. 521 (W.D. Pa. 1979) (agency must actually intend to use information in related future enforcement matter).

4.1.4. In addition to showing that the documents relate to an active, ongoing investigation, the government must also demonstrate the ways in which disclosure could reasonably be expected to result in interference to a particular proceeding. *See Campbell v. HHS*, 682 F.2d 256 (D.C. Cir. 1982); *Center for Auto Safety v. DOJ*, 576 F. Supp. 739 (D.D.C. 1983). *But see Crooker v.*

BATF, No. 85-0615 (D.D.C., Aug. 2, 1985) (where firearms case was still "open," prisoner's arrest file is exempt under 7(A) even with respect to documents already shown to defendant during a parole hearing). The courts have recognized a wide variety of potential harms under Exemption 7(A), particularly where the requester is the target of, or defendant in, an investigation or proceeding. For example, the Supreme Court held, in *Robbins Tire*, that premature release of information to the target of an investigation could allow it to intimidate witnesses. *See also J.P. Stevens & Co., Inc. v. Perry*, 710 F.2d 136, 143 (4th Cir. 1983) ("chilling effect" on potential witnesses, interference with flow of information between agencies, diminished ability to "shape and control investigation," greater difficulty for the agency in performing future investigations); *Gaffney v. BATF*, No. 84-1403 (D.D.C., May 13 and June 28, 1985) (disclosure of information requested by one individual could impede continuing investigations of his "associates" and allow the defendants to "infer the scope of the investigation as to suspects and activities").

4.1.5. In certain situations, an agency may be permitted to make "generic" showings of interference with respect to whole categories of law enforcement records, rather than justify withholding on a case-by-case basis. Thus, the Supreme Court has held "that Congress did not intend to prevent the federal courts from determining that, with respect to particular kinds of enforcement proceedings, disclosure of particular kinds of investigatory records while a case is pending would generally 'interfere with enforcement proceedings.'" *NLRB v. Robbins Tire & Rubber Co.*, 437 U.S. at 236.

4.1.5.1. In *Robbins Tire*, the Supreme Court found that one kind of record—witness statements—would generally be exempt in one kind of enforcement proceeding—NLRB unfair labor practices proceedings—at least until the time of the hearing, because of the unique potential for intimidation of witnesses involved in labor disputes.

4.1.5.2. The Court noted that, under restrictive NLRB discovery rules, witness statements would not be available in NLRB proceedings until a witness actually testified, and then concluded that "pre-hearing disclosure of witnesses' statements would involve the kind of harm that Congress believed would constitute an 'interference' with NLRB enforcement proceedings: that of giving a party litigant earlier and greater access to the Board's case than he would otherwise have." 437 U.S. at 241.

4.1.5.3. Applying the rationale of *Robbins Tire*, courts have permitted a generic demonstration of interference in cases involving NLRB unfair labor practices, *see, e.g., NLRB v. Martins Ferry Hospital Association*, 649 F.2d 445, 449 (6th Cir. 1981) (union authorization cards); *but see Pacific Molasses Co. v. NLRB*, 577 F.2d 1172 (5th Cir. 1978) (investigation report concerning a representation petition is not exempt absent pending labor enforcement proceeding).

4.1.5.4. However, the result in *Robbins Tire* has also been applied in other types of law enforcement proceedings, where the courts have also assumed that interference would result if a litigant were allowed to utilize the FOIA to obtain premature access to the government's evidence and strategy. These cases have involved certain EEOC proceedings, *see J. P. Stevens & Co., Inc. v. Perry, supra* (while all records relating to ongoing enforcement investigations are not entitled to "blanket" protection, an agency may make "generic" showings of interference with respect to certain "categories" of records, such as witness statements and notes of interviews of and correspondence with charging parties); INS proceedings, *Kacilauskas v. DOJ*, 565 F. Supp. 546 (N.D. Ill. 1983); IRS proceedings, *see, e.g., Barney v. IRS*, 618 F.2d 1268 (8th Cir. 1980); FTC investigations, *Fedders Corp. v. FTC, supra*; and Labor audits, *Copus v. Roegeau*, 504 F. Supp. 534 (D.D.C. 1980). *See also Moorefield v. U.S. Secret Service,* 449 U.S. 909 (1980) (generic determination allowed for investigatory records of the Secret Service); *Peterzell v. DOJ, supra* (generic showing of interference permitted with respect to foreign law enforcement proceeding). *But see Wright v. OSHA*, 822 F.2d 642, 646 (7th Cir. 1987) (category of "reference materials" did not provide the court with adequate information to evaluate whether release of the documents may interfere with enforcement proceedings); *Stephenson v. IRS*, 629 F.2d 1140 (5th Cir. 1980) (government affidavit describing the withheld documents in fairly detailed but generic terms was insufficient basis to deny taxpayer's motion for detailed justification, itemization and indexing of the documents); *Agee v. CIA*, 524 F. Supp. 1290 (D.D.C. 1981) (generic determination not allowed for investigatory records of CIA where agency sought to withhold "on the basis of generalized affidavits a variety of documents, compiled in a variety of ways, whose chief common characteristic is their presence in a file concerning an individual under indictment"). The full Eighth Circuit ruled that the FBI's investigation of the disappearance of Jimmy Hoffa was still an ongoing investigation and allowed the agency to assert categorical claims of exemptions for its records. *In Re: DOJ*; *Crancer v. DOJ,* 999 F.2d 1302 (8th Cir. 1993).

4.1.5.5. In *Bevis v. Department of State*, 801 F.2d 1386, 1389-90 (D.C. Cir. 1986), the court articulated a tripartite standard to justify generic determinations for 7(A) claims: "[I]f it wishes to adopt the generic approach, the FBI has a three-fold task. First, it must define its categories functionally. Second, it must conduct a document-by-document review in order to assign documents to the proper category. Finally, it must explain to the court how the release of each category would interfere with enforcement proceedings." *See also Spannaus v. DOJ*, 813 F.2d 1285, 1289 (4th Cir. 1987) (citing similar standards without reference to *Bevis*). *But see Curran v. DOJ*, 813 F.2d 473, 475-76 (1st Cir. 1987) (court did not decide "whether the *Bevis* paradigm or some other (less demanding) set of criteria" should apply in a "generic determination" case, but FBI's use of a "miscellaneous" category that referred to "other sundry items of information" was accepted as "understandable and probably essential" given the range of subjects in the FOIA request).

4.1.5.6. The Eighth Circuit has ruled that *Robbins'* approval of generic claims does not mean a court cannot order a detailed *Vaughn* index of proposed 7(A) withholdings. "District courts must be able to ask [for] this type of document-by-document information. Otherwise, district courts will be nothing more than rubber stamps for the government's decision to deny disclosure. The FOIA does not permit such a limited role for the district courts." *In Re DOJ*, 950 F.2d 530, 536 (8th Cir. 1991). However, this decision was overturned by the full court, *In Re DOJ*, 999 F.2d 1302 (8th Cir. 1993).

4.1.6. Where the FOIA request is made by a third party seeking information to which the target of the investigation already has access, the government will be required to make a more particularized showing of harm or interference to law enforcement proceedings. *Campbell v. HHS, supra. See also Goldschmidt v. Department of Agriculture*, 557 F. Supp. 274 (D.D.C. 1983) (documents sought were already in the possession of the targets of the investigation and agency failed to demonstrate that disclosure would interfere with law enforcement proceedings; assertion that publicity would interfere with enforcement by making a company less willing to negotiate an informal settlement is insufficient); *Cohen v. EPA*, 575 F. Supp. 425 (D.D.C. 1983) (EPA failed to substantiate claim that disclosure of identities of corporations and individuals who are potentially responsible for the cleanup of hazardous waste would "interfere with law enforcement proceedings" by reducing the cooperation of such parties in voluntary cleanup programs); *Center for Auto Safety v. DOJ, supra* (release of documents compiled in connection with an inquiry into whether the Department of Justice should modify a consent decree to reduce the obligations imposed on the defendants in that case would not "interfere with enforcement proceedings," since the underlying enforcement proceeding had already concluded and the Department of Justice failed to substantiate its claim that disclosure would adversely affect future settlement negotiations).

4.1.7. Other courts have held that there is no harm to enforcement proceedings where potential defendants already have access to the requested information. *See, e.g., Coastal States Gas Corp. v. DOE*, 617 F.2d at 870. *But see Alyeska Pipeline Service Co. v. EPA,* 856 F.2d 309 (D.C. Cir. 1988), where the court affirmed withholding of plaintiff's own corporate records provided to EPA by a third party, on grounds that plaintiff was not fully aware of the scope and focus of the agency's investigation and release might result in destruction or alteration of evidence, fabrication of alibis, and witness intimidation.

4.2. Records or information also may be withheld if disclosure would "(B) deprive a person of a right to a fair trial or an impartial adjudication."

4.2.1. The only extant appellate decision on this provision noted the "sparse" caselaw and "scant" legislative history construing it, and cited the Attorney General's Memorandum on the 1974 FOIA amendments for the view that it protects the rights of private persons, including corporations; applies to both civil and criminal proceedings, as well as agency adjudications; and, "was meant to prevent disclosures from conferring an unfair advantage upon one party to an adversary proceeding or leading to prejudicial publicity in pending cases that might inflame jurors or distort administrative judgment." *Washington Post Co. v. DOJ,* 863 F.2d 96, 101 (D.C. Cir. 1988).

4.2.2. The court held that the government, in asserting a 7(B) claim, "bears the burden of showing: (1) that a trial or adjudication is pending or truly imminent; and (2) that it is more probable than not that disclosure of the material sought would seriously interfere with the fairness of those proceedings." *Id.* at 102.

4.2.3. Because the 1986 amendments did not replace "would" with "could reasonably be expected to" in this provision, the court concluded that "Congress made the threshold of 7(B) higher than for most of the other exemptions for law enforcement material." *Id.*

4.3. Records or information may be withheld if disclosure could "(C) reasonably be expected to constitute an unwarranted invasion of personal privacy."

4.3.1. This exemption, like Exemption 6, ordinarily involves a balancing of the public interest in disclosure against the degree of the invasion of privacy which would result from disclosure. *Lesar v. DOJ*, 636 F.2d at 486; *Congressional News Syndicate v. DOJ*, 438 F. Supp. 538, 542 (D.D.C. 1977). *Cf. Department of the Air Force v. Rose*, 425 U.S. 352 (1976). (*See* Chapter 9 on Personal Privacy.)

4.3.2. Unlike Exemption 6, this exemption does not require a showing of a "clearly" unwarranted invasion of personal privacy, and thus it has been interpreted as providing somewhat broader protection for privacy interests than Exemption 6. *Department of the Air Force v. Rose*, 425 U.S. at 378-79 n.16; *Fund for Constitutional Gov't v. National Archives,* 656 F.2d 856, 862 (D.C. Cir. 1981). As with Exemption 6, the balance is tilted in favor of disclosure. *See Congressional News Syndicate v. DOJ*, 438 F. Supp. at 542, *quoting Getman v. NLRB*, 450 F.2d 670, 674 (D.C. Cir. 1971), *stay denied,* 404 U.S. 1204 (1971).

4.3.3. The Supreme Court's decision in *DOJ v. Reporters Comm. for Freedom of the Press*, 489 U.S. 749 (1989), *reversing* 831 F.2d 1124 (D.C. Cir. 1987), has substantially revised the accepted approach to determining and balancing "privacy interests" and "public interests" under the FOIA.

4.3.3.1. Without dissent, the Court held "as a categorical matter that a third party's request for law enforcement records or information about a private citizen can reasonably be expected to invade that citizen's privacy, and that when the request seeks no 'official information' about a government agency, but merely records that the government happens to be storing, the invasion of privacy is 'unwarranted.'" 489 U.S. at 780.

4.3.3.2. The Court concluded that the subject of a "rap sheet"—a record containing the history of arrests, charges, convictions and incarcerations of a particular identified individual—has a "substantial" privacy interest in the FBI's indexed compilation of such records even though the events summarized in a rap sheet have been previously disclosed to the public and may still be accessible in diverse public records.

4.3.3.2.1. Although the Court cited "the common-law and dictionary understanding" of privacy interests, together with state and federal laws and policies restricting disclosure of rap sheets, to support its conclusion, the Court's reasoning was more the product of its assertion that "there is a vast difference between the public records that might be found after a diligent search of courthouse files, county archives, and local police stations throughout the country and a computerized summary located in a single clearinghouse of information." *Id.* at 764.

4.3.3.2.2. The Court, however, did not offer any specific explanation of this "vast difference." Instead, it simply identified the absence of "free availability to the public" as a key "attribute of a privacy interest" and concluded in a tautological fashion that, but for the "federal compilation," the "scattered bits of criminal history" in the rap sheets "would not otherwise be 'freely available' either to the officials who have access to the underlying files or to the general public." *Id.* at 764.

4.3.3.2.3. The Court dismissed the contention that previously public information could not subsequently be withheld under a privacy exemption, noting that "our cases have also recognized the privacy interest inherent in the nondisclosure of certain information even where the information may have been at one time public," and citing its earlier decision under Exemption 6 in *Department of the Air Force v. Rose*, 425 U.S. 352 (1976) as "most apposite." *Id.* at 767.

4.3.3.3. The Court then stated that whether an invasion of privacy is warranted "must turn on the nature of the requested document and its relationship to 'the basic purpose' of the Freedom of Information Act 'to open agency action to the light of public scrutiny,' rather than on the particular purpose for which the document is being requested." *Id.* at 772 (citation omitted).

4.3.3.3.1. In contrast to past statements broadly linking the FOIA's "basic purpose" to "the citizens' right to be informed about 'what their government is up to,'" the Court used this reference to narrowly define "the public interest that the FOIA was enacted to serve." *Id.* at 775. To this end, the Court favorably cited the suggestion that the FOIA was not intended to be "a boon to academic researchers," *id.* at n.20, and distinguished between "details to include in a news story" and "the kind of public interest for which Congress enacted the FOIA." *Id.* at 774. *See also id.* at 775 (Court blurs distinction between the public interest in disclosure and the public interest which warrants a waiver of fees by citing the statutory fee waiver standard, as amended in 1986, to show that "Congress once again expressed the core purpose of the FOIA as 'contribut[ing] significantly to public understanding *of the operations or activities of the government*'") (emphasis added).

4.3.3.3.2. Moreover, while recognizing that "[o]fficial information that sheds light on an agency's performance of its statutory duties falls squarely within [FOIA's] statutory purpose," the Court apparently doubted that a FOIA request for information about a particular private citizen would ever "shed any light on the conduct of any government agency or official." *See id.* at 773 & n.21.

4.3.3.4. Finally, although the Court acknowledged that the reference to an "unwarranted" invasion of privacy requires a court to balance the public interest in disclosure against the privacy interest in nondisclosure, the Court for the first time in the context of a FOIA "privacy" dispute adopted the position that "categorical decisions may be appropriate and individual circumstances disregarded when a case fits into a genus in which the balance characteristically tips in one direction." *Id.* at 776. *See also NLRB v. Robbins Tire & Rubber Co, supra.* The D.C. Circuit reinforced this holding in *Computer Prof'ls for Soc. Responsibility v. Secret Serv.*, 72 F.3d 897 (D.C. Cir. 1996). There, in withholding the names of persons attending a meeting of alleged computer hackers, the court noted that "even if those individuals were not suspects, their public identification with a meeting that reportedly attracted the attention of law enforcement officials would subject them to a degree of interest that would impinge upon their privacy."

4.3.3.4.1. The Court's willingness to permit "categorical balancing" in this context was, in part, based on its curious reading of the intent behind the change in this provision from "would" to "could reasonably be expected to" under the 1986 amendments. *Id.* at 777 n.22. The Court interpreted the Senate's effort to impose "a standard of reasonableness... based on an objective test" for assessing the risk of harm from a particular disclosure as "intended to replace a focus on the effect of a particular disclosure," and concluded that this "amply supports a categorical approach to the balance of private and public interests in Exemption 7(C)." *Id.*

4.3.3.4.2. The Court's citation of *FTC v. Grolier, Inc.*, 462 U.S. 19, 27-28 (1983), an Exemption 5 case, as another example of its acceptance of categorical balancing appears to foreshadow the further application of the categorical approach as the Court emphasized, without irony, that "[o]nly by construing the exemption to provide a categorical rule can the Act's purpose of expediting disclosure by means of workable rules be furthered." *Id.* at 779.

4.3.3.4.3. In applying the categorical approach to rap sheets, the Court concluded that "[t]he privacy interest in maintaining the practical obscurity of rap-sheet information will always be high." *Id.* at 780. But, the Court continued, when the subject of such a record is a private citizen and the information is in the government's control as a compilation, the privacy interest protected by the exemption "is in fact at its apex while the FOIA-based public interest in disclosure is at its nadir." *Id.*.

4.3.3.4.4. Since then, the D.C. Circuit has applied categorical balancing to names and addresses. "We now hold categorically that, unless access to the names and addresses of private individuals appearing in files within the ambit of Exemption 7(C) is necessary in order to confirm or refute compelling evidence that the agency is engaged in illegal activity, such information is exempt from disclosure." *SafeCard Services, Inc. v. SEC,* 926 F.2d 1197, 1206 (D.C. Cir. 1991). The court further noted that except in cases where names and addresses could be used to confirm or deny charges of illegal activity "there is no reason to believe that the incremental public interest in such information would ever be significant." *Id.* at 1206.

4.3.3.5. Lower courts have interpreted the decision as cutting back on disclosure under 7(C). *See Landano v. DOJ,* 956 F.2d 422 (3d Cir. 1992) *vacated and remanded*; *Nadler v. DOJ,* 955 F.2d 1479 (11th Cir. 1992); *KTVY-TV v. United States,* 919 F.2d 1465 (10th Cir. 1990); *Halloran v. VA,* 874 F.2d 315 (5th Cir. 1989); *Albuquerque Publ'g Co. v. DOJ,* 726 F. Supp. 851 (D.D.C. 1989). *But see Rosenfeld v. DOJ,* 761 F. Supp. 1440 (N.D. Cal. 1991) (concluding that there was a heightened public interest in records of questionable FBI monitoring of student groups). *See also Ray v. DOJ,* 908 F.2d 1549 (11th Cir. 1990), *rev'd,* 502 U.S. 164 (1991) ("atypical case" under Exemption 6 where request about private individuals involves public interest in federal immigration policies).

4.3.4. The exemption applies to matters which under normal circumstances "would prove personally embarrassing to an individual of normal sensibilities...." *Committee on Masonic Homes v. NLRB*, 414 F. Supp. 426, 431 (E.D. Pa. 1976), *judgment vacated, rev'd and remanded in part*, 556 F.2d 214 (3d Cir. 1977); *Rural Housing Alliance v. USDA*, 498 F.2d at 77; *Rushford v. Civiletti,* 485 F. Supp. 477, 480 (D.D.C. 1980), *aff'd mem.*, 656 F.2d 900 (D.C. Cir. 1981).

4.3.4.1 Thus, information in a law enforcement agency's file which indicates that a named individual has been investigated for suspected criminal or other wrongful activity is, at least as a threshold matter, sufficient without more to trigger scrutiny under Exemption 7(C). *Stern v. FBI*, 737 F.2d at 91-92 ("individuals have a strong interest in not being associated unwarrantedly with alleged criminal activity"); *Abramson v. FBI,* 566 F. Supp. 1371 (D.D.C. 1983) (public disclosure of the fact that an individual was investigated by the FBI could subject the individual to embarrassment or harassment); *Fund for Constitutional Gov't v. National Archives,* 656 F.2d at 863; *Baez v. DOJ*, 647 F.2d 1328, 1338 (D.C. Cir. 1980). *See also Antonelli v. FBI*, 721 F.2d 615, 618 (7th Cir. 1983) (court upheld FBI's refusal to confirm or deny the existence of records sought in third-party request on grounds that "merely confirming that a particular file exists and stating the applicable exemption could reveal too much information where the requester seeks access to another person's files.... At the least, revealing that a third party has been the subject of FBI investigations is likely to constitute an invasion of that person's privacy that implicates the protections of Exemptions 6 and 7"); *Dunkelberger v. DOJ,* 906 F.2d 779, 781-82 (D.C. Cir. 1990) (FBI agent "has a particular interest in not being associated unwarrantedly with the misconduct alleged"). *But see Detroit Free Press, Inc. v. DOJ*, No. 93-74692 (E.D. Mich., Apr. 25, 1994) (bench order), *aff'd*, 73 F.3d 93 (6th Cir. 1996). There, the judge ruled that mug shots were not protected, noting that "other pictures can be taken by the press under other circumstances in the course of the prosecution, they simply are not private matters, and their appearance at the time of booking may well be of interest in examination of how the Marshal's Office conducts its booking procedures, how government works, essentially, whether the operations of this part of the judicial process are as fair, as open, and as reasonably conducted and appropriately conducted as any other part that has already been thrown open to public scrutiny and for good reason." For a case in which the court ruled the other way based on similar facts, *see Times Picayune Publ'g Co. v. DOJ*, 37 F. Supp. 2d 472 (E.D. La. 1999), which involved mug shots of Dick DeBartolo, the owner of the San Francisco 49ers. *Beck v. DOJ*, 997 F.2d 1489 (D.C. Cir. 1993) (plaintiff must provide evidence that release of records concerning investigation of low-level employees is in public interest before presumption in favor of non-disclosure can be overcome).

4.3.4.2. The D.C. Circuit has ruled that where a plaintiff asserts the government waived its exemption claims by prior public disclosure, the burden of proof shifts to the plaintiff to document what information was actually disclosed. *Davis v. DOJ*, 968 F.2d 1276 (D.C. Cir. 1992).

4.3.4.3. In such cases, the courts may still be required to conduct a balancing of the interests involved. *See, e.g., Emerson v. DOJ*, 603 F. Supp. 459 (D.D.C. 1985); *Lame v. DOJ*, 654 F.2d 917, 923 n.6 (3d Cir. 1981) (there is no *per se* rule that mere connection of an individual with a criminal investigation constitutes unwarranted invasion of privacy);

Common Cause v. National Archives and Records Serv., 628 F.2d 179, 184 (D.C. Cir. 1980); *see also Cohen v. EPA, supra* (information concerning potential responsibility of individuals investigated in connection with hazardous waste does not fall within a protected privacy interest, since it relates to business, not personal, activities and the dumping of hazardous substances is a matter of urgent public concern); *Van Bourg, Allen, Weinberg & Roger v. NLRB*, 751 F.2d 982 (9th Cir. 1985) (affidavits containing details concerning the "personalities, activities, biases and proclivities of employers, union members and officials" are exempt, while affidavits discussing only legitimate union activities without "intimate details" must be disclosed).

4.3.4.4. However, the D.C. Circuit has concluded that the highly intrusive nature of disclosures reflecting the names of individuals who have been investigated but ultimately not charged with criminal activity requires withholding unless "exceptional interests militate in favor of disclosure." *Fund for Constitutional Government*, 656 F.2d at 866. *See also Holy* Spirit *Association v. FBI*, 683 F.2d 562 (D.C. Cir. 1982); *Librach v. FBI,* 587 F.2d 372 (8th Cir.), *cert. denied*, 440 U.S. 910 (1978) (names of persons investigated by FBI for suspected criminal activity are exempt where persons were neither indicted nor tried); *Rushford v. Civiletti*, 485 F. Supp. at 479 (publication of the fact that a federal judge has been the subject of a closed criminal investigation would have a severe impact upon both his personal life and official performance). The D.C. Circuit ruled, in *McCutcheon v. HHS,* 30 F.3d 183 (D.C. Cir. 1994), that names of persons investigated by the Office of Scientific Integrity where no wrongdoing was found and the names of complainants were both protected by Exemption 7(C). The court found that disclosure could "carry a stigma and can damage a career." It noted that even if disclosure would allow the requester to monitor the thoroughness of the agency's work, "we will not force the agency to turn over the names of the complainants simply because someone has accused it of wrongdoing."

4.3.4.5. In *Hunt v. FBI*, 972 F.2d 286, 288 (9th Cir. 1992), the court refused to allow disclosure of the investigation of an FBI agent with all identifiers redacted to a prisoner who had charged the agent with sexual misconduct. The court pointed out that "the agent's identity could be easily traced by anyone having access to the file, and, of course, was known to the requester, Hunt...Disclosure of any material contents of this file, coupled with the public availability of Hunt's FOIA request naming the agent, would make redaction of the file a pointless exercise."

4.3.4.6. In *Lissner v. U.S. Customs Service,* 241 F.3d 1220 (9th Cir. 2001), the court found that information concerning the mitigation of a fine to two police officers charged with smuggling steroids from Mexico was not covered by Exemption 7(C). The court pointed out that police officers had a diminished expectation of privacy and that the lack of any evidence of bad faith on the part of the agency did not necessarily lead to the conclusion that disclosure was not in the public interest.

4.3.4.7. "Exceptional" public interests may include circumstances where the third party is a "public figure." In such cases, the individual has a diminished expectation of privacy, and this factor may tip the 7(C) balance in favor of disclosure. *Common Cause v. National Archives and Records Serv.*, 628 F.2d at 184 (special circumstances to be examined include the fact that the individuals whose privacy interests were invoked were candidates for public office and the records related to campaign contributions that were required by law to be reported publicly); *Congressional News Syndicate v. DOJ*, 438 F. Supp. at 543-544 (names of contributors and recipients of campaign contributions investigated by Watergate Special Prosecution Force are not exempt because of "opprobrium" that attaches to those investigated as part of Watergate inquiry, even though not indicted, in view of policy of Federal Corrupt Practices Act that their names be made public). *But see Fund for Constitutional Gov't v. National Archives,* 656 F.2d at 866 (privacy of individuals investigated but not charged may not be overridden by a "general public curiosity"); *Bast v. DOJ*, 665 F.2d 1251, 1255 (D.C. Cir. 1981) (government officials do not surrender rights to personal privacy when they accept a public appointment).

4.3.4.8. In *Dow Jones & Co. v. DOJ*, No. 94-0527, 1995 WL 6155 (S.D.N.Y. Jan. 5, 1995), the court found that a copy of the suicide note of Vincent Foster available for public inspection at the Department of Justice was not protected by 7(C). The judge noted that "although Mr. Foster's suicide note may be intensely personal, the written word is qualitatively different from an audio recording of the last words of the [*Challenger*] astronauts...[T]he missing pieces of the Note, and therefore the physical look of the Note, are an integral part of the public's interest."

4.3.5. Privacy claims may outlive the individual. In *Favish v. Office of Independent Counsel*, 217 F.3d 1168 (9th Cir. 2000), the court upheld the denial of access to Vince Foster's autopsy photos, noting the pain such disclosure would cause his family. In *Campbell v. DOJ*, 164 F.3d 20 (D.C. Cir. 1998), the court indicated that the privacy interests of deceased individuals should be re-assessed in light of the Supreme Court's ruling in *Swidler & Berlin v. U.S.*, 524 U.S. 399 (1998), which had found the attorney-client privilege could be claimed even when the client was dead. *See also Accuracy in Media, Inc. v. National Park Serv.*, 194 F.3d 120 (D.C. Cir. 1999), which, following the holding in *Campbell*, indicated the privacy interests of Vince Foster's family must be considered.

4.3.6. Some courts have held that the exemption protects the identities of FBI agents and other non-policymaking officials involved in investigations, where their interest in not being harassed in the performance of their official duties outweighs the public interest in disclosure. *See New England Apple Council v. Donovan,* 725 F.2d 139 (1st Cir. 1984) (protection under 7(C) is not limited to cases involving "private facts" or an actual showing of harassment or other harm to government officials); *Ingle v. DOJ*, 698 F.2d 259 (6th Cir. 1983); *Lesar v. DOJ, supra; Baez v. DOJ, supra; Lame v. DOJ, supra.*

4.3.6.1. However, such protection does not apply across the board for identities of FBI agents, and can be overcome where, for example, the performance of a particular agent is called into question. *See Castaneda v. United States,* 757 F.2d 1010 (9th Cir. 1985) ("where it appears that the motives or truthfulness of the investigator are in doubt, the public need for supervision and disclosure is necessarily heightened"); *Lesar v. DOJ, supra; Baez v. DOJ, supra. Compare Cunningham v. FBI,* 501 F. Supp. 898 (D.D.C. 1980) (names of SEC investigators not exempt, since there is a public interest in subjecting them to inquiry) *with Iglesias v. CIA,* 525 F. Supp. 547 (D.D.C. 1981) (agents may be able to provide valuable information in the context of a related civil suit).

4.3.6.2. A lengthy analysis of the balancing process under 7(C) appears in *Stern v. FBI*, 737 F.2d at 91-94, where, in the context of "potential association with notorious and serious allegations of criminal wrongdoing," the D.C. Circuit panel concluded that the balance favored disclosure of the name of a high-level FBI employee "found to have participated deliberately and knowingly in the withholding of damaging information in an important inquiry," but did not favor disclosure of names of lower-level employees "found to have contributed only inadvertently to the wrongdoing under investigation."

4.3.6.3. In *Schmerler v. FBI,* 696 F. Supp. 717 (D.D.C. 1988), the court held that the names of FBI agents involved in a murder investigation more than 50 years ago could not be withheld under 7(C) or (D) where their involvement had been fully revealed by authorized disclosures. The court also ruled that the agency should check not only its case records, but its pension and personnel records to determine whether any of the agents whose names it sought to withhold had died. If the agent is deceased, "a particularized need to continue withholding the information must be presented." However, this decision was later reversed by the D.C. Circuit, *Schmerler v. FBI*, 900 F.2d 333 (D.C. Cir. 1990).

4.3.6.4. An Exemption 7(C) claim for the identity of an FBI supervisor was rejected in *Butler v. DOJ,* No. 86-2255 (D.D.C. Feb. 3, 1994), where the court noted that "FBI agents and other law enforcement personnel 'may not have as great a claim to privacy as that afforded ordinarily to private citizens.'" The court added that "the public interest in seeing that [the plaintiff's] due process rights are protected in his criminal case is significant. Moreover, the defendant has made bald claims, unsupported by any factual evidence, that the release of these names will subject the FBI supervisory personnel to harassment."

4.3.7. In *Manna v. DOJ*, 51 F.3d 1158 (3d Cir. 1995), the Third Circuit ruled that the requester's background as an organized crime figure heightened the privacy concerns in identifying information. However, the dissent noted that "while I agree that this information is a cognizable concern under Exemption 7(F), I disagree with the government that the threat of retaliation is a cognizable concern under Exemption 7(C). Retaliation has nothing to do with privacy, and, moreover, such a construction of Exemption 7(C) would eliminate the need for Exemption 7(F)."

4.3.8. Despite the fact that Exemption 7 contains a separate provision designed to protect the identities of confidential sources (*see* paragraphs on 7(D) in this outline, *infra*), some courts have also invoked the privacy provision of Exemption 7 to withhold the identities of informants who may not technically qualify as "confidential sources" under 7(D). *See, e.g., L & C Marine Transport, Ltd. v. United States,* 740 F.2d 919 (11th Cir. 1984) (employee witnesses interviewed during OSHA investigation are exempt even though identities could ultimately be ascertained through discovery, since the "linking" of the names with their respective witness statements could cause "problems with their jobs and with their livelihoods"); *Kiraly v. FBI*, 728 F.2d 273 (6th Cir. 1984); *New England Apple Council v. Donovan, supra. But see Miller v. Webster*, 483 F. Supp. 883 (N.D. Ill. 1979), *aff'd in part and rev'd in part sub nom. Miller v. Bell*, 661 F.2d 623 (7th Cir. 1981), *cert. denied sub nom. Miller v. Webster*, 456 U.S. 960 (1982) (names of persons interviewed in investigation of alleged wiretap on plaintiff's phone must be disclosed where disclosure reveals nothing of a private nature and interviewees had no expectation of privacy); *Diamond v. FBI*, 532 F. Supp. 216 (S.D.N.Y. 1981), *aff'd*, 707 F.2d 75 (2d Cir. 1983) (7(C) does not apply where source has died, and government is required to determine from those still living whether they oppose release of their names and fact of cooperation with FBI investigation). *See also* those cases which have held Exemption 7(C) inapplicable to witness statements in unfair labor practice proceedings, since the matters involved no personal privacy concerns and statements were made by individuals who could be called to testify publicly at trial. *Associated Dry Goods Corp. v. NLRB,* 455 F. Supp. 802 (S.D.N.Y. 1978); *Poss v. NLRB,* 565 F.2d 654 (10th Cir. 1977). *But see Kiraly v. FBI, supra* (Exemption 7(C) protects records concerning FBI informant who not only testified at trial, but has since died).

4.3.9. In *Providence Journal Co. v. FBI*, 602 F.2d 1010 (1st Cir. 1979), *cert. denied*, 444 U.S. 1071 (1980), the court held that the *manner* of obtaining the information, rather than its *content*, was controlling with respect to applicability of 7(C) where the records were obtained through warrantless electronic surveillance by the FBI. The court reasoned that Title III of the Omnibus Crime Control Act of 1968, which prohibits the disclosure of illegally intercepted information, demonstrated that Congress had already weighed the competing interests and determined that the risk to privacy created by unlawful surveillance outweighed any possible public interest in disclosure.

4.3.10. Corporations do not have the same expectation of privacy as do individuals. *See, e.g., Public Citizen Health Research Group v. HEW*, 477 F. Supp. 595, 603 (D.D.C. 1979).

4.4. Records or information may be withheld if disclosure "(D) could reasonably be expected to disclose the identity of a confidential source, including a State, local, or foreign agency or authority or any private institution which furnished information on a confidential basis, and, in the case of a record of information compiled by criminal law enforcement authority in the course of a criminal investigation, information furnished by a confidential source."

4.4.1. Unlike Exemption 7(A), 7(D) does not require a showing that enforcement proceedings are currently underway, but only that the materials sought were compiled for law enforcement purposes. *Founding Church of Scientology v. Regan*, 670 F.2d 1158 (D.C. Cir. 1981), *cert. denied*, 456 U.S. 976 (1982). This would also presumably be true for Exemptions 7(C), (E) and (F).

4.4.2. The additional requirement in 7(D) that records be "compiled by a criminal law enforcement agency in the course of a criminal investigation" has been interpreted as involving an analysis identical to that used in applying the Exemption 7 threshold test ("investigatory records compiled for law enforcement purposes")—i.e., whether the records were compiled as part of an investigation that has a colorable nexus to the agency's law enforcement duties. *Shaw v. FBI*, 749 F.2d 58 (D.C. Cir. 1984). *See also* 3.5., *supra*. In *Shaw*, the D.C. Circuit also ruled that the crime which makes the inquiry a "criminal investigation" for purposes of 7(D) need not be a crime under *federal* law. "Where, for a federally authorized purpose, a federal criminal investigatory agency has opened an inquiry into a crime perpetrated under the law of another jurisdiction, there seems to us no reason why confidential information would be considered any less deserving of protection." 749 F.2d at 64.

4.4.3. In civil cases, this clause protects the name and other identifying details which might reasonably be found to lead to the disclosure of a "confidential source," when there was an express or implied assurance of confidentiality. H.R. Conf. Rep. No. 93-1380, 93d Cong., 2d Sess. 13 (1974). *See Pope v. United States*, 599 F.2d 1383 (5th Cir. 1979); *Canadian Javelin, Ltd. v. SEC*, 501 F. Supp. 898, 903 (D.D.C. 1980) (agency failed to meet its burden of demonstrating a promise of confidentiality). *Terkel v. Kelly*, 599 F.2d 214 (7th Cir. 1979), *cert. denied,* 444 U.S. 1013 (1980) (remanded for determination of why "symbol nos." would reveal confidential source). *Cf. Nemetz v. Dep't of Treasury,* 446 F. Supp. 102, 105 (N.D. Ill. 1978) (under Privacy Act, § 552a(k)(5), "[e]vidence must be presented based on personal knowledge that an express or implied promise of confidentiality was given to each source sought to be exempted under this provision").

4.4.4. If a record is compiled by the FBI or other criminal law enforcement authority during a criminal investigation, and it contains information furnished by a confidential source, all of that information may be withheld. Prior to enactment of the 1986 FOIA amendments, the provision specified that its protection was limited to "confidential information furnished *only* by the confidential source." H.R. Conf. Rep. No. 93-1380, 93d Cong., 2d Sess. 13 (1974). *See Scherer v. Kelley,* 584 F.2d 170 (7th Cir. 1978); *Nix v. United States*, 572 F.2d 998 (4th Cir. 1978); *Church of Scientology of California v. DOJ*, 612 F.2d 417 (9th Cir. 1979). Courts have held, however, that whether information is protected from disclosure under 7(D) depends on whether the *source* is confidential, not on the contents of the document sought. *See, e.g., Lesar v. DOJ*, 636 F.2d at 492 (once the court determines that the information was supplied by a confidential source "all such information obtained from the confidential source receives protection"); *Shaw v. FBI, supra* (photographs of a public event constitute "confidential information" within the meaning of 7(D) so long as they were supplied by a "confidential source"); *Duffin v. Carlson*, 636 F.2d 709, 712 (D.C. Cir. 1980) (irrelevant whether the information would actually reveal the identity of the confidential source). *See also Radowich v. U.S. Attorney*, 658 F.2d 957 (4th Cir. 1981) (exemption protects information furnished by a confidential source in the course of a criminal investigation, regardless of whether the information, in whole or in part, might have been available from some other source). These results were codified in the 1986 amendments. *See* this chapter, *supra.*

4.4.4.1. The passage of time has no legal bearing on whether information should remain confidential. *Schmerler v. FBI,* 900 F.2d 333, 336 (D.C. Cir. 1990) ("That nearly sixty years have passed since the confidential sources were interviewed and that the sources may have died are of no moment to the analysis. Once the government has demonstrated that the sources are confidential, the statute does not require the government to justify the continued withholding against claims that the confidentiality is no longer warranted or that the public interest weighs in favor of disclosure.").

4.4.5. Similarly, as a result of the 1986 amendments deleting the words "confidential" and "only," an agency conducting a lawful national security intelligence investigation may now also protect in its entirety *any* information furnished by a confidential source.

4.4.6. Over the years, a conflict arose among the federal appellate courts regarding the burden of proof, and the nature of supporting evidence required, for an agency, especially the FBI, to claim that a source is "confidential" within the meaning of this exemption. Although most Circuits had concluded that a presumption of confidentiality arises whenever any individual or institutional source supplies information to the FBI during a criminal investigation, *see, e.g., Nadler v. DOJ,* 955 F.2d 1479, 1484-87 (11th Cir. 1992): *Schmerler v. FBI*, 900 F.2d 333, 337 (D.C. Cir. 1990); *Donovan v. FBI*, 806 F.2d 55 (2d Cir. 1986); and *Miller v. Bell*, 661 F.2d 623, 627 (7th Cir. 1981), *cert. den.*, 456 U.S. 960 (1982), the Third Circuit had rejected this categorical presumption and ruled that the Government must justify a 7(D) claim with "detailed explanations relating to each alleged confidential source." *Landano v. DOJ,* 956 F.2d 422, 435 (3d Cir. 1992), citing *Lame v. DOJ*, 654 F.2d 917, 928 (3d Cir. 1981).

4.4.7. The Supreme Court, in vacating and remanding *Landano*, ruled that a source "should be deemed confidential if the source furnished information with the understanding that the FBI would not divulge the communications except to the extent the Bureau thought necessary for law enforcement purposes." *DOJ v. Landano*, 508 U.S. 165 (1993). The Court rejected the assertion of any categorical presumption, but ruled that a presumption will arise when "more narrowly defined circumstances," such as the nature of the crime investigated and the source's relation to it, "support an inference of confidentiality." *Id.* at 2024.

4.4.7.1. Since *Landano*, courts have found various circumstances in which confidentiality could be implied. Speaking broadly about these circumstances, the Tenth Circuit pointed out, in *Hale v. DOJ*, 99 F.3d 1025 (10th Cir. 1996), that "all crime, of course, has the potential to be intimidating and to engender anxiety in those who testify about it. However, in the absence of an express agreement of confidentiality, the 'nature of the crime' will ordinarily support an inference of confidentiality only when there are discrete aspects of the crime that make it particularly likely that a source reasonably would fear reprisal." In *Williams v. FBI*, 69 F.3d 1155 (D.C. Cir. 1995), the court found that sources supplying information about a group of black militants could be protected both because of the nature of the crimes—rebellion and insurrection, and advocating the overthrow of the government—and closeness of the relationship between the source and the group being investigated. The court noted that "sources were so close to Afro Set that they could supply intelligence information to local law enforcement officials who would have been vulnerable to retaliation if their cooperation had been disclosed."

4.4.7.2. Other courts have identified situations in which an implied assurance of confidentiality would not be present. The D.C. Circuit pointed out in *Computer Prof'ls for Soc. Responsibility v. Secret Serv.*, 72 F.3d at 899, that "the Service offered no evidence that fear of retaliation by [computer] hackers is sufficiently widespread to justify an inference that sources of information relating to computer crimes expect their identities and the information they provide to be kept confidential." Casual business or social relationships with the subject of an investigation are not adequate to imply confidentiality. In *Quinon v. FBI*, 86 F.3d at 1225, the court observed that "it is simply not reasonable to assume, for example, that anyone who provides the FBI with exculpatory information about a professional associate will be 'embarrassed' to have that fact disclosed."

4.4.7.3. While the *Landano* court suggested that certain circumstances related to the nature of the crime could support an implied assurance of confidentiality, *Ortiz v. HHS*, 70 F.3d 729 (2d Cir. 1995), a post-*Landano* decision, found that the anonymity of the source suggested the source would not have come forward without some assurance of confidentiality. The court noted that "under these circumstances, where serious allegations were made by a source who chose to remain anonymous and was privy to information of a personal nature regarding Ortiz which could reasonably have been thought to lead to a criminal investigation, it is reasonable to presume that the information would not have been provided if confidentiality had not been assured."

4.4.8. The term "confidential source" may also apply to institutions as well as individuals. Courts have held that foreign, state or local law enforcement agencies supplying information to the FBI may be considered to be "confidential sources" (and in criminal investigations, all such information kept secret) on the policy ground that their cooperation with the FBI might otherwise be impaired. *Shaw v. FBI, supra; Founding Church of Scientology v. Regan, supra; Lesar v. DOJ, supra; Baez v. DOJ, supra; Church of Scientology of California v. DOJ, supra; Nix v. United States, supra. See also Payne v. DOJ,* 904 F.2d 695 (3d Cir. 1990) (criminal laboratory tests from the FBI requested by a local police department are protected by 7(D)). This body of caselaw was codified by the 1986 amendments. *See* this outline, *supra.*

4.4.9. The NLRB's contention that witnesses in unfair labor practices proceedings are confidential sources under (7)(D) has generally been rejected because there has been no promise of confidentiality, either express or implied. Indeed, witnesses apparently expect their names and testimony to be revealed at hearing. *See, e.g., Van Bourg, Allen, Weinberg & Roger v. NLRB, supra; Nemacolin Mines, Corp. v. NLRB, supra. But see Irons v. FBI,* 811 F.2d 681, 689 (1st Cir. 1987) (court rejected "*per se* potential witness rule" and held that "it was wrong as a matter of law to equate an express or implied agreement to testify, without more, with a waiver" of confidentiality). In later proceedings, the court further clarified that the actual giving of testimony waives that part of the exemption which governs "identity" information, and also waives protection for (1) the subject matter of testimony, and (2) all related information as measured by a hypothetical scope of cross-examination; otherwise, the exemption may still protect other information furnished to the government by the witness in confidence. *Irons v. FBI,* 851 F.2d 532 (1st Cir. 1988). The full court reversed, reasoning that the waiver doctrine should not be applied where there was no indication that the source actually wanted to make public the information that was not in fact made public and the agency opposed disclosure. *Irons v. FBI,* 880 F.2d 1446 (1st Cir. 1989) (en banc). The D.C. Circuit has taken this rationale one step further indicating that testimony creates no waiver of the confidentiality of the information provided *or* of the identity of the source itself. *Parker v. DOJ,* 934 F.2d 375 (D.C. Cir. 1991). *See Burge v. Eastburn,* 934 F.2d 577 (5th Cir. 1991).

4.4.10. Exemption 7(D) has been found to provide protection for an "indirect confidential source," who has had no contact with the defendant agency, but who was assured confidentiality by another law enforcement agency which in turn supplied the information to the defendant. *Sands v. Murphy,* 633 F.2d 968 (1st Cir. 1980).

4.4.11. The Sixth Circuit upheld 7(D) protection for an FBI informant despite the fact that the individual was dead and his identity as an FBI informant was already known, reasoning that "the concern of the court should also be upon the effect a disclosure would have on other informants." *Kiraly v. FBI,* 728 F.2d at 279. *See also Stassi v. DOJ,* No. 78-0538 (D.D.C. Apr. 12, 1979) (information from deceased informant withheld because disclosure, "notwithstanding the fact that [the informant] is deceased, would inhibit other informants from coming forward").

4.4.12. In *Bennett v. DEA,* 155 F. Supp. 2d 36 (D.D.C. 1999), the court ruled that persuasive evidence of a suspicious relationship between the source and the agency provided a public interest in disclosing records about him.

Exemption 7

4.5. Records may also be withheld if production would "(E) disclose techniques and procedures for law enforcement investigations or prosecutions, or would disclose guidelines for law enforcement investigations or prosecutions if such disclosure could reasonably be expected to risk circumvention of the law."

4.5.1. The provision does not exempt all investigative procedures and techniques from disclosure. In particular, it does not protect *routine* techniques and procedures already well known to the public, such as ballistics tests, fingerprinting, and other scientific tests or commonly known techniques. *See* H.R. Conf. Rep. No. 93-1380, 93d Cong., 2d Sess. 12 (1974). This interpretation was not altered by the 1986 amendment. *See* discussion in this outline, *supra. See, e.g. Albuquerque Publ'g Co. v. DOJ,* 726 F. Supp. at 858 (The court ordered agency to explain further why certain techniques are considered unknown to the public, stating that "information pertaining to techniques that are commonly described or depicted in movies, popular novels, stories or magazines, or on television" cannot be withheld. The court included "eavesdropping, wiretapping, and surreptitious tape recording and photographing" within this category.). *Jaffe v. CIA*, 573 F. Supp. 377, 387 (D.D.C. 1983) (7(E) applies to information regarding "obscure or secret techniques"); *Dunway v. Webster*, 519 F. Supp. at 1082-83 (exemption is to be applied only to techniques and procedures generally unknown to the public and, absent any explanation from the government, court would not assume that disclosure would result in revelation of investigative techniques which were so unique as to warrant exemption). *But see Shaver v. Bell*, 433 F. Supp. 438 (N.D. Ga. 1977) (*dictum*: "bait money" falls within 7(E)); *Ott v. Levi*, 419 F. Supp. 750 (E.D. Mo. 1976) (1954 arson laboratory tests exempt); *Malloy v. DOJ*, 457 F. Supp. 543, 545 (D.D.C. 1978) (FBI material on bank security devices and investigative leads exempt); *Martinez v. FBI*, No. 82-1547 (D.D.C. Oct. 11, 1983) (7(E) held applicable to certain procedures even though commonly known, where their use "in concert with other elements of an investigation and in their totality directed toward a specific investigative goal constitute[s] a 'technique' which merits protection to insure its future effectiveness").

4.5.2. Nor does the exemption apply to records which fall within the scope of § 552(a)(2) of the FOIA, such as administrative staff manuals and instructions to staff. *See* legislative history cited above, H.R. Conf. Rep. No. 93-1380, 93d Cong., 2d Sess. 12 (1974). *See also Firestone Tire & Rubber Co. v. Coleman*, 432 F. Supp. 1359 (N.D. Ohio 1976) (memoranda setting forth National Highway Safety Administration's policy regarding sampling plans for tire safety tests are "instructions to staff" and not exempt under 7(E)). *But see Fund for a Conservative Majority v. Federal Election Commission*, No. 84-1342 (D.D.C. Feb. 26, 1985) (staff memoranda recommending an audit of a political committee held exempt under 7(E), as well as under Exemption 2 (internal agency rules), where contested material would reveal which of the FEC's many reporting requirements will be focused on during the review process).

4.5.3. Similarly, FBI records regarding the relocation of witnesses under the Department of Justice's Witness Security Program are exempt because disclosure would jeopardize the effectiveness of the program. *Librach v. FBI*, 587 F.2d 372, 373 (8th Cir. 1978).

4.5.4. The 1986 amendment regarding "guidelines for law enforcement investigations or prosecutions" expanded the scope of subparagraph (E) to codify the D.C. Circuit's *en banc* decision in *Crooker v. BATF,* 670 F.2d 1051 (D.C. Cir. 1981). See discussion in Chapter 4 on Exemption 2.

4.6. Information is protected where disclosure would "(F) endanger the life or physical safety of any individual." The exemption is self-explanatory; however, it was expanded through the 1986 amendments from prior coverage limited to "law enforcement personnel." Cases interpreting the earlier version of the provision applied it to the identities of FBI agents, or other law enforcement personnel, as well as information that might lead to their identities, where their safety would be endangered by disclosure. *See, e.g., Maroscia v. Levi*, 569 F.2d 1000 (7th Cir. 1977); *Scherer v. Kelley*, 584 F.2d at 176; *Shaver v. Bell*, 433 F. Supp. at 441. *See also* discussion of 1986 amendments in this outline, *supra*.

CHAPTER 11

Exemption 8—Records of Financial Institutions

Eleanor H. Smith

1. **Exemption 8 provides that the FOIA does not apply to matters that are: contained in or related to examination, operating, or condition reports prepared by, on behalf of, or for the use of an agency responsible for the regulation or supervision of financial institutions.**

2. **Legislative History.**

2.1 The legislative history explaining Exemption 8 is brief; however, as noted by the court in *Consumers Union v. Heimann*, 589 F.2d 531 (D.C. Cir. 1978), the Senate and House reports "are in striking accord." *Id.* at 534 n.10.

2.2. The Senate Report states that Exemption 8 is: directed specifically to insuring the security of our financial institutions by making available only to the government agencies responsible for the regulation or supervision of such institutions the examination, operating, or condition reports prepared by on behalf of, or for the use of such agencies. S. Rep. No. 813, 89th Cong., 1st Sess. at 10 (1965), reprinted in *Freedom of Information Act Source Book: Legislative Materials, Cases, Articles*, Subcommittee on Administrative Practice and Procedure of the Senate Committee on the Judiciary, U.S. Senate, 93d Cong., 2d Sess. 45 (1974) (hereinafter cited as "*1974 Source Book*").

2.3. The House Report explains the rationale behind the exemption: This exemption is designed to insure the security and integrity of financial institutions, for the sensitive details collected by Government agencies which regulate these institutions could, if indiscriminately disclosed, cause great harm. H. Rep. No. 1497, 89th Cong. 2d Sess. 11 (1966), *reprinted in* 1966 U.S. Code Cong. & Admin. News 2418, 2428, and *1974 Source Book* at 32.

2.4. Although the primary purpose of Congress in adopting Exemption 8 was to "ensure the security of financial institutions" against the possibility that "disclosure of examination, operation, and condition reports containing frank evaluations of the investigated banks might undermine public confidence and cause unwarranted runs of banks," *Consumers Union*, 589 F.2d at 534, courts have noted that a broader, secondary purpose "appears to have been to safeguard the relationship between the banks and their supervising agencies," on grounds that "banks would cooperate less than fully with federal authorities" if "the details of bank examinations were made freely available to the public and to banking competitors." *Id.*

2.5. Exemption 8 has been criticized as both overbroad and superfluous. *See* literature cited in *Consumers Union*, 589 F.2d at 535 n.19.

3. **What are "Financial Institutions?"**

3.1. Neither the Act, its legislative history, nor subsequent case law has specifically defined "financial institutions."

Exemption 8

3.2. One district court implicitly approved the SEC's interpretation of "financial institution" set forth in a rule promulgated pursuant to another statute, 15 U.S.C. § 79(c). The SEC defines the term to include banks, trust companies, investment bankers, and banking associations or firms. *Id.* The court ruled, however, that the term did not extend to national securities exchanges or broker-dealers. *M.A. Schapiro & Co. v. SEC*, 339 F. Supp. 467, 470 (D.D.C. 1972).

3.3. Another district court impliedly approved the Federal Reserve Board's position that Exemption 8 covered bank holding companies and similar institutions that are subject to examination under the Bank Holding Company Act, 12 U.S.C. § 1844(c). *Kaye v. Burns*, 411 F. Supp. 897, 900 (S.D.N.Y. 1976).

3.4. Subsequently, the district court in *Mermelstein v. SEC,* 629 F. Supp. 672 (D.D.C. 1986), contradicted the *Schapiro* court in holding that securities exchanges are "financial institutions" under Exemption 8.

3.4.1. The court in *Mermelstein* dismissed the *Schapiro* court's statement on securities exchanges as "*dicta*" that was based on a definition in an SEC rule promulgated "for an altogether different purpose." *Id.* at 673.

3.4.2. Moreover, the court's review of the Government in the Sunshine Act, a statute which is closely related to the FOIA and which was enacted four years after the *Schapiro* decision, led it to conclude that "Congress never acceded to the *Schapiro* court's restrictive census of 'financial institutions'...but, to the contrary, has since given sufficient indication that it expects securities exchanges to be numbered among them when it comes to ordering public disclosure of matters relating to their regulation." *Id.* at 674. *See also* 5 U.S.C. § 552b(c)(8) and (9)(A); S.Rep. No. 354, 94th Cong., 1st Sess. 24 (1975), *reprinted in Government In The Sunshine Source Book: Legislative History, Texts, and other Documents,* Committees on Government Operations, U.S. Senate and House of Representatives, 94th Cong., 2d Sess. 219 (1976)("*Sunshine Source Book*").

3.4.3. "To the extent it may be of value to the Commission in its supervision of the BSE," the court in *Mermelstein* viewed information concerning disciplinary proceedings by the Boston Stock Exchange against the requester's firm as "squarely within the spirit and purpose of Exemption 8," and refused to conduct an *in camera* review to see if such information was segregable from the rest of an SEC report concerning its inspection of the BSE. *Id.* at 675.

3.5. The legislative history of Exemption 8 suggests that the exemption applies only to reports by federal regulators and supervisors of banks of deposit. H.R. Rep. 1497, *supra*; S.Rep. No. 813, *supra*. However, a panel of the D.C. Circuit, basing its conclusion on the "plain-meaning" rules of statutory construction and a legal dictionary definition of "financial institution," has ruled that Exemption 8 is not limited to depository institutions. *Public Citizen v. Farm Credit Administration,* 938 F.2d 290 (D.C. Cir. 1991). The court reaffirmed that the exemption is not confined to cases in which disclosure of an examination report could cause a run on the examined financial institution. *Id.* at 292-93.

4. **Are the requested records "contained in or related to examination, operating, or condition reports?"**

4.1. The "broad, all-inclusive scope" of this language in Exemption 8 was reaffirmed in *Gregory v. Federal Deposit Insurance Corporation,* 631 F.2d 896, 898 (D.C. Cir. 1980), *citing Consumers Union,* 589 F.2d at 535. The court concluded that "Congress looked to the nature and source of the material and determined to provide absolute protection regardless of the circumstances underlying the regulatory agency's receipt or preparation of examination, operating or condition reports." *Id.* at 898.

4.2. Thus, Exemption 8 has been broadly interpreted as blocking disclosure, even when an institution's financial condition is not at issue or the information sought does not reflect upon financial soundness. *See, e.g., Fagot v. Fed. Deposit Ins. Corp.*, 584 F. Supp. 1168 (D.P.R. 1984) (memoranda showing FDIC action in investigating bank counsel's "claims of irregularities in the bank's procedures").

4.3. Even when the requested records pertain to a bank which has failed and whose financial soundness can thus no longer be harmed disclosure has been blocked on the ground that Exemption 8 "was drawn to protect not simply each individual bank but the integrity of financial institutions as an industry." *Gregory*, 631 F.2d at 898.

4.4. "[T]here is nothing in the legislative history to indicate that Congress...intended Exemption 8 to apply only to the varieties of bank examinations then extant." *Consumers Union*, 589 F.2d at 534. Thus, the court rejected the argument that Exemption 8 does not protect audits conducted under statutes which were enacted *after* the FOIA, imposed new obligations on banks, and provided for audits to ensure compliance; e.g., Truth in Lending Act, Fair Housing Act, Fair Credit Reporting Act, Real Estate Settlement Procedure Act and others.

5. **Are the reports "prepared by, on behalf of, or for the use of an agency responsible for the regulation or supervision of financial institutions"?**

5.1. This requirement of Exemption 8 "does not require that the agency regulate or supervise the particular institution that is the subject of the report." *Public Citizen v. Farm Credit Administration,* 938 F.2d at 293.

5.2. The rationale for this interpretation is simply that the "concerns" regarding disclosure "may be implicated regardless of whether the agency regulates or supervises the financial institution." *Id.*

CHAPTER 12

Exemption 9—Oil Well Data

Allan Robert Adler

1. **Exemption 9 provides that the FOIA does not apply to matters that are: "geological and geophysical information and data, including maps, concerning wells."**

2. **Legislative History.**

2.1. Only the 1966 House Report mentions Exemption 9: "This category was added after witnesses testified that geological maps based on explorations by private oil companies were not covered by 'trade secrets' provisions of present laws. Details of oil and gas findings must be filed with Federal agencies by companies which want to lease Government-owned land. Current regulations of the Bureau of Land Management prohibit disclosure of these details only if the disclosure 'would be prejudicial to the interests of the Government' (43 CFR Part 2). Witnesses contended disclosure of seismic reports and other exploratory findings of oil companies would give speculators an unfair advantage over the companies which spent millions of dollars in exploration. H.R. Rep. No.1497, 89th cong., 2d Sess. 11 (1966), reprinted in *Freedom of Information Act Source Book: Legislative Materials, Cases, Articles (of the 1966 Act)*, Subcommittee on Administrative Practice and Procedure of the Committee on the Judiciary, U.S. Senate, 93d Cong., 2d Sess. 32 (1974)."

2.2. Exemption 9 has been criticized as a "Texas touch," providing blanket protection for oil well materials when such information, insofar as it would be confidential commercial information, is already adequately protected by Exemption 4. *See, e.g., Attorney General's Memorandum on the Public Information Section of the Administrative Procedure Act* at 39 (1967). However, the Interior Department has cited it on occasion to apply to water wells.

3. **Litigation.**

3.1. Exemption 9 is the least invoked, least litigated exemption of the FOIA. In the most recent published judicial opinion construing the language and legislative history of Exemption 9, the district court rejected a claim for withholding the number, locations and depths of an oil company's proposed exploration drill holes based on its view that Congress intended the exemption to be limited in scope "only to well information of a technical or scientific nature." *Black Hills Alliance v. U.S. Forest Service*, 603 F. Supp. 117, 122 (D.S.D. 1984).

3.2. As an indication of its redundancy with respect to Exemption 4, Exemption 9 also generates "reverse" FOIA issues. Extant cases relate to discretionary releases by agencies of material which oil company submitters wish to keep confidential.

3.3. Courts have handled the question of an abuse of discretion by requiring a balancing test as to the public's interest in disclosure.

3.3.1. The double protection available for this narrow category of data has been interpreted as underscoring the need for particular attention of courts in reviewing discretionary releases concerning wells: therefore, "where releasing the information serves no legitimate function, this court will prohibit disclosure." *Pennzoil Co. v. Federal Power Commission*, 534 F.2d 627, 630 (5th Cir. 1976).

3.3.2. Factors determining whether release is an abuse of discretion: *See Pennzoil Co.*, 534 F.2d at 632; *Superior Oil Co. v. Federal Energy Regulatory Commission*, 563 F.2d 191, 205 (5th Cir. 1977).

3.3.2.1. Whether disclosure of detailed information will significantly aid the Commission in fulfilling its statutory functions.

3.3.2.2. Balancing the potential benefits of disclosure against the potential harm both to submitters of the information and to the public by threatening the incentive for energy development.

3.3.2.3. An agency should consider whether public benefit from release might be adequately met by partial disclosure.

CHAPTER 13

Agency

Elaine English and Katherine A. Meyer

1. **Section 552(f) provides: "For the purpose of this section, the term 'agency' as defined in section 551(1) of this title includes any executive department, military department, Government corporation, Government-controlled corporation, or other establishment in the executive branch of the Government (including the Executive Office of the President), or any independent regulatory agency."**

1.1. Section 551(1) of the Administrative Procedures Act defines the term "agency" to mean "each authority of the Government of the United States, whether or not it is within or subject to review by another agency... [with certain limited exceptions]." 5 U.S.C. § 551(1).

1.2. The courts and Congress are expressly excluded from coverage under the Act. § 551(1)(A) and (B). "Congress," as used in § 551(1)(A), does not refer only to the House and Senate but means the entire legislative branch, including individual units of Congress such as the Government Printing Office. *Mayo v. U.S. Government Printing Office*, 9 F.3d 1450, 1451 (9th Cir. 1993).

2. **Legislative History.**

2.1. The 1974 amendments expanded the definition of "agency" to include entities which "may not be considered agencies under § 551(1) of title 5, U.S. Code, but which perform governmental functions and control information of interest to the public." H.R. Rep. No. 876, 93d Cong., 2d Sess. 8-9 (1974). The legislative history indicates that the term "Government-controlled corporation" was employed by Congress to ensure that the disclosure provisions of the FOIA reached those corporations which, while not owned or incorporated by the federal government, receive federal funds and operate under federal control. The Conference Report specifically noted that the Postal Service, Postal Rate Commission, and Amtrak would be included as agencies. *See* H. Rep. No. 1380, 93d Cong., 2d Sess. 14-15 (1974).

2.2. The legislative history makes it clear that corporations which receive federal funds but are neither chartered nor controlled by the federal government, such as the Corporation for Public Broadcasting, are specifically excluded from the Act. H. Rep. No. 1380, 93d Cong., 2d Sess. 15 (1974). *See Forsham v. Harris*, 445 U.S. 169 (1980); *Rocap v. Indiek*, 539 F.2d 174, 178 (D.C. Cir. 1976).

2.3. The legislative history also makes clear that the term "agency" as used in the FOIA does not include "the President's immediate personal staff or units in the Executive Office whose sole function is to advise and assist the President." H. Rep. No. 1380, 93d Cong., 2d Sess. 15 (1974); *Kissinger v. Reporters Committee for Freedom of the Press*, 445 U.S. 136 (1980) (National Security Advisor); *Armstrong v. Executive Office of the President*, 90 F.3d 556 (D.C. Cir. 1996) (National Security Council); *Sweetland v. Walters*, 60 F.3d 852 (D.C. Cir. 1995) (White House Chief Usher); *National Security Archive v. Archivist of the United States*, 909 F.2d 541 (D.C. Cir. 1990) (White House Counsel).

2.3.1. The Conference Report expressly stated that the conferees intended the term "Executive Office of the President" to be interpreted consistent with "the result reached" in *Soucie v. David*, 448 F.2d 1067 (D.C. Cir. 1971). In that case, the court rejected the argument that the Office of Science and Technology's "sole function" was to advise and assist the President, finding instead that its congressionally authorized independent function of evaluating federal scientific programs made it an "agency" subject to the FOIA rather than a part of the President's staff. *See also Rushforth v. Council of Economic Advisors*, 762 F.2d 1038 (D.C. Cir. 1985) (applying the *Soucie* "sole-function" test in ruling that the Council is *not* an "agency" subject to the FOIA); *Pacific Legal Foundation v. Council on Environmental Quality*, 636 F.2d 1259 (D.C. Cir. 1980) (under *Soucie*, Council is an "agency" subject to the FOIA).

2.3.2. Similarly, the exclusion applies only to units within the Executive Office of the President and *not* throughout the Executive Branch. *Crooker v. Office of the Pardon Attorney*, 614 F.2d 825 (2d Cir. 1980).

2.4. A district court judge ruled the White House was subject to the Privacy Act, even though that statute's definition of "agency" is identical to the FOIA definition. His reasoning was that the two statutes were designed to fulfill different goals and that the need to protect the confidentiality of discussions between the President and his advisors, which underlies the exclusion of the EOP from the FOIA, was not present in the Privacy Act. *Alexander v. FBI*, 971 F. Supp. 603 (D.D.C. 1997). Since that time, four other courts have faced the same issue and all have ruled that the EOP is not an agency subject to the Privacy Act because it is not subject to the FOIA. *See Tripp v. EOP*, 200 F.R.D. 140 (D.D.C. 2001); *Flowers v. EOP*, 142 F. Supp. 2d 38 (D.D.C. 2001); *Broaddrick v. EOP*, 139 F. Supp. 2d 55 (D.D.C. 2001); *Falwell v. EOP*, 158 F. Supp. 2d 734 (W.D. Va. 2000).

3. The U.S. Court of Appeals for the D.C. Circuit, in *Washington Research Project, Inc. v. HEW*, 504 F.2d 238, 246 (D.C. Cir. 1974), *cert. denied*, 421 U.S. 963 (1975), has cautioned that, in assessing whether an entity is an agency under this definition, "[t]he unavoidable fact is that each new arrangement must be examined anew and viewed in its own context." *Accord Public Citizen Health Research Group v. HEW*, 668 F.2d 537, 542 (D.C. Cir. 1981). **The critical inquiry is "whether it has any authority in law to make decisions."** 504 F.2d at 248. The Court also noted that, in its earlier decisions on the scope of § 551(1), it found two other factors significant in determining agency status: (1) whether the entity has "substantial independent authority in the exercise of specific functions," *Soucie v. David*, 448 F.2d at 1073; and (2) whether the entity deals directly with those subject to its decisions, *Grumman Aircraft Engineering Corp. v. Renegotiation Board*, 482 F.2d 710, 715 (D.C. Cir. 1973), *rev'd on other grounds*, 421 U.S. 168 (1975).

3.1. The U.S. Court of Appeals for the D.C. Circuit held, in *Energy Research Foundation v. Defense Nuclear Facilities Safety Board*, 917 F.2d 581 (D.C. Cir. 1990), that the Defense Nuclear Facilities Safety Board is an agency within the meaning of FOIA and the Sunshine Act because it is an establishment in the executive branch that has numerous investigatory as well as advisory functions.

3.2. The U.S. Court of Appeals for the D.C. Circuit held that the Presidential Task Force on Regulatory Relief is not an agency under FOIA because it is (1) operationally close to the President; (2) has no delegation of substantially independent authority from the President; and (3) has no separate staff and self-contained structure. *Meyer v. Bush*, 981 F.2d 1288 (D.C. Cir. 1993).

4. **"Independent" Agencies. One issue is whether an entity is sufficiently independent so as not to be treated as an agency. As noted, the legislative history makes clear that the Postal Service and Amtrak are "agencies" for the purposes of the FOIA.**

4.1. The Federal Home Loan Mortgage Corporation is a "government controlled corporation" within the definition because, among other things, it is federally chartered; its Board of Directors is presidentially appointed; it is subject to close governmental supervision and control over its business transactions; and it is empowered to make and enforce bylaws, rules, and regulations as necessary to carry out the purposes of its enabling statute. *Rocap v. Indiek*, 539 F.2d at 180.

4.2. The fact that an entity does business in the private sector does not disqualify it as a government-controlled corporation expressly referenced in the legislative history of § 552(f). (*See* legislative history cited above). *See also Aug v. National Railroad Passenger Corp.*, 425 F. Supp. 946 (D.D.C. 1976). *But see Ehm v. National R.R. Passenger Corp.*, 732 F.2d 1250 (5th Cir. 1984), *cert. denied,* 469 U.S. 982 (1984) ("ultimate Congressional intent is simply unclear" whether Amtrak is an "agency" as a matter of law; however, Amtrak is not a "government-controlled corporation" within subsection 552(e) as a matter of fact).

4.3. The Red Cross is not an "agency" despite the fact that it was established by Congressional charter and its Board of Governors is appointed by the President. *Irwin Memorial Blood Bank v. American Nat'l Red Cross*, 640 F.2d 1051 (9th Cir. 1981). The determining factors in the court's decision were that the U.S. does not appropriate funds to assist the Red Cross; government officials do not direct the every day affairs of the organization; there is *de minimus* federal control of its operations; and, most significantly, the Red Cross operates as a "national society" with autonomous status, owing its allegiance to the alleviation of human suffering, not to any nation.

4.4. The Trust Territory of the Pacific Islands was held not to be an "agency." *Gale v. Andrus*, 643 F.2d 826 (D.C. Cir. 1980). The Court reasoned that although the Trust Territory is supervised by the Department of Interior (which is subject to the FOIA), it performs purely local governmental functions for non-United States citizens and has never become an instrumentality of the U.S. government.

4.5. The Consolidated Rail Corporation (Conrail) cannot be considered an "agency" under subsection 552(f) because "[n]ot only did Congress clearly state its intention for Conrail not to be considered 'an agency or instrumentality of the Federal Government,' but Conrail lacks those attributes of agencies that have been considered significant in this analysis." *Railway Labor Executives' Ass'n v. Consolidated Rail Corp.*, 580 F. Supp. 777, 779 (D.D.C. 1984).

4.6. The Smithsonian Institution is not an agency because it does not fit into any of the definitional categories of FOIA; it is not an establishment in the executive branch because it "simply is not the kind of 'center of gravity in the exercise of administrative power' to which 551(1) refers." *Dong v. Smithsonian Institution*, 125 F.3d 877 (D.C.

Cir. 1997), reversing the earlier holdings in *Cotton v. Adams*, 798 F. Supp. 22 (D.D.C. 1992) and *Dong v. Smithsonian Institution*, 943 F. Supp. 69 (D.D.C. 1996).

4.7. In a case brought under the Federal Advisory Committee Act rather than the FOIA, the U.S. Sentencing Commission was held to be outside the definition of "agency" because Congress so stated when it established the Commission as an independent entity within the judicial branch under the Sentencing Reform Act of 1984. *Washington Legal Foundation v. U.S. Sentencing Commission,* 17 F.3d 1446, 1448-9 (D.C. Cir. 1994).

4.8. A private contractor, even one over which the agency exercises significant authority is not an agency because contractual oversight did not rise to level of control of day-to-day operations necessary to make the contractor a Government controlled corporation. *Gilmore v. DOE*, 4 F. Supp. 2d 912 (N.D. Cal. 1998).

5. Sub-units of Agencies. The Conference Report states that "subdivisions, offices or units within an agency" are not "agencies." However, a sub-unit may be sufficiently independent so as to be treated as an agency.

5.1. As a unit within an executive department (Department of Justice) the Office of the Pardon Attorney is subject to the FOIA. *Crooker v. Office of the Pardon Attorney, supra.*

5.2. The U.S. Parole Board is an agency subject to the FOIA. *Strout v. U.S. Parole Comm'n*, 842 F. Supp. 948, 954 (E.D. Mich.), *affirmed*, 40 F.3d 136 (6th Cir. 1994). *See also Pickus v. U.S. Board of Parole*, 507 F.2d 1107 (D.C. Cir. 1974).

5.3. Regional Boards established by the Renegotiation Board to exercise substantial decision-making power with respect to members of the public are "agencies." *Grumman Aircraft Engineering Corp., supra.*

6. Advisory Groups. Whether groups are agencies is dependent on the specific functions and purpose of each group.

6.1. *Washington Research Project v. HEW* held that "initial review groups" which make recommendations to the National Institutes of Mental Health concerning research grant applications are not "agencies" for purposes of the FOIA because they do not have any legal authority to make decisions, but merely act as consultants. 504 F.2d at 248.

6.2. A university group diabetes program was not an "agency" where it had no independent authority to perform specific governmental functions and was empowered only to make recommendations. *Ciba-Geigy Corp. v. Mathews*, 428 F. Supp. 523, 529 (S.D.N.Y. 1977).

6.3. Professional Standards Review Organizations, which are designated by the Department of HEW to review health care provided under Medicaid and Medicare, and to make final and binding determinations as to whether such care is "necessary" and therefore eligible for federal reimbursement, are not "agencies" because the legislative history demonstrates that the PSRO is to operate independently of the government. *Public Citizen Health Research Group v. Department of HEW*, 668 F.2d at 542-544. *Accord St. Mary's Hospital v. Philadelphia Professional Standards Review Organization, Inc.*, No. 78-2943 (E.D. Pa. 1980).

7. **Congressional Savings Clause. Although expressly excluded from coverage of the FOIA as an agency, Congress is expressly assured under the Act that "[t]his section is not authority to withhold information from Congress." § 552(d).** In a suit brought against two agencies by the ranking member of the House Banking Committee, the court declined to rule on the plaintiff's right to sue, stating that the question of who constitutes "Congress" for the purpose of the savings clause "is largely a matter of self-definition that should be determined by the legislature itself" because, at least in this case, the determination would only affect Congress itself. *Leach v. Resolution Trust Corp.*, 860 F. Supp. 868, 877-8 (D.D.C. 1994).

CHAPTER 14

Agency Records

Elaine English and Katherine A. Meyer

1. The FOIA provides the federal district courts with jurisdiction to compel the disclosure of "agency records." § 552(a)(4)(B).

1.1. Federal court jurisdiction under the FOIA is dependent upon a showing by the requester that a federal agency has (1) "improperly;" (2) "withheld;" (3)"agency records." *Kissinger v. Reporters Committee for Freedom of the Press*, 445 U.S. 136, 150 (1980).

1.2. **The FOIA provides no definition of the term "agency records."** Moreover, "the legislative history yields insignificant insight into Congress' conception of the sorts of materials the Act covers." *McGehee v. CIA*, 697 F.2d 1095, 1106 (D.D.C. 1983), *vacated in part and aff'd in part*, 711 F.2d 1076 (D.C. Cir. 1983). While the EFOIA amendments of 1996 added the term "record" to § 552(f), the reference serves only to clarify that status as a record under the FOIA incorporates any and all formats in which the record may be maintained, including an electronic format.

2. The Supreme Court has established a two-pronged test for determining whether material constitutes an "agency record." *DOJ v. Tax Analysts*, 492 U.S. 136 (1989).

2.1. First, a federal agency must "either create or obtain" the materials at issue. *Id.* at 144, *citing Kissinger, supra*, and *Forsham v. Harris*, 445 U.S. 169 (1980). Under this requirement, the agency must have *possession* of the material at the time of the request in order for the material to qualify as an "agency record."

2.2. Second, the agency "must be in control of the requested materials at the time the FOIA request is made." *Tax Analysts*, 492 U.S. at 145. Moreover, the Court held, "[b]y control we mean that the materials have come into the agency's possession in the legitimate conduct of its official duties." *Id.*

2.3. Applying this test in *Tax Analysts*, the Court held that federal district court tax opinions in the possession of the Tax Division of the Department of Justice are not *court* records (which, in any case, are not subject to the FOIA), but are "agency records" subject to the FOIA, regardless of the fact that they may also be obtained from the courts that rendered them.

3. Evolution of "Possession" and "Control" Tests.

3.1. In *Forsham v. Harris, supra*, the Supreme Court reviewed definitions of the term "record" in the Records Disposal Act, 44 U.S.C. § 3301 *et seq.*, and the Presidential Records Act of 1978, 44 U.S.C. § 2201, in order to determine what Congress contemplated in its use of the term in FOIA.

3.1.1. Based on its reading of "[t]he text, structure, and legislative history of the FOIA itself," the Court held that "an agency must first either create or obtain a record as a prerequisite to it becoming an 'agency record' within the meaning of the FOIA." 445 U.S. at 182.

3.1.2. In *Forsham*, the Court ruled that raw data which was compiled by a group of physicians and scientists and which formed the evidentiary basis for a study that was funded and relied upon by the Department of Health, Education, and Welfare, was nevertheless not an "agency record" under FOIA because the data was never obtained by HEW.

3.2. In *Kissinger v. Reporters Committee for Freedom of the Press, supra*, the Supreme Court declined to hold that notes of telephone conversations by Henry Kissinger were "agency records." The notes were made while Kissinger was National Security Advisor, but they were transferred to the State Department when Kissinger became Secretary of State. 445 U.S. at 157.

3.3. Relying on *Kissinger*, the D.C. Circuit held that the transition team report prepared for President-elect Reagan's HHS was not an "agency record" (although copies of the report were physically located at HHS, the report was not created by HHS; nor was it in the "control of HHS, since the report was never integrated into the records system at HHS, nor was it read or relied upon by any agency officials"); *Wolfe v. HHS*, 711 F.2d 1077 (D.C. Cir. 1983). *See also Illinois Institute for Continuing Legal Education v. Department of Labor*, 545 F. Supp. 1229, 1235 (N.D. Ill. 1982) (Reagan transition team report on Labor Department "has not been prepared or used pursuant to the functioning of the DOL, and hence is not a record of the DOL").

3.4. In *Goland v. CIA*, 607 F.2d 339 (D.C. Cir. 1978), *cert. denied*, 445 U.S. 927 (1980), the Court held that a transcript of secret congressional hearings in the possession of the CIA was not an "agency record" because the circumstances under which the transcript was obtained by the CIA led to the conclusion that it remained under the "control" of Congress. The transcript was of secret hearings, Congress had manifested a clear intent to preserve its secrecy, and the document was released to the agency for internal reference purposes only. Thus, the Court held that whether a congressionally generated document has become an agency record depends on whether, under all the circumstances, "the document has passed from the control of Congress and become property subject to the free disposition of the agency with which the document resides." 607 F.2d at 347. *Accord Dunway v. Webster*, 519 F. Supp. 1059 (N.D. Cal. 1981); *Washington Post Co. v. Department of Defense*, 766 F. Supp. 1 (D.D.C. 1991) (congressional transcript is not an agency record where it was sent to the Department of Defense for corrections only).

3.5. In *Paisley v. CIA*, 712 F.2d 686 (D.C. Cir. 1983), *vacated in part, mot. to intervene granted, reh'g granted*, 724 F.2d 201 (1984), the D.C. Circuit held that the documents created by the FBI pursuant to an investigation initiated by a Senate committee are agency records. The court held that, read together, *Kissinger* and *Goland*, stand for the proposition that the agency to whom the request is directed must have exclusive control of the documents. 712 F.2d at 693. It also held that, under *Goland*, two factors are determinative of whether documents in the possession of an agency remain under the control of Congress: 1) the circumstances attending the document's creation, and 2) the conditions under which it was transferred to the agency. *Id.* at 692. In *Paisley*, the court found that neither factor was satisfied and the mere fact that the documents would not have been created had there not been a congressional investigation is too tenuous a connection to establish congressional control. 712 F.2d at 695-96. *See also Allen v. Department of Defense*, 580 F. Supp. 74 (D.D.C. 1983) (records created at the request of Congress are "agency records"). *But see Navasky v. CIA*, 499 F. Supp. 269 (S.D.N.Y. 1980) (document generated by CIA in response to specific request of a congressional committee, as part of the exercise of its oversight authority and pursuant to express wish that such material not be disclosed without prior approval of that committee, remains under the control of Congress and is therefore exempt from the FOIA).

3.6. In *Ricchio v. Kline*, 773 F.2d 1389 (D.C. Cir. 1985), the court of appeals ruled that public access to the Watergate Special Prosecution Task Force transcripts of tape recordings made by President Nixon is governed exclusively by the Presidential Recordings and Materials Preservation Act, and not at all by the FOIA. The district court had determined that the transcripts are not "agency records," despite the fact that they are in the possession and control of the National Archives, because the Task Force that created them for use as evidence in criminal trials lacked dispositive "control" over them. The appellate court, however, reached its decision without deciding whether the transcripts are "agency records."

3.7. In *Armstrong v. Executive Office of the President*, 877 F. Supp. 750 (D.D.C. 1995), the district court held that the NSC is an agency and creates both agency and presidential records. When documents are created by an individual whose function is to advise and assist the President, the records are Presidential Records, in all other circumstances the records will be agency records. The decision, however, was subsequently reversed. 90 F.3d 556 (D.C. Cir. 1996).

3.7.1. Many of the records management and preservation issues in the case arose under the Federal Records Act, 44 U.S.C. §§ 2101 *et seq.*, 2901 *et seq.*, 3101 *et seq.*, 3301 *et seq.* However, the case also raised the question of whether the National Security Council ("NSC") properly classified many of its records as presidential records, which are unavailable to the public for a period of time, rather than as "agency records" subject to the FOIA. The NSC divided its records into agency and presidential records depending on the process by which the records were created. The guidelines governing the treatment of electronic mail records were inadequate under the federal records statutes. 810 F. Supp. 335, 347-48 (D.D.C. 1993). The D.C. Circuit reversed this ruling, but could not determine on the basis of the existing record whether the government was improperly classifying agency records as presidential ones. Accordingly, the court remanded the case to the district court for further proceedings to determine whether electronic records that would otherwise be subject to the FOIA were improperly being classified as presidential records.

3.7.2. The *Armstrong* case led to another agency records decision in connection with electronic records that were located and printed out for Caspar Weinberger in response to a subpoena in his criminal case. After the criminal proceedings concluded, the records were transferred to the National Archives under a protective order that would have given Mr. Weinberger access but not the public. The plaintiffs in *Armstrong* contended that the records were responsive to their longstanding FOIA request and that a *Vaughn* index should be prepared to facilitate litigation over the plaintiffs' right to access them. The district court agreed that the records are agency records under the FOIA because they were created by federal agencies and they were then in the possession and control of a government agency—the Archives, albeit a different agency than the one that created them. *Armstrong v. Executive Office of the President*, 810 F. Supp. 335 (D.D.C. 1993).

4. **The government bears the burden of proving that a record remains under the "control" of an exempt entity.** *Paisley v. CIA, supra* (the government must provide proof of Congress' specific intent to transfer particular documents under condition that Congress retain control; general and sweeping attempts to retain control are insufficient). *See also Holy Spirit Association v. CIA*, 636 F.2d 838 (D.C. Cir. 1980), *vacated in part as moot*, 455 U.S. 997 (1982) (letter from Clerk of the House of Representatives written after transfer of records does not establish congressional control).

4.1. Prior to *Tax Analysts*, in determining whether an agency had sufficient "control" over a document, courts examined the *purpose* for which the record had been obtained by the agency.

4.1.1. Thus, in *Ryan v. DOJ*, 617 F.2d 781 (D.C. Cir. 1980), the Court held that United States Senators' responses to the Attorney General's questionnaires concerning procedures for recommending judicial nominees were "agency records" because they were under the "control" of the Attorney General. The factors bearing on "control" included the fact that the Senators gave no indication that they wished to limit the AG's use of their responses, or retain any prerogative to maintain control over the records.

4.1.2. In *RCA Global v. FCC*, 524 F. Supp. 579 (D. Del. 1981), the court used a "function" test to determine that subpoenaed documents in the possession of the FCC were "agency records." The subpoenaed documents were in the possession of the FCC in order to help it determine what if any action to take to regulate the company: "That decision is one to be made in the regular course of the FCC business under its enabling legislation, and public scrutiny, subject to appropriate exemptions, of how that decision is made was an objective of the FOIA." *Id.* at 583.

4.1.3. In *St. Paul's Benev. Ed. & Miss. Inst. v. United States*, 506 F. Supp. 822 (N.D. Ga. 1980), the court held that a computer tape voluntarily submitted to the Center for Disease Control by a private company was an agency record because the CDC had a significant involvement in its production and was to have a copy for its own internal use.

4.1.4. In *General Electric Co. v. NRC*, 750 F.2d 1394 (7th Cir. 1984), the court held that a utility company's report concerning criticism of its nuclear plant design was an "agency record" despite the fact that the report had been submitted for a licensing proceeding *in camera* under a protective order and notwithstanding that the proceeding was aborted after the FOIA request for the report was received. The court's conclusion was based upon its finding that the report was "used" by the Commission in carrying out agency duties. *Id.* at 1400-01.

4.1.5. Peel-off labels bearing names and addresses of employees eligible to vote in an upcoming representation election are not "agency records" when, under court order, the labels are to be used by the National Mediation Board for attachment to ballot envelopes only and other uses are precluded. The Board's transitory possession of the labels for this limited, one-time use does not constitute sufficient "control" to render the labels "agency records." *International Brotherhood of Teamsters v. National Mediation Board*, 111 L.R.R.M. (BNA) 2020 (D.D.C. 1982), *aff'd*, 712 F.2d 1495 (D.C. Cir. 1983).

4.1.6. In *Hercules, Inc. v. Marsh*, 839 F.2d 1027 (4th Cir. 1988), the court ruled that an Army ammunition plant telephone directory, which was prepared at the Government's expense and for the Government's use by the government contractor that operated the plant, was an "agency record" under the "indicia of ownership" standard applied in *Ryan v. DOJ, supra.*

4.2. The D.C. Circuit, in *Tax Analysts*, had emphasized that "agency possession and power to disseminate a document are still insufficient by themselves to make it an 'agency record'" and held that "[a]gencies must use or rely on the document to perform agency business, and integrate it into their files, before it may be deemed an 'agency record.'" *Tax Analysts v. DOJ*, 845 F.2d 1060, 1068 (D.C. Cir. 1988), *citing Wolfe v. HHS, supra* and *Lindsey v. U.S. Bureau of Prisons*, 736 F.2d 1462, 1465 (11th Cir. 1984), *vacated*, 469 U.S. 1082 (1984). Although the Supreme Court affirmed the judgment of the appeals court, which it noted was based, in part, on the fact that the Justice Department "routinely uses" the requested tax decisions, 492 U.S. at 141, the Court did not adopt the "use" analysis as part of the "control" test it articulated.

4.3. Thus, after *Tax Analysts*, it appears that the "control" test will be met if the agency can show that the materials came into its possession in the "legitimate conduct of its official duties." 492 U.S. at 145. *See, e.g., Rush v. Department of State*, 716 F. Supp. 598 (S.D. Fla. 1989) (Court held that, although the State Department had never "used" certain correspondence between a former ambassador to Germany and the National Security Adviser, the materials were "agency records" because they were in the possession of the State Department, there was no evidence of "control" by any other entity, and the State Department had exercised unfettered discretion in storing them). *See also Armstrong v. Executive Office of the President*, 810 F. Supp. 335 (D.D.C. 1993) (electronic records printed out for Caspar Weinberger in response to a subpoena in his criminal case and later transferred under a protective order to the National Archives are agency records, in that they were created by federal agencies—albeit a different agency than the one that created them.)

4.4. Following the analysis of *Tax Analysts*, courts have begun to expand the scope of the FOIA to cover records in the possession of a government contractor, in situations where an agency has "control" over the record, notwithstanding the holding of the Supreme Court in *Forsham v. Harris*. *See, e.g., Burka v. HHS*, 87 F.3d 508, 515 (D.C. Cir. 1996) (a data tape in the possession of a government contractor is nevertheless an agency record because the government had considerable supervision over the contract, including over the creation and control of the records and had relied upon the records in developing agency policies). *See also Los Alamos Study Group v. DOE*, No. 97-1412 (D.N.M. July 22, 1998) (contractor records are agency records because agency had indicated intent to retain control over them), and *Chicago Tribune Co. v. HHS*, 1999 WL 299875 (N.D. Ill. May 4, 1999) (records re-analyzing breast cancer study results were in constructive control of agency, therefore, must be turned over to requester).

4.4.1. In 1998, Congress carved out an exception to *Forsham v. Harris* by enacting the Shelby Amendment mandating that agencies with grants to institutions of higher education, hospitals and other non-profit organizations allow access under FOIA to data generated in studies by those contractors when the data is used by the agency in promulgating a regulation. P.L. 105-277 (Oct. 21, 1998).

4.5. In two post-*Tax Analysts* cases involving databases of court opinions and other reference materials, district courts have focused on the kind of "control" an agency must exert over a record. See *Bazier v. U.S. Department of the Air Force*, 887 F. Supp. 225 (N.D. Ca. 1995) (database of Supreme Court cases not an agency record within "control" of the agency because used by agency only for reference purposes and not otherwise incorporated into its activities or records). *Tax Analysts v. DOJ and West Publ'g Co.*, 913 F. Supp. 599 (D.D.C. 1996) (JURIS database is not an agency record because the database is not "subject to the free disposition of the agency" as a result of contractual limitations imposed by provider). On its own initiative, the government later made the Air Force database of federal cases available to the public.

5. **Although the "possession, control, or custody" test has generally been the focus of judicial analysis to determine whether a record obtained by an agency is an "agency record," one court concluded that a dispositive determination may be based on whether the agency had legal authority to obtain the record in the first place.** *Marzen v. HHS*, 632 F. Supp. 785 (N.D. Ill. 1985), *aff'd on other grounds*, 825 F.2d 1148 (7th Cir. 1987).

5.1. The court in *Marzen* reasoned that the *Forsham* line of cases and the FOIA itself rest on the "implicit assumption" that records are obtained by agencies pursuant to legal authority, since "Congress could not have intended to expose to public scrutiny documents that the agency itself had no legal authority to examine." 632 F. Supp. at 798.

5.2. The *Marzen* court noted that this "assumption" is expressly supported by the Privacy Act's requirements that agencies collect, maintain and disclose records only as authorized by statute or executive order. *Id.* at 798-800.

5.3. The *Marzen* court held that "'agency records' do not include records obtained by a governmental authority without legal authority, express or implied, to do so." *Id.* at 802. "Of course," the court continued, "portions of government-generated reports that divulge information obtained from illegally acquired reports could not be disclosed because such disclosure would circumvent the rationale for not disclosing the illegally acquired reports themselves." *Id.*

5.4. The court was "not convinced" that the agency's good-faith belief that it was authorized by statute to obtain the documents should make any difference. *Id.*

5.5. The court of appeals declined to decide whether the documents in question were "agency records" because "however they were obtained—whether in good faith, or by theft in clear contravention of the law"—the appellate court found that they were exempt as investigatory records whose production could interfere with enforcement proceedings. 825 F.2d at 1153.

5.6. It is not clear whether the second-prong of the "control" test articulated by the Supreme Court in *Tax Analysts*—i.e., whether the materials "have come into the agency's possession in the legitimate conduct of its official duties"—was intended by the Court to encompass the "authority to obtain" analysis employed by the court in *Marzen*.

6. **Distinguishing "Agency Records" from Personal Materials of Agency Employees.**

6.1. Appointment materials, such as desk calendars and telephone logs, "that are created solely for an individual's convenience, that contain a mix of personal and business entries, and that may be disposed of at the individual's discretion are not 'agency records' under FOIA." *Bureau of National Affairs, Inc. v. DOJ*, 742 F.2d 1484 (D.C. Cir. 1984).

6.1.1. In a consolidated appeal with *Environmental Defense Fund v. EPA*, Nos. 80-0360, 80-0362 (D.D.C., June 28, 1982), the court was required to determine "under what circumstances can an individual's creation of a record be attributed to the agency, thereby making the material an 'agency record' disclosable under FOIA, rather than personal material not covered by the Act." 742 F.2d at 1489.

6.1.2. The disputed documents were appointment materials of agency officials, including telephone message slips, daily schedule agendas, and desk calendars.

6.1.3. Where a record is created by an employee of a FOIA agency, the court's inquiry must focus "on the totality of the circumstances surrounding the creation, maintenance, and use of the document to determine whether the document is in fact an 'agency record' and not an employee's record that happens to be located physically within an agency." *Id.* at 1492-93. "In this regard, use of the documents by employees other than the author is an important consideration...[and] an inquiry is therefore required into the purpose for which the document was created, the actual use of the document, and the extent to which the creator of the document and other employees acting within the scope of their employment relied upon the document to carry out the business of the agency." *Id.* at 1493.

6.1.4. The court rejected the government's invitation to hold that the treatment of documents for disposal and retention purposes under the various federal records management statutes determines their status under FOIA. "However tempting such a 'bright line' test may be, it cannot be used as the divining rod for the meaning of 'agency records' under FOIA." *Id.*

6.1.5. The court noted that "inclusion of personal information does not, by itself, take material outside the ambit of FOIA," but the presence of such information "may be relevant in determining the author's intended use of the documents at the time he or she created them." *Id.* at 1496.

6.1.6. Applying its analyses to the three kinds of materials at issue, the court concluded that (1) the telephone message slips were not "agency records" because they contained no substantive information, were used only by the official for whom the messages were taken, and there was no way to segregate personal from business calls; (2) the daily agendas were "agency records" because, even though they reflected personal appointments, they were created and circulated to the staff for the express purpose of facilitating daily scheduling of business activities; and (3) the appointment calendars were not "agency records" because, as distinguished from the daily agendas, they were not distributed to other employees and they were created and retained solely for the convenience of individual officials.

6.2. The *Bureau of National Affairs* analysis was subsequently applied and refined in a decision holding that "records of schedule"—typewritten transcriptions of documents compiled on a daily basis by the staff of former Secretary of State Alexander Haig—were "agency records," despite the fact that the Secretary did not have direct access to the records and was never made aware of their existence. *Washington Post Co. v. Department of State*, 632 F. Supp. 607 (D.D.C. 1986).

6.2.1. Employing a bifurcated analysis, the court first examined the "totality of the circumstances" underlying the creation of the records by reference to a four-factor test considering whether (a) the documents were generated within the agency seeking to avoid disclosure; (b) the documents have been placed into agency files; (c) the documents are within the agency's control; and (d) the documents have been used by the agency for an agency purpose. 632 F. Supp. at 612.

6.2.2. Next, the court sought to "draw guidance from the treatment of the disputed documents under the provisions of the various federal records management statutes," reasoning that their qualifications as "agency records" under the applicable statutory definitions "lends support to the conclusion that the materials are similarly 'agency records' for the purposes of FOIA." *Id.*

6.2.3. As preliminary considerations, the court rejected the proposition that the FOIA was intended to encompass only those documents created by mandate of law, and refused to resolve the status of the records solely by reference to the alleged intent of the authors in creating the documents. *Id.* at 612 and n.2.

6.2.4. The court concluded that the non-use of the documents by the official for whose personal use they were purportedly created *supports* the conclusion that the materials are "agency records."

6.2.4.1. The court determined that the use test discussed in *Bureau of National Affairs* does not require that the agency "must *actually* use the document to establish that the requested materials are agency records. Instead, the creation and filing of documents absent indicia of personal use may constitute the 'use' of agency records for an agency purpose." *Id.* at 614 and n.9.

6.2.4.2. The court found that, in contrast to the materials found not to constitute "agency records" in *Bureau of National Affairs*, "[t]he creation, maintenance, and storage of the records of schedule...evidence numerous indicia of record-keeping extraneous to the use of the documents as mere personal work-aids." *Id.* at 615.

6.2.4.3. Although the use of documents solely for personal convenience "strongly reinforces the conclusion" that they are not agency records subject to FOIA, the court concluded that non-use also "weighs in favor of record status" because the alternative would encourage reluctant officials not to maintain records of actual use. *Id.* at 615 and n.12.

6.2.5. Ultimately, the court held that "where the creation and maintenance of a document evinces numerous indicia of agency record-keeping, under circumstances totally lacking in incidents of personal use, the document may be deemed subject to disclosure under the Act." *Id.* at 616.

6.3. In *Gallant v. NLRB*, 26 F.3d 48 (D.C. Cir. 1994), the D.C. Circuit ruled that letters sent by a Board member to drum up support for her renomination were "personal" rather than "agency" records, even though they were on agency letterhead and the Board member used agency staff to work on them. The court noted that "nothing in the record here indicates that [the Board member] created the correspondence with anything other than the purely personal objective of retaining her job." The court added that "even though employing agency resources in the creation of the correspondence is a relevant factor in the agency record analysis, the utilization of agency resources in this case is not as significant as the other factors employed in our precedents, which compel a conclusion that the correspondence was personal, rather than attributable to the agency."

6.4. In *Dow Jones & Co. v. GSA*, 714 F. Supp. 35 (D.D.C. 1989), the court held that a list of business partners of a former GSA Administrator, used to avoid conflicts of interests during the Administrator's period in office, were not "agency records" because the list remained under the personal "control" of the official.

7. Special Materials.

7.1. Presentence Reports.

7.1.1. The issue of whether a presentence report in the possession of the Parole Commission or the Bureau of Prisons is an "agency record" under the FOIA generated a great deal of litigation. *See, e.g., Carson v. DOJ*, 631 F.2d 1008 (D.C. Cir. 1980); *Lykins v. DOJ*, 725 F.2d 1455 (D.C. Cir. 1984); *Berry v. DOJ*, 733 F.2d 1343 (9th Cir. 1984) (each holding that a presentence report is an "agency record").

7.1.2. In *Crooker v. U.S. Parole Comm'n*, 730 F.2d 1 (1st Cir. 1984), *vacated,* 469 U.S. 926 (1985), the court held that a presentence report in the possession of the Parole Commission was a court record, not an "agency record," because the sentencing court exercises "control" over the document. However, the Solicitor General, on behalf of the appellee Parole Commission, conceded in a brief in response to appellants' petition for a writ of certiorari that presentence reports are agency records subject to the FOIA, and the U.S. Supreme Court vacated this judgment and remanded the case to the court of appeals. 469 U.S. 926 (1984). *See Crooker v. U.S. Parole Comm'n*, 760 F.2d 1 (1st Cir. 1985). *See also Cotner v. U.S. Parole Comm'n*, 747 F.2d 1016, 1018 (5th Cir. 1984). The government subsequently asserted Exemption 5 to withhold presentence reports—a claim that was rejected by the Supreme Court in *DOJ v. Julian*, 486 U.S. 1 (1988). *See* Chapter 8 on Agency Memoranda.

7.2. Union authorization cards are "agency records." *Committee on Masonic Homes v. NLRB*, 556 F.2d 214 (3d Cir. 1977).

Agency Records

7.3. *Life* magazine photographs taken at the time of Martin Luther King's assassination were "agency records." *Weisberg v. DOJ*, 631 F.2d 824 (D.C. Cir. 1980) (remanded for copyright question). Similarly, a motion picture was held to be an "agency record" in *Save the Dolphins v. Department of Commerce*, 404 F. Supp. 407, 411 (N.D. Cal. 1975).

7.4. Address labels given to the National Mediation Board by Trans World Airlines for mailing union representation ballots are not "agency records." *TWA v. National Mediation Board*, Nos. 81-0823 and 81-1648 111 L.R.R.M. 2020 (D.D.C. July 30, 1982).

7.5. The Kennedy autopsy records are not agency records subject to FOIA, having been given to the National Archives by the Kennedy family who had "control" over these records. The records are, thus, governed by the deed of gift under which the records were transferred to the government. *Katz v. National Archives & Records Admin.*, 862 F. Supp. 476 (D.D.C. 1994). Similarly, the Kennedy Assassination Records Act (creating a review board for collection, review and dissemination of records relating to the assassination) creates a separate scheme of access which does not directly intersect with FOIA and does not provide a private cause of action to seek review of release of records. *Assassination Archives & Research Center v. DOJ*, 43 F.3d 1542 (D.C. Cir. 1995).

7.6. In direct contrast to the outcome of *Tax Analysts*, a court in California ruled that a database of Supreme Court cases maintained by the Department of the Air Force is not an agency record. Finding the material to be solely a library reference, the court concluded that the agency lacked the necessary indicia of control over the record. *Baizer v. Department of the Air Force*, 1995 WL 1254643 (N.D. Ca. March 10, 1995).

8. Computer Records.

8.1. The FOIA "makes no distinction between records maintained in manual and computer storage systems," *Yeager v. Drug Enforcement Administration*, 678 F.2d 315, 321 (D.C. Cir. 1982), and therefore, in light of the policies underlying the Act's disclosure mandate, it has generally been held that "computer-stored records, whether stored in the central processing unit, on magnetic tape or in some other form, are still 'records' for purposes of the FOIA," and that "the FOIA applies to computer tapes to the same extent it applies to any other documents." *Long v. IRS*, 596 F.2d 362, 365 (9th Cir. 1979) (Kennedy, J.), *cert. denied*, 446 U.S. 917 (1980).

8.2. In the Electronic Freedom of Information Act Amendments of 1996, see Section 6.6 in Chapter 1, supra, Congress confirmed the judicial view of its intended policy by amending § 552(f) to state that "'record' and any other term used in this section in reference to information includes any information that would be an agency record subject to the requirements of this section when maintained by an agency in any format, including an electronic format." Congress also resolved a number of practical issues regarding how the FOIA applies to requests for records in electronic forms or formats.

8.2.1. The 1996 amendments provided that an agency, in making a record available to a person in response to a FOIA request "shall provide the record in any form or format requested by the person if the record is readily reproducible by the agency in that form or format." § 552(a)(3)(B). In thus overruling *Dismukes v.*

Department of the Interior, 603 F. Supp. 760, 763 (D.D.C. 1984), where the court had held that an agency has no obligation under the FOIA to accommodate a requester's preferences, Congress instructed that each agency must "make reasonable efforts to maintain its records in forms or formats that are reproducible" for purposes of this requirement. *Id.* Courts are required to "accord substantial weight" to an agency affidavit concerning the agency's determination as to whether a record is "readily reproducible" in the requested form or format. § 552(a)(4)(B).

8.2.2. The 1996 amendments also defined the terms "search" to include a review of agency records "by automated means" and provided that an agency shall make "reasonable efforts" to search for responsive records "in electronic form or format, except when such efforts would significantly interfere with the operation of the agency's automated information system." § 552(a)(3)(D) and (C), respectively. *See Yeager*, 678 F.2d at 321, *Long*, 596 F.2d at 365, and *Mayock v. INS*, 714 F. Supp. 1558 (N.D. Cal. 1989) for earlier judicial consideration of electronic search issues in the context of the legislative history of the 1974 FOIA amendments and the now-rejected concern that computerized searches may run afoul of the settled principle that agencies are not required by the FOIA to create a record that does not exist in order to satisfy a request.

8.2.3. Congress reaffirmed the importance of agency compliance with FOIA's segregability requirements in electronic contexts, while acknowledging potential practical problems that may arise in applying segregability requirements to the processing of computerized records.

8.2.3.1. The 1996 amendments provided that (1) the "amount of information deleted shall be indicated on the released portion of the record, unless including that indication would harm an interest protected by the exemption in this subsection under which the deletion is made," and (2) the amount of the Information deleted shall be Indicated at the place in the record where such deletion occurred if it is "technically feasible" to do so. § 552(b).

8.2.3.2. Courts are required to "accord substantial weight" to an agency affidavit concerning the agency's determination as to such technical feasibility. § 552(a)(4)(B).

8.2.3.3. For previous judicial consideration regarding the extent to which the computerized form of a record may influence the agency's segregability burden, see *Yeager*, 678 F.2d at 322-323 and n.16 & 17 (rejecting the need to employ "compacting" and "collapsing" techniques) and *Long*, 596 F.2d at 366 (regarding expenses and inconvenience of redaction). *See also Long v. IRS*, 825 F.2d 225 (9th Cir. 1987).

8.3. It remains to be seen how the term "record" added as part of the 1996 amendments will be applied with respect to particular types of electronic records in light of previous caselaw.

8.3.1. In *SDC Development Corp. v. Mathews*, 542 F.2d 1116 (9th Cir. 1976), the court denied a FOIA request for copies of the National Library of Medicine's

MEDLARS computer tapes containing citations and abstracts of some two million articles from some 3000 journals. The court, in an opinion written by then Judge Anthony Kennedy, assumed without explicitly deciding that the materials constituted "agency records," but ruled that they were exempt from disclosure under the FOIA because Congress had provided an alternative statutory scheme to facilitate their public accessibility. The issue was not whether the public would gain access to the tapes but rather whether the FOIA fee structure would apply instead of the higher licensing fees. In keeping with *SDC v. Mathews*, the 1986 amendments allow other statutes to supersede the Act's fee structure where they specifically provide for the setting of fees for particular types of records. *See* § 552(a)(4)(A)(vi).

8.3.2. In *Armstrong v. Bush*, 721 F. Supp. 343 (D.D.C. 1989), *aff'd in part, rev'd in part*, 924 F.2d 282 (D.C. Cir. 1991), the district court rejected the argument that electronic mail systems are not "agency records" because they merely serve as alternatives to communicating through telephone calls or personal visits. On remand, the district court held that electronic mail records are agency records in addition to any hard copy printout because the record, in electronic form, contains additional information. *Armstrong v. Executive Office of the President*, 810 F. Supp. 335 (D.D.C. 1993).

8.3.3. Although computer software appears to be subject to the new definition of "record," Congress did not explicitly address the application of FOIA to computer software in the 1996 amendments.

8.3.3.1. At least one federal court since the enactment of the amendments has found that software developed by an outside contractor for agency use under a restrictive licensing agreement is not an agency record. *Gilmore v. DOE*, 4 F. Supp. 2d 912 (N.D. Cal. 1998).

8.3.3.2. If software should be found to constitute an "agency record," it is likely that questions regarding access to agency software will be determined through consideration of the FOIA's exemptions from disclosure, particularly Exemption 4 regarding confidential business information.

8.3.3.3. The argument that software can be withheld as an internal agency record under Exemption 2 has been rejected where the software is necessary to read computer data. *See Yeager*, 678 F.2d at 318.

8.3.3.4. Computer software cannot be withheld under Exemption 3 based on the Copyright Act, 17 U.S.C. § 101 *et seq.*, because copyright protection is not available for government works and the Act does not meet the requirements to constitute an Exemption 3 statute. *See St. Paul's Benev. Ed. and Miss. Inst. v. United States*, 506 F. Supp. at 830; *Weisberg v. DOJ, supra* (court of appeals remanded for resolution of copyright issue).

8.4. In *Petroleum Information Corp. v. Department of the Interior*, 976 F.2d 1429 (D.C. Cir. 1992), the D.C. Circuit rejected the contention that a computer compilation of paper records did not have to be released because the underlying paper records are public, particularly since the paper records were not in "reasonably accessible form."

See also DeLorme Publ. Co. v. NOAA, 917 F. Supp. 867 (D. Me. 1996) (digitized data used by NOAA in electronic charting system is an agency record subject to disclosure even though agency's paper-format charts were readily available).

9. Handwritten Notes.

9.1. Some courts have considered withholding of handwritten notes under Exemption 5 without discussing whether such notes were properly subject to FOIA as "agency records."

9.1.1. "File notes" and "investigative notes" prepared by NLRB agents and attorneys during unfair labor practice investigation were "neither primary information nor final opinions." *Marathon LeTourneau Co., Marine Division v. NLRB*, 414 F. Supp. 1074, 1081 (S.D. Miss. 1976).

9.1.2. Handwritten notes of NLRB Regional Office attorney that "appear to be records of interviews of the charging parties and reflect only the answers of the charging parties" could not be said to reflect his thought processes for purposes of Exemption 5; however, they were found to be "the equivalent of the statements and affidavits submitted by the charging parties" for purposes of withholding under Exemption 7(C). *Associated Dry Goods Corp. v. NLRB*, 455 F. Supp. 802, 811 (S.D.N.Y. 1978).

9.1.3. NLRB agent's handwritten notes captioned "Memo to file" and other "file notes and investigative notes" were protected under Exemption 5. *Joseph Horne Co. v. NLRB*, 455 F. Supp. 1383, 1387 (W.D. Pa. 1978).

9.1.4. In *Fulbright & Jaworski v. Department of the Treasury*, 545 F. Supp. 615 (D.D.C. 1982), the court held that handwritten notes taken by an agency official during treaty negotiations were protected under Exemption 5.

9.2. Better-reasoned and more recent decisions, however, have discussed the "personal nature" and extent-of-circulation of handwritten notes in preliminary consideration of whether they qualify as "agency records" subject to the FOIA.

9.2.1. In connection with Atomic Energy Commission health, safety and environmental reviews, handwritten materials of staff members that "are not circulated to nor used by anyone other than the authors, and are discarded or retained at the author's sole discretion for their own individual purposes in their own personal files," were expressly found to be "personal notes, rather than agency records." *Porter County Chapter of the Izaak Walton League, Inc. v. Atomic Energy Commission*, 380 F. Supp. 630, 633 (N.D. Ind. 1974). "Disclosure of such personal documents," said the court, "would invade the privacy of and impede the working habits of individual staff members; it would preclude employees from ever committing any thoughts to writing which the author is unprepared, for whatever reason, to disseminate publicly." *Id.*

9.2.2. Citing *Porter County*, the court in *British Airports Authority v. CAB*, 531 F. Supp. 408 (D.D.C. 1982), held that handwritten notes of a senior CAB analyst, though prepared during the course of his official duties, were not "agency records" because the analyst "need not have created them, intended them to be temporary, not permanent, and kept them within his own personal files, with no intent to distribute them through normal agency channels." *Id.* at 416.

9.2.3. However, in *Bureau of National Affairs v. DOJ, supra*, a panel of the D.C. Circuit questioned the court's analysis in *Porter County* as being "based entirely on the *contents* of the notes, not on the agency's control, possession, or use of the notes," suggesting that "the court was applying policies underlying the FOIA exemptions" in concluding that the notes were not agency records. 742 F.2d at 1494 (emphasis supplied).

9.2.4. In *Conoco, Inc. v. DOJ*, 521 F. Supp. 1301 (D. Del. 1981), *aff'd in part, rev'd and remanded in part*, 687 F.2d 724 (3d Cir. 1982), the parties stipulated that 37 handwritten notes of employees of the Energy and Justice Departments assigned to investigate oil price control violations were "memoranda" subject to the FOIA, but disputed whether they were "intra-agency documents" subject to Exemption 5. The court rejected plaintiff's view that "intra-agency" means "circulated within the agency" and held instead that it "includes handwritten notes written by agency employees which remain within the files or confines of the agency." 521 F. Supp. at 1305; *see also* 687 F.2d at 728.

9.2.5. Another court found that handwritten "logs" maintained as indices at the front of Census Bureau notebooks concerning personnel actions, "although undoubtedly work-related, were nevertheless a voluntary piece of unofficial scholarship of an employee who finished them only to facilitate her own performance of her duties, and their disclosure can no more be compelled by a request for them under FOIA made to her employer than could, for example, her desk-side telephone directory or day-book." *AFGE, Local 2782 v. Department of Commerce*, 632 F. Supp. 1272, 1277 (D.D.C. 1986).

10. Request to Agency in Possession, Not to Originating Agency.

10.1. The requester need not seek access from the agency having the original copy or producing the document. *Legal Aid Soc'y of Alameda County v. Shultz*, 349 F. Supp. 771 (N.D. Cal. 1972); *Church of Scientology of California v. Department of the Air Force*, No. 76-1008 (D.D.C. Apr. 12, 1978).

10.2. In *McGehee v. CIA*, 697 F.2d 1095, 1110 (D.C. Cir. 1983), *vacated in part and aff'd in part*, 711 F.2d 1076 (D.C. Cir. 1983), the court stated the principle that "when an agency receives a FOIA request for 'agency records' in its possession it must take responsibility for processing the request. It cannot simply refuse to act on the ground that the documents originated elsewhere." *Accord Paisley v. CIA*, 712 F.2d at 691. However, the court in *McGehee* held that, under some circumstances, it may be proper for the agency to refer the request to the originating agency for direct response to the requester. However, the agency must provide a "reasonable explanation" for its procedure, including a showing that the procedure "significantly improves" the process for determining whether documents are to be released or withheld. 697 F.2d at 1110.

CHAPTER 15

Segregable Portions

Harry A. Hammitt

1. **Following its list of exemption provisions, § 552(b) of the FOIA provides: "Any reasonably segregable portion of a record shall be provided to any person requesting such record after deletion of the portions which are exempt under this subsection. The amount of information deleted shall be indicated on the released portion of the record, unless including that indication would harm an interest protected by the exemption in this subsection under which the deletion is made. If technically feasible, the amount of information deleted shall be indicated at the place in the record where such deletion is made."**

2. **Legislative History.**

2.1. As originally enacted in 1966, FOIA did not specifically require agencies to segregate non-exempt portions of a record from exempt portions for release to the requester.

2.2. The 1974 amendments to FOIA added the present "reasonably segregable" language specifically "to remedy the situation in which an agency seeks to withhold an entire record because a portion of it contains exempt information." *Yeager v. Drug Enforcement Administration*, 678 F.2d 315, 323 & n.18 (D.C. Cir. 1982). *See Arieff v. Department of the Navy*, 712 F.2d 1462, 1466 (D.C. Cir. 1983) ("...the exemptions to the FOIA do not apply wholesale. An item of exempt information does not insulate from disclosure the entire file in which it is contained, or even the entire page on which it appears.").

2.3. Prior to the 1974 amendments, the Supreme Court had held that Exemption 1 did not permit federal judges to inspect classified documents *in camera* "to sift out so-called 'non-secret components.'" If any part of a document or even a file was classified, all of it was exempt. *EPA v. Mink*, 410 U.S. 73, 81, 84 (1973). Also, other courts had interpreted Exemption 7 as a *per se* exemption authorizing withholding of entire investigatory files even when they contained non-exempt records. *See Weisberg v. DOJ*, 489 F.2d 1195 (D.C. Cir. 1973) (*en banc*), *cert. denied*, 416 U.S. 993 (1974).

2.4. In contrast, the Senate report on the 1974 amendments cited with approval several cases in which courts had ordered deletion of exempt information and disclosure of the remainder of the document. S. Rep. No. 854, 93d Cong., 2nd Sess. 31 (1974). *See, e.g., Wellford v. Hardin,* 444 F.2d 21 (4th Cir. 1971); *Grumman Aircraft Engineering Corp. v. Renegotiation Board,* 425 F.2d 578 (D.C. Cir. 1970); *Bristol-Myers Co. v. FTC,* 424 F.2d 935 (D.C. Cir. 1970), *cert. denied*, 400 U.S. 824 (1970).

2.5. The 1974 Senate report further stated: [The segregability requirement] emphasizes what is presently understood by most courts but has gone unheeded by agencies; it would not be enough for the government to refuse disclosure of the record merely because, it or the file it was in, contained such exempt information, since deletion of information would provide full protection for the purposes to be served by the exemption. Thus, the government could not refuse to disclose the requested records merely because it finds in those records some portions which may be exempt. S. Rep. No. 854, 93d Cong., 2d Sess. 32 (1974).

Segregable Portions

3. **The Attorney General's Memorandum on the 1974 Amendments to the Freedom of Information Act ("AG Memo") (*Reprinted in Freedom of Information Act and Amendments of 1974 (P.L. 93-502)—Source Book*, 99th Cong., 1st Sess. (Joint Cmte. Print, Mar. 1975) (1975 *Source Book)* at 507-38) provides further explanation of the term segregability.**

3.1. The Attorney General's Memorandum, explaining Congress's intent to "codify a deletion principle," notes that the language of § 552(b) should be read in conjunction with the *in camera* review provision of § 552(a)(4)(B), which states that a court "may examine the contents of [withheld] agency records *in camera* to determine whether such records or any part thereof shall be withheld under any of the exemptions...." AG Memo, *supra*, at 14, 1975 *Source Book* at 521. *See also Yeager,* 678 F.2d at 320 ("The segregation requirement, in conjunction with *Vaughn* indexing and the provision of the Act that allows *in camera* review of the requested documents, forecloses the possibility that an agency's sweeping claim of blanket exemption for any record or group of records will escape intensive court scrutiny.").

3.2. The AG Memo states that, after deletion of exempt materials from a requested file, "[t]he remaining material...must be released if it is at all intelligible.... [D]oubts about the intelligibility or responsiveness of remaining non-exempt material should be resolved in favor of release." *Id.* at 15.

4. **Claims of non-segregability must be made with the same degree of detail as required for claims of exemption. *See Vaughn v. Rosen (I)*, 484 F.2d 820 (D.C. Cir. 1973), *cert. denied*, 415 U.S. 977 (1974); *Mead Data Central, Inc. v. Department of the Air Force*, 566 F.2d 242, 260 (D.C. Cir. 1977). Moreover, the segregability requirement applies to all documents and all exemptions in the FOIA. *Center for Auto Safety v. EPA*, 731 F.2d 16, 21 (D.C. Cir. 1984).**

4.1. In addition to a statement of its reasons, an agency should also describe what proportion of the information in a document is non-exempt and how that material is dispersed throughout the document. *Mead Data Central*, 566 F.2d at 261. The agency must adequately describe the exempted material, "correlating the claimed exemptions to particular passages in the documents." *Schiller v. NLRB*, 964 F.2d 1205, 1209 (D.C. Cir. 1992). "The focus in the FOIA is information, not documents, and an agency cannot justify withholding an entire document simply by showing that it contains some exempted material." *Id. See Wightman v. BATF*, 755 F.2d 979, 982-983 (1st Cir. 1985).

4.1.1. In *Trans-Pacific Policing Agreement v. U.S. Customs Serv.*, 177 F.3d 1022 (D.C. Cir. 1999), the court ruled that district courts had an obligation to bring up segregability on their own if the issue had not been adequately addressed by the agency. The court ordered a series of numbers identifying shipments to be redacted in such a way that four numbers of the sequence could be disclosed.

4.2. When considering segregability claims, courts also must make "an express finding" as to the issue. "A district court that 'simply approves the withholding of an entire document without entering a finding of segregability or the lack thereof,' errs." *Krikorian v. Department of State*, 984 F.2d 461, 467 (D.C. Cir. 1993), *quoting Powell v. United States Bureau of Prisons,* 927 F.2d 1239, 1242 & n.4 (D.C. Cir. 1991) (criticizing lower court's review where "the magistrate never made an express finding as to segregability but rather simply noted with approval that the '[d]efendant avers that meaningful segregation of the material in the Manual is not feasible'") and *Church of Scientology v. Department of the Army*, 611 F.2d 738, 744 (9th Cir. 1979).

5. **In the Electronic Freedom of Information Act Amendments of 1996, see Section 6.6 in Chapter 1, *supra*, Congress reaffirmed the importance of agency compliance with these segregability requirements, while acknowledging potential risks of harmful disclosure and addressing practical problems that may arise in applying segregability requirements to the processing of computerized records.**

5.1. In amending the segregability language at the end of § 552(b), Congress mandated that "[t]he amount of information deleted shall be indicated on the released portion of the record, unless including that indication would harm an interest protected by the exemption in this subsection under which the deletion is made."

5.2. "If technically feasible," Congress added, "the amount of the information deleted shall be indicated at the place in the record where such deletion is made." The 1996 amendments further provide that courts "shall accord substantial weight" to an agency affidavit concerning the agency's determination as to the "technical feasibility" of indicating the amount of deleted information at the place in the record where the deletion occurred. § 552(a)(4)(B).

5.3. Since agencies are not permitted to charge fees for the cost of deleting exempt portions of records, the cost of editing are not relevant unless "so extreme that segregation of revealable material is unreasonable as a matter of law." *Long v. IRS*, 596 F.2d 362, 367 (9th Cir. 1979), *cert. denied*, 446 U.S. 917 (1980) ("deleting names and addresses did not amount to the production of a new record because the remaining information was 'reasonably segregable'"; court subsequently concluded that "all three of the Longs' disclosure plans would involve editing so extensive as to amount to the creation of new records"). *Compare Long v. IRS*, 825 F.2d 225 (9th Cir. 1987). *See Sherman v. Department of the Army*, 244 F.3d 357 (5th Cir. 2001), where the court upheld the agency's decision to require the requester to pay an estimated $350,000 to $1 million in costs for redacting Social Security numbers from a database of Vietnam medal awardees.

6. **District courts have broad discretion to determine whether *in camera* inspection is necessary to evaluate the government's claim that non-exempt material cannot be segregated from exempt material. *Center for Auto Safety v. EPA*, 731 F.2d 16 (D.C. Cir. 1984).**

6.1. The D.C. Circuit has declined to adopt a *per se* rule that *in camera* review is required where the government concedes that records contain factual material but contends that such material cannot be segregated from deliberative material withheld under Exemption 5. *Id.* This ruling reaffirms the court's discretion to determine when *in camera* review of withheld records is appropriate. *See also Meeropol v. Meese,* 790 F.2d 942 (D.C. Cir. 1986); *Doherty v. DOJ,* 775 F.2d 49, 53 (2nd Cir. 1985); *Mead Data Central*, 566 F.2d at 261-62 ("Requiring a detailed justification for an agency decision that non-exempt material is not segregable will not only cause the agency to reflect on the need for secrecy and improve the adversarial position of FOIA plaintiffs, but it will also enable the courts to conduct their review on an open record and avoid routine reliance on *in camera* inspection.").

Segregable Portions

6.2. The courts are far more reluctant to perform *in camera* inspections in national security cases than in other cases, and the D.C. Circuit has suggested that such review should be performed only where the government's affidavits are deficient. *See Weissman v. CIA,* 565 F.2d 692 (D.C. Cir. 1977); *Phillippi v. CIA,* 655 F.2d 1325 (D.C. Cir. 1981). However, even when an agency asserts the national security exemption to justify its failure to segregate, courts "insist that the affidavits provide a relatively detailed description" of the material withheld. *See Krikorian*, 984 F.2d at 467 (*quoting Goldberg v. Department of State*, 818 F.2d 71, 78 (D.C. Cir. 1987)). In *Krikorian*, where the descriptions in the agency's affidavits were found to be "quite general and may well include segregable material" and used "qualifying language impl[ying] that other portions of the documents may be segregable," the appeals court remanded for a determination "whether more detailed affidavits are appropriate or whether an alternative such as *in camera* review would better strike the balance between protecting sensitive foreign relations material and disclosing non-exempt information as required by the FOIA." 984 F.2d at 467.

6.3. Where *in camera* inspection shows the agency has not disclosed segregable material, that failure has been held to "create[] an appearance of arbitrariness...which in turn presents an issue as to whether the [agency] has properly responded to plaintiff's FOIA request." *Ferguson v. FBI,* 762 F. Supp. 1082, 1094-95 (S.D.N.Y. 1991) (requiring reprocessing of all documents for second *in camera* review), *rev'd on other grounds*, 957 F.2d 1059 (2d Cir. 1992).

7. **The "compilation" or "mosaic" theory of national security information has been held not to violate the segregability provision.** The statutory requirement to disclose "segregable portions" does not mean that unclassified items or portions of a document must be released if a compilation of the individual unclassified items of information viewed together warrants classification of the whole document. *See American Friends Service Committee v. Department of Defense,* 831 F.2d 441, 445 (3d Cir. 1987); *Taylor v. Department of the Army,* 684 F.2d 99, 102-05 (D.C. Cir. 1982); *Halperin v. NSC,* 452 F. Supp. 47 (D.D.C. 1978), *aff'd without opinion,* 612 F.2d 586 (D.C. Cir. 1980).

8. **Because of the subjective nature of many exemption claims by agency officials, administrative appeals of adverse FOIA responses by requesters who cite the segregability requirement often result in the release of additional responsive information.** Even in Exemption 1 cases, the second (and often more senior) agency reviewer required by the administrative appeal process frequently segregates and releases additional information or even entire documents that were withheld by the initial reviewer. Likewise, an agency reviewer who initially denies the information requested may, over time, change his or her mind about the sensitivity of particular records. The process can work in the other direction as well, towards reclassification of previously released records.

CHAPTER 16

Fees and Fee Waivers

Harry A. Hammitt & David L. Sobel

1. **Under the 1986 FOIA amendments, agencies are allowed to charge FOIA requesters three types of fees: (a) the direct cost to the agency to search for documents responsive to the request; (b) the direct cost for the agency to review documents it locates to determine what portions may be released; and (c) duplication costs. *See* § 552 (a)(4)(A). As is discussed below, all, some, or none of these fees may be assessed, depending on the requester's characteristics and the nature of the request.**

2. **Legislative History.**

2.1. As originally enacted in 1966, § 552(a)(3) of the FOIA allowed agencies, via published rules, to set "fees to the extent authorized by statute" for services performed in response to requests.

2.2. Absent specific statutory fee requirements, agencies looked to the Federal User Fee Statute, 31 U.S.C. § 9701, which authorized agency heads to determine "fair and equitable charges" and the guidelines for cost recovery set out in OMB's Circular A-25.

2.3. Years of experience under this approach demonstrated that requesters were being deterred from using the FOIA by the excessive search and duplication fees assessed by some agencies and that there was a "wide disparity among agencies in fees charged for the same types of records." *See* H. Rep. No. 1419, 92d Cong., 2d Sess. 10 (1972), reprinted in *Freedom of Information Act and Amendments of 1974* (P.L. 93-502)—*Source Book,* Joint Committee Print, 94th Congress, 1st Sess. (March 1975) at 3.

2.4. To address these problems, the FOIA's fee provisions were amended in 1974, requiring in § 552(a)(4)(A) that agency fees "be limited to reasonable standard charges for document search and duplication and provide for recovery of only the direct costs of such search and duplication." Conferees on the 1974 amendments intended that the costs of examination or review of records "should not be subject to recovery through assessment of fees" and that "fees should not be used for the purpose of discouraging requests for information or as obstacles to disclosure of requested information." *See* S. Rep. No. 1200, 93d Cong., 2d Sess. (1974) (Conference Report).

2.5. After years of debate regarding the fairness and sufficiency of the policies adopted in the 1974 amendments, Congress in 1986 again amended the FOIA, substantially revising the statutory fee and fee waiver provisions. *See generally* Chapter 1, "Overview," especially hearings cited in discussion of 1986 amendments.

2.6. The current FOIA fee and fee waiver statutory standards, as amended in 1986, require agency promulgation of fee regulations, authorize fee schedule guidance from OMB, provide for limitations on fees, and establish categories of requesters for purposes of assessing fees or granting fee waivers. *See* § 552(a)(4)(A).

3. Agency Regulations and OMB Guidelines.

3.1. Each agency is required to promulgate regulations under notice and comment procedures specifying a fee schedule and procedures for determining fee waivers or reductions, must "conform" to guidelines issued by OMB. § 552(a)(4)(A)(i).

3.2. After notice and comment, OMB issued its "Uniform Fee Schedule and Guidelines." 52 Fed. Reg. 10012 (daily ed. March 27, 1987). OMB's restrictive interpretation of procedural and definitional fee issues raised by the 1986 amendments appears to go far beyond OMB's specific statutory authorization to provide "a uniform schedule of fees for all agencies." However, an appeals court has ruled that an agency is free to adopt verbatim the fee waiver guidelines issued by OMB. Rejecting a claim that the FCC unlawfully delegated to OMB its duty to make an independent determination as to its fee waiver guidelines, the court found "that OMB's express mandate to establish fee schedule guidelines is broad enough to encompass guidelines for determining the assessment of fees for statutory categories." *Media Access Project v. Federal Communications Comm'n*, 883 F.2d 1063, 1069 (D.C. Cir. 1989).

3.3. Although agencies may adopt the OMB guidelines in their regulations, courts nevertheless have rejected narrow agency applications of those regulations that tend to follow the OMB guidelines' lead in restricting grants of fee waivers. Agency regulations based on the OMB guidelines for the "commercial use" and "representative of the news media" requester categories were found by an appeals court, after reviewing the legislative history, to allow fee waivers more broadly than the agency had applied them. *See National Security Archive v. Department of Defense*, 880 F.2d 1381 (D.C. Cir. 1989), *cert. denied*, 494 U.S. 1029 (1990) (reversing agency denial of fee waiver under "representative of the news media" category and finding "commercial use" fees cannot be assessed to requesters who fit into a preferred fee waiver category).

4. General Limitations on Fees and Relation of FOIA to Other Fee Statutes.

4.1. Agencies can provide for the recovery of only the direct costs of search, duplication and review of records responsive to a request. § 552(a)(4)(A)(iv).

4.2. No fee may be charged if the routine costs of collecting and processing the fee will likely equal or exceed the amount assessed. *Id.* at (iv)(I).

4.3. Agencies are required to provide free of charge the first two (2) hours of search time and the first one hundred (100) pages of duplication to all non-commercial requesters.

4.4. Requesters may not avoid legitimate fees by filing multiple requests to artificially "break down" what would reasonably be a single request. *Id.* at (iv)(II). However, the OMB guidelines regarding this provision, which have been adopted nearly verbatim by many agencies, make it clear that the agency must have a "reasonable basis" for believing that a request deliberately has been broken down into several requests solely to avoid payment of fees. Although the guidelines state that proximity in time is a factor to consider in determining whether there is a reasonable basis to aggregate requests, agencies are cautioned that such a presumption is especially difficult to support when requests were made more than thirty days apart. OMB also unequivocally states that "[i]n no case may agencies aggregate multiple requests on unrelated subjects from one requester." OMB Guidelines, Section 9(c).

4.5. Agencies may not require advance payment of any fee unless the requester has previously failed to pay fees in a timely fashion or the agency has determined that the fee will exceed $250 and the requester has not committed to pay assessed fees. § 552(a)(4)(A)(v). *See Vennes v. Internal Revenue Service*, 890 F.2d 419 (8th Cir. 1989) (agency not required to release records to a requester who had not sought waiver and would not commit to pay fees over $250); *Schmanke v. U.S. Postal Service*, No. 89-1551 (D.D.C. Jan. 4, 1990) (agency not required to release 72 boxes of records to a prisoner where he had not paid assessed fees in the past and did not otherwise qualify for a fee waiver). *See also Strout v. U.S. Parole Comm'n*, 40 F.3d 136, 139 (6th Cir. 1994) (agency did not violate restriction on requiring advance payment when it refused to release records until payment was made for search and duplication expenses "already incurred"). Rejecting a claim by the Justice Department that a request filed by Judicial Watch and a similar one filed by Judicial Watch of Florida should be aggregated for search purposes, the court found "this regulation is inapposite." The agency had treated the request by Judicial Watch of Florida as nothing more than an update of the earlier request from Judicial Watch. When the organization sued, the agency claimed the two requests fell within the provisions for aggregation. The court observed that "indeed, the two requests did not subdivide related requests but rather *duplicated* requests, an action poorly calculated to avoid fees." *Judicial Watch of Florida, Inc. v. DOJ,* 102 F. Supp. 2d 6 (D.D.C. 2000).

4.6. The Federal User Fee Statute, 31 U.S.C. § 9701, does not qualify as a superseding statute on fees for records containing information on matters of public interest.

5. Categories of Requesters For Fee and Fee Waiver Purposes.

5.1. "Commercial Use" Requester Fees.

5.1.1. When records are "requested for commercial uses," fees are limited to reasonable standard charges for document search, duplication, and review. § 552(a)(4)(A)(ii)(I).

5.1.2. Creation of the "commercial use" category in the 1986 amendments constituted a significant and controversial change in the law. Never before did the FOIA permit agency assessment of "review costs" against any requester, nor had it distinguished between "commercial" and other users.

5.1.3. Under the 1986 amendments, "review costs" shall include "only the direct costs incurred during the initial examination of a document for the purposes of determining whether the documents must be disclosed...and the purposes of withholding any portions exempt from disclosure." *Id.* at (iv). Review fees "may not include any costs incurred in resolving issues of law or policy that may be raised in the course of processing a request." *Id.* House sponsors of the amendments understood this to mean that "[o]nce a document has been reviewed in response to a request—whether from a commercial requester or otherwise—no charge may be imposed on any subsequent requester for reviewing that document." 132 Cong. Rec. H9463 (daily ed. Oct. 8, 1986) (statement of Reps. English and Kindness).

5.1.4. The 1986 amendments do not explain the intended meaning of the terms "commercial use" or "commercial interest" for purposes of FOIA fees.

Conflicting interpretations of these terms were articulated by the bill's chief Senate sponsors, Senators Leahy and Hatch. *See* 132 Cong. Rec. S16505 (daily ed. Oct. 15, 1986); Chapter 1, "Overview."

5.1.5. The OMB guidelines follow the legislative history's minority view of Senator Hatch to define a "commercial request" as "from or on behalf of one who seeks information for a use or purpose that furthers the commercial, trade, or profit interest of the requester or the person on whose behalf the request is made." OMB Guidelines, Section 6.g. The guidelines also state that to determine if a requester falls within this category, "agencies must determine the use to which a requester will put the documents requested." *Id.*

5.1.6. The court of appeals in *McClellan Ecological Seepage Situation v. Carlucci*, 835 F.2d 1282, 1285 (9th Cir. 1987), followed the D.C. Circuit ruling in an Exemption 4 case, *Public Citizen Health Research Group v. FDA*, 704 F.2d 1280, 1290 (D.C. Cir. 1983), holding that the term "commercial" is to be "given its ordinary meaning when read in conjunction with [the] FOIA." Although the *McClellan* court upheld the agency's "commercial use" regulation (which was based on the OMB Guidelines), it nevertheless found that the requester in question was not a commercial user because the information sought which related to a tort claim for damages against the government, "further[ed] a[n] interest in compensation or retribution, but not an interest in commerce, trade, or profit." *Id. See Muffoleto v. Sessions*, 760 F. Supp. 268, 277-78 (E.D.N.Y. 1991) (reversing FBI's "commercial" treatment of a requester seeking records in connection with his defense of a civil suit).

5.1.7. Clarification of the term "commercial" for FOIA fee purposes was provided in *National Security Archive v. Department of Defense, supra.* The court unanimously reversed the agency's assertion that a requester categorized as a representative of the news media could nevertheless be assessed search and review fees as a commercial requester because it received some remuneration for its publishing activities which incorporated "the fruits of its FOIA requests." Noting that most news media undertakings "are for-profit enterprises," the court rejected the agency's position as "contrary to the manifest purpose of the [FOIA]...and common sense." 880 F.2d at 1387-88.

5.1.8. *National Security Archive* clarifies that agency assessments of "commercial use" search and review fees to requesters who qualify for a preferred fee waiver category, or whose requests are not solely for a private, profit-making purpose violate the FOIA. Thus, for example, a freelance author who supports a request for a fee waiver with proof of a publication contract to show an ability to disseminate information from FOIA materials to the public is not liable for "commercial use" or "commercial interest" fees.

5.2. Fees for non-commercial requesters who do not otherwise qualify for a fee waiver (*see* infra Section 5.3-5.5) are limited to reasonable standard charges for document search and duplication. § 552(a)(4)(A)(ii)(III).

5.3. "Educational or Noncommercial Scientific Institution" Requester Fee Waivers.

5.3.1. When records are not sought for a commercial use and are requested by "an educational or noncommercial scientific institution whose purpose is scholarly or scientific research," agencies may only charge reasonable standard charges for duplication of the documents. § 552(a)(4)(A)(ii)(II).

5.3.2. As is true for the "commercial use" category, FOIA does not define "educational" or "noncommercial scientific" institution, and the legislative history conflicts as to what these terms were intended to mean. *See* 132 Cong. Rec. S14040 (daily ed. Sep. 27, 1986); 132 Cong. Rec. S14298 (daily ed. Sep. 30, 1986); 132 Cong. Rec. S16505 (daily ed. Oct. 15, 1986); 132 Cong. Rec. H9463 (daily ed. Oct. 8, 1986).

5.3.3. The applicable OMB guidelines again tend to reflect the minority views of Senator Hatch rather that the consensus views of the three other key sponsors of the 1986 amendments. OMB narrowly defines "educational institution" as "a preschool, a public or private elementary or secondary school, an institution of graduate higher education...of undergraduate higher education...of professional education...and of vocational education, which operates a program or programs of scholarly research." *See* OMB Guidelines, Section 6.h. Agency adoption of OMB's narrow interpretation of "educational institution" to refer exclusively to schools was upheld in *National Security Archive v. Department of Defense*. After reviewing the conflicting statements in the legislative history and finding them of little assistance in interpreting the statute, the court concluded that an organization is not an "educational institution" for FOIA fee waiver purposes "merely because it intends to make information available to the public." 880 F.2d at 1383-85.

5.3.4. The definition crafted by OMB for "noncommercial scientific institution" is broader than that for an "educational institution." OMB specifically rejected the suggestion from many agencies that "qualifying institutions be limited to those conducting research in the natural sciences," finding "no support in either the statute, the legislative history, or the plain meaning of the term to permit such a narrow reading." OMB Guidelines, Section 6.i. Because OMB's definition includes the social as well as natural sciences, libraries, "think-tanks," and other non-profit organizations that devote time and resources to research and dissemination of information on matters of public interest should consider invoking this "noncommercial scientific institution" category when seeking a fee waiver. *Compare McClellan* holding that public interest group does not qualify for a presumptive waiver of fees under this categorical scheme but must instead satisfy the alternative "public interest" statutory test for waiver of fees. 835 F.2d at 1284.

5.4. "Representative of the News Media" Requester Fee Waivers.

5.4.1. "Fees shall be limited to reasonable standard charges for document duplication when records are not sought for a commercial use and are requested by...a representative of the news media." § 552(a)(4)(A)(ii)(II).

5.4.2. Again, because the statutory language fails to define "representative of the news media," reference to the legislative history is necessary to determine congressional intent. *See, e.g.,* 132 Cong. Rec. S14040 (daily ed. Sep. 27, 1986); 132 Cong. Rec. S14298 (daily ed. Sep. 30, 1986); 132 Cong. Rec.

S16505 (daily ed. Oct. 15, 1986); 132 Cong. Rec. H9463 (daily ed. Oct. 8, 1986).

5.4.3. OMB interprets "representative of the news media" to require affiliation with "an entity that is organized and operated to publish or broadcast news to the public," and defines "news" as information "about current events or of current interest to the public." OMB Guidelines, Section 6.j., *reprinted at* Appendix A-108.

5.4.4. However, in *National Security Archive v. Department of Defense*, the D.C. Circuit unanimously rejected OMB's narrow reading and held that, for purposes of the FOIA's fee waiver provisions, a "representative of the news media" is "a person or entity that gathers information of potential interest to a segment of the public, uses its editorial skills to turn the raw materials into a distinct work, and distributes that work to an audience." 881 F.2d at 1387.

5.4.4.1. In reaching this holding, the court noted that "because one of the purposes of the [FOIA] is to encourage the dissemination of information in Government files...it is critical that the phrase 'representative of the news media' be broadly interpreted if the Act is to work as expected." *Id.* at 1386, *quoting* 132 Cong. Rec. S14298 (daily ed. Sept. 30, 1986) (remarks of Sen. Leahy).

5.4.4.2. The agency regulation at issue in *National Security Archive,* like similar regulations of many other agencies, was drawn nearly verbatim from the OMB Guidelines' interpretation of the term "representative of the news media."

5.4.4.3. One practical effect of *National Security Archive* is that a wide range of authors, freelance journalists, and non-profit and other organizations that put out newsletters or other publications should be granted fee waivers as "representatives of the news media."

5.4.5. Extending the holding of *National Security Archive*, a federal court in Illinois found that a small publisher whose previous business was more akin to that of information retrieval qualified for news media status because it claimed it planned to begin publishing a newsletter. *Hospital and Physician Publ'g Inc v. Dept. of Defense*, No. 98-4117 (S.D. Ill. June 22, 1999).

5.4.6. The public interest group Judicial Watch has been involved in a number of fee status decisions in the district court in Washington, D.C. One judge found that, although the group's website was "self-serving," such a method of dissemination qualified them for news media status under *National Security Archive* and if the status category was to be reined in in light of technological advances, it was Congress who should do so, not the courts. *Judicial Watch v. DOJ*, 133 F. Supp. 2d 52 (D.D.C. 2000). However, several other judges found that Judicial Watch characterized itself in its affidavits as a public interest law firm, not a member of the news media. These judges pointed out that Judicial Watch was perhaps an important source for the media, but the fact that it provided information to the media was an indication that it was not a member of the media itself. The courts also found that the fact Judicial Watch had disseminated information in the past was not relevant to its ability to disseminate the records at issue in the case. *See Judicial Watch v. DOJ*, 122 F. Supp. 2d 5 (D.D.C. 2000), *Judicial Watch v. DOJ*, 122 F. Supp. 2d 13 (D.D.C. 2000), *Judicial Watch v. DOJ*, No. 99-2315 (D.D.C. Aug. 16, 2000), *Judicial Watch v. DOJ*, No. 00-745 (D.D.C. Feb. 12, 2001) ("link between the information requested here and the possibility that plaintiff will eventually publish it in some future work that will contribute to the understanding of a reasonably broad audience is too attenuated."), *Judicial Watch v. Rossotti*, No. 01-1612, 2002 WL 535803 (D.D.C. Mar. 18, 2002), *Judicial Watch v. DOJ*, 185 F. Supp. 2d 54 (D.D.C. 2002).

5.5. Fee Waivers Where Disclosure "Is In the Public Interest."

5.5.1. In addition to establishing the preferred fee categories discussed above, the 1986 amendments provided for fee waivers or reductions "if disclosure of the information is in the public interest because it is likely to contribute significantly to public understanding of the operations or activities of the government and is not primarily in the commercial interest of the requester." § 552(a)(4)(A)(ii)(II).

5.5.1.1. This provision also can operate to waive copying fees that might otherwise be assessed to a preferred fee category requester (who is already entitled to an automatic waiver of all search and review fees).

5.5.1.2. The legislative history of the fee waiver standard established by the 1974 amendments "clearly indicates" that Congress intended to create a public interest/benefit test for granting FOIA fee waivers that was to be "liberally construed," and was "consistently associated with requests from journalists, scholars, and non-profit interest groups who it was intended to benefit." *Ettlinger v. FBI*, 596 F. Supp. 867, 872 (D. Mass. 1984); *National Treasury Employees Union v. Griffin*, 811 F.2d 644, 649 (D.C. Cir. 1987) (legislative history shows "a special solicitude for journalists"); *Lybarger v. Cardwell*, 577 F.2d 764 (1st Cir. 1978).

5.5.2. Sharp conflicts as to the intended scope of the 1986 fee waiver amendments again are visible in the legislative history between the interpretation offered by three of the sponsors—Sen. Leahy and Reps. English and Kindness—and the views of the fourth, Sen. Hatch. *See* 132 Cong. Rec. S14040 (daily ed. September 27, 1986); 132 Cong. Rec. S14298 (daily ed. September 30, 1986); 132 Cong. Rec. S16505 (daily ed. October 15, 1986); 132 Cong. Rec. H9463 (daily ed. October 8, 1986). *See also McClellan*, 835 F.2d at 1284-86 (citing Leahy-English-Kindness consensus).

5.5.3. Any requester, regardless of identity or status, can qualify for a fee waiver under this general standard on a case-by-case basis. Because the requester's intended "use" of the information is key, even a commercial requester possibly could qualify for a public interest fee waiver if, for example, release of the information would expose government fraud or other improprieties. *See* OMB Guidelines, Section 6(g).

5.5.4. In *Friends of the Coast Fork, et al. v. Dept. of Interior*, 110 F.3d 53 (9th Cir. 1997), the Ninth Circuit enunciated a rather broad standard for public interest fee waivers. In granting the plaintiff a waiver, the court said that when a public interest group submitted a persuasive argument pertaining to how it would use the information to further the public interest, then a fee waiver should be granted.

5.5.5. Most fee waiver decisions in recent years in the District of Columbia have involved the public interest group Judicial Watch. One court turned down the group's bid for a fee waiver for a broad topic because it failed to establish a link between the information and the public interest and failed to show how disclosure of the information would further public understanding of government activities and operations. *Judicial Watch v. DOJ*, 122 F. Supp. 2d 13 (D.D.C. 2000). But another judge granted a fee waiver for a more focused request—pertaining to possible political influence in the awarding of a lease for a D.C. office building—after finding the organization had shown how the information would increase public understanding of government activities or operations and that the organization had the ability to disseminate the information widely. *Judicial Watch v. General Services Administration*, No. 98-2223 (D.D.C. Sept. 25, 2000), *Judicial Watch v. DOJ*, 185 F. Supp. 2d 54 (D.D.C. 2002) .

5.5.6. Judge Gladys Kessler rejected DOJ's claim that Judicial Watch was not entitled to a fee waiver for records concerning President Clinton's final pardons because nothing but news clippings would be disclosable without Privacy Act waivers. Kessler indicated that "it is therefore unclear how the Defendant could represent at this early juncture that *all* documents that are likely to be responsive and disclosable to Plaintiff are currently in the public domain." She told the agency it would have to prepare an index indicating "at least one site in the public domain where each document is located or at least one public source from which these documents could be obtained." *Judicial Watch v. DOJ*, Nos. 01-0639 and 01-0720 (D.D.C. Mar. 22, 2002).

6. Department of Justice Guidelines for Public Interest Fee Waivers.

6.1. During the Reagan Administration, the Justice Department issued several sets of guidelines instructing federal agencies how to process fee waiver requests under the public interest standard. The first set, interpreting the 1974 amendments and issued on January 7, 1983, emphasized two policy objectives: (1) fostering "disclosure of non-exempt agency records which will primarily benefit the general public," and (2) "the preservation of public funds where there will be insufficient public benefit derived from disclosure."

6.2. Purportedly merely a "restatement" of policy, the 1983 guidelines' major goal was apparently to urge agencies to collect more fees and be more stringent in granting fee waivers. Critics charged that the guidelines distorted the intent of Congress with respect to the statutory "public interest" fee waiver standard by improperly stressing that "agencies are obligated to safeguard the public treasury." Some courts agreed. *See, e.g., Diamond v. FBI*, 548 F. Supp. 1158, 1160 (S.D.N.Y. 1982) ("Insofar as the agency's determination was based on the risk to the public in waiving fees for prospective authors without a guarantee of future public benefit, it was based on a factor 'not controlling under the terms of the statute' and was, therefore, arbitrary and capricious."); *Fitzgibbon v. CIA,* No. 76-700 (D.D.C. Jan. 10, 1977) (agency's "perceived obligation to the public" to collect FOIA fees is "irrelevant to the purposes of § 552(a)(4)(A)"). *But see Better Government Ass'n v. Department of State,* 780 F.2d 86 (D.C. Cir. 1986) (1983 Justice Department fee waiver guidelines held facially consistent with the FOIA).

6.3. The 1983 guidelines' emphasis on preventing "a drain upon agency appropriations" sharply contrasts with the more access-oriented approach of the guidelines they replaced, which were issued in January 1981 by then-Attorney General Benjamin Civiletti. *See* 20 C.F.R. § 16.9(a) (1981). In the memorandum accompanying those rules, Civiletti noted that "Congress clearly intended that [agency] discretion be exercised generously," yet "the Federal Government often fails to grant fee waivers under the Freedom of Information Act when requesters have demonstrated that sufficient public interest exists to support such waivers."

6.4. The 1983 Justice Department guidelines specified five criteria that agencies were to consider in deciding to grant a fee waiver request: (1) whether there is a genuine public interest in the subject matter of the documents; (2) the value to the public of the records themselves; (3) whether the information is already in the public domain; (4) the requester's identify and qualifications (e.g., the requester's "expertise in the subject and ability and intention to disseminate information to the public"); and (5) the requester's "personal" interest that would be benefited by disclosure, including some commercial benefit, personal use, or use in litigation.

6.5. In a November 12, 1986 memorandum to all federal agencies, the Justice Department provided "Additional Fee Waiver Guidance" stating that an agency was not required to grant a fee waiver to "a library or other record repository (or to a requester who intends to disseminate information to such an institution) based solely upon its status as an institution at which records are generally available."

6.5.1. This memorandum said that such requests, "like those of any other requester, should be considered on a case-by-case basis in light of all relevant information."

6.5.2. The memorandum further instructed that, "where a fee waiver request from an institution or individual is based upon intended dissemination to other institutions, or upon scholarly or other analytic work to be done by another person to whom the requested records (or any information based thereon) ultimately will be made available, an agency may reasonably require the requester to identify specifically a person who will actually use such information in scholarly or other analytic work and to make the same showing that person would have to make to obtain a fee waiver for the records directly, including a representation by that person of intent to perform the work involved."

6.5.3. However, in a colloquy during debate on State Department appropriations legislation, Senator Leahy responded to Senator Kerry's question about the State Department's policy of denying fee waivers to libraries by stating that, for fee waiver purposes, all government agencies "should recognize the vital contributions that libraries and depositories of public records make to the public's understanding of the operations of government. All federal agencies should implement the intended favorable treatment of these organizations under the FOIA." 135 Cong. Rec. S8466 (daily ed. July 20, 1989).

6.6. Following enactment of the 1986 FOIA amendments, the Department of Justice, in an April 2, 1987 memorandum from its Office of Information and Privacy, issued new "FOIA Fee Waiver Policy Guidance." The 1987 guidelines superseded the previous fee waiver guidance of January 1983 and November 1986 and became effective with respect to fee waiver determinations as of April 25, 1987.

6.7. Although the Justice Department's 1987 fee waiver guidance addresses the 1986 revisions to the FOIA's fee waiver standards, their tone and substance is closely consistent with the Department's previous restrictive fee policies and continue to reflect a stated concern for "safeguarding federal funds by granting waivers or reductions only where it is determined that the statutory standard is satisfied."

6.8. The six factors which the Department urges agencies to employ in the determination of fee waiver actions under the 1987 policy guidance are substantially similar to the five criteria of the Department's 1983 policy guidance. These factors include:

6.8.1. A. Disclosure of the Information "is in the Public Interest Because it is Likely to Contribute Significantly to Public Understanding of the Operations or Activities of the Government." (1) The subject of the request: Whether the subject of the requested records concerns "the operations or activities of the government"; (2) The informative value of the information to be disclosed: Whether the disclosure is "likely to contribute" to an understanding of government operations or activities; (3) The contribution to an understanding of the subject by the general public likely to result from disclosure: Whether disclosure of the requested information will contribute to "public understanding"; and (4) The significance of the contribution to public understanding: Whether the disclosure is likely to contribute "significantly" to public understanding of government operations or activities.

6.8.2. B. Disclosure of the Information "is Not Primarily in the Commercial Interest of the Requester." (1) The existence and magnitude of a commercial interest: Whether the requester has a commercial interest which would be furthered by the requested disclosure; and, if so (2) The primary interest in disclosure: Whether the magnitude of the identified commercial interest of the requester is sufficiently large, in comparison with the public interest in disclosure, that disclosure is "primarily in the commercial interest of the requester."

6.9. The Justice Department's fee waiver guidelines do not supplant the statutory waiver standard; they are "advisory" and merely provide agencies with "policy guidance" for its application. However, since most agencies have incorporated the guidelines into their own FOIA regulations and some courts have applied the six factors as the basis for judicial review, *see, e.g., McClellan*, 835 F.2d at 1286, and *Sloman v. DOJ*, 832 F. Supp. 63, 68 (S.D.N.Y. 1993), it is important for requesters who seek a fee waiver to address these concerns in their request letters. Failure to provide this information may result in a delay in processing the request while the agency seeks more detailed justification for the request.

7. Applying public interest fee waiver criteria.

7.1. The burden for satisfying the public interest standard is on the requester. *Larson v. CIA*, 843 F.2d 1481 (D.C. Cir. 1988). *Compare Project on Military Procurement v. Department of the Navy*, 710 F. Supp. 362, 367 (D.D.C. 1989) (contrasting initial burden on plaintiff to establish entitlement to public interest fee waiver with burden on government to justify nondisclosure under the FOIA's exemptions).

7.2. There is no rigid formula for determining whether there is public interest in the subject of the disclosed documents. However, benefit to a population group of some size distinct from the requester alone is sufficient. *Ettlinger*, 596 F. Supp. at 876. *See also Carney v. DOJ*, 19 F.3d 807, 815 (2d Cir. 1994), *cert. denied,* 513 U.S. 823 (1994) (applying "public" to require a sufficient "breadth of benefit" beyond the requester's own interests). *But see National Treasury Employees Union*, 811 F.2d at 648 (court found union's public interest "at best tenuous" and rejected union's "suggestion that its size insures that any benefit to it amounts to a public benefit").

7.3. Court decisions interpreting this provision look to all of the facts and circumstances in determining whether a public interest fee waiver is warranted, but generally agree that simply "establishing a public interest in the subject matter is not sufficient," and that absent a showing of an ability to disseminate the information to the public, the fee waiver request may be denied. *See Larson v. CIA*, 843 F.2d at 1481. *See also McClain v. DOJ*, 13 F.3d 220, 221 (7th Cir. 1993) (fee waiver denied to prisoner who asserted only an intent to give the requested information to unnamed reporters and to public interest groups for whom no interest in the material or ability to disseminate had been shown). The ability to disseminate the information to the public may be shown in a variety of ways, including an intent to give the information to an interested person or group that has the ability to publish it. *See, e.g., Pederson v. Resolution Trust Corp.*, 847 F. Supp. 851, 856-57 (D. Colo. 1994). *But see Larson, id.* at n.5 ("special solicitude" for journalists does not extend to requesters who simply assert an intention to give released records to journalists).

7.4. At least one court that has carefully considered the issue has held that "neither the statute nor the Department of Justice guidelines permit an agency to make a *de novo* determination as to the intrinsic value of the subject matter on which the information is requested." *Ettlinger*, 596 F. Supp. at 875. While the agency may evaluate "whether the subject matter is one in which there is some objectively demonstrable interest by some segment of the public," it may not "substitute its own judgment for that of an objectively reasonable judgment by the requester as to the scholarly, historical or academic value of the particular subject of the requesters' research." *Id.* The *Ettlinger* court exhaustively reviewed cases demonstrating that "courts have consistently overturned agency denials of fee waivers when requestors have made a legitimate, objectively supportable showing of using the requested information for scholarly research into political and historical events." *Id.* *But see Shaw v. FBI*, 604 F. Supp. 342 (D.D.C. 1985) (waiver denial upheld where agency found only "remote and theoretical" connection between records sought and plaintiff's "unorthodox," "amorphous," and "somewhat unique" theory of French mercenaries' involvement in the JFK assassination).

7.5. The Justice Department's focus on the informative value of the records has led it to declare that a fee waiver is appropriate "only if the disclosable contents of the records are in fact informative on the issue found by the agency to be of public interest," and that the public will benefit from disclosure "only if the information released meaningfully contributes to public development or understanding of the subject"; if the information is only of "marginal value in informing the public," then the public benefit "is diminished accordingly." *Common Cause v. IRS*, 646 F.2d 656 (D.C. Cir. 1981). However, in a suit for a waiver of search fees involving a request for historical material admittedly of benefit to the public if released, one court has said that "[t]he statute does not permit a consideration of how many documents will ultimately be released....[A] single document may...substantially enrich the public domain." *Eudey v. CIA*, 478 F. Supp. 1175, 1177 (D.D.C. 1979). *Compare Diamond v. FBI*, 532 F. Supp. 216, 234 (S.D.N.Y. 1981), *aff'd* 707 F.2d 75 (2d Cir. 1983), *cert. denied*, 465 U.S. 1004 (1984) (appropriateness of fee waiver dependent upon court's *in camera* review of documents to assess their "historical significance") *and Ettlinger*, 596 F. Supp. at 876 (FBI abused its discretion by rejecting an objectively supportable assessment of the value and usefulness of the releasable material and substituting its own).

7.6. An agency cannot deny a fee waiver request on the grounds that much of the requested information is likely to be redacted or exempt from disclosure. As one court has observed, "[i]t is unfair and contrary to the spirit of the FOIA to deny a financially limited requester...a fee waiver based on an agency determination [regarding exemption claims] that is speculative and unreviewable." *Project on Military Procurement*, 710 F. Supp. at 367-68. *See also Carney*, 19 F.3d at 815 (fee waiver request should be evaluated based on the face of the request and reasons given in support by the requester; only if request was for "patently exempt" documents would it be proper to deny a fee waiver on the basis of exemption).

7.7. The Justice Department also has instructed agencies to determine whether the requested material has been published "or is otherwise available on the public record." If so, a waiver of copying fees could be denied. *Blakey v. DOJ*, 549 F. Supp. 362, 364-65 (D.D.C. 1982) (copying fee waiver denied). *See also Carney, supra* ("mere fact that particular records have been released to other requesters does not mean that the information contained in the records is readily available to the public;" improper to reject waiver without explaining how these released records were readily available to the public). Courts are split as to whether the fact that records sought by a requester are available in a public reading room precludes a fee waiver. Rejecting agency arguments that the availability of FOIA material in an agency's public reading room "thrust[s] the material into the public domain," one court has stated that the requester's publication of the information sought would be much more likely than the agency's reading room "to contribute significantly to public understanding" of agency practices. *Fitzgibbon v. AID*, 724 F. Supp. 1048, 1051 (D.D.C. 1989). *See also Coalition for Safe Power, Inc. v. DOE*, No. 91-0078 (D.D.C. Sept. 10, 1991) (fee waiver granted to non-profit public interest organization even though document requested was available in agency's public reading room). *But see Sloman*, 832 F. Supp. at 68 ("public's understanding" of material would not be significantly enhanced by release to requester where material is available in agency's public reading room); *Sierra Club Legal Defense Fund, Inc. v. Bibles*, No. C92-1413 WD (W.D. Wa. February 17, 1993), *aff'd*, No. 93-35383 (9th Cir., Aug. 29, 1994) (unpublished memorandum), 34 F.3d 1073 (9th Cir. 1994) (table cite) (fee waiver denied where documents sought were "published or...routinely available in a public reading room or a federal depository library"); *St. Hilaire v. DOJ*, No. 91-0078 (D.D.C. Sept. 10, 1991), *aff'd*, No. 92-5153 (D.C. Cir. Apr. 28, 1994) (fee waiver denied where records were available in the public reading room).

7.8. The 1983 guidelines recommended that requesters describe their qualifications, the nature of their research, and the purposes for which they intend to use requested records. *See, e.g., Blakey v. DOJ*, 549 F. Supp. 362, 364 (D.D.C. 1982) . *See also McClain,* 13 F.3d at 221 (waiver request must be assessed in light of the identity and objective of the actual requester). A "mere representation" that someone is a researcher or "plans to write a book" is insufficient, *Burris v. CIA*, 524 F. Supp. 448 (M.D. Tenn. 1981), although requesters seeking materials in connection with a publication or similar work should be granted a waiver if they identify the public interest in the requested records and can make some showing that the resulting work is likely to be disseminated to the public. *See Larson*, 843 F.2d at 1483; *Ettlinger*, 596 F. Supp. at 877. *See* Section 5.5.4., *supra*.

7.9. The fact that the requester may have some personal interest or pecuniary gain as a result of the release of records is not dispositive of whether there will be a discernible benefit to the public from release of the requested information, nor should it necessarily outweigh the requester's salutary purpose of widely disseminating such information to others. *Ettlinger,* 596 F. Supp. at 877. *See also National Treasury Employees Union,* 811 F.2d at 649 (requiring a requesting union to submit more detail than a journalist to secure a finding of predominant public benefit because, unlike the journalists, a union "may put information to such varied uses, many of which are wholly independent of informing the public, that the relation between public and private benefits is by no means constant"). *See* Section 5.1., *supra,* for criteria for "commercial use" fee category.

7.10. The 1983 Justice Department guidelines declared that a requester's indigence is not by itself sufficient to qualify the requester for a waiver of fees. *See Schmanke, supra* ("indigency is not a basis for an exemption from the fee requirement of the FOIA, nor for a waiver of the requirement by the agency"). *See also Ely v. U.S. Postal Service*, 753 F.2d 163, 165 (D.C. Cir. 1985), *cert. denied*, 471 U.S. 1106 (1985) (holding that Congress rejected waivers based on indigence) and *Durham v. DOJ,* 829 F. Supp. 428 (D.D.C. 1993) (court found that plaintiff "failed to identify how it is in the public interest for the Defendant to provide him with free copies of public court records that are easily accessible and available to everyone else for a fee" and that "indigency alone does not constitute adequate grounds for a fee waiver"). *But see Blue v. Bureau of Prisons*, No. C75-2092A (N.D. Ga. Aug. 23, 1978), *rev'd and remanded*, 570 F.2d 529 (5th Cir. 1978) (fees can be waived for indigents because otherwise fees would be an obstacle to disclosure, contrary to the pro-disclosure thrust of the Act).

8. Judicial Review of Fee Waiver Denials and Exhaustion of Remedies.

8.1. The 1986 FOIA amendments establish that, in an action regarding the waiver of fees, the court shall determine the matter *de novo,* except that its review of the matter shall be limited to the administrative record. § 552(a)(4)(A)(vii). If an appeal to the agency is unsuccessful, a court can review the agency's action and order fees waived.

8.2. Prior to the 1986 amendments, judicial review of fee waiver matters was limited to determining whether the agency's action was an abuse of discretion. *See, e.g.,*

National Treasury Employees Union, 811 F.2d at 647; *Ely v. U.S. Postal Service,* 753 F.2d at 165. Even after the 1986 amendments, courts may still uphold an agency's finding that fee waiver does not satisfy the public interest standard unless the finding is arbitrary or capricious. *McClain,* 13 F.3d at 220-21; *Savage v. CIA*, 826 F.2d 561, 563 (7th Cir. 1987).

8.3. Even if the requester submits information sufficient to support the request for a fee waiver in a court action challenging an agency's denial of the waiver, a court's review of the agency's denial is limited to the facts in the administrative record before the agency. *Oglesby v. Department of the Army*, 920 F.2d 57 (D.C. Cir. 1990). *See Larson,* 843 F.2d at 1483 (letter from newspaper offered as proof of requester's intent to release documents to the press could not be considered by the district court because it had not been part of the record before the agency).

8.4. A requester who does not comply with the procedures established in an agency's fee regulations may be found to have failed to exhaust administrative remedies and be precluded from filing suit to challenge assessed fees. In *Morello v. DOJ*, No. 90-1078 (D.D.C. Oct. 16, 1990), *aff'd*, 948 F.2d 1337 (D.C. Cir. 1991), a requester's suit was dismissed for failure to resolve fee disputes regarding his request, either through a commitment to pay processing fees likely to exceed $250 or by requesting a fee waiver, with the court stating that resolution of fee issues under the FOIA "is a step in the administrative process which must be pursued before resort to judicial remedies." *See also Voinche v. Department of the Air Force*, 983 F.2d 667 (5th Cir. 1993) *cert. denied.*, 510 U.S. 817 (1993) (no exhaustion where fee waivers were not initially sought for all requests and requester neither responded to agency's request for clarification nor sought a final ruling on his waiver request before filing suit).

8.5. Payment of fees after a fee waiver denial has been appealed, in order to quickly obtain the records sought, may be construed as a waiver of the right to challenge the fee waiver denial in court. *See Savage v. FBI*, No. 90-1110 (7th Cir. July 31, 1991). To preserve the right to sue, such payments should be accompanied by a written statement that they are made "under protest" and that the requester reserves the right to pursue judicial remedies.

8.6. A requester can recover attorney fees for successfully litigating an agency's refusal to waive fees. *See Wilson v. DOJ,* No. 87-2415 (D.D.C. May 2, 1989), 1993 U.S. Dist LEXIS 9175 (D.D.C. June 30, 1993), *supra* (attorney fees awarded as "compensation for time spent addressing the fee waiver issue"); *Ettlinger*, 596 F. Supp. at 879. *Cf. Weisberg v. DOJ (II)*, 848 F.2d 1265, 1268-69 (D.C. Cir. 1988) (discussing with approval attorney fee awards for fee waiver issues). *See* Chapter 17 on "Attorney Fees."

9. Requester Guidance for Obtaining Fee Waivers.

9.1. Check the agency's FOIA regulation in the Code of Federal Regulations to see if it mentions any specific criteria that should be addressed, or information that should be provided, when making your fee request.

9.2. Do some homework. Call the agency and try to find out which office actually has the records you seek, how they are filed, how voluminous they are, and how you might narrow your request to locate only the records in which you are truly interested. The more specific you can be in framing your request, the less likely the agency is to respond by saying that your request is too vague or will require hundreds or even thousands of dollars of fees in order for it to respond.

9.3. In the request letter, identify yourself and your organization (if applicable); any relevant experience, expertise or interest in the subject; and, indicate why disclosure of the requested information is likely to contribute significantly to public understanding of the operations or activities of the government.

9.4. Indicate why the records you seek are important and what people or groups are the likely beneficiaries of knowing the contents of the records.

9.5. Explain how you intend to disseminate the contents of the records to the public, such as by publishing an article, book, or similar work, conveying it through public statements or testimony, or by making the information in the documents otherwise accessible to the public. If you have published or otherwise made similar information available to the public in the past, inform the agency about such action.

9.6. If the requested material is likely to be something that others will request, point out the unfairness of requiring the first requester to bear the search costs.

9.7. State your knowledge that the FOIA requires that agencies must waive all fees if the costs of routine collection and processing of the fee are likely to equal or exceed that amount of the fee to be assessed.

9.8. Consider asking to inspect the records, rather than requesting the agency to provide you with copies, especially if you are interested in a great number of documents and suspect that you will simply want to take notes or copy just a few of them. This approach may reduce the potential cost to the agency and provide an incentive to waive the fee entirely, although it may not be feasible if requesters do not have ready access to the site where the records are kept or if the agency wants to make a number of deletions from the requested records.

9.9. As the Justice Department guidelines emphasize, fee waiver requests are committed to the agency's discretion to assess the facts and circumstances in each case to determine whether the statutory standard is satisfied. If, however, the agency determines that the facts and circumstances in a particular case meet the statutory standard, the mandatory language of § 552(a)(4)(A)(iii) states that the documents "shall be furnished without any charge or at a charge reduced below" the established fee.

9.10. If a fee waiver request is denied, it should first be appealed to the agency under the same procedures used to appeal a denial of a request for access to records. *See* discussion in Chapter 2 on "Administrative Process."

9.11. Agencies sometimes significantly overestimate the fees that may ultimately be assessable in processing a particular FOIA request, sometimes overstating by tens of thousands of dollars the actual cost to the agency. A 1990 General Accounting Office study of the government's claim that compliance with the court-ordered release of agency records in *DOJ v. Tax Analysts*, 492 U.S. 136 (1989), would cost $75,000 yearly found that the actual annual cost was closer to $23,500. Thus, before paying in advance any fee estimated to exceed $250 [*see* Section 4.5., *supra*], requesters should contact the agency to determine how those costs were estimated and whether those estimated costs can be reduced. This may include inquiring about the basis for the cost estimate, narrowing or redefining the request, setting a ceiling on the amount of fees you wish to incur and asking that the agency contact you before performing more work on the request, or offering to examine documents located by the agency to determine if they are responsive to the request before they are copied.

9.12. Success in pursuing judicial review of a fee waiver matter can turn on the quality and extent of supporting information a requester provides to the agency initially and on administrative appeal, as well as the rationale given by the agency. One court has suggested that a requester restructure his request to conform to the Justice Department fee waiver guidelines then in effect, *Buriss v. CIA*, 524 F. Supp. at 449, while another court ordered fees waived because it found that the agency had failed to consider a fee waiver request seriously. *Diamond*, 523 F. Supp. at 1160. *But see National Treasury Employees Union*, 811 F.2d at 648 ("The reasonableness of the agency's refusal [to grant a fee waiver] depends on the information before it at the time of its decision, and failure to demonstrate a public interest before the agency cannot be remedied by doing so before a court.... This is not to say that courts should ignore otherwise admissible evidence of a public interest that was not submitted to the agency, however, since such evidence may apprise the court of a controversy already known to the agency.").

Chapter 17
Attorney Fees and Litigation Costs
David C. Vladeck & Harry A. Hammitt

1. **Attorneys' fees and litigation costs under FOIA are governed by § 552(a)(4)(E), which provides: "The court may assess against the United States reasonable attorney fees and other litigation costs reasonably incurred in any case under this section in which the complainant has substantially prevailed."**

2. **Legislative History.**

2.1. The 1974 House bill provided that fees and costs could be assessed at the court's discretion when the agency "has not prevailed." *Freedom of Information Act and Amendments of 1974 (P.L. 93-502) Source Book*, House Committee on Government Operations, Senate Committee on the Judiciary, 94th Cong., 1st Sess. (March 1975) (hereinafter "*1974 Source Book*") at 133). The language was drawn from "similar provisions," citing 42 U.S.C. §§ 2000a-3(b), 2003-5(1) (Titles II and VII of 1964 Civil Rights Act) and 20 U.S.C. § 1617 (Title II of Emergency School Aid Act) (H.R. Rep. No. 876, quoted in *1974 Source Book*, at 127).

2.2. The Senate bill provided that fees and costs could be assessed where "complainant has substantially prevailed." (*1974 Source Book* at 189) (emphasis supplied). Four criteria were specified for the court to "consider" in determining whether to grant an award:

2.2.1. "the benefit to the public, if any, deriving from the case";

2.2.2. "the commercial benefit of the complainant";

2.2.3. "the nature of [the complainant's] interest in the records sought"; and

2.2.4. "whether the government's withholding of the records sought had a reasonable basis in law" *Id.* at 189-90.

2.3. The Conference Report states that the amendment adopted the Senate formulation, applying to cases in which plaintiff has "substantially prevailed," but eliminating the criteria in the Senate bill "because the existing body of law on the award of attorney fees recognizes such factors, [and] a statement of the criteria may be too delimiting and is unnecessary." *Id.* at 226-27.

2.4. Congressional policies for including the attorney fees and cost provision in the FOIA.

2.4.1. "Congress realized that too often the insurmountable barriers presented by court costs and attorney fees to the average person requesting information under the FOIA enabled the government to escape compliance with the law." *Cuneo v. Rumsfeld*, 553 F.2d 1360, 1363-64 (D.C. Cir. 1977).

2.4.2. The Senate Report refers to the traditional role of statutory allowance of attorney fees to plaintiffs "in encouraging individuals 'to seek judicial relief" for the purpose of 'vindicating national policy.'" *Northcross v. Board of Education of the Memphis City Schools*, 412 U.S. 427 (1973). *1974 Source Book* at 170.

2.4.3. Congressional intent underlying the fee provision is also discussed in *LaSalle Extension University v. FTC*, 627 F.2d 481, 484 (D.C. Cir. 1980); *Fenster v. Brown*, 617 F.2d 740, 742-43 (D.C. Cir. 1979); *Blue v. Bureau of Prisons*, 570 F.2d 529, 532-33 (5th Cir. 1978); *Nationwide Building Maintenance, Inc. v. Sampson*, 559 F.2d 704, 710-13 (D.C. Cir. 1977); *Cuneo v. Rumsfeld*, 553 F.2d at 1364; and *Rocap v. Indiek*, 539 F.2d 174, 179 (D.C. Cir. 1976).

3. **Before a court may award attorney fees, it must determine first whether the plaintiff is eligible, and, if so, whether the plaintiff is entitled to such an award.** *See, e.g., GMRI, Inc. v. EEOC*, 149 F.3d 449, 451 (6th Cir. 1998); *Tax Analysts v. DOJ*, 965 F.2d 1092, 1093 (D.C. Cir. 1992); *Weisberg v. DOJ*, 745 F.2d 1476, 1495 (D.C. Cir. 1984); *Union of Concerned Scientists v. NRC*, 824 F.2d 1219, 1222-28 (D.C. Cir. 1987). Under the FOIA, "any person" includes entities as well as individuals, and courts have found that various entities are eligible for attorney fees. *See Texas v. ICC*, 935 F.2d 728 (5th Cir. 1991) (state government); *Church of Scientology, Western United States v. IRS*, 769 F. Supp. 328 (C.D. Cal. 1991) (church).

3.1. A FOIA plaintiff must be found to have "substantially prevailed" in order to be eligible for an award of attorney fees. § 552(a)(4)(e).

3.1.1. The determination of whether the plaintiff has "substantially prevailed" is "largely a question of causation." *Weisberg v. DOJ*, 745 F.2d at 1496; *Church of Scientology v. Harris*, 653 F.2d 584, 587 (D.C. Cir. 1981). Obviously, if the court compels the release of the requested records, the plaintiff has "substantially prevailed."

3.1.2. This requirement can be met even where only some portions of requested materials are ordered released, while other withholding is sustained by the court. *See, e.g., Cook v. Watt*, 597 F. Supp. 552, 555 (D. Alaska 1984) ("[A] batting average calculation, i.e., one release out of nineteen responsive documents withheld, is relevant to the amount of entitlement but not to eligibility for fees for the document disclosed."); *Katz v. DOJ*, 498 F. Supp. 177, 185 (S.D.N.Y. 1979) ("In determining that plaintiff has 'substantially prevailed,' this court has taken into consideration not simply the quantity of the information which it has directed the government to produce, but it has also considered the quality of that information."). *But see Braintree Electric Light Department v. DOE*, 494 F. Supp. 287, 291 (D.D.C. 1980) (plaintiff has not "substantially prevailed" because of the "minimal significance of the compelled disclosure").

3.1.3. The D.C. Circuit's decision in *Oil, Chemical & Atomic Workers International Union, AFL-CIO v. DOE*, 288 F.3d 452 (D.C. Cir. 2002), interprets the Supreme Court's ruling in *Buckhannon Bd. and Care Home, Inc. v. West Virginia Department of Health & Human Resources*, 532 U.S. 598 (2001), as limiting the eligibility for a fee award to only those plaintiffs who prevail by securing a court order. For FOIA litigants, this means that anything short of court action in favor of the plaintiff will deprive the plaintiff of eligibility for a fee award. While it is common for many FOIA suits to be resolved in part or in whole through a settlement with the government during the litigation, such a settlement will not, under the *OCAW* ruling, support an award. *See also Union of Needlestades, Industrial and Textile Employees, AFL-CIO, CLC v. U.S. INS*, 202 F. Supp. 2d 265 (S.D.N.Y. 2002).

3.1.4. Prior to the Supreme Court's decision in *Buckhannon*, the law under FOIA was settled that the government's release of requested materials prior to final judgment ordering disclosure did not necessarily preclude an award of fees. The theory was that if the plaintiff could show that the litigation played a "catalyst" role in prompting the release of records, then the plaintiff would be eligible for a fee award. *E.g., Vermont Low Income Advocacy Council v. Usery*, 546 F.2d 509, 513 (2d Cir. 1976). Of course, if the requester waives his right to attorney fees as part of a settlement, that waiver will be enforced. *National Senior Citizens Law Center v. Social Security Administration*, 849 F.2d 401 (9th Cir. 1988).

3.1.4.1. Before *Buckhannon*, the government's contention that voluntary release precludes award of attorney fees was rejected as "ha[ving] no merit." *Cuneo v. Rumsfeld*, 553 F.2d at 1364 ("Recent court decisions and the legislative history of section 552(a)(4)(E) support...[the conclusion that] a judgment is not an absolute prerequisite to an award of attorney fees."); *see also Fund for Constitutional Gov't v. National Archives*, 656 F.2d 856, 871 (D.C. Cir. 1981); *Church of Scientology v. Harris*, 653 F.2d at 587 ("largely a question of causation—did the institution and prosecution of the litigation cause the agency to release the documents obtained during the pendency of the litigation?").

3.1.4.2. In *Vermont Low Income Advocacy Council v. Usery*, 546 F.2d 509, 513 (2d Cir. 1976), the court agreed with the virtually unanimous consensus that attorney fees could be awarded even if the requested materials were voluntarily disclosed by the government prior to judgment.

3.1.4.2.1. Although affirming the district court decision denying fees (for reasons discussed *infra*), the court of appeals specifically rejected the lower court's rationale. *Vermont Low Income Advocacy Council v. Dunlop*, 71 F.R.D. 343, 346 (D. Vt. 1976) ("an election to favorably settle an action does not transform a compromising litigant into a prevailing party.... To hold otherwise would tend to discourage voluntary compliance after judicial review is undertaken.").

3.1.4.2.2. However, one court has ruled that a plaintiff substantially prevails by compelling an agency to release records on a "priority basis." *Exner v. FBI*, 443 F. Supp. 1349, 1353 (S.D. Cal. 1978), aff'd, 612 F.2d 1202 (9th Cir. 1980).

3.1.5. *Buckhannon* casts substantial doubt on the viability of the catalyst theory in attorney fee litigation across the board, including in fee litigation under FOIA. *Buckhannon* involved an effort by the operator of an assisted living facility to challenge a West Virginia law that required all residents of such facilities to be capable of "self-preservation," that is, being able to move themselves out of situations of danger, including fire. The complaint alleged that the law violated both the Fair Housing Amendment Act of 1988 and the Americans with Disabilities Act of 1990. As soon as the case was filed, the state agreed to stay enforcement of the law. Thereafter, the "self-preservation" law was repealed by the West Virginia legislature and the court, on the state's motion, dismissed the case as moot. Plaintiffs sought fees under both Acts, which permit "prevailing" parties to recover fees and costs. The district court denied the fee request because, unlike every other circuit, the Fourth Circuit had rejected the "catalyst theory." The Court of Appeals affirmed, and the Supreme Court, by a 5-4 vote, affirmed as well.

3.1.5.1. The Court's ruling focuses on the meaning of "prevailed," a word used in FOIA's fee provision as well. The Court holds that a "'prevailing party' is one who has been awarded some relief by the court." *Buckhannon*, 532 U.S. at 1839. The Court rejected the catalyst theory as a basis for a fee award because it "allows an award where there is no judicially sanctioned change in the legal relationship of the parties." *Id.* at 1840. Without some judicial involvement that embodies a change in the legal relationship between the parties, the plaintiff has not "prevailed" in a manner that warrants the imposition of fees.

3.1.5.2. The Court holds out one theory that might provide a means of obtaining fees by a plaintiff who wins as a result of the defendant's capitulation: The Court notes that "voluntary cessation of a challenged practice does not deprive a federal court of its power to determine the legality of the practice unless it is absolutely clear that the allegedly wrongful behavior could not reasonably be expected to recur." *Id.* at 1842-3 (citation and internal quotation omitted). Thus, even where the government relinquishes documents prior to a court order, there may be grounds for the court to issue a ruling for the plaintiff on the merits. *But cf. Students Against Genocide v. Department of State*, 257 F.3d 828, 841 n.14 (D.C. Cir. 2001) (remanding question of whether *Buckhannon* forecloses a fee in a FOIA case that was rendered moot by the government's disclosure of records).

3.1.5.3. Mootness caused by an event manifestly unrelated to litigation may preclude an award. *See, e.g., Misegades & Douglas v. Schuyler*, 456 F.2d 255 (4th Cir. 1972) (FOIA case, decided before 1974 amendments, in which appeal was mooted by release of document in normal course of patent office procedures; but no fee issue was presented).

3.1.5.4. Nothing in *Buckhannon* appears to cast doubt on the rule that, even where no documents are released, plaintiff may be deemed to have "substantially prevailed" if the suit compels an agency to comply with the law. *Halperin v. Department of State*, 565 F.2d 699, 706 n.11 (D.C. Cir. 1977).

3.1.6. Attorney fees may be awarded to FOIA plaintiffs who force governmental publication of records, as well as to those forcing government release of records. *See, e.g., Birkland v. Rotary Plaza, Inc.*, 643 F. Supp. 223 (N.D. Cal. 1986) (HUD meal program policy violated (a)(1) publication requirement).

3.1.7. Attorney fees may also be awarded to FOIA plaintiffs who successfully litigate an agency's refusal to waive fees. *Ettlinger v. FBI*, 596 F. Supp. 867, 879 (D. Mass. 1984). *See also Weisberg v. DOJ (II)*, 848 F.2d 1265, 1268-69 (D.C. Cir. 1988) (*Weisberg II*) (Under the "clearly-erroneous" rule for review of lower court fact-finding, the appellate court refused to upset a finding that the agency decision to waive all copying fees for 60,000 documents resulted from "administrative reconsideration unrelated to this litigation.").

3.1.8. But, even if the plaintiff substantially prevails, an award of attorney fees is not automatic. *See, e.g., Tax Analysts*, 965 F.2d at 1093; *Blue v. Bureau of Prisons*, 570 F.2d at 533 ("attorneys' fees under the FOIA were not to be awarded as a matter of course, as in civil rights cases"); *see also* Conference Committee Report, *1974 Source Book* at 227 "the conferees do not intend to make the award of attorney fees automatic").

3.2. Although a plaintiff has "substantially prevailed" and is thereby eligible for an award, the decision on whether the plaintiff is entitled to actually be awarded attorney fees resides in the discretion of the court. *GMRI, Inc. v. EEOC*, 149 F.3d at 452; *Tax Analysts*, 965 F.2d at 1093; *Cuneo v. Rumsfeld*, 553 F.2d at 1365-68. Based upon Congress' intent that the criteria listed in the Senate Report "are to be considered as part of the existing body of law on the award of attorney fees," *Cuneo v. Rumsfeld, id.*, the court will generally consider the Senate criteria in deciding whether the plaintiff is entitled to such an award. The D.C. Circuit suggested in *LaSalle Extension University v. FTC, supra*, that it might be an abuse of discretion for the district court to fail to consider each of the four factors. 627 F.2d at 484. *See also United Association of Journeymen and Apprentices of the Plumbing and Pipefitting Industry, Local 598 v. Department of the Army, Corps of Engineers*, 841 F.2d 1459, 1464 (9th Cir. 1988). *But see Crooker v. U.S. Parole Comm'n*, 776 F.2d 366, 369 (1st Cir. 1985) (One factor alone is not dispositive, and the criteria are intended to provide guidance and direction, rather than "airtight standards"). In addition, these criteria have been expressly accepted as relevant factors by every other circuit that has considered the question. *See e.g., American Commercial Barge Lines v. NLRB*, 758 F.2d 1109, 1111 (6th Cir. 1985); *Church of Scientology of California v. U.S. Postal Service*, 700 F.2d 486, 490 (9th Cir. 1983); *Aviation Data Service v. FAA*, 687 F.2d 1319, 1321 (10th Cir. 1982); *Stein v. DOJ*, 662 F.2d 1245, 1262 (7th Cir. 1981); *Lovell v. Alderete*, 630 F.2d 428, 431-32 (5th Cir. 1980); *Education/Instruccion v. HUD*, 649 F.2d 4, 7 (1st Cir. 1981); *Crooker v. Dep't of Treasury*, 634 F.2d 48 (2d Cir. 1980).

3.2.1. The "public benefit" factor speaks for an award where the complainant's victory is "likely to add to the fund of information that citizens may use in making in making vital political choices." *Cotton v. Heyman*, 63 F.3d 1115, 1120 (D.C. Cir. 1995) (citations omitted); *see also Tax Analysts*, 965 F.2d at 1094-96 (finding that a public benefit test was meet by for-profit tax journal that disseminated information to subscribers); *Fenster v. Brown*, 617 F.2d at 744 (citations omitted). "Public benefit" could be demonstrated by, among other things, a "newsman... seeking information to be used in a publication or a public interest group... seeking information to further a project benefiting the general public." *1974 Source Book* at 171 (Senate Report). *See e.g., Church of*

Scientology of California v. U.S. Postal Service, 700 F.2d at 493; *Blue v. Bureau of Prisons*, 570 F.2d at 533-34; *OCAW v. DOE*, 141 F. Supp. 2d 1, 7 (D.D.C. 2001); *Des Moines Register & Tribune Co. v. DOJ*, 563 F. Supp. 82 (D.D.C. 1983); *Nixon v. Sampson*, 437 F. Supp. 654 (D.D.C. 1977), *rev'd*, 591 F.2d 944 (D.C. Cir. 1978) (awarding $77,000 to attorneys in Nixon tape case). An award is possible even when the information is not of general significance, so long as plaintiff is not seeking it solely for commercial purposes. *Simon v. United States*, 587 F. Supp. 1029 (D.D.C. 1984) (suit for personal files); *but see Public Law Education Institute v. DOJ*, 556 F. Supp. 476 (D.D.C. 1983), *aff'd on other grounds*, 744 F.2d 181 (D.C. Cir. 1984) (publisher of the *Military Law Reporter* denied fees in part because seeking documents to use in publication was commercial interest). In some cases, the "public benefit" may simply be "the vindication of the Act itself." *Seegull Mfg. Co. v. NLRB*, 741 F.2d 882, 886 (6th Cir. 1984).

3.2.2. "Commercial benefit to the complainant" might preclude an award if the beneficiary is a "large corporate interest (or a representative of such an interest)." *1974 Source Book* at 171. However, commercial benefit would not bar recovery "where the complainant was indigent or a nonprofit public interest group." *Id. Compare Chamberlain v. Kurtz*, 589 F.2d 827, 842 (5th Cir. 1979), *cert. denied*, 444 U.S. 842 (1979) (award not appropriate where court found "virtually no benefit to the public accruing from this litigation" and the plaintiff's "personal pecuniary and commercial interest in this litigation is large") with *Blue v. Bureau of Prisons*, 570 F.2d at 534 (abuse of discretion for judge to consider only the "public benefit" criterion in determining to award no attorney fees to indigent requester-prisoner); *see also Aronson v. HUD*, 866 F.2d 1, 3 (1st Cir. 1989), *appeal after remand*, 869 F.2d 646 (1st Cir. 1989). In *Cuneo v. Rumsfeld, supra*, plaintiff was a lawyer specializing in government contract law attempting to obtain the Manual of the Defense Contract Audit Agency. The court of appeals suggested, without deciding, that his private commercial interests may have been the incentive for the lawsuit. 553 F.2d at 1368. "If the potential for private commercial benefit was sufficient incentive to encourage Cuneo to pursue his FOIA claim the policy objectives of section 552(a)(4)(E) would be met and it would not be improper for the trial court to deny his request for attorney fees." *Id.* This rationale is used to deny fees where a requester receives a strong commercial benefit from the records. *See Frye v. U.S. EPA*, No. 90-3041 (D.D.C. Mar. 31, 1992); *LaSalle Extension University v. FTC, supra*; *Fenster v. Brown, supra*; *Werner-Continental, Inc. v. Farkas*, 478 F. Supp. 815, 817 (S.D. Ohio 1979), *aff'd*, 661 F.2d 935 (6th Cir. 1981); *Kendland Co. v. Department of the Navy*, 599 F. Supp. 936 (D. Me. 1984). Conversely, it has been held that a finding of no commercial benefit to the plaintiff should weigh in favor of a fee award "since the award section of the Act was intended to encourage complainants who lack substantial pecuniary incentives to pursue their claims." *Local 598*, 841 F.2d at 1461-62, citing *Lovell*, 630 F.2d at 433 & n.6.

3.2.3. "Nature of the [complainant's] interest" is "closely related [to] and often considered together" with the commercial benefit criterion. *Tax Analysts v. DOJ*, 965 F.2d 1092, 1095 (D.C. Cir. 1992); *See Local 598*, 841 F.2d at 1462. Favored interests are "scholarly, journalistic or public-interest oriented." *1974*

Source Book at 171. *See Long v. IRS*, 932 F.2d 1309, 1316 (9th Cir.), *amended*, 91 Daily Journal D.A.R. 6973 (9th Cir. 1991), where the lower court's ruling that the plaintiff's scholarly interest weighed against her recovery of fees was held "wrong as a matter of law and an abuse of discretion."

3.2.3.1. Even where a plaintiff has "substantially prevailed" and is therefore "eligible" for an award of attorney fees, a purely or even primarily private interest will weigh against "entitlement" to an award. *See, e.g., Republic of New Afrika v. FBI*, 645 F. Supp. 117, 121 (D.D.C. 1986) (group's motive was to exonerate its members of criminal charges and circumvent civil discovery to bolster claims in damage suit); *New England Apple Council v. Donovan*, 640 F. Supp. 16 (D. Mass. 1985) (public benefit "marginal at best" where group sought to show investigation of members was unwarranted, but did not allege fraud or improper motives). *But see Cazalas v. DOJ*, 709 F.2d 1051 (5th Cir. 1983) (acknowledgment of requester's "strong personal interest" in obtaining documents allegedly proving sex discrimination in her dismissal as Assistant U.S. Attorney "is not necessarily inconsistent with an equally strong public interest in also receiving these items," since "it is in the 'public interest" to discover, if true, that the Department of Justice is less than entirely just in its dealings"); *Seegull Mfg. Co. v. NLRB*, 741 F.2d at 886 ("the Act does not exclude corporations or the wealthy from obtaining fees where such would be otherwise proper").

3.2.4. "Reasonable basis" for the government's withholding is perhaps the most difficult criterion to apply because it often requires an examination into the merits of the government's claim in cases where there has been no ruling on the merits. Recent decisions of the D.C. Circuit suggest that this prong will be difficult for requesters to overcome. In *Chesapeake Bay Found. v. Department of Agriculture*, 108 F.3d 375, 376 (D.C. Cir. 1997) the court held that the requester was not entitled to fees where the government's withholding decision "had a reasonable basis" in law even though the case was resolved prior to a court ruling on the merits. And in *Cotton v. Heyman*, 63 F.3d 1115 (D.C. Cir. 1995), the court reversed a fee award to a requester which came after the requester had prevailed on the merits, because, although the court rejected the government's position that the Smithsonian Institution was not an "agency" subject to FOIA, that ruling was open to challenge in subsequent cases and the Smithsonian's position was a reasonable one even though it was rejected. *Id.* at 1122-23. *See also Local 598*, 841 F.2d at 1466 n.2 (Skopil, J., concurring) for cases and "legislative history indicat[ing] that Congress thought that fees should not be awarded when the government had 'a colorable basis' for withholding information." It bears noting that in both *Chesapeake Bay* and *Cotton*, the court concluded that the information released did not further the public interest. In cases where the courts find disclosure in the public interest, an adverse ruling on the reasonableness of the government's position will not necessarily foreclose a fee award. As the Senate Report put it, "for example, a newsman would 'ordinarily recover fees even where the government's defense had a reasonable basis in law, while corporate interests might recover where the withholding was without such basis.'" *1974 Sourcebook* at 172. *See American*

Commercial Barge Lines Co. v. NLRB, 758 F.2d at 1114; *Education/Instruccion v. HUD*, 649 F.2d at 8; *Fenster v. Brown*, 617 F.2d 740, 742 (D.C. Cir. 1979); *Cuneo v. Rumsfeld*, 553 F.2d at 1365.

3.2.4.3. In *Local 598, supra*, the majority ruled that a "lack of clarity in the law" regarding the application of Exemption 6 would not excuse or make "reasonable" an agency's reliance upon "inapposite authority" and its "failure to consider other authority that tended to support disclosure" of the records at issue. 841 F.2d at 1463-64.

3.2.4.4. Although plausible and not indicative of bad faith, the State Department's representations that records were not produced more quickly due to processing backlogs, confusion, and administrative error were "practical explanations, not reasonable legal bases" for withholding. *Miller v. Department of State*, 779 F.2d 1378, 1390 (8th Cir. 1985). "The FOIA does not contain a statutory exception for administrative inefficiency. When a private citizen is obliged to seek legal services in order to wrest from the government information which the government had no legal reason to withhold from him, he is entitled under the Act to be reimbursed for the cost to which he has been put." *Id.*

3.2.4.5. While a decision to award attorney fees is generally reviewed under an abuse of discretion standard, a *de novo* standard applies to the court's evaluation of the government's legal argument. *Pierce v. Underwood*, 487 U.S. 552, 565 (1988) (case under Equal Access to Justice Act); *American Commercial Barge Lines Co. v. NLRB*, 758 F.2d at 1111.

4. Miscellaneous Attorney Fees Issues.

4.1. Calculation of Fee Award.

4.1.1. Evaluation of fees is based on the "lodestar," which is the number of hours the lawyers reasonably spent on the case multiplied by the lawyers' hourly rates. *See generally Hensley v. Eckerhart*, 461 U.S. 424, 433 (1983); *Dixie Fuel Co. v. Callahan*, 136 F. Supp. 2d 659, 666-67 (E.D. Ky. 2001); *Consumers Union v. Federal Reserve System*, 410 F. Supp. 63, 64 (D.D.C. 1975). A lawyer's hourly rate is measured by its "fair market value," which is determined by the prevailing local rate or the attorney's actual billing rate, whichever is higher, as well as "the quality of the attorney's work." *See generally Johnson v. Georgia Highway Express, Inc.*, 488 F.2d 714, 717-19 (5th Cir. 1974) (enumerating fee calculation factors in civil rights cases); *Evans v. Sheraton Park Hotel*, 503 F.2d 177, 187-88 (D.C. Cir. 1974), cited with approval in *Copeland v. Marshall*, 641 F.2d 880, 889 (D.C. Cir. 1980) (*en banc*). The *Copeland* decision established the first-step practice of calculating a "lodestar" figure by multiplying reasonable hourly rates for the attorneys to whom fees are to be awarded by the number of hours reasonably expended on the litigation by each attorney, and, in addition, removed any doubt that public interest lawyers are entitled to fees calculated at "market rates." 641 F.2d at 900. *See also New York Gaslight Club v. Carey*, 447 U.S. 54, 70-71 n.9 (1980); *Save Our Cumberland Mountains, Inc. v. Hodel*, 857 F.2d 1516 (D.C. Cir. 1988), *vacated sub nom. Save Our Cumberland Mountains, Inc. v. Lujan*, 963 F.2d 1541 (D.C. Cir. 1992), *cert. denied sub nom. Save Our Cumberland Mountains, Inc. v. Babbitt*, 507 U.S. 911 (1993).

4.1.2. In *National Ass'n of Concerned Veterans v. Secretary of Defense*, 675 F.2d 1319 (D.C. Cir. 1982), the panel laid down detailed standards setting forth the evidence that fee applicants are required to submit in order to prove the "prevailing rates." Among other things, the panel noted that fee applicants must furnish (a) affidavits reciting the precise fees that attorneys with similar qualifications have received from fee-paying clients in similar cases; (b) affidavits detailing the actual rate that applicant's counsel can command in the market; (c) specific evidence of the attorney's actual billing practices during the relevant time period; and (d) recent fees awarded to attorneys of comparable reputation and experience performing similar work, provided that the applicant demonstrates that the fee awards were based on actual evidence of prevailing rates. The panel also set guidelines concerning the documentation fee applicants must supply to prove the reasonableness of the hours for which compensation is sought, and made it clear that fees will be denied to applicants who fail to support their claims with adequate time records. In an amendment to its opinion dated July 15, 1982, the panel also clarified the government's role in fee litigation, noting that "once the fee applicant has provided support for the requested rate, the burden falls on the Government to go forward with evidence that the rate is erroneous. And when the Government attempts to rebut the case for a requested rate, it must do so with equally specific countervailing evidence." The analysis in *Concerned Veterans* was refined by the court in *Jordan v. DOJ*, 691 F.2d 514 (D.C. Cir. 1982). There the court reversed the district court's outright denial of fees and discussed at length the documentation required of fee applicants, including the appropriate contents of supporting affidavits and the type of time records that will be required.

4.1.3. *Concerned Veterans* also holds that an award should not compensate the plaintiff "for nonproductive time or for time expended on issues on which plaintiff did not prevail," 675 F.2d at 1327, so long as the rejected claims are "truly fractionable." *Id.* at n.13. *See generally* the Supreme Court's discussion in *Hensley v. Eckerhart*, 461 U.S. at 434-36 of "results obtained" and other considerations that may lead the court to adjust the award upward or downward for a "prevailing plaintiff." *See also Weisberg II*, 848 F.2d at 1272 (lower court's reduction of compensable hours is reviewable only for abuse of discretion); *Des Moines Register & Tribune Co. v. DOJ*, 563 F. Supp. at 85 (court reduced award amount requested to the extent of time devoted to unsuccessful opposition to the agency's motion for summary judgment). *But see Badhwar v. Department of the Air Force*, 629 F. Supp. 478 (D.D.C. 1986) (court granted fees for work on legal theory which it found unnecessary to consider, and on withholding issues plaintiff did not win).

4.1.4. In one case, the Ninth Circuit implicitly limited a lower court's authority to reduce the lodestar figure. *Long v. IRS*, 932 F.2d 1309, 1316 (9th Cir. 1991).

4.1.5. *Anderson v. Dep't of Treasury*, 648 F.2d 1 (D.C. Cir. 1979), *supplemental opinion and denial of rehearsing en banc sub nom. National Treasury Employees Union v. Dep't of Treasury*, 656 F.2d 848 (D.C. Cir. 1981), carves out a limited exception to the general rule regarding hourly rate. In *Anderson*, the court ruled that salaried attorneys working for a labor union were not entitled to fees based on the prevailing rate, but rather were only entitled to compensation to the extent of reimbursing their employer for salaries and costs. The Court was careful to stress that where fees were to be plowed back into litigation by a public interest group, the general rule articulated in *Copeland, supra*, would govern. 656 F.2d at 855.

4.1.6. Based upon decisions construing an identical attorney fees provision in the Privacy Act, 5 U.S.C. § 552a(g)(2)(B), the FOIA has been held to preclude an award for costs and fees incurred in administrative proceedings, since it refers only to "litigation" costs. § 552(a)(4)(E). *Newport Aeronautical Sales v. Department of the Navy*, No. 84-0120 slip op. (D.D.C. Apr. 17, 1985), citing *Kennedy v. Andrus*, 459 F. Supp. 240, 243 (D.D.C. 1978), *aff'd without opinion*, 612 F.2d 586 (D.C. Cir. 1980) and *Associated General Contractors, Northern Nevada Chapter v. EPA*, 488 F. Supp. 861, 864 (D. Nev. 1980). *See also Weisberg*, 745 F.2d at 1476, 1496-97 (remanding for determination of whether release was due to litigation or the administrative process). However, one judge has, without comment, awarded $150.00 for "work at the administrative level." *Mahler v. IRS*, No. 79-3238 (D.D.C. Mar. 28, 1980). It should also be noted that attorney fees and costs are available in other administrative proceedings intended by Congress to provide a non-judicial forum for "enforcement of individual rights." *Fitzgerald v. U.S. Civil Service Commission*, 407 F. Supp. 380, 386-87 (D.D.C. 1975), *rev'd*, 544 F.2d 1186 (D.C. Cir. 1977) (Civil Service Commission may award fees and costs for reinstatement and backpay proceeding). *See generally*, *Turner v. FCC*, 514 F.2d 1354 (D.C. Cir. 1975) (agency cannot grant attorney fees to a party in proceedings absent specific statutory authority).

4.2. Interim Fee Awards.

4.2.1. There has also been litigation over the propriety of interim fee awards. In a number of cases, district courts have held that, under certain circumstances, interim awards are appropriate. In *Powell v. DOJ*, 569 F. Supp. 1192 (N.D. Cal. 1983), the court awarded an interim fee of over $20,000 to compensate counsel for the initial phase of the litigation. The court ruled that the first stage of the action—forcing the disclosure of all non-exempt documents responsive to the request—was final and binding and would not be affected by further litigation. That fact, coupled with the financial pressure placed on plaintiff's counsel by the litigation, mitigated in favor of an interim fee award. In so ruling, the court relied on *Biberman v. FBI*, 496 F. Supp. 263 (S.D.N.Y. 1980), which had held that the legislative history of the FOIA fee provision supported the conclusion that interim fee awards were authorized in protracted cases where an interim award is "necessary to the continuation of litigation which has proved meritorious at the time of the application." *See also Allen v. Department of Defense*, 713 F. Supp. 7, 12 (D.D.C. 1989) (collecting cases).

4.2.2. There is one district court decision to the contrary. *Letelier v. DOJ*, 6 Media L. Rep. (BNA) 2140 (D.D.C. 1980). The opinion in *Powell*, however, addresses the flaws in the *Letelier* opinion at length, and it is likely that even the D.C. courts would reexamine the question in light of *Powell*. *See, e.g., Badhwar v.*

Department of the Air Force, 629 F. Supp. 478 (D.D.C. 1986) (interim award granted).

4.2.3. In *Rosenfeld v. United States*, 859 F.2d 717, 723-24 (9th Cir. 1988), the court cited the "thorough analyses" in *Powell* and *Biberman*, and upheld interim fee awards as a matter of "clear Congressional intent" because they "so clearly further the purpose of the FOIA fee provision." The court, in its own lengthy analysis, ruled that an interim award is not an appealable final order. *Id.* at 720-22.

4.2.4. The D.C. Circuit has ruled the government may not appeal an interim fee award, nor may it invoke the collateral order doctrine or mandamus to obtain interlocutory review of an interim fee award. In *National Ass'n of Criminal Def. Lawyers v. DOJ*, 182 F.3d 981 (D.C. Cir. 1999), the Justice Department sought review of an interim fee in a case seeking access to materials relating to the Department's investigation into allegations of improprieties at the FBI crime laboratory. After finding that the protracted litigation posed a financial hardship on plaintiff's counsel and that the litigation had already resulted in the release of one report and the expedition in processing the remaining documents, the district court held that plaintiff was entitled to an interim fee. 182 F.3d at 984. In rejecting the Department's appeal, the D.C. Circuit first noted that there was no final order giving rise to appellate jurisdiction. It next rejected the government's argument that the collateral order doctrine permitted the appeal because the government would not be irreparably injured by delaying review of the fee question until the case had been concluded in the district court. *Id.* at 984-85. The same considerations led the court to deny the government's mandamus petition, finding that the government failed to show irreparable harm and that the propriety of the interim award could be reviewed once a final order had been entered. *Id.*

4.3. Compensation for Delay.

4.3.1. Increasing an attorney's fee award to compensate counsel for delay in receiving payment might seem appropriate because the hourly rate used for the "lodestar" represents the prevailing rate for clients who typically pay legal bills promptly, whereas court-awarded fees are normally received long after legal services are rendered. The purpose would be to compensate the attorney for the money he could have earned from earlier receipt and investment of the funds.

4.3.2. However, such upward adjustment of the "lodestar" to compensate for delay has been held to be "functionally equivalent" to an interest award, which cannot be recovered against the Government in the absence of an express waiver of sovereign immunity under the longstanding "no-interest rule." *Library of Congress v. Shaw*, 478 U.S. 310 (1986).

4.3.3. Although the *Shaw* decision construes the attorney's fee provision in Title VII of the Civil Rights Act of 1964, the Court's conclusion that the requisite waiver of immunity cannot be found in the legislative history of that statute or read into its stipulation for "reasonable" awards would apparently apply to the FOIA's analogous "fee-shifting" provision. *See e.g., Weisberg II*, 848 F.2d at 1272 (because *Shaw* would require explicit statutory authorization for fee enhancement to compensate for delay, such compensation is unavailable under FOIA).

4.3.4. One court, in examining the *Shaw* decision, noted that calculation of the "lodestar" by the use of current rather than historical rates, or historical rates that were based on expected delay, would compensate for delay in a manner that was not specifically disapproved by the Supreme Court and would simplify the task of trying to determine prevailing market rates over a period of years in long-running cases. *McKenzie v. Kennickell*, 645 F. Supp. 437, 443 (D.D.C. 1986), citing *Shaw*, 478 U.S. at 314. Evidently, the Supreme Court may agree with this approach. *See Pennsylvania v. Delaware Valley Citizens Cncl for Clean Air*, 483 U.S. 711 (1987) (*Delaware Valley II*) (White, J., writing for the plurality). *See also Thompson v. Kennickell*, 836 F.2d 616, 619 (D.C. Cir. 1988).

4.4. Compensation for Risking Contingency Fees.

4.4.1. In *Delaware Valley II, supra* (so-called because of a previous decision in the same case), the Supreme Court divided sharply over the question of what enhancements, if any, were appropriate in a contingency fee case. Two factions split 4-4, and hence Justice O'Connor's concurring opinion provides a majority on the key issues. Her opinion makes clear that the "novelty" or "difficulty" of the issues presented did not warrant an adjustment, since those factors were presumably built into the lodestar. 483 U.S. at 731-34. However, she did not rule out an enhancement because of the contingent nature of the payment. Thus, her opinion makes clear that in some cases an enhancement would be warranted if the plaintiff could show that, without an adjustment, the plaintiff would have had "substantial difficulties" obtaining competent counsel. *Id.*

4.4.2. However, in *King v. Palmer*, 950 F.2d 771 (D.C. Cir. 1991), *cert. denied*, 503 U.S. 918, *and cert. denied sub nom. King v. Ridley*, 505 U.S. 1229 (1992), a divided D.C. Circuit refused to accept Justice O'Connor's concurrence as the controlling opinion, on the grounds that it is at odds with the plurality's view that contingency enhancements are never available. *Id.* at 782-83. With the appeals court split 7 to 4, the majority was "unable to derive a governing rule" from *Delaware Valley II*, and concluded that "the appropriate course is to hold that contingency enhancements will not be available in this Circuit." *Id.* at 784. *See id.* at 784-85 for standards in other circuits that have interpreted *Delaware Valley II* to permit the awarding of contingency enhancements to compensate the prevailing party's counsel for the initial risk of loss in agreeing to take a case in certain circumstances.

4.5. Settlement Conditioned Upon Waiver of Attorney Fees.

4.5.1. In *Evans v. Jeff D.*, 475 U.S. 717 (1986), the Supreme Court rejected the argument that the Civil Rights Attorney's Fee Awards Act of 1976 prohibited settlements conditioned on the "coercive" waiver of a plaintiff's statutory eligibility for attorney fees.

4.5.2. "[W]hile it is undoubtedly true that Congress expected fee-shifting to attract competent counsel to represent citizens deprived of their civil rights, it neither bestowed fee awards upon attorneys nor rendered them nonwaivable or nonnegotiable; instead, it added them to the arsenal of remedies available to combat violations of civil rights, a goal not invariably inconsistent with conditioning settlement on the merits on a waiver of statutory attorney's fees." *Id.* at 726.

4.5.3. A footnote to the Court's majority opinion refers to "fee-shifting" provisions in over fifty other federal statutes, presumably including the FOIA, and it is likely that the Government will seize the opportunity to apply the *Jeff D.* rationale to FOIA cases. *See id.* at 726 n.22.

4.5.4. Courts have upheld settlements embodying waivers of fees. *See National Senior Citizens Law Center v. Social Security Administration*, 849 F.2d 401, 402-03 (9th Cir. 1988).

4.6. Pro Se Fee Awards.

4.6.1. Although there are some old D.C. Circuit decisions holding that pro se plaintiffs may be awarded fees, *Holly v. Acree*, 72 F.R.D. 115, 116 (D.D.C. 1976), *aff'd sub nom. Holly v. Chasen*, 569 F.2d 160 (D.C. Cir. 1977); *Cox v. DOJ*, 601 F.2d 1, 5-6 (D.C. Cir. 1979); *Crooker v. Dep't of Treasury*, 663 F.2d 140 (D.C. Cir. 1980), the weight of authority has long been that pro se litigants may not recover a fee under FOIA. *See Crooker v. DOJ*, 632 F.2d 916, 920 (1st Cir. 1980); *Cunningham v. FBI*, 664 F.2d 383 (3d Cir. 1981); *Barrett v. Bureau of Customs*, 651 F.2d 1087 (5th Cir. 1981), *cert. denied*, 455 U.S. 950 (1982); *Falcone v. IRS*, 714 F.2d 646 (6th Cir. 1983), *cert. denied*, 466 U.S. 908 (1984); *Wolfel v. United States*, 711 F.2d 66 (6th Cir. 1983); *DeBold v. Stimson*, 735 F.2d 1037 (7th Cir. 1984); *Carter v. Veterans Administration*, 780 F.2d 1479 (9th Cir. 1986). *See also Burke v. DOJ*, 432 F. Supp. 251 (D. Kan. 1976), *aff'd*, 559 F.2d 1182 (10th Cir. 1977); *Clarkson v. IRS*, 678 F.2d 1368 (11th Cir. 1982).

4.6.2. In 1991, the Supreme Court ruled in *Kay v. Ehrler*, 499 U.S. 432 (1991) that an attorney who represented himself in a successful civil rights case could not recover attorney's fees under 42 U.S.C. § 1988. In the wake of *Kay*, lower courts have held that several different fee-shifting statutes, including FOIA, preclude awards of fees to all persons who appear pro se. In 1993, the D.C. Circuit held that based on *Kay*, a pro se non-attorney plaintiff who prevailed in a FOIA action could not obtain attorney's fees. *See Benavides v. Bureau of Prisons*, 993 F.2d 257 (D.C. Cir. 1993), *cert. denied*, 510 U.S. 996 (1993).

4.6.4. The rationale of *Kay* has also been applied to lawyers who litigate FOIA cases in their own name. In *Burka v. HHS*, 142 F.3d 1286 (D.C. Cir. 1998), the D.C. Circuit concluded that *Kay* compelled the conclusion that a lawyer who successfully litigated a FOIA case pro se, although on behalf of an unnamed client, was not entitled to fees. *Id.* at 1290-91; *see also Kooritzky v. Herman*, 178 F.3d 1315 (D.C. Cir. 1999) (finding that *Kay* foreclosed a fee award to a pro se lawyer plaintiff under the Equal Access to Justice Act). *Kay*, as applied by the D.C. Circuit in *Burka*, casts doubt on prior rulings awarding fees to pro se lawyer plaintiffs under FOIA. *See, e.g., Lawrence v. Bowsher*, 931 F.2d 1579 (D.C. Cir. 1991);

Attorney Fees and Litigation Costs

4.7. Litigation Costs.

4.7.1. In *Baez v. DOJ*, 684 F.2d 999 (D.C. Cir. 1982) (*en banc*), the court endorsed the general presumption that the prevailing party is entitled to costs, and held that it applies with equal force in the FOIA context. *See* Rule 39, Fed. R. App. P. The three dissenting judges adhered to the views set forth in the vacated panel opinion, 647 F.2d 1328 (D.C. Cir. 1980), which had held that costs could be assessed against a non-prevailing plaintiff only where the plaintiff's suit, or appeal, was frivolous, unreasonable, or without foundation.

4.7.2. Even a pro se FOIA litigant can generally claim reimbursement for "litigation costs actually incurred." *Crooker v. DOJ*, 632 F.2d at 921. In *Kuzma v. U.S. Postal Service*, 725 F.2d 16, 17 (2d Cir. 1984), the Second Circuit denied a request for attorney fees but granted a pro se litigant's claim for costs and reimbursements totaling $110.04 after the government informed the court that it had no objection to the claim. Similarly, in *DeBold v. Stimson, supra*, the Seventh Circuit, after refusing to award attorney fees to a non attorney pro se litigant, nevertheless held him entitled to "litigation costs reasonably incurred," reasoning that a pro se litigant "is made whole thereby, serving as a small incentive to pursue litigation if no attorney may be found to represent the litigant." 735 F.2d at 1043. *See also Carter v. Veterans Administration, supra* and *Clarkson v. IRS*, 678 F.2d 1368, 1371 (11th Cir. 1982) (similarly distinguishing Barrett rationale for denying fee recovery).

4.7.3. In *Kuzma v. IRS*, 821 F.2d 930 (2d Cir. 1987), the court ruled that an award of costs pursuant to the FOIA is not limited to those authorized under the "taxable costs" provision of 28 U.S.C. § 1920 because the phrase "other litigation costs" was intended by Congress to add to the scope of costs already recoverable under § 1920. In assessing which of the claimed costs qualified for recovery as "other litigation costs reasonably incurred," the court excluded "law books readily available in libraries," but approved recovery of costs for photocopying, postage, covers, exhibits, typing, transportation and parking fees as "reasonable costs of litigation." *Id.* at 933.

4.7.4. In *Seegull Mfg. Co. v. NLRB*, 735 F.2d 971 (6th Cir. 1984), an award of attorney fees was affirmed based on the court's view that the agency's "continued arbitrary and capricious implementation of...self-serving guidelines" promulgated in violation of the Administrative Procedures Act "is a display of bureaucratic arrogance." Finding the agency's appeal of the award to be "frivolous, unreasonable and groundless on its face," the court assessed double costs against the NLRB pursuant to Federal Rule of Appellate Procedure 38. *Id.* at 974. This opinion was vacated and replaced by a later opinion, 741 F.2d 882, which affirmed the award of attorney fees but did not assess double costs.

CHAPTER 18

Records Exclusions

Allan Robert Adler

1. The General Effect of "Exclusion" Authority.

1.1. The 1986 FOIA amendments added a new subsection (c) to the FOIA establishing that, in certain circumstances, a criminal law enforcement agency which receives a request for (1) records concerning an ongoing and undisclosed criminal investigation; (2) informant records maintained under an informant's name or personal identifier; or, (3) classified FBI records pertaining to a foreign intelligence, counterintelligence, or international terrorism investigation, "may treat the records as not subject to the requirement of this section." *See generally* discussion of 1986 amendments at section 6 of Chapter 1, Overview.

1.2. In its report on S.774, the Senate Judiciary Committee stated that an earlier version of the informant records provision enacted in these amendments "operates as an exclusion" in the sense that "the agency would have no obligation to acknowledge the existence of such records in response to such a request." Report at 25, discussed at section 6.5 of Chapter 1, Overview.

1.3. Senator Leahy and Reps. English and Kindness confirmed that the intended purpose of these provisions is to statutorily authorize, as requested in testimony by the Director of the FBI, a "Glomar response," or a refusal to confirm or deny the existence of the requested records, in the specific circumstances indicated. *See* 132 Cong. Rec. S14297 (daily ed. Sept. 30, 1986) (statement of Senator Leahy); 132 Cong. Rec. H9467 (daily ed. Oct. 8, 1986) (statement of Reps. English and Kindness); House hearings, *supra* Chapter 1 at 888-95, 906-09 (testimony and letter for the record by FBI Director William Webster). They further indicated that the provisions are to operate subject to established judicial interpretations in CIA "Glomar" cases. Moreover, the "explicit understanding of the amendment's sponsors" was that notice of the authority to refuse to confirm or deny would be included in every FOIA response by agencies permitted to exercise such authority, as agreed to by Justice Department officials and the House subcommittee staff during their discussions of the draft bill from which the provisions were derived. Statements of Leahy, English, and Kindness, *supra*.

1.4. However, Senator Hatch, in a later statement following final Senate passage of the House-amended provision, stated that the effect of the exclusions would be "somewhat analogous" to "Glomarization," but "their operation, both administratively and in court, will of necessity be different" in that agencies would invoke them "without the specific knowledge of the requester" and would respond to court challenges with the automatic filing of an *in camera* affidavit, "regardless of whether the exclusion was in fact employed in that case." 132 Cong. Rec. S16505 (daily ed. Oct. 15, 1986.)

1.5. Senator Hatch's interpretation was adopted by the Department of Justice, which interprets the exclusion provisions as authorizing a "no records" response informing the FOIA requester that there are no records responsive to his request. The Department offered no explanation for rejecting the Leahy-English-Kindness statements of intent. *See Attorney General's Memorandum on the 1986 Amendments to the Freedom of Information Act* 18-30 (December 1987).

Records Exclusions

1.6. Although the Justice Department's "Freedom of Information Act Guide" states that "the decision to employ an exclusion in response to a particular request must not be reflected on anything made available to the requester," the Department acknowledges that providing a "no records" response as part of an exclusion strategy "does not insulate the agency from either administrative or judicial review of the agency's action." *See* "Freedom of Information Act Guide and Privacy Act Overview," Office of Information and Privacy, Office of Policy Development, U.S. Department of Justice, at 463 (May 2000 ed.).

1.6.1. Administrative or judicial review may occur when the recipient of a "no records" response believes that the agency failed to conduct an adequate search for the requested records, or when the recipient suspects that the agency has resorted to the exclusion mechanism and seeks a determination of whether the exclusion, if in fact used, has been properly asserted. *See, e.g., Beauman v. FBI*, No. 92-7603 (C.D. Cal. Apr. 28, 1993) (In upholding the adequacy of an FBI search which found no records concerning the plaintiff, the court addressed the plaintiff's concern that the FBI was relying on the (C)(1) exclusion. After reviewing an *in camera* FBI affidavit, the court stated that "without confirming or denying that any such exclusion was actually invoked by the defendant, the Court finds and concludes that if an exclusion was in fact employed, it was, and remains, amply justified.").

1.6.2. Because an agency's "no records" response has been held to be an "adverse determination" requiring the agency to notify the requester of administrative appeal rights under § 552(a)(6)(A)(i), *Oglesby v. Department of the Army*, 920 F.2d 57, 67 (D.C. Cir. 1990), the Justice Department guide advises agencies to "accept any clear request for review of the possible use of an exclusion and specifically address it in evaluating and responding to the appeal." *See* "Guide," *supra*, at 463.

1.6.3. In a case where the Government had refused to confirm or deny the existence of records regarding two individuals whose status as informants had allegedly been confirmed by the Government at trial, the trial court was held to have erred for failing to consider whether subsections (c)(2) applied and barred the use of such a response. *Benavides v. DEA*, 968 F.2d 1243 (D.C. Cir. 1992). However, upon the Government's petition for rehearing, the appellate court modified its earlier ruling to clarify that it had not "authoritatively construed" (c)(2) insofar as determining whether it requires a *Glomar* response, as Senator Leahy and Reps. English and Kindness maintained, or a "not found" response, as Senator Hatch and the Department of Justice have claimed. 976 F.2d 751 (D.C. Cir. 1992).

2. Records whose disclosure would interfere with criminal proceedings of which the subject is not aware.

2.1. Subsection (c)(1) permits agencies to refuse to acknowledge the existence of records when their disclosure could reasonably be expected to interfere with a criminal law enforcement proceeding under (b)(7)(A), and there is reason to believe that the subject of the proceedings is not aware of its pendency.

2.2. "While the agency is thus able to prevent a tip-off of investigatory activity to someone using the FOIA to find out if such activity is underway, its authority to do so is narrowly drawn and closely circumscribed." 132 Cong. Rec. S14297 (daily ed. Sept. 30, 1986) (statement of Senator Leahy). "Thus the provision gives agencies no new substantive withholding authority, since it does not apply to records that are not already exempt from disclosure and it would not be available to an agency when there is reason to believe that the subject of an investigation or proceeding is aware of its pendency." *Id., see also* 132 Cong. Rec. H9468 (daily ed. Oct. 8, 1986) (statement of Reps. English and Kindness).

2.3. Certain "publicly demonstrable facts" will carry a heavy presumption of the subject's awareness of proceedings which the agency must rebut with "clear and convincing evidence" if the records are to remain outside the scope of the Act. 132 Cong. Rec. H9467 (daily ed. Oct. 8, 1986) (statement of Reps. English and Kindness). Among those facts are public statements by law enforcement officials relating to an ongoing or contemplated investigation; returns of subpoenas and search warrants against subjects or other persons from whom the subject could reasonably be expected to learn of the subpoenas or search warrants; public statements by subjects or persons associated with subjects; arrests of subjects or persons associated with subjects; grand jury investigations of which subjects and/or the general public are aware; and, any other incident or statement that brings the existence of an investigation to public attention. *Id.* A showing by a requester that an agency had in its possession such publicly demonstrable facts, but withheld records from normal search and review processes without justification will "raise a strong inference" of arbitrary and capricious withholding under subsection (a)(4)(F) of the Act. *Id.* at H9468.

3. Informant record requested by a third-party according to the name or personal identifier by which it is maintained.

3.1. Subsection (c)(2) permits agencies to refuse to acknowledge the existence of informant records that are maintained by a criminal law enforcement agency under an informant's name or other personal identifier, when the records are requested by a third party who specifically refers to them by such name or personal identifier.

3.2. Referring to a virtually identical provision in S. 774, the Senate Judiciary Committee confirmed that such an "exclusion" means "the agency would have no obligation to acknowledge the existence of such records in response to such request." Report at 25. The Committee also noted the obvious limitations of the exclusion for informant records: "Where the requester is the informant himself, or a third party who describes the responsive records without reference to the informant's name or personal identifier, the records are subject to ordinary consideration under the provisions of the FOIA." *Id.*

3.3. Senator Leahy and Reps. English and Kindness noted a further limitation on this provision in that an agency must acknowledge the existence or nonexistence of such records when the informant's status as an informant has been "officially confirmed." 132 Cong. Rec. S14297 (daily ed. Sept. 30, 1986) (statement of Senator Leahy): 132 Cong. Rec. H9467 (daily ed. Oct. 8, 1986) (statement of Reps. English and Kindness).

4. Classified records of the FBI pertaining to foreign intelligence, counterintelligence or international terrorism.

Records Exclusions

4.1. Subsection (c)(3) permits the FBI to refuse to acknowledge the existence of records maintained by the FBI pertaining to foreign intelligence, counterintelligence, or international terrorism, to the extent that the fact of the existence of such records itself remains properly classified information.

4.2. The terms "foreign intelligence" and "counterintelligence" are defined in Section 3.4. of Executive Order 12333 on U.S. Intelligence Activities and the term "international terrorism" is defined in the Foreign Intelligence Surveillance Act, 50 U.S.C. § 1801(c).

4.3. Like the (c)(1) exclusion regarding ongoing criminal law enforcement proceedings, this provision "permits the FBI to avoid confirmation of the investigatory status of specific individuals or incidents in the context of activities regarding foreign intelligence, counterintelligence, or international terrorism." 132 Cong. Rec. H9467 (daily ed. Oct. 8, 1986) (statement of Reps. English and Kindness). Moreover, this provision, based directly on the circumstances of the "Glomar response" as developed in CIA caselaw and prescribed in Section 3.7(a) of Executive Order 12958 on Classified National Security Information, gives no new substantive withholding authority to the FBI since it applies only to records that are properly classified as national security information and, therefore, already exempt from disclosure pursuant to Exemption 1 of the FOIA. *Id., see also* 132 Cong. Rec. S14297 (daily ed. Sept. 30, 1986) (statement of Senator Leahy).

CHAPTER 19
The Electronic Freedom of Information Act Amendments of 1996

Chris Jay Hoofnagle

1. Introduction.

1.1. The Electronic Freedom of Information Act Amendments of 1996 ("EFOIA"), Pub. L. 104-231, 110 Stat. 3048, were signed by President Bill Clinton on October 2, 1996, and most of its provisions became effective on March 31, 1997. EFOIA has not been amended since enactment.

1.2. Congress enacted the EFOIA for two primary purposes: to specify that the FOIA applied to agency records stored in electronic formats and to change administrative process to address long delays and backlogs in agency production of documents. H.R. Rep. No. 104-795, at 11-14 (1996).

2. Legislative History.

2.1. The legislative history of the EFOIA Amendments is included in Chapter 1, section 6.6. *See* Appendix A for the House Report accompanying the EFOIA.

3. Definition of "Record."

3.1. The EFOIA Amendments specified that electronic documents are records for purposes of the FOIA. The term "record" was redefined to include "any information that would be an agency record subject to the requirements of this section when maintained by an agency in any format, including an electronic format." § 552(f)(2). This provision became effective on March 31, 1997.

3.1.1. This definition is to be construed broadly, and includes computer tapes, disks, CD-ROMs, digital media, microfiche, microforms, databases, and yet-to-be invented technologies that are developed to store, maintain, or produce information. H.R. Rep. No. 104-795, at 19-20 (1996).

3.1.2. "No matter how it is preserved, information that passes the threshold test of being an agency record, remains an agency record." *Id.* at 20.

4. Information Availability in Electronic Format.

4.1. The EFOIA Amendments call for the creation of "electronic reading rooms." An electronic reading room is a system that gives the public access to records by "electronic means," preferably online. § 552(a)(2). Agencies were required to create web sites for electronic reading rooms by November 1, 1997.

4.2. The EFOIA places a burden on agencies to publish certain records electronically. These are: final opinions in the adjudication of administrative cases, specific agency policy statements, administrative staff manuals that affect the public, a reference guide detailing records maintained by the agency and procedures to use FOIA, and the agency's annual report that includes statistics related to the agency's processing of requests. § 552(a)(2).

EFOIA Amendments

4.2.1. The guide for use of FOIA should "explain in clear and simple language" the types of records available, why some records are exempt, and how the agency determines whether records should be released. The guide should also explain how to make a request, the expected time for agency response, the requestor's rights under the law, and a brief summary of recent agency FOIA litigation. H.R. Rep. No. 104-795, at 30 (1996).

4.3. The EFOIA requires agencies to place records that are likely to "become the subject of subsequent requests" in the electronic reading room. § 552(a)(2)(D). This requirement applies only to records that are processed and released after November 1, 1996. By December 31, 1999, all agencies were required to publish an electronic index of all frequently requested material, whether the actual records are online or only available in paper form.

4.3.1. In determining whether records are likely to be requested frequently, agency personnel should use their knowledge of past requests to decide whether the materials are likely to be the subject of future requests. *Electronic FOIA Amendments Implementation Guidance Outline,* FOIA Update, U.S. Department of Justice Office of Information and Privacy, Vol. 19, No. 1, Winter 1998, at http://www.usdoj.gov/oip/foia_updates/Vol_XIX_1/ xixpage3.htm.

4.3.2. Records "on a popular topic, such as the assassinations of public figures" should be included in the electronic reading room. H.R. Rep. No. 104-795, at 21 (1996).

4.3.3. The purpose of including these popular records in the reading room is to help reduce the number of requests for the same records, and to help requestors determine what records have been released previously. *Id.*

4.4. Records that are posted in the electronic reading room must also be made available in the agency's conventional reading room. OIP Guidance: Amendment Implementation Questions, FOIA Update, U.S. Department of Justice Office of Information and Privacy, Vol. 18, No. 1, Winter 1997 at http://www.usdoj.gov/oip/foia_updates/ Vol_XVIII_1/page3.htm.

4.5. The EFOIA requires an agency to make "reasonable efforts" in searching for records in electronic "form or format." Reasonable efforts do not include those that "would significantly interfere with the operation of the agency's automated information system." § 552(a)(3)(C). This provision became effective on March 31, 1997.

4.6. Compliance with the EFOIA Amendments has been poor. In a 1998 study of 135 federal web sites, OMB Watch found that 57 agencies had no EFOIA presence, and found that no agency had fully complied with the 1996 law. OMB WATCH, ARMING THE PEOPLE "...WITH THE POWER KNOWLEDGE GIVES:" A REPORT ON THE IMPLEMENTATION OF THE ELECTRONIC FREEDOM OF INFORMATION AMENDMENTS OF 1996," (Apr. 1998). A 1999 study also conducted by OMB Watch found that no agency examined had fully implemented EFOIA. OMB WATCH, A PEOPLE ARMED?, (1999) at http://www.ombwatch.org/info/efoia/efoiareport.html; *see also Hearing on the Implementation of the Electronic Freedom of Information Act Amendments of 1996* Before the Subcomm. On Gov't Management, Info. & Tech. of the House Comm. On Gov't Reform, 105 Cong., June 9, 1998, at http://www.house.gov/reform/

gmit/hearings/testimony/980609h.htm; Martin E. Halstuk, *Speed Bumps on the Information Superhighway: A Study of Federal Agency Compliance with the Electronic Freedom of Information Act of 1996*, 5 Comm. L. & Pol'y 423 (2000).

4.6.1. In 1998, Public Citizen sued a group of federal agencies for failure to comply with requirements set by the EFOIA Amendments. Specifically, Public Citizen alleged that the agencies were violating § 552(g) by not making available indexes of major record systems and descriptions of those of information systems. The court held in that case that the agencies were violating § 552(g) and issued an injunction preventing the agencies from excluding broad categories of information from the indexing and description requirements. *Public Citizen, Inc. v. OMB*, 127 F. Supp. 2d 1 (D.D.C. 2000).

4.6.2. In what amounted to a symbolic victory, the court found that OMB's guidance on "major information systems" under the Paperwork Reduction Act was too narrow to be applied in the context of the EFOIA requirements. While many agencies were doing no more than pointing to the Government Information Locator Service (GILS), the court agreed with Public Citizen that "major information systems" at the agency level could include such categories as word-processing documents.

5. Honoring Form or Format Requests.

5.1. The EFOIA allows requesters to specify the format in which responsive documents are delivered. When an agency produces documents, the agency "shall provide the record in any form or format requested by the person if the record is readily reproducible by the agency in that form or format." § 552(a)(3)(B).

5.2. Requests for documents in a new form or format will be considered on a case-by-case basis by the agency to determine whether the records are "readily reproducible." A court will afford "substantial weight to an agency's determination as to technical feasibility" for reproduction in new formats. § 552(a)(4)(B).

6. Time Limits for Response to Requests.

6.1. The EFOIA doubled the time allotted to an agency to make a determination on a request. An agency must determine within twenty (20) business days whether to comply with the request and provide notice to the requestor of the determination. § 552(a)(6)(A)(i).

6.1.1. Despite the Congressional intent to address agency backlogs and to speed response times, courts have not compelled agencies to comply with the twenty-day requirement. "[I]t is commonly accepted that no federal agency can meet the impossibly rigorous timetable set forth in the statute…" *Natural Resources Defense Council v. DOE*, 191 F. Supp. 2d 41 (D.D.C. 2002).

6.2. The EFOIA allows agencies to create "multitrack" processing systems. Such systems enhance processing of requests by allowing smaller requests to be addressed quickly through an alternative multitrack system rather than by the standard "first in-first out" system. § 552(a)(6)(D)(i). Further, individuals have the option to limit the scope of their requests consistent with agency regulation in order to enjoy faster multitrack processing. § 552(a)(6)(D)(ii). These provisions became effective on March 31, 1997.

EFOIA Amendments

6.3. The EFOIA allows agencies to take an additional ten (10) working days in answering requests involving "unusual circumstances" upon notice to the requestor. § 552(a)(6)(B)(i). Unusual circumstances include requests that require searches of field offices or other remote offices, requests that produce voluminous responsive records, and requests that require consultation with other components or agencies that have a "substantial interest in the determination of the request." § 552(a)(6)(B)(iii).

6.3.1. In some situations, the additional ten working days still will not provide the agency adequate time to process the request. In such cases, the agency must notify the requester of the additional time required and allow the requester to "reasonably modify" the scope of the request. The agency may also negotiate "an alternative time frame for processing the request or a modified request" with the requestor. § 552(a)(6)(B)(ii). A court will consider a refusal to "reasonably modify" the scope of a request as a factor in determining whether "exceptional circumstances" exist. § 552(a)(6)(C)(iii).

6.3.2. Agencies should seek extensions beyond the additional ten days "only in rare instances." H.R. Rep. No. 104-795, at 24 (1996).

6.4. "Exceptional circumstances," situations where there is both a backlog of requests and "reasonable progress in reducing" the backlog, can allow an agency more time to comply with a request. § 552(a)(6)(C)(ii). Prior to the EFOIA Amendments, a court could extend extra time to an agency in complying with a request where a backlog prevented timely compliance. The EFOIA Amendments prevent an agency from using a backlog of requests alone as a condition to show "exceptional circumstances." This provision became effective on October 2, 1997.

6.4.1. Other factors that can justify "exceptional circumstances" include the amount of material classified, the size and complexity of other requests processed by the agency, resources being devoted to the declassification of classified material of public interest, or the number of requests for records made by courts or administrative tribunals. H.R. Rep. No. 104-795, at 24-25 (1996).

6.4.2. A large backlog of requests and inadequate resources to complete the requests does not constitute "exceptional circumstances." *Donham v. DOE,* 192 F. Supp. 2d 877 (S. D. Ill. 2002).

6.4.3. Exceptional circumstances were found where an agency was deluged with an unexpected number of FOIA requests, was experiencing personnel shortages, and was preparing to relocate the office. Additionally, the agency demonstrated due diligence in attempting to reduce backlogs by establishing new databases and document scanning methods. *Emerson v. CIA*, No. 99-0274 (TFH), 1999 U.S. Dist. LEXIS 19511 (D.D.C. 1999).

6.5. Even in cases where a court rejects an agency's defense of "exceptional circumstances," most courts have not ordered agencies to comply immediately with litigants' requests. Courts have reasoned that doing so would advantage litigants over non-litigants, and result in a delay of other FOIA requests. Instead, courts have set deadlines and monitored compliance over time. For instance, in a case where the Department of Energy failed to complete two requests after two years, the court ordered the agency to complete a partially finished request and file a schedule for completion for the other request within twenty-four business days. *Donham v. DOE*, 192 F. Supp. 2d 877 (S. D. Ill. 2002).

7. Expedited Processing (See Appendix F for a sample expedited processing request).

7.1. EFOIA requires agencies to promulgate regulations to allow expedited processing of requests where the requester can show a "compelling need" for records. § 552(a)(6)(E)(i).

7.1.1. Agencies may promulgate regulations that are broader than provided under the EFOIA. H.R. Rep. No. 104-795, at 26 (1996). A requestor should check the agency's regulations for expedited processing criteria that may exceed the rights of the EFOIA.

7.1.2. Expedited processing "is intended to be limited to circumstances in which a delay in obtaining information can reasonably be foreseen to cause a significant adverse consequence to a recognized interest." H.R. Rep. No. 104-795, at 26 (1996).

7.2. The FOIA defines two categories of requestors that can show compelling needs: first, where the requestor shows that failing to obtain the records on an expedited basis could "reasonably be expected to pose an imminent threat to the life or physical safety of an individual." § 552(a)(6)(E)(v)(I).

7.2.1. Under the first category of compelling need requests, a reasonable person should be able to appreciate an imminent threat to life or physical safety posed by a failure to obtain the records. H.R. Rep. No. 104-795, at 26 (1996).

7.2.1.1. A mere allegation that agency documents contain information that may exculpate a requestor facing criminal prosecution will not justify expedited processing. The requestor must make an "adequate showing" that the documents sought contain materially exculpatory information. *Williams v. FBI*, 2000 U.S. Dist. LEXIS 17493 (D.D.C. 2000); *Edmond v. U.S. Attorney*, 959 F. Supp. 1 (D.D.C. 1997).

7.3. The second category of compelling need exists when a request is made by a "person primarily engaged in disseminating information" who has some "urgency to inform the public concerning actual or alleged Federal Government activity." § 552(a)(6)(E)(v)(II). This provision became effective on October 2, 1997.

7.3.1. This category requires that the requestor's main activity be information dissemination. However, information dissemination does not have to be the requestor's sole activity. H.R. Rep. No. 104-795, at 26 (1996).

7.3.2. The D.C. Circuit established a three-part test for determining whether there is an "urgency to inform the public concerning actual or alleged Federal Government activity." First, a court must consider whether the request "concerns a matter of current exigency to the American public;" second, whether "the consequences of delaying a response would compromise a significant recognized interest;" and last, whether "the request concerns federal government activity." The court also noted that the credibility of the requestor is a relevant consideration in finding compelling need. *Al-Fayed v. CIA*, 254 F.3d 300 (D.C. Cir. 2001).

7.3.3. A number of cases have subjected the "compelling needs" test to judicial review in the context of requestors who are primarily engaged in disseminating information.

7.3.3.1. A court first reviewed the 1996 expedited processing provisions in a case where the Electronic Privacy Information Center (EPIC) sought Federal Bureau of Information (FBI) documents relating to the Carnivore Internet surveillance program. In its request for expedited processing, EPIC noted that over fifty news articles had appeared in the Lexis-Nexis news database regarding Carnivore, the House Judiciary Committee scheduled hearings, and several prominent U.S. newspapers published editorials on Carnivore. EPIC brought suit after the FBI failed to respond to the request for expedited processing. After litigation was initiated, the agency granted expedited processing. The court retained jurisdiction to supervise the release of documents, but refused to require the agency to complete the request in twenty days. *Electronic Privacy Information Center v. DOJ*, No. 00-1849 (JR), (D.D.C. Aug. 2, 2000).

7.3.3.2. Expedited processing was denied twice in a case involving requests for intelligence information regarding the 1997 death of British Princess Diana and Dodi Al-Fayed. The agencies determined that expedited processing should be denied because there was no compelling need to respond, that a delay in release of the information would not reduce its value, and that the subject of the requests no longer concerned issues of widespread media interest. Although the court noted that news coverage surrounding the deaths was extensive and that the requestor was primarily engaged in disseminating information, the court held that the agencies acted properly in denying expedited processing. The court also considered that granting expedited processing would delay other requests already in the queue, and that such delay may be against the public interest. *Al-Fayed v. CIA*, No. 00-2092 (CKK), 2000 U.S. Dist. LEXIS 21476 (D.D.C. 2000). On appeal, the Circuit Court affirmed the denial of expedited processing, and set forth the three-part test (*supra* at 6.3.2) for determining "compelling need" by requestors primarily engaged in dissemination of information. *Al-Fayed v. CIA*, 254 F.3d 300 (D.C. Cir. 2001).

7.3.3.3. A court denied expedited processing to Linda Tripp, a figure involved in the scandal involving former President Clinton and White House intern Monica Lewinsky. In that case, Tripp requested information relating to her employment and a bid for potential employment. In denying her request for expedited processing the court noted that the information requested was three years old and was not the subject of any breaking news story. Additionally, although Tripp had previously provided information to the media, she was not currently "primarily engaged" in the activity of disseminating information. *Tripp v. Dept. of Defense*, 193 F. Supp. 2d 229 (D.D.C. 2001).

7.3.3.4. Expedited processing was ordered in a case involving a request for documents concerning energy policy and President Bush's Energy Task Force. Without applying the analysis set forth in *Al-Fayed* or the considerations of the House Report, the court concluded that the request concerned material of "extraordinary public interest." The court noted that the terrorist attacks of September 11, 2001, the secrecy involved in the activities of the task force, and Congressional interest in the task force demonstrated enormous public concern. *Natural Resources Defense Council v. DOE*, 191 F. Supp. 2d 41 (D.D.C. 2002). A request for the same documents by another organization was also granted expedited processing. *Judicial Watch, Inc. v. DOE*, 191 F. Supp. 2d 138 (D.D.C. 2002).

7.4. An agency must notify the requestor of its determination to grant expedited processing within ten (10) calendar days of the request. § 552(a)(6)(E)(ii)(I). The postmark of the request may determine the start date of the ten-day period. *Congress Enacts FOIA Amendments*, FOIA Update, U.S. Department of Justice Office of Information and Privacy, Vol. 17, No. 4, Fall 1996 at http://www.usdoj.gov/oip/foia_updates/Vol_XVII_4/page1.htm.

7.5. If the agency grants the expedited request, the agency must process and disclose responsive records "as soon as practicable." § 552(a)(6)(E)(iii).

7.6. If the agency denies expedited processing, the agency must give "expeditious consideration of administrative appeals of such determinations." § 552(a)(6)(E)(ii)(II). Judicial review of a denial of expedited processing will be limited to the administrative record generated by the requester and agency. Accordingly, it is important for requestors to build an administrative record in the request for expedited processing or the appeals process. Requestors should "explain in detail their basis for seeking" expedited processing. H.R. Rep. No. 104-795, at 26 (1996).

7.6.1. A denial of a request for expedited processing authorizes judicial review. A requestor does not have to exhaust administrative remedies by appealing a denial of expedited processing before bringing suit. *Al-Fayed v. CIA*, No. 00-2092 (CKK), 2000 U.S. Dist. LEXIS 21476 (D.D.C. 2000).

7.6.2. However, once an agency completes a response to a request, the court does not have jurisdiction to examine a denial for expedited processing. § 552(a)(6)(E)(iv); *Judicial Watch, Inc. v. United States Naval Observatory*, No. 01-1293 (D.D.C. Sept. 4, 2001).

7.6.3. A court will review an agency denial of expedited processing *de novo*. *Al-Fayed v. CIA*, 254 F.3d 300 (D.C. Cir. 2001).

7.7. Requestors must certify that their request for expedited processing is true. § 552(a)(6)(E)(vi). This can be accomplished by including the following statement: "I hereby affirm that the foregoing is true and correct to the best of my knowledge and belief."

EFOIA Amendments

8. Computer Redaction.

8.1. Where an agency has withheld portions of documents, the EFOIA requires notice to the requester of the amount of information withheld, except where this notice would harm an interest protected by any of the exemptions recognized under § 552(b). If possible, the agency should indicate where the deletions from the record were made. § 552(b). Courts are to "accord substantial weight" to agency determinations regarding the technical feasibility of indicating where records have been redacted. § 552(a)(4)(B).

8.2. Where entire records are withheld, the agency must notify the requestor of the estimated volume of withheld records. § 552(a)(6)(F). In small-volume cases, the agency must provide an exact page count of withheld documents. Estimates are acceptable in large-volume cases. This provision became effective on October 2, 1997.

9. Reporting Requirements.

9.1. The EFOIA also changed a number of annual reporting requirements for agencies. Each agency must submit a report annually to the Attorney General by February 1 covering the following statistics:

9.1.1. The number of determinations not to comply with requests for records and the justifications for these denials. § 552(e)(1)(A).

9.1.2. The number of appeals made under § 552(a)(6) and their dispositions. If the appeal is denied, the agency must also report the reason for the denial. § 552(e)(1)(B).

9.1.3. A list of all statutes used to withhold information under exemption (b)(3) and the nature of those determinations to withhold. This list must include a description of the information withheld. Additionally, the agency must report whether a court has upheld the decision of the agency to withhold documents under the (b)(3) statute. § 552(e)(1)(B)(ii).

9.1.4. The number of requests pending before the agency as of September 30 of the preceding year, and the median number of days that those requests had been pending. § 552(e)(1)(C).

9.1.5. The number of requests received by the agency and the number of requests processed. § 552(e)(1)(D).

9.1.6. The median number of days taken by the agency to process different types of requests. § 552(e)(1)(E).

9.1.7. The total amount of fees collected by the agency for processing requests. § 552(e)(1)(F).

9.1.8. The number of full-time staff devoted to processing requests under FOIA, and the total amount expended by the agency in processing requests. § 552(e)(1)(G).

9.2. These reports are to be included in the agency's electronic reading room if possible. § 552(e)(2).

9.3. The Attorney General is to make these reports available through a single electronic portal. § 552(e)(3).

9.4. The Attorney General is required to compile a report by April 1 of each year including:

9.4.1. A listing of the number of cases arising under FOIA;

9.4.2. The exemption involved in each case;

9.4.3. The disposition of the case, and the cost, fees, and penalties assessed. The list of penalties assessed must include attorney's fees and litigation costs awarded under subparagraphs (E), (F), and (G) of subsection (a)(4).

9.4.4. A description of efforts undertaken by the Department of Justice to encourage agencies' compliance with the FOIA. § 552(e)(5).

10. **The 11th Circuit has ruled that the EFOIA has not altered the privacy balancing test under exemption (b)(7).** In that case, the requestor sought lists from the U.S. Customs Services of individuals who had their property seized. Citing *FLRA v. Department of Defense*, 977 F.2d 545 (11th Cir. 1992) and *DOJ v. Reporters Comm. for Freedom of the Press*, 489 U.S. 749 (1989), the circuit court upheld the determination that privacy interests in the lists trumped the public interest in disclosure.

CHAPTER 20

Using the FOIA as an Alternative or Adjunct to Civil or Criminal Discovery

Allan Robert Adler and Harry A. Hammitt

1. Introduction.

1.1. Despite numerous judicial statements to the effect that "the Freedom of Information Act was not intended to serve as a substitute for... discovery," *see, e.g., Fruehauf Corp. v. Thornton*, 507 F.2d 1253, 1254 (6th Cir. 1974) (*per curiam*), it is clear that the FOIA can be and has been profitably used for discovery of government documents for use in both administrative and court proceedings. The confusion on this point may have been engendered by statements such as the one made by the Supreme Court in *Renegotiation Board v. Bannercraft Clothing Co.*, 415 U.S. 1, 24 (1974), in which the Court noted that "[d]iscovery for litigation purposes is not an expressly indicated purpose of the Act." Although the Court's statement is correct, the Court failed to note that the FOIA contains no express statement as to its use for any purpose.

1.2. As is apparent from the requirement of § 552(a)(3) that records be made available to "any person" upon request, the FOIA is "litigation neutral," i.e., in its main structure the FOIA does not contemplate considerations of the requester's identity or intended use of agency records. Thus, the Supreme Court stated the correct rule as to the effect of a litigant's use of the FOIA as a discovery tool in *NLRB v. Sears, Roebuck & Co.*, 421 U.S. 132, 143 n.10 (1975), when the Court stated that Sears' rights under the Act "are neither increased nor decreased by reason of the fact that it claims an interest in the Advice and Appeals Memoranda greater than that shared by the average member of the public."

1.3. The FOIA and civil and criminal discovery provide independent schemes for obtaining federal agency documents. Thus, there is no requirement that a FOIA plaintiff involved in criminal litigation exhaust the criminal discovery process as a prerequisite to disclosure under the FOIA. *See Hawkes v. IRS*, 467 F.2d 787, 792-93 & n.6 (6th Cir. 1972). By the same token, the mere fact that a particular agency record falls within the ambit of one of the exemptions to the FOIA does not furnish a defense to a request for production made in civil or criminal discovery. *See Baldridge v. Shapiro*, 455 U.S. 345, 360 n.15 (1982). Conversely, the fact that information is privileged from discovery in civil litigation does not necessarily mean that it is exempt from disclosure under the FOIA. *See Washington Post Co. v. HHS*, 690 F.2d 252 (D.C. Cir. 1982), and *Playboy Enterprises, Inc. v. DOJ*, 677 F.2d 931, 936 (D.C. Cir. 1982) ("That for one reason or another a document may be exempt from discovery does not mean that it will be exempt from a demand under FOIA."). *See also Friedman v. Bache Halsey Stuart Shields, Inc.*, 738 F.2d 1336, 1344 (D.C. Cir. 1984) ("The FOIA acts as a 'floor' when discovery of government documents is sought in the course of civil litigation.").

1.4. In general, "FOIA rights are unaffected by the requester's involvement in other litigation; an individual may therefore obtain under FOIA information that may be useful in non-FOIA litigation, even when the documents sought could not be obtained through discovery." *North v. Walsh*, 881 F.2d 1088, 1099 (D.C. Cir. 1989).

Using FOIA for Discovery

2. **Certain differences between the FOIA and the rules of civil discovery may, in some cases, make the FOIA an attractive alternative or adjunct to civil discovery.**

2.1. A FOIA request may be filed by "any person" (§ 552(a)(3)). Civil discovery requests, on the other hand, must be filed by a "party" to a pending action. *See* Rule 26(b)(1) of the Federal Rules of Civil Procedure.

2.2. A FOIA requester is entitled to obtain disclosure of any nonexempt agency records responsive to his request without making any showing of need or relevancy. Civil discovery, on the other hand, is limited to that which is "relevant to the subject matter involved in the pending action." *See* Fed. R. Civ. P. 26(b)(1); *Baldridge v. Shapiro*, 455 U.S. at 360 (contrasting the discovery provisions of the Federal Rules of Civil Procedure with the broad statutory grant of disclosure under the FOIA based on the former's focus on the litigant's "need" for the information). A good illustration of how a litigant's rights to obtain disclosure of federal agency documents can vary depending on whether the disclosure is sought under the FOIA or under civil discovery is found in *Firestone Tire & Rubber Co. v. Coleman*, 432 F. Supp. 1359, 1364-65 & 1371-73 (N.D. Ohio 1976).

2.3. A FOIA request theoretically would be the faster way to obtain copies of federal agency records since a FOIA request may be made by a simple letter which, when received, places the agency under a statutory obligation to respond within "20 days (except Saturdays, Sundays, and legal public holidays)." *See* § 552(a)(6)(A)(i). (Agency delays, however, often make the FOIA process slower than discovery.) A discovery request, on the other hand, obviously may not be filed until after "commencement" of an action. Additionally, except upon a motion made pursuant to the provisions of either Rule 30(b)(3) or Rule 34(b), a plaintiff involved in a civil action may not compel production of documents via discovery until thirty days after commencement of an action.

2.4. If a FOIA requester prevails, documents are released to the requester without any restrictions as to their use. *See Baldridge v. Shapiro*, 455 U.S. at 350 n.4 (The Supreme Court, in the course of discussing a district court disclosure order that had been conditioned on the disclosed records being used solely by persons sworn to secrecy, stated: "We note in passing that there is no provision in the FOIA statute for this procedure."). In civil discovery, of course, release of sensitive documents is often conditioned on compliance with strict terms of a protective order issued by the court pursuant to Rule 26(c). In *Schiffer v. FBI*, 78 F.3d 1405 (9th Cir. 1996), the court indicated that the lower court had erred by limiting Schiffer's ability to disseminate records disclosed to him under FOIA. Finding such a limitation would go beyond the language of the statute, the court observed that no limits could be placed on records once disclosed. However, the court found the records here were exempt.

2.5. The plaintiff in a FOIA suit does not risk bearing any portion of the government's litigation costs or expenses if his suit is unsuccessful. In civil discovery, on the other hand, attorney's fees and costs may be assessed against a party unsuccessfully moving for an order compelling discovery of documents. *See* Fed. R. Civ. P. 37(a)(4).

2.6. Because the issues in discovery proceedings differ significantly from the issues in a FOIA action, the general rule of "issue preclusion" would not bar a FOIA action for documents which were earlier sought by subpoena during grand jury proceedings.

North v. Walsh, 881 F.2d at 1095. *See also Hoover v. Department of the Interior,* 611 F.2d 1132, 1137 (5th Cir. 1980) (district court erred in dismissing FOIA action on the grounds that the same issue was pending in a contemporaneous condemnation action).

3. Tactical Considerations in Using the FOIA as an Alternative or Adjunct to Civil Discovery.

3.1. Perhaps the key advantages of the FOIA over civil discovery result from the FOIA's lack of any requirement for a showing of relevancy of the records sought to a particular pending action. Thus, the FOIA may be the only way to discover government documents during certain phases of an agency's investigation or compliance proceeding when discovery is typically not permitted under agency procedural rules. Moreover, agency discovery rules are often so strict that a litigant may not even be able to discover the existence of arguably relevant documents. The FOIA at least permits the identification of such arguably relevant documents, and, even though the records may not be disclosable because of the exemptions of § 552(b), the FOIA requester may later be able to obtain disclosure of the documents through civil discovery by making a demonstration of relevancy and need sufficient to override any applicable privileges.

3.2. Although most FOIA requests used for discovery probably seek disclosure of agency records for use in litigating against the government, the possible uses of the FOIA as an alternative or adjunct to discovery in civil litigation against private parties should not be overlooked. If the opposing party in civil litigation is a large corporation, for instance, there is a high likelihood that some "agency" subject to the FOIA maintains records concerning the corporation's business activities, some of which may be helpful in litigation against them. A key advantage to using the FOIA, rather than civil discovery, in this context is that the FOIA requester's civil opponent usually would not be a party to the FOIA administrative or court proceeding, and, unless the request seeks confidential business data of the opponent, the opponent typically would not even learn that the FOIA request had been filed. This creates the possibility that the litigant could use the FOIA to obtain an *ex parte* look at agency records without bringing any possibly unfavorable records to his opponent's attention.

4. Examples of FOIA Use as an Adjunct to Civil Discovery Include:

4.1. *Weber Aircraft Corp. v. United States*, 688 F.2d 638 (9th Cir. 1982), *rev'd*, 465 U.S. 792 (1984) (certain manufacturers and designers of parachute and pilot ejection systems of an Air Force plane that crashed sought Air Force accident reports for use in defending a personal injury suit brought by an Air Force pilot).

4.2. *Campbell v. HHS*, 682 F.2d 256, 257-58 (D.C. Cir. 1982) (a "whistleblower" discharged by a drug company after he made allegations that his employer had failed to report to the FDA adverse reaction data and toxicological information relating to certain drugs sought some of his former employer's filings with the FDA to support his state court suit for retaliatory discharge). *See also Borrell v. United States International Communications Agency*, 682 F.2d 981, 983 (D.C. Cir. 1982).

4.3. *County of Madison, N.Y. v. DOJ*, 641 F.2d 1036, 1038 (1st Cir. 1981) (attorney representing a county in a suit brought against it by the Oneida Indian Nation sought Justice Department records relating to a tentative settlement of a related suit brought by the Oneida Indian Nation against the United States).

4.4. *Carlisle Tire and Rubber Co., v. U.S. Customs Service*, 663 F.2d 210, 211 (D.C. Cir. 1980) (company involved in litigation before the Customs Court sought records relating to Customs Service's countervailing duty determinations as to certain imported bicycle tires and tubes).

4.5. *Thomas v. EPA*, 554 F. Supp. 418 (W.D.N.Y. 1983) (attorney representing plaintiffs in a state court class action suit against the Volkswagen Company sought EPA records relating to a recall of certain Volkswagen Rabbits).

5. Although civil and criminal discovery are substantially similar in points of comparison with the FOIA, there is one key difference between civil and criminal discovery that has special implications for use of the FOIA as an alternative or adjunct to criminal discovery. In civil discovery, once the proponent of discovery demonstrates that documents sought are "relevant to the subject matter involved in the pending action," the documents are presumptively disclosable unless the opponent of the discovery carries the burden of proving the applicability of some privilege. *See* Fed. R. Civ. P. 26(b) and 26(c). Conversely, in criminal discovery, the criminal defendant usually must demonstrate not only the relevance of documents sought, but also that the request for documents is "reasonable" and that the documents are within the scope of criminal discovery. *See* Fed. R. Crim. P. 16(a). Moreover, under Fed. R. Crim. P. 16(b), a criminal defendant's request for discovery may trigger reciprocal discovery in favor of the government.

6. Tactical Considerations in Using the FOIA as an Alternative or Adjunct to Criminal Discovery.

6.1. The chief advantages of using the FOIA as an alternative or adjunct to criminal discovery result from the absence of any standing or relevancy requirements in the FOIA, as well as the differences in timing and burden of proof between the FOIA and criminal discovery. Thus, the FOIA may be the only way for the criminal practitioner to obtain marginally relevant but potentially useful prosecutorial documents such as policy guidelines, prosecutorial workbooks, and statistical files. *See Jordan v. DOJ*, 591 F.2d 753, 755-56, 781-82 (D.C. Cir. 1978) (*en banc*) (charging manuals, rules and guidelines relating to prosecutorial discretion).

6.2. Courts, however, will not permit FOIA requests in this context to interfere with "the orderly and efficient operation of the criminal justice system" which, at least in part, depends upon adherence to the rules of criminal discovery. In *United States v. U.S. District Court, C.D. California, Los Angeles*, 717 F.2d 478 (9th Cir. 1983), the court of appeals issued a writ of mandamus vacating the trial court's order requiring the government to respond to defendant John DeLorean's 18 FOIA requests without regard to the materiality or relevancy of the materials sought. "The necessary consequence of the trial court's ruling would be that, as a routine discovery device in criminal cases within this circuit, counsel would request disclosure under the Freedom of Information Act, a substantial displacement of the balance established for criminal discovery by Rule 16. The harm to the Government in allowing FOIA discovery to override Rule 16 would be substantial in this case and in all later criminal cases. Under the trial court's order, the prosecution, instead of concentrating on the criminal case, would be compelled to devote its scarce resources to screen and process FOIA material." *Id.* at

481. *See also United States v. Murdock*, 548 F.2d 599, 602 (5th Cir. 1977); *Fruehauf Corp. v. Thornton*, 507 F.2d at 1254.

6.3. In addition to rejecting an "issue preclusion" argument, the court in *North v. Walsh* rejected the argument that a FOIA action for records unsuccessfully sought by subpoena during grand jury proceedings was barred by the doctrine of "claim preclusion." The court ruled that the plaintiff could not have invoked the FOIA in the grand jury proceeding, and was not obligated to file a separate FOIA action and then move for consolidation with the non-FOIA proceeding "in order to avert the risk of claim preclusion." 881 F.2d at 1094-95.

6.4. The mere existence of a court order sealing records presented as evidence in a criminal case was held insufficient to justify withholding under the FOIA. *Morgan v. DOJ*, 923 F.2d 195 (D.C. Cir. 1991). The court ruled that whether the criminal defendant's FOIA litigation is an impermissible collateral attack on the trial court's sealing order depends on the intended effect of the sealing order, noting that "only those orders intended to operate as the functional equivalent of an injunction prohibiting disclosure" can justify agency withholding of records that do not fall within any FOIA exemptions. *Id.* at 199.

6.5. An agency is not required to determine whether records sought pursuant to a FOIA request constitute exculpatory material which must be released to a criminal defendant under the Due Process requirements of *Brady v. Maryland*, 373 U.S. 83 (1963), nor is an agency required by the FOIA to forego a statutory exemption simply because the record at issue has been identified as possibly exculpatory. *Johnson v. DOJ*, 758 F. Supp. 2, 5 (D.D.C. 1991).

CHAPTER 21
Litigation Strategy in FOIA Cases
Eric R. Glitzenstein, Katherine A. Meyer and Amy Atwood

1. Exhaustion of Administrative Remedies.

1.1. FOIA requesters must exhaust their administrative remedies before filing suit to obtain agency records. *Oglesby v. Department of the Army*, 920 F.2d 57, 61-2 (D.C. Cir. 1990); *Spannaus v. DOJ*, 824 F.2d 52, 59 (D.C. Cir. 1987); *Hedley v. United States*, 594 F.2d 1043, 1044 (5th Cir. 1979). *Accord Sherer v. Balkema*, 840 F.2d 437 (7th Cir. 1988); *Brumley v. Department of Labor*, 767 F.2d 444 (8th Cir. 1985); *Stebbins v. Nationwide Mut. Ins. Co.*, 757 F.2d 364 (D.C. Cir. 1985). Thus, FOIA plaintiffs must make a written request for records to the relevant federal agency, and that request must either be denied or not acted on by the agency within the FOIA's time limits before a lawsuit can be filed.

1.1.1. As soon as the initial request and subsequent appeal to the agency are both denied, the requester has exhausted administrative remedies and may seek review in federal court. *Oglesby*, 920 F.2d at 61; *Pollack v. DOJ*, 49 F.3d 115, 118 (4th Cir. 1995), *cert. denied*, 516 U.S. 843 (1995).

1.1.2. A requester must exhaust for all aspects of the request. In *Dettman v. DOJ*, 802 F.2d 1472 (D.C. Cir. 1986), a panel of the D.C. Circuit found that the FBI improperly responded to a first-party request when it processed only those portions of "see" reference files containing specific references to the plaintiff. However, the court refused to rule on the issue because the plaintiff failed to challenge the FBI's processing policy for such files when it was explained to her at the administrative level.

1.1.2.1. In *Hamilton Securities Group, Inc. v. Department of Housing and Urban Development*, 106 F. Supp. 2d 23, 26-27 (D.D.C. 2000), *aff'd*, 2001 WL 238162 (D.C. Cir. Feb. 23, 2001), the district court applied the "*Dettman* analysis" to rule that the requester had not completely exhausted his administrative remedies, when he failed to appeal all of the bases upon which his request was initially denied. Thus, where the agency notified the requester in writing of its narrow construction of the request, but the requester's counsel did not appeal that construction, the court held that the requester did not exhaust remedies with respect to any records beyond those covered by the request as construed by the agency.

1.1.2.2. In *Halpern v. FBI*, 181 F.3d 279 (2d Cir. 1999), the Second Circuit held that where the agency had informed the requester that it had not processed records that "cross-referenced" individuals about whom records were sought, and the requester did not ask it to do so, the plaintiff had not exhausted his administrative remedies for those records.

1.1.2.3. A requester must also exhaust his or her administrative remedies with respect to field offices as well as headquarters. *See Kowalczyk v.*

DOJ, 73 F.3d 386 (D.C. Cir. 1996) (headquarters had no obligation to search field offices absent some indication by requester that responsive records would be found there); *accord*, *Voinche v. FBI*, 1997 WL 411685 (D.C. Cir. June 19, 1997).

1.1.3. In the alternative, the requester is deemed to have exhausted administrative remedies where the agency fails to comply with any of the FOIA's time limits for response. Thus, requesters may seek immediate judicial review where the agency takes more than 20 working days to make a determination on the initial request or more than 20 working days to act on an appeal, except where the agency demonstrates the existence of unusual circumstances allowing it to extend the time limits by not more than 10 working days. 5 U.S.C. § 552(a)(6)(A) & (a)(6)(B). Alternatively, a requester can file an appeal to the "constructive" denial of her request, when she does not receive a response within 20 working days, and then wait for the appeal to run before filing suit. However, once the requester receives any response to the initial request which advises the requester of a right to appeal, she must exhaust the appeal process before filing suit. *Oglesby*, 920 F.2d at 61; *Lewis v. Glickman*, 1996 WL 39398 (E.D. La. Jan. 31, 1996); *Judicial Watch, Inc. v. United States Naval Observatory*, 160 F. Supp. 2d 111 (D.D.C. 2001).

1.1.4. It is sometimes an effective strategy for a FOIA requester to proceed to court as soon as the Act's time limits expire or soon thereafter. If an agency is intentionally delaying its response, filing suit can put needed pressure on agency officials to expeditiously process the request. If, however, the agency is processing the request in good faith and legitimately needs to take additional time to complete processing, it is generally unwise and unproductive to rush into court merely because the FOIA's time limits have elapsed. To effectively assess which course of action to pursue, the requester should establish a dialogue with the agency official responsible for processing the request.

1.2. Even if an agency has violated the FOIA's time limits and suit is filed, this does not guarantee that the court will establish a strict deadline for the agency's response to the request. Under subsection (a)(6)(C) of the FOIA, "if the Government can show exceptional circumstances exist and that the agency is exercising due diligence in responding to the request, the court may retain jurisdiction and allow the agency additional time" to process the request.

1.2.1. A massive backlog of FOIA requests at an agency with sufficient resources to process them in a timely manner can constitute "exceptional circumstances" justifying additional time for an agency to complete processing of a request. *Open America v. Watergate Special Prosecution Force*, 547 F.2d 605 (D.C. Cir. 1976); *Exner v. FBI*, 542 F.2d 1121 (9th Cir. 1976). Moreover, both cases hold that a "first-in, first-out" system for processing requests can constitute "due diligence" under subsection (a)(6)(C).

1.2.2. *Open America* and *Exner* differ in terms of the effect that the requester's filing suit can have on his or her place in line, with *Open America* holding that filing suit should have absolutely no bearing on the requester's place in line and *Exner* holding that filing suit can, in the discretion of the district court, move a requester "up the line."

1.2.3. In *Fiduccia v. DOJ*, 185 F.3d 1035, 1040 (9th Cir. 1999), the Ninth Circuit qualified *Exner*, rejecting the proposition that there is an automatic "litigation preference" for requesters who sue agencies. Thus, the Court indicated that whether an FOIA plaintiff moves "up the line" falls within the discretion of the district court judge and depends on whether there are "appropriate circumstances" for doing so. *Id.* The Court found that there were no such "appropriate circumstances" where the requesters did not argue or show entitlement to expedited processing. *Id.* at 1041.

1.2.4. Indeed, even *Open America* recognized that a FOIA litigator should be given priority where an "exceptional need or urgency" for the records can be shown. 547 F.2d at 615-16; *The Nation Magazine v. Department of State*, 805 F. Supp. 68, 73 (D.D.C. 1992). To show this, the requester must show a "genuine need and reason for urgency in gaining access to Government records ahead of prior applicants for information." *Lisee v. CIA*, 741 F. Supp. 988, 989 (D.D.C. 1990), *quoting Open America*, 547 F.2d at 615-16); *accord, Edmond v. U.S. Attorney*, 959 F. Supp. 1 (D.D.C. 1997) (to "demonstrate such urgency," the requester "must show potential jeopardy to his or her personal safety, or to substantial due process rights"). Obviously, this is a difficult standard to satisfy and most requesters have been unsuccessful in claiming an "exceptional need or urgency" for requested records. *Lisse*, 741 F. Supp. 988 (author seeking records to meet publication schedule did not demonstrate "exceptional need"); *Edmond*, 959 F. Supp. 1 (prisoner seeking records to aid him in overturning his criminal conviction did not establish exceptional need or urgency; prisoners must provide an "adequate showing" that it is "likely" that the documents "contain materially exculpatory information"); *Fiduccia*, 185 F.3d at 1041 (requester's failure to argue or show entitlement to expedited processing precluded court from ordering the agency to move the requester "up the line" for processing); *Ohaegbu v. FBI*, 936 F. Supp. 7 (D.D.C. 1996) (requester did not show "urgent need"); *accord, Jimenez v. FBI*, 938 F. Supp. 21, 31-2 (D.D.C. 1996). *But see Cleaver v. Kelley*, 427 F. Supp. 80 (D.D.C. 1976) (plaintiff's need for records to be used in his upcoming criminal trial on murder and assault charges did constitute exceptional circumstances requiring expedited processing). In *Morrow v. FBI*, 2 F.3d 642 (5th Cir. 1993), the court vacated a trial court's dismissal of a death row inmate's FOIA case that had been filed as soon as the time for a response expired, and remanded the case with directions that the FBI must demonstrate that it exercised due diligence in not processing the request within that time period. *See also Electronic Privacy Information Center v. FBI*, 865 F. Supp. 1 (D.D.C. 1994) (court rejected FBI's motion for stay based on backlog claim, finding *Open America* "inapposite" where contested records were previously reviewed for release of summary); *Fiduccia*, 185 F.3d 1035 (FBI failed to show "exceptional circumstances" for delay when it asked for eight years to process request because of the large number of pages covered by the request).

1.2.5. Noting that, "to the extent that the FBI takes unjustified positions in FOIA proceedings, it generates its own burdens and increases delays," one district court granted the requester's motion for expedited response, notwithstanding *Open America*, on grounds that "when the agency's position on a specific FOIA document production or fee waiver request has been determined to be unjustified ... the resulting special impact on the particular request warrants some degree of priority attention to that request." *Ettlinger v. FBI*, 596 F. Supp. 867, 879 (D. Mass. 1984).

1.2.6. Subsection (a)(6)(C) does not authorize a court to dismiss an action when the court determines that the agency should receive additional time to process the request. The plaintiff should ask the court to exercise close supervision over the case to ensure that the request is processed in a reasonable period of time. Courts are generally receptive to such requests since they do not want cases sitting on their dockets for extended periods. In turn, persuading a court to closely monitor an agency's processing of a request will encourage the agency to process the request more expeditiously than it otherwise would. However, a district court's refusal to order an agency to expedite processing of a request is not an appealable interlocutory order. *Summers v. DOJ*, 925 F.2d 450 (D.C. Cir. 1991).

1.2.7. In *Mayock v. INS*, 714 F. Supp. 1558 (N.D. Cal. 1989), the court held that the Immigration and Naturalization Service must meet the statutory deadline for responding to a FOIA request where requested records were needed to defend against deportation and where there was no evidence that the INS had sought sufficient funds to process FOIA requests. This ruling was reversed and remanded for factual findings regarding the extent to which the government had sought FOIA funding, as well as the urgency of the requesters' need for the records. 938 F.2d 1006 (9th Cir. 1991). *See also Gilmore v. National Security Agency*, 76 F.3d 386 (9th Cir. 1995) (routine delay, regardless of the complexity of the request, does not constitute exceptional circumstances).

2. Jurisdiction.

2.1. The FOIA provides that a federal district court "has jurisdiction to enjoin the agency from withholding agency records and to order the production of any agency records improperly withheld from the complainant." § 552(a)(4)(B). This subsection has been construed as providing jurisdiction not only over requests for records made under the FOIA's general disclosure provision, subsection 552(a)(3), but also over the affirmative disclosure provisions found in the Act, i.e., subsections 552(a)(1) (requiring that certain types of records be routinely "published" by agencies) and 552(a)(2) (requiring that other types of records be made available for public inspection and copying). *See American Mail Line, Ltd. v. Gulick*, 411 F.2d 696 (D.C. Cir. 1969). This subsection also confers jurisdiction over fee questions, *i.e.*, whether an agency is charging excessive fees for a particular request, *Long v. IRS*, 596 F.2d 362 (9th Cir. 1979) *cert. denied*, 446 U.S. 917 (1980), and whether an agency has properly denied a request for a fee waiver. *Fitzgibbon v. CIA*, No. 76-700 (D.D.C. Jan. 10, 1977).

2.2. In *Kissinger v. Reporters Committee for Freedom of the Press*, 445 U.S. 136 (1980), the Supreme Court construed the FOIA's jurisdictional provision to require a showing that the agency has (1) improperly, (2) withheld, (3) agency records. All three of these conditions must be satisfied for jurisdiction to exist. *Id.* at 150.

2.2.1. The D.C. Circuit has held that an agency process for dealing with particular records constitutes "withholding" if "its net effect is significantly to impair the requester's ability to obtain the records or significantly to increase the amount of time he must wait to obtain them." *McGehee v. CIA*, 697 F.2d 1095, 1110 (D.C. Cir. 1982). Thus, an agency process for referring documents to other agencies, which will substantially delay processing of the request, constitutes "withholding" under the FOIA's jurisdictional provision; *see also infra* at 4.4.2.1.- 4.2.2.2.

2.2.2. The Supreme Court has ruled that an agency's withholding of records is not "improper" under the FOIA where a court of competent jurisdiction over the subject matter and over the parties has issued a valid injunction prohibiting the disclosure of the same records. *GTE Sylvania, Inc. v. Consumers Union of the United States, Inc.* 445 U.S. 375 (1980); *see also Wagar v. DOJ*, 846 F.2d 1040, 1047 (6th Cir. 1988) (the nondisclosure order need not be based on FOIA exemptions); *accord, Brown & Williamson Tobacco Corp. v. FTC*, 710 F.2d 1165, 1177 (6th Cir. 1983) (rejecting argument that court sealing should have been limited to documents not available under FOIA exemptions). *But see Morgan v. DOJ*, 923 F.2d 195 (D.C. Cir. 1991) (notes that were sealed in a criminal case may still be subject to FOIA). In contrast, where a federal district court has simply declared a "policy" or issued a general "order" that pre-sentence reports are not to be disclosed and there is no formal proceeding before the court in which the affected parties are involved, an agency's withholding is not rendered "proper" by virtue of the policy or order. *Lykins v. DOJ*, 725 F.2d 1455 (D.C. Cir. 1984); *see also U.S. Intern Trade Com'n v. Tenneco West*, 822 F.2d 73, 80 (D.C. Cir. 1987) (the district court cannot "rely upon *GTE Sylvania* to support the appropriateness of the protective order itself").

2.2.3. In *DOJ v. Tax Analysts*, 492 U.S. 136 (1989), the Supreme Court held that a document is an "agency record" for purposes of meeting the jurisdictional requirement if it (1) is in the possession of a federal agency and (2) came into the agency's possession "in the legitimate conduct of the [the agency's] official duties." *See* Chapter 14 on Agency Records.

2.2.4. The D.C. Circuit has held that an agency's use of the date of the request as a "cut-off" date is an improper withholding of records. *See Public Citizen v. Department of State*, 276 F.3d 634, 642 (D.C. Cir. 2002) (agency's use of a "cut-off policy" to process FOIA requests held "unreasonable because it force[d] the requester to 'periodically… resubmit the identical request in order to get more recent records'") (internal citation omitted); *see also McGehee v. CIA*, 697 F.2d at 1102-03 (holding that the FOIA does not support the use of a time-of-request cut-off date for all requests).

2.3. Although the D.C. Circuit has ruled that district courts have jurisdiction to review agency regulations concerning access to records, *McGehee v. CIA*, 697 F.2d 1095; *Webb v. HHS*, 696 F.2d 101 (D.C. Cir. 1982), the court has restricted such review to instances where there is a "live dispute" over denial of access to particular documents. *Id.* at 108; *see also Better Government Ass'n v. Department of State*, 780 F.2d 86 (D.C. Cir. 1986) (challenge to Justice Department fee waiver guidelines as applied to specific requests dismissed as moot where government ultimately waived the fees, but arguments concerning facial validity of the guidelines were ripe for review); *Irons v. FBI*, 571 F. Supp. 1241 (D. Mass. 1983) (FBI regulation, requiring requester to agree to pay anticipated fees before request will be deemed to have been received, held valid). However, while in *Public Citizen v. Department of State*, the D.C. Circuit refused to review a claim that an agency promulgated its "cut-off policy without the notice and opportunity for comment" as required under the Administrative Procedure Act, and held that the "cut-off policy is procedural and thus covered by the APA's exemption from notice and comment for 'rules of agency organization, procedure, or practice,'" 276 F.3d at 640, the Court nevertheless went on to hold that the policy was "unreasonable." *Id.* at 643.

2.4. Obtaining relief as to a specific request under the FOIA will not moot a claim that an agency policy or practice will impair the requester's lawful access to information. *Payne Enterprises, Inc. v. United States*, 837 F.2d 486, 491 (D.C. Cir. 1988), *citing Perry v. Block*, 684 F.2d 121, 125 (D.C. Cir. 1982) and *Better Government Assn.*, 780 F.2d at 91. Where the requester alleges that the agency follows an "impermissible practice" in evaluating FOIA requests, "[t]he fact that the practice at issue is informal, rather than articulated in regulations or an official statement of policy, is irrelevant to determining whether a challenge to that policy or practice is moot." *Id.* For discussion of "ripeness," *see Payne Enterprises*, 837 F.2d at 492-94; *see also Public Citizen v. Department of State*, 276 F.3d at 641-42 (agency's cut-off policy was ripe for review).

2.5. Statute of Limitations—Although the FOIA itself contains no time limitation for bringing suit against an agency, the general federal statute of limitations, 28 U.S.C. § 2401(a), barring civil actions against the U.S. "unless the complaint is filed within six years after the right of action first occurs," has been held by the D.C. Circuit to be applicable to FOIA suits. *Spannaus v. DOJ*, 824 F.2d at 55, 56.

2.5.1. As a jurisdictional prerequisite, the statute of limitations cannot be waived by the government, nor relaxed by the courts for equitable considerations. *Id.*

2.5.2. Although the question was not before the court in *Spannaus*, the district court stated in *dicta* that "it is at least arguable that *res judicata* would apply where a plaintiff seeks to challenge an agency's response to a FOIA request that is in all material respects identical to an earlier request... where that earlier request was the subject of a lawsuit previously dismissed as untimely." *Spannaus v. DOJ*, 643 F. Supp. 698, 702 (D.D.C. 1986).

2.5.3. When an agency makes no response to a request within six years and no administrative appeal has been made, the statute of limitations is deemed to have expired because the six year period began to toll after the agency failed to meet the initial time period for responding to the requester; no suit may be filed even if the agency subsequently responds and the requester exhausts her administrative remedies. *Spannaus*, 824 F.2d at 60-61. The court acknowledged that the requester can simply make a new request and file a lawsuit then. *Id.*

2.5.4. As a practical matter, since "any person" may request the same records, the statute of limitations could not be a bar to gaining access, since a requester can simply interest someone else in requesting the same records.

2.6. Survivability—The FOIA itself is silent on the issue of whether a FOIA lawsuit survives the death of the plaintiff. However, the D.C. Circuit has held that legal next-of-kin may be substituted in a FOIA suit if the original requester dies. *Sinito v. DOJ*, 176 F.3d 512 (D.C. Cir. 1999).

3. Choice of Forum.

3.1. The FOIA provides that requesters may file suit in (1) the district where the plaintiff resides or has its principal place of business; (2) the district where the agency records are located; or (3) the District of Columbia. § 552(a)(4)(B). *See East Tennessee Research Corp. v. TVA*, 416 F. Supp. 988 (D.D.C. 1976), *voluntarily dismissed and vacated*, 424 F. Supp. 1329 (D.D.C. 1976) (government-controlled corporation can be sued in D.C. even though it does not do business there and records are not located there); *Murphy v. TVA*, 559 F. Supp. 58 (D.D.C. 1983) (same); *Jones v. NRC*, 654 F. Supp. 130 (D.D.C. 1987) (declining to follow the two preceding TVA cases).

3.2. Congress purposefully selected D.C. as an appropriate forum for all FOIA cases, and therefore the United States District Court for the District of Columbia should not transfer FOIA cases to other jurisdictions under 28 U.S.C. § 1404(a). *See In Re Scott*, 709 F.2d 717 (D.C. Cir. 1983) (trial judge abused his discretion by transferring prisoner's *pro se* FOIA cases to Georgia on grounds that too many prisoner suits are filed in the District of Columbia); *accord*, *In Re Wilton Chatman-Bey*, 718 F.2d 484 (D.C. Cir. 1983). *See also Lykins*, 725 F.2d at 1462 n.7 (to allow Virginia District Court's policy to control prisoner's access to his presentence report would run counter to Congress' "express statutory intention" that the District of Columbia be a preferred forum for the resolution of FOIA lawsuits). In *Environmental Crimes Project v. EPA*, 928 F. Supp. 1 (D.D.C. 1995), the D.C. district court held that, while the "interest of justice clearly favor[ed] transfer" of a FOIA action to a Nevada court, the case would not be transferred absent "'precise' information" in the record "concerning the location of the records sought." *Id.* at 2, *quoting In Re Scott*.

3.3. Because the vast majority of FOIA lawsuits are filed in the District of Columbia, the district court and court of appeals there have developed a substantial body of expertise in FOIA matters that may be lacking in other jurisdictions. However, since the mid-1980s, the rulings of the D.C. Circuit have tended to favor the government and not the requester. Some other Circuits, especially the Ninth, have tended to enforce the FOIA more favorably for requesters. *Compare Wiener v. FBI*, 943 F.2d 972 (9th Cir. 1991), *cert. denied*, 120 L. Ed. 2d 886, 505 U.S. 1212 (1992) and *Fiduccia*, 185 F.3d 1035, *with Dow Jones & Co. v. DOJ*, 917 F.2d 571 (D.C. Cir. 1990) (*reh'g en banc denied*); *Spirko v. United States Postal Service*, 147 F.3d 992 (D.C. Cir. 1998).

4. The Complaint.

4.1. The FOIA complaint should generally be a brief, simple document stating the facts regarding the records requested, the facts that demonstrate that the plaintiff has exhausted administrative remedies, the denial of access by the federal agency defendant (or an allegation that the agency failed to comply with the Act's time limits), the impropriety of the agency's action under the FOIA, and the relief requested (*i.e.*, disclosure of the requested records. *See* Sample complaint, Appendix F.

4.1.1. However, in some cases, it may be useful to expand the complaint to tell the story behind the lawsuit, especially when the case is of interest to the media.

Litigation Strategy

4.2. Only the named FOIA requester(s) can bring a FOIA suit. *See, e.g.*, *McDonnell v. U.S.*, 4 F.3d 1227, 1236-1239 (3d Cir. 1993); *cf.*, *Burka v. HHS*, 142 F.3d 1286, 1290-91 (D.C. Cir. 1998).

4.2.1. Proper Defendants

4.2.1.1. A federal agency must always be named as a defendant in an FOIA lawsuit. *See, e.g., Oil, Chemical & Atomic Workers International Union, AFL-CIO v. DOE*, 141 F. Supp. 2d 1, 4 (D.D.C. 2001) (original defendant, a wholly-owned government corporation, substituted with defendant government agency after transfer of the government's ownership to the private sector). There is no need or justification for also naming the federal official who is responsible for the denial of information. § 552(a)(4)(B); *Jefferson v. Reno*, 123 F. Supp. 2d 1, 3 (D.D.C. 2000).

4.2.1.2. If documents have been referred from one agency to another for response, it is advisable to name both agencies as defendants. This will ensure that the proper custodian of the records is before the court. *See generally Peralta v. U.S. Attorney's Office*, 136 F.3d 169 (D.C. Cir. 1998) (demonstrating the procedural problems that can arise in litigation when the agency to which the request has been referred has not been named as a party defendant); *see also generally McGehee v. CIA*, 697 F.2d 1095. If the plaintiff learns after the lawsuit has been filed that referral of records was made, the plaintiff should add the agency receiving the referral as a defendant as soon as possible, either by amending the complaint or by filing a motion to add the agency as a defendant under Rule 19 of the Federal Rules of Civil Procedure.

4.2.1.2.1. The D.C. Circuit has observed that an agency's referral of a request to another agency may "result in the improper 'withholding'" of the requested records. *See Peralta*, 136 F.3d at 175. This inquiry focuses on whether "the 'net effect [of the referral procedure] is significantly to impair the requester's ability to obtain the records or significantly to increase the amount of time he must wait to obtain them.'" *Id., quoting McGehee*, 697 F.2d at 1110. While the *Peralta* court noted that "there is no 'bright line' test for evaluating a given referral procedure," a court should also consider "whether the originating agency has the 'intent to control' the contested records, and whether the referral is 'prompt and public.'" *Id., quoting McGehee*, 697 F.2d at 1111-12; *Paisley v. CIA*, 712 F.2d 686, 691-92 (D.C. Cir. 1983).

4.2.1.2.2. In *Peralta*, the court specifically remanded to the district court the question of whether the decision of the U.S. Attorney's Office to refer the case to the FBI was justified, stating that the inquiry was required in light of *McGehee* and *Paisley*. *Peralta*, 136 F3d at 175.

4.2.2. If documents have been withheld on the grounds that they contain confidential commercial information, it is generally good practice to name the business submitter of the information as a defendant, if the court has jurisdiction over the submitter. Such parties will almost invariably be permitted to intervene in any event, and naming them as defendants will ensure that they are subject to the full range of discovery applicable to parties.

4.3. Relief—In addition to asking for the routine order for the production of records withheld by the government, the Complaint may also seek:

4.3.1. Expedition of the lawsuit. Subsection 552(a)(4)(D), which provided that, except as to cases the court considers to be of greater importance, FOIA lawsuits should be "expedited in every way," was repealed by Section 402(2) of the Federal Courts Civil Priorities Act of 1984, P.L. 98-620, Title IV, 98 Stat. 3357. However, both the definition and legislative history of the "good cause" standard, with which Congress replaced numerous statutory provisions directing civil docket priorities, makes clear that, as a practical matter, FOIA cases will continue to be accorded priority to the same extent provided under the repealed laws. *See* 28 U.S.C. § 1657, as added by Section 401 of P.L. 98-620; H. Rpt. No. 985, 98th Cong. 2d Sess. 5-6 (1984); 130 Cong. Rec. S12930 (1984) (colloquy between Senators Leahy and Dole). As discussed, the requester must show that there is an "exceptional need or urgency" for the agency to process its request for access to the records before other requesters. *See supra* at 1.2.4., *quoting Open America*, 547 F.2d at 615-16.

4.3.2. An award of attorney's fees and costs, pursuant to subsection (a)(4)(E);

4.3.3. A request for a written finding by the court that the circumstances surrounding the withholding raise questions whether there has been arbitrary or capricious agency action and a referral of the matter to the Special Counsel for investigation, pursuant to subsection (a)(4)(F);

4.3.4. A request for an injunction preventing an agency from relying on an invalid regulation or practice in its future processing of FOIA requests. *See* discussion of *McGehee* and *Webb v. HHS, supra* at 2.3. *See also Payne Enterprises* (lower court abused its discretion in denying equitable relief to requester in face of persistent agency non-compliance with the FOIA).

4.4. *See In Re Powell*, 851 F.2d 427 (D.C. Cir. 1988), regarding allegations that multiple FOIA suits by certain individuals were "frivolous" and constitute "harassment" of both the agencies and the courts. In reversing the lower court's injunction against further filings by these litigants, the appellate court noted that the record "does not suggest a case in which the 'orderly and expeditious administration of justice' has been so impeded as to require such an extreme sanction." *Id.* at 434. "Mere litigiousness alone" does not support the issuance of an injunction against litigants, which should be imposed in "only the most egregious cases." *Id.*; *but see Schwarz v. USDA*, No. 01-1464 (D.D.C. June 29, 2001) (because of her history of "frivolous" claims and litigation "abuses," which constituted "harassment," FOIA plaintiff was enjoined from filing any further civil actions without first obtaining leave of the court).

5. **The Answer.**

5.1. The FOIA provides that "the defendant shall serve an answer or otherwise plead to any complaint made under this subsection within *thirty days* after service upon the defendant… unless the court otherwise directs for good cause shown." § 552(a)(4)(C) (emphasis added). This cuts in half the amount of time normally afforded to the government to answer complaints in civil suits.

5.2. The government's answer to a FOIA complaint generally will not provide any useful information to the court or the requester. Requesters should not regard the answer as an opportunity to learn much about the government's claims of exemption or the support for such claims.

6. **Motion for Summary Judgment.**

6.1. As in any civil case, plaintiffs in FOIA cases may move for summary judgment twenty days after service of the complaint has been accomplished. Fed. R. Civ. P. 56(a). In deciding whether to make such a motion, it is important to keep the following in mind:

6.1.1. Judicial review of withholding under FOIA is *de novo*, rather than a narrower standard of review such as an "arbitrary or capricious" or "substantial evidence" test. § 552(a)(4)(B). This means that the district court must develop its own record to determine whether documents are properly being withheld, instead of merely relying on the administrative record. On the other hand, the agency is not restricted to the rationales for withholding that are advanced in the administrative phase, and may raise new claims of exemption and new arguments in support of those claims after suit has been filed. *See generally* the discussion of *de novo* judicial review and summary judgment in *Washington Post Co. v. Department of State*, 840 F.2d 26, 29-35 (D.C. Cir. 1988), *vacated*, 898 F.2d 793 (D.C. Cir. 1990).

6.1.1.1. The D.C. Circuit has held that review on appeal of an agency's denial of a request for expedited processing shall also be *de novo*, "rather than defer to agency determinations." *Al-Fayed v. CIA*, 254 F.3d 300, 304-07 (D.C. Cir. 2001).

6.1.1.2. However, review of an agency's denial of a request for a fee waiver, while *de novo*, is based on the administrative record that was before the agency at the time it made its decision. *See* Chapter 16 on Fees and Fee Waivers.

6.1.2. In light of these general principles, there are some FOIA cases where an immediate summary judgment motion (without attempting to take any discovery) is appropriate. Specifically, when the requester has sufficient knowledge of the nature and content of the records sought, as well as the government's justification for withholding the records, the plaintiff can file a summary judgment motion contending that the government cannot satisfy its burden of proving that the documents are exempt from disclosure. *See Vaughn v. Rosen (II)*, 523 F.2d 1136, 1147-48 (D.C. Cir. 1975); *see also, e.g., Carlton v. Department of Interior*, No. 97-2105 (D.D.C. Sep. 3, 1998) (where agency failed to carry its burden, the court ordered the agency to disclose the records to the requester).

6.1.3. In such cases, the plaintiff should be prepared to submit affidavits and evidence demonstrating that the government cannot meet part of its burden of proof. For example, where the government is claiming Exemption 6 and must show that disclosure would "constitute a clearly unwarranted invasion of personal privacy," and the claim must therefore do a balancing of the privacy interest against the public interest, the plaintiff should supply the court with as much evidence of the public's interest in the subject matter as possible—e.g., newspaper articles, Congressional testimony, websites, etc.

6.1.4. In contrast, where the requester has only vague knowledge of the types of records that are responsive to the request, or of the government's rationale for withholding them, it would be unwise for plaintiff to move for summary judgment. In addition, in cases where the requester's argument is that withheld information is already in the "public domain," the D.C. Circuit has held that the requester "carries the burden of production on that issue," although the ultimate burden of persuasion" remains with the government. *Davis v. DOJ*, 968 F.2d 1276, 1279 (D.C. Cir. 1992); *Niagara Mohawk Power Corp. v. DOE*, 169 F.3d 16, 19 (D.C. Cir. 1999).

6.1.5. When the government files a summary judgment motion with an affidavit that does not provide enough information to demonstrate that the withheld records are exempt from disclosure, the plaintiff may:

6.1.5.1. File an opposition to the government's motion for summary judgment along with a Rule 56(f) affidavit, contending that discovery is needed for plaintiff to effectively respond to the government's supporting affidavits. This is generally the correct course of action where the plaintiff needs discovery to challenge specific factual assertions that underlie the government's claims of exemption.

6.1.5.2. File a cross motion for summary judgment, contending that the government's proffered justifications for withholding are not adequate to sustain its burden of proof under the FOIA. This is generally the correct course of action where the government's affidavits are conclusory and fail to establish that specific records are exempt from disclosure. *See, e.g.*, *Coastal States Gas Corp. v. DOE*, 617 F.2d 854, 861 (D.C. Cir. 1980); *Parke Davis & Co. v. Califano*, 623 F.2d 1, 6-7 (6th Cir. 1980); *see also Carlton v. Department of Interior*, No. 97-2105 (D.D.C. Sep. 3, 1998) (where agency failed to carry its burden, documents were ordered to be disclosed to the requester).

6.2. The D.C. Circuit has indicated the circumstances in which summary judgment typically may or may not be appropriate in FOIA cases.

6.2.1. In *Washington Post Co. v. Department of State*, the court ruled that summary judgment is inappropriate "when the litigants quarrel over key factual premises for a determination" regarding "the probable consequences of releasing particular information." 840 F.2d at 30. Similarly, in *Niagara Mohawk Power Corp.*, 169 F.3d 16, the D.C. Circuit held that summary judgment was not appropriate where a material fact existed as to whether the agency's disclosure would impair its ability to collect such information, pursuant to analysis under Exemption 4. *Id.* at 18.

6.2.2. However, in *Alyeska Pipeline Service Co. v. EPA*, 856 F.2d 309, 313 (D.C. Cir. 1988), the court refused to allow the plaintiff "to cull from *Washington Post* the proposition that anytime the parties' affidavits disagree on the probable consequences of a disclosure, summary judgment is barred."

6.2.2.1. The court warned that "many unmeritorious FOIA cases could not be disposed of prior to a trial" if any motion for summary judgment "could readily be defeated by submission of a counter-affidavit that merely draws from a single set of uncontroverted facts a conclusion different from that reached by the [moving party]." *Id.*

6.2.2.2. "To be sure," said the court, "if material facts are genuinely in issue or, though undisputed, are susceptible to divergent inferences bearing upon an issue critical to disposition of the case, summary judgment is not available. But if on the other hand, neither of these two scenarios is present, a motion for summary judgment adequately underpinned is not defeated simply by a bare opinion or an unaided claim that a factual controversy persists." *Id.* at 314.

6.2.3. The majority in *Washington Post* rejected Judge Bork's dissenting view that the court must defer to the agency's assessment of the threat of harm from disclosure because such a determination was unsuited to the judicial process. 840 F.2d at 40 (Bork, dissenting). "This thesis," the court concluded, "ignores the lengthening record of satisfactory judicial performance in adjudication of questions of predictive fact under FOIA." *Id.* at 31.

6.2.4. The D.C. district court has granted summary judgment for government agencies on the basis that the requester had "abandoned" its request by failing to respond to the agency's invitation to narrow the request or otherwise prosecute the case. *See Judicial Watch of Florida, Inc. v. DOJ*, 159 F. Supp. 2d 763 (D.D.C. 2001).

7. Discovery—Plaintiffs in FOIA cases suffer the inherent handicap of not knowing the contents of the documents at issue. Discovery is necessary to provide plaintiffs with the information they need to advance the pro-disclosure position and establish a record sufficient to permit the courts to resolve FOIA disputes.

7.1. The "*Vaughn* Index." To permit adversarial testing of the government's claims of exemption without compromising the confidential nature of the requested records, the U.S. Court of Appeals for the D.C. Circuit established specific discovery procedures to be employed in an FOIA case. *Vaughn v. Rosen (I)*, 484 F.2d 820 (D.C. Cir. 1973), *cert. denied*, 415 U.S. 977 (1974). The *Vaughn* procedures, which have been adopted by virtually all of the circuits, require the government to provide the FOIA plaintiff and the court an itemized "index" of the withheld records that describes each record or withheld portion and gives a detailed justification of the agency's grounds for withholding, correlating each exemption claimed with the record or portion to which it assertedly applies.

7.1.1. Courts have qualified those circumstances and FOIA exemptions for which a *Vaughn* index is required.

7.1.1.1. For example, the Ninth Circuit has said that "a *Vaughn* index is not required where it is not needed to restore the traditional adversary process." *Fiduccia*, 185 F.3d at 1042, *quoting Wiener*, 943 F.2d at 978 n.5; *accord, Minier v. CIA*, 88 F.3d 796, 804 (9th Cir. 1996) ("when a FOIA requester has sufficient information to present a full legal argument, there is no need for a *Vaughn* index"). The Seventh Circuit has held that a *Vaughn* index is "generally not required in Exemption 7(A) cases," because the government need only show that the records are covered by generic categories the disclosure of which always interferes with an ongoing enforcement pending. *Solar Sources, Inc. v. United States*, 142 F.3d 1033, 1040 (7th Cir. 1998). *See also, e.g., In Re DOJ*, 950 F.2d 530 (8th Cir. 1991), *vacated, and remanded sub nom. Crancer v. DOJ*, 999 F.2d 1302 (8th Cir. 1993) (*en banc*) (refusing to require *Vaughn* index and permitting functional generic categorical classification of documents).

7.1.1.2. As the D.C. Circuit has observed, several holdings from the Supreme Court and the D.C. Circuit have permitted "generic, categorical showings" to satisfy the government's burden of proof rather than requiring a *Vaughn* index. *See Maydak v. DOJ*, 218 F.3d 760, 766 (D.C. Cir. 2000), *citing DOJ v. Landano*, 508 U.S. 165, 179-80 (1993) (discussing circumstances in which the government can substantiate a claim of Exemption 7(D) generically); *DOJ v. Reporters Comm. for Freedom of the Press*, 489 U.S. 749, 777-80 (1989) (holding that the categorical approach to Exemption 7(A), as articulated in *NLRB v. Robbins Tire & Rubber Co.*, 437 U.S. 214 (1978) is appropriate for Exemption 7(C), and citing *FTC v. Grolier, Inc.*, 462 U.S. 19 (1983), as establishing the same for Exemption 5); *Church of Scientology v. IRS*, 792 F.2d 146 (D.C. Cir. 1986) (permitting the IRS to support its Exemption 3 claim generically with affidavits instead of a *Vaughn* index); *see also Brinton v. Department of State*, 636 F.2d 600, 606 (D.C. Cir. 1980) (allowing the agency's invocation of Exemption 5 on the basis of affidavits and no *Vaughn* index). In *Maydak*, the D.C. Circuit reiterated that "when...a claimed FOIA exemption consists of a generic exclusion, dependent upon the category of records rather than the subject matter which each individual record contains, resort to a *Vaughn* index is futile." *Maydak*, 218 F.3d at 766, *quoting Church of Scientology*, 792 F.2d at 152.

7.1.1.3. Generally, courts are thus moving toward the view that "it is the function, not the form, which is important" in meeting the *Vaughn* requirement. *Halpern*, 181 F.3d at 290, *citing Keys v. DOJ*, 830 F.2d 337, 349 (D.C. Cir. 1987) (Second Circuit observing that "a number of courts, including our own, have eschewed rigid adherence to any particular indexing format under the *Vaughn* standard, opting instead for a functional approach"); *Hinton v. DOJ*, 844 F.2d 126 (3d Cir. 1988). "All that is required, and it is the least that is required, is that the requester and the trial judge be able to derive from the index a clear explanation of why each document or portion of a document withheld is putatively exempt from disclosure." *Id.; see also Keys* ("it is the function, not the form, of the index that is important"). *But see King v. DOJ*, 830 F.2d 210, 221 (D.C. Cir. 1987) ("a system is only as good as its results, and the vital result must be an adequate representation of context which, when combined with descriptions of deletions, enables de novo review of the propriety of withholding"); *id.* at 225 ("The measure of a *Vaughn* index is its descriptive accuracy, and we are willing to accept innovations in its form so long, but only so long, as they contribute to that end."); *cf. Fiduccia*, 185 F.3d at 1043-44 (agency's disclosure of redacted documents, in lieu of a *Vaughn* index, provided district court judge and the requester with the context from which they could adequately deduce what the agency was withholding).

7.1.2. A *Vaughn* index is nevertheless an important tool for plaintiffs in FOIA litigation, and the plaintiff should obtain a *Vaughn* index as early as possible by (a) agreement with the government, (b) filing a *Vaughn* motion, or (c) filing interrogatories pursuant to Rule 33 of the Federal Rules of Civil Procedure. The government inevitably argues that it need not submit a *Vaughn* index until it is prepared to file its dispositive motion on the merits. In response, the plaintiffs' lawyer should insist on a *Vaughn* index as the rudimentary basis for which the plaintiff can begin to prepare its case, or, alternatively request that the government be required to submit its "dispositive motion," with a sworn affidavit that meets the minimum requirements of *Vaughn*, by a date certain.

7.1.3. Although there is "no set formula" for a *Vaughn* index, *Hinton*, 844 F.2d at 129, the D.C. Circuit has provided further instruction on the basic requirements of an adequate *Vaughn* index. *See, e.g., Ray v. Turner*, 587 F.2d 1187, 1191 (D.C. Cir. 1978). For an excellent discussion of those requirements *see Founding Church of Scientology v. Bell*, 603 F.2d 945, 949 (D.C. Cir. 1979). where the court held that there are "three indispensable elements": (1) The index should be contained in one document, complete in itself. (2) The index must adequately describe each withheld document or deletion from a released document. (3) The index must state the exemption claimed for each deletion or withheld document, and explain why the exemption is relevant. Of course, the explanation of the exemption claim and the descriptions of withheld material need not be so detailed as to reveal that which the agency wishes to conceal, but they must be sufficiently specific to permit a reasoned judgment as to whether the material is actually exempt under FOIA. Although the court recognized that these requirements place an administrative burden on the agencies, it concluded that "less exacting standards would not satisfy the FOIA's unambiguous policy in favor of the fullest possible disclosure of government records." 603 F.2d at 949. *See also Wiener*, 943 F.2d 972; *Davin v. DOJ*, 60 F.3d 1043 (3d Cir. 1995) (excellent discussion of purpose of *Vaughn* index); *Oglesby v. Department of the Army*, 79 F.3d 1172 (D.C. Cir. 1996) (*Vaughn* index must include "functional description" of document).

7.1.4. Since *Bell*, courts have reiterated and further delineated the minimum requirements for a *Vaughn* index. These cases have generally focused on the tendency of agencies to create "boilerplate" *Vaughn* indices. For example, the

D.C. Circuit has said that the *Vaughn* index "'must show, with reasonable specificity, why the documents fall within the exemption.'" *Campbell v. DOJ*, 164 F.3d 20, 30 (D.C. Cir. 1998), *quoting Hayden v. NSA*, 608 F.2d 1381, 1387 (D.C. Cir. 1979); *see also PHE, Inc. v. DOJ*, 983 F.2d 248, 250 (D.C. Cir. 1993), *quoting King*, 830 F.2d 210, 224 (D.C. Cir. 1987) ("[A]n affidavit that contains merely a 'categorical description of redacted material coupled with a categorical indication of anticipated consequences of disclosure is clearly inadequate.'"). Thus, "affidavits will not suffice if the agency's claims are conclusory, merely reciting statutory standards, or if they are too vague or sweeping." *Id.* In *Campbell*, the D.C. Circuit held that an agency's *Vaughn* index was insufficient where it "fail[ed] to draw any connection between the documents at issue and the general standards that govern" the exemption claimed. Similarly, the Ninth Circuit has held that a *Vaughn* index is "boilerplate" if "[n]o effort is made to tailor the explanation to the specific document withheld." *Wiener*, 943 F.2d at 978-79.

7.1.5. In cases involving national security information withheld under Exemption 1, agencies have been permitted to make a part of their *Vaughn* showing through *in camera* affidavits. *See Allen v. CIA*, 636 F.2d 1287, 1298 n. 63 (D.C. Cir. 1980) (stating that such procedures "should be employed only where absolutely necessary"); and *Phillippi v. CIA*, 546 F.2d 1009, 1013 (D.C. Cir. 1976) (district courts are required to create as complete a public record as possible before allowing *in camera* submissions).

7.1.6. In cases involving law enforcement and national security claims by the FBI, the agency has discarded the standard *Vaughn* showing in favor of submitting copies of released materials with deletions marked by codes that are explained through reference to an accompanying code catalogue and affidavit. *Compare King*, 830 F.2d 210 (discussing at length the inadequacy of the FBI's submission for purposes of the *de novo* review responsibility of the court) *with Keys*, 830 F.2d at 350 (D.C. Cir. 1987) (court found code system served "more efficiently and clearly than would the classical *Vaughn* index," distinguishing *King* finding as based on lack of "contextual description for documents or substantial portions of documents withheld in their entirety"). *See also Canning v. DOJ*, 848 F. Supp. 1037, 1043-45 (D.D.C. 1994) (rejecting *King*-based challenge to coded *Vaughn* showing) and *Branch v. FBI*, 658 F. Supp. 204, 207 (D.D.C. 1987) ("coded format effectively serves same function as *Vaughn* index"). *But see Wiener* (rejecting "boilerplate" explanations that were not tailored to the specific documents withheld); *Davin* (rejecting coded *Vaughn* index as inadequate).

7.1.7. However, the D.C. Circuit has rejected an agency's argument that providing too much detail in a declaration would risk disclosure of the very information that the agency was trying to protect under the national security exemption, saying that while it is true that "requiring too much detail in a declaration could defeat the point of the exemption," *Campbell*, 164 F.3d at 31, *citing Hayden*, 608 F.2d at 1385, "in most cases the agency should not have difficulty describing the context and nature of the withheld information without revealing its substance." *Id.* Similarly, the Second Circuit has ruled that the FBI's mere assertions in its *Vaughn* index that requested information was exempt would "automatically reveal... United States intelligence-gathering capabilities" failed to "provide the kind of fact-specific justification" for withholding. *See Halpern*, 181 F.3d at 293. In addition, where the information at issue "appears to describe no more than routine FBI surveillance and monitoring techniques," "[s]uch activity no doubt generates material that may properly be classified and withheld under FOIA, but it is implausible to baldly assert that such material is so sensitive that the FBI is incapable of providing any descriptive information." *Id.*

7.2. Although the normal federal discovery rules for civil cases apply to FOIA cases, it is usually an uphill battle for plaintiffs to obtain discovery, since the courts generally allow the defendant agency to file supplemental declarations to fill evidentiary gaps identified by the plaintiff. Thus, as a general matter, "[d]iscovery is not favored in lawsuits under the FOIA." *See Judicial Watch v. DOJ*, 185 F. Supp. 2d 54, 64 (D.D.C. 2002); *see also id.* ("when an agency's affidavits or declarations are deficient regarding the adequacy of its search,... the courts generally will request that the agency supplement its supporting declarations" instead of allowing discovery); *cf. Accuracy in Media, Inc. v. National Park Serv.*, 194 F.3d 120, 125 (D.C. Cir. 1999) (requests for discovery cannot be based on "mere speculation"). Nevertheless, a *Vaughn* motion should force the government to provide a description of the documents at issue. Additional discovery by way of interrogatories, depositions, requests for admissions, etc. may be useful:

7.2.1. to expand the government's generalized or ambiguous description of the records, or to test the basis for the government's claim that the documents are exempt from disclosure. *See Renegotiation Board v. Grumman Aircraft Eng. Corp.*, 421 U.S. 168, 181 (1975) (Court noted that plaintiff was permitted to depose an agency official regarding the question of whether the documents at issue were final agency opinions); *Tax Analysts v. IRS*, 214 F.3d 179, 185 (D.C. Cir. 2000) (discovery necessary to develop factual record); *Schaffer v. Kissinger*, 505 F.2d 389, 391 (D.C. Cir. 1974) (district court's grant of summary judgment reversed and remanded with instructions that plaintiffs be permitted to undertake discovery relating to whether the records in question had been "properly classified" in accordance with an Executive Order as is required by the terms of Exemption 1); *Cooper v. Department of the Navy*, 558 F.2d 274 (5th Cir. 1977), *modified*, 594 F.2d 484, 486 (1979), *cert. denied*, 444 U.S. 926 (1979) (FOIA plaintiff established by oral depositions of Navy personnel that portions of a secret Navy report on the investigation of a helicopter accident had been circulated without authorization and that the Navy had thus waived its right to withhold certain portions of the report under FOIA exemptions).

7.2.2. to challenge the adequacy of the agency's search for responsive documents.

7.2.2.1. Discovery as to the adequacy of the agency's search is crucial to the FOIA plaintiff and to the proper judicial administration of the FOIA. *See Founding Church of Scientology of Washington v. NSA*, 610 F.2d 824, 836-37 (D.C. Cir. 1979) ("To accept its claim of inability to retrieve the requested documents in the circumstances presented is to raise the specter of easy circumvention of the Freedom of Information Act... and if, in the face of well-defined requests and positive indications of overlooked materials, an agency can so easily avoid adversary scrutiny of its search techniques, the Act will inevitably become nugatory."); *see also Weisberg v. DOJ*, 543 F.2d 308, 311 (D.C. Cir. 1976); *Schaffer v. Kissinger*, 505 F.2d at 391; *Phillippi v. CIA*, 546 F.2d at 1014 & n.12.

7.2.2.2. The established standard for the adequacy of an agency's search efforts is "reasonableness," and the district court must "expressly conclude that the search was adequate or that it satisfied the reasonableness standard." *Krikorian v. Department of State*, 897 F.2d 461 (D.C. Cir. 1993). *See also Truitt v. Department of State*, 897 F.2d 540 (D.C. Cir. 1990); *Founding Church of Scientology of Washington v. NSA*, 610 F.2d at 837; *Goland v. CIA*, 607 F.2d 339, 353 (D.C. Cir. 1978), *reh'g denied*, 607 F.2d 367, *cert. denied*, 445 U.S. 927 (1980). Where challenged, the facts concerning the adequacy of the search will be viewed in the light most favorable to the requester. *Zemansky v. EPA*, 767 F.2d 569, 571 (9th Cir. 1985), *citing Weisberg v. Webster*, 749 F.2d 864 (D.C. Cir. 1984); *The Nation Magazine v. U.S. Customs Serv.*, 71 F.3d 885 (D.C. Cir. 1995). However, the issue is not whether other responsive documents might exist, but whether the search for them was reasonably conducted, and an agency is not required to reorganize its files in response to a request. *Goland v. CIA*, 607 F.2d 339; *Miller v. Department of State*, 779 F.2d 1378, 1383-87 (8th Cir. 1985). However, when "an agency becomes reasonably clear as to the materials desired, FOIA's text and legislative history make plain the agency's obligation to bring them forth." *Truitt v. Department of State. But see Fitzgibbon v. U.S. Secret Service*, 747 F. Supp. 51 (D.D.C. 1990) (fact that agency located fewer documents than anticipated by requester does not render search "unreasonable"); *Accuracy in Media, Inc. v. National Park Serv.*, 194 F.3d 120, 125 (D.C. Cir. 1999) (plaintiff was not entitled to take additional discovery where its claim of the need to do so "rest[ed] on highly speculative criticism of the [agency's] search").

7.2.2.3. Normally an agency is permitted to establish the adequacy of its search through affidavits. *See, e.g., Perry v. Block*, 684 F.2d 121. There, the court held that, "in the absence of countervailing evidence or apparent inconsistency of proof, affidavits that explain in reasonable detail the scope and method of the search conducted by the agency will suffice to demonstrate compliance with the obligations imposed by the FOIA." *Id.* at 127. *See also SafeCard Services, Inc. v. SEC*, 926 F.2d 1197 (D.C. Cir. 1991).

7.2.2.4. However, where the agency's description of its search is conclusory, or the record raises serious doubts as to the completeness of the agency's search, or there is evidence of agency bad faith, summary judgment for the government based on affidavits alone is inappropriate. *Perry v. Block*, , 684 F.2d 121; *see also Exxon Corp. v. FTC*, 466 F. Supp. 1088, 1094 (D.D.C. 1978), *aff'd*, 663 F.2d 120 (D.C. Cir. 1980); *The Nation Magazine v. U.S. Customs Serv.*, 71 F.3d 885. In such cases, the plaintiff is entitled to discovery to ascertain the nature and scope of the search undertaken by the agency. *See, e.g., Neugent v. Department of Interior*, 640 F.2d 386 (D.C. Cir. 1981); *Weisberg v. DOJ*, 543 F.2d 308; *Founding Church of Scientology of Washington v. NSA*, 610 F.2d 824.

7.2.2.5. The most effective ways to challenge the inadequacy of the agency's search for records are: to show the existence of responsive records that were neither disclosed nor identified by the agency in its *Vaughn* index; to show that because of the way the request is worded and the circumstances surrounding the subject matter of the request, additional records would normally have been generated; or to show that the agency failed to search a particular repository of records that would likely contain responsive records.

7.2.3. to obtain information from the submitter of the documents on whose behalf the government may claim the applicability of Exemption 4 (trade secrets and confidential commercial information), e.g., to determine whether the information is maintained in secrecy, how commercially valuable it is, or whether it is truly the end product of either innovation or substantial effort. *See* Chapter 6 on Business Information.

7.2.4. to obtain information concerning the government's assertion that records withheld for privacy grounds were submitted to the government with an expectation of confidentiality.

7.3. The discovery sought in a FOIA case must be relevant to the issue in the FOIA case itself—e.g., disclosure of government records. Thus, discovery cannot be used to obtain unrelated information. *See, e.g., Giza v. Secretary of Health Ed. & Welfare*, 628 F.2d 748, 751 (1st Cir. 1980) (plaintiffs could not use discovery in FOIA cases to obtain a deposition from the government's expert on allegedly defective birth control pills for use in plaintiff's wrongful birth suit pending in state court); *DiViaio v. Kelley*, 571 F.2d 538, 542 (10th Cir. 1978) (prisoner's attempt in a FOIA case to obtain "general discovery" concerning whether the CIA had ever photographed him and disseminated such photographs outside the agency rejected as being a "demand not countenanced by the scope and reach of the Freedom of Information Act").

7.4. The government may be permitted to engage in discovery "to uncover facts which will enable it to meet its burden of proving either the adequacy of its search or the exempt status of requested documents." *Weisberg v. Webster*, 749 F.2d 864, 868 (D.C. Cir. 1984). The need for such discovery will be infrequent, however, since "in the usual FOIA case, the government will be in possession of all such evidence." *Id.*

7.5. Of course, the district court has discretion to limit discovery in FOIA cases, as in other civil cases, and to enter summary judgment on the basis of affidavits. *Simmons v. DOJ*, 796 F.2d 709, 711-12 (4th Cir. 1986), *citing Goland v. CIA*, *supra*. *See also Teich v. FDA*, 751 F. Supp. 243 (D.D.C. 1990) (district judge granted motion to strike submitter's affidavits in Exemption 4 case where submitter refused to lift protective order barring experts from testifying on behalf of plaintiffs).

7.6. An order limiting discovery will be overturned by the appellate court only if it was "'clearly unreasonable, arbitrary, or fanciful.'" *Landmark Legal Found. v. IRS*, 267 F.3d 1132, 1138 (D.C. Cir. 2001), *quoting Northrop Corp. v. McDonnell Douglas Corp.*, 751 F.2d 395, 399 (D.C. Cir. 1984).

8. The FOIA provides that the court "may examine the contents of such agency records *in camera* to determine whether such records or any part thereof shall be withheld." § 552(a)(4)(B). This provision has been construed as giving courts the authority to review not only the documents themselves but also *in camera* affidavits submitted by the government in support of its claims of exemption. These two different types of *in camera* submissions raise different issues.

8.1. *In Camera* Inspection of Withheld Records.

8.1.1. The trial court has broad discretion to review the requested records *in camera* to test the government's claims of exemption. *See Spirko*, 147 F.3d at 996, *citing Lam Lek Chong v. DEA*, 929 F.2d 729, 735 (D.C. Cir. 1991); *Robbins Tire*, 437 U.S. at 224. *See generally Carter v. Department of Commerce*, 830 F.2d 388, 392-94 (D.C. Cir. 1987). In *Spirko*, the D.C. Circuit ruled that the lower court did not err when it dispensed with a *Vaughn* index and reviewed records *in camera* instead. *Id.* Such an inspection, however, does not relieve the government of its obligation to provide the detailed justification for withholding required under *Vaughn*. *See PHE*, 983 F.2d at 259. Rather, *in camera* review of the records to warrant summary judgment in the government's favor, is most profitably done in conjunction with a *Vaughn* index to ensure that the government is accurately describing the withheld materials and is correlating asserted exemptions to specific portions of withheld documents. When done in this way, *in camera* review of records can be an important tool in the FOIA plaintiff's arsenal.

8.1.2. The D.C. Circuit has noted that "'*in camera* inspection may be particularly appropriate when either the agency affidavits are insufficiently detailed to permit meaningful review of exemption claims or there is evidence of bad faith on the part of the agency,' when the number of withheld documents is relatively small, and 'when the dispute turns on the contents of the withheld documents, and not the parties' interpretations of those documents.'" *Spirko*, 147 F.3d at 996, *quoting Quinon v. FBI*, 86 F.3d 1222, 1228 (D.C. Cir. 1996).

8.1.3. The Ninth Circuit has held that *in camera* review, "may be required in any particular case, depending on the circumstances." *Fiduccia*, 185 F.3d at 1043-43. In *Wiener*, the Ninth Circuit held that *in camera* review of documents is inappropriate until "after 'the government has submitted as detailed public affidavits and testimony as possible.'" *Wiener*, 943 F.2d at 979, *quoting Doyle v. FBI*, 722 F.2d 554, 556 (9th Cir. 1983). The *Wiener* court required the more detailed public *Vaughn* index even though the district court had already reviewed the documents *in camera*.

8.1.4. However, the D.C. Circuit has expressly held that it has declined to adopt a *per se* rule that district courts *must* conduct *in camera* review. *See Spirko*, 147 F.3d 992. Thus, the *Spirko* court ruled that the district court "'should first offer the agency the opportunity to demonstrate, through detailed affidavits and oral testimony, that the withheld information is clearly exempt and contains no segregable, nonexempt portions,'" *id.* at 997, *quoting Allen*, 636 F.2d at 1299-1300, but that if the agency then "fails to provide a sufficiently detailed explanation to enable the district court to make a *de novo* determination of the agency's claims of exemption, the district court then has several options," including *in camera* inspection, ordering the agency to prepare further affidavits, or allowing discovery. *Id.*

8.1.5. Courts may inspect documents *in camera* where the government argues that they are subject to Exemption 1, the FOIA's national security exemption. *See, e.g., Ray v. Turner, supra*; *see also Campbell*, 164 F.3d at 31 & n.9, *quoting Simon v. DOJ*, 980 F.2d 782, 784 (D.C. Cir. 1992) (in "special circumstances," when including "even minimal detail" in a *Vaughn* index would reveal "sensitive information," "'the solution is for the court to review the document *in camera*'"). In fact, the FOIA's provision for *in camera* review was enacted for the express purpose of overruling the Supreme Court's holding in *EPA v. Mink*, 410 U.S. 73, 81 (1973), that district courts could not review *in camera* records subject to a national security claim. Even so, the courts are far more reluctant to perform *in camera* inspections in national security cases than in other cases, and the D.C. Circuit has suggested that such review should be performed only where the government's affidavits are deficient. *See Weissman v. CIA*, 565 F.2d 692 (D.C. Cir. 1977); *Phillippi v. CIA, supra; accord, Campbell v. DOJ*, 164 F.3d at 31 (when agency affidavits in support of national security exemption as basis for withholding documents are "facially inadequate," the district court can review the documents *in camera* or require the agency to prepare new affidavits; the favored course is to require new affidavits).

8.1.6. In the context of a *Vaughn* index or *in camera* inspection, or in combination with both, a "sampling" of documents claimed to be exempt from disclosure can helpfully reduce a voluminous FOIA exemption case to a manageable number of items that can be individually evaluated for an extrapolation of the court's conclusions to the larger body of materials. Courts may allow sampling procedures where "the number of documents is excessive and it would not realistically be possible to review each and every one." *See Weisberg v. DOJ*, 745 F.2d 1476, 1490 (D.C. Cir. 1984).

8.1.6.1. Representative sampling.

8.1.6.1.1. With "representative sampling," the agency assures the Court and the plaintiff that it is addressing a selection of records that are typical of *all* of the records that have been withheld. Hence, "[i]f the sample is well-chosen, a court can, with some confidence, 'extrapolate its conclusions from the representative sample to the larger group of withheld materials.'" *Bonner v. Department of State*, 928 F.2d 1148, 1151 (D.C. Cir. 1991), *quoting Fensterwald v. CIA*, 443 F. Supp. 667, 669 (D.D.C. 1977); *see also Campaign for Responsible Transplantation v. FDA*, 186 F. Supp. 2d 29 (D.D.C. 2001) (holding that a representative *Vaughn* index was appropriate); *Bonner*, 928 F.2d at 1153 ("Representative sampling tests the propriety of the agency's FOIA processing.").

8.1.6.1.2. Sampling "involves a trade-off between," on one hand, "the high degree of confidence that comes from examining every item for which exemption is claimed, and," on the other hand, limitations of time and resources that constrain agencies, courts, and FOIA requesters alike." *Bonner*, 928, F.2d 1151. Accordingly, "the technique will yield satisfactory results only if the sample employed is sufficiently representative, and if the documents in the sample are treated in a consistent manner." *Id.*

8.1.6.1.3. Since the plaintiff usually does not know the nature of all of the records that have been withheld, it is important to get a declaration from the agency that affirms that the representative sample is indeed "representative" of all withheld records. On the other hand, if the plaintiff has some basis for actually choosing which records should be used for the representative sample, it would be wise to insist on making the choice. *See Campaign for Responsible Transplantation*, 186 F. Supp. at 34.

8.1.6.1.4. The D.C. Circuit Court of Appeals has indicated that a 25 percent "error rate" for exemptions claimed for withheld material is "unacceptably high" and, in such situations, the agency "must... reprocess all of the... documents at issue." *Bonner*, 928 F.2d at 1153-54; *see also id.* at 1153, *quoting Meeropol v. Meese*, 790 F.2d 942, 960 (D.C. Cir. 1986) ("[i]f the sample uncovers no excisions or withholding improper when made, then the agency's action ordinarily should be upheld," but "an error rate of 25% in a representative sample is 'unacceptably high'").

8.1.6.2. Random sampling.

8.1.6.2.1. Another way to choose the representative sample is through a "random" selection process, where the parties agree that the government will address, e.g., every third or tenth record at issue. This can sometimes be a better way of ensuring that the sample used is truly "representative." In contrast to representative sampling— which generally applies when the records being withheld are "essentially uniform," *Campaign for Responsible Transplantation*, 180 F. Supp. 2d at 34—random sampling seeks to provide the agency with the opportunity to demonstrate that each claimed exemption has been lawfully applied to the records being withheld, regardless of their uniformity. *See, e.g., Meeropol*, 790 F.2d 942; *accord*, *Jones v. FBI*, 41 F.3d 238, 241, 243 (6th Cir. 1994). However, an obvious and significant drawback of random sampling is that, where an agency proves that exemptions lawfully apply to records or portions of records included in the sample, the remainder of the withheld records may forever escape scrutiny by the requester and the Court.

8.2. *In Camera* Affidavits.

8.2.1. Unlike *in camera* inspection of the requested records, *in camera* affidavits submitted by the government are almost never to the plaintiff's advantage. Such affidavits constitute *ex parte* arguments in support of the government's claims of exemption and should therefore be resisted in almost all circumstances.

8.2.2. The courts have held that *in camera* affidavits may be employed only where "absolutely necessary," *Allen v. CIA*, 636 F.2d at 1298 n. 63, and have expressed "grave reservations regarding non-public presentations absent sensitive national security concerns." *Campbell v. HHS*, 682 F.2d 256, 265 (D.C. Cir. 1982). In essence, the government can only submit *in camera* affidavits where it demonstrates that the interests of the adversary process are outweighed" by other crucial interests. *Lykins*, 725 F.2d at 1465. In order to make such a showing, the government must demonstrate that:

8.2.2.1. it has provided as much information as possible on the public record. *Lykins*, 725 F.2d at 1455; *Yeager v. Drug Enforcement Administration*, 678 F.2d 315, 324 (D.C. Cir. 1982); and,

8.2.2.2. its exemption claims "cannot be evaluated without information beyond that contained in the public affidavits and in the records themselves." *Arieff v. Department of the Navy*, 712 F.2d 1462, 1471 (D.C. Cir. 1983).

8.2.3. If a district court decides that an *in camera* affidavit is warranted, it should ensure that the justification for such a determination is evident on the public record. *Yeager*, 678 F.2d at 325; *Phillippi*, 546 F.2d at 1013. In addition, after reviewing the affidavit along with the full record, the court should make available to the public as much of it as possible without jeopardizing the government's legitimate interest in secrecy. *Lykins; Hayden*, 608 F.2d at 1388.

8.2.4. While the D.C. Circuit has suggested that access to an *in camera* submission by plaintiff's counsel and experts is within the discretion of the district judge, *Hayden*, its most recent pronouncement on the subject declares that such "discretion is significantly constrained." *Arieff*, 712 F.2d at 1469. Thus, the court stated that "when an affidavit disclosing information assertedly exempt from production under the FOIA is proffered, we think that the district court—at least as a general matter—is limited to the stark choice of receiving it *ex parte* and *in camera*, or receiving it not at all." *Id.* at 1470. Given this "stark choice," FOIA plaintiffs should vigorously oppose the government's filing of *in camera* affidavits in virtually all circumstances.

8.2.5. In one Exemption 4 case, a court struck from the record the company's affidavits setting forth the evidence of competitive injury when the company refused to waive protective orders that had been entered in private product liability actions and which prohibited individuals who had seen documents at issue in the FOIA case from presenting *in camera* testimony to the judge about the contents of the documents. *Teich v. FDA*, 751 F. Supp. 243 (D.D.C. 1990).

9. Segregability.

9.1. The D.C. Circuit has held that the segregability requirements in the statute—i.e., that the agency must disclose all reasonably segregable non-exempt information must be addressed in the district court, regardless of whether a party raises it. *Trans-Pacific Policing Agreement v. U.S. Customs Serv.*, 17 F.3d 1022, 1028 (D.C. Cir. 1999), *citing Kimberlin v. DOJ*, 139 F.3d 944, 949-50 (D.C. Cir. 1998). *See* Chapter 15 on Segregable Portions.

9.2. *Trans-Pacific* established that "the district court ha[s] an affirmative duty to consider *sua sponte* whether the agency could have segregated the exempt portions of the requested records despite the plaintiff's failure to expressly suggest such action." *Maydak*, 218 F.3d at 768; *PHE*, 983 F.2d at 252; *Schiller v. NLRB*, 964 F.2d 1205, 1209-10 (D.D.C. 1992); *Public Citizen Health Research Group v. FDA*, 185 F.3d 898, 907 (D.C. Cir. 1999). Similarly, the D.C. Circuit recently suggested that in light of *McGehee*, 697 F.2d at 110, and *Paisley*, 712 F.2d 686, 691-92 (D.C. Cir. 1983), the district court may also be required to determine whether an agency's referral of a request to another agency was appropriate. *See Peralta*, 136 F.3d at 175.

10. Trials.

10.1. Trials may be required in a FOIA case when there are material facts in dispute. *See, e.g., Irons v. Bell*, 596 F.2d 468, 471-72 (1st Cir. 1979); *National Ass'n of Government Employees v. Campbell*, 593 F.2d 1023, 1027 (D.C. Cir. 1978) on remand, No. 76-1041 (D.D.C. April 17, 1980).

10.2. Trials have been required most often in Exemption 4 cases where the issue is whether a document qualifies as a "trade secret" or confidential commercial information. *See Sears, Roebuck & Co. v. GSA*, 553 F.2d 1378, 1382 (D.C. Cir. 1977); *National Ass'n of Government Employees v. Campbell*, 593 F.2d 1023 (D.C. Cir. 1978), *on remand*, No. 76-1041 (D.D.C. Apr. 17, 1980); *Green v. Department of Commerce*, 468 F. Supp. 691, 693 (D.D.C. 1979), *appeal dism'd*, 618 F.2d 836 (D.C. Cir. 1980).

10.3. The district court judge presides as the trier of fact who may hear testimony from expert witnesses for all sides, including the government, the submitter of the documents, and the FOIA plaintiff. Because the government bears the burden of proof and the court must decide the matter *de novo*, it may be possible for the plaintiff to prevail without producing any expert testimony, by simply resting its case on the fact that the government did not carry its burden of proof. *See Green v. Department of Commerce, supra* (government failed to sustain its burden of proof on Exemption 4 claims at trial, even when plaintiff produced no expert testimony of its own). However, this is an extremely risky strategy, and should be employed only where expert testimony is unavailable or it is clear from discovery that the government cannot meet its evidentiary burden.

11. Motion for Reconsideration or Clarification (Rules 52(b), 59(b), and 60(b) of the Federal Rules of Civil Procedure). To permit a plaintiff to properly argue its case on appeal, the trial court which enters an order declaring documents to be exempt from disclosure should provide the same kind of elaboration contemplated under *Vaughn*. *See Schartz v. IRS*, 511 F.2d 1303, 1305 (D.C. Cir. 1974) (district court abused its discretion by refusing a request for clarification of the legal basis of its opinion). *See also Coastal States*, 644 F.2d at 980

(requirement for district court to articulate explicitly the legal basis as well as the findings, necessary to demonstrate that the documents are exempt or disclosable is implicit in the statutory duty of *de novo* review).

12. Attorney Fees.

12.1. Before filing a request with the court, an effort should be made to reach a settlement with the government on the question of plaintiffs' entitlement to attorneys' fees. The plaintiff does not have to file an application for attorneys' fees within 10 days of judgment under Rule 59(c), but must do so within a reasonable period of time. *See White v. New Hampshire Department of Employment Security*, 455 U.S. 445 (1982).

12.2. The FOIA provides that "[t]he court may assess against the United States reasonable attorney fees and other litigation costs reasonably incurred" in any FOIA case "in which the complainant has substantially prevailed." § 552(a)(4)(E). Whether a complainant has "substantially prevailed" has traditionally required a determination of whether the complainant is both "eligible" and "entitled" to an award. *See* Chapter 17 on Attorney Fees.

12.3. Where the agency discloses records after the suit has been filed, but without a court order requiring it do so, the requester is usually considered a "prevailing" party. *See, e.g., Oil, Chemical & Atomic Workers International Union, AFL-CIO v. DOE*, 141 F. Supp. 2d at 4; *Burka v. HHS*, 142 F.3d at 1288. However, the applicability to the FOIA of *Buckhannon Bd. and Care Home, Inc. v. West Virginia Department of Health & Human Res.*—in which the Supreme Court held that fee-shifting provisions in two federal statutes require a party to secure either a judgment on the merits or a court-ordered consent decree in order to qualify as a "prevailing party," *see Buckhannon*, 532 U.S. 598, 622 (2001)—has recently been established. In ruling that *Buckhannon* applied equally to FOIA's attorney's fees provisions, the D.C. Circuit, in *Oil, Chemical & Atomic Workers International Union, AFL-CIO v. DOE*, 2002 WL 959825 (D.C. Cir. 2002) concluded that plaintiffs were not eligible for an award of fees because there had never been a court order issued in favor of the plaintiffs.

13. Sanctions.

13.1. Subsection 552(a)(4)(F) provides that "[w]henever the court orders the production of any agency records improperly withheld from the complainant and assesses against the United States reasonable attorney's fees and other litigation costs, and the court additionally issues a written finding that the circumstances surrounding the withholding raise questions whether agency personnel acted arbitrarily or capriciously with respect to the withholding, the Special Counsel shall promptly initiate a proceeding to determine whether disciplinary action is warranted against the officer or employee who was primarily responsible for the withholding."

13.2. This provision was included in the 1974 FOIA Amendments to instill a notion of individual accountability for wrongful withholding. *See Rocap v. Indiek*, 539 F.2d 174 (D.C. Cir. 1976). The Civil Service Reform Act of 1978, P.L. 95-454, substituted references to the Special Counsel for references to the Civil Service Commission. *See* Chapter 2 on Administrative Process.

13.3. A proceeding for sanctions against an officer or employee may be initiated by the Special Counsel only if the following conditions are met in the original FOIA action:

13.3.1. The court must order production of agency records improperly withheld. § 552(a)(4)(F). *See Jefferson v. Reno*, 123 F. Supp. 2d at 3; *Lovell v. Alderete*, 630 F.2d 428, 431 (5th Cir. 1980); *Perry v. Block*, 684 F.2d at 125 & n. 19, 129, 130 (*dictum*); *Wilder v. Commissioner of Internal Revenue Service*, 601 F. Supp. 241, 243 (M.D. Ala. 1984); *Simm v. Department of Labor*, No. 83-3780 (D.D.C. Mar. 21, 1984); *Emery v. Laise*, 421 F. Supp. 91 (D.D.C. 1976), *aff'd without opinion sub nom. Emery v. Reinhardt*, No. 76-1973 (D.C. Cir. Oct. 27, 1977).

13.3.2. The court must assess reasonable attorney's fees and other litigation costs against the United States. Section 552(a)(4)(F). *See Lovell v. Alderete, supra*; *Emery v. Laise*, 421 F. Supp. 91 (D.D.C. 1976).

13.3.3. The court must issue a written finding that "the circumstances surrounding that withholding raise questions whether agency personnel acted arbitrarily or capriciously with respect to the withholding." Section 552(a)(4)(F). *See Lovell v. Alderete, supra*; *Holly v. Acree*, 72 F.R.D. 115 (D.D.C. 1976), *aff'd sub nom. Holly v. Chasen*, 569 F.2d 160 (D.C. Cir. 1977).

13.4. To date, there has been only one case in which a court has made a finding that agency officials may have acted arbitrarily or capriciously. *Holly v. Acree, supra*. However, the Civil Service Commission declined to take any disciplinary action in the case. While the court ultimately upheld the CSC's determination, it rejected the government's argument that this action by the CSC was not subject to judicial review. *Id.*; *see also Jaffe v. CIA*, 573 F. Supp. 377 (D.D.C. 1983) (agency's failure to comply fully with three *Vaughn* orders does not warrant a finding of contempt or sanctions where non-compliance may be attributable merely to an "inherent tendency to resist disclosure").

13.5. Even where there has been no court order compelling the release of documents because the documents have been released by the government prior to the issuance of an order, the court may take the allegation of arbitrary and capricious withholding into account in determining the appropriate amount of attorney fees to be awarded. *See Simm v. Department of Labor*, No. 83-3780 (D.D.C. Mar. 21, 1984).

13.6. A court may also rely on its "inherent authority" to impose monetary penalties for violation of a court order when it finds that a party has "'acted in bad faith, vexatiously, wantonly, or for oppressive reasons.'" *Jefferson v. Reno*, 123 F. Supp. 2d at 6-7, *quoting Alexander v. FBI*, 186 F.R.D. 6, 10 (D.D.C. 1998). In *Jefferson v. Reno*, the court determined that imposing sanctions pursuant to the FOIA's provision was "premature because the court's findings necessary to impose such sanctions must await the production of important withheld records." *Id.* at 3, *citing Perry v. Block*, 684 F.2d at 125, n. 19. However, the court nonetheless imposed "a punitive fine" on the agency for failure to comply with a court order and left the door open for additional sanctions pursuant to the court's "inherent authority" and the FOIA's provision for sanctions. The judge later reconsidered the fine imposed and removed it altogether.

14. Appeals.

14.1. In a FOIA case, a "final decision" that is appealable under 28 U.S.C. § 1291 is an order by the district court either requiring or denying release of documents. *See Green*, 618 F.2d at 841.

14.1.1. Courts will generally not entertain interlocutory appeals by FOIA plaintiffs (under 28 US.C. § 1292) where the district court's order does not "affect predominantly all of the merits of the case" and denial of relief would not cause the plaintiffs "serious perhaps irreparable injury." *Center for National Security Studies v. CIA*, 711 F.2d 409, 411-14 (D.C. Cir. 1983) (dismissing an appeal from a district court's order dealing with only one of twelve categories of documents at issue); *accord*, *Summers v. DOJ*, 999 F.2d 570 n.1 (D.C. Cir. 1993); *Pineiro v. Pension Benefit Guaranty Corp.*, 2001 WL 1339000 (2d. Cir. Oct. 25, 2001) (dismissing interlocutory appeal from the denial of a motion to dismiss to allow further development of factual record in district court). *See also Yeager*, 678 F.2d at 319 n.10 (plaintiff's separate challenge to district court's order concerning the processing of computer-stored agency records is not appealable, although challenge to district court's ruling upholding the agency's non-disclosure of the records is appealable).

14.1.2. On the other hand, a district court's order requiring disclosure, even if interlocutory, is generally appealable under 28 U.S.C. § 1292(a). See *Coastal States*, 644 F.2d at 974 (court of appeals took interlocutory appeal of order granting plaintiff's motion for partial judgment to produce certain documents, since effect of order would moot the government's exemption claims); *accord Miller v. Bell*, 661 F.2d 623, 625 (7th Cir. 1981) (*per curiam*), *cert. denied sub nom. Miller v. Webster*, 456 U.S. 960 (1982).

14.1.3. Even absent an order requiring disclosure, the government may be able to get interlocutory review of a district court's order requiring it to process a FOIA request. *See Open America*, 547 F.2d at 608 n.8; *Exner*, 542 F.2d at 1122 (court of appeals took interlocutory appeal of case involving priority processing issue).

14.1.4. In *Rosenfeld v. United States*, 859 F.2d 717 (9th Cir. 1988), the court held that an interim attorney fee award under FOIA was not an appealable interlocutory order under 28 U.S.C. § 1292 (a)(1) because the government could not meet its burden of showing irreparable harm.

14.1.5. Standard of Review—The D.C. Circuit and the Second Circuit Courts of Appeal have held that the FOIA's *de novo* standard of review applies on appeal as well, although neither party may submit any additional evidence once the case is on appeal, without permission of the court. *See Halpern*, 181 F.3d at 287-88 (adopting pure *de novo* standard of review as "more faithful to the text, purpose, and history of FOIA"); *see also id., quoting Summers v. DOJ*, 140 F.3d 1077, 1080 (D.C. Cir. 1998) ("'[O]ur task on appeal is the same as the task faced by the district court—reviewing the record *de novo* to determine whether genuine issues of material fact would preclude summary judgment,' i.e., 'whether the agency has sustained its burden of demonstrating that the documents requested ... are exempt from disclosure under the FOIA.'").

14.1.5.1. However, the Third Circuit has held that a two-step standard of review is appropriate on appeal, i.e., review first to determine whether the district court had an adequate factual basis for its determination and then "clear error" review of the district court's determination. *See Sheet Metal Workers Int'l Ass'n, Local Union #19 v. Department of Veterans Affairs*, 135 F.3d 891, 896 & n.3 (3d Cir. 1998). Appeals courts review district court's findings of law *de novo*. *See Al-Fayed v. CIA*, 254 F.3d at 308, *citing Summers v. DOJ*, 140 F.3d at 1080.

14.1.5.2. Review of lower court's findings of fact—such as those which are developed in the course of a motion for a preliminary injunction—is for clear error. *Id.*; *Fiduccia*, 185 F.3d at 1040.

14.2. Raising New Exemptions

14.2.1. An issue that sometimes arises on appeal is whether the government can rely on an exemption which it did not raise in the district court. As a general matter appellate courts will not allow the agency to raise a new exemption and the failure to raise the exemption at the district court level will be considered a waiver of that exemption by the government. *See Maydak*, 218 F.3d at 768 (rejecting government's argument that "public policy concerns about disclosing information that would otherwise be exempt" where government failed to raise the exemptions in the district court); *Niagara Mohawk Power Corp.*, 169 F.3d at 20 (defendant's new argument on appeal, which it had "effectively disavowed" in the district court, was not entertained by the D.C. Circuit, since doing so "would be grossly unfair" to plaintiff); *Jordan v. DOJ*, 591 F.2d 753, 779-80 (D.C. Cir. 1978) (*en banc*). *See also Ray v. Department of State*, 908 F.2d 1549, 1557 (11th Cir. 1990), *rev'd on other grounds*, 502 U.S. 164 (1991).

14.2.2. Similarly, a plaintiff cannot raise new arguments on appeal—e.g., the D.C. Circuit has held that on appeal, a requester cannot raise the issue of inadequacy of search for the first time. *See Isley v. Executive Office for the U.S. Attorneys*, 203 F.3d 52, 1999 WL 1021934, *7 (D.C. Cir. 1999), *citing Felch v. Air Florida, Inc.*, 866 F.2d 1521, 1525 (D.C. Cir. 1989) (because the question of whether a genuine issue of material fact existed regarding the reasonableness of the search conducted by the agencies "was never presented to the district court," appellant was barred from pursuing the matter on appeal).

14.2.3. In *Jordan*, the court noted that an appellate court has residual discretion to remand the case to allow the district court to consider an exemption not previously raised, but only after extraordinary circumstances. *Accord Fendler v. U.S. Parole Comm'n*, 774 F.2d 975, 978 (9th Cir. 1985), *Ryan v. DOJ*, 617 F.2d 781, 792 (D.C. Cir. 1980); *Crooker v. U.S. Bureau of Prisons*, No. 83-1838 (D.C. Cir. Apr. 10, 1984). The court in *Jordan* indicated that such circumstances would exist where, "through pure mistake," the government's attorney had not invoked the correct exemption and the "the value of the material which otherwise would be subject to disclosure was obviously high, e.g., confidential information compromising the nation's foreign relations or national security, and it appeared highly likely was intended to be protected by one of the nine enumerated exemptions." 591 F.2d at 780. The court also speculated that the appellate court could exercise its discretion where the government is forced to raise an exemption for the first time on appeal because of a "substantial change in the factual context of the case or because of an interim development in applicable legal doctrine." *Id.*

14.2.4. One district court has extended the *Jordan* rationale to prohibit the government raising various grounds for withholding in a piecemeal fashion in the district court. *American Broadcasting Companies, Inc. v. United States Information Agency*, 599 F. Supp. 756 (D.D.C. 1984). *See also Curcio v. FBI*, No. 89-0941, 1990 U.S. Dist. LEXIS 14738 (D.D.C. Nov. 2, 1990) (decision not to raise exemptions was "tactical decision" that does not support the basic requirement that the agency "assess all claims of exemption during initial district court proceedings").

14.2.5. However, the "interim legal developments" exception to the *Jordan* rule is only applicable where the assertion of the exemption originally had been "barred by legal doctrine" and only later became available; it does not apply "when the exemption was available but the government, as the result of a deliberate, tactical decision, simply chose not to assert it," nor does it include a loss on appeal in the very case where the government seeks to belatedly raise an exemption. *Lykins v. Asst. Attorney General*, 608 F. Supp. 693, 695 (D.D.C. 1984); *accord, Maydak,*, 218 F.3d at 768 (holding that "there has been no substantial change in the factual or legal context of this case, and thus there is no reason for us to deviate from our usual rule of requiring the government to assert all its FOIA exemption claims in the original district court proceedings"); *Crooker v. U.S. Parole Comm'n*, 760 F.2d 1 (1st Cir. 1985). *But compare Cotner v. U.S. Parole Comm'n*, 747 F.2d 1016 (5th Cir. 1984) (reached opposite result from *Crook*er on identical facts).

14.2.6. The government's assertion of a new exemption claim in district court after remand has been held to be permissible as consistent with the *Jordan* rationale because the requester has full opportunity to oppose and thus suffers no "unfairness" or surprise. *Lame v. DOJ*, 767 F.2d 66, 71 n.7 (3d Cir. 1985). However, it is not an abuse of discretion for the district court to reject an exemption claim that is raised for the first time after judgment when failure to oppose requester's summary judgment motion was due to "inadvertence and negligence" of government counsel. *Schanen v. DOJ*, 762 F.2d 805 (9th Cir. 1985). On rehearing, the panel in *Schanen* adhered to its earlier holding but ordered the requested documents withheld after *in camera* review led it to conclude release "would endanger the lives and well-being of agents and informants." Order of July 9, 1986.

14.2.7. A divided panel of the D.C. Circuit applied the "extraordinary circumstances" and "interim legal development" exceptions to the *Jordan* rule in a controversial rule in a controversial decision rejecting the government's reliance on a purported "invitation" by the appellate court to raise an Exemption 4 "privilege" defense for the first time on remand. *Washington Post Co. v. HHS*, 795 F.2d 205 (D.C. Cir. 1986) (per Scalia, J.).

14.2.7.1. In *Washington Post*, the court expressed surprise that the government had not asserted the "privilege" defense in the district court, and proceeded to discuss how such an assertion should be analyzed "in case the issue is raised on remand." 690 F.2d 252, 267 (D.C. Cir. 1982).

14.2.7.2. "We do not think that our *dictum* in *Washington Post* can properly be considered an 'extraordinary circumstance' justifying an exception to the rule that the government must assert all of its exemptions in the original proceedings before the district court...That language can assuredly be interpreted as merely recognizing the possibility that an Exemption 4 'privilege' defense might properly be raised on remand, and as inviting HHS to raise (and the district court to consider) the defense only if its ultimate assertion could be justified." *Washington Post v. HHS*, 795 F.2d at 208.

14.2.7.3. The dissent in *Washington Post* believed that the panel's earlier opinion "clearly invited" the government to assert the "privilege" defense, with instructions that "could [not] be reasonably read as anything less than a direction that the district court consider the merits of a privilege claim should the government choose to raise on remand." 795 F.2d at 209 (Starr, J., dissenting).

15. Remands.

15.1. Appeals courts may remand FOIA cases "for further development of the record in light of matters that did not arise until the case was...on appeal." *See, e.g., Trans-Pacific Policing Agreement, supra*, 17 F.3d at 1029) (remanding to district court "for a determination as to whether the requested information fell within" a "newly-minted" definition for "confidential" as used in Exemption 4).

15.2. The D.C. Circuit has stated that "on remand the agency may again attempt to meet its statutory burden." *Campbell*, 164 F.3d at 33, *citing Summers*, 140 F.3d at 1083. In *Peralta*, the D.C. Circuit indicated that, in certain circumstances, a plaintiff may be able to raise new arguments on remand. *See Peralta*, 136 F.3d at 176 & n.4, 5.

15.3. Where a new administration's executive order governing national security superseded an executive order from a prior administration, the new executive order governs the review on remand. *Campbell*, 164 F.3d at 31 & n.11. However, "principles of finality weigh against ordering a new review under a new order," thus, superseding executive orders govern review only when the court orders it "on other grounds." *Id.*

CHAPTER 22

The Privacy Act

Harry A. Hammitt

1. **Introduction.**

1.1. The Privacy Act of 1974, P.L. 93-579, 88 Stat.1896, became effective on September 27, 1975. The Act is codified at 5 U.S.C. § 552a (not to be confused with the first subsection of the FOIA, which is 5 U.S.C. § 552(a)).

1.2. The Congressional findings in support of the Act, set forth in full here, indicate the breadth of Congressional purpose:

1.2.1. "The privacy of an individual is directly affected by the collection, maintenance, use and dissemination of personal information by Federal agencies;

1.2.2. "The increasing use of computers and sophisticated information technology, while essential to the efficient operations of the Government, has greatly magnified the harm to individual privacy that can occur from any collection, maintenance, use or dissemination of personal information;

1.2.3. "The opportunities for an individual to secure employment, insurance, and credit, and his right to due process, and other legal protections are endangered by the misuse of certain information systems;

1.2.4. "The right to privacy is a personal and fundamental right protected by the Constitution of the United States; and

1.2.5. "In order to protect the privacy of individuals identified in information systems maintained by Federal agencies, it is necessary and proper for the Congress to regulate the collection, maintenance, use, and dissemination of information by such agencies."

1.3. To accomplish those purposes, the Act provides:

1.3.1. Restrictions on disclosure, and redisclosure, of personally identifiable records;

1.3.2. "Fair information practices" which require affected agencies to comply with statutory norms for the collection, maintenance, and dissemination of records;

1.3.3. A system for access by individuals to records about themselves, with exceptions;

1.3.4. A system for amendment of records about individuals upon a showing that they are not accurate, relevant, timely, or complete;

1.3.5. Limitations upon the use of Social Security Numbers for identification; and

1.3.6. Authorization for a Privacy Protection Study Commission to study the problems addressed by the Act and to make recommendations.

2. Legislative History.

2.1. The legislative history of the Act is exhaustively collected in *Legislative History of the Privacy Act of 1974*, S. 3418 (Pub. L. 93-579): *Source Book on Privacy*, Joint Committee Print of Senate and House Committees on Government Operations, 94th Cong., 2d Sess., September 1976 (hereafter *"Privacy Source Book"*).

2.2. The Act is the product of a merger of two very different bills from the Senate and the House.

2.2.1. S. 3418, 93d Cong., 2d Sess. (120 Cong. Rec. S6741, May 1, 1974). *See Privacy Source Book* at 3.

2.2.1.1. S. 3418 would have established a Federal Privacy Board with sweeping powers to oversee the collection, maintenance, and dissemination of individually identifiable information by both the public and private sectors. However, most of these provisions did not become law.

2.2.1.2. The bill also defined fair information practices, most of which were eventually enacted.

2.2.1.3. The bill was passed by the Senate on November 21, 1974, after consideration of amendments. 120 Cong. Rec. 36917.

2.2.2. H.R. 16373, 93d Cong., 2d Sess., unlike the Senate bill, had the support of the Administration. It was introduced on August 12, 1974. *See Privacy Source Book* at 239.

2.2.2.1. The focus of the House bill, as reported by committee, was on access to and correction of records, as well as standards for data collection and maintenance. *See* H.R. Rep. No. 93-1416, 93d Cong., 2d Sess., *Privacy Source Book* at 294.

2.2.2.2. On the same day that the full Senate acted on S.3418, the House passed H.R. 16373 by a vote of 353 to 1, after two days of floor debate. 120 Cong. Rec. H36976.

2.2.3. After the Thanksgiving recess and because of "the lateness of the session," the bills were not reconciled by a conference committee, as would have been the usual procedure. Instead, both houses accepted a compromise bill negotiated by the staffs of the two committees and a few interested members. The description of the amendments that made the two bills identical (thus avoiding a conference committee) was inserted into the record on both sides, and both houses passed identical bills. Thus, many of the most important provisions of the bill are not explained by committee reports. The only record of the final negotiations leading to the bill actually adopted is a staff memorandum entitled "Analysis of House and Senate Compromise Amendments to the Federal Privacy Act" (hereafter "Analysis of Compromise Amendments"). *See* 120 Cong. Rec. 40445, Dec. 17, 1974; *see also Privacy Source Book* at 858.

2.2.4. The bill was signed by President Ford on Dec. 31, 1974.

2.2.5. The Act provided two important ways by which further policy guidance could be developed:

2.2.5.1. The Act instructs the Office of Management and Budget to develop guidelines for the implementation of the Act throughout the Executive Branch. Those guidelines are contained in OMB Circular No. A-108. They are referred to here as "the OMB Guidelines."

2.2.5.1.1. The OMB Guidelines are available at 40 Fed. Reg. 28948, 28965 (July 9, 1975).

2.2.5.1.2. The OMB Guidelines are entitled to the usual deference accorded the interpretations of the agency charged with administration of a statute. *Perry v. FBI*, 759 F.2d 1271, 1276 n.7 (7th Cir. 1985), *rev'd en banc on other grounds*, 781 F.2d 1294, *cert. denied*, 479 U.S. 814 (1986), citing *Bartell v. FAA*, 725 F.2d 1403, 1408 n.9 (D.C. Cir. 1984) and *Albright v. United States (I)*, 631 F.2d 915, 919 n.5 (D.C. Cir. 1980).

2.2.5.2. The Privacy Protection Study Commission, created by the Act to study the issues raised by the Act and to recommend further legislation, completed its thorough and informative report and produced a summary volume called *Personal Privacy In An Information Society: The Report of the Privacy Protection Study Commission*, July 1977, Gov't Printing Office Stock No.052-003-00395-3 (hereafter Privacy Protection Report).

3. Privacy Act Definitions.

3.1. "Record"— § 552a(a)(4).

3.1.1. A "record" is any item or collection of information about an individual which is maintained by an agency and which contains that individual's name or other identifying particular. *See White v. Civil Service Comm'n*, 589 F.2d 713 (D.C. Cir. 1978).

3.1.1.1. While at least two courts have suggested that a "record" does not mean all personal information but only "sensitive" information, *Houston v. Dep't of Treasury*, 494 F. Supp. 24 (D.D.C. 1979), the OMB Guidelines impose no such limitation and the idea has not played an important role in the interpretation of the Act.

3.1.1.2. The Act affects records compiled before the Act's effective date as long as some action judicially reviewable under the Act (such as maintenance of the record, or refusal to permit access or amendment) takes place after that date. *Doe v. United States Civil Service Comm'n.*, 483 F. Supp. 539, 556 (S.D.N.Y. 1980).

3.1.2. Such a record is accessible even to the extent it contains information on another person. *Voelker v. IRS*, 646 F.2d 332 (8th Cir. 1981). *See also Topuridze v. U.S. Information Agency,* 772 F. Supp. 662, 666 (D.D.C. 1991) (Subject of letter must be given access, even though letter also contains information about its author, because the letter was located in subject's file. "Were the court to accept USIA's 'dual record' argument, it could lead to results contrary to the purposes of the Privacy Act. Only the government would have access to a record pertaining to more than one individual."). *But see DePlanche v. Califano*, 549 F. Supp. 685 (W.D. Mich. 1982), where requester was denied material in file retrievable by his Social Security Number because it was not "about" him within the meaning of § 552a(a)(4), nor was it information "pertaining to" him within the meaning of § 552a(d)(1); the court distinguished *Voelker* on grounds that information there arguably pertained to both the requester *and* a third-party. *See also Unt v. Aerospace Corp.*, 765 F.2d 1440, 1448-49 (9th Cir. 1985) (despite a vigorous dissent that the majority's interpretation of "about" is "illogical, contrary to the legislative intent, and defies the caselaw's consistent concern with the actual effect of a record on a person's employment when assessing that record's nature or subject," *id.* at 1450, a letter written by an employee, which contained allegations of mismanagement against his employer that led to his dismissal, was held not to be a "record" because it was "about" the corporation and reflected "only indirectly on any quality or characteristic" of the employee).

3.1.3. The Third Circuit rejected the argument that an out-of-date address and a time card were not records because they contained no "meaningful" information about the individual. *Quinn v. Stone*, 978 F.2d 126 (3d Cir. 1992). The court found that "the meaningful privacy interest in a particular piece of information may be lessened by the passage of time, but such an interest is unlikely to be extinguished." *Id.* at 132. The court noted that the time card "does reveal a 'quality or characteristic' about that person. Time card information regarding taking time off from work as compensation for overtime, as sick leave or for vacation can easily be considered descriptive of an individual." *Id.* at 133.

3.1.4. The D.C. Circuit defined "record" narrowly in *Tobey v. NLRB*, 40 F.3d 469 (D.C. Cir. 1994). The court found that a database used for case-tracking purposes, that could be searched by the initials of agency examiners, was not a record under the Privacy Act because it was not "about" an individual. The court pointed out that "admittedly, the system also includes the number of initials the field examiner assigned to the case. But this no more means the information is 'about' the individual than it means the information is 'about' the date on which the case settled."

3.1.5. Opinions based on records are not records. *FDIC v. Dye*, 642 F.2d 833, 836 n.5 (5th Cir. 1981).

3.1.6. The OMB Guidelines emphasize that "record" is to be construed broadly to include any tangible item of information (at 28951). *See also* Analysis of Compromise Amendments, *Privacy Source Book* at 866 ("a record can include as little as one descriptive item about an individual").

3.1.7. The OMB Guidelines at 28952 explain that an "identifying particular" means any datum (name, number) or other descriptor (fingerprint, voice print, photograph) which can be used to identify an individual.

3.2. "System of Records"—§ 552a(a)(5).

3.2.1. Most provisions of the Act apply only to records maintained in a "system of records." *See, e.g., Boyd v. Secretary of the Navy*, 709 F.2d 684 (11th Cir. 1983). But some, depending on the language and history, do not; it has been held, for example, that subsection (e)(7), concerning records on the exercise of First Amendment rights, applies to a "record" even if it is not incorporated in a "system of records." *Clarkson v. IRS*, 678 F.2d 1368, 1374-77 (11th Cir. 1982); *Albright v. United States (I)*, 631 F.2d at 918-20. On the other hand, the Ninth Circuit has held that the rights to seek correction of records and damages for determinations based on erroneous records are limited to records maintained in a system of records. *Baker v. Department of the Navy,* 814 F.2d 1381 (9th Cir. 1987), *cert. denied*, 484 U.S. 963 (1987). Likewise in *Kalmin v. Department of the Navy,* 605 F. Supp. 1492 (D.D.C. 1985), the court held that the plaintiff did not have a right of access to records not maintained in a "system of records," even though the records had been used to make adverse determinations about the plaintiff. *See also Bettersworth v. FDIC*, 248 F.3d 386 (5th Cir. 2001), for an example of a court finding records pertaining to an individual were not Privacy Act records because they were kept in files pertaining to the banks for which the individual had worked, rather than a file under his own name.

3.2.2. A "system of records" is a group of records under the control of an agency "from which information is retrieved by the name of the individual or by some identifying number, symbol, or other identifying particular assigned to the individual." § 552a(a)(5).

3.2.3. The requirement that the records be "under the control of an agency" was intended to serve two purposes:

3.2.3.1. to determine possession and establish accountability; and,

3.2.3.2. "to separate agency records from records which are maintained personally by employees of an agency but which are not agency records," such as "uncirculated personal notes, papers and records which are retained or discarded at the author's discretion and over which the agency exercises no control or dominion." OMB Guidelines at 28952.

3.2.4. According to OMB, the definition requires that the records *actually be retrieved* by reference to a personal identifier, not merely that a capability for such retrieval exists. OMB Guidelines at 28952. *See Smiertka v. Dep't of Treasury*, 447 F. Supp. 221, 228 (D.D.C. 1978), *remanded*, 604 F.2d 698 (D.C. Cir. 1979) ("[I]nformation pertaining to the requester...need not be disclosed unless the information is retrievable by means of requester's own name or other personal identifier. That it can be easily retrieved in some other way by some other identifier is wholly beside the point."). *See also Wren v. Heckler*, 744 F.2d 86, 89 (10th Cir. 1984).

3.2.4.1. This approach can obviously be used to circumvent the rights of individuals under the Act. For example, in *Baker v. Department of the Navy, supra*, the Navy admitted that it had used erroneous records to make adverse employment determinations about the plaintiff, but argued that the plaintiff had no Privacy Act rights because the records were being maintained in the file of the plaintiff's subordinate, rather than plaintiff's own file. The Ninth Circuit upheld this argument, acknowledging its apparent inconsistency with the objectives of the Act, but suggesting that any relief must come from Congress. A similar result was reached in *Kalmin v. Department of the Navy, supra.*

3.2.4.2. Both *Baker* and *Kalmin* suggest, however, that a plaintiff could obtain judicial relief by demonstrating that an agency had acted in bad faith, i.e., that it had intentionally ignored its own filing procedures. Yet neither court indicated how a plaintiff could make such a showing.

3.2.5. The Privacy Protection Study Commission was critical of the "system of records" limitation.

3.2.5.1. It excludes records that are not retrieved by personal identifiers but contain much personal information. For example, a description of a corporate officer in documents evaluating a corporation, filed only by the name of the corporation, would be a record that is not in a "system of records" and therefore not subject to many provisions of the Act.

3.2.5.2. Modern computer technology will enable even more personal records to be kept and retrieved outside of "systems of records."

3.2.5.3. The requirement thus undermines the objective of the Act to afford access to all records about an individual. The Commission's Report cites examples of record-maintenance practices changed to evade the Act in just this manner. *Report* at 503-04.

3.2.6. Private notes, e.g., supervisor's "memory refreshers," need not be placed within "a system of records" and therefore made subject to the Privacy Act, if they are kept private and are not used in decisions affecting the employment status of an employee. *Chapman v. NASA (I)*, 682 F.2d 526 (5th Cir. 1982). *See also Boyd v. Secretary of the Navy*, 709 F.2d at 686. *But see Kalmin v. Department of the Navy, supra* (documents held to be "private notes" for Privacy Act, despite agency assertion of FOIA exemption based on predecisional use in course of deliberations on personnel status of plaintiff).

3.2.7. In *Manuel v. VA Hospital,* 857 F.2d 1112 (6th Cir. 1988), the court rejected the argument that the agency violated the Act by failing to place in its system of records documents generated by special undercover investigators and used to impeach the requester's testimony at an administrative hearing concerning another individual's civil service claims.

3.2.7.1. The court held that the Act places no affirmative duty on agency employees to place individual records in a system of records at the request of an individual, "particularly in the situation where documents are involved which are not part of an official agency investigation into activities of the individual requesting the records, and where the records requested do not have an adverse effect on the individual." *Id.* at 1118-19. *See also Wren v. Heckler,* 744 F.2d at 89.

3.2.7.2. Since both the access and wrongful disclosure provisions apply only to an agency's system of records, not to all records, the court noted that the Act "permits the situation whereby an employee may be deprived of his or her rights when an agency, or its custodian of records, purposely or with malice, misdirects or prevents information from getting into the system." *Id.* Although it acknowledged that "potential for abuse obviously does exist," the court concluded that "it is the responsibility of Congress to fill in these gaps within the Privacy Act and clarify those areas and situations in which records must be placed within the agency's system of records." *Id.*

3.3. "Maintain"—§ 552a(a)(3).

3.3.1. The meaning of "maintain" is far broader than first appears. It is defined in the Act to include collection, use, and dissemination, as well as simply keeping records. *Id.*

3.3.2. A record may be improperly "maintain[ed]" if it is improperly collected, independent of its subsequent use or dissemination. *Albright v. United States (I)*, 631 F.2d at 918.

3.3.3. Destruction of an official record does not itself create a cause of action because "the Privacy Act was created to protect individuals against invasion of their privacy flowing from the misuse of existing files, not to mandate...that files be created and maintained." *Tufts v. Department of the Air Force*, 793 F.2d 259, 261 (10th Cir. 1986). However, if the destruction of the record renders the file "inaccurate" or "incomplete," a cause of action is thereby created.

3.4. "Individual"—§ 552a(a)(2).

3.4.1. The Act defines "individual" as "a citizen of the United States or an alien lawfully admitted for permanent residence." *Id.*

3.4.2. Thus the Privacy Act, unlike the FOIA, is specifically intended to exclude foreign nationals, except for permanent resident aliens. *See* S. Rep. No. 1183, 93d Cong., 2d Sess., *Privacy Source Book* at 232; *Raven v. Panama Canal Co.*, 583 F.2d 169 (5th Cir. 1978), *cert. denied*, 440 U.S. 980 (1979). This means that all foreign nationals, except permanent resident aliens, have no rights under the Act and that their records are not protected by the Privacy Act.

3.4.3. Corporations are not covered by the Privacy Act. *St. Michael's Convalescent Hosp. v. California*, 643 F.2d 1369, 1373 (9th Cir. 1981); *Dresser Industries, Inc. v. United States*, 596 F.2d 1231 (5th Cir. 1979), *cert. denied,* 444 U.S. 1044 (1980); *OKC Corp. v. Williams*, 461 F. Supp. 540 (N.D. Tex. 1978). Nor may a corporation sue under the Act on behalf of its employees. *Dresser Industries*, 596 F.2d at 1238.

3.4.4. Decisions are split as to the "individual" character of the entrepreneur.

3.4.4.1. OMB Guidelines distinguish "between individuals acting in a personal capacity and individuals acting in an entrepreneurial capacity..." The latter are not covered. OMB Guidelines at 28951.

3.4.4.2. One district court has, without much analysis, agreed with the Guidelines. *Shermco Industries, Inc. v. Secretary of the Air Force*, 452 F. Supp. 306, 315 (N.D. Tex. 1978), *rev'd on other grounds*, 613 F.2d 1314 (5th Cir. 1980).

3.4.4.3. Three other district courts, after extensive discussion, have rejected the Guidelines as not binding and have rejected the "entrepreneurial exclusion." *Metadure Corp. v. United States*, 490 F. Supp. 1368, 1373-74 (S.D.N.Y. 1980); *Zeller v. United States* 467 F. Supp. 487, 499 (E.D.N.Y. 1979); *Florida Medical Ass'n v. HEW*, 479 F. Supp. 1291, 1307-11 (M.D. Fla. 1979). *See also St. Michael's Convalescent Hosp.*, 643 F.2d at 1373 (*dictum*).

3.4.5. This subsection allows the parent of any minor, or the guardian of any incompetent, to act in that person's behalf.

3.5. "Agency"—§ 552a(a)(1).

3.5.1. The Privacy Act adopts the FOIA's definition of "agency." (*See* discussion in Chapter 13 on Agency. *But see Ehm v. National R.R. Passenger Corp.*, 732 F.2d 1250 (5th Cir. 1984), *cert. denied,* 469 U.S. 982 (1984) (Amtrak not an agency for Privacy Act purposes, even though it is subject to the FOIA).

3.5.2. There was considerable litigation over whether or not the White House was covered by the Privacy Act. In *Alexander v. FBI*, 971 F. Supp. 603 (D.D.C. 1997), Judge Royce Lamberth ruled the Privacy Act applied to the White House even though the FOIA, from which the Privacy Act's definition of "agency" comes, did not. He noted that "the concerns of FOIA and the Privacy Act are quite different" and added that "there is no need to ignore the plain language of the statute and limit the word 'agency' as has been done under FOIA." However, when three other judges in Washington faced the same issue, they unanimously agreed that if the White House is not an agency under FOIA, then it cannot be an agency under the Privacy Act either. *See Tripp v. EOP*, 200 F.R.D. 140 (D.D.C. 2001), *Flowers v. EOP*, 142 F. Supp. 2d 38 (D.D.C. 2001); and *Broaddrick v. EOP*, 139 F. Supp. 2d 55 (D.D.C. 2001).

3.5.3. In addition, government contractors and their employees are covered by the civil and criminal penalties of the Privacy Act, if the agency provides by contract for the "operation by or on behalf of the agency of a system of records to accomplish an agency function..." In that case the agency "shall...cause" the requirements of the Act to apply. *See* Subsection 552a(m); OMB Guidelines at 28976. *See also* Subsection 552a(i).

3.5.4. State agencies are not included even though they receive federal funds. *St. Michael's Convalescent Hosp.*, 643 F.2d at 1373.

4. The Restriction on Disclosures.

4.1. Introduction.

4.1.1. The general rule is that there is to be no disclosure of any record in a system of records "except pursuant to a written request by, or with the prior written consent of," the subject. § 552a(b). *See generally Local 2047, A.F.G.E. v. Defense General Supply Center*, 423 F. Supp. 481, 483 (E.D. Va. 1976), *aff'd.*, 573 F.2d 184 (4th Cir. 1978); *Zeller v. United States*, 467 F. Supp. at 503.

4.1.2. "The Act does not define 'disclosure', leaving the meaning of that term to case law development." *Krowitz v. Department of Agriculture, U.S. Forest Service,* 641 F. Supp. 1536, 1542 (W.D. Mich. 1986). Generally, courts have read the term in connection with the Act's purpose "to preclude a system of records from serving as the *source* of personal information about a person which is then disclosed without the person's consent." *Olberding v. Department of Defense*, 564 F. Supp. 907, 913 (S.D. Iowa 1982), *aff'd*, 709 F.2d 621 (8th Cir. 1983) (emphasis in original).

4.1.3. The Privacy Act also does not define the word "consent," but it has been held in this context not to require the "intentional relinquishment of a known right or privilege" that must be found to validate consent to a waiver of the Sixth Amendment right to counsel in a criminal trial. *Doe v. GSA*, 544 F. Supp. 530, 541 (D. Md. 1982) ("not dispositive" that plaintiff challenging the disclosure pursuant to his earlier consent "may not have actually known that records would be released, or that he could have withheld his consent to such release"). Questions of consent under subsection 552a(b) more closely involve the scope and detail, rather than the voluntariness, of the authorization for release. *See Perry v. FBI*, 759 F.2d at 1276 (release "not so vague or general" that it is questionable whether subject knew what he was authorizing or whether FBI knew what documents it could lawfully release). *See also Thomas v. VA*, 467 F. Supp. 458 (D. Conn. 1979) (consent was both agency and record specific, and claim of involuntariness was "unsupported by the record").

4.1.4. The wrongful disclosure provision applies only to an agency's systems of records, not all agency records. *Bartell v. FAA,* 725 F.2d at 1408, n.10. *Accord Hanley v. DOJ,* 623 F.2d 1138, 1139 (6th Cir. 1980); *Doyle v. Behan,* 670 F.2d 535, 538-39 (5th Cir. 1982).

4.1.5. The general rule is subject to twelve exceptions, some of which are quite broad.

4.2. The Scope of the Restriction.

4.2.1. Disclosure is prohibited to any person or agency. Subsection 552a(b).

4.2.2. Disclosure includes any means of communication —written, oral, electronic, or mechanical. OMB Guidelines at 28953.

4.2.3. One district court adopted a *de minimus* rule excluding particularly innocuous disclosures. *Harper v. United States*, 423 F. Supp. 192, 197 (D.S.C. 1976). This issue is better analyzed under subsection (g)(1)(D), which requires a showing of "adverse effect" to support a civil remedy for wrongful disclosure.

4.2.4. Courts have generally supported a "retrieval rule" which limits the Privacy Act's coverage to prohibit only non-consensual disclosure of information that has been "retrieved" from a protected record. *See, e.g., Thomas v. DOE*, 719 F.2d 342 (10th Cir. 1983); *Olberding v. Department of Defense*, 709 F.2d at 622. However, in 1984, the D.C. Circuit in *Bartell v. FAA, supra*, declined to apply the previously unanimous "retrieval" rule to the facts before it, concluding that the rationale behind the "retrieval" rule did not support "reading out of the Act's coverage" a situation "where an agency official uses the government's 'sophisticated...information collecting methods' to acquire personal information for inclusion in a record and then discloses that information in an unauthorized fashion without actually physically retrieving it from the record system." 725 F.2d at 1410.

4.2.4.1. Although the *Bartell* opinion emphatically states that "an absolute policy of limiting the Act's coverage to information physically retrieved from a record would make little sense in terms of its underlying purpose," *id.* at 1409, one court has concluded that, upon close examination, "*Bartell's* holding is so inextricably intertwined with the peculiar factual situation in that case that it was not intended and should not be permitted to generally displace the previously unanimous 'retrieval' rule." *Krowitz*, 641 F. Supp. at 1543-44 n.7.

4.2.4.2. The D.C. Circuit has underscored that records have to actually be retrieved to create a system of records. Rejecting the notion that the ability to retrieve could trigger Privacy Act rights, the court noted that "where information about individuals is only being gathered as an administrative adjunct to a grant-making program which focuses on businesses and where the agency has presented evidence that it has no practice if retrieving information keyed to individuals, the agency should not be viewed as maintaining a system of records. On the other hand, where an agency—such as the FBI—is compiling information about individuals primarily for investigatory purposes, Privacy Act concerns are at their zenith, and if there is evidence of even a few retrievals of information keyed to individuals' names, it may well be the case that the agency is maintaining a system of records." *Henke v. Department of Commerce*, 83 F.3d 1453 (D.C. Cir. 1996).

4.2.4.3. The Fourth Circuit disagreed with the D.C. Circuit's ruling in *Henke*. In *Williams v. Department of Veterans Affairs*, 104 F.3d 670 (4th Cir. 1997), the court observed that "common computer utility programs exist that can locate the occurrence of names or client numbers even if not contained in the filename. We find that the narrow *Henke* rationale—that since this document was not in practice actually retrieved 'by the name of the individual or by some identifying number' it cannot be a record within a 'system of records'—unconvincing in these circumstances where there appears to exist already a formal system of records."

4.2.5. Oral disclosures from memory are included within the restriction. *Fitzpatrick v. IRS*, 665 F.2d 327 (11th Cir. 1982).

4.2.6. When a release consists merely of information to which the general public already has access, *FDIC v. Dye,* 642 F.2d at 836, or which the recipient of the release already knows, *King v. Califano,* 471 F. Supp. 180, 181 (D.D.C. 1979), the Privacy Act is not violated.

4.2.6.1. *See Hollis v. Department of the Army,* 856 F.2d 1541, 1545 (D.C. Cir. 1988) (Act not violated by nonconsensual disclosure of soldier's child-support payment records to former wife who, as designated recipient of the allotments and payee of checks received, "learned nothing from the transmittal record of which she was not already aware").

4.2.6.2 The D.C. Circuit refused to expand *Hollis* to cover disclosures to anyone who may have some personal knowledge of the contents of the disclosed record. In *Pilon v. DOJ*, 73 F.3d 1111 (D.C. Cir. 1996), the court emphasized the need for restrictions on the ability to disclose based on personal knowledge, pointing out that under the government's argument "having seen the document once under permissible circumstances, the employee can never violate the Act in retrieving it and making whatever use he pleases of it. Moreover, according to the Department's interpretation of 'disclose,' once in possession of the documents for a second time, the same employee could resign his position with the agency, take the document with him and (as a private citizen) release the document broadly without anyone incurring liability under the Privacy Act."

4.2.6.3. However, availability of a record from another source can be a factor in finding that the agency did not violate the Privacy Act. The Second Circuit ruled in *Devine v. USA*, 202 F.3d 547 (2d Cir. 2000), that the Justice Department did not violate the Privacy Act when it posted an Inspector General's report on its website after the contents of the report had been made public by members of Congress.

4.3. The Twelve Exceptions.

4.3.1. "to those officers and employees of the agency which maintains the record who have a need for the record in the performance of their duties"—§ 552a(b)(1).

4.3.1.1. This exception was intended to authorize internal use for the purpose for which the record was collected, not to justify every internal agency use simply because the users work for the same department. *See* Guidelines at 28954; *Privacy Source Book* at 305. *See Howard v. Marsh*, 785 F.2d 645 (8th Cir. 1986); *Hernandez v. Alexander*, 671 F.2d 402, 410 (10th Cir. 1982); *Beller v. Middendorf*, 632 F.2d 788, 798 n.6 (9th Cir. 1980), *cert. denied sub nom., Beller v. Lehman*, 452 U.S. 905 (1981). *See also Bigelow v. Department of Defense*, 217 F.3d 875 (D.C. Cir. 2000), where the court found Bigelow's supervisor had a need to know the contents of the plaintiff's personnel security file to help assess his trustworthiness.

4.3.1.2. A defense made under this subsection has been held to raise factual issues which cannot be resolved on a motion to dismiss. *Olberding v. Department of Defense, supra.*

4.3.2. "required under Section 552 of this title"—§ 552a(b)(2).

4.3.2.1. Section 552 (of Title 5 of the U.S. Code) is the Freedom of Information Act.

4.3.2.2. Since any record properly requested under the FOIA and not exempt under one or more of the FOIA's nine exemptions must be disclosed, this provision applies to all such records. *See Brown v. FBI*, 658 F.2d 71, 73-74 (2d Cir. 1981).

4.3.2.3. The FOIA exemptions are not mandatory. An agency can choose to release a record that is exempt under FOIA. *See Chrysler Corp. v. Brown*, 441 U.S. 281 (1979). But such a release would not be "required" within the meaning of this subsection.

4.3.2.4. *See* generally the discussion of the overlap between the FOIA and the Privacy Act's access provisions, *infra*.

4.3.2.5. One circuit has held that the Privacy Act, like the FOIA, is irrelevant to confidentiality issues concerning tax return information because 26 U.S.C. § 6103, "while not explicitly amending the Privacy Act, was apparently intended to override any inconsistent provisions of prior statutes, including the Privacy Act." *Cheek v. IRS*, 703 F.2d 271 (7th Cir. 1983). *See* Chapter 5 on Information Exempted by Other Statutes, for contrary holdings regarding § 6103 and the FOIA.

4.3.2.6. This subsection is not a defense; it is inapplicable unless there is an actual FOIA request. *Bartell v. FAA*, 725 F.2d at 1412. *See generally Crooker v. U.S. Parole Comm'n*, 730 F.2d 1, 10 (1st Cir. 1984); *Kiraly v. FBI*, 728 F.2d 273, 275 (6th Cir. 1984). *But see Cochran v. United States*, 770 F.2d 949 (11th Cir. 1985) (FOIA exception applicable where reporters made oral inquiries for facts of investigation, but filed no written request).

4.3.2.7. The Supreme Court resolved a split in the circuits when it ruled, in *Department of Defense v. FLRA*, 510 U.S. 487 (1994), that names and addresses of covered federal employees are not available to union representatives because release would be prohibited by the Privacy Act. The Court, relying on its earlier ruling in *DOJ v. Reporters Committee*, 489 U.S. 749 (1989), found such information would no longer be available. It found irrelevant that the unions had requested the information through the Federal Service Labor-Management Relations Statute because application of that statute still referenced the Privacy Act and required an analysis of subsection (b)(2). Justice Ruth Ginsburg, concurring, said she felt bound by the *Reporters Committee* holding, but observed that "it is...doubtful that Congress intended a privacy interest, appraised by most courts as relatively modest, to trump the legislature's firmly-declared interest in promoting federal-sector collective bargaining. I do not agree with the Court that the *Reporters Committee* rule yielding these anomalies is indubitably commanded by FOIA."

4.3.3. "for a routine use as defined in subsection (a)(7) of this section and described under subsection (e)(4)(D) of this section"—§ 552a(b)(3).

4.3.3.1. The "routine use" exception is the most important of the twelve.

4.3.3.2. A "routine use" is defined in subsection (a)(7) to mean "with respect to the disclosure of a record, the use of such record for a purpose which is compatible with the purpose for which it was collected." *See Swenson v. U.S. Postal Service,* 890 F.2d 1075 (9th Cir. 1989).

4.3.3.3. Subsection (e)(4)(D) requires that each "routine use" be published in the Federal Register, at least annually, for each system of records. Thus, "the scope of routine uses is confined by the published definitions." *Doe v. Naval Air Station, Pensacola, Fla.*, 768 F.2d 1229, 1231 (11th Cir. 1985). *See Covert v. Herrington,* 876 F.2d 751 (9th Cir. 1989) in which the court found a disclosure improper because the agency had not provided an appropriate "routine use" listing on the form used to collect the data.

4.3.3.4. According to the Analysis of Compromise Amendments, the "routine use" exception was included to permit the non-consensual intra- or inter-agency transfer of information where such transfer was for "housekeeping" or was "necessarily frequent," but also was intended "to discourage the unnecessary exchange of information to another person or to agencies who may not be as sensitive to the collection agency's reasons for using and interpreting the material." *Id., Privacy Source Book* at 859-60.

4.3.3.5. Congressman Moorhead, principal author of the House bill, stated on the floor that the term was intended to include "all of the proper and necessary uses even if any such use occurs infrequently." 120 Cong. Rec. H10962 (Nov. 21, 1974); *see also* OMB Guidelines at 28963.

4.3.3.6. The language of the exception, in light of its legislative history, is quite elastic. Agencies, limited only by the publication requirement, are thus free to treat as a routine use any disclosure which is arguably "compatible" with the original purpose for collecting the information. While some agencies have been restrained, others have carried this authority to extremes—some of which were criticized in the report of the Privacy Protection Study Commission. *Privacy Protection Report* at 516-21.

4.3.3.7. A typical routine use, which interacts with the seventh exemption, is disclosure of information to law enforcement agencies when an agency suspects misconduct by administrators of, or participants in, government programs. *See, e.g., United States v. Miller*, 643 F.2d 713, 715 (10th Cir. 1981). *See also Hastings v. Judicial Conference of the United States,* 770 F.2d 1093 (D.C. Cir. 1985), *cert. denied,* 477 U.S. 904 (1986) (disclosures by Justice Department officials to Investigation Committee concerning criminal proceedings against a judge). *But see Doe v. Naval Air Station, Pensacola, Fla.*, 768 F.2d at 1232 (release from vehicle registration system to outside law enforcement agencies to assist criminal investigation held improper where published routine uses clearly relate to parking control, insurance verification, etc.). The Third Circuit struck down the Navy's broad routine use exemptions which allowed disclosures based on relevance. The court said "if the numerous government agencies which collect information about individuals are free to share their information with others, bound only by the standard of relevance to the recipient agency, the purpose of the limitation in [the Privacy Act] may be nullified." *Britt v. Naval Investigative Service,* 886 F.2d 544 (3d Cir. 1989). However, the Fourth Circuit upheld a routine use of the FAA allowing the agency to release law enforcement investigation reports to interested parties. *Alphin v. FAA,* 902 F.2d 27 (4th Cir. 1990).

4.3.3.8. The notice of routine use need not be so specific as, for example, to name statutes under which prosecution might result. *United States v. Annunziato*, 643 F.2d 676, 678 (9th Cir. 1981), *cert. denied*, 452 U.S. 966 (1981). *See also United States v. Berney*, 713 F.2d 568, 572-73 (10th Cir. 1983) and *United States v. Rickman*, 638 F.2d 182, 183 (10th Cir. 1980) (not a valid defense in tax prosecutions).

4.3.3.9. The D.C. Circuit has suggested that the terms of a collective bargaining agreement may bind the agency to publish a routine use notice that would allow the union access to information necessary to perform its functions. *United States Postal Service v. National Ass'n of Letter Carriers,* 9 F.3d 138 (D.C. Cir. 1993).

4.3.4. "to the Bureau of the Census for purposes of planning or carrying out a census or survey or related activity pursuant to the provisions of title 13"—§ 552a(b)(4). *Cf. Baldridge v. Shapiro*, 455 U.S. 345 (1982).

4.3.5. "to a recipient who has provided the agency with advance adequate written assurance that the record will be used solely as a statistical research or reporting record, and the record is to be transferred in a form that is not individually identifiable"—§ 552a(b)(5). The OMB Guidelines suggest that this exception is limited to records which, even in combination, cannot be used to identify individuals. *Id.* at 28954.

4.3.6. "to the National Archives of the United States as a record which has sufficient historical or other value to warrant its continued preservation by the United States Government, or for evaluation by the Archivist of the United States or his designee to determine whether the record has such value"—§ 552a(b)(6).

4.3.7. "to another agency or to an instrumentality of any governmental jurisdiction within or under the control of the United States for a civil or criminal law enforcement activity if the activity is authorized by law, and if the head of the agency or instrumentality has made a written request to the agency which maintains the record specifying the particular portion desired and the law enforcement activity for which the record is sought"— § 552a(b)(7).

4.3.7.1. The OMB Guidelines discourage blanket requests for all records of a particular type. *Id.* at 28955.

4.3.7.2. The Privacy Protection Study Commission reported widespread evasion of this subsection by means of the routine use provision in subsection (b)(3). *Privacy Protection Report* at 517-19.

4.3.7.3. Disclosure is not authorized under subsection (b)(7) absent a written request from the head of the receiving agency. *Doe v. DiGenova*, 779 F.2d 74, 85 (D.C. Cir. 1985).

4.3.8. "to a person pursuant to a showing of compelling circumstances affecting the health or safety of an individual if upon such disclosure notification is transmitted to the last known address of such individual"—§ 552a(b)(8).

4.3.9. "to either House of Congress, or, to the extent of matter within its jurisdiction, any committee or subcommittee thereof, any joint committee of Congress or subcommittee of any such joint committee"—§ 552a(b)(9). This exception applies to Congress and its committees, not to individual members. *Swenson v. U.S. Postal Service,* 890 F.2d 1075 (9th Cir. 1989).

4.3.10. "to the Comptroller General, or any of his authorized representatives, in the course of the performance of the duties of the General Accounting Office"—§ 552a(b)(10)

4.3.11. "pursuant to the order of a court of competent jurisdiction." § 552a(b)(11). Requests for court orders under this subsection should be evaluated by balancing the need for the disclosure against the potential harm to the subject of the disclosure. *Perry v. State Farm Fire & Casualty Co.*, 734 F.2d 1441, 1447 (11th Cir. 1984) (order denied because normal discovery procedures were available to obtain the records). Subpoenas—grand jury or otherwise—are not subsection (b)(11) "orders" unless they are "specifically approved by a court." *Doe v. DiGenova*, 779 F.2d at 85. Thus, a subpoena routinely issued by a court clerk is not an "order" within the meaning of this subsection. *Stiles v. Atlanta Gas Light Co.*, 453 F. Supp. 798, 800 (N.D. Ga. 1978).

4.3.11.1. Because certain information is routinely needed in deciding veterans' appeals, the U.S. Court of Veterans Appeals granted the Department of Veterans Affairs a standing order to routinely release information protected by the Privacy Act during the course of appeals before the court. *In Re A Motion for a Standing Order,* No. 90-85 (U.S. Ct. Vet. App. July 2, 1990).

4.3.12. "to a consumer reporting agency in accordance with Section 3711(f) of Title 31." § 552a(b)(12).

4.4. At least one Circuit has held that disclosure without the subject's consent is not an intentional or willful violation of § 552a(b) for purposes of an action for damages under § 552a(g)(1)(D), where disclosure is according to agency regulations which had not been challenged. *Wisdom v. HUD*, 713 F.2d 422 (8th Cir. 1983); *Bruce v. United States*, 621 F.2d 914 (8th Cir. 1980).

5. Accounting of Disclosures.

5.1. For the purposes of informing individuals about disclosures made, tracing data to be corrected, and monitoring agency compliance, the Act requires in § 552a(c) that each agency keep an accounting of disclosures made under subsection(b).

5.2. The accounting must include the date, nature, and purpose of the disclosure, and the name and address of the recipient. It must be kept for at least five years or the life of the record, whichever is longer.

5.3. An individual must be given access to the accounting of disclosures concerning the individual's records.

5.4. Exceptions.

5.4.1. An accounting need not be kept of disclosures under subsections (b)(1) (intra-agency) or (b)(2) (FOIA).

5.4.2. An accounting must be kept of disclosures under subsection (b)(7) (law enforcement requests), but access to the accounting need not be granted.

5.5. The accounting must be used to inform recipients of corrections or amendments made under other provisions of the Act (*see infra*).

5.6. Agencies entitled to general or specific exemptions from the Privacy Act (*see infra*) may exempt themselves from the requirement of access, but not from the requirement of making and keeping the accounting.

5.7. The Privacy Protection Study Commission reported that the accounting of disclosures provision is "widely regarded as the statute's single most burdensome provision." *Privacy Protection Report* at 525. Many agencies simply ignore it.

6. Agency Recordkeeping Requirements.

6.1. Each agency must comply with certain general principles of recordkeeping set forth in subsection (e) of the Act. *See, e.g., Wisdom v. HUD*, 713 F.2d at 424.

6.2. The Specific Requirements:

6.2.1. Subsection (e)(1)—An agency must "maintain in its records only such information about an individual as is relevant and necessary to accomplish a purpose of the agency required to be accomplished by statute or by executive order of the President."

6.2.1.1. The meaning of "relevant and necessary," as well as such terms as "accurate," "timely," and "complete" is not settled by judicial interpretation. *See* discussion under subsection (e)(5), *infra*.

6.2.1.2. The Senate Committee Report, *Privacy Source Book* at 203, sheds this light: The standards of relevancy here relate to the constitutionality and legality of the entire information program, as well as the reasonableness of maintenance of any particular piece of personal information, given the statutory jurisdiction of the agency. The standards of accuracy, completeness, and timeliness, as well as relevancy, are directed to the quality of the information in an individual's own file. The section thus looks to a double-pronged consideration, first to the authorized needs of the agency, and second, to the scope of the administrative need for information in order to make a decision on that individual.

6.2.1.3. *See also* OMB Guidelines at 28965; *Zeller v. United States*, 467 F. Supp. at 502.

6.2.2. Subsection (e)(2)—Each agency must "collect information to the greatest extent practicable directly from the subject individual when the information may result in adverse determinations about an individual's rights, benefits and privileges under Federal programs." *Privacy Source Book* at 863; OMB Guidelines at 28961. In the most definitive analysis of this provision to date, the D.C. Circuit ruled that the Justice Department violated subsection (e)(2) when it contacted the Pennsylvania State Bar to determine if an employee had actually taken the bar exam, but did not first contact the individual directly in an effort to get definitive proof from him. The court specifically rejected the argument that doubts about the plaintiff's credibility justified seeking information first from a third party, noting that "in the context of an investigation that is seeking objective, unalterable information, reasonable questions about a subject's credibility cannot relieve an agency from its responsibility to collect that information first from the subject." *Waters v. Thornburgh,* 888 F.2d 870, 873 (D.C. Cir. 1989).

6.2.2.1. The Fourth Circuit found, in *Olivares v. NASA*, 103 F.3d 119 (4th Cir. 1996), that the agency was justified in checking directly with a university to confirm Olivares' degree status. The court concluded the fact Olivares continued to insist that the information on his original employment application was correct, allowed the agency to use the waiver of consent in the application as the basis for contacting the school.

6.2.2.2. The credibility of the individual may also be a determining factor. For example, in *Hudson v. Reno*, 130 F.3d 1193 (6th Cir. 1997), the court found the agency did not violate (e)(2) when it failed to collect information directly from Hudson where she had been accused of making false statements and there was evidence that she was intimidating and threatening people in her office.

6.2.3. Subsection (e)(3)—Each agency must inform an individual from whom it proposes to collect information of its statutory authority, whether response is voluntary or mandatory, the principal purposes and routine uses of the information, and the effects of refusal to provide it.

6.2.3.1. "Nothing in the Privacy Act requires agencies to employ the exact language of the statute to give effective notice." *United States v. Wilber*, 696 F.2d 79, 80 (8th Cir. 1982).

6.2.3.2. The Privacy Act does not require notice of a specific criminal penalty for failure to comply with the duty to pay tax. *United States v. Bell*, 734 F.2d 1311, 1318 (8th Cir. 1984), citing *United States v. Wilber*,

696 F.2d at 80; *United States v. Annunziato*, 643 F.2d at 678; *United States v. Rickman*, 638 F.2d at 183; *Field v. Brown*, 610 F.2d 981, 987-88 (D.C. Cir. 1989), *cert. denied*, 446 U.S. 939 (1979). *Accord United States v. Dack*, 747 F.2d 1172, 1176 n.5 (7th Cir. 1984).

6.2.3.3. In *Usher v. Secretary of Health and Human Services*, 721 F.2d 854, 856 (1st Cir. 1983), concerning Social Security Administration forms that requested information from landlords of benefit recipients without indicating the purposes and routine uses of such information, the court could simply "see no basis in the statute for an agency's refusing to give the information specified" in subsection (e)(3). Yet the court denied plaintiff's damage claim because there was no "adverse effect" from SSA's failure to provide such information.

6.2.4. Subsection (e)(4)—Each agency must publish, at least annually in the Federal Register, notice of the existence of each system of records it maintains, as well as information about that system including the name and location, the categories of records and sources of records in it, the routine uses of the information, and the procedures by which access and correction can be had.

6.2.5. Subsection (e)(5)—Each agency must "maintain all records which are used by the agency in making any determination about any individual with such accuracy, relevance, timeliness and completeness as is reasonably necessary to assure fairness to the individual in determination."

6.2.5.1. In *Hass v. U.S. Air Force*, 848 F. Supp. 926 (D. Kan. 1994), in explaining meaning of accuracy requirements, the court distinguished the agency's inaccurate recording of information—which would be a violation—from its correct recording of information that turned out to be inaccurate—which would not violate (e)(5).

6.2.5.2. In *Manuel v. VA Hospital, supra,* the court held that subsection (e)(5) obligations were not violated by the agency's failure to place certain documents into its system of records, since there was no "determination" about the plaintiff made by the agency based on the disputed documents. 857 F.2d at 1120.

6.2.5.3. The D.C. Circuit found that the Bureau of Prisons had violated subsection (e)(5) by failing to correct information in a prisoner's file showing that he had been involved in a robbery when it had been later shown that he was not involved. In *Sellers v. Bureau of Prisons*, 959 F.2d 1423 (D.C. Cir. 1992), the court distinguished this situation from that in *Doe v. United States*, 821 F.2d 694 (D.C. Cir. 1987), in which the court had found that appending a statement of disagreement was fair where the only two witnesses to an interview disagreed about what happened. In *Sellers*, the court noted, the truth of the matter could be reasonably verified and was not subject to interpretation, and to the extent that the Bureau had not bothered to verify such information it was in violation of (e)(5).

6.2.5.4. In *Fendler v. U.S. Bureau of Prisons,* 846 F.2d 550 (9th Cir. 1988), the court found that, despite alleged inaccuracies in the pre-sentence reports which the Bureau sent to the Parole Commission, the Bureau had met its duty under subsection (e)(5) to "assure fairness" to the subject of the report by allowing the individual to append his 17-page rebuttal to the report presented to the Commission. *See also Deters v. U.S. Parole Comm'n*, 85 F.3d 655 (D.C. Cir. 1996), in which the court found the Commission had not violated (e)(5) by appending Deters' statement of disagreement to his pre-sentence investigation report. The court noted that "no fact-finder could determine on this record that the Commission 'flagrantly disregarded' Deters' Privacy Act rights when it supplemented his file with his rebuttal to the PSI and offered him a hearing that would have addressed the accuracy of the PSI."

6.2.5.5. The D.C. Circuit has ruled that where the statute creates a specific channel for redress of violations, claims of a violation of subsection (e)(5) cannot be used to bypass those channels. *Doe v. FBI,* 936 F.2d 1346 (D.C. Cir. 1991).

6.2.6. Subsection (e)(6)—Except for disclosures under the FOIA, each agency must, prior to dissemination of a record, "make reasonable efforts to assure that such records are accurate, complete, timely, and relevant for agency purposes." (*See* comments under subsection (e)(1)).

6.2.7. Subsection (e)(7)—Each agency shall "maintain no record describing how any individual exercises rights guaranteed by the First Amendment, unless expressly authorized by statute or by the individual about whom the record is maintained or unless pertinent to and within the scope of an authorized law enforcement activity."

6.2.7.1. *See Privacy Source Book* at 929-31 for explanatory House floor debate.

6.2.7.2. The OMB Guidelines exhort agencies to "apply the broadest reasonable interpretation" of this prohibition. *Id.* at 28965.

6.2.7.3. For a violation of subsection (e)(7) to occur, "the documents involved must implicate an individual's first amendment rights." *Boyd v. Secretary of the Navy*, 709 F.2d at 684, where the court, relying on the Supreme Court's ruling in *Connick v. Myers*, 461 U.S. 138 (1983), held that a memorandum of a meeting in which a disgruntled employee was told to "follow the chain of command," reflected a "valid restriction on the time, place and manner" of the employee's expression of grievance and therefore did not involve any First Amendment or Privacy Act infringement. *See also Reuber v. United States*, 829 F.2d 133, 142-43 (D.C. Cir. 1987).

6.2.7.4. The authority to monitor First Amendment activities is separate from the authority to keep records concerning it. *Clarkson v. IRS*, 678 F.2d at 1374-75.

6.2.7.5. The subsection is violated unless records of the surveillance are authorized by statute, made and kept pursuant to consent, or part of an authorized law enforcement activity. *Albright v. United States (I)*, 631

F.2d at 921 (secret videotape of employee grievance meeting violates subsection (e)(7)). Recordkeeping is not part of an authorized law enforcement activity if it is "unconnected to any investigation of past, present or anticipated violations of the statutes which the agency is authorized to enforce...." *Clarkson v. IRS*, 678 F.2d at 1375. However, the exemption for records "pertinent to and within the scope of an authorized law enforcement activity" is not limited to investigation of past, present or future criminal activity; rather, it applies if there is a "direct nexus to an authorized criminal, civil or administrative law enforcement activity." *Jabara v. Webster*, 691 F.2d 272, 280 (6th Cir. 1982). Moreover, an employer's determination whether an employee is performing his job adequately has been held to constitute an authorized law enforcement activity under subsection (e)(7). *Nagel v. HEW*, 725 F.2d 1438 (D.C. Cir. 1984). "A federal agency does not violate the Act if it records, for evaluative or disciplinary purposes, statements made by employees while at work." *Id.* at 1441. *See also MacPherson v. IRS*, 803 F.2d 479 (9th Cir. 1986) (strong policy concerns on both sides "may balance differently in different cases," so court declined to fashion "hard and fast standard" for determining applicability of law enforcement exemption).

6.2.7.6. In *Patterson v. FBI*, 893 F.2d 595 (3d Cir. 1990), the Third Circuit expressly rejected the argument that, in order to invoke the law enforcement exception, an agency must demonstrate a "substantial relationship" between the records and the governmental activity. Instead, the court concluded that an agency need only show that the records were "relevant" to a law enforcement activity.

6.2.7.6.1. In *J. Roderick MacArthur Foundation v. FBI*, 102 F.3d 600 (D.C. Cir. 1996), the court indicated that there were very few circumstances under which records collected by a law enforcement agency would violate (e)(7). The court noted that "the Act refers not to a 'law enforcement investigation' but to an 'authorized law enforcement activity.' Materials may continue to be relevant to a law enforcement activity long after a particular investigation undertaken pursuant to that activity has been closed."

6.2.7.7. A plaintiff is entitled to contest the purpose of surveillance activities and the extent to which records of them are maintained. *Clarkson v. IRS*, 678 F.2d at 1375. *See also MacPherson v. IRS, supra*, and *England v. Commissioner*, 798 F.2d 350 (9th Cir. 1986) (both cases rejecting Privacy Act violations in connection with IRS actions to track "tax protestors").

6.2.7.8. A record maintained in violation of subsection (e)(7) is subject to the Privacy Act even though not kept in a "system of records." *Boyd v. Secretary of the Navy*, 709 F.2d at 687; *Clarkson v. IRS*, 678 F.2d at 1373-77; *Albright v. United States (I)*, 631 F.2d at 918-20.

6.2.7.9. Expungement of such a record is usually the appropriate remedy for violation of subsection (e)(7). *See Hobson v. Wilson*, 737 F.2d 1, 65-66 (D.C. Cir. 1984); *Clarkson v. IRS*, 678 F.2d at 1376-77; *Albright v. United States (I)*, 631 F.2d at 921. In *Becker v. IRS*, 34 F.3d 398 (7th Cir. 1994), the Seventh Circuit ordered the IRS to expunge articles collected about the Beckers' tax protest activities. The court noted that "we have examined the material, and any thought that it could be helpful in future enforcement activity concerning the Beckers is untenable. The material consists of newspaper articles dating from the middle to late 1980s, with no reference to the Beckers; any potential advantage to having these documents in the Beckers' files, at some uncertain date, is minuscule."

6.2.8. Subsection (e)(8) requires "reasonable efforts to serve notice on an individual when any record on such individual is made available to any person under compulsory legal process when such process becomes a matter of public record."

6.2.9. Subsection (e)(9) requires agencies to establish rules of conduct and provide instruction for personnel engaged in using affected records.

6.2.10. Subsection (e)(10) requires appropriate "administrative, technical, and physical safeguards" for the security of affected records.

6.2.11. Subsection (e)(11) requires 30 days' notice in the Federal Register of new uses and intended uses of affected records.

7. Access to Records under the Privacy Act.

7.1. For the purpose of enabling individuals to correct records about themselves (*see infra*), subsection (d) of the Privacy Act provides that an agency must grant an individual an opportunity to see and copy records concerning him or herself. Subsections (j) and (k) permit agencies to exempt certain kinds of records or systems of records from such access. Thus, the Privacy Act establishes a system of access which is not unlike the access granted by the FOIA, although for a different purpose. The relationship between the two systems of access and exemption was reconciled in 1984 when Congress passed the CIA Information Act. P.L. 98-477, 98 Stat. 2209.

7.2. Relationship to the Freedom of Information Act.

7.2.1. The FOIA permits access to records that are not maintained by the requester's identifiers and are therefore not "records" in "systems of records" within the meaning of the Privacy Act. The FOIA plainly and exclusively applies to such records.

7.2.2. In those rare cases in which a record would be available under the Privacy Act but exempt under the FOIA, the former is clear: the Privacy Act applies. § 552a(t).

7.2.3. Although there was a serious split of opinion over whether or not the Privacy Act is a FOIA Exemption 3 statute (*see* Chapter 5 on Information Exempted by Other Statutes. Congress put the argument to rest in the CIA Information Act, amending subsection (t) by indicating the Privacy Act did not diminish access rights available under FOIA. *See DOJ v. Provenzano*, 469 U.S. 14 (1989).

7.3. Privacy Act Access Rights.

7.3.1. The central provision is § 552a(d)(1), which provides that each agency maintaining a system of records must: upon request by any individual to gain access to his record or to any information pertaining to him which is contained in the system, permit him and, upon his request, a person of his own choosing to accompany him, to review the record and have a copy made of all or any portion thereof in a form comprehensible to him...

7.3.2. No reason need be given or should be sought; the reason for the request is irrelevant. *FTC v. Shaffner*, 626 F.2d 32 (7th Cir. 1980); *Smiertka v. Dep't of Treasury*, 447 F. Supp. at 221; OMB Guidelines at 28957.

7.3.3. Like the wrongful disclosure provision, the access rights under the Privacy Act apply only to an agency's system of records, not to all agency records. *See, e.g., Manuel v. VA Hospital,* 857 F.2d at 1117.

7.4. Privacy Act Access Procedures.

7.4.1. Request letter.

7.4.1.1. Like the FOIA, the Privacy Act's access procedures are properly invoked by a request letter.

7.4.1.2. The letter should be marked to the attention of the agency's "FOIA/Privacy Unit," should usually make its request under both Acts, should if possible identify the system of records (from the Federal Register) sought to be searched, and should be as narrow as the requester can make it.

7.4.1.3. The Act requires that agencies have procedures to identify the requester, § 552a(f)(2), in order to avoid giving one individual's records to another. Thus, the letter should contain the requester's full name, address, a notarized signature, and such other identifying information that the requester is willing to divulge as will help the agency. The OMB Guidelines urge that requirements to verify identity "be kept to a minimum." *Id.* at 28957.

7.4.1.4. An attorney requesting on behalf of a client should submit a notarized authorization.

7.4.2. Procedures vary from agency to agency. The Privacy Act requires that each agency establish and publish its procedures, and disclose them to a requester. § 552a(f).

7.4.3. Time limits for response are not set forth in the Privacy Act. The Guidelines say that the agency "should" acknowledge the request within ten business days, advising whether and to what extent access will be granted, and provide access within 30 business days, and if there is "good cause" for further delay, so advise the requester. *Id.* at 28957-78.

7.4.4. No administrative appeal is required by the Privacy Act. Many agencies voluntarily offer such a process, but one district court has held that exhausting that remedy is not required before instituting suit. *Mervin v. Bonfanti*, 410 F. Supp. 1205 (D.D.C. 1976). *See also Diederich v. Department of the Army*, 878 F.2d 646 (2d Cir. 1989), ruling that the plaintiff could proceed to court without going through an administrative appeals process. "[T]o require further exhaustion would not only contradict the plain words of the statute but also would undercut Congress' clear intent to provide speedy disposition of these claims." *Id.* at 648. However, the original remedy required by statute must be exhausted, and both should be pursued. *See* "Exhaustion of Administrative Remedies", *infra*.

7.4.5. Costs may be charged for copying, but not for search. § 552a(f)(5).

7.4.6. The access provisions contain a special exemption from access, not grouped with the other exemptions (*see* relationship to FOIA, *supra*; exemptions, *infra*), providing that nothing in the Privacy Act shall require an agency to grant access to "any information compiled in reasonable anticipation of a civil action proceeding." § 552a(d)(5). Unlike the other exemptions, this one is self-executing and does not depend upon an agency regulation. *Smiertka v. Dep't of Treasury, supra*. It has been held not to be confined to an attorney's work product. *Hernandez v. Alexander*, 671 F.2d at 408.

7.4.7. Subsection (f)(3) allows agencies to institute special procedures for access to an individual's medical records. The D.C. Circuit has ruled that such procedures, which usually require that the records be reviewed by a physician who then determines if release could cause harm to the individual, can be used only to explain the records to the individual, and cannot be used to deny ultimate access to the subject-individual. *Benavides v. Bureau of Prisons*, 995 F.2d 269 (D.C. Cir. 1993). *See also Bavido v. Apfel*, 215 F.3d 743 (7th Cir. 2000).

7.4.8. The D.C. Circuit has ruled that § 6103 of the Internal Revenue Code provides the sole means of access to individual tax return records, superseding more general rights of access in the Privacy Act. *Lake v. Rubin*, 162 F.3d 113 (D.C. Cir. 1998).

8. Amendment and Correction.

8.1. In general.

8.1.1. Subsection (d)(2) of the Privacy Act requires that agencies permit an individual to request amendment of a record pertaining to that individual on the ground that the record is not "accurate, relevant, timely, or complete."

8.1.2. Rules must be promulgated for the processing of such requests. Subsection (f)(4).

8.1.3. Upon receiving a proper request, the agency must either—

8.1.3.1. amend or correct the record as requested, or

8.1.3.2. refuse, explain why, and describe procedures available for the review and challenge of that refusal. Subsection (d)(2)(A) and (B). *See Baker v. Department of the Navy*, 814 F.2d at 1384-85 (Privacy Act remedies of amendment or expungement apply only for records that are accessible under the Privacy Act because they are individually keyed to the requester; an individual's ability to obtain access to a record under the FOIA will not provide any remedies under the Privacy Act).

8.1.4. May opinion and evaluation be corrected?

8.1.4.1. The Ninth Circuit has apparently held that an agency has the power to limit by regulation the errors that can be corrected to "factual" errors. *Blevins v. Plummer*, 613 F.2d 767, 768 n.3 (9th Cir. 1980). Due to the failure of counsel to argue the point thoroughly, the decision may not be of great precedential value. *Id. But see Bernson v. ICC*, 625 F. Supp. 10, 13 (D. Mass. 1984) (opinions, recommendations or judgments by ICC employees "cannot be made more accurate" by the court, nor can the court order that those opinions be amended "to reflect the plaintiff's versions of the facts").

8.1.4.2. At least absent such a regulation, other courts permit the correction of erroneous opinions and judgments as well as facts. *See, e.g., R.R. v. Department of the Army,* 482 F. Supp. 770, 773-74 (D.D.C. 1980) *(dictum); Turner v. Department of the Army*, 447 F. Supp. 1207, 1213 (D.D.C. 1978), *aff'd*, 593 F.2d 1372 (D.C. Cir. 1979).

8.1.4.3. Since plaintiffs have experienced some difficulties in proving that opinions are based upon particular factual errors, *see R.R. v. Department of the Army, supra*, discovery should be sought from those who formed opinions.

8.1.5. The Privacy Act contemplates "expungement [of inaccuracies] and not merely redress by supplement." *R.R. v. Department of the Army*, 482 F. Supp. at 774. *See also Smith v. Nixon*, 807 F.2d 197, 204 (D.C. Cir. 1986); *Doe v. United States Air Force,* 812 F.2d 738, 740-741 (D.C. Cir. 1987); *Hobson v. Wilson*, 737 F.2d at 65. However, the courts will only invoke their equity power "to order the expungement of Government records where *necessary* to vindicate rights secured by the Constitution or by statute." *Fendler v. U.S. Bureau of Prisons,* 846 F.2d at 554 (emphasis added) (expungement of information in presentence report not "necessary" where information "does not pose a real and immediate threat" to parolee).

8.1.6. The D.C. Circuit has also ruled that § 6103 of the Internal Revenue Code provides the only means of amending inaccurate tax return records, superseding the more general amendment rights under the Privacy Act. *Gardner v. USA*, 213 F.3d 735 (D.C. Cir. 2000).

8.2. Procedures.

8.2.1. Although an application in person will be entertained, a request letter is better for the requester and the agency. In at least one case, an oral request has been held sufficient. *Ligouri v. Alexander*, 495 F. Supp. 641 (S.D.N.Y. 1980).

8.2.2. Time limits.

8.2.2.1. The request must be acknowledged within ten working days, and the choice to amend or refuse must be made "promptly." Subsection (d)(2)(A) and (B).

8.2.2.2. The appeal must be decided within 30 working days, or "good cause" for extension shown and explained to the requester. Subsection (d)(3).

8.2.3. An appeal procedure is required by statute. Subsection (d)(3). The OMB Guidelines suggest that, at this point, the reviewing officer may elect to hold a hearing. *Id.* at 28959.

8.2.4. Statement of disagreement.

8.2.4.1. If the appeal is denied, the requester has the right to file a "concise statement setting forth the reasons for his disagreement with the refusal of the agency." Subsection (d)(3).

8.2.4.2. That statement, along with an agency response, must be disseminated to recipients of the record to the extent known from the accounting of disclosures. Subsection (d)(4).

8.2.4.3. "Congress...*mandated that any individual,* no matter how incredible his or her version of events, be allowed to supplement the record." *Doe v. United States*, 781 F.2d 907, 915 (D.C. Cir. 1986) (emphasis in original).

9. Privacy Act Exemptions.

9.1. Introduction.

9.1.1. There are two kinds of exemptions in the Privacy Act. The general exemptions in subsection (j) and the specific exemptions in subsection (k) are each of a different nature with different consequences. Even now there is very little caselaw interpreting the exemptions due to their overlap with those of the FOIA. *See* discussion *supra*. What the two kinds of Privacy Act exemptions have in common is that they are discretionary on the part of the agency, and are not effective until they are invoked by publication in the Federal Register.

9.1.2. The exemptions must be narrowly construed and their requirements strictly met. *Hernandez v. Alexander,* 671 F.2d at 406-07 (*dictum*). *But see Shapiro v. Drug Enforcement Administration,* 721 F.2d 215 (7th Cir. 1983) (exemption (j)(2) does not require that a regulation's rationale for exempting a record from disclosure apply in each particular case).

9.2. The General Exemptions—Subsection (j).

9.2.1. A general exemption, if properly invoked, excuses the exempt systems of records not only from the access provision of the Act, but also from all of the Act's other provisions except:

9.2.1.1. the limitations on disclosure in subsection (b);

9.2.1.2. some of the accounting of disclosure provisions, subsection (c)(1) and (2);

9.2.1.3. some record keeping requirements, subsections (e)(4)(A-F), and (e)(6,7,9,10, and 11);

9.2.1.4. civil remedies included in subsection (g)(1)(C) and (D); and,

9.2.1.5. the criminal penalties, subsection (i).

9.2.2. The general exemption does not excuse noncompliance with the partial prohibition on gathering information concerning the exercise of First Amendment rights. § 552a(e)(7).

9.2.3. While some courts have indicated in *dicta* that agencies may employ the general exemptions under subsection (j) to exempt themselves from the Privacy Act's civil remedies provision, *see, e.g., Kimberlin v. DOJ*, 788 F.2d 434, 436 n.2 (7th Cir. 1986) *and Ryan v. DOJ*, 595 F.2d 954, 958 (4th Cir. 1979), a panel of the D.C. Circuit rejected that view as "a completely anomalous use of the exemption provision that makes the Act a foolishness." *Tijerina v. Walters*, 821 F.2d 789, 797 (D.C. Cir. 1987). *See also* H.R. Rep. No. 93-1416, *Privacy Source Book* at 294.

9.2.4. An agency seeking to exempt itself under subsection (j) from particular requirements of the Privacy Act must state its reasons when it adopts the necessary regulation, and will be bound accordingly. *Compare Alexander v. United States,* 787 F.2d 1349, 1351 (9th Cir. 1986) (agency clearly and expressly invoked exemption from both subsection (e)(5) obligations and subsection (g) enforcement liability) *with Fendler v. U.S. Bureau of Prisons,* 846 F.2d at 553-554 (agency justification for exemption from subsection (g) cannot be read as implied exemption from subsection (e)(5) obligations or their enforcement under (g)(1)(C)).

9.2.5. General exemptions are available for systems of records which are:

9.2.5.1. Subsection (j)(1)—maintained by the Central Intelligence Agency; or

9.2.5.2. Subsection (j)(2)—maintained by an agency which performs as its principal function any activity pertaining to the enforcement of the criminal laws, *and* which consist of: (A) information compiled for the purpose of identifying individual criminal offenders and alleged offenders and consisting only of identifying data and notations of arrests, the nature and disposition of criminal charges, sentencing, confinement, release, and parole and probation status; (B) information compiled for the purpose of a criminal investigation, including reports of informants and investigators, and associated with an identifiable individual; or (C) reports identifiable to an individual compiled at any stage of the process of enforcement of the criminal laws, from arrest or indictment through release from supervision.

9.2.5.2.1. Prisons are law enforcement agencies for the purpose of this subsection. *Duffin v. Carlson*, 636 F.2d 709 (D.C. Cir. 1980).

9.2.5.2.2. The "any stage" of criminal law enforcement scope of (j)(2)(c) is illustrated by decisions upholding the provision's applicability to FBI "rap sheets." *Alexander v. United States, supra*; *Fendler v. U.S. Parole Comm'n*, 774 F.2d 975 (9th Cir. 1985).

9.2.5.2.3. An agency's ability to exempt non-law enforcement records in a law enforcement system of records depends on (1) whether such records were compiled for law enforcement purposes, and (2) the reasons the agency has stated for exempting the system of records. *Doe v. FBI,* 718 F. Supp. 90 (D.D.C. 1989), *aff'd in part, rev'd in part*, 936 F.2d 1346 (D.C. Cir. 1991).

9.3. The Specific Exemptions—Subsection (k).

9.3.1. The specific exemptions focus more on the nature of the records in the system of records than on the agency, and are available to any agency.

9.3.2. A properly invoked specific exemption excuses the exempt system of records from compliance with *only* the following requirements of the Act:

9.3.2.1. Access to accounting of disclosures, subsection (c)(3);

9.3.2.2. All access and amendment provisions, subsection (d);

9.3.2.3. Some of the agency record keeping requirements, subsection (e)(1) and (4) (G, H and I); and

9.3.2.4. Some of the rules requiring publication of public notices, subsection (f).

9.3.3. Specific exemption is available for a system of records which falls into one or more of the following seven categories:

9.3.3.1. Subsection (k)(1)—subject to the provisions of § 552(b)(1) (the FOIA's exemption for properly classified information). The Senate report contains this explanation: This section is not intended to provide a blanket exemption to all information systems or files maintained by an agency which deal with national defense and foreign policy information. Many personnel files and other systems may not be subject to security classification or may not cause damage to the national defense or foreign policy simply by permitting the subjects of such files to inspect them and seek changes in their contents under this

Act. S. Rep. No. 93-1183, *supra; Privacy Source Book* at 227; *see also* OMB Guidelines at 28972.

9.3.3.2. Subsection (k)(2)—"investigatory material compiled for law enforcement purposes, other than material within the scope of subsection (j)(2) of this section: Provided, however, that if any individual is denied any right, privilege, or benefit that he would otherwise be entitled by Federal law, or for which he would otherwise be eligible, as a result of the maintenance of such material, such material shall be provided to such individual, except to the extent that the disclosure of such material would reveal the identity of a source who furnished information to the government under an express promise that the identity of the source would be held in confidence, or, prior to the effective date of this section, under an implied promise that the identity of the source would be held in confidence."

9.3.3.2.1. The language "information compiled for the purposes of a criminal investigation" has been held to be narrower than the analogous FOIA language "investigatory records compiled for law enforcement purposes," which was in exemption 7 of the FOIA prior to the 1986 FOIA amendments. *Von Tempske v. HHS,* 2 G.D.S. (P-H), Sec. 82,091 (W.D. Mo. 1981). *See also Greentree v. U.S. Customs Service*, 674 F.2d 74, 75, 89 (D.C. Cir. 1982) (*dictum*). *See* Chapter 10 on Law Enforcement Records.

9.3.3.2.2. The OMB Guidelines at 28973 suggest otherwise.

9.3.3.2.3. In an action seeking amendment of records compiled by the FBI during an investigation pursuant to a statute requiring a "loyalty check" for all federal job applicants, the court refused to hold that all records generated in an employment investigation fall within the law enforcement records exemption, since this would "read (k)(5)...out of the statute." *Vymetalik v. FBI*, 785 F.2d 1090, 1096 (D.C. Cir. 1986).

9.3.3.3. Subsection (k)(3)—maintained in connection with protection of the President and other VIPs accorded special protection by statute;

9.3.3.4. Subsection (k)(4)—"required by statute to be maintained and used solely as statistical records";

9.3.3.5. Subsection (k)(5)—"investigatory material compiled solely for the purpose of determining suitability, eligibility, or qualifications for Federal civilian employment, military service, Federal contracts, or access to classified information, but only to the extent that the disclosure of such material would reveal the identity of a source who furnished information to the Government under an express promise that the identity of the source would be held in confidence, or, prior to the effective date of this section, under an implied promise that the identity of the source would be held in confidence."

9.3.3.5.1. Under this exemption, the agency must segregate and release material which would not identify the source. *Nemetz v. Dep't of Treasury*, 446 F. Supp. 102, 105 (N.D. Ill. 1978); *see also Privacy Source Book* at 860.

9.3.3.5.2. One court has held the content of material exempt even where the source's identity is known to the requester. *Volz v. DOJ*, 619 F.2d 49 (10th Cir. 1980). Another court has suggested the contrary rule. *Doe v. United States Civil Service Comm'n*, 483 F. Supp. at 576-77. *See also Vymetalik v. FBI*, 785 F.2d at 1096 (amendment request is not barred where records have already been disclosed).

9.3.3.5.3. The exemption is not limited to those who gave derogatory information, *Londrigan v. FBI (I)*, 670 F.2d 1164 (D.C. Cir. 1981), and includes the collection of information for continued as well as original employment. *Hernandez v. Alexander*, 671 F.2d at 406.

9.3.3.5.4. Withholding the identities of those giving information does not deny due process, even if the information leads to dismissal. *Hernandez v. Alexander*, 671 F.2d at 407.

9.3.3.5.5. The exemption applies equally to actions for access to records and for correction of records. *See, e.g., Doe v. United States Civil Service Comm'n*, 483 F. Supp. at 577-78.

9.3.3.5.6. A generalized showing based on an affidavit not indicating personal knowledge is insufficient to support exemption, as is the claim that an implied promise can be proved simply by describing those who were interviewed by the FBI. *Londrigan v. FBI (I), supra.*

9.3.3.5.7. Protection under this exemption depends upon whether the information was collected before or after the effective date of the Act. *See Londrigan v. FBI (II)*, 722 F.2d 840, 843 (D.C. Cir. 1983) (exemption shielding informants' identities is "tightly-contained" for post-Act investigations, requiring express promise of confidentiality to warrant exemption; it is "less strict" for investigations antedating the Act, permitting nondisclosure based upon implied promise of confidentiality).

9.3.3.5.8. It is unclear whether this exemption can be used to withhold sources used during the course of making decisions on federal grant applications.

9.3.3.5.9. The D.C. Circuit has ruled that (k)(5) protects the confidentiality of sources involved in awarding federal grants as well as contracts. In *Henke v. Department of*

Commerce, 83 F.3d 1453 (D.C. Cir. 1996), the court agreed that the National Science Foundation could protect the names of peer reviewers who assessed grant proposals. The court concluded that "we find nothing in the record to substantiate the plaintiffs' suggestion that Congress was more concerned with the suitability and qualifications of procurement contract applicants than with those of grant applicants. Indeed, a good argument can be made in support of the reverse proposition: inasmuch as an agency has less day-to-day control over a grantee than it does over a contractor who performs under a procurement contract, the agency has a stronger interest in determining up front that the grant recipient is qualified and competent."

9.3.3.6. Subsection (k)(6)—"testing or examination material used solely to determine individual qualifications for appointment or promotion in the Federal service the disclosure of which would compromise the objectivity or fairness of the testing or examination process";

9.3.3.7. Subsection (k)(7)—"evaluation material used to determine potential for promotion in the armed services, but only to the extent that the disclosure of such material would reveal the identity of a source who furnished information to the Government under an express promise that the identity of the source would be held in confidence, or, prior to the effective date of this section, under an implied promise that the identity of the source would be held in confidence." *See May v. Department of the Air Force*, 800 F.2d 1402, 1403 (5th Cir. 1986) (court ordered handwritten personnel evaluation to be typed or copied by a third party for release, so that material could be disclosed without revealing the identity of the source).

10. Judicial Review of Privacy Act Violations.

10.1. The judicial review provisions of the Privacy Act—subsection (g)—set forth four agency actions over which a federal district court has jurisdiction: refusal to grant access; refusal to amend or correct a record; failure to maintain a record with accuracy, relevance, timeliness or completeness; and failure to comply with any other provision of the Act. While these four subsections have much in common, there are also important differences among them.

10.2. Rules applicable to all Privacy Act actions.

10.2.1 Venue is proper where the plaintiff resides, or has a principal place of business, or where the records are situated, or in the District of Columbia. Subsection (g)(5).

10.2.2. The remedies of the Privacy Act are not retroactive. *Ibid. But see* discussion of "record," *supra*.

10.2.3. Administrative remedies must be exhausted both in access cases and in correction cases, *Nagel v. HEW*, 725 F.2d at 1441; *Dickson v. OPM,* 828 F.2d 32 (D.C. Cir. 1987); but not where an individual seeks damages pursuant to subsection (g)(4). *Nagel*, 725 F.2d at 1441 n.2; *see also Haase v. Sessions,* 893 F.2d 370 (D.C. Cir. 1990); *Diederich v. Department of the Army,* 878 F.2d 646 (2d Cir. 1989) (where statute does not require exhaustion, courts will not read an exhaustion obligation into the law).

10.2.4. The private right of civil action created by the Privacy Act is specifically limited to actions against *agencies of the United States Government.*

10.2.4.1. The civil remedy provisions of the statute do not apply against private individuals, *Bruce v. United States*, 621 F.2d 914, 916 n.2 (8th Cir. 1980); state agencies, *St. Michael's Convalescent Hospital*, 643 F.2d at 1373; private entities, *Irwin Memorial Blood Bank v. American Nat'l Red Cross*, 640 F.2d 1051, 1057-58 (9th Cir. 1981) (American National Red Cross) and *United States v. Miller*, 643 F.2d at 715 n.1 (national banks); or state and local officials, *Polchowski v. Gorris*, 714 F.2d 749, 752 (7th Cir. 1983). *See also Unt v. Aerospace Corp.*, 765 F.2d at 1448 ("mere fact that [private corporation] receives funding and is regulated to some extent by the federal government does not bring it within the reaches of the Act").

10.2.4.2. Only the agency is a proper defendant; an individual official or employee is not. *Brown-Bey v. United States*, 720 F.2d 467, 469 (7th Cir. 1983); *Windsor v. The Tennessean*, 719 F.2d 155, 160 (6th Cir. 1983); *Wren v. Harris*, 675 F.2d 1144, 1148 n.8 (10th Cir. 1982); *Bruce v. United States*, 621 F.2d at 916 n.2; *Parks v. IRS*, 618 F.2d 677, 684 (10th Cir. 1980).

10.2.4.3. A district court judge found the *Feres* doctrine—which prohibits service personnel from suing the military for injuries sustained while on duty—prohibited a female Navy aviator from suing for an alleged improper disclosure of her personnel evaluation report. *Cummings v. Department of the Navy*, 116 F. Supp. 2d 76 (D.D.C. 2000). However, the D.C. Circuit reversed the decision. *Cummings v. Department of the Navy*, 279 F.3d 1051 (D.C. Cir. 2002).

10.2.5. There is a statute of limitations requiring that an action be brought within two years from the date on which the cause of action arose, or within two years after the discovery of a willful misrepresentation by the agency that is material to its liability. Subsection (g)(5). *See Diliberti v. United States*, 817 F.2d 1259, 1262-64 (7th Cir. 1987) (failure to file within statute of limitations is jurisdictional, thus untimely filing deprives federal courts of subject matter jurisdiction). *Accord Tijerina v. Walters*, 821 F.2d 789, 797 (D.C. Cir. 1987); *Akutowicz v. United States,* 859 F.2d 1122 (2d Cir. 1988). *See also Englerius v. Veterans Administration,* 837 F.2d 895 (9th Cir. 1988) (statute of limitations begins to run when plaintiff knows or had reason to know of violation); *Bowyer v. Department of the Air Force,* 875 F.2d 632 (7th Cir. 1989) (same); *Bergman v. United States*, 751 F.2d 314, 317 (10th Cir. 1984) (rejecting argument that new cause of action arose upon each and every subsequent adverse determination based upon the same erroneous records that plaintiff failed for five years to challenge in court); *Jarrell v. U.S. Postal Service*, 753 F.2d 1088, 1092 (D.C. Cir. 1985) (summary judgment inappropriate where issue of fact as to when cause of action arose). (The statute of limitations under the FOIA is six years.)

10.3. Actions for refusal of access to records.

10.3.1. The court has authority to enjoin the agency from withholding the documents and to order them produced. Subsection (g)(1) and (3)(A).

10.3.2 The court may examine the documents *in camera*, and shall determine the matter *de novo*. The burden of proof is on the agency. *Id.*

10.3.3. No proof of actual injury is required.

10.3.4. The D.C. Circuit has indicated that the level of detail required to state a claim alleging a Privacy Act violation is minimal. Reversing a district court ruling that the plaintiff had failed to show what records the agency had improperly disclosed, the appeals court noted that "the complaint claimed that 'records' concerning [the plaintiff] were wrongfully disclosed, which necessarily means that information in records had been revealed. Nothing more was required to survive a motion to dismiss for failure to state a claim." *Kreiger v. Fadely*, 211 F.3d 134 (D.C. Cir. 2000).

10.4. Actions for refusal to correct or amend a record.

10.4.1. The court has power to order the correction or amendment as requested or to fashion other appropriate relief, including expungement. Subsection (g)(2)(A).

10.4.2. The court shall examine the matter *de novo*. *Id.* Although a *de novo* determination of an amendment request is required, the Privacy Act "does not contemplate that a court will constitute itself as a personnel rating authority to substitute its judgment for the evaluation of performance conducted by a government employee's superior." *Hewitt v. Grabicki*, 794 F.2d 1373, 1378 (9th Cir. 1986). "The trial court should, however, carefully review the record to eliminate clear mistakes of fact, inaccurate opinions based solely upon such erroneous facts, and plainly irresponsible judgments of performance or character." *Id., citing R.R. v. Department of the Army*, 482 F. Supp. at 773-74. The agency must initially make a determination as to its records' accuracy and then the district court "must put itself in the agency's place and ask if the records in question satisfy the Privacy Act's requirement of accuracy." *Doe v. United States*, 821 F.2d at 698.

10.4.3. The burden of proof is on the plaintiff. *Mervin v. FTC*, 591 F.2d 821, 827 (D.C. Cir. 1978); OMB Guidelines at 28969.

10.4.4. No provision for an award for damages is made. *Thurston v. United States*, 810 F.2d 438, 447 (4th Cir. 1987).

10.4.5. Courts have consistently indicated the Privacy Act cannot be used as an alternative to statutory grievance procedures, such as those contained in the Civil Service Reform Act. The Ninth Circuit has noted that allowing plaintiffs to attack employment decisions under the Privacy Act would frustrate "Congress's decision to assign to the [Office of Special Counsel] the task of policing alleged prohibited personnel practices. A disgruntled federal employee would need only to argue that her employer failed to comply with the Privacy Act to obtain judicial review of an employment decision." *Houlihan v. OPM,* 909 F.2d 383 (9th Cir. 1990); *see also Stephens v. HHS*, 901 F.2d 1571 (11th Cir. 1990).

10.4.5.1. While an action to correct derogatory employment files (by expunging them) may be useful in contesting the firing of, or failure to promote, a federal employee, a court may properly postpone such Privacy Act claims until the appeal from the firing is heard. *White v. Civil Service Comm'n*, 589 F.2d at 715-19.

10.4.5.2. The D.C. Circuit refused to allow amendment of military records to show a different assignment. The court noted that "choosing to seek amendment of his records under the Privacy Act, before the Army Privacy Review Board, rather than proceeding before the Correction Board, is inconsistent with the heightened deference Congress intended the courts to accord determinations of the Correction Board." *Cargill v. Marsh,* 902 F.2d 1006 (D.C. Cir. 1990).

10.4.5.3. The D.C. Circuit has ruled that a former agency employee was essentially using the Privacy Act as a substitute for CSRA relief when he asked the agency to change his job description to better reflect his actual duties while at the agency. The court noted that "this seems to us a distinction without a difference.... Were Kleiman successful, the agency either would have to amend the forms to state he actually had been employed as a Program Analyst, or place another document in his file stating that, in the government's view, the unamended forms were erroneous. Either way, Kleiman would have achieved the same impermissible result—a collateral attack on the original personnel decision, bypassing the 'exhaustive remedial scheme provided by Congress' in the CSRA." *Kleiman v. DOE*, 956 F.2d 335, 338 (D.C. Cir. 1992).

10.4.6. A judge cannot review sensitive agency claims by employing admission of classified affidavits or an *in camera* hearing with government personnel, without providing the plaintiff an adequate opportunity to rebut such evidence. *Strang v. U.S. Arms Control and Disarmament Agency,* 920 F.2d 30, 32 (D.C. Cir. 1990). The court specifically indicated the judge should "receive evidence from both sides." The court also remanded the case so the lower court could assess claims that the plaintiff was "justifiably ignorant" of agency procedural requirements and that "her state of mind should be reflected in the agency's records."

10.5. Actions for violation of the standard of "accurate, relevant, timely or complete"—subsection (g)(1)(C).

10.5.1. The subsection allows action for damages where an agency fails: ...to maintain any record concerning any individual with such accuracy, relevance, timeliness and completeness as is necessary to assure fairness in any determination relating to...the individual that may be made on the basis of such record, and consequently a determination is made which is adverse to the individual.

10.5.2. Perfect records are not required, and agencies are not strictly liable for inaccuracies. Subsection (g)(1)(C) must be read together with subsection (e)(5); reasonableness is the standard. *DeBold v. Stimson*, 735 F.2d 1037, 1041 (7th Cir. 1984); *Edison v. Department of the Army*, 672 F.2d 840, 843 (11th Cir. 1982); *Smiertka v. Dep't of Treasury*, 447 F. Supp. at 225.

10.5.3. Actions under this subsection and subsection (g)(4) damage suits, unlike actions to amend, do not require *de novo* review. *White v. OPM*, 787 F.2d 660, 663 (D.C. Cir. 1986) ("This inquiry is necessarily distinct from any undertaken by the agency—no damage claim can be brought directly against the agency—but it is not *de novo* review.").

10.5.4. The D.C. Circuit has held that an action lies under subsection (g)(1)(C) against an agency which creates and disseminates inaccurate records to another agency, which then makes an adverse determination based on the records. *See Dickson v. OPM,* 828 F.2d 32 (D.C. Cir. 1987). The court distinguished *Perry v. FBI,* 759 F.2d at 1275, which held that such an action could not be brought under § (e)(5). The lesson of these cases is to make certain to plead a violation under subsection (g)(1)(C) in any situation where the agency creating and disseminating the records is *not* the same agency that actually used the records.

10.5.5. Unlike actions to redress refusal of access or amendment, these actions require a showing of adverse effect to the plaintiff.

10.5.5.1. However, "adverse effect" has been interpreted as less severe a requirement than many of the Supreme Court's more restrictive standing decisions. *See Parks v. IRS, supra. See also Usher v. Secretary of Health and Human Services*, 721 F.2d at 856. *But see Harper v. United States*, 423 F. Supp. at 192, 196-97.

10.5.5.2. The plaintiff must prove that the adverse effect was proximately caused by the violation of the Privacy Act. *See Edison v. Department of the Army*, 672 F.2d at 842, 845.

10.5.6. In addition, a plaintiff under this subsection must show, to obtain damages, that the agency's action was "intentional and willful." Subsection (g)(4).

10.5.6.1. The Analysis of Compromise Amendments explains the meaning of "intentional or willful" as follows: In a suit for damages, the amendment reflects a belief that a finding of willful, arbitrary or capricious action is too harsh a standard of proof for an individual to exercise the rights granted by this legislation. Thus the standard for recovery of damages was reduced to "willful or intentional" action by an agency. On a continuum between negligence and the very high standard of willful, arbitrary or capricious conduct, this standard is viewed as only somewhat greater than gross negligence. *Privacy Source Book* at 862.

10.5.6.2. The courts have struggled to ascertain what "somewhat greater than negligence" means. While no hard and fast rules have been agreed on, there is a consensus that the plaintiff need not prove "premeditated malice" to prevail, and that reckless or conscious disregard for the plaintiff's Privacy Act rights is sufficient for damages. On the other hand, mere carelessness or sloppiness is not sufficient. *See generally Laningham v. U.S. Navy*, 813 F.2d 1236, 1242 (D.C. Cir. 1987); *Albright v. United States (II)*, 732 F.2d 181, 189-90 (D.C. Cir. 1984); *Edison v. Department of the Army*, 672 F.2d at 846. *See also Andrews v. VA*, 838 F.2d 418, 425 (10th Cir. 1988) (action must, at minimum, constitute "reckless behavior"); *Waters v. Thornburgh,* 888 F.2d 870 (D.C. Cir. 1989); *Doe v. FBI,* 718 F. Supp. 90 (D.D.C. 1989) (finding that "sloppiness was not intentional and willful"); *Rose v. United States,* 905 F.2d 1257 (9th Cir. 1990) (Postal Service's failure to provide employee with appropriate worker's compensation forms may have been negligent, but does not meet willful and intentional standard); *Dickson v. OPM,* No. 83-3503 (D.D.C. Aug. 27, 1991) (failure of OPM officials to follow internal guidelines in handling Dickson's file is not enough to show willfulness); *but see Covert v. Herrington,* 876 F.2d 751 (9th Cir. 1989). *See also Connelly v. Comptroller of the Currency,* No. 4-84-3783, slip. op. at 32 (S.D Tex., June 3, 1991) (judge ruled that an agency employee evaluating a candidate's credentials for becoming president of a newly chartered bank had "maintained and restricted his examination to a minimal record that violated the standard of fairness required by the Privacy Act").

10.5.6.3. Some courts have found it appropriate in Privacy Act cases to rule on issues of intent and motive at the summary judgment stage, rather than to leave these issues for trial. *See, e.g., Hill v. U.S. Air Force*, 795 F.2d 1067, 1070 (D.C. Cir. 1986); *Moskiewiez v. Department of Agriculture*, 791 F.2d 561, 566 (7th Cir. 1986). But some cases have indicated that questions of whether actions were "intentional or willful" should be resolved in a trial, if there are disputed issues of fact. *Waters v. Thornburgh, supra.*

10.5.7. Injunctive relief is not available to remedy violations of subsection (g)(1)(C).

10.5.8. Damages may not be available under this standard after the time at which an agency has volunteered, after criticism, to destroy the records. *Albright v. United States (I)*, 631 F.2d at 921. At minimum, actions taken after the Privacy Act violation—either to rectify or compound the violation—can be taken into consideration in determining whether the violation was intentional or willful. *Waters v. Thornburgh, supra.*

10.5.9. "Actual damages sustained" under subsection (g)(4)(A) has been narrowly interpreted by some courts to include only out-of-pocket expenses, not mental suffering. *Fitzpatrick v. IRS, supra; Albright v. United States*, 558 F. Supp. 260 (D.D.C. 1982). *But see Johnson v. Dep't of Treasury*, 700 F.2d 971 (5th Cir. 1983) ("actual damages" include damages for physical and mental injury for which there is competent evidence, as well as out-of-pocket expenses). In any event, the alleged violation of the Act must *cause* the damages complained of. *Molerio v. FBI*, 749 F.2d 815, 826 (D.C. Cir. 1984), *citing Albright v. United States (II)*, 732 F.2d at 186.

10.6. Actions for Violation of any other Provisions of the Act.—Subsection (g)(1)(D).

10.6.1. This sort of action also requires a showing of adverse effect, and that the agency acted intentionally and willfully (see discussion *supra*) to support an award of damages. Damages are not less than $1000. Subsection (g)(4)(A). For example, the Ninth Circuit found the actions of an administrative judge, in disclosing that a staff attorney had previously been criticized for his productivity although the criticism was later ordered removed from the agency's records, was a willful and intentional disclosure under Privacy Act standards. The court noted that "the ALJ disclosed the information regarding the [performance improvement plan] without any ground for believing it to be lawful and in flagrant disregard of the rights of [the plaintiff] under the Privacy Act." *Wilborn v. HHS*, 49 F.3d 597 (9th Cir. 1995).

10.6.2. With adequate showing of causation, emotional trauma alone is sufficient to qualify as an "adverse effect" under subsection (g)(1)(D). *Albright v. United States (II)*, 732 F.2d at 186. In such circumstances, the court would "consider the extent to which non-economic injuries or damages other than out-of-pocket expenses could qualify as 'actual damages'" under § (g)(4). *Id.* For example, in *Henson v. NASA*, 14 F.3d 1143 (6th Cir. 1994) a supervisor had required a staff doctor to brief employees on the medical condition of a returning employee. The information was disclosed from her worker's compensation file and the Sixth Circuit found that it had been disclosed to persons who had no need to know the information. In finding for the plaintiff, the court noted that "Henson has presented a motive for [her supervisor] to intentionally divulge private information—retaliation for contradicting him about asbestos problems at the Lewis Research Center. In addition, [the doctor's] affidavit stated that [the supervisor] compelled him, against his own wishes, to discuss privileged medical information contained in Henson's worker's compensation file. Henson does not need to prove damages because the Act provides for a statutory minimum of $1000."

10.6.3. A single violation of the Privacy Act will be counted as one violation for purposes of awarding the $1,000 statutory minimum. For instance, although a letter was sent in violation of the Privacy Act to 4,500 agents of the Bureau of Alcohol, Tobacco and Firearms, it constituted a single violation. *See Tomasello v. Rubin*, 167 F.3d 612 (D.C. Cir. 1999).

10.6.4. The Privacy Act does not specifically authorize remedies other than damages for violations in actions under subsection (g)(1)(D), and courts have held that injunctive relief is not available unless specifically authorized under the Act. *See, e.g., Doe v. Stephens,* 851 F.2d 1457, 1463 (D.C. Cir. 1988) ("Act does not authorize entry of injunctive relief requiring return of the medical records to Doe, exclusion of information from the grand jury, or a ban on disclosure by the U.S. Attorney and his staff."). *See also Hastings v. Judicial Conference of the United States*, 770 F.2d at 1104; *Clarkson v. IRS,* 678 F.2d at 1375 n.11.

10.6.5. The damages action, like the correction action, can be useful in litigating the actual cause of a federal employee's termination, but relief under the Privacy Act is limited to the remedies specifically stated in the statute. *Edison v. Department of the Army*, 672 F.2d at 845-47. *See also Hubbard v. EPA*, 809

F.2d 1 (D.C. Cir. 1986) (Privacy Act claims cannot be used to remedy personnel management decisions). Employment, promotion, and transfer, for example, cannot be ordered.

10.6.6. The Privacy Act does not preempt relief under the Federal Tort Claims Act or applicable state statutes. The Third Circuit allowed a suit under FTCA and the Pennsylvania Mental Health Procedures Act to continue after concluding that "it is evident that Congress did not intend, by enacting the Privacy Act, to limit the privacy rights of individuals, nor did it intend to limit their remedies for invasions of those privacy interests." *O'Donnell v. United States,* 891 F.2d 1079 (3d Cir. 1989). *But see Mittleman v. Dep't of Treasury,* 773 F. Supp. 442, 454 (D.D.C. 1991) ("The Privacy Act provides a comprehensive scheme for addressing plaintiff's concerns about the inaccuracy of the records and about disclosure of them to third parties. In establishing the Privacy Act, Congress has undertaken to balance the individual interests of the subjects with the interest in protecting certain records and assuring an efficient government....[T]he court concludes that plaintiff's constitutional claims regarding her records and any disclosures by defendants about those records are barred."). *See also Williams v. Department of Veterans Affairs*, 879 F. Supp. 578 (E.D. Va. 1995).

10.7. Attorney Fees and Costs.

10.7.1. In all Privacy Act actions, the plaintiff who has "substantially prevailed" may, in the discretion of the court, be awarded reasonable attorney fees as well as costs, subsection (g)(3)(B). This means that in actions under subsections (g)(1)(C) and (g)(1)(D) the plaintiff must prove intentional or willful conduct in order to obtain attorney fees. *See Haase v. Sessions,* 893 F.2d 370 (D.C. Cir. 1990) (barring plaintiff from recovering attorney fees in a subsection (e)(7) case because plaintiff did not prove intentional or willful action). However, the Supreme Court's decision in *Buckhannon Bd. & Care Home, Inc. v. W. Va. Dep't of Health & Human Resources*, 532 U.S. 598 (2001), which establishes a narrow rule of interpretations for the term "prevail," has already been found to apply to FOIA (*see Oil, Chem & Atomic Workers Union v. DOE*, 288 F.3d 452, (D.C. Cir. 2002)) and most certainly applies to Privacy Act cases as well. See discussion in Chapter 17 on Attorney Fees.

10.7.2. This fee power does not extend to authorizing fees for administrative proceedings under the Privacy Act. *Kennedy v. Andrus*, 459 F. Supp. 240 (D.D.C. 1978).

10.7.3. Criteria for fee awards.

10.7.3.1. The statutory language is the same as that of the attorney fees provision of the FOIA, and the criteria for awarding fees, at least in a records access case, have been held to be the same. *Barrett v. Bureau of Customs*, 651 F.2d 1087, 1088 (5th Cir. 1981). They are: 1. the benefit to the public deriving from the case; 2. the commercial benefit to the complainant; 3. the nature of complainant's interest in the records sought; and 4. whether the government's withholding had a reasonable basis in law.

10.7.3.2. The D.C. Circuit has ruled, in *Blazy v. Tenet*, 194 F.3d 90 (D.C. Cir. 1999), that the four-factor criteria for an award of attorney's fees under FOIA does not apply in a Privacy Act case because the purpose of the Privacy Act is to vindicate a private right while FOIA focuses on benefits to a larger public.

10.7.3.3. The Eleventh Circuit has held that a more general twelve-part test is applicable in a damages case, and has required a detailed explanation of a fee award from a district court. *Fitzpatrick v. IRS*, 665 F.2d at 331-33.

10.7.4. A union may not recover above-cost fees for the services of its salaried lawyers to a member pursuant to a group legal plan. *National Treasury Employees Union v. Dep't of Treasury*, 656 F.2d 848 (D.C. Cir. 1981).

10.7.5. A *pro se* attorney litigant is entitled to fees. *Cazalas v. DOJ*, 709 F.2d 1051, 1057 & n.3 (5th Cir. 1983). However, such an award is almost certainly no longer available after the Supreme Court's decision in *Kay v. Ehrler*, 499 U.S. 432 (1991).

11. Social Security Numbers.

11.1. A federal, state or local government agency may not deny an individual a right, benefit, or privilege because such individual refuses to disclose his or her Social Security Number. (Pub. L. 93-579, Section 7; 5 U.S.C. § 552a note) unless disclosure is required by federal statute, or disclosure was required under any federal, state or local statute or regulation adopted *prior* to January 1, 1975, to verify the identity of an individual.

11.1.1. Requiring welfare recipients to obtain and provide SSNs of children does not violate the Privacy Act because it is required by federal statute. *McElrath v. Califano*, 615 F.2d 434 (7th Cir. 1980); *Green v. Philbrook*, 576 F.2d 440 (2d Cir. 1978).

11.1.2. An attack on requirements of SSNs to measure eligibility for SSI was rejected on the ground that the practice is authorized by statute. *Tierney v. Schweiker*, 718 F.2d 449 (D.C. Cir. 1983).

11.2. The Tax Reform Act of 1976, Pub. L. 94-455, Section 1211, 42 U.S.C. § 405(c)(2)(C), allows a state or political subdivision to require the disclosure of SSNs to establish the identity of any person affected by

11.2.1. Any tax law (*see also* 26 U.S.C. § 7852);

11.2.2. Any general public assistance law;

11.2.3. Any drivers license law; or,

11.2.4. Any motor vehicle registration law. State coercion of the SSN in administering refunds of traffic fines may not come within these last two exceptions. *Doyle v. Wilson*, 529 F. Supp. 1343, 1348-50 (D. Del. 1982) (*dictum*).

11.3. In requesting SSNs, any federal, state and local government agency must inform the individual, Pub. L. 93-579, Section 7(b), concerning:

11.3.1. Whether disclosure is mandatory or voluntary;

11.3.2. The authority for soliciting the SSN; and

11.3.3. The uses to be made of the SSN.

11.4. The Fourth Circuit has held that the use of Social Security Numbers as a condition for voting is impermissible under both the Privacy Act and the Constitution. *Greidinger v. Davis*, 988 F.2d 1344 (4th Cir. 1993), *rev'g*, 782 F. Supp. 1106 (E.D. Va. 1992) (plaintiff's "fundamental right to vote is substantially burdened to the extent the statutes at issue permit disclosure of his SSN").

11.4.1. Two cases challenging the use of Social Security numbers for voter registration purposes were decided differently based on when the state first required the collection. In Louisiana, the court struck down the use of an SSN for registration purposes because the requirement post-dated January 1, 1975. *See McKay v. Fowler*, No. 97-3127, 1997 WL 266717 (E.D. La. May 16, 1997). By contrast, in Tennessee, the court upheld the collection requirement because it pre-dated January 1, 1975. *See McKay v. Thompson*, 226 F.3d 752 (6th Cir. 2000).

11.5. President Franklin Roosevelt's Executive Order No. 9397, authorizing the widespread use of SSNs as identifiers, has been held for these purposes to be the equivalent of a federal regulation. *Brookens v. United States*, 627 F.2d 494 (D.C. Cir. 1980).

11.6. *See also Alcaraz v. Block*, 746 F.2d 593 (9th Cir. 1984) (standard for required notice when requesting SSNs); *Doe v. Sharp*, 491 F. Supp. 346 (D. Mass. 1980); *Greater Cleveland Welfare Rights Org. v. Bauer*, 462 F. Supp. 1313 (N.D. Ohio 1978); *Chambers v. Klein*, 419 F. Supp. 569 (D.N.J. 1976), *aff'd in part*, 564 F.2d 89 (3d Cir. 1977).

11.7. A district court in New Jersey concluded that Rutgers University, part of the state university system, was not an "agency" for purposes of Section 7 of the Privacy Act and thus was not subject to liability for any violation of that section. *Krebbs v. Rutgers*, 797 F. Supp. 1246 (D.N.J. 1992). *But see Robert Doe, a/k/a Virginia Privacy Litigation v. Herman*, 1999 US Dist LEXIS 17302 (W.D. Va, Oct. 29, 1999), where the court found the Labor Department's practice of including SSNs on Black Lung hearing schedules violated Section 7.

12. Miscellaneous Provisions.

12.1. Criminal Penalties.

12.1.1. Any agency employee who willfully does either of the following is punishable as a misdemeanant and can be fined up to $5000:

12.1.1.1. Makes a disclosure knowing it to be in violation of the Act. § 552a(i)(1); or

12.1.1.2. Maintains a system of records without meeting the notice requirements of subsection (e)(4). § 552a(i)(2).

12.1.2. Any person who knowingly and willfully requests or obtains a record concerning an individual from an agency under false pretenses can be punished similarly. § 552a(i)(3).

12.2. Mailing Lists. An individual's name and address may not be sold or rented by an agency unless such action is specifically authorized by law. This provision shall not be construed to require the withholding of names and addresses otherwise permitted to be made public. § 552a(n).

12.3. Biannual reports. Biannual reports are required to be made by the President to the Congress, listing separately for each agency the number of records in any system exempted by the agencies, the reasons therefore, and "such other information as indicates efforts to administer fully" the Act. § 552a(p).

12.4. Records transferred to the National Archives are exempt from all provisions of the Act except those relating to notice in the Federal Register and to the behavior of agency employees. § 552a(l).

13. The Computer Matching and Privacy Protection Act of 1988.

13.1. In 1988, Congress amended the Privacy Act to regulate the computerized matching of personal information that is covered by the Privacy Act. H. Rep. No. 802, 100th Cong., 2d Sess. 1 (House Committee on Government Operations). For more legislative history information, *see* Appendix B, Legislative History of the Privacy Act.

13.2. The Computer Matching and Privacy Protection Act of 1988 (P.L. 100-503) requires federal agencies that disclose computerized records containing personal information to follow certain procedures intended to give individuals greater protection in the form of notice and appeal rights and to create an oversight mechanism to ensure agency compliance. H. Rep. No. 802 at 1-2. Congress intended the amendment to clarify that computer matching is covered by the Privacy Act and that agencies engaged in matching activities may no longer rely solely on the "routine use" exemption to authorize matches. *Id.* at pp. 21-22.

13.2.1. The first computer matching program, "Project Match," was instituted in 1977 to detect federal employees who were illegally receiving welfare. Proponents of the matching program claimed that matching was justified under the Privacy Act's "routine use" exemption which authorizes the disclosure of records for a purpose compatible with the purpose for which it was originally collected. Detecting waste, fraud and abuse in government programs, they argued, was a legitimate government purpose and thus compatible with the original purpose for which records were collected.

13.2.2. Opponents of computer matching criticized the disclosures as violations of the Privacy Act's basic principle that information collected for one purpose should not be used for a different purpose without the individuals consent. Opponents claimed that the "routine use" exemption could not be invoked to authorize matching because Congress intended the exemption to apply only to "housekeeping measures and necessarily frequent" interagency transfers of information. The proponents prevailed and matching programs proliferated. *Id.* at p. 5.

13.3. The Computer Matching Act does not erect substantive barriers to matching, but it mandates a series of procedures that agencies must comply with if the matching programs involve information contained in a "system of records," as defined by the Privacy Act.

13.3.1. Such matching programs must be established by means of matching agreements entered into by both the source and the recipient agency, including matches between a federal and state agency or a federal agency and a private entity. § 552a(o). The agreements must be approved by Data Integrity Boards established in each agency. § 552a(u).

13.3.2. Under the Act's definition of "matching program," the following matches are excluded from the scope of the Act: any match not involving federal records; matches performed to support research or statistical activities if the results of the match are not used to make decisions concerning the rights, benefits or privileges of specified individuals; matches performed by agencies that perform as its principal function the enforcement of criminal laws, but only those performed subsequent to the initiation of an investigation of a specific person; certain matches conducted by the IRS; internal agency matching activities if not used for the purpose of taking any adverse action against a federal employee; and matches performed for background checks for security clearances of federal personnel or for foreign counterintelligence purposes. § 552a(a).

13.3.3. No agency may disclose information for use in a matching program except pursuant to a written matching agreement that specifies the purpose, legal authority and cost-benefit justification for the match, including a detailed description of the program. § 552a(o)(1)(A-C).

13.3.4. Affected individuals must be given actual written notice that information they divulge may be subject to verification and disclosure through matching programs. § 552a(o)(1)(D). Agencies must agree that records will not be redisclosed or duplicated and the recipient agency must agree to destroy or return records received for the match. § 552a(o)(1)(F,H). Matching agreements must be made available to the public on request and must be provided to Congress. § 552a(o)(2)(A).

13.4. Each federal agency involved in a matching must establish a Data Integrity Board, composed of senior agency officials, to oversee and implement the Computer Matching Act. 552a(u)(1-2).

13.4.1. The Board's function is to review, and approve or disapprove, all matching agreements, and provide a cost-benefit analysis of each program. § 552a(u)(3). The Board must oversee matching programs and provide the agency with guidance in interpreting the law. § 552a(u)(3)(F).

13.4.2. The Board must submit an annual report to the agency head. *Id.* OMB must then consolidate the reports and submit them to the appropriate Congressional committees. § 552a(u)(6).

13.4.3. A Board's disapproval of a matching program may be appealed to OMB for review. § 552a(u)(5).

13.5. A crucial protection in the Computer Matching Act provides that no agency may suspend, terminate, deny or reduce an individual's benefits on the basis of a match until the agency independently verifies the information. § 552a(p). After information is verified, no adverse action may be taken until the individual is given 30 days notice of the match results and an opportunity to contest the results. § 552a(p)(2)(D).

13.5.1. The Computer Matching and Privacy Protection Amendments of 1990 created an alternative to independent verification. Independent verification is no longer necessary if the Data Integrity Board of the recipient agency or, in the case of a non-federal agency, the Board of the source agency determines that (1) the information is limited to identification and amount paid by the source agency under a federal benefits program, and (2) there is a high degree of confidence that the information provided to the recipient agency is accurate. The amendment also changed the 30-day notice provision by substituting the time established for the program at issue by statute or regulation. If no time period is provided by statute or regulation, a 30-day notice period would be provided.

13.6. However, the Act does not make available any remedy (i.e., injunctive relief or damages) other than those which are already provided by the terms of the Privacy Act.

13.7. The Act became effective July 19, 1989, nine months after it became law. The Act required OMB to develop guidelines and regulations by June 19, 1989 for agencies to use in implementing the Act. *See* "Final Guidance Interpreting the Provisions of Public Law 100-503, the Computer Matching and Privacy Protection Act of 1988," 54 Fed. Reg. 25,818 (1989).

CHAPTER 23
Government in the Sunshine Act
Eleanor H. Smith

1. Introduction.

1.1. The Government in the Sunshine Act ("Sunshine Act"), Pub. L. 94-409, 90 Stat. 1241, was enacted on September 13, 1976, and became effective on March 12, 1977. The Act is codified at 5 U.S.C. § 552b. In 1995 Congress amended the Sunshine Act. Pub. L. 104-66, § 3002, Dec. 21, 1995, 109 Stat. 734.

1.2. "Congress enacted the Sunshine Act to open the deliberations of multi-member federal agencies to public view." *Common Cause v. Nuclear Regulatory Comm'n*, 674 F.2d 921, 928 (D.C. Cir. 1982); *see also Clark-Cowlitz Joint Operating Agency v. FERC*, 798 F.2d 499, 501 (D.C. Cir. 1986).

2. Legislative History.

2.1. The initial legislative history of the Sunshine Act is collected in *Government in the Sunshine Source Book: Legislative History, Texts, and other Documents*, Committees on Government Operations, U.S. Senate and House of Representatives, 94th Cong., 2d Sess. (1976) (hereafter "*Sunshine Source Book*").

2.2. The Sunshine Act is "founded on the proposition that the government should conduct the public's business in public." S. Rep. No. 354, 94th Cong., 1st Sess. 1, *reprinted in Sunshine Source Book*, at 196; *see also* Conf. Rep. No. 1178, 94th Cong., 2d Sess. 9 (1976), *reprinted in* 1976 U.S. Code Cong. & Admin. News 2183, 2245, *Sunshine Source Book* at 791.

2.3. Congress intended the Sunshine Act to "enhance greatly" public access to and understanding of government decision-making beyond that offered by the Freedom of Information Act ("FOIA"). S. Rep. No. 354 at 5, *reprinted in Sunshine Source Book* at 200. "Documents disclosed under the FOIA represent a record of what has already transpired. Yet up to now the public has not had a full opportunity to learn how or why government official[s] make the important policy decisions which they do. All too often the meetings at which such decisions are made are closed to the public. Interested persons must content themselves with elementary minutes, or background papers tangentially related to the official agenda. Formal statements in support of agency actions are frequently too brief, or too general, to fully explain the Commission's reasoning, or the compromises that were made. As a result, the public may not understand the reasons an agency has acted in a certain way, or even what exactly it has decided to do. By requiring important decisions to be made openly, this bill will create better understanding of agency decisions." *Id.*

3. What is an "Agency" for Purposes of the Sunshine Act?

3.1. Section 552b(a)(1) states that, for purposes of the Sunshine Act, the term "agency" means any agency, as defined in section 552(e) of this title, headed by a collegial body composed of two or more individual members, a majority of whom are appointed to such position by the President with the advice and consent of the Senate, and any subdivision thereof authorized to act on behalf of the agency. § 552b(a). Section

552(e) of Title 5, redesignated § 552(f) by P.L. 99-570, provides the definition of "agency" for the Freedom of Information Act. § 552(f). For a recent analysis of "agency," see *Energy Research Foundation v. Defense Nuclear Facilities Safety Board,* 917 F.2d 581 (D.C. Cir. 1990), in which the D.C. Circuit applied the Sunshine Act to the defendant board.

3.2. The Sunshine Act "is not concerned with an agency in the broad sense of that word." *Symons v. Chrysler Corporation Loan Guarantee Board*, 670 F.2d 238, 243 (D.C. Cir. 1981), quoting *Hunt v. NRC*, 611 F.2d 332, 336 n.2 (10th Cir. 1979), *cert. denied*, 445 U.S. 906 (1980).

3.3. The Sunshine Act applies only to an agency which is (1) subject to the FOIA, and (2) headed by a body of two or more members, (a) a majority of whom are chosen by the President, (b) with the advice and consent of the Senate. § 552b(a)(1); H.R. Rep. No. 880(part 1), 94th Cong., 2d Sess. 3 (1976), *reprinted in* 1976 U.S. Code Cong. & Admin. News at 2185, *Sunshine Source Book* at 514; S. Rep. No. 354 at 10, *reprinted in Sunshine Source Book* at 205. Lists of agencies that Congress intended to be covered by the Sunshine Act appear in the legislative history to the Act. H.R. Rep. No. 880 (part 1) at 12-14, *reprinted in* 1976 U.S. Code Cong. & Admin. News at 2193-96, *Sunshine Source Book* at 562-64; S. Rep. No. 354, at 15-16, *reprinted in Sunshine Source Book* at 210-11.

3.4. If an agency is not subject to the FOIA, then it is not subject to the Sunshine Act. *Rushforth v. Council of Economic Advisors*, 762 F.2d 1038, 1044 (D.C. Cir. 1985).

3.5. The Sunshine Act applies only to an agency headed by a collegial body.

3.5.1. The Senate Report explains: Multi-headed agencies operate on the principle of give-and-take discussion between agency heads. There is a tradition of public dissent; though the agency takes a final action, it does not necessarily speak with one voice. The agency heads are high public officials, having been selected and confirmed through a process very different from that used for staff members. Their deliberative process can be appropriately exposed to public scrutiny in order to give citizens an awareness of the process and rationale of decision-making. S. Rep. No. 354 at 17, *reprinted in Sunshine Source Book* at 212.

3.5.2. An agency is subject to the Sunshine Act although the day-to-day management of the agency may be under the authority of a single individual, rather than the collegial body that governs the agency. Conf. Rep. No. 1178, 94th Cong., 2d Sess. at 10 (1976), *reprinted in* 1976 U.S. Code Cong. & Admin. News 2246, *Sunshine Source Book* at 792; *see also* H.R. Rep. No. 880 (part 1), at 7-8, *reprinted in Sunshine Source Book* at 518-19; S. Rep. No. 354 at 15, *reprinted in Source Book* at 210. The U.S. Postal Service and Amtrak are examples of such agencies. Conf. Rep. No. 1178 at 10, *reprinted in Sunshine Source Book* at 792.

3.5.3. The Sunshine Act and the Federal Advisory Committee Act, 5 U.S.C. App. II, are mutually exclusive; that is, an entity may be an agency or an advisory committee, but it cannot be both. S. Rep. No. 354 at 14, *reprinted in Sunshine Source Book* at 210. *See* Chapter 24 on Federal Advisory Committee Act.

3.6. The President must appoint members of the collegial body.

3.6.1. A board whose members are not appointed by the President is not an agency subject to the Sunshine Act. *Hunt*, 611 F.2d at 335.

3.6.2. The President must have appointed the majority of the members to the collegial body that heads an agency, with the advice and consent of the Senate, for that agency to be subject to the Sunshine Act. *Symons,* 670 F.2d at 241 (the fact that the President appointed members of the Chrysler Corporation Loan Guarantee Board to other high government offices is not enough to subject that Board to the Sunshine Act).

3.7. The Sunshine Act applies to subdivisions of the collegial body.

3.7.1. The House Report explains that: a subdivision of an agency covered under section 552b is covered if it is authorized to act on behalf of the agency. Panels, or regional boards of an agency, are covered if authorized to act on behalf of the agency, even if their action is not final in nature. Thus, panels or boards authorized to submit recommendations, or to conduct hearings on behalf of the agency are required to comply with the provisions of section 552b. H.R. Rep. No. 880 (part 1) at 7, *reprinted in* 1976 U.S. Code Cong. & Admin. News at 2188-89, *Sunshine Source Book* at 518.

3.7.2. The term "any subdivision thereof" means a subdivision of the "collegial body." *Hunt*, 611 F.2d at 336 n.2.

3.7.3. The Sunshine Act may apply to an interagency meeting if a majority of the members from one or more of the agencies attend the meeting. S. Rep. No. 354, *supra*, at 18, reprinted in *Sunshine Source Book* at 213.

3.7.4. A quorum of a subcommittee of the Federal Communications Commission, which was attending an international conference, was held to be an agency subject to the Sunshine Act, but only with regard to "matters that are within that subdivision's formally delegated authority to take official action for the agency." *FCC v. ITT World Communications*, 466 U.S. 463, 465-66 (1984).

3.7.5. Congress may specify by statute that the Sunshine Act applies to an agency. *See* 39 U.S.C. § 410(b) (Act applies to the United States Postal Service Board of Governors).

3.8. If a governmental unit is an agency under the Sunshine Act for some purposes, it is an agency subject to the Act for all purposes. *Energy Research,* 917 F.2d at 583; *Pacific Legal Foundation v. Council on Environmental Quality*, 636 F.2d 1259, 1264 (D.C. Cir. 1980).

3.9. State agencies are not subject to the Sunshine Act. *See Proffitt v. Davis*, 707 F. Supp. 182, 188 (E.D. Pa. 1989).

4. The term "member" means an individual who belongs to a collegial body heading an agency. *See* § 552b(a)(3); *see also* H.R. Rep. No. 880 (part 1) at 8, *reprinted in* 1976 U.S. Code Cong. & Admin. News at 2189-90, *Sunshine Source Book* at 519.

5. What is a "meeting" for Purposes of the Sunshine Act?

5.1. Section 552b(a)(2) states that for purposes of the Sunshine Act, the term "meeting" means the deliberations of at least the number of individual agency members required to take action on behalf of the agency where such deliberations determine or result in the joint conduct or disposition of official agency business, but does not include deliberations required or permitted by subsection (d) or (e). § 552b(a)(2). Subsections (d) and (e) concern procedures to close a meeting or portion of a meeting and to notify the public of a meeting. § 552b(d) & (e).

5.2. Legislative History.

5.2.1. The Senate Report explains that: The definition of "meetings" includes the conduct, as well as the disposition, of official agency matters. It is not sufficient for the purposes of open government to merely have the public witness final agency votes. The meetings opened by Section 201(a) are not intended to be merely reruns staged for the public after agency members have discussed the issue in private and predetermined their views. The whole decision-making process, not merely its results, must be exposed to public scrutiny. S. Rep. No. 354 at 18, *reprinted in Sunshine Source Book* at 214.

5.2.2. Similarly, the House Report states that "meetings" include not only sessions at which formal action is taken, but also those at which a quorum of members deliberates regarding the conduct or disposition of agency business. H.R. Rep. 880 (part 1) at 3, *reprinted in* 1976 U.S. Code Cong. & Admin. News at 2185.

5.2.3. The Conference Committee adopted the Senate definition, as explained in the Senate report, except that the word "concern" was replaced by the words "determine or result in." The Conference Report also made clear that the definition of "meeting" included "conference telephone calls if they involve the requisite number of members and otherwise come within the definition." Conf. Rep. No. 1178 at 11, *reprinted in* 1976 U.S. Code Cong. & Admin. News 2246-47, *Sunshine Source Book* at 793.

5.3. About the term "meeting" under the Sunshine Act the Supreme Court said: This statutory language contemplates discussions that effectively predetermine official actions. Such discussions must be sufficiently focused on discrete proposals or issues as to cause or to be likely to cause the individual participating members to form reasonably firm positions regarding matters pending or likely to arise before the agency. *FCC v. ITT World Communications, Inc.*, 466 U.S. 463 (1984). The D.C. Circuit recently upheld an agency regulation that defines "meeting" in the language used by the Supreme Court in *ITT* to describe a Sunshine Act "meeting." *National Resource Defense Council v. Nuclear Regulatory Commission*, 216 F.3d 1180, 1189 (D.C. Cir. 2000).

5.4. An agency need not label deliberations and discussions among agency members that determine or result in joint conduct or disposition of official agency business a "meeting" in order for them to be subject to the Sunshine Act. *Pacific Legal Foundation*, 636 F.2d at 1266.

5.5. An agency may not limit its open meetings to those in which an affirmative vote of two members is required by statute, regulation, executive order, or internal agency procedure. *Pacific Legal Foundation*, 636 F.2d at 1265.

5.6. Deliberations of a quorum of an agency subdivision upon matters outside that subdivision's formally delegated authority are not "meetings" subject to the Sunshine Act. *ITT World Communications*, 466 U.S. at 473.

5.7. Sessions of an international gathering attended by commissioners of an agency, but over which that agency has no control, are not "meetings" of an agency. *ITT World Communications*, 466 U.S. at 473-74.

5.8. The definition of "meeting" does not include a meeting at which only the scheduling of a future meeting is discussed. *Washington Association for Television & Children v. FCC*, 665 F.2d 1264, 1272 (D.C. Cir. 1981).

6. The Sunshine Act Provides Public Access to Agency Meetings.

6.1. Except as provided by subsection (c) of the Sunshine Act, "every portion of every meeting of an agency shall be open to public observation." § 552b(b); *Pacific Legal Foundation*, 636 F.2d at 1265 (the language of the Act's open meeting requirement is "sweeping, unqualified, and mandatory"). Accordingly, unless exempt, an agency meeting must be open, regardless of whether the public has requested to attend. *Pan American World Airways, Inc. v. CAB*, 684 F.2d 31, 35 (D.C. Cir. 1982).

6.2. Section 552b(b) "established a general presumption that agency meetings should be held in the open." *Common Cause*, 674 F.2d at 928-29.

6.3. While the Sunshine Act provides the public with a right to observe agency meetings, it does not provide a right of public participation at such meetings. *We the People, Inc. of the U.S. v. Nuclear Regulatory Commission,* 746 F. Supp. 213, 217 (D.D.C. 1990) (Sunshine Act does not manifest a Congressional intention to make an agency meeting a public forum).

6.4. The Sunshine Act's open meeting requirement "'shall not apply to any portion of an agency meeting...where the agency properly determines that such portion or portions of its meeting' fall within one or more of ten, narrow exemptions." *Pan American*, 684 F.2d at 35, quoting § 552b(c) .

6.5. The burden is on the agency to prove that its action to close a meeting was lawful. § 552b(h)(1); *Pan American*, 684 F.2d at 35; *Common Cause*, 674 F.2d at 932.

6.6. Exemptions.

6.6.1. The exemptions to the Sunshine Act must be narrowly construed. *Common Cause*, 674 F.2d at 932; *Philadelphia Newspapers Inc. v. Nuclear Regulatory Commission*, 727 F.2d 1195, 1200 (D.C. Cir. 1984).

6.6.2. "[E]ven if an exception is applicable, the agency must nevertheless hold the meeting in open session if it finds that the public interest so requires." *Common Cause*, 674 F.2d at 929 n.18, *citing* § 552b(c).

6.6.3. The Sunshine Act has 10 exemptions, of which seven employ language patterned after that of exemptions 1-4 and 6-8 of the FOIA, bear those same numbers, and generally should be interpreted in the same way. H.R. Rep. No. 880 (part 1), at 9-13, *reprinted in* 1976 U.S. Code Cong. & Admin. News at 2190-95, *Sunshine Source Book* at 520-24; H.R. Rep. No. 880 (part 2), 94th Cong., 2d Sess. 4, 15, *reprinted in* 1976 U.S. Code Cong. & Admin. News at 2213, 2224-25, *Sunshine Source Book* at 554, 565; Conf. Rep. No. 1178 at 14-15, *reprinted in* 1976 U.S. Code Cong. & Admin. News at 2249-51, *Sunshine Source Book* at 796-97, *see also* S. Rep. No. 354 at 20-27, *reprinted in Source Book* at 215-22.

6.6.4. The Sunshine Act has no parallel to exemption 5 of the FOIA, which incorporates the traditional discovery privileges. *See* § 552(b)(5). The Sunshine Act does not incorporate a deliberative process privilege. *Common Cause*, 674 F.2d at 928-30. "[T]he Sunshine Act was designed to open the predecisional process in multi-member agencies to the public." *Id.* at 929; *see also Public Citizen v. National Economic Commission*, 703 F. Supp. 113, 117 (D.D.C. 1989) (FACA case holding that exemption 9(B) of the Sunshine Act does not include a deliberative process privilege).

6.6.5. The Sunshine Act also omits the FOIA exemption that protects geological or geophysical data. *See* § 552(b)(9).

6.6.6. Exemption 5 to the Sunshine Act relates to agency discussions that "involve accusing any person of a crime, or formally censuring any person." § 552b(c)(5). The House Report states that "the discussion must relate to a specified person or persons, and, if a possible criminal violation is at issue, a specific crime or crimes." Further, the agency must be considering a possible action of a formal nature against the person in question. H. R. Rep. No. 880 (part 1) at 10, *reprinted in* 1976 U.S. Code Cong. & Admin. News at 2191-92, *Sunshine Source Book* at 521; *see also* S. Rep. No. 354 at 22, *reprinted in Sunshine Source Book* at 217.

6.6.7. Exemption 9.

6.6.7.1. Exemption 9 permits an agency to close a meeting, or portions of a meeting, where the agency properly determines that disclosure of information to be discussed is likely to disclose information the premature disclosure of which could

6.6.7.1.1. (A) in the case of an agency which regulates currencies, securities, commodities, or financial institutions, be likely to (i) lead to significant financial speculation in currencies, securities, or commodities, or (ii) significantly endanger the stability of any financial institution; or

6.6.7.1.2. (B) in the case of any agency, be likely to significantly frustrate implementation of a proposed agency action, except that subparagraph (B) shall not apply in any instance where the agency has already disclosed to the public the content or nature of its proposed action, or where the agency is required by law to make such disclosure on its own initiative prior to taking final agency action on such proposal. § 552b(c)(9).

6.6.7.2. Exemption 9(B) permits agencies to close meetings to prevent "premature disclosure" of information whose disclosure would be likely to "significantly frustrate implementation of a proposed agency action." The D. C. Circuit has interpreted this exemption to protect only those discussions that "would permit either financial gain at government expense or circumvention of agency regulation." *Common Cause*, 674 F.2d at 934.

6.6.7.3. Exemption 9(B) does not apply "'in any instance where the agency has already disclosed to the public the content or nature of its proposed action.'" *Common Cause*, 674 F.2d at 936, quoting exemption 9(B).

6.6.7.4. The Conference Report explains that an unauthorized "leak" would not render information unprotectable under exemption 9(B). Conf. Rep. No. 1178 at 15, *reprinted in* 1976 U.S. Code Cong. & Admin. News at 2250-51, *Sunshine Source Book* at 797.

6.6.8. Exemption 10.

6.6.8.1. Exemption 10 states that an agency may close a meeting to prevent the disclosure of information likely to specifically concern the agency's issuance of a subpoena, or the agency's participation in a civil action or proceeding, an action in a foreign court or international tribunal, or an arbitration, or the initiation, conduct, or disposition by the agency of a particular case of formal agency adjudication pursuant to the procedures in [5 U.S.C. § 554] or otherwise involving a determination on the record after opportunity for a hearing. § 552b(c)(10).

6.6.8.2. An agency need not disclose policy discussions that are incidental to discussion of litigation strategy. *Clark-Cowlitz*, 798 F.2d at 502.

6.6.8.3. Exemption 10 has no temporal limitation, so transcripts and minutes of meetings may be withheld under exemption 10 although the litigation discussed has ended. *Clark-Cowlitz*, 798 F.2d at 503.

6.6.8.4. Exemption 10 applies to discussion by an agency board of whether to initiate or participate in adjudicatory proceedings. *A.G. Becker, Inc. v. Board of Governors*, 502 F. Supp. 378 (D.D.C. 1980) (meeting to consider whether to issue a cease and desist order and whether to declare certain actions by the industry subject to its regulation illegal).

6.6.8.5. Exemption 10 may be properly invoked for meetings concerning issues that are the subject of, or subject to, formal agency adjudication, although they are outside the formal adjudicatory process itself. *Philadelphia Newspapers*, 727 F.2d at 1199-1202; *Shurberg Broadcasting of Hartford, Inc. v. FCC*, 617 F. Supp. 825, 830 (D.D.C. 1985).

6.6.8.6. Congress intended exemption 10 to cover "rulemaking involving a determination on the record after opportunity for a hearing, in other words, to include all cases for which the procedures of [5 U.S.C. §§] 556 and 557 were required." *Time, Inc. v. U.S. Postal Service*, 667 F.2d 329, 334 (2d Cir. 1981).

6.6.9. Other Exemptions.

6.6.9.1. Exemption 2, which concerns internal agency matters, does not apply to agency budget discussions relating to personnel cutbacks or performance. *Common Cause*, 674 F.2d at 938.

6.6.9.2. Exemption 6, which protects against unwarranted invasions of personal privacy, does not "shelter substandard performance by government executives" discussed during budget deliberations. *Common Cause*, 674 F.2d at 938.

6.6.9.3. 42 U.S.C. §§ 2286d(a) and (g)(3) are withholding statutes under Exemption 3, such that the Defense Nuclear Facilities Safety Board may close those portions of its meetings at which it discusses recommendations that will be sent to the Secretary of Defense or the President. *National Resources Defense Council v. Defense Nuclear Regulatory Safety Board*, 969 F.2d 1248, 1252 (D.C. Cir. 1992), *cert. denied*, 508 U.S. 906 (1993).

6.7. Segregation of non-exempt portions of a meeting.

6.7.1. The Sunshine Act requires agencies to segregate any exempt discussions at a meeting from any non-exempt discussions. *See, e.g., Philadelphia Newspapers*, 727 F.2d at 1201; *Pan American*, 684 F.2d at 35; *Common Cause*, 674 F.2d at 929, 936 n.46.

6.7.2. "[T]he Sunshine Act provides for an examination of each item of business to ascertain whether it may be closed under the terms of one of ten specific exemptions." *Common Cause*, 674 F.2d at 932; *see also Philadelphia Newspapers*, 727 F.2d at 1200.

6.7.3. An agency may not close an entire meeting because it will arguably discuss some exempt topic, "even if discussion of the exempt topic might come up at various points throughout the meeting." *Philadelphia Newspapers*, 727 F.2d at 1201.

6.7.4. Agency may not, by regulation, exempt an entire category of its business from the Sunshine Act's open-meeting requirements. *Pacific Legal Foundation*, 636 F.2d at 1265 (regulations exempting advice to the President held invalid).

7. The Sunshine Act Prohibits Agencies From Conducting Business Other Than In Accordance With the Act's Provisions.

7.1. Section (b) states that members of a collegial body heading an agency "shall not jointly conduct or dispose of business other than in accordance with [the Sunshine Act]." § 552b(b).

7.2. The Sunshine Act does not require agencies to hold meetings. *See, e.g., Railroad Com'n of Texas v. United States*, 765 F.2d 221, 230 (D.C. Cir. 1985); *Pacific Legal*

Foundation, 636 F.2d at 1266; *Amrep v. FTC,* 768 F.2d 1171, 1178 (10th Cir. 1985); *Republic Airlines v. CAB*, 756 F.2d 1304, 1319 (8th Cir. 1985); *Communications Systems v. FCC*, 595 F.2d 797, 801 (D.C. Cir. 1978).

7.3. "This prohibition does not prevent agency members from considering individually business that is circulated to them sequentially in writing." Conf. Rep. No. 1178 at 11, *reprinted in* 1976 U.S. Code Cong. & Admin. News at 2246-47, *Sunshine Source Book* at 793; *see, e.g., Communications Systems*, 595 F.2d at 799; *Amrep v. FTC*, 768 F.2d 1171 (10th Cir. 1985).

8. What Procedures Must An Agency Follow to Close A Meeting?

8.1. An agency may not close any portion of a meeting without a majority of the members of an agency voting to close that portion. § 552b(d)(1).

8.2. However, a single vote may be taken with respect to a series of meetings, a portion or portions of which are proposed to be closed to the public, "so long as each meeting in the series involves the same particular matters and is scheduled to be held no more than thirty days after the initial meeting in such series." *Id.*

8.3. The vote of each member must be recorded and no proxies are allowed. *Id.*

8.4. Any person whose interests may be directly affected by a portion of a meeting may request the agency to close that portion to the public because the agency is likely to discuss matters relating to personal privacy, criminal accusation, or law enforcement information, exempt under Exemptions 5, 6, or 7. § 552b(d)(2). Conf. Rep. No.1178 at 16, *reprinted in* 1976 U.S. Code Cong. & Admin. News at 2251-52, *Sunshine Act Source Book* at 797-98. An agency must take a recorded vote on such a request if asked to do so by any one of its members. *Id.*

8.5. Each time an agency votes to close a meeting or portion of a meeting, within one day of the vote, the agency must make publicly available a full written explanation of its decision along with a list of all persons expected to attend the meeting and their affiliations. § 552b(d)(3).

8.6. Within one day following each unsuccessful vote to close a meeting, the agency must make publicly available a record of each member's vote. *Id.*

8.7. Expedited Procedures.

8.7.1. Section 552b(d)(4) provides for expedited procedures to close meetings for any agency that may close a majority of its meetings pursuant to Exemptions 4, 8, 9, and/or 10, and that has promulgated regulations to permit it to close meetings or portions of a meeting by a recorded vote of the majority of its members at the beginning of such meeting, or portion thereof. The regulations must also require the agency to provide the public with the vote of each member. § 552b(d)(4).

8.7.2. Those agencies invoking § 552b(d)(4) must publicly announce the time, place, and subject matter of the meeting and of each portion thereof "at the earliest practicable time." Other provisions of § 552b(d) and 552b(e) do not apply. *Id.*

8.7.3. Congress intended § 552b(d)(4) to apply primarily "to agencies which regulate financial institutions, securities, and commodities, and which will often have to conduct their sensitive business in private, and on short notice. It will also apply to agencies whose primary or sole task is to conduct cases of adjudication.'" *A.G. Becker*, 502 F. Supp. at 383, *quoting* S. Rep. No. 354, *supra*, at 28-29.

8.7.4. Determination of whether notice was provided at the earliest possible time must be performed on a case by case basis. *A.G. Becker*, 502 F. Supp. at 384.

8.7.5. Absent extraordinary circumstances, notice must precede commencement of the meeting. *A.G. Becker*, 502 F. Supp. at 385 (agency violated statute by delaying notice until after meeting occurred).

8.7.6. Ordinarily, the earliest practicable time is at the time the agenda for the meeting is established. *A.G. Becker*, 502 F. Supp. at 385-86. An agency must provide a detailed justification for providing notice later than when the agenda for the meeting is established. *Id.* at 385.

9. What Notice Must Be Provided By An Agency About A Meeting?

9.1. Section 552b(e)(1) requires that an agency announce, at least a week in advance of a meeting, the meeting's subject matter, time, place, and whether the meeting will be open or closed. § 552b(e)(1). Subsection (e)(1) also requires that the notice provide the name and phone number of the official designated by the agency to respond to requests for information about the meeting. *Id.*

9.2. By a recorded vote of the majority of an agency's members, shorter notice may be provided, but the notice must be provided "at the earliest practicable time." § 552b(e)(1); *Coalition for Legal Services v. Legal Services Corp.*, 597 F. Supp. 198 (D.D.C. 1984) (the exception to the seven-day notice requirement for business necessity is intended to apply only to emergency and late-breaking items).

9.3. At least one court has enjoined a meeting for failure of the agency to provide adequate notice. *Coalition for Legal Services*, 597 F. Supp. at 200.

9.4. No change in the time and place of a meeting may occur after public notice, unless the agency publicly announces such change at the earliest practicable time. § 552b(e)(2).

9.5. To effect any change in the subject matter of, or public access to, a meeting following public notice of such meeting, (1) a majority of the agency membership must, by recorded vote, determine "that agency business requires the change and that no earlier announcement of the change was possible," and (2), the agency must notify the public of such change and each member's vote upon such change at the earliest practicable time. § 552b(e)(2).

9.6. Notice of each meeting as required by § 552b(e)(1) & (2) must be published in the Federal Register. § 552b(e)(3).

10. The Sunshine Act Requires Agencies to Maintain Transcripts or Minutes of Meetings.

10.1. Section 552b(f)(1) requires agencies to: maintain a complete transcript or electronic recording adequate to record fully the proceedings of each meeting, or portion of a meeting, closed to the public [pursuant to exemptions 1-7 and 9(B)]. § 552(f)(1). Otherwise the agency must maintain such a transcript or recording or a set of minutes. *Id.*

10.2. The Sunshine Act requires agencies to provide prompt public access to such transcripts, recordings, and minutes. *Id.*

10.2.1. The public may obtain a copy of a transcript, recording or minutes at the actual cost of duplication or transcription.

10.3. Transcripts, minutes or electronic recordings of meetings may be withheld from public disclosure only if they are exempt under one of the Act's 10 exemptions. § 552b(k). Otherwise, nothing in the Sunshine Act expands or limits any person's rights of access under the Freedom of Information Act, 5 U.S.C. § 552. *Id.*

10.4. Agencies may not use any provision of the Sunshine Act to withhold from any individual any record, including transcripts, records, or minutes required by the Act.

10.5. Information from transcripts, electronic recordings, and minutes may not be withheld from public disclosure unless a majority of the agency's membership votes that the information may be withheld under subsection (c). § 552b(d)(1). Information regarding the "same particular matters" may be voted on at once. *Id.* The vote to withhold information must be recorded and no proxies are allowed. *Id.*

10.6. Transcripts, recordings, and minutes must disclose the identity of each speaker. *Id.*

10.7. An agency is required to maintain a complete verbatim copy of each transcript, a complete copy of each set of minutes, and a complete copy of each electronic recording of a meeting, or portion of a meeting, closed to the public, for at least 2 years, or until 1 year after the conclusion of an agency proceeding with respect to which the meeting or portion was held, whichever is later. § 552b(f).

10.8. Chapter 33 of Title 44 of the U.S. Code ("Disposal of Records") does not apply to transcripts, minutes, or electronic recordings of agency meetings. § 552b(k).

10.9. Courts may not require an agency to maintain complete records of all closed, non-Sunshine Act discussions. *NRDC v. NRC*, 216 F.3d at 1190.

11. Actions to Challenge Agency Regulations Implementing the Sunshine Act or Failure to Promulgate Such Regulations.

11.1. Section 552b(g) requires each agency subject to the Sunshine Act to promulgate regulations implementing the Act's requirements after notice and comment. § 552b(g).

11.2. Section 552b(g) provides for judicial review of an agency's failure to promulgate regulations implementing the Sunshine Act provisions (b)-(f), and failure to promulgate regulations in accordance with those provisions. *Id.*

11.3. Jurisdiction for an action to force an agency to promulgate regulations is in the United States District Court for the District of Columbia, and any person has standing to sue. *Id. Rushforth*, 762 F.2d at 1939 n.3.

11.4. Challenges to Existing Regulations.

11.4.1. Section 552b(g) applies to challenges to an agency rule on its face. *See, e.g., Pacific Legal Foundation,* 636 F.2d at 1259; *Johnston v. NRC*, 766 F.2d 1182, 1185 (7th Cir. 1985).

11.4.2. Any person has standing to challenge a regulation implementing requirements (b)-(f) of the Sunshine Act. *Johnston*, 766 F.2d at 1186.

11.4.3. Jurisdiction for § 552b(g) challenges to set aside regulations lies exclusively in the United States Court of Appeals for the District of Columbia. *Johnston*, 766 F.2d at 1190.

11.4.4. No deference is due to agency construction of other statutes in light of the Sunshine Act. *NRDC v. Defense Nuclear Facilities Safety Bd.*, 969 F.2d 1248, 1250-51 (D.C. Cir. 1992) (regulating Exemption 3).

12. Actions to Enforce Requirements of Subsections (b)-(f).

12.1. Suits Brought Under The Sunshine Act Alone.

12.1.1. Section 552b(h)(1) grants district courts jurisdiction to "enforce requirements of subsections (b) through (f) of this section by declaratory judgment, injunctive relief, or other relief as may be appropriate." *See, e.g., ITT World Communications*, 466 U.S. at 463.

12.1.2. To state a cause of action under § 552b(h), a complaint under the Sunshine Act must allege that an agency scheduled a meeting to be closed or closed a meeting. *Johnston*, 766 F.2d at 1188.

12.1.3. Any person has standing to sue under § 552b(h)(1). *Johnston*, 766 F.2d at 1187, *citing* S. Rep. No. 354 at 34, *reprinted in Sunshine Source Book* at 229.

12.1.4. Jurisdiction under subsection (h)(1) is exclusively in the federal district courts. § 552b(h).

12.1.5. Venue is proper in the district where the agency meeting is held or in which the agency has its headquarters, or in the District of Columbia. *Id.*

12.1.6. The time to file suit is set out in the statute. Actions may be brought prior to, or within 60 days after, the meeting out of which the violation of this section arises, unless the agency fails to properly announce the meeting, in which case an action may be filed within 60 days after such announcement is provided. § 552(h)(1).

12.1.6.1. The House Report explains that: [a]s with subsections (d) and (e), any public announcement must be made in a manner calculated to assure its wide dissemination in order to qualify as a "public announcement" as that term is used herein. H.R. Rep. No. 880 (part 1) at 16, *reprinted in* 1976 U.S. Code Cong. & Admin. News at 2197-98, *Sunshine Source Book* at 527.

12.1.6.2. The Senate Report clarifies that: If an agency provides no public announcement at all, the 60-day requirement is inapplicable. S. Rep. No. 354 at 33, *reprinted in Sunshine Source Book* at 228.

12.1.6.3. The plaintiff need not exhaust any administrative remedies. H.R. Rep. No. 880 (part 1) at 16, 1976 U.S. Code Cong. & Admin. News at 2225-26, *reprinted in Sunshine Source Book* at 527.

12.1.7. If jurisdiction is based solely on subsection (h)(1), the Sunshine Act does not authorize a court to set aside, enjoin, or invalidate any agency action (other than an action to close a meeting or to withhold information under this section) taken or discussed at any agency meeting out of which the violation of this section arose. § 552b(h)(2); *Investment Co. Institute v. FDIC*, 728 F.2d 518 (D.C. Cir. 1984).

12.1.8. One of the following standards will apply in actions challenging whether a meeting may properly be closed, or information withheld, under one or more of the Sunshine Act's exemptions: If an agency's decision to close a meeting is challenged *before* a meeting is held, then a court must employ a foreseeability standard under which the agency must show that it is "more likely than not that exempt matters would be discussed at the closed portion or portions of the meeting." *Common Cause*, 674 F.2d at 929 n.19. If an agency's decision to close a meeting is challenged *after* the meeting is held, then a court must base its decision on the discussions that actually occurred. Only those portions of a transcript in which exempt matters were discussed may be withheld. *Id., citing* § 552b(f)(2).

12.1.9. An action under subsection (h)(1) is not rendered moot when a meeting is held and the transcript of it is released if the violation claimed is "capable of repetition, yet evading review." *Common Cause*, 674 F.2d at 924 n.6 (internal quotation omitted) (similar meetings). On the other hand, if the agency corrects an isolated violation, then the action is moot. *Coalition for Legal Services*, 597 F. Supp. at 200 (relief sought for single violation of subsection (e)).

12.2. Actions Brought In Conjunction With Other Statutes.

12.2.1. Section 552b(h)(2) states in relevant part: Any federal court otherwise authorized by law to review agency action may, at the application of a person properly participating in the proceeding pursuant to other applicable law, inquire into violations by the agency of the requirements of this section and afford such relief as it deems appropriate. § 552b(h)(2).

12.2.2. The Conference Report sets out the guidelines for when a court should invalidate agency action because of Sunshine Act violations: The conferees do not intend the authority granted to the Federal courts by the first sentence of subsection (h)(2) to be employed to set aside agency action taken other than under section 552b solely because of a violation of section 552b in any case where the violation is unintentional and not prejudicial to the rights of any person participating in the review proceeding. Agency action should not be set aside for a violation of section 552b unless that violation is of a serious nature. Conf. Rep. No. 1178 at 23 reprinted in 1976 U.S. Code Cong. & Admin. News 2258-59, *Sunshine Source Book* at 805.

12.2.3 Subsection (h)(2) does not create an independent right of action, and it may be invoked only on "the application of any person properly participating in the proceeding." *See, e.g., Washington Association for Television & Children*, 665 F.2d at 1264 (challenge to the FCC definition of "agency" combined with challenge to FCC approval of transfer of control of television station); *Communications Systems,* 595 F.2d at 797 (challenge to FCC practice of conducting business by circulating papers, rather than holding a meeting, included in petition for review of FCC refusal to authorize conversion of a radio station from a Class B to a Class C station).

12.2.4. The D.C. Circuit has concluded that: "[r]elease of transcripts, not invalidation of the agency's substantive actions," is the remedy generally appropriate for disregard of the Sunshine Act. *See, e.g., Braniff Master Executive Council v. CAB*, 693 F.2d 220, 226 (D.C. Cir. 1982); *Pan American*, 684 F.2d at 36; *Consolidated Aluminum Corp v. TVA*, 462 F. Supp. 464, 478 (M.D. Tenn. 1978).

12.2.5. Circumstances that might require a court to set aside an agency action taken in violation of the Sunshine Act are where the violation was intentional, prejudicial and of a serious nature. *Railroad Com'n of Texas v. United States*, 765 F.2d at 231.

13. The Sunshine Act Provides for the Recovery of Attorney Fees and Costs.

13.1. Section 552b(i) states: The court may assess against any party reasonable attorney fees and other litigation costs reasonably incurred by any other party who substantially prevails in any action brought in accordance with the provisions of subsection (g) and (h) of this section, except that costs may be assessed against the plaintiff only where the court finds that the suit was initiated by the plaintiff primarily for frivolous or dilatory purposes. In the case of assessment of costs against an agency, the costs may be assessed by the court against the United States.

13.2. The House Report warns: "The provision for liability on the part of the plaintiff... should rarely have to be used, and any invocation of it should be attended by notice, an opportunity to be heard, and any other applicable aspects of due process of law." H. Rep. No. 880 (part 1) at 18, *reprinted in* 1976 U.S. Code Cong. & Admin. News at 2199-2200, *Sunshine Source Book* at 529.

13.3. The application of the Supreme Court's ruling in *Buckhannon Bd. and Care Home, Inc. v. West Virginia Department of Health & Human Res.*, 532 U.S. 598 (2001) regarding "prevailing" will affect awards of attorney's fees under the Sunshine Act. *See* Chapter 17 on Attorney Fees.

14. Miscellaneous.

14.1. Each agency must report annually to Congress with respect to its compliance with the Sunshine Act. § 552b(j). This report shall include changes to agency policy and procedures; tabulation of the number of meetings held, the exemptions applied to close meetings and the days of public notice provided to close meetings; descriptions of litigation and complaints concerning agency implementation of the Sunshine Act; and explanations of any changes in the law affecting agency Sunshine Act responsibilities.

14.2. A person's good faith belief that the government has violated the Sunshine Act is not a legal defense to the charge of impeding and disrupting the performance of official duties by government employees. *United States v. Rankin*, 616 F.2d 1168, 1170 (10th Cir. 1980).

CHAPTER 24
Federal Advisory Committee Act
Eleanor H. Smith

1. Introduction.

1.1. The Federal Advisory Committee Act ("FACA"), Pub. L. 92-463, 86 Stat. 770 (1972), was enacted on October 6, 1972, and became effective on January 4, 1973. The Act is codified at 5 U.S.C. App. II, and it has been amended four times since enactment. Pub. L. 94-409, § 5(c), Sept. 13,1976, 90 Stat. 1247; Pub. L. 96-523, § 2, Dec, 12, 1980, 94 Stat. 3040; Pub. L. 97-375, Title II § 201(c), Dec. 21, 1982, 96 Stat. 1822; and Pub. L. 105-153, Dec. 17, 1997, 111 Stat. 2689.

1.2. Congress enacted FACA "to control the advisory committee process and to open to public scrutiny the manner in which government agencies obtain advice from private individuals." *National Anti-Hunger Coalition v. Executive Committee of the President's Private Sector Survey on Cost Control*, 711 F.2d 1071, 1072 (D.C. Cir. 1983), quoting *Food Chemical News v. Davis*, 378 F. Supp. 1048, 1051 (D.D.C. 1974); *see also* 5 U.S.C. App. II § 2; *Public Citizen v. DOJ*, 491 U.S. 440, 459 (1989); S. Rep. No. 92-1098 at 6, *reprinted in FACA Source Book, infra* at 156.

1.3. "FACA was enacted to cure specific ills, above all the wasteful expenditure of public funds for worthless committee meetings and biased proposals." *Public Citizen v. DOJ*, 491 U.S. at 453. H.R. Rep. 92-1017, *reprinted in* U.S. Code Cong. & Admin. News 3496, *FACA Source Book, infra* at 276.

1.4. The General Services Administration ("GSA") "is responsible for all matters relating to advisory committees." 5 U.S.C. App. II § 7(a). GSA promulgated regulations implementing FACA in 1983. 41 C.F.R. Part 101-6. GSA took over this responsibility from the Office of Management and Budget pursuant to Reorganization Plan No. 1 of 1977, § 5F, 42 F.R. 56, 101; 91 Stat. 1634, and effective November 20, 1977.

2. Legislative History.

2.1. The initial legislative history of FACA is collected in *Federal Advisory Committee Act (Public Law 92-463) and Source Book: Legislative History, Texts, and other Documents*, Subcommittee on Energy, Nuclear Proliferation, and Federal Services of the Committee on Governmental Affairs, United States Senate, 95th Cong., 2d Sess., July 1978 (hereafter *FACA Source Book*).

2.2. FACA has its origins in Executive Order ("E.O.") 11,007, which governed the functioning of advisory committees from 1962 until FACA's passage in 1972. *Public Citizen v. DOJ*, 491 U.S. at 457. While FACA incorporated many of the provisions of E.O. 11,007, it has a broader application than E.O. 11,007. *Id.* at 2567-68; H.R. Rep. No. 91-1731, 91st Cong., 2d Sess. 9-10 (1970), *reprinted in FACA Source Book* at 214; H.R. Rep. No. 92-1017, 92d Cong., 2d Sess. 4 (1972), *reprinted in* 1972 U.S. Code Cong. & Admin. News 3491, 3493-94, *FACA Source Book* at 273-74; S. Rep. No. 92-1098, 92d Cong., 1st Sess. 3-5, 7 (1972), *reprinted in FACA Source Book* at 153-5, 157. Not only did FACA add requirements, but it also applies to "Presidential advisory committees," which E.O. 11,007 did not. *Id.* "Presidential advisory committees" are committees that advise the President. 5 U.S.C. App. II § 3(4).

2.3. FACA was intended to protect against undue influence by special interest groups over government decision-making. The House Report explained: "One of the greatest dangers in the unregulated use of advisory committees is that special interest groups may use their membership on such bodies to promote their private concerns. Testimony... pointed out the danger of allowing special interest groups to exert undue influence upon the government through the dominance of advisory committees which deal with matters in which they have vested interests." H.R. Rep. 92-1017 *reprinted in* 1972 U.S. Code Cong. & Admin. News 3496, *FACA Source Book* at 276.

2.4. Congress also intended FACA to open the advisory committee process to public scrutiny: The lack of public scrutiny of the activities of advisory committees was found to pose the danger that subjective influences not in the public interest could be exerted on the federal decision-makers. S. Rep. No. 92-1098 at 6, *reprinted in FACA Sourcebook* at 156.

3. What is an "Advisory Committee?"

3.1. FACA defines an advisory committee to mean "any committee, board, commission, council, conference, panel, task force, or other similar group, or any subcommittee or other subgroup thereof..., which is (A) established by statute or reorganization plan, or (B) established or utilized by the President, or (C) established or utilized by one or more agencies, in the interest of obtaining advice or recommendations for the President or one or more agencies or officers of the federal government, except that such term excludes (i) the Advisory Commission on Intergovernmental Relations, (ii) the Commission on Government Procurement, and (iii) any committee which is composed wholly of full-time officers or employees of the federal government." 5. U.S.C. App. II § 3(2); *see also* 41 C.F.R. § 101-6.1003. Accordingly, to be an advisory committee subject to FACA, the committee must be either "established" or "utilized" by the executive branch to obtain advice. These terms are not mutually exclusive.

3.2. Legislative history.

3.2.1. The original House bill referred simply to advisory committees "established" in the interest of obtaining advice for the President or any agency, but the House Report made clear that this definition also included: those committees which may have been organized before their advice was sought by the President or any agency in the same manner as an advisory committee formed by the President himself or the agency itself. H.R. Rep. 1017 *reprinted in* 1972 U.S. Code Cong. & Admin. News 3494; *FACA Source Book* at 274. The House Report further explained that "[i]t would be contrary to the purpose and intent of this bill if independent entities used as advisory bodies were to be exempted from the provisions of this bill." *Id.; see also Lombardo v. Handler*, 397 F. Supp. 792, 798 (D.D.C. 1975), *aff'd without opinion*, 546 F.2d 1043 (D.C. Cir. 1976), *cert. denied*, 431 U.S. 932 (1977).

3.2.2. The House Report also indicated that a contractor or consultant would not be subject to FACA because neither is a "committee, board, commission, council...or similar group..." H.R. Rep. 1017, *reprinted in* 1972 U.S. Code Cong. & Admin. News 3494, *FACA Source Book* at 274.

3.2.3. The Senate bill defined an advisory committee as "any committee...established or organized for the purpose of furnishing advice, recommendations, or information to any office or agency." S. Rep. No. 1098 *reprinted in FACA Source Book* at 158. This language was used with the intention "to interpret the words 'established' and 'organized' in the most liberal sense, so that when an officer brings together a group by formal or informal means, by contract or other arrangement, and whether or not federal money is expended, to obtain advice and information, such group is covered by the provisions of the bill." Id.

3.2.4. The Conference Committee adopted the House bill with modification, adding "or utilized" to that bill's definition of advisory committee. The Conference Report states that FACA "does not apply to persons or organizations which have contractual relationships with federal agencies nor to advisory committees not directly established by or for such agencies." *Conf. Rep. No. 92-1403, supra*, at 2-3, *reprinted in* 1972 U.S. Code Cong. & Admin. News 3509, *FACA Source Book* at 323-4.

3.3. "Established" Advisory Committees.

3.3.1. An advisory committee can be "established" only by a statute, the President, or an agency. 5 U.S.C. App. II § 3(2) & 9(a).

3.3.2. Although the FACA does not define "established," the term can be understood from other provisions of the Act to refer to committees that the government has brought into being. 5 U.S.C. App. II § 5(b) (referring to "legislation establishing, or authorizing the establishment of any advisory committee") and § 5(c) (referring to advisory committees "creat[ed]" by the executive).

3.3.3. Guided by the Supreme Court's decision in *Public Citizen v. DOJ, supra*, the D.C. Circuit has interpreted "established" more narrowly to mean only those advisory committees that the government itself has "organized" or "formed." *Food Chemical News v. Young*, 900 F.2d 328, 332 (D.C. Cir. 1990).

3.3.4. Before an advisory committee is established by an agency, "the head of the agency" must have determined "as a matter of formal record," after consultation with the Administrator of GSA, and with timely notice published in the Federal Register, that the advisory committee is "in the public interest in connection with the performance of duties imposed on that agency by law." 41 C.F.R. § 101-6.1015(a).

3.3.5. The D.C. Circuit has been unreceptive to finding that an agency has established an advisory committee pursuant to a contract. *Compare Food Chemical News v. Young*, 900 F.2d at 332, *with Lombardo*, 397 F. Supp. at 797.

3.3.6. A committee is not established by statute as an advisory committee where the relevant statute does not refer to any committee. "The term 'established' does not include committees which merely can be said to owe their existence to legislation." *Lombardo*, 397 F. Supp. at 796.

Federal Advisory Committee Act

3.4. "Utilized" Advisory Committees.

3.4.1. An advisory committee may be "utilized" by the President or one or more agencies. 5 U.S.C. App. II § 3(2).

3.4.2. Prior to the Supreme Court's decision in *Public Citizen v. DOJ*, *supra*, both the executive and the courts uniformly applied a functional definition to "utilized" advisory committees, applying FACA to groups of private individuals used by the executive branch to obtain advice. *See, e.g.* 41 C.F.R. § 101-6.1003 and *Center for Auto Safety v. Tiemann*, 414 F. Supp. 215, 223 (D.D.C. 1976), *remanded on other grounds sub. nom. Center for Auto Safety v. Cox*, 580 F.2d 689 (D.C. Cir. 1978) (group is utilized as an advisory committee if it provides specific draft regulations); *National Nutritional Foods Ass'n v. Califano*, 603 F.2d 327, 336 and n.10, 329 (2d Cir. 1979) (group "utilized" to obtain advice with respect to whether or how to regulate a substance).

3.4.3. In *Public Citizen v. DOJ*, the only Supreme Court case to interpret any aspect of FACA, a majority of the Court held that the American Bar Association's Standing Committee on the Federal Judiciary—which for years has rendered advice concerning candidates for nomination to the federal bench—is not an advisory committee "utilized by" the Department of Justice. 491 U.S. at 467.

3.4.3.1. The Court was most concerned with the potential collision between FACA and the President's appointment power under the Constitution. *Id.* at 455, 465-67. While calling it a "close question whether FACA should be construed to apply to the [ABA] committee," the majority decided that constitutional considerations ultimately "tip[ped] the balance decisively against FACA's application." *Id.* at 465. However, three members of the Court concluded that the ABA Committee is "utilized by" the Department, but that to apply FACA to the Committee would be unconstitutional. *Id.* at 467-89.

3.4.3.2. The Majority cited three main factors behind its decision. First, the ABA Committee was not a committee formed "at the federal government's prompting." *Id.* at 457, 460. Second, the Department of Justice had no control over the Committee by way of contract or otherwise. *Id.* at 457-458, 460. Third, the ABA Committee received no government funds. *Id.* at 457, 460. The absence of these factors led the majority to conclude that the ABA Committee was not "closely tied" to the federal government, and therefore, not "utilized" as an advisory committee.

3.4.3.3. The Court indicated, in dicta, that the term "utilized" appears to have been added simply to clarify that FACA applies to advisory committees established by the federal government in the general sense of that term, encompassing groups formed indirectly by quasi-public organizations, such as the National Academy of Sciences, "for" public agencies as well as "by" such agencies themselves. *Id.* at 462. The Court equated quasi-public entities with those that are "closely tied" to the federal government, but failed to offer any other example of a quasi-public entity other than the National Academy of Sciences.

3.4.4. Relying on *Public Citizen v. DOJ*, the D.C. Circuit held that a National Academy of Sciences committee that prepares work product relied upon by a federal agency is an advisory committee *Animal Legal Defense Fund v. Shalala*, 104 F.3d 424 (D.C. Cir. 1997), *rehearing en banc denied*, 114 F.3d 1209 (D.C. Cir. 1997). Congress thereafter amended FACA to exempt from the definition of "advisory committee" the committees of the National Academy of Sciences and to require them nevertheless to meet certain FACA requirements before any agency may use their advice. *See infra* 3.5.12.

3.4.5. Also relying upon *Public Citizen v. DOJ*, the D.C. Circuit held that a committee is not "utilized" for purposes of FACA where it is created by a wholly private organization and is not amenable to any management by any federal agency or by any private or semi-private entity the federal government helped bring into being. *Food Chemical News v. Young*. 900 F.2d 328 (D.C. Cir. 1990).

3.4.6. An advisory committee is not "utilized" for advice if the agency shows no preference for the committee's advice and that advice is subject to substantial review and revision by the contractor before it is received by the government. *Lombardo*, 397 F. Supp. at 800.

3.4.7. "Utilized" advisory committees include those committees that existed prior to an agency's use of them to obtain advice. *Center for Auto Safety v. Cox, supra*, *see also* H.R. Rep. No. 1017 at 4, *reprinted in 1972 U.S. Code Cong. & Admin. News* at 3494: FACA *Source Book* at 274.

3.4.8. FACA applies to one-time meetings at which an agency seeks a committee's advice. *National Nutritional Foods Ass'n v. Califano*, 603 F.2d 327, 329-30 (2d Cir. 1979); *see also* *Food Chemical News v. Davis*, 378 F. Supp. 1050-52 (D.D.C. 1974).

3.4.9. Activities that a committee performs unrelated to advising the executive branch are not subject to FACA. *Center for Auto Safety v. Cox*, 580 F.2d at 694, *quoting Center for Auto Safety v. Tiemann*, 414 F. Supp. at 225 n. 11.

3.4.10. FACA does not interfere with the First Amendment rights of independent committees "utilized" by the executive branch for advice, *Center for Auto Safety v. Cox*, 580 F.2d at 694, because the committee and "its members remain free to communicate their views."

3.5. Entities Not Subject to FACA.

3.5.1. FACA does not apply to any committee that may advise the legislative or judicial branches of government, but does not advise the executive branch. 5 U.S.C. App. II 3(2). *Washington Legal Foundation v. U.S. Sentencing Commission*, 17 F.3d 1446, 1450 (D.C. Cir. 1994) (U.S. Sentencing Commission is not subject to FACA).

3.5.2. "[a]ny committee that is composed wholly of full-time, permanent part-time, officers or employees of the Federal Government," is specifically excluded from the definition of advisory committee provided in § 3(2) of the Act. *Id.*

3.5.2.1. The First Lady is a *de facto* "full-time officer or employee of the Federal Government" for purposes of FACA. *Association of*

American Physicians and Surgeons v. Hillary Rodham Clinton, 997 F.2d 898, 911 (D.C. Cir. 1993).

3.5.2.2. An outside consultant to a committee composed of full-time officers and employees of the federal government may render the committee subject to FACA if the involvement and role of the outside consultant are functionally indistinguishable from those of the committee's members. *Clinton*, 997 F.2d at 915.

3.5.2.3. The exemption for committees composed wholly of full-time officers or employees of federal government does not apply to a committee of state and federal employees. *Center for Auto Safety v. Tiemann, supra.*

3.5.3. FACA does not apply to any advisory committee established by an Act of Congress for which Congress has specifically provided an exemption from FACA. 5 U.S.C. App. II § 4(b).

3.5.4. FACA does not apply to any advisory committee established or utilized by the Central Intelligence Agency or the Federal Reserve System. 5 U.S.C. App. II § 4(b).

3.5.5. FACA does not apply to any "local civic group whose primary function is that of rendering a public service with respect to a federal program, or any state or local committee, council, board, commission, or similar group established to advise or make recommendations to state or local officials or agencies." 5 U.S.C. § 4(c). However, the American Association of State Highway and Transportation Officials is not exempt from FACA under § 4(c). *Center for Auto Safety v. Cox*, 580 F.2d at 693 (nationally oriented committee that exists to offer advice to the federal government).

3.5.6. A committee that has some advisory functions may nevertheless fail to be an advisory committee if its functions are primarily operational. *Judicial Watch v. Clinton*, 76 F.3d 1232, 1233 (D.C. Cir. 1996); *Sofamor Danek Group v. Gaus*, 61 F.3d 929, 933 (D.C. Cir. 1995) ("panel is operational, developing guidelines for health care practitioners, rather than advisory to the federal government"); *Public Citizen v. Commission on the Bicentennial of the U.S. Constitution*, 622 F. Supp. 753, 757-59 (D.D.C. 1985).

3.5.7. FACA does not apply to committees that provide advice that is not directed to governmental policy. *Judicial Watch v. Clinton*, 76 F.3d at 1233.

3.5.8. Task forces that support an advisory committee are not themselves advisory committees subject to FACA if they do not advise the executive branch or have authority to do so. *National Anti-Hunger Coalition*, 711 F.2d 1071 (*dicta* indicates that FACA would apply if advisory committee was merely "rubber stamping the task forces' recommendations," *Id.* at 1075-76); *See also* 41 C.F.R. § 101-6.1004(k). Heightened scrutiny is required to determine whether FACA applies to a task force that supports a committee not itself subject to FACA. *Clinton*, 997 F.2d at 913.

3.5.9. FACA does not apply when individuals, rather than a group, provide their advice. *National Resources Defense Council v. Herrington*, 637 F. Supp. 116 (D.D.C. 1986); *see also* 41 C.F.R. § 101-6.1004(h) & (i).

3.5.10. FACA "was not intended to apply to all amorphous, ad hoc groups meetings," or to "impede casual, informal contacts by the President or his immediate staff with interested segments of the population...." *Nader v. Baroody*, 396 F. Supp. 1231, 1233-34 (D.D.C. 1975); *see also National Anti-Hunger Coalition*, 711 F.2d at 1073 n.1. Instead Congress intended FACA to apply to "groups having some sort of established structure and defined purpose as 'advisory committees,'" and which receive a governmental "request for specific recommendations on a particular matter of governmental policy." *Id; see also Grigsby Branford Co. v. A.H. Williams & Co.*, 869 F. Supp. 984 (D.D.C. 1994).

3.5.11. A private group is not an advisory committee where the group seeks advice from an agency about a program it intends to implement voluntarily and about which the agency has no authority to regulate. *Consumers Union v. HEW*, 409 F.2d 466 (D.C. Cir. 1976).

3.5.12. In 1997, Congress amended FACA to define "advisory committee" to not apply to "any committee that is created by the National Academy of Sciences or the National Academy of Public Administration." 5 U.S.C. App. II 3(2).

3.5.12.1. However, an agency may not use any advice provided by NAS or NAPA that was developed by use of a committee created by that academy under an agreement with an agency unless certain FACA requirements are met. The NAS or the NAPA may not use the advice of such a committee unless:

3.5.12.2. (1) there is no "actual management or control" by an agent or officer of the Federal Government;

3.5.12.3. (2) in the case of committees created after December 17, 1997, the committee membership was appointed in accordance with § 15(b)(1) of FACA; and

3.5.12.4. (3) the Committee otherwise complied with § 15(b)(1) of § 15, as appropriate for the NAS or the NAPA.

3.5.12.4.1. The requirements of § 15(b)(1) include (1) public notice of committee members, avoidance of conflicts of interest by committee members, committee membership that is "fairly balanced" and independent judgment by the Academy in its final report;

3.5.12.4.2. (2) public notice and access to committee meeting;

3.5.12.4.3. (3) public access to materials provided to the committee by persons outside the Academy subject to FOIA's exemptions;

3.5.12.4.4. (4) public access to a summary of any committee meeting that is not a data gathering meeting, subject to FOIA's exemptions;

3.5.12.4.5. (5) public access to the Academy's final report, or, if necessary, an abbreviated version of the report that does not disclose information exempt under FOIA; and, in the case of NAS,

3.5.12.4.6. (6) public access to the names of the principal reviewers of any draft report who are outside the Academy. These special procedures apply retroactively from December 17, 1997, except for advice subject to judicial action before that date, i.e., the advice subject to disclosure as a result of *Animal Legal Defense Fund, Inc. v. Shalala*, 104 F.3d 424 (D.C. Cir. 1997). *See supra* 3.4.4.

4. What May an Advisory Committee Do?

4.1. "An advisory committee shall be utilized solely for advisory functions," unless a statute or the President has specifically provided otherwise. 5 U.S.C. App. II § 9(b).

4.2. Only the President or an officer of the federal government may determine any action to be taken or policy to be expressed with respect to reports or recommendations by advisory committees. *Id.*

4.3. FACA explicitly prescribes the function of advisory committees to preclude further use of such committees to make government decisions. The legislative history shows that: A number of committees observed by both the House and the Senate inquiries have been allowed to take on a quasi-decision-making status for a variety of reasons which may include neglect, prestige, technical expertise, academic competence, industry pressure, or even political feasibility. S. Rep. 1098 at 13-14, *reprinted in FACA Source Book* at 163-64.

5. Who May Advisory Committees Advise?

5.1. Any agency within the meaning of 5 U.S.C. § 551(1) must comply with FACA. 5 U.S.C. App. II § 3(3); *Lombardo*, 397 F. Supp. at 792.

5.2. FACA also applies to committees that advise the President, known as "Presidential Advisory Committees." 5 U.S.C. App. II §§ 3(2) & (4).

5.2.2. A Presidential advisory committee need not be created by the President. H.R. Rep. No. 1017, 1972 U.S. Code Cong. & Admin. News 3495; *FACA Source Book* at 275.

5.2.3. Provisions governing Presidential Advisory Committees and the President's obligations with respect to them are set out in 5 U.S.C. App. II § 6. In particular, § 6(b) requires the President to report to Congress, within a year of the submission of a public report by a Presidential advisory committee, either the President's proposals for action or his reasons for inaction, with regard to the recommendations contained in the committee's report. 5 U.S.C. App. II § 6(b).

5.2.4. Provision of advisory committee report to Congress, as well as to an agency, does not remove committee from FACA. *Californian Forestry Assoc. v. U.S. Forest Service*, 102 F.3d 609, 612 (D.C. Cir. 1996).

6. FACA Requires that the Membership of an Advisory Committee be "Fairly Balanced."

6.1. Section 5(b) of FACA requires: the membership of the advisory committee to be fairly balanced in terms of points of view represented and the functions to be performed by the advisory committee. 5. U.S.C. App. II § 5(b).

6.2. The purpose of this requirement is to prevent undue influence on agency decision-making by special interest groups, *see* H.R. Rep. No. 1017 at 6; *reprinted in* 1972 U.S. Code Cong. & Admin. News at 3496, *FACA Source Book* at 276; S. Rep. No. 1098 at 4-5,9-10, *reprinted in FACA Source Book* at 154-55, 159-60. The Fifth Circuit and D.C. Circuit have held this requirement justiciable. *Cargill, Inc. v. United States*, 173 F.3d 323, 334 (5th Cir. 1999). *See Public Citizen v. National Advisory Committee on Microbiological Criteria for Foods*, 886 F.2d 419 (D.C. Cir. 1989); *National Anti-Hunger Coalition v. Executive Committee*, 711 F.2d 1071 (D.C. Cir. 1983). "Agencies have considerable discretion to determine whether an advisory committee is fundamentally balanced and adequately staffed." *Cargill*, 173 F.3d at 336; *Microbiological Criteria*, 886 F.2d at 424 (Friedman, J., concurring) and 434 (Edwards, J. concurring in part and dissenting in part) (defense may be due to "difficulty of determining what precisely constitutes a 'fair balance.'"). It appears, however, that no court has ordered a change in an advisory committee's membership, and only one court has issued any relief under this provision. *National Anti-Hunger Coalition v. Executive Committee of the President's Private Sector Survey on Cost Control*, 566 F. Supp. 1515 (D.D.C. 1983) .

6.3. The problems with this provision are highlighted by the three opinions issued in the D.C. Circuit's *Microbiological* decision, 886 F.2d at 419, which concerned an advisory committee that lacked any consumer representation although it was considering regulations to make food products safe. *Microbiological, supra.* One judge concluded that the provision was so vague that it was not violated, another that it was so vague that it could not be enforced, and the third judge concluded that the provision was violated. *See* section 7.3., *infra*.

6.4. Does § 5(b)(2) apply to all advisory committees?

6.4.1. By its terms, § 5(b)(2) applies to any advisory committee established by legislation. It also applies by incorporation to advisory committees established by the President and agencies. 5 U.S.C. App. II § 5(c); *National Anti-Hunger Coalition*, 711 F.2d at 1073 n.1.

6.4.2. No court has yet resolved whether a "utilized" advisory committee must be "fairly balanced." However, a district court has indicated that the provision would apply to a utilized advisory committee. *Food Chemical News v. Davis*, 378 F. Supp. at 1052 ("The government's consideration of such sensitive issues must not be unduly weighted by input from the private commercial sector, lest the government fall victim to the devastating harm of being regulated by those whom the government is supposed to regulate in the public interest.").

6.5. Plaintiffs alleging that their interests are unrepresented on an advisory committee considering those interests may have standing to sue. "When the [fair balance] requirement is ignored, persons having a direct interest in the committee's purpose suffer injury-in-fact sufficient to confer standing to sue." *National Anti-Hunger Coalition*, 711 F.2d at 1074 n.2. *Compare, id., Public Citizen v. DOJ*, 491 U.S. at 451 n.7, *Microbiological*, 886 F.2d at 420-21, 431, 434, *Washington Legal Foundation v. American Bar Association Standing Committee on Federal Judiciary*, 648 F. Supp. 1353, 1358 (D.D.C. 1986) *with Public Citizen v. HHS*, 795 F. Supp. 1212, 1222 (D.D.C. 1992), *Metcalf v. National Petroleum Council*, 553 F.2d 176, 186-89 (D.C. Cir. 1977), *Mulqueeny v. National Comm'n on the Observance of International Women's Year*, 549 F.2d 1115 (7th Cir. 1977), *Physician's Ed. Network v. HEW*, 653 F.2d 621 (D.C. Cir. 1981).

6.6. What constitutes "balance"?

6.6.1. Whether an advisory committee's membership is balanced depends on whether it "represents[s] a fair balance of viewpoints given the functions to be performed." *National Anti-Hunger Coalition*, 711 F.2d at 1074 and n.2. The GSA has also interpreted the balanced representation provision to require agencies to "consider for membership a cross-section of interested persons and groups with demonstrated professional or personal qualifications or experience to contribute to the functions and tasks to be performed." 41 C.F.R. § 101-6.1007(a)(2)(iii).

6.6.2. The House Report on FACA gave the following example of an advisory committee that was not "fairly balanced": When [an advisory committee] met with government officials to consider a proposed national industrial wastes inventory questionnaire, only representatives of industry were present. No representatives of conservation, environment, clean water, consumer, or other public interest groups were present. This lack of balanced representation of different points of view and the heavy representation of parties whose private interests could influence their recommendation should be prohibited by the provision contained in [FACA]. H.R. Rep. No. 92-1017, *supra*, at 6, *reprinted in* 1972 U.S. Code Cong. & Admin. News at 3496, *FACA Source Book* at 276.

6.6.3. If an advisory committee is not fairly balanced, then the recommendations that it has issued are "*ultra vires* and illegal because of the lack of fair balance." *National Anti-Hunger Coalition v. Executive Committee of the President's Private Sector Survey on Cost Control*, 566 F. Supp. 1515, 1516-17 (D.D.C. 1983), *amending judgment, dismissing complaint*, 557 F. Supp. 524 (D.D.C. 1983).

7. Authority Creating Advisory Committee Must Take Appropriate Measures to Avoid Undue Influence over Advisory Committee's Activities.

7.1. Section 5(b)(3) states that the authority creating an advisory committee must make: appropriate provisions to assure that the advice and recommendations of the advisory committee will not be inappropriately influenced by the appointing authority or by any special interest, but will instead be the result of the advisory committee's independent judgment.

7.2. This provision has been the subject of little judicial attention since FACA's enactment in 1972.

7.3. The D.C. Circuit divided in its only decision to consider the application of § 5(b)(3). *Microbiological, supra.* Judge Friedman concluded that § 5(b)(3) was not violated although a committee considering food safety issues was composed of 18 members of which 10 were either employed by or had financial ties to the food industry. 886 F.2d at 425-26. Judge Silberman found the section non-justifiable. *Id.* at 430-31. Judge Edwards did not state an opinion with regard to this provision.

7.4. While FACA does not speak specifically of conflict of interest reporting by advisory committee members, such reporting would be a means for an authority creating an advisory committee to assure that advice and recommendations from its advisory committees are not unduly influenced by the appointing authority or by special interests.

7.4.1. There are reporting requirements applicable to advisory committee members under the Ethics in Government Act. 18 U.S.C. App. 4 §§ 201-7; E.O. No. 11,222 § 306; *see also* E.O. No. 12,565 § 403; E.O. No. 12,674 § 201(d). These requirements apply to "special government employees," who are officers or employees of the executive branch and who are "retained, designated, appointed, or employed to perform, with or without compensation...temporary duties either on a full-time or intermittent basis" for a period of 130 days or less during a 365-day period. *Id.*

7.4.2. Conflict of interest forms and the regulations of the Office of Personnel Management give the agencies discretion to release the forms to the public by providing that "[a]n agency may not disclose information from a statement except as OPM or the agency head may determine for good cause shown." 5 C.F.R. § 735.410.

8. Each Advisory Committee Must be Chartered Before It May Take Any Action.

8.1. Before an advisory committee meets or takes any action, a charter for it must be filed with (1) the Administrator of GSA, in the case of Presidential advisory committees, or (2) with the head of the agency to whom the advisory committee reports, as well as with the standing committees of the Senate and of the House of Representatives having legislative jurisdiction over such agency. 5 U.S.C. App. II § 9(c). Advisory Committee may not lawfully "meet or take action" if the requests of § 9 have not been met. *Cargill v. United States*, 173 F.3d 323, 330 (5th Cir. 1999).

8.2. A copy of any such charter must also be furnished to the Library of Congress. *Id.; see also* 41 C.F.R. § 101-6.1013.

8.3. Among other things, each charter must contain the following information: the committee's objectives and the scope of its activities; the period of time necessary for the committee to carry out its purposes; the agency responsible for providing the necessary support for the committee; a description of the duties for which the committee is responsible, and, if such duties are not solely advisory, a specification of the authority for such functions. 5 U.S.C. App. II § 9(c).

8.4. Failure to comply with FACA's procedural prerequisites for convening an advisory committee, recited in §§ 9(a)-(c) of the Act, "cannot be employed as a subterfuge for avoiding the Act's public access requirements." *Food Chemical News v. Davis*, 378 F. Supp. at 1051).

9. Public Access.

9.1. Notice of Advisory Committee Meetings.

9.1.1. Section 10(a)(2) requires that timely notice of each advisory committee meeting be published in the Federal Register, unless the President determines otherwise for reasons of national security. Timely notice requires that notice of a meeting must be published in the Federal Register 15 days prior to that meeting. 41 C.F.R. § 101-6.1015(b)(1); *Bureau of National Affairs v. President's Council of Advisors of Science and Technology*, C.A. 92-1088 (D.D.C. 1993) (stipulation of liability for failure to provide timely notice of advisory committee meetings).

9.1.2. The notice must include the proper name of the committee, the time, place, and purpose of the meeting, a summary of the agenda, and whether all or part of the meeting is open to the public or closed, and if closed, the reasons why, citing the exemption(s) in the Government in the Sunshine Act relied upon for closure. *Id.*

9.1.3. "This requirement, like those contained in section 10(b), is designed to assure public access to deliberations of advisory committees." H.R. Rep. No. 1017, reprinted in 1972 U.S. Code Cong. & Admin. News 3500, *FACA Source Book* at 280-81.

9.1.4. GSA regulations provide for less than timely notice of an advisory committee meeting under "exceptional circumstances," which must be stated in the Federal Register notice. 41 C.F.R. § 101-6.1015(b)(2).

9.2. Public Access to and Participation in Advisory Committee Meetings.

9.2.1. "Each advisory committee meeting shall be open to the public." 5 U.S.C. App. II § 10(a)(1).

9.2.2. "Interested persons shall be permitted to attend, appear before, or file statements with any advisory committee, subject to such reasonable rules or regulations as the Administrator shall prescribe." 5 U.S.C. App. II § 10(a)(3); *see also* 41 C.F.R. § 101-6.1021.

9.2.2.1. This provision does not create a right of public participation. *Gates v. Schlesinger*, 366 F. Supp. 797, 801 (D.D.C. 1973).

9.2.2.2. The public has no right to compel an agency to convene an advisory committee for a meeting, even where the committee's charter states that it will meet a specific number of times a year. Advisory committees render advice at the pleasure of governmental agencies and, therefore, the agencies are at liberty to not have them meet. *Dabney v. Reagan*, 559 F. Supp. 861, 865 (S.D.N.Y. 1982) (concerning §§ 10(b)(e) & (f)).

9.2.3. The public access requirement sections 10(a)(1) & 10(a)(3) do not apply "to any portion of any advisory committee meeting where the President, or the head of the agency to which the advisory committee reports, determines that such portion of such meeting may be closed to the public in accordance with subsection (c) of § 552b of Title 5." 5 U.S.C. App. II § 10(d). 5 U.S.C. § 552b(c) specifies the ten exemptions in the Government in the Sunshine Act.

9.2.4. "Any such determination shall be in writing and shall contain the reasons for such determination." 5 U.S.C. App. II § 10(d); *Nader v. Dunlop*, 370 F. Supp. 177 (D.D.C. 1973).

9.2.5. If a determination is made pursuant to § 10(d), the advisory committee "shall issue a report at least annually setting forth a summary of its activities and such related matters as would be informative to the public consistent with the policy of section 552(b)"—i.e., the nine exemptions to the Freedom of Information Act.

9.2.6. The government bears the burden of proof that a meeting or portion of a meeting is exempt from the open meeting requirement. *Public Citizen v. National Economic Commission*, 703 F. Supp. 113, 117, 119 (D.D.C. 1989); *Nader*, 370 F. Supp. at 177.

9.2.7. Exemption 9(B) of the Government in the Sunshine Act does not incorporate any deliberative process privilege. *Id.*

9.2.8. FACA originally incorporated only the exemptions of the Freedom of Information Act. Pub. L. 92-463, 86 Stat. 775, § 10(d) (1972). Congress amended FACA at the time it passed the Government in the Sunshine Act to provide that exemptions of the Sunshine Act apply to advisory committee meetings. 5 U.S.C. § 552b, Pub. L. 94-409, 90 Stat. 1247, § 5(c) (1976). This change prevented further application of the deliberative process privilege of Exemption 5 of the FOIA to close meetings, specifically overruling *Aviation Consumer Action Project v. Washburn*, 535 F.2d 101 (D.C. Cir. 1976). Conf. Rep. No. 94-1178, 94th Cong., 2d Sess. at 26 (1976); *reprinted in* 1976 U.S. Code Cong. & Admin. News 2183, 2262, *Government in the Sunshine Source Book: Legislative History, Texts, and other Documents*, Committees on Government Operations, U.S. Senate and House of Representatives, 94th cong, 2d Sess. 808 (1976).

9.3. Public Access to Advisory Committee Records.

9.3.1. Section 10(b) states that: "[r]ecords, reports, transcripts, minutes, appendices, working papers, drafts, studies, agenda, or other documents which were made available to or prepared by each advisory committee shall be available for public inspection and copying at a single location in the offices of the advisory committee or the agency to which the advisory committee reports until the advisory committee ceases to exist." 5. U.S.C. App. II § 10(b).

9.3.2. Section 10(b) materials must be made available for public inspection and copying before or on the date of the advisory committee meeting to which they apply. However, an agency may require a FOIA request for advisory committee records reasonably claimed by it to be exempt from public disclosure. *Food Chemical News v. HHS*, 980 F.2d 1468 (D.C. Cir. 1992).

9.3.3. The agency to which the advisory committee reports must "assemble and maintain the reports, records, and other papers" of a committee during its existence, and comply with the provisions of the Freedom of Information Act with respect to these records. 5 U.S.C. App. II § 8(b)(2) & (3).

9.3.4. The D.C. Circuit has concluded that FACA does not require an entity receiving a request for records over which it has neither possession nor control to forward that request to the appropriate entity. *National Security Archive v. Archivist of the United States*, 909 F.2d 541 (D.C. Cir. 1990).

9.3.5. Exemptions.

9.3.4.1. FACA's right of access to advisory committee records is subject to the same nine exemptions that apply to access to agency records under the Freedom of Information Act, 5 U.S.C. § 552(b).

9.3.4.2. The Ninth Circuit has held that the Ethics in Government Act is an Exemption 3 statute under the FOIA, requiring nondisclosure of financial statements of members of an advisory committee of the Environmental Protection Agency. *Meyerhoff v. EPA*, 958 F.2d 1498 (9th Cir. 1992), *affirming* 728 F. Supp. 613 (N.D. Cal. 1990).

9.3.4.3. Exemption 5 does not apply to draft reports, working papers and other documents made available to or prepared by or for an advisory committee. *See, e.g.*, *Food Chemical News v. Advisory Committee on the Food and Drug Administration*, 760 F. Supp. 220 (D.D.C. 1991), *affirmed as clarified sub nom. Food Chemical News v. HHS*, 980 F.2d 1468 (D.C. Cir. 1992); *ACLU v. Attorney General's Commission on Pornography*, C.A. No. 86-0893 (D.D.C. 1986); *Bureau of National Affairs v. President's Council of Advisors of Science and Technology*, C.A. 92-1088 (D.D.C. 1993) (stipulation required public disclosure).

9.3.6. "Detailed minutes of each meeting of each advisory committee shall be kept and shall contain a record of the persons present, a complete and accurate description of matters discussed and conclusions reached, and copies of all reports received, issued, or approved by the advisory committee." 5 U.S.C. App. II § 10(c). These transcripts must be made available to the public upon request.

9.3.7. At least eight copies of each report made by each advisory committee, and, where appropriate, background papers prepared by consultants, must be available for public inspection and use at the Library of Congress. 5 U.S.C. App. II § 13.

9.4. Any person has standing to challenge denial to him of access to advisory committee meetings and records. *Public Citizen v. DOJ*, 491 U.S. at 450-51.

10. Government Supervision of Advisory Committees.

10.1. The General Services Administration is "responsible for all matters relating to advisory committees." 5 U.S.C. App. II § 7(a)-(d). *See supra* 1.6.

10.2. Agency Supervision.

10.2.1. An agency must exercise control and supervision over the establishment, procedures, and accomplishments of its advisory committees. 5 U.S.C. App. II § 8(b)(1). In this regard, an agency must keep complete records of the nature and extent of its advisory committees' activities and use of funds. 5 U.S.C. App. II § 12(a).

10.2.2. Each agency must provide support for its advisory committees, as well as maintain and make their records available to the public. 5 U.S.C. App. II §§ 12(b), 8(b) & (3).

10.2.3. Each meeting of an advisory committee must be chaired or attended by a designated government officer or employee. 5 U.S.C. App. II § 10(e). That officer or employee is authorized to adjourn any meeting upon a determination that to do so is in the public interest. *Id.* In addition, the government officer or employee must call or approve of that meeting and, unless the committee is a Presidential advisory committee, must approve the agenda. 5 U.S.C. App. II § 10(f).

10.2.3.1. Agency decision whether to adjourn an advisory committee meeting is committed to agency discretion. *Claybrook v. Slater*, 111 F.3d 904, 907 (D.C. Cir. 1997).

10.2.4. Each agency is responsible for providing support services to its advisory committees. 5 U.S.C. App. II § 12(b).

10.3. Congressional Oversight.

10.3.1. The standing committees of each house of Congress must review the necessity of advisory committees under their jurisdiction on an ongoing basis. 5 U.S.C. App. II § 5(a).

10.3.2. Each year the President must report to Congress on the activities, status, and changes in the composition of advisory committees in existence during the preceding calendar year. 5 U.S.C. App. II § 6(c).

11. Termination of Advisory Committees.

11.1. Each advisory committee has a two-year life span unless a different period is specified by statute or the committee's creating authority takes appropriate action to renew its existence. 5 U.S.C. App. II § 14(a); H.R. Rep. No. 1017, *reprinted in* 1972 U.S. Code Cong. & Admin. News 3492, 3499; *FACA Source Book* at 272, 279.

11.2. Appropriate action must be taken for the renewal prior to the expiration of the advisory committee's two-year term. A renewal may be for a period of up to two years. 5 U.S.C. App. II § 14(b) & (c).

11.3. A new charter must be filed for each advisory committee each time it is renewed. 5 U.S.C. App. II § 14(b).

12. Filing a Complaint.

12.1. A FACA violation may be addressed by a complaint brought under the Administrative Procedure Act, 5 U.S.C. § 706. While FACA does not explicitly provide a cause of action, the courts have recognized a private right of action under FACA. *See, e.g., Washington Legal Foundation*, 648 F. Supp. at 1361; *but see Judicial Watch v. National Energy Policy Development Group*, C.A. 01-530 (EGS) (D.D.C. July 11, 2002) (citing *Alexander v. Sandoval*, 532 U.S. 275 (2001)).

12.2. The complaint should be succinct, stating the material facts, the agency's alleged noncompliance with FACA, and the requested relief. *See* sample complaint in Appendix F.

12.3. Who is the Proper Party to Sue?

12.3.1. The agency to whom the advisory committee reports is a proper defendant. *Cf. Public Citizen v. DOJ, supra.*

12.3.2. A private party that is not established, appointed, or financed by the government is not a proper party. *Washington Legal Foundation v. American Bar Ass'n*, 648 F. Supp. at 1359-61.

12.4. As to proper venue, plaintiffs may at least sue where the defendant is located. *Public Citizen v. DOJ, supra.*

12.5. Relief.

12.5.1. Plaintiffs may sue for declaratory and injunctive relief. See, e.g., *National Anti-Hunger Coalition*, 566 F. Supp. at 1516-17; *Public Citizen v. National Economic Commission*, 703 F. Supp. at 120; *Cargill*, 173 F.3d at 340. *Alabama-Tombigbee Rivers Coalition v. Department of Interior*, 26 F.3d 1103 (11th Cir. 1994) declaring that "the fact that an instance of noncompliance with FACA seems trivial and inconsequential should not deter the court from granting some type of injunctive relief."

12.5.2. Relief should also include reasonable attorney fees and costs. FACA does not contain any provision expressly authorizing an award of attorney fees to parties that successfully challenge noncompliance with the Act. In practice, attorneys have relied upon the Equal Access to Justice Act, 28 U.S.C. § 2412(d), to recover attorney fees.

12.5.3. An injunction against agency use of an advisory committee report may be requested. 5 U.S.C. App. II § 3; *Alabama-Tombigbee Rivers Coalition v. Department of Interior*, 26 F.3d 1103 (11th Cir. 1994) (court enjoined agency use of report prepared in violation of FACA). The D.C. Circuit regards a use injunction as a "remedy of last resort." *NRDC v. Pena*, 147 F.3d 1012, 1025 (D.C. Cir. 1998). In evaluating a request for a use injunction, the D.C. Circuit has advised the district court to consider whether there has been a delay in seeking this relief and, if so, who caused it, the plaintiff or the defendant; whether the defendant otherwise acted to deprive the plaintiff of effective relief; whether an injunction would serve "FACA's principal purposes—(1) avoidance of wasteful expenditures and (2) public accountability—and if so, to what extent. *NRDC v. Pena*, 147 F.3d at 1025-27.

12.6. Standing

12.6.1. In *Public Citizen v. DOJ*, 491 U.S. 440 (1989), the Supreme Court held that the "refusal to permit appellants to scrutinize the ABA committee's activities to the extent FACA allows constitutes a sufficiently distinct injury to provide standing to sue." 491 U.S. at 449. The Court further held that the "[a]ppellants' potential gains are undoubtedly sufficient to give them standing." *Id.* at 451. These potential gains included a ruling that would require the advisory committee "to file a charter and give notice of its meetings," public attendance at some committee meetings, and public access to some committee records. *Id.* at 450.

12.6.2. Member of an advisory committee has standing to sue for violation of FACA founded on the committee's failure to provide her with information required under the Act. *Cummock v. Gore*, 180 F.3d 282 (D.C. Cir. 1999) (duly appointed advisory committee member has special rights of access to committee records and has right to fully participate in the work of the committee).

12.6.3. Declaratory relief addresses failure by agency to make public records until they are no longer useful to requester. *Byrd v. EPA*, 174 F.3d 239, 242 (D.C. Cir. 1999). A declaration that the agency violated FACA would give requestor "ammunition for [his] attack on the Committee's findings." *NRDC v. Pena*, 147 F.3d at 1026 n. 6. Such a declaration could also cause the agency to change its practices to conform with FACA. *Byrd*, 174 F.3d at 242.

12.6.4. Plaintiffs seeking to enjoin an agency from using an advisory committee report must show that the agency's use of the report will cause them Article III injury in fact. *NRDC v. Pena*, 147 F.3d 1012, 1020 (D.C. Cir. 1998). Injunctive relief is remedial and calls for allegations regarding the likely reoccurrence of FACA violations. *Id.* at 1021. In this regard an agency's ongoing refusal to provide public access to committee records does not support standing to sue for an injunction against agency use of the committee's final report. *Id.*

12.6.5. Standing requires allegation of non-speculative causal connection between the alleged injury and the allegedly improper conduct. *Compare*, *Alabama-Tombigbee Rivers Coalition v. Department of Interior*, 26 F.3d 1103 (11th Cir. 1994) and *Florida Association of Medical Equipment Dealers v. Aptel*, 194 F.3d 1227, 1229-30 (11th Cir. 1999).

12.6.6. Person affected by work of advisory committee has standing to challenge filing of advisory committee's charter with wrong congressional committee. *Cargill v. United States*, 173 F.3d 323, 330 (5th Cir. 1999).

13. Discovery.

13.1. Plaintiffs are entitled to take discovery or streamline request for equitable relief to address jurisdictional requirements. *NRDC v. Pena*, 147 F.3d at 1022.

14. Mootness.

14.1. Allegations of tardiness of release of advisory committee records defeats claim of mootness based on release of records. *Byrd v. EPA*, 174 F.3d 239, 242 (D.C. Cir. 1999).

15. Miscellaneous.

15.1. A court has granted qualified immunity to members of an advisory committee accused of violating the First Amendment rights of others to speak. *Playboy Enterprises, Inc. v. Meese*, 746 F. Supp. 154 (D.D.C. 1990).

APPENDIX A
Text of the Freedom of Information Act

This appendix is available online at http://www.epic.org/foia/21/appendixa.html

The FOIA, originally enacted in 1966 and amended in 1974, 1976, 1986, and 1996, is codified as Section 552 of Title 5 of the United States Code (5 U.S.C. § 552). Its current complete text follows.

§ 552. Public information; agency rules, opinions, orders, records, and proceedings

(a) Each agency shall make available to the public information as follows:

(1) Each agency shall separately state and currently publish in the Federal Register for the guidance of the public—

(A) descriptions of its central and field organization and the established places at which, the employees (and in the case of a uniformed service, the members) from whom, and the methods whereby, the public may obtain information, make submittals or requests, or obtain decisions;

(B) statements of the general course and method by which its functions are channeled and determined, including the nature and requirements of all formal and informal procedures available;

(C) rules of procedure, descriptions of forms available or the places at which forms may be obtained, and instructions as to the scope and contents of all papers, reports, or examinations;

(D) substantive rules of general applicability adopted as authorized by law, and statements of general policy or interpretations of general applicability formulated and adopted by the agency; and

(E) each amendment, revision, or repeal of the foregoing.

Except to the extent that a person has actual and timely notice of the terms thereof, a person may not in any manner be required to resort to, or be adversely affected by, a matter required to be published in the Federal Register and not so published. For the purpose of this paragraph, matter reasonably available to the class of persons affected thereby is deemed published in the Federal Register when incorporated by reference therein with the approval of the Director of the Federal Register.

(2) Each agency, in accordance with published rules, shall make available for public inspection and copying—

(A) final opinions, including concurring and dissenting opinions, as well as orders, made in the adjudication of cases;

(B) those statements of policy and interpretations which have been adopted by the agency and are not published in the Federal Register;

(C) administrative staff manuals and instructions to staff that affect a member of the public;

(D) copies of all records, regardless of form or format, which have been released to any person under paragraph (3) and which, because of the nature of their subject matter, the agency determines have become or are likely to become the subject of subsequent requests for substantially the same records; and

(E) a general index of the records referred to under subparagraph (D);

unless the materials are promptly published and copies offered for sale. For records created on or after November 1, 1996, within one year after such date, each agency shall make such records available, including by computer telecommunications or, if computer telecommunications means have not been established by the agency, by other electronic means. To the extent required to prevent a clearly unwarranted invasion of personal privacy, an agency may delete identifying details when it makes available or publishes an opinion, statement of policy, interpretation, staff manual, instruction, or copies of records referred to in subparagraph (D). However, in each case the justification for the deletion shall be explained fully in writing, and the extent of such deletion shall be indicated on the portion of the record which is made available or published, unless including that indication would harm an interest protected by the exemption in subsection (b) under which the deletion is made. If technically feasible, the extent of the deletion shall be indicated at the place in the record where the deletion was made. Each agency shall also maintain and make available for public inspection and copying current indexes providing identifying information for the public as to any matter issued, adopted, or promulgated after July 4, 1967, and required by this paragraph to be made available or published. Each agency shall promptly publish, quarterly or more frequently, and distribute (by sale or otherwise) copies of each index or supplements thereto unless it determines by order published in the Federal Register that the publication would be unnecessary and impracticable, in which case the agency shall nonetheless provide copies of an index on request at a cost not to exceed the direct cost of duplication. Each agency shall make the index referred to in subparagraph (E) available by computer telecommunications by December 31, 1999. A final order, opinion, statement of policy, interpretation, or staff manual or instruction that affects a member of the public may be relied on, used, or cited as precedent by an agency against a party other than an agency only if—

(i) it has been indexed and either made available or published as provided by this paragraph; or

(ii) the party has actual and timely notice of the terms thereof.

(3)(A) Except with respect to the records made available under paragraphs (1) and (2) of this subsection, each agency, upon any request for records which (i) reasonably describes such records and (ii) is made in accordance with published rules stating the time, place, fees (if any), and procedures to be followed, shall make the records promptly available to any person.

(B) In making any record available to a person under this paragraph, an agency shall provide the record in any form or format requested by the person if the record is readily reproducible by the agency in that form or format. Each agency shall make reasonable efforts to maintain its records in forms or formats that are reproducible for purposes of this section.

(C) In responding under this paragraph to a request for records, an agency shall make reasonable efforts to search for the records in electronic form or format, except when such efforts would significantly interfere with the operation of the agency's automated information system.

(D) For purposes of this paragraph, the term "search" means to review, manually or by automated means, agency records for the purpose of locating those records which are responsive to a request.

(4)(A)(i) In order to carry out the provisions of this section, each agency shall promulgate regulations, pursuant to notice and receipt of public comment, specifying the schedule of fees applicable to the processing of requests under this section and establishing procedures and guidelines for determining when such fees should be waived or reduced. Such schedule shall conform to the guidelines which shall be promulgated, pursuant to notice and receipt of public comment, by the Director of the Office of Management and Budget and which shall provide for a uniform schedule of fees for all agencies.

(ii) Such agency regulations shall provide that—

(I) fees shall be limited to reasonable standard charges for document search, duplication, and review, when records are requested for commercial use;

(II) fees shall be limited to reasonable standard charges for document duplication when records are not sought for commercial use and the request is made by an educational or noncommercial scientific institution, whose purpose is scholarly or scientific research; or a representative of the news media; and

(III) for any request not described in (I) or (II), fees shall be limited to reasonable standard charges for document search and duplication.

(iii) Documents shall be furnished without any charge or at a charge reduced below the fees established under clause (ii) if disclosure of the information is in the public interest because it is likely to contribute significantly to public understanding of the operations or activities of the government and is not primarily in the commercial interest of the requester.

(iv) Fee schedules shall provide for the recovery of only the direct costs of search, duplication, or review. Review costs shall include only the direct costs incurred during the initial examination of a document for the purposes of determining whether the documents must be disclosed under this section and for the purposes of withholding any portions exempt from disclosure under this section. Review costs may not include any costs incurred in resolving issues of law or policy that may be raised in the course of processing a request under this section. No fee may be charged by any agency under this section—

(I) if the costs of routine collection and processing of the fee are likely to equal or exceed the amount of the fee; or

(II) for any request described in clause (ii)(II) or (III) of this subparagraph for the first two hours of search time or for the first one hundred pages of duplication.

(v) No agency may require advance payment of any fee unless the requester has previously failed to pay fees in a timely fashion, or the agency has determined that the fee will exceed $250.

(vi) Nothing in this subparagraph shall supersede fees chargeable under a statute specifically providing for setting the level of fees for particular types of records.

(vii) In any action by a requester regarding the waiver of fees under this section, the court shall determine the matter de novo, provided that the court's review of the matter shall be limited to the record before the agency.

(B) On complaint, the district court of the United States in the district in which the complainant resides, or has his principal place of business, or in which the agency records are situated, or in the District of Columbia, has jurisdiction to enjoin the agency from withholding agency records and to order the production of any agency records improperly withheld from the complainant. In such a case the court shall determine the matter de novo, and may examine the contents of such agency records in camera to determine whether such records or any part thereof shall be withheld under any of the exemptions set forth in subsection (b) of this section, and the burden is on the agency to sustain its action. In addition to any other matters to which a court accords substantial weight, a court shall accord substantial weight to an affidavit of an agency concerning the agency's determination as to technical feasibility under paragraph (2)(C) and subsection (b) and reproducibility under paragraph (3)(B).

(C) Notwithstanding any other provision of law, the defendant shall serve an answer or otherwise plead to any complaint made under this subsection within thirty days after service upon the defendant of the pleading in which such complaint is made, unless the court other wise directs for good cause is shown.

(D) Repealed by Pub. L. 98-620, Title IV, 402(2), Nov. 8, 1984, 98 Stat. 3335, 3357.

(E) The court may assess against the United States reasonable attorney fees and other litigation costs reasonably incurred in any case under this section in which the complainant has substantially prevailed.

(F) Whenever the court orders the production of any agency records improperly withheld from the complainant and assesses against the United States reasonable attorney fees and other litigation costs, and the court additionally issues a written finding that the circumstances surrounding the withholding raise questions whether agency personnel acted arbitrarily or capriciously with respect to the withholding, the Special Counsel shall promptly initiate a proceeding to determine whether disciplinary action is warranted against the officer or employee who was primarily responsible for the withholding. The Special Counsel, after investigation and consideration of the evidence submitted, shall submit his findings and recommendations to the administrative authority of the agency concerned and shall send copies of the findings and recommendations to the officer or employee or his representative. The administrative authority shall take the corrective action that the Special Counsel recommends.

(G) In the event of noncompliance with the order of the court, the district court may punish for contempt the responsible employee, and in the case of a uniformed service, the responsible member.

(5) Each agency having more than one member shall maintain and make available for public inspection a record of the final votes of each member in every agency proceeding.

(6)(A) Each agency, upon any request for records made under paragraph (1), (2), or (3) of this subsection, shall—

(i) determine within twenty days (excepting Saturdays, Sundays, and legal public holidays) after the receipt of any such request whether to comply with such request and shall immediately notify the person making such request of such determination and the reasons therefor, and of the right of such person to appeal to the head of the agency any adverse determination; and

(ii) make a determination with respect to any appeal within twenty days (excepting Saturdays, Sundays, and legal public holidays) after the receipt of such appeal. If on appeal the denial of the request for records is in whole or in part upheld, the agency shall notify the person making such request of the provisions for judicial review of that determination under paragraph (4) of this subsection.

(B)(i) In unusual circumstances as specified in this subparagraph, the time limits prescribed in either clause (i) or clause (ii) of subparagraph (A) may be extended by written notice to the person making such request setting forth the unusual circumstances for such extension and the date on which a determination is expected to be dispatched. No such notice shall specify a date that would result in an extension for more than ten working days, except as provided in clause (ii) of this subparagraph.

(ii) With respect to a request for which a written notice under clause (i) extends the time limits prescribed under clause (i) of subparagraph (A), the agency shall notify the person making the request if the request cannot be processed within the time limit specified in that clause and shall provide the person an opportunity to limit the scope of the request so that it may be processed within that time limit or an opportunity to arrange with the agency an alternative time frame for processing the request or a modified request. Refusal by the person to reasonably modify the request or arrange such an alternative time frame shall be considered as a factor in determining whether exceptional circumstances exist for purposes of subparagraph (C).

(iii) As used in this subparagraph, "unusual circumstances" means, but only to the extent reasonably necessary to the proper processing of the particular requests—

(I) the need to search for and collect the requested records from field facilities or other establishments that are separate from the office processing the request;

(II) the need to search for, collect, and appropriately examine a voluminous amount of separate and distinct records which are demanded in a single request; or

(III) the need for consultation, which shall be conducted with all practicable speed, with another agency having a substantial interest in the determination of the request or among two or more components of the agency having substantial subject matter interest therein.

(iv) Each agency may promulgate regulations, pursuant to notice and receipt of public comment, providing for the aggregation of certain requests by the same requestor, or by a group of requestors acting in concert, if the agency reasonably believes that such requests actually constitute a single request, which would otherwise satisfy the unusual circumstances specified in this subparagraph, and the requests involve clearly related matters. Multiple requests involving unrelated matters shall not be aggregated.

(C)(i) Any person making a request to any agency for records under paragraph (1), (2), or (3) of this subsection shall be deemed to have exhausted his administrative remedies with respect to such request if the agency fails to comply with the applicable time limit provisions of this paragraph. If the Government can show exceptional circumstances exist and that the agency is exercising due diligence in responding to the request, the court may retain jurisdiction and allow the agency additional time to complete its review of the records. Upon any determination by an agency to comply with a request for records, the records shall be made promptly available to such person making such request. Any notification of denial of any request for records under this subsection shall set forth the names and titles or positions of each person responsible for the denial of such request.

(ii) For purposes of this subparagraph, the term "exceptional circumstances" does not include a delay that results from a predictable agency workload of requests under this section, unless the agency demonstrates reasonable progress in reducing its backlog of pending requests.

(iii) Refusal by a person to reasonably modify the scope of a request or arrange an alternative time frame for processing the request (or a modified request) under clause (ii) after being given an opportunity to do so by the agency to whom the person made the request shall be considered as a factor in determining whether exceptional circumstances exist for purposes of this subparagraph.

(D)(i) Each agency may promulgate regulations, pursuant to notice and receipt of public comment, providing for multitrack processing of requests for records based on the amount of work or time (or both) involved in processing requests.

(ii) Regulations under this subparagraph may provide a person making a request that does not qualify for the fastest multitrack processing an opportunity to limit the scope of the request in order to qualify for faster processing.

(iii) This subparagraph shall not be considered to affect the requirement under subparagraph (C) to exercise due diligence.

(E)(i) Each agency shall promulgate regulations, pursuant to notice and receipt of public comment, providing for expedited processing of requests for records—

(I) in cases in which the person requesting the records demonstrates a compelling need; and

(II) in other cases determined by the agency.

(ii) Notwithstanding clause (i), regulations under this subparagraph must ensure—

(I) that a determination of whether to provide expedited processing shall be made, and notice of the determination shall be provided to the person making the request, within 10 days after the date of the request; and

(II) expeditious consideration of administrative appeals of such determinations of whether to provide expedited processing.

(iii) An agency shall process as soon as practicable any request for records to which the agency has granted expedited processing under this subparagraph. Agency action to deny or affirm denial of a request for expedited processing pursuant to this subparagraph, and failure by an agency to respond in a timely manner to such a request shall be subject to judicial review under paragraph (4), except that the judicial review shall be based on the record before the agency at the time of the determination.

(iv) A district court of the United States shall not have jurisdiction to review an agency denial of expedited processing of a request for records after the agency has provided a complete response to the request.

(v) For purposes of this subparagraph, the term "compelling need" means—

(I) that a failure to obtain requested records on an expedited basis under this paragraph could reasonably be expected to pose an imminent threat to the life or physical safety of an individual; or

(II) with respect to a request made by a person primarily engaged in disseminating information, urgency to inform the public concerning actual or alleged Federal Government activity.

(vi) A demonstration of a compelling need by a person making a request for expedited processing shall be made by a statement certified by such person to be true and correct to the best of such person's knowledge and belief.

(F) In denying a request for records, in whole or in part, an agency shall make a reasonable effort to estimate the volume of any requested matter the provision of which is denied, and shall provide any such estimate to the person making the request, unless providing such estimate would harm an interest protected by the exemption in subsection (b) pursuant to which the denial is made.

(b) This section does not apply to matters that are—

(1)(A) specifically authorized under criteria established by an Executive order to be kept secret in the interest of national defense or foreign policy and (B) are in fact properly classified pursuant to such Executive order;

(2) related solely to the internal personnel rules and practices of an agency;

(3) specifically exempted from disclosure by statute (other than section 552b of this title), provided that such statute (A) requires that the matters be withheld from the public in such a manner as to leave no discretion on the issue, or (B) establishes particular criteria for withholding or refers to particular types of matters to be withheld;

(4) trade secrets and commercial or financial information obtained from a person and privileged or confidential;

(5) inter-agency or intra-agency memorandums or letters which would not be available by law to a party other than an agency in litigation with the agency;

(6) personnel and medical files and similar files the disclosure of which would constitute a clearly unwarranted invasion of personal privacy;

(7) records or information compiled for law enforcement purposes, but only to the extent that the production of such law enforcement records or information (A) could reasonably be expected to interfere with enforcement proceedings, (B) would deprive a person of a right to a fair trial or an impartial adjudication, (C) could reasonably be expected to constitute an unwarranted invasion of personal privacy, (D) could reasonably be expected to disclose the identity of a confidential source, including a State, local, or foreign agency or authority or any private institution which furnished information on a confidential basis, and, in the case of a record or information compiled by a criminal law enforcement authority in the course of a criminal investigation or by an agency conducting a lawful national security intelligence investigation, information furnished by a confidential source, (E) would disclose techniques and procedures for law enforcement investigations or prosecutions, or would disclose guidelines for law enforcement investigations or prosecutions if such disclosure could reasonably be expected to risk circumvention of the law, or (F) could reasonably be expected to endanger the life or physical safety of any individual;

(8) contained in or related to examination, operating, or condition reports prepared by, on behalf of, or for the use of an agency responsible for the regulation or supervision of financial institutions; or

(9) geological and geophysical information and data, including maps, concerning wells.

Any reasonably segregable portion of a record shall be provided to any person requesting such record after deletion of the portions which are exempt under this subsection. The amount of information deleted shall be indicated on the released portion of the record, unless including that indication would harm an interest protected by the exemption in this subsection under which the deletion is made. If technically feasible, the amount of the information deleted shall be indicated at the place in the record where such deletion is made.

(c)(1) Whenever a request is made which involves access to records described in subsection (b)(7)(A) and—

(A) the investigation or proceeding involves a possible violation of criminal law; and

(B) there is reason to believe that (i) the subject of the investigation or proceeding is not aware of its pendency, and (ii) disclosure of the existence of the records could reasonably be expected to interfere with enforcement proceedings, the agency may, during only such time as that circumstance continues, treat the records as not subject to the requirements of this section.

(2) Whenever informant records maintained by a criminal law enforcement agency under an informant's name or personal identifier are requested by a third party according to the informant's name or personal identifier, the agency may treat the records as not subject to the requirements of this section unless the informant's status as an informant has been officially confirmed.

(3) Whenever a request is made which involves access to records maintained by the Federal Bureau of Investigation pertaining to foreign intelligence or counterintelligence, or international terrorism, and the existence of the records is classified information as provided in subsection (b)(1), the Bureau may, as long as the existence of the records remains classified information, treat the records as not subject to the requirements of this section.

(d) This section does not authorize the withholding of information or limit the availability of records to the public, except as specifically stated in this section. This section is not authority to withhold information from Congress.

(e)(1) On or before February 1 of each year, each agency shall submit to the Attorney General of the United States a report which shall cover the preceding fiscal year and which shall include—

(A) the number of determinations made by the agency not to comply with requests for records made to such agency under subsection (a) and the reasons for each such determination;

(B)(i) the number of appeals made by persons under subsection (a)(6), the result of such appeals, and the reason for the action upon each appeal that results in a denial of information; and

(ii) a complete list of all statutes that the agency relies upon to authorize the agency to withhold information under subsection (b)(3), a description of whether a court has upheld the decision of the agency to withhold information under each such statute, and a concise description of the scope of any information withheld;

(C) the number of requests for records pending before the agency as of September 30 of the preceding year, and the median number of days that such requests had been pending before the agency as of that date;

(D) the number of requests for records received by the agency and the number of requests which the agency processed;

(E) the median number of days taken by the agency to process different types of requests;

(F) the total amount of fees collected by the agency for processing requests; and

(G) the number of full-time staff of the agency devoted to processing requests for records under this section, and the total amount expended by the agency for processing such requests.

(2) Each agency shall make each such report available to the public including by computer telecommunications, or if computer telecommunications means have not been established by the agency, by other electronic means.

(3) The Attorney General of the United States shall make each report which has been made available by electronic means available at a single electronic access point. The Attorney General of the United States shall notify the Chairman and ranking minority member of the Committee on Government

Reform and Oversight of the House of Representatives and the Chairman and ranking minority member of the Committees on Governmental Affairs and the Judiciary of the Senate, no later than April 1 of the year in which each such report is issued, that such reports are available by electronic means.

(4) The Attorney General of the United States, in consultation with the Director of the Office of Management and Budget, shall develop reporting and performance guidelines in connection with reports required by this subsection by October 1, 1997, and may establish additional requirements for such reports as the Attorney General determines may be useful.

(5) The Attorney General of the United States shall submit an annual report on or before April 1 of each calendar year which shall include for the prior calendar year a listing of the number of cases arising under this section, the exemption involved in each case, the disposition of such case, and the cost, fees, and penalties assessed under subparagraphs (E), (F), and (G) of subsection (a)(4). Such report shall also include a description of the efforts undertaken by the Department of Justice to encourage agency compliance with this section.

(f) For purposes of this section, the term—

(1) "agency" as defined in section 551(1) of this title includes any executive department, military department, Government corporation, Government controlled corporation, or other establishment in the executive branch of the Government (including the Executive Office of the President), or any independent regulatory agency; and

(2) "record" and any other term used in this section in reference to information includes any information that would be an agency record subject to the requirements of this section when maintained by an agency in any format, including an electronic format.

(g) The head of each agency shall prepare and make publicly available upon request, reference material or a guide for requesting records or information from the agency, subject to the exemptions in subsection (b), including—

(1) an index of all major information systems of the agency;

(2) a description of major information and record locator systems maintained by the agency; and

(3) a handbook for obtaining various types and categories of public information from the agency pursuant to chapter 35 of title 44, and under this section.

Legislative History of the FOIA

1966 Act

The most significant legislative materials concerning the original FOIA have been reprinted in Subcomm. on Adm. Prac. And Proc. Of the Senate Comm. on the Judiciary, *Freedom of Information Act Source Book: Legislative Materials, Cases, Articles*, S. Doc. 93-82, 93d Cong., 2d Sess. (Comm. Print 1974)(commonly "Source Book" or "1966 Source Book").

1. Hearings:

Senate Committee on the Judiciary, Hearings on S. 1160, May 12, 13, 14, and 21, 1965.
Senate Committee on the Judiciary, Hearings on S. 1663, July 21, 22, and 23, 1964.

House Committee on Government Operations, Hearings on H.R. 5012, March 30 and 31, April 1, 2, and 5, 1956 (and Appendix).

2. Senate Passage—88th Congress:

S. Rep. No.1219, 88th Cong. 2d Sess. (S. 1666).
Considered and passed Senate, July 28, 1964, 110 Cong. Rec. 17086.
On motion to reconsider, July 31, 1964, 110 Cong. Rec. 17666.

3. Reports on S. 1160—89th Congress:

S. Rep. No. 813, 89th Cong. 1st Sess., Committee on the Judiciary, October 4, 1965.
H. Rep. No. 1497, 89th Cong. 2d Sess., Committee on Government Operations, May 9, 1966.

4. Floor Consideration of S. 1160—89th Congress:

Considered and passed Senate, October 13, 1965, 111 Cong. Rec. 26820.
Considered and passed House, June 20, 1966, 112 Cong. Rec. 13007.

1974 Amendments

The most significant legislative materials concerning the 1974 amendments to the FOIA have been reprinted in Subcomm. on Govt. information and Individual Rights of the House Comm. on Govt. Op. et al., *Freedom of Information Act and Amendments of 1974. (PL. 93-502) Source Book: Legislative History, Texts, and other Documents*, 94th Cong. 1st Sess. (Joint Comm. Print 1975)(commonly "1974 Source Book").

1. Hearings:

House Committee on Government Operations, May 2, 7, 8, 10, and 16, 1973.
Senate Committee on the Judiciary, April 10, 11, 12, May 8, 9, 10, 16, June 7, 8, 11, and 26, 1972 (and Appendix).

2. House Reports:

H. Rep. No. 93-876 accompanying H.R. 12471 (Comm. on Gov't Op.) and No. 93-1380 (Comm. of Conference).

3. Senate Reports:

S. Rep. No. 93-854 accompanying S. 2543 (Comm. on the Judiciary) and No. 93-1200 (Comm. of Conference).

4. Congressional Record, Vol. 120 (1974):

March 14, considered and passed House.
May 30, considered and passed Senate, amendment in lieu of S. 2543.
October 1, Senate agreed to conference report.
October 7, House agreed to conference report.

5. Weekly Compilation of Presidential Documents, Vol. 10, No. 42:

October 17, vetoed; Presidential message.

6. Congressional Record, Vol. 120 (1974):

November 20, House overrode veto.
November 21, Senate overrode veto.

1976 Amendments

Note: Congress, in passing the "Government in the Sunshine Act," P.L. 94-409, 94th Cong, 2d Sess. S.5, Sept. 13, 1976, 90 Stat. 1241, amended section 552(b)(3), the FOIA exemption relating to other statutes. The pages citied in the legislative history are those pages related specifically to the amendment of the third exemption to the FOIA.

1. House Reports:

H. Rep. No. 94-880, Part I (Comm. on Gov't Op.) 9-10, 22-23, 25.
H. Rep. No. 94-880, Part II (Comm. on the Judiciary) pp. 34, 7, 14, 16, 25.
H. Rep. No. 94-1441 (Comm. of Conference).

2. Senate Reports:

S. Rep. No. 94-354, to accompany S. 5 (Comm. on Gov't Op.), and No. 94-1441 (Comm. of Conference).

3. Congressional Record, daily ed. (1976):

July 28, pp. 7867, 7871-73, 7886, 7897-98: considered and passed House.
July 29, pp. E4187089: remarks of Rep. McCloskey.
August 31, pp. H9258-62: House agreed to Conference Report S15043-45: Senate agreed to Conference Report.

4. Weekly Compilation of Presidential Documents, Vol. 12 (1976) No. 42: p. 1334:

Sept. 13, 1976, signed; Presidential statements.

1978 Amendments

Note: Congress, in passing the Civil Service Report Act, P.L. 95-454, 95th Cong. 2d Sess., S. 2640, 91 Stat. 1111, amended subsection 552(a)(4)(F) to substitute reference to "Special Counsel" for references to the "Civil Service Commission.")

1. House Reports:

H. Rep. No. 95-1403 (Post Office and Civil Service Comm.).
H. Rep. No. 95-1717 (Conference Comm.).

2. Senate Reports:

S. Rep. No. 95-969 (Governmental Affairs Comm.).
S. Rep. No. 95-1272 (Conference Comm.).
See 1978 U.S. Code Cong. and Adm. News, p. 2723.

1984 Amendments

Note: Congress, in passing legislation that included much of a proposed Federal Courts Civil Priorities Act (H.R. 5645) as passed by the House, P.L. 98-620, Title IV, Subtitle A 98th Cong., 2d Sess., 98 Stat. 3356, struck out subsection 552(a)(4)(D) which provided for expedited docketing and hearing of FOIA cases in precedence over other cases no considered of greater importance.

1. House Report:

H. Rep. No. 98-985 (Judiciary Comm.)
See 1984 U.S. Code Cong. and Admin. News, p. 5779.

1986 Amendments

Note: These FOIA amendments were enacted as provisions of the Anti-Drug Abuse Act of 1986, P.L. 99-570, Title I, Subtitle N, Sec. 1801-1804. Because they were adopted initially as Senate floor amendments, there is no mention of them in the numerous committee reports that are cited as part of the legislative history of the public law. The amendments are explained, however, in several floor statements prepared by their individual co-sponsors.

1. Congressional Consideration:

(All cites are to pages of daily edition of Vol. 132 Congressional Record.)
S 13648, 13660-61 (Sept. 25, 1986) [Introduction of Senate Bill (S. 2878)].
S 14033 (Sept. 27, 1986) (Leahy Amendment and Statement).
S 14038-40 (Sept. 27, 1986) (Hatch Statement).
S 14252 (Sept. 30, 1986) (Denton Statement).
S 14295-300 (Sept. 30, 1986) (Leahy Statement).
S 14277-78 (Sept. 30, 1986) (Senate Technical Amendments).
H 9462-68 (Oct. 8, 1986) (English/Kindness Statements).
H 9497-98 (Oct. 8, 1986) (House Approves Amendments).
E 3596 (Oct. 10, 1986) (Correction to English Statement of Oct. 8, 1986).
S 15956 (Oct. 10 1986) (Senate Amendment to House Amendment).
S 16496-97 (Oct. 10, 1986) (Leahy-Kerry Colloquy).
S 16502 (Oct. 15, 1986) (Senate Approves Amendments/Final Text of the FOIA Changes).
S 16504-05 (Oct 15, 1986) (Hatch Statement).
SH 11233-34 (Oct. 17, 1986) (House Amendment to Senate Amendment/Final Text of the FOIA Changes).
H 10787 (Oct. 17, 1986) (House Approves Amendments).
S 16921 (Oct. 17, 1986) (Senate Concurs in House Amendments).

Appendix A

1996 Amendments

Note: These FOIA amendments were enacted as provisions of the Electronic Freedom of Information Act Amendments of 1996, P.L.104-231, 110 Stat. 3048, based on separate Senate (S.1090) and House (H.R.3802) bills that were informally reconciled by their primary sponsors without the need of a formal House-Senate conference. The "Findings and Purposes" section which appears in the Public Law was not codified as part of the statutory text of the amended FOIA.

1. House Report:

No.104-175 accompanying H.R.3802 (Committee on Government Reform and Oversight)

2. Senate Report:

No.104-272 accompanying S.1090 (Committee on the Judiciary)

3. Congressional Record, daily ed.

S 10888-10891 (July 28, 1995) (Text and Introductory Remarks: S.1090)
E 1280-1281 (July 12, 1996) (Text and Introductory Remarks: H.R. 3802)
H 10447-10449 (September 17, 1996) (House passage of H.R.3802)
S 10713-10715 (September 17, 1996) (Senate passage of S.1090, as amended by substitution of H.R.3802)

Conference Report on the 1974 Amendments

93d Congress 2d Session

Senate Report No. 93-1200

FREEDOM OF INFORMATION ACT AMENDMENTS

October 1, 1974 Ordered to be printed

MR. KENNEDY, from the committee of conference, submitted the following

CONFERENCE REPORT

[To accompany H.R. 12471]

The committee of conference on the disagreeing votes of the two Houses on the amendment of the Senate to the bill (H.R. 12471) to amend section 552 of title 5, United States Code, known as the Freedom of Information Act, having met, after full and free conference, have agreed to recommend and do recommend to their respective Houses as follows:

That the House recede from its disagreement to the amendment of the Senate and agree to the same with an amendment as follows:

In lieu of the matter proposed to be inserted by the Senate amendment insert the following:

That (a) the fourth sentence of section 552(a)(2) of title 5, United States Code, is amended to read as follows: "Each agency shall also maintain and make available for public inspection and copying current indexes providing identifying information for the public as to any matter issued, adopted, or promulgated after July 4, 1967, and required by this paragraph to be made available or published in the Federal Register that the publication would be unnecessary and impracticable, in which case the agency shall nonetheless provide copies of such index on request at a cost not to exceed the direct cost of duplication."

(b)(1) Section 552(a)(3) of title 5, United States Code is amended to read as follows:

"(3) Except with respect to the records made available under paragraphs (1) and (2) of this subsection each agency, upon any request for records which (A) reasonably describes such records and (B) is made in accordance with published rules stating the time, place, fees (if any), and procedures to be followed, shall make the records promptly available to any person."

(2) Section 552(a) of title 5, United States Code, is amended by redesignating paragraph (4), and all references thereto, as paragraph (5) and by inserting immediately after paragraph (3) the following new paragraph:

"(4)(A) In order to carry out the provisions of this section, each agency shall promulgate regulations, pursuant to notice and receipt of public comment, specifying a uniform schedule of fees applicable to all constituent units of such agency. Such fees shall be limited to reasonable standard charges for document search and duplication and provide for recovery of only the direct costs of such search and duplication. Documents shall be furnished without charge or at a reduced charge where the agency determines that waiver or reduction of the fee is in the public interest because furnishing the information can be considered as primarily benefiting the general public."

"(B) On complaint, the district court of the United States in the district in which the complainant resides, or has his principal place of business, or in which the agency records are situated, or in the District of Columbia, has jurisdiction to enjoin the agency from withholding agency records and to order the production of any agency records improperly withheld from the complainant. In such a case the court shall determine the matter de novo, and may examine the contents of such agency records in camera to determine whether such records or any part thereof shall be withheld under any of the exemptions set forth in subsection (b) of this section, and the burden is on the agency to sustain its action."

"(C) Notwithstanding any other provision of law, the defendant shall serve an answer or otherwise plead to any complaint made under this subsection within thirty days after service upon the defendant of the pleading in which such complaint is made unless the court otherwise directs for good cause shown."

"(D) Except as to cases the court considers of greater importance, proceedings before the district court, as authorized by this subsection, and appeals therefrom, take precedence on the docket over all cases and shall be assigned for hearing and trial or for argument at the earliest practicable date and expedited in every way."

"(E) The court may assess against the United States reasonable attorney fees and other litigation costs reasonably incurred in any case under this section in which the complainant has substantially prevailed."

"(F) Whenever the court orders the production of any agency records improperly withheld from the complainant and assesses against the United States reasonable attorney fees and other litigation costs, and the court additionally issues a written finding that the circumstances surrounding the withholding raise questions whether agency personnel acted arbitrarily or capriciously with respect to the withholding, the Civil Service Commission shall promptly initiate a proceeding to determine whether disciplinary action is warranted against the officer or employee who was primarily responsible for the withholding. The Commission, after investigation and consideration of the evidence submitted, shall submit its findings and recommendations to the administrative authority to the agency concerned and shall send copies of the findings and recommendations to the officer or employee or his representative. The administrative authority shall take the corrective action that the Commission recommends."

"(G) In the event of noncompliance with the order of the court, the district court may punish for contempt the responsible employee, and in the case of a uniformed service, the responsible member."

(c) Section 552(a) of title 5, United States Code, is amended by adding at the end thereof the following paragraph:

"(6)(A) Each agency, upon any request for records made under paragraph (1), (2), or (3) of this subsection, shall—

"(i) determine within ten days (excepting Saturdays, Sundays, and legal public holidays) after the receipt of any such request whether to comply with such request and shall immediately notify the person making such request of such determination and the reasons therefore, and of the right of such person to appeal to the head of the agency any adverse determination; and

"(ii) make a determination with respect to any appeal within twenty days (excepting Saturdays, Sundays, and legal public holidays) after the receipt of such appeal. If on appeal the denial of the request for records is in whole or in part upheld, the agency shall notify the person making such request of the provisions for judicial review of that determination under paragraph (4) of this subsection."

"(B) In unusual circumstances as specified in this subparagraph, the time limits prescribed in either clause (i) or clause (ii) of subparagraph (A) may be extended by written notice to the person making such request setting forth the reasons for such extension and the date on which a determination is expected to be dispatched. No such notice shall specify a date that would result in an extension for more than ten working days. As used in this subparagraph, 'unusual circumstances' means, but only to the extent reasonable necessary to the proper processing of the particular request—

"(i) the need to search for and collect the requested records from field facilities or other establishments that are separate from the office processing the request;

"(ii) the need to search for, collect, and appropriately examine a voluminous amount of separate and distinct records which are demanded in a single request; or

"(iii) the need for consultation, which shall be conducted with all practicable speed, with another agency having a substantial interest in the determination of the request or among two or more components of the agency having substantial subject-matter interest therein."

"(C) Any person making a request to any agency for records under paragraph (1), (2), or (3) of this subsection shall be deemed to have exhausted his administrative remedies with respect to such request if the agency fails to comply with the applicable time limit provisions of this paragraph. If the Government can show exceptional circumstances exist and that the agency is exercising due diligence in responding to the request, the court may retain jurisdiction and allow the agency additional time to complete its review of the records. Upon any determination by an agency to comply with a request for records, the records shall be made promptly available to such person making such request. Any notification of denial of any request for records under this subsection shall set forth the names and titles or positions of each person responsible for the denial of such request."

SEC. 2. (a) Section 552(b)(1) of title 5, United States Code, is amended to read as follows:

"(1) (A) Specifically authorized under criteria established by an Executive order to be kept secret in the interest of national defense or foreign policy and (B) are in fact properly classified pursuant to such Executive order;"

(b) Section 552(b)(7) of title 5, United States Code, is amended to read as follows:

"(7) investigatory records compiled for law enforcement purposes, but only to the extent that the production of such records would (A) interfere with enforcement proceedings, (B) deprive a person of a right to a fair trial or an impartial adjudication , (C) constitute an unwarranted invasion of personal privacy, (D) disclose the identity of a criminal law enforcement authority in the course of a criminal investigation, or by an agency conducting a lawful national security intelligence investigation, confidential information furnished only be the confidential source (E) disclose investigative techniques and procedures, or (F) endanger the life or physical safety of law enforcement personnel;"

(c) Section 552)b) of title 5, United States Code, is amended by adding at the end the following: "Any reasonable segregable portion of a record shall be provided to any person requesting such record after deletion of the portions which are exempt under this subsection."

SEC. 3 Section 552 of title 5, United States Code, is amended by adding at the end thereof the following new subsections:

"(d) On or before March 1 of each calendar year, each agency shall submit a report covering the preceding calendar year to the Speaker of the House of Representatives and President of the Senate for referral to the appropriate committees of the Congress. The report shall include-

Appendix A

"(1) the number of determinations made by such agency not to comply with requests for records made to such agency under subsection (a) and the reasons for each such determinations;

"(2) the number of appeals made by persons under subsection (a)(6), the result of such appeals, and the reason for the action upon each appeal that results in a denial of information;

"(3) the names and titles or positions of each person responsible for the denial of records requested under this section, and the number of instances of participation for each;

"(4) the results of each proceeding conducted pursuant to subsection (a)(4)(F), including a report of the disciplinary action taken against the officer or employee who was primarily responsible for improperly withholding records or an explanation of why disciplinary action was not taken;

"(5) a copy of every rule made by such agency regarding this section;

"(6) a copy of the fee schedule and the total amount of fees collected by the agency for making records available under this section; and

"(7) such other information as indicates efforts to administer fully this section."

The Attorney General shall submit an annual report on or before March of each calendar year which shall include for the prior calendar year a listing of the number of cases arising under this section, the exemption involved in each case, the disposition of such cases, and the cost, fees, and penalties assessed under subsections (a)(4)(E), (F), and (G). Such report shall also include a description of the efforts undertaken by the Department of Justice to encourage agency compliance with this section.

"(e) For purposes of this section, the term 'agency' as defined in section 551(1) of this title includes any executive department, military department, Government corporation, Government controlled corporation, or other establishment in the executive branch of the Government (including the Executive Office of the President), or any independent regulatory agency."

SEC. 4. The amendments made by this Act shall take effect on the ninetieth day beginning after the date of enactment of this Act.

And the House agrees to the same.

EDWARD KENNEDY,
PHILIP A. HART,
BIRCH BAYH,
QUENTIN BURDICK,
JOHN TUNNEY,
CHARLES McC. MATHIAS, JR.,
Managers on the Part of the Senate.

CHET HOLIFIELD,
WILLIAM S. MOORHEAD,
JOHN E. MOSS,
BILL ALEXANDER,
FRANK HORTON,
JOHN N. ERLENBORN,
PAUL McCLOSKEY,
Managers on the Part of the House.

Joint Explanatory Statement of the Committee of Conference

The managers on the part of the House and the Senate at the conference on the disagreeing votes of the two houses on the amendment of the Senate to the bill (H.R.12471) to amend section 552 of title 5, United States Code, known as the Freedom of Information Act, submit the following joint statement to the House and the Senate in explanation of the effect of the action agreed upon by the managers and recommended in the accompanying conference report:

The Senate amendment struck out all of the House bill after the enacting clause and inserted a substitute text.

The House recedes from its disagreement to the amendment of the Senate with an amendment which is a substitute for the House bill and the Senate amendment. The differences between the House bill, the Senate amendment, and the substitute agreed to in conference are noted below, except for clerical corrections, conforming changes made necessary by agreements reached by the conferees, and minor drafting and clarifying changes.

Index Publication

The House bill added language to the present Freedom of Information law to require the publication and distribution (by sale or otherwise) of agency indexes identifying information for the public as to any matter issued, adopted, or promulgated after July 4, 1967, which is required by U.S.C. 552(a)(2) to be made available or published. This includes final opinions, orders, agency statements of policy and interpretations not published in the *Federal Register*, and administrative staff manuals and agency staff instructions that affect the public unless they are otherwise published and copies offered for sale to the public. Such published indexes would be required for the July 4, 1967, period to date. Where agency indexes are now published by commercial firms, as they are in some instances, such publication would satisfy the requirements of this amendment so long as they are made readily available for public use by the agency.

The Senate amendment contained similar provisions, indicating that the publication of indexes should be on a quarterly or more frequent basis, but provided that if an agency determined by an order published in the *Federal Register* that its publication of any index would be "unnecessary and impracticable," it would not actually be required to publish the index. However, it would nonetheless be required to provide copies of such index on request at a cost comparable to that charged had the index been published.

The conference substitute follows the Senate amendment, except that if the agency determines not to publish its index, it shall provide copies on request to any person at a cost not to exceed the direct cost of duplication.

Identifiable Records

Present law requires that a request for information from an agency be for "identifiable records." The House bill provided that the request only "reasonably describe" the records being sought.

The Senate amendment contained similar language, but added a provision that when agency records furnished a person are demonstrated to be of "general public concern," the agency shall also make them available for public inspection and purchase, unless the agency can demonstrate that they could subsequently be denied to another individual under exemptions contained in subsection (b) of the Freedom of Information Act.

The conference substitute follows the House bill. With respect to the Senate proviso dealing with agency records of "general public interest," the conferees wish to make clear such language was eliminated only because they conclude that all agencies are presently obligated under the Freedom of

Information Act to pursue such a policy and that all agencies should effect this policy through regulation.

Search and Copying Fees

The Senate amendment contained a provision, not included in the House bill, directing the Director of the Office of Management and Budget to promulgate regulations establishing a uniform schedule of fees for agency search and copying of records made available to a person upon request under the law. It also provided that an agency could furnish the records requested without charge or at a reduced charge if it determined that such action would be in the public interest. It further provided that no fees should ordinarily be charged if the person requesting the records was an indigent if such fees would amount to less than $3, if the records were not located by the agency, or if they were determined to be exempt from disclosure under subsection (b) of the law.

The conference substitute follows the Senate amendment, except that each agency would be required to issue its own regulations for the recovery of only the direct costs of search and duplication—not including examination or review of records—instead of having such regulations promulgated by the Office of Management and Budget. In addition, the conference substitute retains the agency's discretionary public-interest waiver authority but eliminates the specific categories of situations where fees should not be charged.

By eliminating the list of specific categories, the conferees do not intend to imply that agencies should actually charge fees in those categories. Rather, they felt, such matters are properly the subject for individual agency determination in regulations implementing the Freedom of Information law. The conferees intend that fees should not be used for the purpose of discouraging requests for information or as obstacles to disclosure of requested information.

Court Review

The House bill clarifies the present Freedom of Information law with respect to *de novo* review requirements by Federal courts under section 552(a)(3) by specifically authorizing the court to examine *in camera* any requested records in dispute to determine whether the records are—as claimed by an agency—exempt from mandatory disclosure under any of the nine categories of section 552(b) of the law.

The Senate amendment contained a similar provision authorizing *in camera* review by Federal courts and added another provision, not contained in the House bill, to authorize Freedom of Information suits to be brought in the Federal courts in the District of Columbia, even in cases where the agency records were located elsewhere.

The conference substitute follows the Senate amendment, providing that in determining *de novo* whether agency records have been properly withheld, the court may examine records *in camera* in making its determination under any of the nine categories of exemptions under section 552(b) of the law. In *Environmental Protection Agency v. Mink, et al.,* 410 U.S. 73 (1973), the Supreme Court ruled that *in camera* inspection of documents withheld under section 552(b)(1) of the law, authorizing the withholding of classified information, would ordinarily be precluded in Freedom of Information cases, unless Congress directed otherwise. H.R. 12471 amends the present law to permit such *in camera* examination at the discretion of the court. While in camera examination need not be automatic, in many situations it will plainly be necessary and appropriate. Before the court orders in camera inspection, the Government should be given the opportunity to establish by means of testimony or detailed affidavits that the documents are clearly exempt from disclosure. The burden remains on the Government under this law.

Response to Complaints

The House bill requires that the defendant to a complaint under the Freedom of Information law serve a responsive pleading within 20 days after service, unless the court directed otherwise for good cause shown.

The Senate amendment contained a similar provision, except that it would give the defendant 40 days to file an answer.

The conference substitute would give the defendant 30 days to respond, unless the court directs otherwise for good cause shown.

Expedited Appeals

The Senate amendment included a provision, not contained in the House bill, to give precedence on appeal to cases brought under the Freedom of Information law, except as to cases on the docket which the court considers of greater importance.

The conference substitute follows the Senate amendment.

Assessment of Attorney Fees and Costs

The House bill provided that a Federal court may, in its discretion, assess reasonable attorney fees and other litigation costs reasonably incurred by the complainant in Freedom of Information cases in which the Federal Government had not prevailed.

The Senate amendment also contained a similar provision applying to cases in which the complainant had "substantially prevailed," but added certain criteria for consideration by the court in making such awards, including the benefit to the public deriving from the case, the commercial benefit to the complainant and the nature of his interest in the Federal records sought, and whether the Government's withholding of the records sought had "a reasonable basis in law."

The conference substitute follows the Senate amendment, except that the statutory criteria for court award of attorney fees and litigation costs were eliminated. By eliminating these criteria, the conferees do not intend to make the award of attorney fees automatic or to preclude the courts, in exercising their discretion as to awarding such fees, to take into consideration such criteria. Instead, the conferees believe that because the existing body of law on the award of attorney fees recognizes such factors, a statement of the criteria may be too delimiting and is unnecessary.

Sanction

The Senate amendment contained a provision, not included in the House bill, authorizing the court in Freedom of Information cases to impose a sanction of up to 60 days suspension from employment against a Federal employee or official who the court found to have been responsible for withholding the requested records without reasonable basis in law.

The conference substitute follows the Senate amendment, except that the court is authorized to make a finding whether the circumstances surrounding the withholding raise questions whether agency personnel acted arbitrarily or capriciously with respect to the withholding. If the court so finds, the Civil Service Commission must promptly initiate a proceeding to determine whether disciplinary action is warranted against the responsible officer or employee. The commission's findings and recommendations are to be submitted to the appropriate administrative authority of the agency concerned and to the responsible official or employee, and the administrative authority shall promptly take the disciplinary action recommended by the commission. This section applies to all persons employed by agencies under this law.

Administrative Deadlines

The House bill required that an agency make a determination whether or not to comply with a request for records within 10 days (excepting Saturdays, Sundays, and legal public holidays) and to notify the person making the request of such determination and the reasons therefor, and the right of such person to appeal any adverse determination to the head of the agency. It also required that agencies make a final determination on any appeal of an adverse determination within 20 days (excepting Saturdays, Sundays, and legal public holidays) after the date of receipt of the appeal by the agency. Further, any person would be deemed to have exhausted his administrative remedies if the agency fails to comply with either of the two time deadlines.

The Senate amendment contained similar provision but authorized certain other administrative actions to extend these deadlines for another 30 working days under specified types of situations, if requested by an agency head and approved by the Attorney General. It also would grant an agency, under specified "unusual circumstances," a 10-working-day extension upon notification to the person requesting the records. In addition, an agency could transfer part of the number of days from one category to another and authorize the court to allow still additional time for the agency to respond to the request. The Senate amendment also provided that any agency's notification of denial of any request for records set forth the names and titles or positions of each person responsible for the denial. It further allowed the court, in a Freedom of Information action, to allow the government additional time if "exceptional circumstances" were present and if the agency was exercising "due diligence in responding to the request."

The conference substitute generally adopts the 10- and 20-day administrative time deadlines of the Senate amendment for "unusual circumstances" in situations where the agency must search for and collect the requested records from field facilities separate from the office processing the request, where the agency must search for, collect, and examine a voluminous amount of separate and distinct records demanded in a single request, or where the agency has a need to consult with another agency or agency unit having a substantial interest in the determination because of the subject matter. This 10-day extension may be invoked by the agency only once—either during initial review of the request or during appellate review.

The 30-working-day certification provision of the Senate amendment has been eliminated, but the conference substitute retains the Senate language requiring that any agency's notification to a person of the denial of any request for records set forth the names and titles or positions of each person responsible for the denial. The conferees intend that this listing include those persons responsible for the original, as well as the appellate, determination to deny the information requested. The conferees intend that consultations between an agency unit and the agency's legal staff, the public information staff, or the Department of Justice should not be considered the basis for an extension under the subsection.

The conference substitute also retains the Senate language giving the court authority to allow the agency additional time to examine requested records in exceptional circumstances where the agency was exercising due diligence in responding to the request and had been since the request was received.

National Defense and Foreign Policy Exemption (b)(1)

The House bill amended subsection (b)(1) of the Freedom of Information law to permit the withholding of information "authorized under the criteria established by an Executive order to be kept secret in the interest of the national defense or foreign policy."

The Senate amendment contained similar language but added "statute" to the exemption provision.

The conference substitute combines language of both House and Senate bills to permit the withholding of information where it is "specifically authorized under criteria established by an Executive order to be kept secret in the interest of national defense or foreign policy" and is "in fact, properly classified" pursuant to both procedural and substantive criteria contained in such Executive order.

When linked with the authority conferred upon the Federal courts in this conference substitute for *in camera* examination of contested records as part of their *de novo* determination in Freedom of Information cases, this clarifies Congressional intent to override the Supreme Court's holding in the case of *E.P.A. v. Mink, et al. supra*, with respect to *in camera* review of classified documents.

However, the conferees recognize that the Executive departments responsible for national defense and foreign policy matters have unique insights into what adverse affects might occur as a result of public disclosure of a particular classified record. Accordingly, the conferees expect that Federal courts, in making *de novo* determinations in section 552(b)(1) cases under the Freedom of Information law, will accord substantial weight to an agency's affidavit concerning the details of the classified status of the disputed record.

Restricted Data (42 U.S.C. 2162), communication information (18 U.S.C. 798), and intelligence sources and methods (50 U.S.C. 403(d)(3) and (g)), for example, may be classified and exempted under section 552(b)(3) of the Freedom of Information Act. When such information is subjected to court review, the court should recognize that if such information is classified pursuant to one of the above statutes, it shall be exempted under this law.

Investigatory Records

The Senate amendment contained an amendment to subsection (b)(7) of the Freedom of Information law, not included in the House bill, that would clarify Congressional intent disapproving certain court interpretations which have tended to expand the scope of agency authority to withhold certain "investigatory files compiled for law enforcement purposes." The Senate amendment would permit an agency to withhold investigatory records compiled for law enforcement purposes only to the extent that the production of such records would interfere with enforcement proceedings, deprive a person of a right to a fair trial or an impartial adjudication, constitute a clearly unwarranted invasion of personal privacy, disclose the identity of an informer, or disclose investigative techniques and procedures.

The conference substitute follows the Senate amendment except for the substitution of "confidential source" for "informer," the addition of language protecting information compiled by a criminal law enforcement authority from a confidential source in the course of a criminal investigation or by an agency conducting a lawful national security intelligence investigation, the deletion of the word "clearly" relating to avoidance of an "unwarranted invasion of personal privacy," and the addition of a category allowing withholding of information whose disclosure "would endanger the life or physical safety of law enforcement personnel."

The substitution of the term "confidential source" in section 552(b)(7)(D) is to make clear that the identity of a person other than a paid informer may be protected if the person provided information under an express assurance of confidentiality or in circumstances from which such an assurance could be reasonably inferred. Under this category, in every case where the investigatory records sought were compiled for law enforcement purposes—either civil or criminal in nature—the agency can withhold the names, addresses, and other information that would reveal the identity of a confidential source who furnished the information. However, where the records are compiled by a criminal law enforcement authority, *all* of the information furnished only by a confidential source may be withheld if the information was compiled in the course of a criminal investigation. In addition, where the records are compiled by an agency conducting a lawful national security intelligence investigation, all of the information furnished only by a confidential source may also be withheld. The conferees intend the term "criminal law enforcement authority" to be narrowly construed to include the Federal Bureau of Investigation and similar investigative authorities. Likewise, "national security" is to be strictly construed to refer to military security, national defense, or foreign policy. The term "intelligence" in section 552(b)(7)(D) is intended to apply to positive intelligence-gathering activities, counterintelligence activities, and background security investigations by governmental units which have authority to conduct such functions. By "an agency" the conferees intend to include criminal law enforcement authorities as well as other agencies. Personnel, regulatory, and civil enforcement investigations are covered by the first clause authorizing withholding of information what would reveal the identity of a confidential source but are not encompassed by the second clause authorizing withholding of all confidential information under the specified circumstances.

The conferees also wish to make clear that disclosure of information about a person to that person does not constitute an invasion of his privacy. Finally, the conferees express approval of the present Justice Department policy waiving legal exemptions for withholding historic investigatory records over 15 years old, and they encourage its continuation.

Segregable Portions of Records

The Senate amendment contained a provision, not included in the House bill, providing that any reasonably segregable portion of a record shall be provided to any person requesting such record after the deletion of portions which may be exempted under subsection (b) of the Freedom of Information law.

The conference substitute follows the Senate amendment.

Annual Reports by Agencies

The House bill provided that each agency submit an annual report, on or before March 1 of each calendar year, to the Speaker of the House and the President of the Senate, for referral to the appropriate committees of the Congress. Such report shall include statistical information on the number of agency determinations to withhold information requested under the Freedom of Information law; the reasons for such withholding; the number of appeals of such adverse determinations with the result and reasons for each; a copy of every rule made by the agency in connection with this law; a copy of the agency fee schedule with the total amount of fees collected by the agency during the year; and other information indicating efforts to properly administer the Freedom of Information law.

The Senate amendment contained similar provisions and added two requirements not contained in the House bill, (1) that each agency report list those officials responsible for each denial of records and the numbers of cases in which each participated during the year and (2) that the Attorney General also submit a separate annual report on or before March 1 of each calendar year listing the number of cases arising under the Freedom of Information law, the exemption involved in each such case, the disposition of the case, and the costs, fees, and penalties assessed under the law. The Attorney General's report shall also include a description of Justice Department efforts to encourage agency compliance with the law.

The conference substitute incorporates the major provisions of the House bill and two Senate amendments. With respect to the annual reporting by each agency of the names and titles or positions of each person responsible for the denial of records requested under the Freedom of Information law and the number of instances of participation for each, the conferees wish to make clear that such listing include those persons responsible for the original determination to deny the information requested in each case as well as all other agency employees or officials who were responsible for determinations at subsequent stages in the decision.

Expansion of Agency Definition

The House bill extends the applicability of the Freedom of Information law to include any executive department, military department, Government corporation, Government-controlled corporation, or other establishment in the executive branch of Government (including the Executive Office of the President), or any independent regulatory agency.

The Senate amendment provided that for purposes of the Freedom of Information law the term agency included any agency defined in section 551(l) of title 5, United States Code, and in addition included the United States Postal Service, the Postal Rate Commission, and any other authority of the Government of the United States which is a corporation and which receives any appropriated funds.

The conference substitute follows the House bill. The conferees stated that they intend to include within the definition of "agency" those entities encompassed by 5 U.S.C. 551 and other entities including the United States Postal Service, the Postal Rate Commission, and government corporations or government-controlled corporations now in existence or which may be created in the future. They do not intend to include corporations which receive appropriated funds but are neither chartered by the Federal Government nor controlled by it, such as the Corporation for Public Broadcasting. Expansion of the definition of "agency" in this subsection is intended to broaden applicability of the Freedom of Information Act but it is not intended that the term "agency" be applied to subdivisions, offices or units within an agency.

With respect to the meaning of the term "Executive Office of the President" the conferees intend the result reached in *Soucie v. David*, 448 F.2d 1067 (C.A.D.C. 1971). The term is not to be interpreted as including the President's immediate personal staff or units in the Executive Office whose sole function is to advise and assist the President.

Effective Date

Both the House bill and the Senate amendment provided for an effective date of 90 days after the date of enactment of these amendments to the Freedom of Information law.

The conference substitute adopts the language of the Senate amendment.

EDWARD KENNEDY,
PHILIP A. HART,
BIRCH BAYH,
QUENTIN N. BURDICK,
JOHN TUNNEY,
CHARLES McC. MATHIAS, JR.,
Managers on the Part of the Senate.

CHET HOLIFIELD,
WILLIAM S. MOORHEAD,
JOHN E. MOSS,
BILL ALEXANDER,
FRANK HORTON,
JOHN N. ERLENBORN,
PAUL McCLOSKEY,
Managers on the Part of the House.

1996 EFOIA Amendments House Report (Excerpts)

IV. EXPLANATION OF THE BILL

A. Overview

The highlights of the Electronic Freedom of Information Amendments include:

Electronic records.— Records which are subject to the FOIA shall be made available under the FOIA when the records are maintained in electronic format. This clarifies existing practice by making the statute explicit on this point.

Format Requests.— Requestors may request records in any form or format in which the agency maintains those records. Agencies must make a "reasonable effort" to comply with requests to furnish records in other formats.

Redaction.— Agencies redacting electronic records (deleting part of a record to prevent disclosure of material covered by an exemption) must note the location and the extent of any deletions made on a record. This provision, however, applies only if the agencies have the technology to comply with it.

Expedited Processing.— Certain categories of requestors would receive priority treatment of their requests if failure to obtain information in a timely manner would pose a significant harm. The first category of requestors entitled to this special processing includes those who could reasonably expect that delay could pose an imminent threat to the life or physical safety of an individual. The second category includes requests, made by a person primarily engaged in the dissemination of information to the public, and involving compelling urgency to inform the public.

Multitrack processing.— Agencies will be able to establish processes for processing requests of various sizes on different tracks. Because of this procedure, larger numbers of requests for smaller amounts of material will be completed more quickly. Requestors will also have an incentive to frame narrower requests.

Agency Backlogs.— Agencies can no longer delay responding to FOIA requests because of "exceptional circumstances" simply as a result from a predictable agency request workload. This strengthens the requirement that agencies respond to requests on time.

Deadlines.— The deadline for responding to FOIA is extended to 20 workdays from the current 10 workday requirement for initial determinations.

Reporting requirements.— The legislation expands certain reporting requirements, and requires agencies to make more information available through electronic means.

B. Section by Section

Section 1. Short title

The Act should be cited as the "Electronic Freedom of Information Act Amendments of 1996."

Section 2. Findings and purposes

The findings make clear that Congress enacted the FOIA to require Federal agencies to make records available to the public through public inspection and at the request of any person for any public or private use. They further acknowledge the increase in the Government's use of computers and encourages agencies to use new technology to enhance public access to Government information.

Appendix A

Section 3. Application of requirements to electronic format information

The section explicitly states that a "record" under the FOIA includes electronically stored information. This articulates the existing general policy under the FOIA that all Government records are subject to the Act, regardless of the form in which they are stored by the agency. The Department of Justice agrees that computer database records are agency records subject to the FOIA. \31\ The bill defines "record" to "include any information that would be an agency record subject to the requirements of this section if maintained by an agency in any format, including an electronic format."

\31\See "Department of Justice Report on 'Electronic Record' Issues Under the Freedom of Information Act," Senate Hearing 102 1098, 102d Cong., 2d Sess. P. 33, 1992. This section clarifies the meaning of the term "record" and similar terminology used in the FOIA. Several important points are worth making.

Breadth of Policy.—First, the FOIA usually uses the term "record," but other terms are also used occasionally, including "information" and "matter." The terms are used interchangeable. The section makes clear a comprehensive policy that records in electronic formats are agency records subject to the Act. The language of the section should leave no doubt about the breadth of the policy. As noted previously, a number of statutes set Federal Government information policy. This bill is not intended to be dispositive of all aspects of those policies. For example, matter not previously subject to FOIA when maintained in a non-electronic format is not made subject to FOIA by this bill.

Storage Media.—Second, the section clarifies that a record in electronic format can be requested just like a record on paper or any other format, and within enumerated exceptions, can potentially be fully disclosed under the law. The format in which data is maintained is not relevant under the FOIA. Computer tapes, computer disks, CD ROMs, and all other digital or electronic media are records. Microfiche and microforms are records. When other, yet-to-be invented technologies are developed to store, maintain, produce, or otherwise record information, these will be records as well. When determining whether information is subject to the FOIA, the form or format in which it is maintained is not relevant to the decision.

The requirements for the disclosure of information exist elsewhere in the Act. No matter how it is preserved, information that passes the threshold test of being an agency record, remains a record. This provision should restrain agencies from evading the clear intent of the FOIA by deeming some forms of data as not being agency records and not subject to the law. The primary focus should always be on whether information is subject to disclosure or is exempt, rather than the form or format it is stored in. This provision, however, does not broaden the concept of agency record. The information maintained on a computer is a record, but the computer is not.

Rejected Definitions.—Third, the Committee rejects the definition of record in the substitute to S. 90, as reported by the Senate Committee on the Judiciary on April 25, 1996. The Senate bill had incorporated a definition of record drawn from the Records Disposal Act. \32\

\32\44 U.S.C. *3301 (1994).

A case in point comes from the decision in *SDC Development Corp. v. Mathews*. \33\ The decision has previously been sharply criticized by this Committee and its holding is inconsistent with the policies expressed in this legislation. \34\ The Court found that an agency-created computer database of research abstracts was not an agency record because it was library material. The court used the library material exclusion in the Records Disposal Act as an excuse to place these records beyond the reach of the FOIA. H.R. 3802 makes clear, contrary to *SDC v. Mathews*, that information an agency has created and is directly or indirectly disseminating remains subject to the FOIA in any of its forms or formats. \35\

\33\542 F.2d 1116 (9th Cir. 1976).

\34\See House Committee on Government Operations, Electronic Collection and Dissemination of Information by Federal Agencies: A Policy Overview, 99th Cong., 2d Sess. 32 36 (1986).

\35\A recent scholarly article examines the background and policy of the Records Disposal Act and the FOIA. It provides a more extensive discussion of the Court's misreading of the FOIA, the Records Disposal Act and the Copyright Act. See Robert Gellman, Twin Evils: Government Copyright and Copyright-Like Controls Over Government Information, 45 Syracuse Law Review 999, 1036 1046 (1995).

Section 4. Information made available in electronic format and indexation of records

This section of the bill requires that materials, such as agency opinions and policy statements, which an agency must "make available for public inspection and copying," pursuant to Section 552(a)(2), and which are created on or after November 1, 1996, be made available by computer telecommunications, and in hard copy, within one year after the date of enactment. If an agency does not have the means established to make these materials available on-line, then the information should be made available in another electronic form, e.g., CD ROM or disc. The bill would thus treat (a)(2) materials in the same manner as it treats (a)(1) materials, which under the Government Printing Office Electronic Information Access Enhancement Act of 1993 \36\ are required, via the Federal Register, to be made available on-line.

\36\44 U.S.C. 4101 (1993).

This section would also increase the information made available under Section 552(a)(2). Specifically, agencies would be required to make available for public inspection and copying, in the same manner as other materials made available under Section 552(a)(2), copies of records released in response to FOIA requests that the agency determines have been or will likely be the subject of additional requests. In addition, they would be required to make available a general index of these previously-released records. By December 31, 1999, this index should be made available by computer telecommunications. Since not all individuals have access to computer networks or are near agency public reading rooms, requestors would still be able to access previously-released FOIA records through the normal FOIA process.

As a practical matter, this would mean that copies of previously-released records on a popular topic, such as the assassinations of public figures, would subsequently be treated as (a)(2) materials, made available for public inspection and copying. This would help to reduce the number of multiple FOIA requests for the same records requiring separate agency responses. Likewise, the general index would help requestors in determining which records have been the subject of prior FOIA requests. By diverting some potential FOIA requests for previously-released records with this index, agencies can better use their FOIA resources to fulfill new requests.

This section also makes clear that to prevent a clearly unwarranted invasion of personal privacy, an agency may delete identifying details when it makes available or publishes the index and copies of previously-released records.

Finally, this section would require an agency to indicate the extent of any deletion from the previously-released records. This provision is consistent with the "Computer Redaction" section of the bill. Both provisions similarly temper this requirement by giving agencies the flexibility to show that marking the place on the record where the deletion was made was not technically feasible. Agencies need not reveal information about deletions if such disclosure would harm an interest protected by an exemption.

Section 5. Honoring form or format requests

This section requires agencies to help requestors by providing information in the form requested, including requests for the electronic form of records, if the agency can readily reproduce it in that form. The section would overrule *Dismukes v. Department of the Interior*, which held that an agency "has no obligation under the FOIA to accommodate plaintiff's preference [but] need only provide responsive, nonexempt information in a reasonably accessible form." \37\

\37\603 F. Supp. 760, 763 (D.D.C. 1984)

This section also requires agencies to make reasonable efforts to search for records kept in an electronic format. An unreasonable effort would significantly interfere with the operations of the agency or the agency's use of its computers. Electronic searches should not result in any greater expenditure of agency resources than would have occurred with a conventional paper-based search for documents.

The bill defines "search" as a "review, manually or by automated means," of "agency records for the purpose of locating those records responsive to a request." Under the FOIA, an agency need not create documents that do not exist. Computer records found in a database rather than in a file cabinet may require the application of codes or some form of programming to retrieve the information. Under the definition of "search" in the bill, the review of computerized records would not amount to the creation of records. Otherwise, it would be virtually impossible to get records maintained completely in an electronic format, like computer database information, because some manipulation of the information likely would be necessary to search the records.

Current law provides that most requestors receive the first two hours of search time for free. Ten years ago, computer time was expensive and carefully metered. Today, computer time is generally no longer a scarce resource. Except in unusual cases, the cost of computer time should not be a factor in calculating the two free hours of search time. Often, searching by computer will reduce costs because computer searches are generally faster, more thorough and more accurate, than manual searches. In those unusual cases, where the cost of conducting a computerized search significantly detracts from the agencies'' ordinary operations, no more than the dollar equivalent of two hours manual search time shall be allowed for two hours free search time. For any searches conducted beyond the first two hours, an agency shall only charge the direct costs of conducting such searches.

Section 6. Standard for judicial review

Section 5 requires a court to accord substantial weight to an agency's determination as to both the technical feasibility of redacting non-releasable material at the place on the record where the deletion was made, under paragraphs (2)(C) and subsection (b), as amended by this Act, and the reproducibility of the requested form or format of records, under paragraph (3)(B), as amended by this Act. This deference is warranted because agencies are the most familiar with the availability of their own technical resources to process, redact, and reproduce records.

This section does not affect the extent of judicial deference that a court may or may not extend to an agency on any other matter. There is no intent with this provision, either expressly or by implication, to affect the deference or weight which a court may extend to an agency determination or an agency affidavit on any other matter. The provision applies narrowly to agency determinations with regard to technical feasibility.

Section 7. Ensuring timely response to requests

The bill addresses the single most frequent complaint about the operation of the FOIA: agency delays in responding to FOIA requests. This section encourages agencies to employ better records management systems and to set priorities for using their FOIA resources.

In underscoring the requirement that agencies respond to requests in a timely manner, the Committee does not intend to weaken any interests protected by the FOIA exemptions. Agencies processing some requests may need additional time to adequately review requested material to protect those exemption interests. For example, processing some requests may require additional time in order to properly screen material against the inadvertent disclosure of material covered by the national security exemption.

Multitrack First-In First-Out Processing.—An agency commitment to process requests on a first-in, first-out basis has been held to satisfy the requirement that an agency exercise due diligence in dealing with backlogs of FOIA requests. Processing requests solely on a FIFO basis, however, may result in lengthy delays for simple requests. The prior receipt and processing of complex requests delays other requests, increasing agency backlogs. The bill would permit agencies to promulgate regulations starting multitrack processing systems, and makes clear that agencies should exercise due diligence within each track. Agencies would also be required to give requestors the opportunity to limit the scope of their requests to qualify for processing under a faster track.

Unusual Circumstances.—The FOIA currently permits an agency in "unusual circumstances" to extend for a maximum of ten working days the statutory time limit for responding to a FOIA request, upon written notice to the requestor setting forth the reason for such extension. The FOIA enumerates various reasons for such an extension. These reasons include the need to search for and collect requested records from multiple offices, the volume of records requested, and the need for consultation with other components within the agency.

An extra ten days may still provide an insufficient time for an agency to respond to unusually burdensome FOIA requests. The bill provides a mechanism to deal with such requests, which an agency would not be able to process even with an extra ten days. For such requests, the bill requires an agency to inform the requestor that the request cannot be processed within the statutory time limits and provide an opportunity for the requestor to limit the scope of the request so that it may be processed within statutory time limits, and/or arrange with the agency a negotiated deadline for processing the request. In the event that the requestor refuses to reasonably limit the request's scope or agree upon a time frame and then seeks judicial review, that refusal shall be considered as a factor in determining whether "exceptional circumstances" exist under subparagraph (6)(C).

The Committee believes that the FOIA works best when requestors and agencies work together to define and fulfill reasonable requests. When a requestor can modify a request to make it easier for the agency to process it, this benefits everyone. Still, there will be circumstances in which a requestor and an agency cannot agree upon a modification that will speed processing. As long as a request meets the legal standards of the FOIA, each requestor has the right to frame his or her own request. If an agency determines by an objective standard that a requestor has unreasonably refused to modify a request, and a court concurs, then the court shall consider that refusal when determining whether exceptional circumstances exist.

However, if an agency determines on its own that a requestor has unreasonably refused to modify a request, the agency may not otherwise discriminate against that request or requestor. The request must be processed as it would have been had no modification been sought. An agency may not maintain a separate queue of "unreasonable" requests, nor may an agency constantly move "unreasonable" requests to the back of the queue. The Committee cautions agencies against using this limited test of "reasonableness" in any way other than the narrow way that the statute provides.

This provision does not relieve an agency of the responsibility of making a diligent, good-faith effort to complete its review of an initial request within the statutory time frame. An agency should seek an extension beyond the additional ten days already provided in "unusual circumstances" only in rare instances. This procedure will achieve one of the bill's important goals of encouraging a dialogue between an agency and a requestor. This enhances the opportunity of a requestor to obtain at least some of the records sought in a timely fashion, and could alleviate some of the agency's burden in responding to a request that could not otherwise be processed within the statutory time limits. In addition, it could provide a requestor with some certainty as to a time frame for processing his or her request.

Appendix A

Exceptional Circumstances. —The Freedom of Information Act provides that, in "exceptional circumstances," a court may extend the statutory time limits for an agency to respond to a FOIA request, but does not specify what those circumstances are. The bill would clarify that routine, predictable agency backlogs for FOIA requests do not constitute exceptional circumstances for purposes of the Act. This is consistent with the holding in *Open America v. Watergate Special Prosecution Force*, \38\ where the court held that an unforeseen 3,000 percent increase in FOIA requests in one year, which created a massive backlog in an agency with insufficient resources to process those requests in a timely manner, can constitute "exceptional circumstances." Routine backlogs of requests for records under the FOIA should not give agencies an automatic excuse to ignore the time limits, since this provides a disincentive for agencies to clear up those backlogs. Nevertheless, the bill makes clear that a court shall consider an agency's efforts to reduce the number of pending requests in determining whether exceptional circumstances exist. Agencies may also make a showing of exceptional circumstances based on the amount of material classified, based on the size and complexity of other requests processed by the agency, based on the resources being devoted to the declassification of classified material of public interest, or based on the number of requests for records by courts or administrative tribunals.

\38\547 F.2d 605 (D.C. Cir. 1976)

Aggregation of Requests. —The amendments reported out of Committee had reflected an implicit assumption that agency regulations may permit the aggregation of requests by the same requestor, or requestors that an agency reasonably believes are acting in concert. An amendment clarifying this point is anticipated to be considered on the House floor.

Any aggregation must involve such clearly related material that should be considered as a single request. Multiple requests involving unrelated matters should not be aggregated. Existing agency procedures regarding entitlement for fee waivers already permit agencies to aggregate some multiple requests.

The purpose of this aggregation is to ensure the equitable treatment of similarly situated requestors. Aggregation would depend upon the factual circumstances of the requests, and particularly whether multiple requests were being used primarily to obtain a procedural advantage over other requests or requestors. Multiple or related requests could also be aggregated with requests seeking similar information for the purposes of negotiating the scope of the request and schedule. Where multiple requestors have not acted in concert, such aggregation must be with their consent. Applying the same principles, agencies should not aggregate groups of requests simply to delay responding to requests. For example, the filing of a subsequent request should not affect the processing of an initial request by the same requestor.

Section 8. Time period for agency consideration of requests

The bill contains provisions designed to address the needs of both agencies and requestors for more workable deadlines for processing FOIA requests.

Expedited Processing. —The bill would require agencies to promulgate regulations authorizing expedited access to requesters who show a "compelling need" for a speedy response. The agency would be required to decide whether to grant the request for expedited access within ten days and then notify the requestor of the decision. The requestor would bear the burden of showing that expedition is appropriate. This section limits judicial review to the same record before the agency on the determination of whether to grant expedited access. Moreover, the section provides that the Federal courts will not have jurisdiction to review an agency's denial of an expedited access request if the agency has already provided a complete response to the request for records. The latter provision does not limit a court's ability to consider a requestor's application for the award of attorney's fees.

A "compelling need" warranting faster FOIA processing would exist in two categories of circumstances. In the first category, the failure to obtain the records within an expedited deadline poses an imminent threat to an individual's life or physical safety. The second category requires a request by someone "primarily engaged in disseminating information" and "urgency to inform the public concerning actual or alleged Federal government activity." The section also permits agencies to elect to offer expedited processing in other circumstances.

The agencies are directed to establish rules and regulations for processing requests for expedited access. By requiring a "compelling need," the expedited access procedure is intended to be limited to circumstances in which a delay in obtaining information can reasonably be foreseen to cause a significant adverse consequence to a recognized interest.

Agency officials will be required to make factual and subjective judgments about the circumstances cited by requestors to qualify them for "expedited processing." To do so the requestors will need to explain in detail their basis for seeking such treatment. Agency discretion should be exercised with fairness and diligence. The credibility of a requestor who makes repeated claims for expedited processing that are determined to lack factual foundation may be taken into account when the same requestor makes additional requests.

The specified categories for compelling need are intended to be narrowly applied. A threat to an individual's life or physical safety qualifying for expedited access should be imminent. A reasonable person should be able to appreciate that a delay in obtaining the requested information poses such a threat. A person "primarily engaged" in the dissemination of information should not include individuals who are engaged only incidentally in the dissemination of information. The standard of "primarily engaged" requires that information dissemination be the main activity of the requestor, although it need not be their sole occupation. A requestor who only incidentally engages in information dissemination, besides other activities, would not satisfy this requirement.

The standard of "urgency to inform" requires that the information requested should pertain to a matter of a current exigency to the American public and that a reasonable person might conclude that the consequences of delaying a response to a FOIA request would compromise a significant recognized interest. The public's right to know, although a significant and important value, would not by itself be sufficient to satisfy this standard.

Some agencies, such as the Department of Justice, already employ expedited access procedures that, in some respects, have a broader criteria for expedited access than contained in Section 7. \39\ Agencies are given latitude to expand the criteria for expedited access, "in other cases determined by the agency." However, the expedited processing procedure should be invoked in the circumstances as enumerated in the bill. Given the finite resources generally available for fulfilling FOIA requests, unduly generous use of the expedited processing procedure would unfairly disadvantage other requestors who do not qualify for its treatment.

\39\The Department of Justice's procedures for expedited access permits it if a delay would result in the loss of substantial due process rights and the information sought is not otherwise available in a timely manner.

Expansion of Agency Response Time. —To help Federal agencies in reducing their backlog of FOIA requests, the bill would double the time limit for an agency to respond to FOIA requests from ten days to twenty days. Attorney General Janet Reno has acknowledged the inability of most Federal agencies to comply with the ten-day rule "as a serious problem" stemming principally from "too few resources in the face of too heavy a workload." \40\

\40\Reno, Janet, Attorney General, Memorandum for Heads of Departments and Agencies, October 4, 1993, "The Freedom of Information Act."

Estimation of Matter Denied. —The bill would require agencies when denying a FOIA request to try to estimate the volume of any denied material and provide that estimate to the requestor, unless doing so would harm an interest protected by an exemption.

Section 9. Computer redaction

The ease with which information on the computer may be redacted makes the determination of whether a few words or 30 pages have been withheld by an agency at times impossible. The amendments require agencies to identify the location of deletions in the released portion of the record and, where technologically feasible, to show the deletion at the place on the record where they made the deletion, unless including that indication would harm an interest protected by an exemption.

Section 10. Report to the Congress

This section would add to the information an agency is already required to publish as part of its annual report. Specifically, agencies would be required to publish in their annual reports information regarding denials of requested records, appeals, a complete list of statutes upon which the agency relies to withhold information under Section 552 (b)(3), which exempts information that is specifically exempted from disclosure by other statutes, the number of backlogged FOIA requests, the number of days taken to process requests, the amount of fees collected, and the number of staff devoted to processing FOIA requests. The annual reports would be required to be made available to the public, including by computer telecommunications means. If an agency does not have the means established to make the report available on-line, then the report should be made available in another electronic form. The Attorney General is required to make each report available at a single electronic access point, and advise the Chairmen and ranking members of the Senate Committee on the Judiciary and the House Committee on Government Reform and Oversight that such reports are available.

Congress has undertaken several recent initiatives focused on streamlining government, making government processes more efficient, and improving the availability of government information. The Government Performance and Results Act requires a system of evaluation measures based on performance and results. The Paperwork Reduction Act of 1995 reexamines government information in the light of recent technological developments. Also, the Reports Elimination Act eliminates hundreds of reports to Congress required in a statute. Other pending legislation is likely to eliminate more than 200 statutorily required reports to Congress from the General Accounting Office.

In the spirit of these reforms, the Committee considered the reporting requirements of the Freedom of Information Act. Some new requirements were added to make the reports more useful to the public and to Congress. For the public, the FOIA reports should answer certain common questions, such as: How does one request documents? How does the Government respond to those requests, including an explanation of the reasons for not honoring a request? And, how long does it usually take for a request to be processed? For Congress, these reports should furnish a view of the agency workload and any backlog. The reports should identify the progress the agency is making toward eliminating that backlog. They should report on the resources devoted to answering FOIA requests, allowing for meaningful comparisons among agencies about performance. Someone unfamiliar with the FOIA process should be able to understand a report without resorting to reading the statute. Jargon such as "(b)(3) exemptions" should be replaced with more understandable language substituted. Guidance should be given to the agencies so that all reports contain terms with identical meanings.

Besides revising the contents of the reports to make them more useful, the Committee changed the timing and reporting period of the reports. Both changes were done to reduce the burden on the agencies, though it meant a delay in providing information and descriptive language to the public and Congress. FOIA reports have previously reported on a calendar year and have been due on March 1st of the following year. This bill changes the reporting period to a fiscal year to make it easier for agencies to compile the budget and staffing information required. This bill also gives agencies more time to prepare the reports from two to four months. Of course, agencies should strive to make their reports available sooner. In addition, the Committee has provided an additional two months to the Department of Justice to coordinate electronic access to these reports.

This bill also requires the availability of all FOIA reports by electronic means. The Committee anticipates that the Department of Justice will establish a home page for reaching all agency reports through a single site. Until a single site of electronic access is available for all reports, the Committee expects the Attorney General will forward to Congress print copies of all reports not available electronically. Agencies that do not provide electronic access should also make print reports available to the public, including distribution to Depository Libraries.

In drafting this legislation, the Committee rewrote the entire reporting section of the Freedom of Information Act. This was done to make it easier for the public to understand the new reporting requirements, without constant reference to existing law.

Three reporting requirements were added to aid the public and Congress to understand the work flow in each agency. Beginning in 1998, agencies will be required to report:

> How many requests have not been resolved to the requestors' satisfaction at the end of the reporting period? What is the median number of days those appeals have been pending?
> What is the number of requests received during the year, and the number of requests processed during the year?
> What is the median number of days taken to process requests of different types? What is the volume of requests coming into the agency annually, and the number of requests processed by the agency that year? These requirements will give the public and Congress clear measures of any backlog that exists. This will allow Congress to monitor progress in responding to FOIA requests across time. It will help the public understand how long it takes an agency to respond to a request.

The Committee has requested that agencies provide the median number of days requests have been in the backlog queue, and the median number of days necessary to complete the processing of requests. The Committee elected to use medians as a statistical measure because of their appropriateness when the measure being summarized does not have a normal distribution, or when a few cases of extreme value would skew an average. For example, a few requests for excessively large numbers of documents could artificially inflate the average time taken to fill a request. Of course, if agencies determine that the average time is a better measure of their performance, they can include that in the report along with the median. Medians are simple to calculate, simply requiring a distribution of the number of days each request has been pending, and do not increase the reporting burden on agencies. The Committee appreciates that some agencies with decentralized FOIA operations may have trouble in calculating a precise agency-wide median. In such circumstances reasonable estimates may be used. Finally, this bill requires that agencies report the number of staff assigned to processing FOIA requests, and their budget for processing FOIA requests.

Much comment is made of the adequacy of agency resources to comply with the statutory requirements of the FOIA. Effective future congressional oversight of the FOIA requires more detailed information about the level of resources that agencies devote to FOIA, the effectiveness of their utilization and the level of resources that might be required for agencies to fully comply with the FOIA. Agencies should inform Congress of the additional resources needed to fully comply with the FOIA. In the absence of such information on budget requests and management initiatives, the complaint by agencies that Congress has denied the resources necessary to comply with the statutory deadlines is unsupportable.

The Committee has rewritten the FOIA reporting requirements to make them more useful to the public and to Congress, and to make the information in them more accessible. With those goals in mind, we expect that the Department of Justice, in consultation with the Office of Management and Budget, will provide guidelines to the agencies so that all reports use common terminology and follow a similar format. The Attorney General and the Director of the Office of Management and Budget are required to develop reporting guidelines for the annual reports by October 1, 1997.

Appendix A

Section 11. Reference materials and guides

This section requires agencies to make publicly available, upon request, reference material or a guide for requesting records or information from an agency. This guide would include an index and description of all major information systems of an agency, and a handbook for obtaining various types and categories of public information from an agency.

The guide is intended to be a short and simple explanation for the public of what the Freedom of Information Act is designed to do, and how a member of the public can use it to access government records. Each agency should explain in clear and simple language, the types of records that can be obtained from the agency through FOIA requests, why some records cannot, by law, be made available, and how the agency makes the determination of whether or not a record can be released.

Each agency guide should explain how to make a FOIA request, and how long a requestor can expect to wait for a reply from the agency. In addition, the guide should explain the requestor's rights under the law to appeal to the courts to rectify agency action. The guide should give a brief history of recent litigation it has been involved in, and the resolution of those cases. If an agency requires that certain requests, such as applications for expedited access, be completed on agency forms, then the forms should be part of the guide.

The guide is intended to supplement other information locator systems, like the Government Information Locator System (GILS) called for in the Paperwork Reduction Act of 1995. 41 Thus, the guide should reference those systems and explain how a requestor can obtain more information about them. Of course, any agency specific locator systems should be similarly referenced in the guide. 41The Paperwork Reduction Act consists of (P.L. 96 511, 94 Stat. 2812) as amended by the Paperwork Reduction Act of 1986 (section 101(m) [Title VIII, Part A] of P.L. 99 500 and P.L. 99 591, 100 Stat. 1783) and The Paperwork Reduction Act of 1995 (P.L. 104 13, 109 Stat. 163). The Paperwork Reduction Act is codified at Chapter 35 of Title 44 of the United States Code.

It is expected that OMB will assist the agencies in assuring that all guides follow a common format so that a requestor picking up guides from two or more agencies can easily find the information they are seeking. Similarly, OMB should assure that all agencies use common terminology in describing record systems, how to file a FOIA request, and in describing other locator systems.

All guides should be available through electronic means, and should be linked to the annual reports. A citizen picking up a FOIA guide should learn how to access the annual reports. Similarly, any potential requestor reading an annual report should learn about the guide, and how to access it.

Section 12. Effective date

To provide agencies with time to implement new requirements under the Act, sections 7 and 8 shall become effective one year after the date of enactment. These sections concern multitrack and expedited processing, unusual and exceptional circumstances, the doubling of the statutory time period for responding to FOIA requests, and estimating the amount of material to which access is denied. The remainder of the bill will take effect 180 days after enactment.

Statement of Attorney General Ashcroft Regarding Implementation of FOIA

October 12, 2001
Memorandum for Heads of all Federal Departments and Agencies

From: John Ashcroft, Attorney General
Subject: The Freedom of Information Act

As you know, the Department of Justice and this Administration are committed to full compliance with the Freedom of Information Act (FOIA), 5 U.S.C. § 552 (2000). It is only through a well-informed citizenry that the leaders of our nation remain accountable to the governed and the American people can be assured that neither fraud nor government waste is concealed.

The Department of Justice and this Administration are equally committed to protecting other fundamental values that are held by our society. Among them are safeguarding our national security, enhancing the effectiveness of our law enforcement agencies, protecting sensitive business information and, not least, preserving personal privacy.

Our citizens have a strong interest as well in a government that is fully functional and efficient. Congress and the courts have long recognized that certain legal privileges ensure candid and complete agency deliberations without fear that they will be made public. Other privileges ensure that lawyers' deliberations and communications are kept private. No leader can operate effectively without confidential advice and counsel. Exemption 5 of the FOIA, 5 U.S.C. § 552(b)(5), incorporates these privileges and the sound policies underlying them.

I encourage your agency to carefully consider the protection of all such values and interests when making disclosure determinations under the FOIA. Any discretionary decision by your agency to disclose information protected under the FOIA should be made only after full and deliberate consideration of the institutional, commercial, and personal privacy interests that could be implicated by disclosure of the information.

In making these decisions, you should consult with the Department of Justice's Office of Information and Privacy when significant FOIA issues arise, as well as with our Civil Division on FOIA litigation matters. When you carefully consider FOIA requests and decide to withhold records, in whole or in part, you can be assured that the Department of Justice will defend your decisions unless they lack a sound legal basis or present an unwarranted risk of adverse impact on the ability of other agencies to protect other important records.

This memorandum supersedes the Department of Justice's FOIA Memorandum of October 4, 1993, and it likewise creates no substantive or procedural right enforceable at law.

APPENDIX B
Text of the Privacy Act of 1974

This appendix is available online at http://www.epic.org/foia/21/appendixb.html

The Privacy Act, Public Law 93-579 (93rd Congress, S. 3418), was enacted on December 31st, 1974.

Congressional Findings and Statement of Purpose

(a) The Congress finds that—

(1) the privacy of an individual is directly affected by the collection, maintenance, use, and dissemination of personal information by Federal agencies;

(2) the increasing use of computers and sophisticated information technology, while essential to the efficient operations of the Government, has greatly magnified the harm to individual privacy that can occur from any collection, maintenance, use, or dissemination of personal information;

(3) the opportunities for an individual to secure employment, insurance, and credit, and his right to due process, and other legal protections are endangered by the misuse of certain information systems;

(4) the right to privacy is a personal and fundamental right protected by the Constitution of the United States; and

(5) in order to protect the privacy of individuals identified in information systems maintained by Federal agencies, it is necessary and proper for the Congress to regulate the collection, maintenance, use, and dissemination of information by such agencies.

(b) The purpose of this Act is to provide certain safeguards for an individual against an invasion of personal privacy by requiring Federal agencies, except as otherwise provided by law, to—

(1) permit an individual to determine what records pertaining to him are collected, maintained, used, or disseminated by such agencies;

(2) permit an individual to prevent records pertaining to him obtained by such agencies for a particular purpose from being used or made available for another purpose without his consent;

(3) permit an individual to gain access to information pertaining to him in Federal agency records, to have a copy made of all or any portion thereof, and to correct or amend such records;

(4) collect, maintain, use, or disseminate any record of identifiable personal information in a manner that assures that such action is for a necessary and lawful purpose, that the information is current and accurate for its intended use, and that adequate safeguards are provided to prevent misuse of such information;

(5) permit exemptions from the requirements with respect to records provided in this Act only in those cases where there is an important public policy need for such exemption as has been determined by specific statutory authority; and

(6) be subject to civil suit for any damages which occur as a result of willful or intentional action which violates any individual's rights under this Act.

Appendix B

5 U.S.C. § 552a Public information; agency rules, opinions, orders, records, and proceedings

(a) Definitions

For purposes of this section—

(1) the term "agency" means agency as defined in section 552(e) \1\ of this title;

(2) the term "individual" means a citizen of the United States or an alien lawfully admitted for permanent residence;

(3) the term "maintain" includes maintain, collect, use, or disseminate;

(4) the term "record" means any item, collection, or grouping of information about an individual that is maintained by an agency, including, but not limited to, his education, financial transactions, medical history, and criminal or employment history and that contains his name, or the identifying number, symbol, or other identifying particular assigned to the individual, such as a finger or voice print or a photograph;

(5) the term "system of records" means a group of any records under the control of any agency from which information is retrieved by the name of the individual or by some identifying number, symbol, or other identifying particular assigned to the individual;

(6) the term "statistical record" means a record in a system of records maintained for statistical research or reporting purposes only and not used in whole or in part in making any determination about an identifiable individual, except as provided by section 8 of title 13;

(7) the term "routine use" means, with respect to the disclosure of a record, the use of such record for a purpose which is compatible with the purpose for which it was collected;

(8) the term "matching program"—

(A) means any computerized comparison of—

(i) two or more automated systems of records or a system of records with non-Federal records for the purpose of—

(I) establishing or verifying the eligibility of, or continuing compliance with statutory and regulatory requirements by, applicants for, recipients or beneficiaries of, participants in, or providers of services with respect to, cash or in-kind assistance or payments under Federal benefit programs, or

(II) recouping payments or delinquent debts under such Federal benefit programs, or

(ii) two or more automated Federal personnel or payroll systems of records or a system of Federal personnel or payroll records with non-Federal records,

(B) but does not include—

(i) matches performed to produce aggregate statistical data without any personal identifiers;

(ii) matches performed to support any research or statistical project, the specific data of which may not be used to make decisions concerning the rights, benefits, or privileges of specific individuals;

(iii) matches performed, by an agency (or component thereof) which performs as its principal function any activity pertaining to the enforcement of criminal laws, subsequent to the initiation of a specific criminal or civil law enforcement investigation of a named person or persons for the purpose of gathering evidence against such person or persons;

(iv) matches of tax information (I) pursuant to section 6103(d) of the Internal Revenue Code of 1986, (II) for purposes of tax administration as defined in section 6103(b)(4) of such Code, (III) for the purpose of intercepting a tax refund due an individual under authority granted by section 464 or 1137 of the Social Security Act; or (IV) for the purpose of intercepting a tax refund due an individual under any other tax refund intercept program authorized by statute which has been determined by the Director of the Office of Management and Budget to contain verification, notice, and hearing requirements that are substantially similar to the procedures in section 1137 of the Social Security Act;

(v) matches—

(I) using records predominantly relating to Federal personnel, that are performed for routine administrative purposes (subject to guidance provided by the Director of the Office of Management and Budget pursuant to subsection (v)); or

(II) conducted by an agency using only records from systems of records maintained by that agency; if the purpose of the match is not to take any adverse financial, personnel, disciplinary, or other adverse action against Federal personnel;

(vi) matches performed for foreign counterintelligence purposes or to produce background checks for security clearances of Federal personnel or Federal contractor personnel; or

(vii) matches performed pursuant to section 6103(l)(12) of the Internal Revenue Code of 1986 and section 1144 of the Social Security Act;

(9) the term "recipient agency" means any agency, or contractor thereof, receiving records contained in a system of records from a source agency for use in a matching program;

(10) the term "non-Federal agency" means any State or local government, or agency thereof, which receives records contained in a system of records from a source agency for use in a matching program;

(11) the term "source agency" means any agency which discloses records contained in a system of records to be used in a matching program, or any State or local government, or agency thereof, which discloses records to be used in a matching program;

(12) the term "Federal benefit program" means any program administered or funded by the Federal Government, or by any agent or State on behalf of the Federal Government, providing cash or in-kind assistance in the form of payments, grants, loans, or loan guarantees to individuals; and

(13) the term "Federal personnel" means officers and employees of the Government of the United States, members of the uniformed services (including members of the Reserve Components), individuals entitled to receive immediate or deferred retirement benefits under any retirement program of the Government of the United States (including survivor benefits).

(b) Conditions of Disclosure

No agency shall disclose any record which is contained in a system of records by any means of communication to any person, or to another agency, except pursuant to a written request by, or with the prior written consent of, the individual to whom the record pertains, unless disclosure of the record would be—

(1) to those officers and employees of the agency which maintains the record who have a need for the record in the performance of their duties;

(2) required under section 552 of this title;

(3) for a routine use as defined in subsection (a)(7) of this section and described under subsection (e)(4)(D) of this section;

(4) to the Bureau of the Census for purposes of planning or carrying out a census or survey or related activity pursuant to the provisions of title 13;

(5) to a recipient who has provided the agency with advance adequate written assurance that the record will be used solely as a statistical research or reporting record, and the record is to be transferred in a form that is not individually identifiable;

(6) to the National Archives and Records Administration as a record which has sufficient historical or other value to warrant its continued preservation by the United States Government, or for evaluation by the Archivist of the United States or the designee of the Archivist to determine whether the record has such value;

(7) to another agency or to an instrumentality of any governmental jurisdiction within or under the control of the United States for a civil or criminal law enforcement activity if the activity is authorized by law, and if the head of the agency or instrumentality has made a written request to the agency which maintains the record specifying the particular portion desired and the law enforcement activity for which the record is sought;

(8) to a person pursuant to a showing of compelling circumstances affecting the health or safety of an individual if upon such disclosure notification is transmitted to the last known address of such individual;

(9) to either House of Congress, or, to the extent of matter within its jurisdiction, any committee or subcommittee thereof, any joint committee of Congress or subcommittee of any such joint committee;

(10) to the Comptroller General, or any of his authorized representatives, in the course of the performance of the duties of the General Accounting Office;

(11) pursuant to the order of a court of competent jurisdiction; or

(12) to a consumer reporting agency in accordance with section 3711(f) of title 31.

(c) Accounting of Certain Disclosures

Each agency, with respect to each system of records under its control, shall—

(1) except for disclosures made under subsections (b)(1) or (b)(2) of this section, keep an accurate accounting of—

(A) the date, nature, and purpose of each disclosure of a record to any person or to another agency made under subsection (b) of this section; and

(B) the name and address of the person or agency to whom the disclosure is made;

(2) retain the accounting made under paragraph (1) of this subsection for at least five years or the life of the record, whichever is longer, after the disclosure for which the accounting is made;

(3) except for disclosures made under subsection (b)(7) of this section, make the accounting made under paragraph (1) of this subsection available to the individual named in the record at his request; and

(4) inform any person or other agency about any correction or notation of dispute made by the agency in accordance with subsection (d) of this section of any record that has been disclosed to the person or agency if an accounting of the disclosure was made.

(d) Access to Records

Each agency that maintains a system of records shall—

(1) upon request by any individual to gain access to his record or to any information pertaining to him which is contained in the system, permit him and upon his request, a person of his own choosing to accompany him, to review the record and have a copy made of all or any portion thereof in a form comprehensible to him, except that the agency may require the individual to furnish a written statement authorizing discussion of that individual's record in the accompanying person's presence;

(2) permit the individual to request amendment of a record pertaining to him and—

(A) not later than 10 days (excluding Saturdays, Sundays, and legal public holidays) after the date of receipt of such request, acknowledge in writing such receipt; and

(B) promptly, either—

(i) make any correction of any portion thereof which the individual believes is not accurate, relevant, timely, or complete; or

(ii) inform the individual of its refusal to amend the record in accordance with his request, the reason for the refusal, the procedures established by the agency for the individual to request a review of that refusal by the head of the agency or an officer designated by the head of the agency, and the name and business address of that official;

(3) permit the individual who disagrees with the refusal of the agency to amend his record to request a review of such refusal, and not later than 30 days (excluding Saturdays, Sundays, and legal public holidays) from the date on which the individual requests such review, complete such review and make a final determination unless, for good cause shown, the head of the agency extends such 30-day period; and if, after his review, the reviewing official also refuses to amend the record in accordance with the request, permit the individual to file with the agency a concise statement setting forth the reasons for his disagreement with the refusal of the agency, and notify the individual of the provisions for judicial review of the reviewing official's determination under subsection (g)(1)(A) of this section;

(4) in any disclosure, containing information about which the individual has filed a statement of disagreement, occurring after the filing of the statement under paragraph (3) of this subsection, clearly note any portion of the record which is disputed and provide copies of the statement and, if the agency deems it appropriate, copies of a concise statement of the reasons of the agency for not making the amendments requested, to persons or other agencies to whom the disputed record has been disclosed; and

(5) nothing in this section shall allow an individual access to any information compiled in reasonable anticipation of a civil action or proceeding.

(e) Agency Requirements

Each agency that maintains a system of records shall—

(1) maintain in its records only such information about an individual as is relevant and necessary to accomplish a purpose of the agency required to be accomplished by statute or by executive order of the President;

(2) collect information to the greatest extent practicable directly from the subject individual when the information may result in adverse determinations about an individual's rights, benefits, and privileges under Federal programs;

(3) inform each individual whom it asks to supply information, on the form which it uses to collect the information or on a separate form that can be retained by the individual—

(A) the authority (whether granted by statute, or by executive order of the President) which authorizes the solicitation of the information and whether disclosure of such information is mandatory or voluntary;

(B) the principal purpose or purposes for which the information is intended to be used;

(C) the routine uses which may be made of the information, as published pursuant to paragraph (4)(D) of this subsection; and

(D) the effects on him, if any, of not providing all or any part of the requested information;

(4) subject to the provisions of paragraph (11) of this subsection, publish in the Federal Register upon establishment or revision a notice of the existence and character of the system of records, which notice shall include—

(A) the name and location of the system;

(B) the categories of individuals on whom records are maintained in the system;

(C) the categories of records maintained in the system;

(D) each routine use of the records contained in the system, including the categories of users and the purpose of such use;

(E) the policies and practices of the agency regarding storage, retrievability, access controls, retention, and disposal of the records;

(F) the title and business address of the agency official who is responsible for the system of records;

(G) the agency procedures whereby an individual can be notified at his request if the system of records contains a record pertaining to him;

(H) the agency procedures whereby an individual can be notified at his request how he can gain access to any record pertaining to him contained in the system of records, and how he can contest its content; and

(I) the categories of sources of records in the system;

(5) maintain all records which are used by the agency in making any determination about any individual with such accuracy, relevance, timeliness, and completeness as is reasonably necessary to assure fairness to the individual in the determination;

(6) prior to disseminating any record about an individual to any person other than an agency, unless the dissemination is made pursuant to subsection (b)(2) of this section, make reasonable efforts to assure that such records are accurate, complete, timely, and relevant for agency purposes;

(7) maintain no record describing how any individual exercises rights guaranteed by the First Amendment unless expressly authorized by statute or by the individual about whom the record is maintained or unless pertinent to and within the scope of an authorized law enforcement activity;

(8) make reasonable efforts to serve notice on an individual when any record on such individual is made available to any person under compulsory legal process when such process becomes a matter of public record;

(9) establish rules of conduct for persons involved in the design, development, operation, or maintenance of any system of records, or in maintaining any record, and instruct each such person with respect to such rules and the requirements of this section, including any other rules and procedures adopted pursuant to this section and the penalties for noncompliance;

(10) establish appropriate administrative, technical, and physical safeguards to insure the security and confidentiality of records and to protect against any anticipated threats or hazards to their security or integrity which could result in substantial harm, embarrassment, inconvenience, or unfairness to any individual on whom information is maintained;

(11) at least 30 days prior to publication of information under paragraph (4)(D) of this subsection, publish in the Federal Register notice of any new use or intended use of the information in the system, and provide an opportunity for interested persons to submit written data, views, or arguments to the agency; and

(12) if such agency is a recipient agency or a source agency in a matching program with a non-Federal agency, with respect to any establishment or revision of a matching program, at least 30 days prior to conducting such program, publish in the Federal Register notice of such establishment or revision.

(f) Agency Rules

In order to carry out the provisions of this section, each agency that maintains a system of records shall promulgate rules, in accordance with the requirements (including general notice) of section 553 of this title, which shall—

(1) establish procedures whereby an individual can be notified in response to his request if any system of records named by the individual contains a record pertaining to him;

(2) define reasonable times, places, and requirements for identifying an individual who requests his record or information pertaining to him before the agency shall make the record or information available to the individual;

(3) establish procedures for the disclosure to an individual upon his request of his record or information pertaining to him, including special procedure, if deemed necessary, for the disclosure to an individual of medical records, including psychological records, pertaining to him;

(4) establish procedures for reviewing a request from an individual concerning the amendment of any record or information pertaining to the individual, for making a determination on the request, for an appeal within the agency of an initial adverse agency determination, and for whatever additional means may be necessary for each individual to be able to exercise fully his rights under this section; and

(5) establish fees to be charged, if any, to any individual for making copies of his record, excluding the cost of any search for and review of the record.
The Office of the Federal Register shall biennially compile and publish the rules promulgated under this subsection and agency notices published under subsection (e)(4) of this section in a form available to the public at low cost.

(g) Civil Remedies

(1) Whenever any agency

(A) makes a determination under subsection (d)(3) of this section not to amend an individual's record in accordance with his request, or fails to make such review in conformity with that subsection;

(B) refuses to comply with an individual request under subsection (d)(1) of this section;

(C) fails to maintain any record concerning any individual with such accuracy, relevance, timeliness, and completeness as is necessary to assure fairness in any determination relating to the qualifications, character, rights, or opportunities of, or benefits to the individual that may be made on the basis of such record, and consequently a determination is made which is adverse to the individual; or

(D) fails to comply with any other provision of this section, or any rule promulgated thereunder, in such a way as to have an adverse effect on an individual, the individual may bring a civil action against the agency, and the district courts of the United States shall have jurisdiction in the matters under the provisions of this subsection.

(2)(A) In any suit brought under the provisions of subsection (g)(1)(A) of this section, the court may order the agency to amend the individual's record in accordance with his request or in such other way as the court may direct. In such a case the court shall determine the matter de novo.

(B) The court may assess against the United States reasonable attorney fees and other litigation costs reasonably incurred in any case under this paragraph in which the complainant has substantially prevailed.

(3)(A) In any suit brought under the provisions of subsection (g)(1)(B) of this section, the court may enjoin the agency from withholding the records and order the production to the complainant of any agency records improperly withheld from him. In such a case the court shall determine the matter de novo, and may examine the contents of any agency records in camera to determine whether the records or any portion thereof may be withheld under any of the exemptions set forth in subsection (k) of this section, and the burden is on the agency to sustain its action.

(B) The court may assess against the United States reasonable attorney fees and other litigation costs reasonably incurred in any case under this paragraph in which the complainant has substantially prevailed.

(4) In any suit brought under the provisions of subsection (g)(1)(C) or (D) of this section in which the court determines that the agency acted in a manner which was intentional or willful, the United States shall be liable to the individual in an amount equal to the sum of—

(A) actual damages sustained by the individual as a result of the refusal or failure, but in no case shall a person entitled to recovery receive less than the sum of $1,000; and

(B) the costs of the action together with reasonable attorney fees as determined by the court.

(5) An action to enforce any liability created under this section may be brought in the district court of the United States in the district in which the complainant resides, or has his principal place of business, or in which the agency records are situated, or in the District of Columbia, without regard to the amount in controversy, within two years from the date on which the cause of action arises, except that where an agency has materially and willfully misrepresented any information required under this section to be disclosed to an individual and the information so misrepresented is material to establishment of the liability of the agency to the individual under this section, the action may be brought at any time within two years after discovery by the individual of the misrepresentation. Nothing in this section shall be construed to authorize any civil action by reason of any injury sustained as the result of a disclosure of a record prior to September 27, 1975.

(h) Rights of Legal Guardians

For the purposes of this section, the parent of any minor, or the legal guardian of any individual who has been declared to be incompetent due to physical or mental incapacity or age by a court of competent jurisdiction, may act on behalf of the individual.

(i) Criminal Penalties.

(1) Any officer or employee of an agency, who by virtue of his employment or official position, has possession of, or access to, agency records which contain individually identifiable information the disclosure of which is prohibited by this section or by rules or regulations established thereunder, and who knowing that disclosure of the specific material is so prohibited, willfully discloses the material in any manner to any person or agency not entitled to receive it, shall be guilty of a misdemeanor and fined not more than $5,000.

(2) Any officer or employee of any agency who willfully maintains a system of records without meeting the notice requirements of subsection (e)(4) of this section shall be guilty of a misdemeanor and fined not more than $5,000.

(3) Any person who knowingly and willfully requests or obtains any record concerning an individual from an agency under false pretenses shall be guilty of a misdemeanor and fined not more than $5,000.

(j) General Exemptions

The head of any agency may promulgate rules, in accordance with the requirements (including general notice) of sections 553(b)(1), (2), and (3), (c), and (e) of this title, to exempt any system of records within the agency from any part of this section except subsections (b), (c)(1) and (2), (e)(4)(A) through (F), (e)(6), (7), (9), (10), and (11), and (i) if the system of records is—

(1) maintained by the Central Intelligence Agency; or

(2) maintained by an agency or component thereof which performs as its principal function any activity pertaining to the enforcement of criminal laws, including police efforts to prevent, control, or reduce crime or to apprehend criminals, and the activities of prosecutors, courts, correctional, probation, pardon, or parole authorities, and which consists of (A) information compiled for the purpose of identifying individual criminal offenders and alleged offenders and consisting only of identifying data and notations of arrests, the nature and disposition of criminal charges, sentencing,

confinement, release, and parole and probation status; (B) information compiled for the purpose of a criminal investigation, including reports of informants and investigators, and associated with an identifiable individual; or (C) reports identifiable to an individual compiled at any stage of the process of enforcement of the criminal laws from arrest or indictment through release from supervision.

At the time rules are adopted under this subsection, the agency shall include in the statement required under section 553(c) of this title, the reasons why the system of records is to be exempted from a provision of this section.

(k) Specific Exemptions

The head of any agency may promulgate rules, in accordance with the requirements (including general notice) of sections 553(b)(1), (2), and (3), (c), and (e) of this title, to exempt any system of records within the agency from subsections (c)(3), (d), (e)(1), (e)(4)(G), (H), and (I) and (f) of this section if the system of records is—

(1) subject to the provisions of section 552(b)(1) of this title;

(2) investigatory material compiled for law enforcement purposes, other than material within the scope of subsection (j)(2) of this section: Provided, however, That if any individual is denied any right, privilege, or benefit that he would otherwise be entitled by Federal law, or for which he would otherwise be eligible, as a result of the maintenance of such material, such material shall be provided to such individual, except to the extent that the disclosure of such material would reveal the identity of a source who furnished information to the Government under an express promise that the identity of the source would be held in confidence, or, prior to the effective date of this section, under an implied promise that the identity of the source would be held in confidence;

(3) maintained in connection with providing protective services to the President of the United States or other individuals pursuant to section 3056 of title 18;

(4) required by statute to be maintained and used solely as statistical records;

(5) investigatory material compiled solely for the purpose of determining suitability, eligibility, or qualifications for Federal civilian employment, military service, Federal contracts, or access to classified information, but only to the extent that the disclosure of such material would reveal the identity of a source who furnished information to the Government under an express promise that the identity of the source would be held in confidence, or, prior to the effective date of this section, under an implied promise that the identity of the source would be held in confidence;

(6) testing or examination material used solely to determine individual qualifications for appointment or promotion in the Federal service the disclosure of which would compromise the objectivity or fairness of the testing or examination process; or

(7) evaluation material used to determine potential for promotion in the armed services, but only to the extent that the disclosure of such material would reveal the identity of a source who furnished information to the Government under an express promise that the identity of the source would be held in confidence, or, prior to the effective date of this section, under an implied promise that the identity of the source would be held in confidence.

At the time rules are adopted under this subsection, the agency shall include in the statement required under section 553(c) of this title, the reasons why the system of records is to be exempted from a provision of this section.

(l) Archival Records

Each agency record which is accepted by the Archivist of the United States for storage, processing, and servicing in accordance with section 3103 of title 44 shall, for the purposes of this section, be considered to be maintained by the agency which deposited the record and shall be subject to the provisions of this section. The Archivist of the United States shall not disclose the record except to the agency which maintains the record, or under rules established by that agency which are not inconsistent with the provisions of this section.

(2) Each agency record pertaining to an identifiable individual which was transferred to the National Archives of the United States as a record which has sufficient historical or other value to warrant its continued preservation by the United States Government, prior to the effective date of this section, shall, for the purposes of this section, be considered to be maintained by the National Archives and shall not be subject to the provisions of this section, except that a statement generally describing such records (modeled after the requirements relating to records subject to subsections (e)(4)(A) through (G) of this section) shall be published in the Federal Register.

(3) Each agency record pertaining to an identifiable individual which is transferred to the National Archives of the United States as a record which has sufficient historical or other value to warrant its continued preservation by the United States Government, on or after the effective date of this section, shall, for the purposes of this section, be considered to be maintained by the National Archives and shall be exempt from the requirements of this section except subsections (e)(4)(A) through (G) and (e)(9) of this section.

(m) Government Contractors

(1)When an agency provides by a contract for the operation by or on behalf of the agency of a system of records to accomplish an agency function, the agency shall, consistent with its authority, cause the requirements of this section to be applied to such system. For purposes of subsection (i) of this section any such contractor and any employee of such contractor, if such contract is agreed to on or after the effective date of this section, shall be considered to be an employee of an agency.

(2) A consumer reporting agency to which a record is disclosed under section 3711(f) of title 31 shall not be considered a contractor for the purposes of this section.

(n) Mailing Lists

An individual's name and address may not be sold or rented by an agency unless such action is specifically authorized by law. This provision shall not be construed to require the withholding of names and addresses otherwise permitted to be made public.

(o) Matching Agreements

(1) No record which is contained in a system of records may be disclosed to a recipient agency or non-Federal agency for use in a computer matching program except pursuant to a written agreement between the source agency and the recipient agency or non-Federal agency specifying—

(A) the purpose and legal authority for conducting the program;

(B) the justification for the program and the anticipated results, including a specific estimate of any savings;

(C) a description of the records that will be matched, including each data element that will be used, the approximate number of records that will be matched, and the projected starting and completion dates of the matching program;

(D) procedures for providing individualized notice at the time of application, and notice periodically thereafter as directed by the Data Integrity Board of such agency (subject to guidance provided by the Director of the Office of Management and Budget pursuant to subsection (v)), to—

(i) applicants for and recipients of financial assistance or payments under Federal benefit programs, and

(ii) applicants for and holders of positions as Federal personnel, that any information provided by such applicants, recipients, holders, and individuals may be subject to verification through matching programs;

(E) procedures for verifying information produced in such matching program as required by subsection (p);

(F) procedures for the retention and timely destruction of identifiable records created by a recipient agency or non-Federal agency in such matching program;

(G) procedures for ensuring the administrative, technical, and physical security of the records matched and the results of such programs;

(H) prohibitions on duplication and redisclosure of records provided by the source agency within or outside the recipient agency or the non-Federal agency, except where required by law or essential to the conduct of the matching program;

(I) procedures governing the use by a recipient agency or non-Federal agency of records provided in a matching program by a source agency, including procedures governing return of the records to the source agency or destruction of records used in such program;

(J) information on assessments that have been made on the accuracy of the records that will be used in such matching program; and

(K) that the Comptroller General may have access to all records of a recipient agency or a non-Federal agency that the Comptroller General deems necessary in order to monitor or verify compliance with the agreement.

(2)(A) A copy of each agreement entered into pursuant to paragraph (1) shall—

(i) be transmitted to the Committee on Governmental Affairs of the Senate and the Committee on Government Operations of the House of Representatives; and

(ii) be available upon request to the public.

(B) No such agreement shall be effective until 30 days after the date on which such a copy is transmitted pursuant to subparagraph (A)(i).

(C) Such an agreement shall remain in effect only for such period, not to exceed 18 months, as the Data Integrity Board of the agency determines is appropriate in light of the purposes, and length of time necessary for the conduct, of the matching program.

(D) Within 3 months prior to the expiration of such an agreement pursuant to subparagraph (C), the Data Integrity Board of the agency may, without additional review, renew the matching agreement for a current, ongoing matching program for not more than one additional year if—

(i) such program will be conducted without any change; and

(ii) each party to the agreement certifies to the Board in writing that the program has been conducted in compliance with the agreement.

(p) Verification and Opportunity to Contest Findings

(1) In order to protect any individual whose records are used in a matching program, no recipient agency, non-Federal agency, or source agency may suspend, terminate, reduce, or make a final denial of any financial assistance or payment under a Federal benefit program to such individual, or take other adverse action against such individual, as a result of information produced by such matching program, until—

(A)(i) the agency has independently verified the information; or

(ii) the Data Integrity Board of the agency, or in the case of a non-Federal agency the Data Integrity Board of the source agency, determines in accordance with guidance issued by the Director of the Office of Management and Budget that—

(I) the information is limited to identification and amount of benefits paid by the source agency under a Federal benefit program; and

(II) there is a high degree of confidence that the information provided to the recipient agency is accurate;

(B) the individual receives a notice from the agency containing a statement of its findings and informing the individual of the opportunity to contest such findings; and

(C)(i) the expiration of any time period established for the program by statute or regulation for the individual to respond to that notice; or

(ii) in the case of a program for which no such period is established, the end of the 30-day period beginning on the date on which notice under subparagraph (B) is mailed or otherwise provided to the individual.

(2) Independent verification referred to in paragraph (1) requires investigation and confirmation of specific information relating to an individual that is used as a basis for an adverse action against the individual, including where applicable investigation and confirmation of—

(A) the amount of any asset or income involved;

(B) whether such individual actually has or had access to such asset or income for such individual's own use; and

(C) the period or periods when the individual actually had such asset or income.

(3) Notwithstanding paragraph (1), an agency may take any appropriate action otherwise prohibited by such paragraph if the agency determines that the public health or public safety may be adversely affected or significantly threatened during any notice period required by such paragraph.

(q) Sanctions

(1) Notwithstanding any other provision of law, no source agency may disclose any record which is contained in a system of records to a recipient agency or non-Federal agency for a matching program if such source agency has reason to believe that the requirements of subsection (p), or any

matching agreement entered into pursuant to subsection (o), or both, are not being met by such recipient agency.

(2) No source agency may renew a matching agreement unless—

(A) the recipient agency or non-Federal agency has certified that it has complied with the provisions of that agreement; and

(B) the source agency has no reason to believe that the certification is inaccurate.

(r) Report on New Systems and Matching Programs

Each agency that proposes to establish or make a significant change in a system of records or a matching program shall provide adequate advance notice of any such proposal (in duplicate) to the Committee on Government Operations of the House of Representatives, the Committee on Governmental Affairs of the Senate, and the Office of Management and Budget in order to permit an evaluation of the probable or potential effect of such proposal on the privacy or other rights of individuals.

(s) Biennial Report

The President shall biennially submit to the Speaker of the House of Representatives and the President pro tempore of the Senate a report—

(1) describing the actions of the Director of the Office of Management and Budget pursuant to section 6 of the Privacy Act of 1974 during the preceding 2 years;

(2) describing the exercise of individual rights of access and amendment under this section during such years;

(3) identifying changes in or additions to systems of records;

(4) containing such other information concerning administration of this section as may be necessary or useful to the Congress in reviewing the effectiveness of this section in carrying out the purposes of the Privacy Act of 1974.

(t) Effect of Other Laws

(1) No agency shall rely on any exemption contained in section 552 of this title to withhold from an individual any record which is otherwise accessible to such individual under the provisions of this section.

(2) No agency shall rely on any exemption in this section to withhold from an individual any record which is otherwise accessible to such individual under the provisions of section 552 of this title.

(u) Data Integrity Boards

(1) Every agency conducting or participating in a matching program shall establish a Data Integrity Board to oversee and coordinate among the various components of such agency the agency's implementation of this section.

(2) Each Data Integrity Board shall consist of senior officials designated by the head of the agency, and shall include any senior official designated by the head of the agency as responsible for implementation of this section, and the inspector general of the agency, if any. The inspector general shall not serve as chairman of the Data Integrity Board.

(3) Each Data Integrity Board—

(A) shall review, approve, and maintain all written agreements for receipt or disclosure of agency records for matching programs to ensure compliance with subsection (o), and all relevant statutes, regulations, and guidelines;

(B) shall review all matching programs in which the agency has participated during the year, either as a source agency or recipient agency, determine compliance with applicable laws, regulations, guidelines, and agency agreements, and assess the costs and benefits of such programs;

(C) shall review all recurring matching programs in which the agency has participated during the year, either as a source agency or recipient agency, for continued justification for such disclosures;

(D) shall compile an annual report, which shall be submitted to the head of the agency and the Office of Management and Budget and made available to the public on request, describing the matching activities of the agency, including—

(i) matching programs in which the agency has participated as a source agency or recipient agency;

(ii) matching agreements proposed under subsection (o) that were disapproved by the Board;

(iii) any changes in membership or structure of the Board in the preceding year;

(iv) the reasons for any waiver of the requirement in paragraph (4) of this section for completion and submission of a cost-benefit analysis prior to the approval of a matching program;

(v) any violations of matching agreements that have been alleged or identified and any corrective action taken; and

(vi) any other information required by the Director of the Office of Management and Budget to be included in such report;

(E) shall serve as a clearinghouse for receiving and providing information on the accuracy, completeness, and reliability of records used in matching programs;

(F) shall provide interpretation and guidance to agency components and personnel on the requirements of this section for matching programs;

(G) shall review agency recordkeeping and disposal policies and practices for matching programs to assure compliance with this section; and

(H) may review and report on any agency matching activities that are not matching programs.

(4)(A) Except as provided in subparagraphs (B) and (C), a Data Integrity Board shall not approve any written agreement for a matching program unless the agency has completed and submitted to such Board a cost-benefit analysis of the proposed program and such analysis demonstrates that the program is likely to be cost effective.

(B) The Board may waive the requirements of subparagraph (A) of this paragraph if it determines in writing, in accordance with guidelines prescribed by the Director of the Office of Management and Budget, that a cost-benefit analysis is not required.

(C) A cost-benefit analysis shall not be required under subparagraph (A) prior to the initial approval of a written agreement for a matching program that is specifically required by statute. Any subsequent written agreement for such a program shall not be approved by the Data Integrity Board unless the agency has submitted a cost-benefit analysis of the program as conducted under the preceding approval of such agreement.

(5)(A) If a matching agreement is disapproved by a Data Integrity Board, any party to such agreement may appeal the disapproval to the Director of the Office of Management and Budget. Timely notice of the filing of such an appeal shall be provided by the Director of the Office of Management and Budget to the Committee on Governmental Affairs of the Senate and the Committee on Government Operations of the House of Representatives.

(B) The Director of the Office of Management and Budget may approve a matching agreement notwithstanding the disapproval of a Data Integrity Board if the Director determines that—

(i) the matching program will be consistent with all applicable legal, regulatory, and policy requirements;

(ii) there is adequate evidence that the matching agreement will be cost-effective; and

(iii) the matching program is in the public interest.

(C) The decision of the Director to approve a matching agreement shall not take effect until 30 days after it is reported to committees described in subparagraph (A).

(D) If the Data Integrity Board and the Director of the Office of Management and Budget disapprove a matching program proposed by the inspector general of an agency, the inspector general may report the disapproval to the head of the agency and to the Congress.

(6) In the reports required by paragraphs (3)(D), agency matching activities that are not matching programs may be reported on an aggregate basis, if and to the extent necessary to protect ongoing law enforcement or counterintelligence investigations.

(v) Office of Management and Budget Responsibilities

The Director of the Office of Management and Budget shall—

(1) develop and, after notice and opportunity for public comment, prescribe guidelines and regulations for the use of agencies in implementing the provisions of this section; and

(2) provide continuing assistance to and oversight of the implementation of this section by agencies.

Section 7 Disclosure of Social Security Number

(a)(1) It shall be unlawful for any Federal, State or local government agency to deny to any individual any right, benefit, or privilege provided by law because of such individual's refusal to disclose his social security account number.

(2) the provisions of paragraph (1) of this subsection shall not apply with respect to—

(A) any disclosure which is required by Federal statute, or

(B) the disclosure of a social security number to any Federal, State, or local agency maintaining a system of records in existence and operating before January 1, 1975, if such disclosure was required under statute or regulation adopted prior to such date to verify the identity of an individual.

(b) Any Federal, State, or local government agency which requests an individual to disclose his social security account number shall inform that individual whether that disclosure is mandatory or voluntary, by what statutory or other authority such number is solicited, and what uses will be made of it.

Sec. 6 Functions of the Director of the Office of Management and Budget.

(b) Implementation Guidance for Amendments— The Director shall, pursuant to section 552a(v) of Title 5, United States Code, develop guidelines and regulations for the use of agencies in implementing the amendments made by this Act not later than 8 months after the date of enactment of this Act.

Sec. 9 Rules of Construction.

Nothing in the amendments made by this Act shall be construed to authorize—

(1) the establishment or maintenance by any agency of a national data bank that combines, merges, or links information on individuals maintained in systems of records by other Federal agencies;

(2) the direct linking of computerized systems of records maintained by Federal agencies;

(3) the computer matching of records not otherwise authorized by law; or

(4) the disclosure of records for computer matching except to a Federal, State, or local agency.

Sec. 10 Effective Dates.

(a) In General—Except as provided in subsection (b), the amendments made by this Act shall take effect 9 months after the date of enactment of this Act.

(b) Exceptions—The amendment made by sections 3(b) [Notice of Matching Programs—Report to Congress and the Office of Management and Budget], 6 [Functions of the Director of the Office of Management and Budget], 7 [Compilation of Rules and Notices] and 8 [Annual Report] of this Act shall take effect upon enactment.

Legislative History of The Privacy Act of 1974

For complete legislative history of the original Act, see *Legislative History of the Privacy Act of 1974, S. 3418 (Pub.L.93-579): Source Book on Privacy,* Joint Committee Print of Sen. Comm. on Governmental Affairs and House Comm. on Governmental Operations, 94th Cong., 2d Sess. (September 1976).

HOUSE REPORT No. 93-1416 accompanying H.R. 16373 (Comm. on Government Operations. SENATE REPORT No. 93-1183 (Comm. on Government Operations). CONGRESSIONAL RECORD, Vol. 120 (1974):

Nov. 21, 1974—S. 3418 was considered and passed by Senate. 120 CONG. REC. 36917.
November 21, 1974—H.R. 16373 was considered and passed by House. 120 CONG. REC. 36976.
Dec. 11, 1974—S. 3418 was considered and passed by House, amended in lieu of H.R. 16373.
Dec. 17, 1974—Senate concurred in House amendment to S. 3418 with amendments. 120 CONG. REC. 40445.
Dec. 18, 1974—House concurred in Senate amendments.

WEEKLY COMPILATION OF PRESIDENTIAL DOCUMENTS, Vol. 11, No. 1: Jan. 1, Presidential statement.

1982 Amendments

Note: Congress, in passing the Debt Collection Act of 1982, P.L. 97-365, 97th Cong., 2d Sess., H.R. 4613, 96 Stat. 1749, amended subsection 552a(e)(4) to substitute "upon establishment or revision" for "at least annually," and amended subsection 552a(m) to redesignate the existing provision as par. (1) and add Par. (2).

1. House Report:

   H. Rep. No. 97-496 (Ways and Means Committee)

2. Senate Reports:

   S. Rep. No. 97-287 (Finance Committee)
   S. Rep. No. 97-378 (Governmental Affairs Committee)

See 1982 U.S. Code Cong. and Adm. News, p. 3377.

Note: Congress, in passing the Congressional Reports Elimination Act of 1982, P.L. 97-375, 97th Cong., 2d Sess., H.R. 6005, 96 Stat. 1819, amended subsection 552a(p) to substitute annual reporting requirements for existing requirements for consolidated reports to be filed by June 30 of each calendar year.

1. House Report:

   H. Rep. No. 97-804 (Government Operations Committee). *See* 1982 U.S., Code Cong. and Adm. News, p. 3435.

1983 Amendment

Note: Congress, in its revision of title 31 to reflect changes in laws relating to money and finance, P.L. 97-452, 97th Cong., 2d Sess., 96 Stat. 2467, amended subsections 552a(b)(12) and (m)(2) to substitute "section 3711(f) of title 31" for "section 3(d) of the Federal Claims Collection Act of 1966 (31 U.S.C. 952(d))."

Appendix B

Neither the Senate nor the House submitted a report with this legislation, but a detailed explanation was prepared by the Office of Law Revision Counsel. 128 Cong. Rec. H 9528 (1982).

See 1982 U.S. Code Cong. and Adm. News, p. 4301.

1984 Amendments

Note: Congress, in enacting the National Archives and Records Administration Act of 1984, P.L. 98-497, 98th Cong., 2d. Sess., S. 905, 98 Stat. 2280, amended subsections 552a(b)(6) and (l)(1) generally by substituting references to the "Archivist of the United States" for the "Administrator of General Services."

1. House Reports:

   H. Rep. No. 98-707 (Government Operations Committee).
   H. Rep. No. 98-1124 (Conference Committee).

2. Senate Report:

   S. Rep. No. 98-373 (Governmental Affairs Committee).

See 1984 U.S. Code Cong. and Adm. News, p. 3865.

Note: Congress, in enacting the Central Intelligence Information Act, P.L. 98-477, 98th Cong., 2d Sess., HR. 5164, 98 Stat. 2209, amended subsection 552a(q) to redesignate that provision as (q)(1) and add another provision (q)(2) which clarified that Privacy Act exemptions do not constitute authority to withhold records from a requester who would otherwise have access to them under the FOIA.

1. House Reports:

   H. Rep. No. 98-726 (I) (Intelligence Comm.).
   H. Rep. No. 98-726 (II) (Government Operations Comm.).

2. Senate Report:

   S. Rep. No. 98-305 (Intelligence Comm.).

See 1984 U.S. Code Cong. and Adm. News, p. 3741.

1988 Amendments

Congress enacted the Computer Matching and Privacy Protection Act of 1988, P.L. 100-503, 102 Stat. 2507-2514.

1. House Report:

   H. Rep. No. 100-802 on H.R. 4699 (House Comm. on Gov't Op.).

2. Congressional Record:

   134 Cong. Rec. H 3716 (English Statement).
   134 Cong. Rec. H 6091 (H.R. 4699 Passed in House by Voice Vote).
   134 Cong. Rec. H 6068-91 (English/McCandless Statements).
   134 Cong. Rec. S 12995 (Senate Concurred in House Amendment with an Amendment).

Subsequent Amendments

Pub. L. 101-508, title VII, Sec. 7201(b)(1), Nov. 5, 1990, 104 Stat. 1388-334
Pub. L. 103-66, title XIII, Sec. 13581(c), Aug. 10, 1993, 107 Stat. 611
Pub. L. 104-193, title I, Sec. 110(w), Aug. 22, 1996, 110 Stat. 2175
Pub. L. 104-226, Sec. 1(b)(3), Oct. 2, 1996, 110 Stat. 3033
Pub. L. 104-316, title I, Sec. 115(g)(2)(B), Oct. 19, 1996, 110 Stat. 3835
Pub. L. 105-34, title X, Sec. 1026(b)(2), Aug. 5, 1997, 111 Stat. 925
Pub. L. 105-362, title XIII, Sec. 1301(d), Nov. 10, 1998, 112 Stat. 3293
Pub. L. 106-170, title IV, Sec. 402(a)(2), Dec. 17, 1999, 113 Stat. 1908.

APPENDIX C
Text of the Government in the Sunshine Act

This appendix is available online at http://www.epic.org/foia/21/appendixc.html

Public Law 94-409, 90 Stat. 1241, was enacted on September 13, 1976, and codified at 5 U.S.C. § 552(b).

Sec. 552b.—Open meetings

(a) For purposes of this section—

(1) the term "agency" means any agency, as defined in section 552(e) [1] of this title, headed by a collegial body composed of two or more individual members, a majority of whom are appointed to such position by the President with the advice and consent of the Senate, and any subdivision thereof authorized to act on behalf of the agency;

(2) the term "meeting" means the deliberations of at least the number of individual agency members required to take action on behalf of the agency where such deliberations determine or result in the joint conduct or disposition of official agency business, but does not include deliberations required or permitted by subsection (d) or (e); and

(3) the term "member" means an individual who belongs to a collegial body heading an agency.

(b) Members shall not jointly conduct or dispose of agency business other than in accordance with this section. Except as provided in subsection (c), every portion of every meeting of an agency shall be open to public observation.

(c) Except in a case where the agency finds that the public interest requires otherwise, the second sentence of subsection (b) shall not apply to any portion of an agency meeting, and the requirements of subsections (d) and (e) shall not apply to any information pertaining to such meeting otherwise required by this section to be disclosed to the public, where the agency properly determines that such portion or portions of its meeting or the disclosure of such information is likely to—

(1) disclose matters that are

(A) specifically authorized under criteria established by an Executive order to be kept secret in the interests of national defense or foreign policy and

(B) in fact properly classified pursuant to such Executive order;

(2) relate solely to the internal personnel rules and practices of an agency;

(3) disclose matters specifically exempted from disclosure by statute (other than section 552 of this title), provided that such statute

(A) requires that the matters be withheld from the public in such a manner as to leave no discretion on the issue, or

(B) establishes particular criteria for withholding or refers to particular types of matters to be withheld;

(4) disclose trade secrets and commercial or financial information obtained from a person and privileged or confidential;

(5) involve accusing any person of a crime, or formally censuring any person;

(6) disclose information of a personal nature where disclosure would constitute a clearly unwarranted invasion of personal privacy;

(7) disclose investigatory records compiled for law enforcement purposes, or information which if written would be contained in such records, but only to the extent that the production of such records or information would

(A) interfere with enforcement proceedings,

(B) deprive a person of a right to a fair trial or an impartial adjudication,

(C) constitute an unwarranted invasion of personal privacy,

(D) disclose the identity of a confidential source and, in the case of a record compiled by a criminal law enforcement authority in the course of a criminal investigation, or by an agency conducting a lawful national security intelligence investigation, confidential information furnished only by the confidential source,

(E) disclose investigative techniques and procedures, or

(F) endanger the life or physical safety of law enforcement personnel;

(8) disclose information contained in or related to examination, operating, or condition reports prepared by, on behalf of, or for the use of an agency responsible for the regulation or supervision of financial institutions;

(9) disclose information the premature disclosure of which would—

(A) in the case of an agency which regulates currencies, securities, commodities, or financial institutions, be likely to

(i) lead to significant financial speculation in currencies, securities, or commodities, or

(ii) significantly endanger the stability of any financial institution; or

(B) in the case of any agency, be likely to significantly frustrate implementation of a proposed agency action,

except that subparagraph (B) shall not apply in any instance where the agency has already disclosed to the public the content or nature of its proposed action, or where the agency is required by law to make such disclosure on its own initiative prior to taking final agency action on such proposal; or

(10) specifically concern the agency's issuance of a subpoena, or the agency's participation in a civil action or proceeding, an action in a foreign court or international tribunal, or an arbitration, or the initiation, conduct, or disposition by the agency of a particular case of formal agency adjudication pursuant to the procedures in section 554 of this title or otherwise involving a determination on the record after opportunity for a hearing.

(d)(1) Action under subsection (c) shall be taken only when a majority of the entire membership of the agency (as defined in subsection (a)(1)) votes to take such action. A separate vote of the agency members shall be taken with respect to each agency meeting a portion or portions of which are proposed to be closed to the public pursuant to subsection (c), or with respect to any information which is proposed to be withheld under subsection (c). A single vote may be taken with respect to a series of meetings, a portion or portions of which are proposed to be closed to the public, or with respect to any information concerning such series of meetings, so long as each meeting in such series involves the same particular matters and is scheduled to be held no more than thirty days after the initial meeting in such series. The vote of each agency member participating in such vote shall be recorded and no proxies shall be allowed.

(2) Whenever any person whose interests may be directly affected by a portion of a meeting requests that the agency close such portion to the public for any of the reasons referred to in paragraph (5), (6), or (7) of subsection (c), the agency, upon request of any one of its members, shall vote by recorded vote whether to close such meeting.

(3) Within one day of any vote taken pursuant to paragraph (1) or (2), the agency shall make publicly available a written copy of such vote reflecting the vote of each member on the question. If a portion of a meeting is to be closed to the public, the agency shall, within one day of the vote taken pursuant to paragraph (1) or (2) of this subsection, make publicly available a full written explanation of its action closing the portion together with a list of all persons expected to attend the meeting and their affiliation.

(4) Any agency, a majority of whose meetings may properly be closed to the public pursuant to paragraph (4), (8), (9)(A), or (10) of subsection (c), or any combination thereof, may provide by regulation for the closing of such meetings or portions thereof in the event that a majority of the members of the agency votes by recorded vote at the beginning of such meeting, or portion thereof, to close the exempt portion or portions of the meeting, and a copy of such vote, reflecting the vote of each member on the question, is made available to the public. The provisions of paragraphs (1), (2), and (3) of this subsection and subsection (e) shall not apply to any portion of a meeting to which such regulations apply: Provided, That the agency shall, except to the extent that such information is exempt from disclosure under the provisions of subsection (c), provide the public with public announcement of the time, place, and subject matter of the meeting and of each portion thereof at the earliest practicable time.

(e)(1) In the case of each meeting, the agency shall make public announcement, at least one week before the meeting, of the time, place, and subject matter of the meeting, whether it is to be open or closed to the public, and the name and phone number of the official designated by the agency to respond to requests for information about the meeting. Such announcement shall be made unless a majority of the members of the agency determines by a recorded vote that agency business requires that such meeting be called at an earlier date, in which case the agency shall make public announcement of the time, place, and subject matter of such meeting, and whether open or closed to the public, at the earliest practicable time.

(2) The time or place of a meeting may be changed following the public announcement required by paragraph (1) only if the agency publicly announces such change at the earliest practicable time. The subject matter of a meeting, or the determination of the agency to open or close a meeting, or portion of a meeting, to the public, may be changed following the public announcement required by this subsection only if

(A) a majority of the entire membership of the agency determines by a recorded vote that agency business so requires and that no earlier announcement of the change was possible, and

(B) the agency publicly announces such change and the vote of each member upon such change at the earliest practicable time.

(3) Immediately following each public announcement required by this subsection, notice of the time, place, and subject matter of a meeting, whether the meeting is open or closed, any change in one of the preceding, and the name and phone number of the official designated by the agency to respond to requests for information about the meeting, shall also be submitted for publication in the Federal Register.

(f)(1) For every meeting closed pursuant to paragraphs (1) through (10) of subsection (c), the General Counsel or chief legal officer of the agency shall publicly certify that, in his or her opinion, the meeting may be closed to the public and shall state each relevant exemptive provision. A copy of such certification, together with a statement from the presiding officer of the meeting setting forth the time and place of the meeting, and the persons present, shall be retained by the agency. The agency shall maintain a complete transcript or electronic recording adequate to record fully the proceedings of each meeting, or portion of a meeting, closed to the public, except that in the case of a meeting, or portion of a meeting, closed to the public pursuant to paragraph (8), (9)(A), or (10) of subsection (c), the agency shall maintain either such a transcript or recording, or a set of minutes. Such minutes shall fully and clearly describe all matters discussed and shall provide a full and accurate summary of any actions taken, and the reasons therefor, including a description of each of the views expressed on any item and the record of any rollcall vote (reflecting the vote of each member on the question). All documents considered in connection with any action shall be identified in such minutes.

(2) The agency shall make promptly available to the public, in a place easily accessible to the public, the transcript, electronic recording, or minutes (as required by paragraph (1)) of the discussion of any item on the agenda, or of any item of the testimony of any witness received at the meeting, except for such item or items of such discussion or testimony as the agency determines to contain information which may be withheld under subsection (c). Copies of such transcript, or minutes, or a transcription of such recording disclosing the identity of each speaker, shall be furnished to any person at the actual cost of duplication or transcription. The agency shall maintain a complete verbatim copy of the transcript, a complete copy of the minutes, or a complete electronic recording of each meeting, or portion of a meeting, closed to the public, for a period of at least two years after such meeting, or until one year after the conclusion of any agency proceeding with respect to which the meeting or portion was held, whichever occurs later.

(g) Each agency subject to the requirements of this section shall, within 180 days after the date of enactment of this section, following consultation with the Office of the Chairman of the Administrative Conference of the United States and published notice in the Federal Register of at least thirty days and opportunity for written comment by any person, promulgate regulations to implement the requirements of subsections (b) through (f) of this section. Any person may bring a proceeding in the United States District Court for the District of Columbia to require an agency to promulgate such regulations if such agency has not promulgated such regulations within the time period specified herein. Subject to any limitations of time provided by law, any person may bring a proceeding in the United States Court of Appeals for the District of Columbia to set aside agency regulations issued pursuant to this subsection that are not in accord with the requirements of subsections (b) through (f) of this section and to require the promulgation of regulations that are in accord with such subsections.

(h)(1) The district courts of the United States shall have jurisdiction to enforce the requirements of subsections (b) through (f) of this section by declaratory judgment, injunctive relief, or other relief as may be appropriate. Such actions may be brought by any person against an agency prior to, or within sixty days after, the meeting out of which the violation of this section arises, except that if public announcement of such meeting is not initially provided by the agency in accordance with the requirements of this section, such action may be instituted pursuant to this section at any time prior to sixty days after any public announcement of such meeting. Such actions may be brought in the district court of the United States for the district in which the agency meeting is held or in which the agency in question has its headquarters, or in the District Court for the District of Columbia. In such actions a defendant shall serve his answer within thirty days after the service of the complaint. The burden is on the defendant to sustain his action. In deciding such cases the court may examine in camera any portion of the transcript, electronic recording, or minutes of a meeting closed to the public, and may take such additional evidence as it deems necessary. The court, having due regard for orderly administration and the public interest, as well as the interests of the parties, may grant such equitable relief as it deems appropriate, including granting an injunction against future violations of this section or ordering the agency to make available to the public such portion of the transcript, recording, or minutes of a meeting as is not authorized to be withheld under subsection (c) of this section.

(2) Any Federal court otherwise authorized by law to review agency action may, at the application of any person properly participating in the proceeding pursuant to other applicable law, inquire into violations by the agency of the requirements of this section and afford such relief as it deems appropriate. Nothing in this section authorizes any Federal court having jurisdiction solely on the basis of paragraph (1) to set aside, enjoin, or invalidate any agency action (other than an action to close a meeting or to withhold information under this section) taken or discussed at any agency meeting out of which the violation of this section arose.

(i) The court may assess against any party reasonable attorney fees and other litigation costs reasonably incurred by any other party who substantially prevails in any action brought in accordance with the provisions of subsection (g) or (h) of this section, except that costs may be assessed against the plaintiff only where the court finds that the suit was initiated by the plaintiff primarily for frivolous or dilatory purposes. In the case of assessment of costs against an agency, the costs may be assessed by the court against the United States.

(j) Each agency subject to the requirements of this section shall annually report to the Congress regarding the following:

(1) The changes in the policies and procedures of the agency under this section that have occurred during the preceding 1-year period.

(2) A tabulation of the number of meetings held, the exemptions applied to close meetings, and the days of public notice provided to close meetings.

(3) A brief description of litigation or formal complaints concerning the implementation of this section by the agency.

(4) A brief explanation of any changes in law that have affected the responsibilities of the agency under this section.

(k) Nothing herein expands or limits the present rights of any person under section 552 of this title, except that the exemptions set forth in subsection (c) of this section shall govern in the case of any request made pursuant to section 552 to copy or inspect the transcripts, recordings, or minutes described in subsection (f) of this section. The requirements of chapter 33 of title 44, United States Code, shall not apply to the transcripts, recordings, and minutes described in subsection (f) of this section.

(l) This section does not constitute authority to withhold any information from Congress, and does not authorize the closing of any agency meeting or portion thereof required by any other provision of law to be open.

(m) Nothing in this section authorizes any agency to withhold from any individual any record, including transcripts, recordings, or minutes required by this section, which is otherwise accessible to such individual under section 552a of this title.

Legislative History—The Government in the Sunshine Act

For complete legislative history of the Act, see *Government in the Sunshine Act Source Book: Legislative History, Texts, and other Documents*, Committees on Government Operations, U.S. Senate and House of Representatives, 94th Cong., 2d Sess. (1976), or see 1976 U.S. Code Cong. & Admin. News 2183 et seq.

1. Senate Action:

Introduction of S.5, 121 Cong. Rec. S59-64 (January 15, 1975).
S.5 reported by Senate Committee on Government Operations, July 31, 1975 (S. Rpt. 94-354).
S.5 reported by Senate Committee on Rules and Administration, September 18, 1975 (S. Rpt. 94-381).
Floor Consideration and Passage of S.5, 121 CONG.REC. S19372-19378 (November 5, 1975), 121 CONG.REC. S19432-19447 (November 6, 1975).

2. House Action:

Introduction of H.R.5075, 122 CONG.REC. H1939-1942 (March 18, 1975).
Introduction of H.R.11656, 122 CONG.REC. (March 8, 1976).

1995 Amendment

Congress, in enacting the Federal Reports Elimination and Sunset Act of 1995, Pub. L. 104-66, 109 Stat. 734, altered requirements under subsection (j) regarding the reporting requirements of agencies.

APPENDIX D
Text of the Federal Advisory Committee Act

This appendix is available online at http://www.epic.org/foia/21/appendixd.html

The FACA is codified at 5 U.S.C. §§ App. 1 et seq..

Sec. 2. (a) The Congress finds that there are numerous committees, boards, commissions, councils, and similar groups which have been established to advise officers and agencies in the executive branch of the Federal Government and that they are frequently a useful and beneficial means of furnishing expert advice, ideas, and diverse opinions to the Federal Government.

(b) The Congress further finds and declares that -

(1) the need for many existing advisory committees has not been adequately reviewed:

(2) new advisory committees should be established only when they are determined to be essential and their number should be kept to the minimum necessary;

(3) advisory committees should be terminated when they are no longer carrying out the purposes for which they were established;

(4) standards and uniform procedures should govern the establishment, operation, administration, and duration of advisory committees;

(5) the Congress and the public should be kept informed with respect to the number, purpose, membership, activities, and cost of advisory committees; and

(6) the function of advisory committees should be advisory only, and that all matters under their consideration should be determined, in accordance with law, by the official, agency, or officer involved.

Sec. 3. For the purpose of this Act —

(1) The term "Administrator" means the Administrator of General Services.

(2) The term "advisory committee" means any committee, board, commission, council, conference, panel, task force, or other similar group, or any subcommittee or other subgroup thereof (hereafter in this paragraph referred to as "committee"), which is -

(A) established by statute or reorganization plan, or

(B) established or utilized by the President, or

(C) established or utilized by one or more agencies, in the interest of obtaining advice or recommendations for the President or one or more agencies or officers of the Federal Government, except that such term excludes

(i) any committee that is composed wholly of full-time, or permanent part-time, officers or employees of the Federal Government, and

(ii) any committee that is created by the National Academy of Sciences or the National Academy of Public Administration.

(3) The term "agency" has the same meaning as in section 551(1) of title 5, United States Code.

(4) The term "Presidential advisory committee" means an advisory committee which advises the President.

Sec. 4. (a) The provisions of this Act or of any rule, order, or regulation promulgated under this Act shall apply to each advisory committee except to the extent that any Act of Congress establishing any such advisory committee specifically provides otherwise.

(b) Nothing in this Act shall be construed to apply to any advisory committee established or utilized by -

(1) the Central Intelligence Agency; or

(2) the Federal Reserve System.

(c) Nothing in this Act shall be construed to apply to any local civic group whose primary function is that of rendering a public service with respect to a Federal program, or any State or local committee, council, board, commission, or similar group established to advise or make recommendations to State or local officials or agencies.

Sec. 5. (a) In the exercise of its legislative review function, each standing committee of the Senate and the House of Representatives shall make a continuing review of the activities of each advisory committee under its jurisdiction to determine whether such advisory committee should be abolished or merged with any other advisory committee, whether the responsibilities of such advisory committee should be revised, and whether such advisory committee performs a necessary function not already being performed. Each such standing committee shall take appropriate action to obtain the enactment of legislation necessary to carry out the purpose of this subsection.

(b) In considering legislation establishing, or authorizing the establishment of any advisory committee, each standing committee of the Senate and of the House of Representatives shall determine, and report such determination to the Senate or to the House of Representatives, as the case may be, whether the functions of the proposed advisory committee are being or could be performed by one or more agencies or by an advisory committee already in existence, or by enlarging the mandate of an existing advisory committee. Any such legislation shall -

(1) contain a clearly defined purpose for the advisory committee;

(2) require the membership of the advisory committee to be fairly balanced in terms of the points of view represented and the functions to be performed by the advisory committee;

(3) contain appropriate provisions to assure that the advice and recommendations of the advisory committee will not be inappropriately influenced by the appointing authority or by any special interest, but will instead be the result of the advisory committee's independent judgment;

(4) contain provisions dealing with authorization of appropriations, the date for submission of reports (if any), the duration of the advisory committee, and the publication of reports and other materials, to the extent that the standing committee determines the provisions of section 10 of this Act to be inadequate; and

(5) contain provisions which will assure that the advisory committee will have adequate staff (either supplied by an agency or employed by it), will be provided adequate quarters, and will have funds available to meet its other necessary expenses.

(c) To the extent they are applicable, the guidelines set out in subsection (b) of this section shall be followed by the President, agency heads, or other Federal officials in creating an advisory committee.

Sec. 6. (a) The President may delegate responsibility for evaluating and taking action, where appropriate, with respect to all public recommendations made to him by Presidential advisory committees.

(b) Within one year after a Presidential advisory committee has submitted a public report to the President, the President or his delegate shall make a report to the Congress stating either his proposals for action or his reasons for inaction, with respect to the recommendations contained in the public report.

(c) The President shall, not later than December 31 of each year, make an annual report to the Congress on the activities, status, and changes in the composition of advisory committees in existence during the preceding fiscal year. The report shall contain the name of every advisory committee, the date of and authority for its creation, its termination date or the date it is to make a report, its functions, a reference to the reports it has submitted, a statement of whether it is an ad hoc or continuing body, the dates of its meetings, the names and occupations of its current members, and the total estimated annual cost to the United States to fund, service, supply, and maintain such committee. Such report shall include a list of those advisory committees abolished by the President, and in the case of advisory committees established by statute, a list of those advisory committees which the President recommends be abolished together with his reasons therefor. The President shall exclude from this report any information which, in his judgment, should be withheld for reasons of national security, and he shall include in such report a statement that such information is excluded.

Sec. 7. (a) The Administrator shall establish and maintain within the General Services Administration a Committee Management Secretariat, which shall be responsible for all matters relating to advisory committees.

(b) The Administrator shall, immediately after October 6, 1972, institute a comprehensive review of the activities and responsibilities of each advisory committee to determine -

(1) whether such committee is carrying out its purpose;
(2) whether, consistent with the provisions of applicable statutes, the responsibilities assigned to it should be revised;
(3) whether it should be merged with other advisory committees; or
(4) whether it should be abolished.
The Administrator may from time to time request such information as he deems necessary to carry out his functions under this subsection. Upon the completion of the Administrator's review he shall make recommendations to the President and to either the agency head or the Congress with respect to action he believes should be taken. Thereafter, the Administrator shall carry out a similar review annually. Agency heads shall cooperate with the Administrator in making the reviews required by this subsection.

(c) The Administrator shall prescribe administrative guidelines and management controls applicable to advisory committees, and, to the maximum extent feasible, provide advice, assistance, and guidance to advisory committees to improve their performance. In carrying out his functions under this subsection, the Administrator shall consider the recommendations of each agency head with respect to means of improving the performance of advisory committees whose duties are related to such agency.

(d)(1) The Administrator, after study and consultation with the Director of the Office of Personnel Management, shall establish guidelines with respect to uniform fair rates of pay for comparable services of members, staffs, and consultants of advisory committees in a manner which gives appropriate recognition to the responsibilities and qualifications required and other relevant factors. Such regulations shall provide that -

(A) no member of any advisory committee or of the staff of any advisory committee shall receive compensation at a rate in excess of the rate specified for GS-18 of the General Schedule under section 5332 of title 5, United States Code;

(B) such members, while engaged in the performance of their duties away from their homes or regular places of business, may be allowed travel expenses, including per diem in lieu of subsistence, as authorized by section 5703 of title 5, United States Code, for persons employed intermittently in the Government service; and

(C) such members -

(i) who are blind or deaf or who otherwise qualify as handicapped individuals (within the meaning of section 501 of the Rehabilitation Act of 1973 (29 U.S.C. 794)), and

(ii) who do not otherwise qualify for assistance under section 3102 of title 5, United States Code, by reason of being an employee of an agency (within the meaning of section 3102(a)(1) of such title 5), may be provided services pursuant to section 3102 of such title 5 while in performance of their advisory committee duties.

(2) Nothing in this subsection shall prevent -

(A) an individual who (without regard to his service with an advisory committee) is a full-time employee of the United States, or

(B) an individual who immediately before his service with an advisory committee was such an employee, from receiving compensation at the rate at which he otherwise would be compensated (or was compensated) as a full-time employee of the United States.

(e) The Administrator shall include in budget recommendations a summary of the amounts he deems necessary for the expenses of advisory committees, including the expenses for publication of reports where appropriate.

Sec. 8. (a) Each agency head shall establish uniform administrative guidelines and management controls for advisory committees established by that agency, which shall be consistent with directives of the Administrator under section 7 and section 10. Each agency shall maintain systematic information on the nature, functions, and operations of each advisory committee within its jurisdiction.

(b) The head of each agency which has an advisory committee shall designate an Advisory Committee Management Officer who shall -

(1) exercise control and supervision over the establishment, procedures, and accomplishments of advisory committees established by that agency;

(2) assemble and maintain the reports, records, and other papers of any such committee during its existence; and

(3) carry out, on behalf of that agency, the provisions of section 552 of title 5, United States Code, with respect to such reports, records, and other papers.

Sec. 9. (a) No advisory committee shall be established unless such establishment is -

(1) specifically authorized by statute or by the President; or

(2) determined as a matter of formal record, by the head of the agency involved after consultation with the Administrator, with timely notice published in the Federal Register, to be in the public interest in connection with the performance of duties imposed on that agency by law.

(b) Unless otherwise specifically provided by statute or Presidential directive, advisory committees shall be utilized solely for advisory functions. Determinations of action to be taken and policy to be expressed with respect to matters upon which an advisory committee reports or makes recommendations shall be made solely by the President or an officer of the Federal Government.

(c) No advisory committee shall meet or take any action until an advisory committee charter has been filed with

(1) the Administrator, in the case of Presidential advisory committees, or

(2) with the head of the agency to whom any advisory committee reports and with the standing committees of the Senate and of the House of Representatives having legislative jurisdiction of such agency. Such charter shall contain the following information:

(A) the committee's official designation;

(B) the committee's objectives and the scope of its activity;

(C) the period of time necessary for the committee to carry out its purposes;

(D) the agency or official to whom the committee reports;

(E) the agency responsible for providing the necessary support for the committee;

(F) a description of the duties for which the committee is responsible, and, if such duties are not solely advisory, a specification of the authority for such functions;

(G) the estimated annual operating costs in dollars and man-years for such committee;

(H) the estimated number and frequency of committee meetings;

(I) the committee's termination date, if less than two years from the date of the committee's establishment; and

(J) the date the charter is filed.
A copy of any such charter shall also be furnished to the Library of Congress.

Sec. 10. (a)(1) Each advisory committee meeting shall be open to the public.

(2) Except when the President determines otherwise for reasons of national security, timely notice of each such meeting shall be published in the Federal Register, and the Administrator shall prescribe regulations to provide for other types of public notice to insure that all interested persons are notified of such meeting prior thereto.

(3) Interested persons shall be permitted to attend, appear before, or file statements with any advisory committee, subject to such reasonable rules or regulations as the Administrator may prescribe.

(b) Subject to section 552 of title 5, United States Code, the records, reports, transcripts, minutes, appendixes, working papers, drafts, studies, agenda, or other documents which were made available to or prepared for or by each advisory committee shall be available for public inspection and copying at a single location in the offices of the advisory committee or the agency to which the advisory committee reports until the advisory committee ceases to exist.

(c) Detailed minutes of each meeting of each advisory committee shall be kept and shall contain a record of the persons present, a complete and accurate description of matters discussed and conclusions reached, and copies of all reports received, issued, or approved by the advisory committee. The accuracy of all minutes shall be certified to by the chairman of the advisory committee.

(d) Subsections (a)(1) and (a)(3) of this section shall not apply to any portion of an advisory committee meeting where the President, or the head of the agency to which the advisory committee reports, determines that such portion of such meeting may be closed to the public in accordance with subsection (c) of section 552b of title 5, United States Code. Any such determination shall be in writing and shall contain the reasons for such determination. If such a determination is made, the advisory committee shall issue a report at least annually setting forth a summary of its activities and such related matters as would be informative to the public consistent with the policy of section 552(b) of title 5, United States Code.

(e) There shall be designated an officer or employee of the Federal Government to chair or attend each meeting of each advisory committee. The officer or employee so designated is authorized, whenever he determines it to be in the public interest, to adjourn any such meeting. No advisory committee shall conduct any meeting in the absence of that officer or employee.

(f) Advisory committees shall not hold any meetings except at the call of, or with the advance approval of, a designated officer or employee of the Federal Government, and in the case of advisory committees (other than Presidential advisory committees), with an agenda approved by such officer or employee.

Sec. 11. (a) Except where prohibited by contractual agreements entered into prior to the effective date of this Act, agencies and advisory committees shall make available to any person, at actual cost of duplication, copies of transcripts of agency proceedings or advisory committee meetings.

(b) As used in this section "agency proceeding" means any proceeding as defined in section 551(12) of title 5, United States Code.

Sec. 12. (a) Each agency shall keep records as will fully disclose the disposition of any funds which may be at the disposal of its advisory committees and the nature and extent of their activities.
The General Services Administration, or such other agency as the President may designate, shall maintain financial records with respect to Presidential advisory committees. The Comptroller General of the United States, or any of his authorized representatives, shall have access, for the purpose of audit and examination, to any such records.

(b) Each agency shall be responsible for providing support services for each advisory committee established by or reporting to it unless the establishing authority provides otherwise. Where any such advisory committee reports to more than one agency, only one agency shall be responsible for support services at any one time.
In the case of Presidential advisory committees, such services may be provided by the General Services Administration.

Sec. 13. Subject to section 552 of title 5, United States Code, the Administrator shall provide for the filing with the Library of Congress of at least eight copies of each report made by every advisory committee and, where appropriate, background papers prepared by consultants. The Librarian of Congress shall establish a depository for such reports and papers where they shall be available to public inspection and use.

Sec. 14. (a)(1) Each advisory committee which is in existence on the effective date of this Act shall terminate not later than the expiration of the two-year period following such effective date unless -

(A) in the case of an advisory committee established by the President or an officer of the Federal Government, such advisory committee is renewed by the President or that officer by appropriate action prior to the expiration of such two-year period; or

(B) in the case of an advisory committee established by an Act of Congress, its duration is otherwise provided for by law.

(2) Each advisory committee established after such effective date shall terminate not later than the expiration of the two-year period beginning on the date of its establishment unless -

(A) in the case of an advisory committee established by the President or an officer of the Federal Government such advisory committee is renewed by the President or such officer by appropriate action prior to the end of such period; or

(B) in the case of an advisory committee established by an Act of Congress, its duration is otherwise provided for by law.

(b)(1) Upon the renewal of any advisory committee, such advisory committee shall file a charter in accordance with section 9(c).

(2) Any advisory committee established by an Act of Congress shall file a charter in accordance with such section upon the expiration of each successive two-year period following the date of enactment of the Act establishing such advisory committee.

(3) No advisory committee required under this subsection to file a charter shall take any action (other than preparation and filing of such charter) prior to the date on which such charter is filed.

(c) Any advisory committee which is renewed by the President or any officer of the Federal Government may be continued only for successive two-year periods by appropriate action taken by the President or such officer prior to the date on which such advisory committee would otherwise terminate.

Sec. 15. (a) In General.—An agency may not use any advice or recommendation provided by the National Academy of Sciences or National Academy of Public Administration that was developed by use of a committee created by that academy under an agreement with an agency, unless -

(1) the committee was not subject to any actual management or control by an agency or an officer of the Federal Government;

(2) in the case of a committee created after the date of the enactment of the Federal Advisory Committee Act Amendments of 1997, the membership of the committee was appointed in accordance with the requirements described in subsection (b)(1); and

(3) in developing the advice or recommendation, the academy complied with -

(A) subsection (b)(2) through (6), in the case of any advice or recommendation provided by the National Academy of Sciences; or

(B) subsection (b)(2) and (5), in the case of any advice or recommendation provided by the National Academy of Public Administration.

(b) Requirements.—The requirements referred to in subsection (a) are as follows:

(1) The Academy shall determine and provide public notice of the names and brief biographies of individuals that the Academy appoints or intends to appoint to serve on the committee. The

Academy shall determine and provide a reasonable opportunity for the public to comment on such appointments before they are made or, if the Academy determines such prior comment is not practicable, in the period immediately following the appointments. The Academy shall make its best efforts to ensure that

(A) no individual appointed to serve on the committee has a conflict of interest that is relevant to the functions to be performed, unless such conflict is promptly and publicly disclosed and the Academy determines that the conflict is unavoidable,

(B) the committee membership is fairly balanced as determined by the Academy to be appropriate for the functions to be performed, and

(C) the final report of the Academy will be the result of the Academy's independent judgment. The Academy shall require that individuals that the Academy appoints or intends to appoint to serve on the committee inform the Academy of the individual's conflicts of interest that are relevant to the functions to be performed.

(2) The Academy shall determine and provide public notice of committee meetings that will be open to the public.

(3) The Academy shall ensure that meetings of the committee to gather data from individuals who are not officials, agents, or employees of the Academy are open to the public, unless the Academy determines that a meeting would disclose matters described in section 552(b) of title 5, United States Code. The Academy shall make available to the public, at reasonable charge if appropriate, written materials presented to the committee by individuals who are not officials, agents, or employees of the Academy, unless the Academy determines that making material available would disclose matters described in that section.

(4) The Academy shall make available to the public as soon as practicable, at reasonable charge if appropriate, a brief summary of any committee meeting that is not a data gathering meeting, unless the Academy determines that the summary would disclose matters described in section 552(b) of title 5, United States Code. The summary shall identify the committee members present, the topics discussed, materials made available to the committee, and such other matters that the Academy determines should be included.

(5) The Academy shall make available to the public its final report, at reasonable charge if appropriate, unless the Academy determines that the report would disclose matters described in section 552(b) of title 5, United States Code. If the Academy determines that the report would disclose matters described in that section, the Academy shall make public an abbreviated version of the report that does not disclose those matters.

(6) After publication of the final report, the Academy shall make publicly available the names of the principal reviewers who reviewed the report in draft form and who are not officials, agents, or employees of the Academy.

(c) Regulations.—The Administrator of General Services may issue regulations implementing this section.

Sec. 16. Except as provided in section 7(b), this Act shall become effective upon the expiration of ninety days following October 6, 1972.

Legislative History—The Federal Advisory Committee Act

For complete legislative history, *see Federal Advisory Committee Act (Pub.L. 92-463) Source Book: Legislative History, Texts, and other Documents*, Subcommittee on Energy, Nuclear Proliferation, and Senate 95th Cong., 2d Sess. (July 1978) or 1972 U.S. Cong. Code and Admin. News 3491 et seq.

1. House Action

Report of House Committee on Government Operations, No. 1731, 91st Cong., 2d Sess (1970) (H. Rpt. 91-1731).
Introduction of H.R.4383, 117 CONG.REC. 2750 (February 17, 1971).
H.R. 4383 reported by House Committee on Government Operations, (H. Rpt. 92-1017).
Floor Consideration and Passage of H.R. 4383, 118 CONG.REC. H4272-4286 (May 9, 1972).

2. Senate Action

Introduction of S.33529, 118 CONG.REC. (1972)
S.3529 reported by Senate Committee on Government Operations, (S. Rpt. 92-1098).
Floor Consideration and Passage of S. 3529 and amended H.R. 4383, 118 CONG.REC. S14644-14655 (September 12, 1972).

3. Conference Action

H. Rpt. 92-1403 (Conference Report) adopted by the Senate, 118 CONG.REC. S15285-15286 (September 19, 1972).
H. Rpt. 92-1403 (Conference Report) adopted by the House, 118 CONG.REC H8610-8611 (September 20, 1972).

Subsequent Amendments

P. L. 94-409, SEC. 5(C), SEPT. 13, 1976, 90 Stat. 1247.
P. L. 96-523, SEC. 2, DEC. 12, 1980, 94 Stat. 3040.
P. L. 97-375, TITLE II, SEC. 201(C), DEC. 21, 1982, 96 Stat. 1822.
P. L. 105-153, SEC. 2(A), (B), DEC. 17, 1997, 111 Stat. 2689.

APPENDIX E
Executive Orders and Regulations

Executive Order 12958
Classified National Security Information

This appendix is available online at http://www.epic.org/foia/21/appendixe.html

This order prescribes a uniform system for classifying, safeguarding, and declassifying national security information. Our democratic principles require that the American people be informed of the activities of their Government. Also, our Nation's progress depends on the free flow of information. Nevertheless, throughout our history, the national interest has required that certain information be maintained in confidence in order to protect our citizens, our democratic institutions, and our participation within the community of nations. Protecting information critical to our Nation's security remains a priority. In recent years, however, dramatic changes have altered, although not eliminated, the national security threats that we confront. These changes provide a greater opportunity to emphasize our commitment to open Government.

Now, Therefore, by the authority vested in me as President by the Constitution and the laws of the United States of America, it is hereby ordered as follows:

Part 1 Original Classification

Section 1.1. Definitions. For purposes of this order:

(a) "National security" means the national defense or foreign relations of the United States.

(b) "Information" means any knowledge that can be communicated or documentary material, regardless of its physical form or characteristics, that is owned by, produced by or for, or is under the control of the United States Government. "Control" means the authority of the agency that originates information, or its successor in function, to regulate access to the information.

(c) "Classified national security information" (hereafter "classified information") means information that has been determined pursuant to this order or any predecessor order to require protection against unauthorized disclosure and is marked to indicate its classified status when in documentary form.

(d) "Foreign Government Information" means:

(1) information provided to the United States Government by a foreign government or governments, an international organization of governments, or any element thereof, with the expectation that the information, the source of the information, or both, are to be held in confidence;

(2) information produced by the United States pursuant to or as a result of a joint arrangement with a foreign government or governments, or an international organization of governments, or any element thereof, requiring that the information, the arrangement, or both, are to be held in confidence; or

(3) information received and treated as "Foreign Government Information" under the terms of a predecessor order.

(e) "Classification" means the act or process by which information is determined to be classified information.

(f) "Original classification" means an initial determination that information requires, in the interest of national security, protection against unauthorized disclosure.

(g) "Original classification authority" means an individual authorized in writing, either by the President, or by agency heads or other officials designated by the President, to classify information in the first instance.

(h) "Unauthorized disclosure" means a communication or physical transfer of classified information to an unauthorized recipient.

(i) "Agency" means any "Executive agency," as defined in 5 U.S.C. 105, and any other entity within the executive branch that comes into the possession of classified information.

(j) "Senior agency official" means the official designated by the agency head under section 5.6(c) of this order to direct and administer the agency's program under which information is classified, safeguarded, and declassified.

(k) "Confidential source" means any individual or organization that has provided, or that may reasonably be expected to provide, information to the United States on matters pertaining to the national security with the expectation that the information or relationship, or both, are to be held in confidence.

(l) "Damage to the national security" means harm to the national defense or foreign relations of the United States from the unauthorized disclosure of information, to include the sensitivity, value, and utility of that information.

Sec. 1.2. Classification Standards. (a) Information may be originally classified under the terms of this order only if all of the following conditions are met:

(1) an original classification authority is classifying the information;

(2) the information is owned by, produced by or for, or is under the control of the United States Government;

(3) the information falls within one or more of the categories of information listed in section 1.5 of this order; and

(4) the original classification authority determines that the unauthorized disclosure of the information reasonably could be expected to result in damage to the national security and the original classification authority is able to identify or describe the damage.

(b) If there is significant doubt about the need to classify information, it shall not be classified. This provision does not:

(1) amplify or modify the substantive criteria or procedures for classification; or

(2) create any substantive or procedural rights subject to judicial review.

(c) Classified information shall not be declassified automatically as a result of any unauthorized disclosure of identical or similar information.

Sec. 1.3. Classification Levels. (a) Information may be classified at one of the following three levels:

(1) "Top Secret" shall be applied to information, the unauthorized disclosure of which reasonably could be expected to cause exceptionally grave damage to the national security that the original classification authority is able to identify or describe.

(2) "Secret" shall be applied to information, the unauthorized disclosure of which reasonably could be expected to cause serious damage to the national security that the original classification authority is able to identify or describe.

(3) "Confidential" shall be applied to information, the unauthorized disclosure of which reasonably could be expected to cause damage to the national security that the original classification authority is able to identify or describe.

(b) Except as otherwise provided by statute, no other terms shall be used to identify United States classified information.

(c) If there is significant doubt about the appropriate level of classification, it shall be classified at the lower level.

Sec. 1.4. Classification Authority. (a) The authority to classify information originally may be exercised only by:

(1) the President;

(2) agency heads and officials designated by the President in the Federal Register; or

(3) United States Government officials delegated this authority pursuant to paragraph (c), below.

(b) Officials authorized to classify information at a specified level are also authorized to classify information at a lower level.

(c) Delegation of original classification authority.

(1) Delegations of original classification authority shall be limited to the minimum required to administer this order. Agency heads are responsible for ensuring that designated subordinate officials have a demonstrable and continuing need to exercise this authority.

(2) "Top Secret" original classification authority may be delegated only by the President or by an agency head or official designated pursuant to paragraph (a)(2), above.

(3) "Secret" or "Confidential" original classification authority may be delegated only by the President; an agency head or official designated pursuant to paragraph (a)(2), above; or the senior agency official, provided that official has been delegated "Top Secret" original classification authority by the agency head.

(4) Each delegation of original classification authority shall be in writing and the authority shall not be redelegated except as provided in this order. Each delegation shall identify the official by name or position title.

(d) Original classification authorities must receive training in original classification as provided in this order and its implementing directives.

(e) Exceptional cases. When an employee, contractor, licensee, certificate holder, or grantee of an agency that does not have original classification authority originates information believed by that person to require classification, the information shall be protected in a manner consistent with this order and its implementing directives. The information shall be transmitted promptly as provided under this order or its implementing directives to the agency that has appropriate subject matter interest and classification authority with respect to this information. That agency shall decide within 30 days whether to classify this information. If it is not clear which agency has classification responsibility for this information, it shall be sent to the Director of the Information Security Oversight Office. The Director shall determine the agency having primary subject matter interest and forward the information, with appropriate recommendations, to that agency for a classification determination.

Sec. 1.5. Classification Categories.

Information may not be considered for classification unless it concerns:

(a) military plans, weapons systems, or operations;

(b) foreign government information;

(c) intelligence activities (including special activities), intelligence sources or methods, or cryptology;

(d) foreign relations or foreign activities of the United States, including confidential sources;

(e) scientific, technological, or economic matters relating to the national security;

(f) United States Government programs for safeguarding nuclear materials or facilities; or (g) vulnerabilities or capabilities of systems, installations, projects or plans relating to the national security.

Sec. 1.6. Duration of Classification. (a) At the time of original classification, the original classification authority shall attempt to establish a specific date or event for declassification based upon the duration of the national security sensitivity of the information. The date or event shall not exceed the time frame in paragraph (b), below.

(b) If the original classification authority cannot determine an earlier specific date or event for declassification, information shall be marked for declassification 10 years from the date of the original decision, except as provided in paragraph (d), below.

(c) An original classification authority may extend the duration of classification or reclassify specific information for successive periods not to exceed 10 years at a time if such action is consistent with the standards and procedures established under this order. This provision does not apply to information contained in records that are more than 25 years old and have been determined to have permanent historical value under title 44, United States Code.

(d) At the time of original classification, the original classification authority may exempt from declassification within 10 years specific information, the unauthorized disclosure of which could reasonably be expected to cause damage to the national security for a period greater than that provided in paragraph (b), above, and the release of which could reasonably be expected to:

(1) reveal an intelligence source, method, or activity, or a cryptologic system or activity;

(2) reveal information that would assist in the development or use of weapons of mass destruction;

(3) reveal information that would impair the development or use of technology within a United States weapons system;

(4) reveal United States military plans, or national security emergency preparedness plans;

(5) reveal foreign government information;

(6) damage relations between the United States and a foreign government, reveal a confidential source, or seriously undermine diplomatic activities that are reasonably expected to be ongoing for a period greater than that provided in paragraph (b), above;

(7) impair the ability of responsible United States Government officials to protect the President, the Vice President, and other individuals for whom protection services, in the interest of national security, are authorized; or

(8) violate a statute, treaty, or international agreement.

(e) Information marked for an indefinite duration of classification under predecessor orders, for example, "Originating Agency's Determination Required," or information classified under predecessor orders that contains no declassification instructions shall be declassified in accordance with part 3 of this Order.

Sec. 1.7. Identification and Markings. (a) At the time of original classification, the following shall appear on the face of each classified document, or shall be applied to other classified media in an appropriate manner:

(1) one of the three classification levels defined in section 1.3 of this order;

(2) the identity, by name or personal identifier and position, of the original classification authority;

(3) the agency and office of origin, if not otherwise evident;

(4) declassification instructions, which shall indicate one of the following:

(A) the date or event for declassification, as prescribed in section 1.6(a) or section 1.6(e); or

(B) the date that is 10 years from the date of original classification, as prescribed in section 1.6(b); or

(C) the exemption category from declassification, as prescribed in section 1.6(d); and

(5) a concise reason for classification which, at a minimum, cites the applicable classification categories in section 1.5 of this order.

(b) Specific information contained in paragraph (a), above, may be excluded if it would reveal additional classified information.

(c) Each classified document shall, by marking or other means, indicate which portions are classified, with the applicable classification level, which portions are exempt from declassification under section 1.6(d) of this order, and which portions are unclassified. In accordance with standards prescribed in directives issued under this order, the Director of the Information Security Oversight Office may grant waivers of this requirement for specified classes of documents or information. The Director shall revoke any waiver upon a finding of abuse.

(d) Markings implementing the provisions of this order, including abbreviations and requirements to safeguard classified working papers, shall conform to the standards prescribed in implementing directives issued pursuant to this order.

(e) Foreign government information shall retain its original classification markings or shall be assigned a U.S. classification that provides a degree of protection at least equivalent to that required by the entity that furnished the information.

(f) Information assigned a level of classification under this or predecessor orders shall be considered as classified at that level of classification despite the omission of other required markings. Whenever such information is used in the derivative classification process or is reviewed for possible declassification, holders of such information shall coordinate with an appropriate classification authority for the application of omitted markings.

(g) The classification authority shall, whenever practicable, use a classified addendum whenever classified information constitutes a small portion of an otherwise unclassified document.

Sec. 1.8. Classification Prohibitions and Limitations. (a) In no ease shall information be classified in order to:

(1) conceal violations of law, inefficiency, or administrative error;

(2) prevent embarrassment to a person, organization, or agency;

(3) restrain competition; or

(4) prevent or delay the release of information that does not require protection in the interest of national security.

(b) Basic scientific research information not clearly related to the national security may not be classified.

(c) Information may not be reclassified after it has been declassified and released to the public under proper authority.

(d) Information that has not previously been disclosed to the public under proper authority may be classified or reclassified after an agency has received a request for it under the Freedom of Information Act (5 U.S.C. 552) or the Privacy Act of 1974 (5 U.S.C. 552a), or the mandatory review provisions of section 3.6 of this order only if such classification meets the requirements of this order and is accomplished on a document-by-document basis with the personal participation or under the direction of the agency head, the deputy agency head, or the senior agency official designated under section 5.6 of this order. This provision does not apply to classified information contained in records that are more than 25 years old and have been determined to have permanent historical value under title 44, United States Code.

(e) Compilations of items of information which are individually unclassified may be classified if the compiled information reveals an additional association or relationship that:

(1) meets the standards for classification under this order; and

(2) is not otherwise revealed in the individual items of information. As used in this order, "compilation" means an aggregation of pre-existing unclassified items of information.

Sec. 1.9. Classification Challenges. (a) Authorized holders of information who, in good faith, believe that its classification status is improper are encouraged and expected to challenge the classification status of the information in accordance with agency procedures established under paragraph (b), below.

(b) In accordance with implementing directives issued pursuant to this order, an agency head or senior agency official shall establish procedures under which authorized holders of information are encouraged and expected to challenge the classification of information that they believe is improperly classified or unclassified. These procedures shall assure that:

(1) individuals are not subject to retribution for bringing such actions;

(2) an opportunity is provided for review by an impartial official or panel; and

(3) individuals are advised of their right to appeal agency decisions to the Interagency Security Classification Appeals Panel established by section 5.4 of this order.

Part 2 Derivative Classification

Sec. 2.1. Definitions. For purposes of this order: (a) "Derivative classification" means the incorporating, paraphrasing, restating or generating in new form information that is already classified, and marking the newly developed material consistent with the classification markings that apply to the source information. Derivative classification includes the classification of information based on classification guidance. The duplication or reproduction of existing classified information is not derivative classification.

(b) "Classification guidance" means any instruction or source that prescribes the classification of specific information.

(c) "Classification guide" means a documentary form of classification guidance issued by an original classification authority that identifies the elements of information regarding a specific subject that must be classified and establishes the level and duration of classification for each such element.

(d) "Source document" means an existing document that contains classified information that is incorporated, paraphrased, restated, or generated in new form into a new document.

(e) "Multiple sources" means two or more source documents, classification guides, or a combination of both.

Sec. 2.2. Use of Derivative Classification.

(a) Persons who only reproduce, extract, or summarize classified information, or who only apply classification markings derived from source material or as directed by a classification guide, need not possess original classification authority.

(b) Persons who apply derivative classification markings shall:

(1) observe and respect original classification decisions; and

(2) carry forward to any newly created documents the pertinent classification markings. For information derivatively classified based on multiple sources, the derivative classifier shall carry forward: (A) the date or event for declassification that corresponds to the longest period of classification among the sources; and

(B) a listing of these sources on or attached to the official file or record copy.

Sec. 2.3. Classification Guides. (a) Agencies with original classification authority shall prepare classification guides to facilitate the proper and uniform derivative classification of information. These guides shall conform to standards contained in directives issued under this order.

(b) Each guide shall be approved personally and in writing by an official who:

(1) has program or supervisory responsibility over the information or is the senior agency official; and

(2) is authorized to classify information originally at the highest level of classification prescribed in the guide.

(c) Agencies shall establish procedures to assure that classification guides are reviewed and updated as provided in directives issued under this order.

Part 3 Declassification and Downgrading

Sec. 3.1. Definitions. For purposes of this order: (a) "Declassification" means the authorized change in the status of information from classified information to unclassified information.

(b) "Automatic declassification" means the declassification of information based solely upon:

(1) the occurrence of a specific date or event as determined by the original classification authority; or

(2) the expiration of a maximum time frame for duration of classification established under this order.

(c) "Declassification authority" means:

(1) the official who authorized the original classification, if that official is still serving in the same position;

(2)the originator's current successor in function;

(3) a supervisory official of either; or

(4) officials delegated declassification authority in writing by the agency head or the senior agency official.

(d) "Mandatory declassification review" means the review for declassification of classified information in response to a request for declassification that meets the requirements under section 3.6 of this order.

(e) "Systematic declassification review" means the review for declassification of classified information contained in records that have been determined by the Archivist of the United States ("Archivist") to have permanent historical value in accordance with chapter 33 of title 44, United States Code.

(f) "Declassification guide" means written instructions issued by a declassification authority that describes the elements of information regarding a specific subject that may be declassified and the elements that must remain classified.

(g) "Downgrading" means a determination by a declassification authority that information classified and safeguarded at a specified level shall be classified and safeguarded at a lower level.

(h) "File series" means documentary material, regardless of its physical form or characteristics, that is arranged in accordance with a filing system or maintained as a unit because it pertains to the same function or activity.

Sec. 3.2. Authority for Declassification.

(a) Information shall be declassified as soon as it no longer meets the standards for classification under this order.

(b) It is presumed that information that continues to meet the classification requirements under this order requires continued protection. In some exceptional cases, however, the need to protect such information may be outweighed by the public interest in disclosure of the information, and in these cases the information should be declassified. When such questions arise, they shall be referred to the agency head or the senior agency official. That official will determine, as an exercise of discretion, whether the public interest in disclosure outweighs the damage to national security that might reasonably be expected from disclosure. This provision does not:

(1) amplify or modify the substantive criteria or procedures for classification; or

(2) create any substantive or procedural rights subject to judicial review.

(c) If the Director of the Information Security Oversight Office determines that information is classified in violation of this order, the Director may require the information to be declassified by the agency that originated the classification. Any such decision by the Director may be appealed to the President through the Assistant to the President for National Security Affairs. The information shall remain classified pending a prompt decision on the appeal.

(d) The provisions of this section shall also apply to agencies that, under the terms of this order, do not have original classification authority, but had such authority under predecessor orders.

Sec. 3.3. Transferred Information. (a) In the case of classified information transferred in conjunction with a transfer of functions, and not merely for storage purposes, the receiving agency shall be deemed to be the originating agency for purposes of this order.

(b) In the ease of classified information that is not officially transferred as described in paragraph (a), above, but that originated in an agency that has ceased to exist and for which there is no successor agency, each agency in possession of such information shall be deemed to be the originating agency for purposes of this order. Such information may be declassified or downgraded by the agency in possession after consultation with any other agency that has an interest in the subject matter of the information.

(c) Classified information accessioned into the National Archives and Records Administration ("National Archives") as of the effective date of this order shall be declassified or downgraded by the Archivist in accordance with this order, the directives issued pursuant to this order, agency declassification guides, and any existing procedural agreement between the Archivist and the relevant agency head.

(d) The originating agency shall take all reasonable steps to declassify classified information contained in records determined to have permanent historical value before they are accessioned into the National Archives. However, the Archivist may require that records containing classified information be accessioned into the National Archives when necessary to comply with the provisions of the Federal Records Act. This provision does not apply to information being transferred to the Archivist pursuant to section 2203 of title 44, United States Code, or information for which the National Archives and Records Administration serves as the custodian of the records of an agency or organization that goes out of existence.

(e) To the extent practicable, agencies shall adopt a system of records management that will facilitate the public release of documents at the time such documents are declassified pursuant to the provisions for automatic declassification in sections 1.6 and 3.4 of this order.

Appendix E

Sec. 3.4. Automatic Declassification. (a) Subject to paragraph (b), below, within 5 years from the date of this order, all classified information contained in records that (1) are more than 25 years old, and (2) have been determined to have permanent historical value under title 44, United States Code, shall be automatically declassified whether or not the records have been reviewed. Subsequently, all classified information in such records shall be automatically declassified no longer than 25 years from the date of its original classification, except as provided in paragraph (b), below.

(b) An agency head may exempt from automatic declassification under paragraph (a), above, specific information, the release of which should be expected to:

(1) reveal the identity of a confidential human source, or reveal information about the application of an intelligence source or method, or reveal the identity of a human intelligence source when the unauthorized disclosure of that source would clearly and demonstrably damage the national security interests of the United States;

(2) reveal information that would assist in the development or use of weapons of mass destruction;

(3) reveal information that would impair U.S. cryptologic systems or activities;

(4) reveal information that would impair the application of state of the art technology within a U.S. weapon system;

(5) reveal actual U.S. military war plans that remain in effect;

(6) reveal information that would seriously and demonstrably impair relations between the United States and a foreign government, or seriously and demonstrably undermine ongoing diplomatic activities of the United States;

(7) reveal information that would clearly and demonstrably impair the current ability of United States Government officials to protect the President, Vice President, and other officials for whom protection services, in the interest of national security, are authorized;

(8) reveal information that would seriously and demonstrably impair current national security emergency preparedness plans; or

(9) violate a statute, treaty, or international agreement.

(c) No later than the effective date of this order, an agency head shall notify the President through the Assistant to the President for National Security Affairs of any specific file series of records for which a review or assessment has determined that the information within those file series almost invariably fails within one or more of the exemption categories listed in paragraph (b), above, and which the agency proposes to exempt from automatic declassification. The notification shall include:

(1) a description of the file series;

(2) an explanation of why the information within the file series is almost invariably exempt from automatic declassification and why the information must remain classified for a longer period of time; and

(3) except for the identity of a confidential human source or a human intelligence source, as prodded in paragraph (b), above, a specific date or event for declassification of the information. The President may direct the agency head not to exempt the file series or to declassify the information within that series at an earlier date than recommended.

(d) At least 180 days before information is automatically declassified under this section, an agency head or senior agency official shall notify the Director of the Information Security Oversight Office, serving as Executive Secretary of the Interagency Security Classification Appeals Panel, of any specific information beyond that included in a notification to the President under paragraph (c), above, that the agency proposes to exempt from automatic declassification. The notification shall include:

(1) a description of the information;

(2) an explanation of why the information is exempt from automatic declassification and must remain classified for a longer period of time; and

(3) except for the identity of a confidential human source or a human intelligence source, as provided in paragraph (b), above, a specific date or event for declassification of the information. The Panel may direct the agency not to exempt the information or to declassify it at an earlier date than recommended. The agency head may appeal such a decision to the President through the Assistant to the President for National Security Affairs. The information will remain classified while such an appeal is pending.

(e) No later than the effective date of this order, the agency head or senior agency official shall provide the Director of the Information Security Oversight Office with a plan for compliance with the requirements of this section, including the establishment of interim target dates. Each such plan shall include the requirement that the agency declassify at least 15 percent of the records affected by this section no later than 1 year from the effective date of this order, and similar commitments for subsequent years until the effective date for automatic declassification.

(f) Information exempted from automatic declassification under this section shall remain subject to the mandatory and systematic declassification review provisions of this order.

(g) The Secretary of State shall determine when the United States should commence negotiations with the appropriate officials of a foreign government or international organization of governments to modify any treaty or international agreement that requires the classification of information contained in records affected by this section for a period longer than 25 years from the date of its creation, unless the treaty or international agreement pertains to information that may otherwise remain classified beyond 25 years under this section.

Sec. 3.5. Systematic Declassification Review. (a) Each agency that has originated classified information under this order or its predecessors shall establish and conduct a program for systematic declassification review. This program shall apply to historically valuable records exempted from automatic declassification under section 3.4 of this order. Agencies shall prioritize the systematic review of records based upon:

(1) recommendations of the Information Security Policy Advisory Council, established in section 5.5 of this order, on specific subject areas for systematic review concentration; or

(2) the degree of researcher interest and the likelihood of declassification upon review.

(b) The Archivist shall conduct a systematic declassification review program for classified information:

(1) accessioned into the National Archives as of the effective date of this order; (2) information transferred to the Archivist pursuant to section 2203 of title 44, United States Code; and (3) information for which the National Archives and Records Administration serves as the custodian of the records of an agency or organization that has gone out of existence. This program shall apply to pertinent records no later than 25 years from the date of their creation. The Archivist shall establish priorities for the

systematic review of these records based upon the recommendations of the Information Security Policy Advisory Council; or the degree of researcher interest and the likelihood of declassification upon review. These records shall be reviewed in accordance with the standards of this order, its implementing directives, and declassification guides provided to the Archivist by each agency that originated the records. The Director of the Information Security Oversight Office shall assure that agencies provide the Archivist with adequate and current declassification guides.

(c) After consultation with affected agencies, the Secretary of Defense may establish special procedures for systematic review for declassification of classified cryptologic information, and the Director of Central Intelligence may establish special procedures for systematic review for declassification of classified information pertaining to intelligence activities (including special activities), or intelligence sources or methods.

Sec. 3.6. Mandatory Declassification Review. (a) Except as provided in paragraph (b), below, all information classified under this order or predecessor orders shall be subject to a review for declassification by the originating agency if:

(1) the request for a review describes the document or material containing the information with sufficient specificity to enable the agency to locate it with a reasonable amount of effort;

(2) the information is not exempted from search and review under the Central Intelligence Agency Information Act; and

(3) the information has not been reviewed for declassification within the past 2 years. If the agency has reviewed the information within the past 2 years, or the information is the subject of pending litigation, the agency shall inform the requester of this fact and of the requester's appeal rights.

(b) Information originated by:

(1) the incumbent President;

(2) the incumbent President's White House Staff;

(3) committees, commissions, or boards appointed by the incumbent President; or

(4) other entities within the Executive Office of the President that solely advise and assist the incumbent President is exempted from the provisions of paragraph (a), above. However, the Archivist shall have the authority to review, downgrade, and declassify information of former Presidents under the control of the Archivist pursuant to sections 2107, 2111, 2111 note, or 2203 of title 44, United States Code. Review procedures developed by the Archivist shall provide for consultation with agencies having primary subject matter interest and shall be consistent with the provisions of applicable laws or lawful agreements that pertain to the respective Presidential papers or records. Agencies with primary subject matter interest shall be notified promptly of the Archivist's decision. Any final decision by the Archivist may be appealed by the requester or an agency to the Interagency Security Classification Appeals Panel. The information shall remain classified pending a prompt decision on the appeal.

(c) Agencies conducting a mandatory review for declassification shall declassify information that no longer meets the standards for classification under this order. They shall release this information unless withholding is otherwise authorized and warranted under applicable law.

(d) In accordance with directives issued pursuant to this order, agency heads shall develop procedures to process requests for the mandatory review of classified information. These procedures shall apply to information classified under this or predecessor orders. They also shall provide a means for administratively appealing a denial of a mandatory review request, and for notifying the requester of the right to appeal a final agency decision to the Interagency Security Classification Appeals Panel.

(e) After consultation with affected agencies, the Secretary of Defense shall develop special procedures for the review of cryptologic information, the Director of Central Intelligence shall develop special procedures for the review of information pertaining to intelligence activities (including special activities), or intelligence sources or methods, and the Archivist shall develop special procedures for the review of information accessioned into the National Archives.

Sec. 3.7. Processing Requests and Reviews. In response to a request for information under the Freedom of Information Act, the Privacy Act of 1974, or the mandatory review provisions of this order, or pursuant to the automatic declassification or systematic review provisions of this order:

(a) An agency may refuse to confirm or deny the existence or nonexistence of requested information whenever the fact of its existence or nonexistence is itself classified under this order.

(b) When an agency receives any request for documents in its custody that contain information that was originally classified by another agency, or comes across such documents in the process of the automatic declassification or systematic review provisions of this order, it shall refer copies of any request and the pertinent documents to the originating agency for processing, and may, after consultation with the originating agency, inform any requester of the referral unless such association is itself classified under this order. In cases in which the originating agency determines in writing that a response under paragraph (a), above, is required, the referring agency shall respond to the requester in accordance with that paragraph.

Sec. 3.8. Declassification Database. (a) The Archivist in conjunction with the Director of the Information Security Oversight Office and those agencies that originate classified information, shall establish a Government-wide database of information that has been declassified. The Archivist shall also explore other possible uses of technology to facilitate the declassification process.

(b) Agency heads shall fully cooperate with the Archivist in these efforts.

(c) Except as otherwise authorized and warranted by law, all declassified information contained within the database established under paragraph (a), above, shall be available to the public.

Part 4 Safeguarding

Sec. 4.1. Definitions. For purposes of this order: (a) "Safeguarding" means measures and controls that are prescribed to protect classified information.

(b) "Access" means the ability or opportunity to gain knowledge of classified information.

(c) "Need-to-know" means a determination made by an authorized holder of classified information that a prospective recipient requires access to specific classified information in order to perform or assist in a lawful and authorized governmental function.

(d) "Automated information system" means an assembly of computer hardware, software, or firmware configured to collect, create, communicate, compute, disseminate, process, store, or control data or information.

(e) "Integrity" means the state that exists when information is unchanged from its source and has not been accidentally or intentionally modified, altered, or destroyed.

(f) "Network" means a system of two or more computers that can exchange data or information.

(g) "Telecommunications" means the preparation, transmission, or communication of information by electronic means.

(h) "Special access program" means a program established for a specific class of classified information that imposes safeguarding and access requirements that exceed those normally required for information at the same classification level.

Sec. 4.2. General Restrictions on Access. (a) A person may have access to classified information provided that:

(1) a favorable determination of eligibility for access has been made by an agency head or the agency head's designee;

(2) the person has signed an approved nondisclosure agreement; and

(3) the person has a need-to-know the information.

(b) Classified information shall remain under the control of the originating agency or its successor in function. An agency shall not disclose information originally classified by another agency without its authorization. An official or employee leaving agency service may not remove classified information from the agency's control.

(c) Classified information may not be removed from official premises without proper authorization.

(d) Persons authorized to disseminate classified information outside the executive branch shall assure the protection of the information in a manner equivalent to that provided within the executive branch.

(e) Consistent with law, directives, and regulation, an agency head or senior agency official shall establish uniform procedures to ensure that automated information systems, including networks and telecommunications systems, that collect, create, communicate, compute, disseminate, process, or store classified information have controls that:

(1) prevent access by unauthorized persons; and (2) ensure the integrity of the information.

(f) Consistent with law, directives, and regulation, each agency head or senior agency official shall establish controls to ensure that classified information is used, processed, stored, reproduced, transmitted, and destroyed under conditions that provide adequate protection and prevent access by unauthorized persons.

(g) Consistent with directives issued pursuant to this order, an agency shall safeguard foreign government information under standards that provide a degree of protection at least equivalent to that required by the government or international organization of governments that furnished the information. When adequate to achieve equivalency, these standards may be less restrictive than the safeguarding standards that ordinarily apply to United States "Confidential" information, including allowing access to individuals with a need-to-know who have not otherwise been cleared for access to classified information or executed an approved nondisclosure agreement.

(h) Except as provided by statute or directives issued pursuant to this order, classified information originating in one agency may not be disseminated outside any other agency to which it has been made available without the consent of the originating agency. An agency head or senior agency official may waive this requirement for specific information originated within that agency. For purposes of this section, the Department of Defense shall be considered one agency.

Sec. 4.3. Distribution Controls. (a) Each agency shall establish controls over the distribution of classified information to assure that it is distributed only to organizations or individuals eligible for access who also have a need-to-know the information.

(b) Each agency shall update, at least annually, the automatic, routine, or recurring distribution of classified information that they distribute. Recipients shall cooperate fully with distributors who are updating distribution lists and shall notify distributors whenever a relevant change in status occurs.

Sec. 4.4. Special Access Programs. (a) Establishment of special access programs. Unless otherwise authorized by the President, only the Secretaries of State, Defense and Energy, and the Director of Central Intelligence, or the principal deputy of each, may create a special access program. For special access programs pertaining to intelligence activities (including special activities, but not including military operational, strategic and tactical programs), or intelligence sources or methods, this function will be exercised by the Director of Central Intelligence. These officials shall keep the number of these programs at an absolute minimum, and shall establish them only upon a specific finding that:

(1) the vulnerability of, or threat to, specific information is exceptional; and

(2) the normal criteria for determining eligibility for access applicable to information classified at the same level are not deemed sufficient to protect the information from unauthorized disclosure; or (3) the program is required by statute.

(b) Requirements and Limitations. (1) Special access programs shall be limited to programs in which the number of persons who will have access ordinarily will be reasonably small and commensurate with the objective of providing enhanced protection for the information involved.

(2) Each agency head shall establish and maintain a system of accounting for special access programs consistent with directives issued pursuant to this order.

(3) Special access programs shall be subject to the oversight program established under section 5.6(c) of this order. In addition, the Director of the Information Security Oversight Office shall be afforded access to these programs, in accordance with the security requirements of each program, in order to perform the functions assigned to the Information Security Oversight Office under this order. An agency head may limit access to a special access program to the Director and no more than one other employee of the Information Security Oversight Office; or, for special access programs that are extraordinarily sensitive and vulnerable, to the Director only.

(4) The agency head or principal deputy shall review annually each special access program to determine whether it continues to meet the requirements of this order.

(5) Upon request, an agency shall brief the Assistant to the President for National Security Affairs, or his or her designee, on any or all of the agency's special access programs.

(c) Within 180 days after the effective date of this order, each agency head or principal deputy shall review all existing special access programs under the agency's jurisdiction. These officials shall terminate any special access programs that do not clearly meet the provisions of this order. Each existing special access program that an agency head or principal deputy validates shall be treated as if it were established on the effective date of this order.

(d) Nothing in this order shall supersede any requirement made by or under 10 U.S.C. 119.

Sec. 4.5. Access by Historical Researchers and Former Presidential Appointees. (a) The requirement in section 4.2(a)(3) of this order that access to classified information may be granted only to individuals who have a need-to-know the information may be waived for persons who:

(1) are engaged in historical research projects; or

(2) previously have occupied policy-making positions to which they were appointed by the President.

(b) Waivers under this section may be granted only if the agency head or senior agency official of the originating agency:

(1) determines in writing that access is consistent with the interest of national security;

(2) takes appropriate steps to protect classified information from unauthorized disclosure or compromise, and ensures that the information is safe-guarded in a manner consistent with this order; and

(3) limits the access granted to former Presidential appointees to items that the person originated, reviewed, signed, or received while serving as a Presidential appointee.

Part 5 Implementation and Review

Sec. 5.1. Definitions. For purposes of this order: (a) "Self-inspection" means the internal review and evaluation of individual agency activities and the agency as a whole with respect to the implementation of the program established under this order and its implementing directives.

(b) "Violation" means:

(1) any knowing, willful, or negligent action that could reasonably be expected to result in an unauthorized disclosure of classified information;

(2) any knowing, willful, or negligent action to classify or continue the classification of information contrary to the requirements of this order or its implementing directives; or

(3) any knowing, willful, or negligent action to create or continue a special access program contrary to the requirements of this order.

(c) "Infraction" means any knowing, willful, or negligent action contrary to the requirements of this order or its implementing directives that does not comprise a "violation," as defined above.

Sec. 5.2. Program Direction. (a) The Director of the Office of Management and Budget, in consultation with the Assistant to the President for National Security Affairs and the co-chairs of the Security Policy Board, shall issue such directives as are necessary to implement this order. These directives shall be binding upon the agencies. Directives issued by the Director of the Office of Management and Budget shall establish standards for:

(1) classification and marking principles;

(2) agency security education and training programs;

(3) agency self-inspection programs; and

(4) classification and declassification guides.

(b) The Director of the Office of Management and Budget shall delegate the implementation and monitorship functions of this program to the Director of the Information Security Oversight Office.

(c) The Security Policy Board, established by a Presidential Decision Directive, shall make a recommendation to the President through the Assistant to the President for National Security Affairs with respect to the issuance of a Presidential directive on safeguarding classified information. The Presidential directive shall pertain to the handling, storage, distribution, transmittal, and destruction of and accounting for classified information.

Sec. 5.3. Information Security Oversight Office. (a) There is established within the Office of Management and Budget an Information Security Oversight Office. The Director of the Office of Management and Budget shall appoint the Director of the Information Security Oversight Office, subject to the approval of the President.

(b) Under the direction of the Director of the Office of Management and Budget acting in consultation with the Assistant to the President for National Security Affairs, the Director of the Information Security Oversight Office shall:

(1) develop directives for the implementation of this order;

(2) oversee agency actions to ensure compliance with this order and its implementing directives;

(3) review and approve agency implementing regulations and agency guides for systematic declassification review prior to their issuance by the agency;

(4) have the authority to conduct on-site reviews of each agency's program established under this order, and to require of each agency those reports, information, and other cooperation that may be necessary to fulfill its responsibilities. If granting access to specific categories of classified information would pose an exceptional national security risk, the affected agency head or the senior agency official shall submit a written justification recommending the denial of access to the Director of the Office of Management and Budget within 60 days of the request for access. Access shall be denied pending a prompt decision by the Director of the Office of Management and Budget, who shall consult on this decision with the Assistant to the President for National Security Affairs;

(5) review requests for original classification authority from agencies or officials not granted original classification authority and, if deemed appropriate, recommend Presidential approval through the Director of the office of Management and Budget;

(6) consider and take action on complaints and suggestions from persons within or outside the Government with respect to the administration of the program established under this order;

(7) have the authority to prescribe, after consultation with affected agencies, standardization of forms or procedures that will promote the implementation of the program established under this order;

(8) report at least annually to the President on the implementation of this order; and

(9) convene and chair interagency meetings to discuss matters pertaining to the program established by this order.

See. 5.4. Interagency Security Classification Appeals Panel. (a) Establishment and Administration.

(1) There is established an Interagency Security Classification Appeals Panel ("Panel"). The Secretaries of State and Defense, the Attorney General, the Director of Central Intelligence, the Archivist of the United States, and the Assistant to the President for National Security Affairs shall each appoint a senior level representative to serve as a member of the Panel. The President shall select the Chair of the Panel from among the Panel members.

(2) A vacancy on the Panel shall be filled as quickly as possible as provided in paragraph (1), above.

(3) The Director of the Information Security Oversight Office shall serve as the Executive Secretary. The staff of the Information Security Oversight Office shall provide program and administrative support for the Panel.

(4) The members and staff of the Panel shall be required to meet eligibility for access standards in order to fulfill the Panel's functions.

(5) The Panel shall meet at the call of the Chair. The Chair shall schedule meetings as may be necessary for the Panel to fulfill its functions in a timely manner.

(6) The Information Security Oversight Office shall include in its reports to the President a summary of the Panel's activities.

(b) Functions. The Panel shall:

(1) decide on appeals by persons who have filed classification challenges under section 1.9 of this order;

(2) approve, deny, or amend agency exemptions from automatic declassification as provided in section 3.4 of this order; and

(3) decide on appeals by persons or entities who have filed requests for mandatory declassification review under section 3.6 of this order.

(c) Rules and Procedures. The Panel shall issue bylaws, which shall be published in the Federal Register no later than 120 days from the effective date of this order. The bylaws shall establish the rules and procedures that the Panel will follow in accepting, considering, and issuing decisions on appeals. The rules and procedures of the Panel shall provide that the Panel will consider appeals only on actions in which: (1) the appellant has exhausted his or her administrative remedies within the responsible agency; (2) there is no current action pending on the issue within the federal courts; and (3) the information has not been the subject of review by the federal courts or the Panel within the past 2 years.

(d) Agency heads will cooperate fully with the Panel so that it can fulfill its functions in a timely and fully informed manner. An agency head may appeal a decision of the Panel to the President through the Assistant to the President for National Security Affairs. The Panel will report to the President through the Assistant to the President for National Security Affairs any instance in which it believes that an agency head is not cooperating fully with the Panel.

(e) The Appeals Panel is established for the sole purpose of advising and assisting the President in the discharge of his constitutional and discretionary authority to protect the national security of the United States. Panel decisions are committed to the discretion of the Panel, unless reversed by the President.

Sec. 5.5. Information Security Policy Advisory Council. (a) Establishment. There is established an Information Security Policy Advisory Council ("Council"). The Council shall be composed of seven members appointed by the President for staggered terms not to exceed 4 years, from among persons who have demonstrated interest and expertise in an area related to the subject matter of this order and are not otherwise employees of the Federal Government. The President shall appoint the Council Chair from among the members. The Council shall comply with the Federal Advisory Committee Act, as amended, 5 U.S.C. App. 2.

(b) Functions. The Council shall:

(1) advise the President, the Assistant to the President for National Security Affairs, the Director of the Office of Management and Budget, or such other executive branch officials as it deems appropriate, on policies established under this order or its implementing directives, including recommended changes to those policies;

(2) provide recommendations to agency heads for specific subject areas for systematic declassification review; and

(3) serve as a forum to discuss policy issues in dispute.

(c) Meetings. The Council shall meet at least twice each calendar year, and as determined by the Assistant to the President for National Security Affairs or the Director of the Office of Management and Budget.

(d) Administration.

(1) Each Council member may be compensated at a rate of pay not to exceed the daily equivalent of the annual rate of basic pay in effect for grade GS-18 of the general schedule under section 5376 of title 5, United States Code, for each day during which that member is engaged in the actual performance of the duties of the Council.

(2) While away from their homes or regular place of business in the actual performance of the duties of the Council, members may be allowed travel expenses, including per diem in lieu of subsistence, as authorized by law for persons serving intermittently in the Government service (5 U.S.C. 5703(b)).

(3) To the extent permitted by law and subject to the availability of funds, the Information Security Oversight Office shall provide the Council with administrative services, facilities, staff, and other support services necessary for the performance of its functions.

(4) Notwithstanding any other Executive order, the functions of the President under the Federal Advisory Committee Act, as amended, that are applicable to the Council, except that of reporting to the Congress, shall be performed by the Director of the Information Security Oversight Office in accordance with the guidelines and procedures established by the General Services Administration.

Sec. 5.6. General Responsibilities. Heads of agencies that originate or handle classified information shall: (a) demonstrate personal commitment and commit senior management to the successful implementation of the program established under this order;

(b) commit necessary resources to the effective implementation of the program established under this order; and

(c) designate a senior agency official to direct and administer the program, whose responsibilities shall include:

(1) overseeing the agency's program established under this order, provided, an agency head may designate a separate official to oversee special access programs authorized under this order. This official shall provide a full accounting of the agency's special access programs at least annually;

(2) promulgating implementing regulations, which shall be published in the Federal Register to the extent that they affect members of the public;

(3) establishing and maintaining security education and training programs;

(4) establishing and maintaining an ongoing self-inspection program, which shall include the periodic review and assessment of the agency's classified product;

(5) establishing procedures to prevent unnecessary access to classified information, including procedures that: (i) require that a need for access to classified information is established before initiating administrative clearance procedures; and (ii) ensure that the number of persons granted access to classified information is limited to the minimum consistent with operational and security requirements and needs;

(6) developing special contingency plans for the safeguarding of classified information used in or near hostile or potentially hostile areas;

(7) assuring that the performance contract or other system used to rate civilian or military personnel performance includes the management of classified information as a critical element or item to be evaluated in the rating of: (i) original classification authorities; (ii) security managers or security specialists; and (iii) all other personnel whose duties significantly involve the creation or handling of classified information;

(8) accounting for the costs associated with the implementation of this order, which shall be reported to the Director of the Information Security Oversight Office for publication; and

(9) assigning in a prompt manner agency personnel to respond to any request, appeal, challenge, complaint, or suggestion arising out of this order that pertains to classified information that originated in a component of the agency that no longer exists and for which there is no clear successor in function.

Sec. 5.7. Sanctions. (a) If the Director of the Information Security Oversight Office finds that a violation of this order or its implementing directives may have occurred, the Director shall make a report to the head of the agency or to the senior agency official so that corrective steps, if appropriate, may be taken.

(b) Officers and employees of the United States Government, and its contractors, licensees, certificate holders, and grantees shall be subject to appropriate sanctions if they knowingly, willfully, or negligently:

(1) disclose to unauthorized persons information properly classified under this order or predecessor orders;

(2) classify or continue the classification of information in violation of this order or any implementing directive;

(3) create or continue a special access program contrary to the requirements of this order; or

(4) contravene any other provision of this order or its implementing directives.

(c) Sanctions may include reprimand, suspension without pay, removal, termination of classification authority, loss or denial of access to classified information, or other sanctions in accordance with applicable law and agency regulation.

(d) The agency head, senior agency official, or other supervisory official shall, at a minimum, promptly remove the classification authority of any individual who demonstrates reckless disregard or a pattern of error in applying the classification standards of this order.

(e) The agency head or senior agency official shall:

(1) take appropriate and prompt corrective action when a violation or infraction under, paragraph (b), above, occurs; and

(2) notify the Director of the Information Security Oversight Office when a violation under paragraph (b)(1), (2) or (3), above, occurs.

Part 6 General Provisions

See. 6.1. General Provisions. (a) Nothing in this order shall supersede any requirement made by or under the Atomic Energy Act of 1954, as amended, or the National Security Act of 1947, as amended. "Restricted Data" and "Formerly Restricted Data" shall be handled, protected, classified, downgraded, and declassified in conformity with the provisions of the Atomic Energy Act of 1954, as amended, and regulations issued under that Act.

(b) The Attorney General, upon request by the head of an agency or the Director of the Information Security Oversight Office, shall render an interpretation of this order with respect to any question arising in the course of its administration.

(c) Nothing in this order limits the protection afforded any information by other provisions of law, including the exemptions to the Freedom of Information Act, the Privacy Act, and the National Security Act of 1947, as amended. This order is not intended, and should not be construed, to create any right or benefit, substantive or procedural, enforceable at law by a party against the United States, its agencies, its officers, or its employees. The foregoing is in addition to the specific provisos set forth in sections 1.2(b), 3.2(b) and 5.4(e) of this order.

(d) Executive Order No. 12356 of April 6, 1982, is revoked as of the effective date of this order.

Sec. 6.2. Effective Date. This order shall become effective 180 days from the date of this order.

William J. Clinton
The White House, April 17, 1995.

Executive Order 13142
Amendment to Executive Order 12958
Classified National Security Information

By the authority vested in me as President by the Constitution and the laws of the United States of America, and in order to extend and establish specific dates for the time within which all classified information contained in records more than 25 years old that have been determined to have historical value under title 44, United States Code, should be automatically declassified, and to establish the Information Security Oversight Office within the National Archives and Records Administration, it is hereby ordered that Executive Order 12958 is amended as follows:

Section 1. In the first sentence of section 3.4(a) of Executive Order 12958, the words "within five years from the date of this order" are deleted and the words "within six and one half years from the date of this order" are inserted in lieu thereof.

Sec. 2. The following new language is inserted at the end of section 3.4(a): "For records otherwise subject to this paragraph for which a review or assessment conducted by the agency and confirmed by the Information Security Oversight Office has determined that they: (1) contain information that was created by or is under the control of more than one agency, or (2) are within file series containing information that almost invariably pertains to intelligence sources or methods, all classified information in such records shall be automatically declassified, whether or not the records have been reviewed, within 8 years from the date of this order, except as provided in paragraph (b), below. For records that contain information that becomes subject to automatic declassification after the dates otherwise established in this paragraph, all classified information in such records shall be automatically declassified, whether or not the records have been reviewed on December 31 of the year that is 25 years from the origin of the information, except as provided in paragraph (b), below."

Sec. 3. Subsections (a) and (b) of section 5.2 are amended to read as follows:

"(a) The Director of the Information Security Oversight Office, under the direction of the Archivist of the United States and in consultation with the Assistant to the President for National Security Affairs and the co-chairs of the Security Policy Board, shall issue such directives as are necessary to implement this order. These directives shall be binding upon the agencies. Directives issued by the Director of the Information Security Oversight Office shall establish standards for:

(1) classification and marking principles;

(2) agency security education and training programs;

(3) agency self-inspection programs; and

(4) classification and declassification guides.

(b) The Archivist of the United States shall delegate the implementation and monitorship functions of this program to the Director of the Information Security Oversight Office."

Sec. 4. Subsection (a) and the introductory clause and item (4) of subsection (b) of section 5.3 are amended as follows:

(a) Subsection (a) shall read "(a) There is established within the National Archives and Records Administration an Information Security Oversight Office. The Archivist of the United States shall appoint the Director of the Information Security Oversight Office, subject to the approval of the President."

(b) The introductory clause of subsection (b) shall read "Under the direction of the Archivist of the United States, acting in consultation with the Assistant to the President for National Security Affairs, the Director of the Information Security Oversight Office shall:".

(c) Item (4) of subsection (b) shall read "(4) have the authority to conduct on-site reviews of each agency's program established under this order, and to require of each agency those reports, information, and other cooperation that may be necessary to fulfill its responsibilities. If granting access to specific categories of classified information would pose an exceptional national security risk, the affected agency head or the senior agency official shall submit a written justification recommending the denial of access to the President through the Assistant to the President for National Security Affairs within 60 days of the request for access. Access shall be denied pending the response,".

WILLIAM J. CLINTON
THE WHITE HOUSE,
November 19, 1999.

Executive Order 12600
Predisclosure Notification Procedures for Confidential Commercial Information

By the authority vested in me as President by the Constitution and statutes of the United States of America and in order to provide predisclosure notification procedures under the Freedom of Information Act concerning confidential commercial information, and to make existing agency notification provisions more uniform, it is hereby ordered as follows:

Section 1

The head of each Executive department and agency subject to the Freedom of Information Act shall, to the extent permitted by law, establish procedures to notify submitters of records containing confidential commercial information as described in section 3 of this Order, when those records are requested under the Freedom of Information Act (FOIA), 5 U.S.C. 552, as amended, if after reviewing the request, the responsive records, and any appeal by the requester, the department or agency determines that it may be required to disclose the records. Such notice requires that an agency use good-faith efforts to advise submitters of confidential commercial information of the procedures of this Order. Further, where notification of a voluminous number of submitters is required, such notification may be accomplished by posting or publishing the notice in a place reasonably calculated to accomplish notification.

Section 2

For Purposes of this Order, the following definitions apply:

(a) "Confidential commercial information" means records provided to the government by a submitter that arguably contain material exempt from release under exemption 4 of the Freedom of Information Act, 5 U.S.C. 552(b)(4), because disclosure could reasonably be expected to cause substantial competitive harm.

(b)"Submitter" means any person or entity who provides confidential commercial information to the government. The term "submitter" includes, but is not limited to, corporations, state governments, and foreign governments.

Section 3

(a) For confidential commercial information submitted prior to January 1, 1988, the head of each Executive department or agency shall, to the extent permitted by law, provide a submitter with notice pursuant to section 1 whenever:

(i) the records are less than 10 years old and the information has been designated by the submitter as confidential commercial information; or

(ii) the department or agency has reason to believe that disclosure of the information could reasonably be expected to cause substantial competitive harm.

(b) For confidential commercial information submitted on or after January 1, 1988, the head of each Executive department or agency shall, to the extent permitted by law, establish procedures to permit submitters of confidential commercial information to designate, at the time the information is submitted to the Federal government or a reasonable time thereafter, any information the disclosure of which the submitter claims could reasonably be expected to cause substantial competitive harm. Such agency procedures may provide for the expiration, after a specified period of time or changes in circumstances, of designations of competitive harm made by submitters. Additionally, such procedures may permit the agency to designate specific classes of information that will be treated by the agency as if the information has been so designated by the submitter. The head of each Executive department or agency shall, to the extent permitted by law, provided the submitter notice in accordance with section 1 of this Order whenever the department or agency determines that it may be required to disclose records:

(i) designated pursuant to this subsection; or

(ii) the disclosure of which the department or agency has reason to believe could reasonably be expected to cause substantial competitive harm.

Section 4

When notification is made pursuant to section 1, each agency's procedures shall, to the extent permitted by law, afford the submitter a reasonable period of time in which the submitter or its designee may object to the disclosure of any specified portion of the information and to state all grounds upon which disclosure is opposed.

Section 5

Each agency shall give careful consideration to all such specified grounds for nondisclosure prior to making an administrative determination of the issue. In all instances when the agency determines to disclose requested records, its procedures shall provide that the agency give the submitter a written statement briefly explaining why the submitter's objections are not sustained. Such statements shall, to the extent permitted by law, be provided a reasonable number of days prior to a specified disclosure date.

Section 6

Whenever a FOIA requester brings suit seeking to compel disclosure of confidential commercial information, each agency's procedures shall require that the submitter be promptly notified.

Section 7

The designation and notification procedures required by this Order shall be established by regulations, after notice and public comment. If similar procedures or regulations already exist, they should be reviewed for conformity and revised where necessary. Existing procedures or regulations need not be modified if they are in compliance with this Order.

Section 8

The notice requirements of this Order need not be followed if:

(a) The agency determines that the information should not be disclosed;

(b) The information has been published or has been officially made available to the public;

(c) Disclosure of the information is required by law [other than 5 U.S.C. 552];

(d) The disclosure is required by an agency rule that (1) was adopted pursuant to notice and public comment, (2) specifies narrow classes of records submitted to the agency that are to be released under the Freedom of Information Act, and (3) provides in exceptional circumstances for notice when the submitter provides written justification, at the time the information is submitted or a reasonable time thereafter, that disclosure of the information could reasonably be expected to cause substantial competitive harm;

(e) The information requested is not designated by the submitter as exempt from disclosure in accordance with agency regulations promulgated pursuant to section 7, when the submitter had an opportunity to do so at the time of submission of the information or a reasonable time thereafter, unless the agency has substantial reason to believe that disclosure of the information would result in competitive harm; or

(f) The designation made by the submitter in accordance with agency regulations promulgated pursuant to section 7 appears obviously frivolous; except that, in such case, the agency must provide the submitter with written notice of any final administrative disclosure determination within a reasonable number of days prior to the specified disclosure date.

Section 9

Whenever an agency notifies a submitter that it may be required to disclose information pursuant to section 1 of this Order, the agency shall also notify the requester that notice and an opportunity to comment are being provided the submitter. Whenever an agency notifies a submitter of a final decision pursuant to section 5 of this Order, the agency shall also notify the requester.

Section 10

This Order is intended only to improve the internal management of the Federal government, and is not intended to create any right or benefit, substantive or procedural, enforceable at law by a party against the United States, its agencies, its officers, or any person.

Ronald Reagan
The White House
June 23, 1987

APPENDIX F
Sample Legal Documents

This appendix is available online at http://www.epic.org/foia/21/appendixf.html

Sample Freedom of Information Act Request

July 12, 2000

FOI/Privacy Acts Section
Office of Public & Congressional Affairs
Federal Bureau of Investigation
9th & Constitution Ave., N.W.
Washington, DC 20535

Re: Freedom of Information Request

Dear Sir or Madam:

This letter constitutes a request under the Freedom of Information Act ("FOIA"), 5 U.S.C. § 552, and is submitted on behalf of Electronic Privacy Information Center ("EPIC").

We request the release of all FBI records concerning the system known as "Carnivore" and a device known as "EtherPeek" for the interception and/or review of electronic mail (e-mail) messages.

For purposes of FOIA fee assessments, we request that EPIC be placed in the category of "news media" requester. The organization publishes a weekly electronic newsletter that is available to the general public, and any information obtained as a result of this request will be disseminated through that publication. We note that other agencies have recognized that EPIC qualifies for "news media" status. We also request a waiver of all processing fees, as release of this information will contribute significantly to the public's understanding of the activities and operations of the government.

As the FOIA requires, I will look forward to your response within twenty (20) working days.

Thank you.

Sincerely,

David L. Sobel
General Counsel
Electronic Privacy Information Center

Sample Request for Expedited Processing

July 18, 2000

BY MESSENGER DELIVERY

Myron Marlin
Director of Public Affairs
Office of Public Affairs
U.S. Department of Justice
Room 1128
950 Pennsylvania Avenue, NW.
Washington DC 20530-0001

REQUEST FOR EXPEDITED FOIA PROCESSING

Dear Mr. Marlin:

This is a request for expedited processing of a Freedom of Information Act ("FOIA") request, made pursuant to 28 CFR 16.5(d)(1). On July 12, 2000, I submitted an FOIA request (copy attached) to the Federal Bureau of Investigation ("FBI") seeking the disclosure of "all FBI records concerning the system known as 'Carnivore' and a device known as 'EtherPeek' for the interception and/or review of electronic mail (e-mail) messages."

I believe this request meets the criteria for expedited processing under 28 CFR 16.5(d)(1)(iv), as "[a] matter of widespread and exceptional media interest in which there exist possible questions about the government's integrity which affect public confidence." 28 CFR 16.5(d)(1)(iv).

Through use of the Carnivore system, the FBI reportedly obtains a vast amount of private communications, far in excess of the material it is lawfully authorized to obtain. Release of the requested records would indicate the scope of material Carnivore intercepts and whether the Bureau has any mechanisms in place to limit data collection in keeping with Fourth Amendment and statutory requirements.

There can be no question that the FBI's use of the Carnivore system to intercept electronic mail messages has engendered "widespread and exceptional media interest" since the Wall Street Journal first disclosed the activity on July 11. Accordingly to Lexis-Nexis, more than 50 articles have appeared in the U.S. press since that disclosure, and the Attorney General was closely questioned on the matter at her weekly news briefing on July 13. CNN has reported that "[a]n FBI spokesman says the Bureau has been so inundated with requests on this issue, it may call a news briefing to answer everybody's questions all at once."

It is equally clear that "there exist possible questions about the government's integrity which affect public confidence." Such questions are exemplified in a St. Petersburg Times editorial of July 17:

> The FBI... is trying to take a bite out of Americans' privacy on the Internet. It has started using a rapacious computer program known as "Carnivore" to do cyberspace snooping on investigative targets. The program is attached to the target's Internet service provider. There, it absorbs and analyzes all the traffic or "packets" traveling through the ISP, not just the communications of the suspect. The FBI claims Carnivore can be programmed to spit out as little information as the addresses of those receiving the suspect's e-mails. The problem is, Carnivore also could be used to retain much more, and no one but the government would know.

Appendix F

> . . . The FBI says, "Trust us: We'll only collect what we should." But there is little reassuring about the way Carnivore may snack on our electronic conversations. The agency might sound like a protective parent, but its newest snooping tool is all Big Brother.

Likewise, the Christian Science Monitor notes in an editorial published today, "The potential for abuse is greater with Carnivore than with a simple phone tap. The program's capabilities are potentially sweeping."

The American public is deeply concerned about potential government intrusions into personal affairs, particularly private communications. While the Attorney General and FBI spokesmen have acknowledged and addressed these concerns, there is no substitute for the disclosure of internal Bureau records concerning the use of the Carnivore system. Indeed, the very purpose of the FOIA is to lessen the public's dependence on official agency statements and open the underlying documentation to public scrutiny. This is clearly an instance in which expedited processing of an FOIA request is warranted.

For your information, the Electronic Privacy Information Center ("EPIC") is a non-profit educational organization that disseminates information on privacy issues to the public. We accomplish that mission through our heavily-visited website and a bi-weekly electronic newsletter that is sent to more than 13,000 recipients, many of whom cover Internet privacy issues for a variety of news outlets. Indeed, EPIC has been recognized as a "representative of the news media" for fee assessment purposes by every federal agency that has received our FOIA requests.

Thank you for your consideration of this request. As applicable Department regulations provide, I will anticipate your determination within ten (10) calendar days.

Under penalty of perjury, I hereby affirm that the foregoing is true and correct to the best of my knowledge and belief.

David L. Sobel
General Counsel
Electronic Privacy Information Center

Sample Freedom of Information Act Complaint

UNITED STATES DISTRICT COURT
FOR THE DISTRICT OF COLUMBIA

ELECTRONIC PRIVACY INFORMATION CENTER)
1718 Connecticut Ave. NW.)
Suite 200)
Washington, DC 20009)
)
Plaintiff,)
)
v.) C.A. No. 02-0063
)
U.S. DEPARTMENT OF JUSTICE)
950 Pennsylvania Avenue, NW)
Washington, DC 20530-0001)
)
and)
)
U.S. DEPARTMENT OF THE TREASURY)
1500 Pennsylvania Avenue, NW)
Washington, D.C. 20220)
)
Defendants.)
)

COMPLAINT FOR INJUNCTIVE RELIEF

1. This is an action under the Freedom of Information Act, 5 U.S.C. § 552, for injunctive and other appropriate relief and seeking the disclosure and release of agency records improperly withheld from plaintiff by defendant Department of Justice ("DOJ") and its components Federal Bureau of Investigation ("FBI"), United States Marshals Service ("USMS"), Drug Enforcement Agency ("DEA"), Immigration and Naturalization Service ("INS"), and defendant U.S. Treasury ("Treasury") and its components Internal Revenue Service ("IRS"), and Bureau of Alcohol, Tobacco & Firearms ("ATF").

Jurisdiction and Venue

2. This Court has both subject matter jurisdiction over this action and personal jurisdiction over the parties pursuant to 5 U.S.C. § 552(a)(4)(B). This court also has jurisdiction over this action pursuant to 28 U.S.C. § 1331. Venue lies in this district under 5 U.S.C. § 552(a)(4)(B).

3. Plaintiff Electronic Privacy Information Center ("EPIC") is a public interest non-profit research organization in Washington, DC. It was established in 1994 to focus public attention on emerging civil liberties issues and to protect privacy, the First Amendment, and constitutional values. EPIC's activities include the review of federal data collection and data sharing policies to determine their possible impacts on civil liberties and privacy interests. Among its other activities, EPIC has prepared reports and presented testimony on privacy issues and has participated in and organized conferences on privacy.

4. Defendant DOJ is a Department of the Executive Branch of the United States Government, and includes component entities FBI, USMS, DEA, and INS. The DOJ is an agency within the meaning of 5 U.S.C. § 552(f).

5. Defendant Treasury is a Department of the Executive Branch of the United States Government, and includes component entities IRS and ATF. The Treasury is an agency within the meaning of 5 U.S.C. § 552(f).

Government Agencies' Acquisition of Private Sector Personal Information

6. On April 13, 2001, the Wall Street Journal reported that executive branch agencies were purchasing "troves of personal data from the private sector." Glenn R. Simpson, *Big Brother-in-Law, If the FBI Hopes to Get the Goods on You, It May Ask ChoicePoint*, Wall St. J., April 13, 2001 at A1.

7. The article quoted government sources for the proposition that DOJ, FBI, USMS, INS, and IRS employees had electronic access to citizens' assets, phone numbers, driving records, and other personal information from their desktop computers.

8. The article reported that ChoicePoint, a publicly-held company, and its competitors were supplying citizens' personal information to at least thirty-five federal government agencies.

9. The use of private sector databases of personal information enables the government to obtain detailed information on citizens while avoiding the creation of files that would implicate protections provided under the Privacy Act of 1974, 5 § U.S.C. 552a.

Plaintiff's FOIA Requests and Defendants' Failure to Respond

10. By separate letters to DOJ, FBI, USMS, DEA, INS, IRS, and ATF dated June 22, 2001, plaintiff submitted Freedom of Information Act ("FOIA") requests for "all records relating to transactions, communications, and contracts concerning businesses that sell individuals' personal information." A copy of the news article referenced in paragraphs 6-8, supra, accompanied the request.

Defendant DOJ's Failure to Timely Comply with Plaintiff's Request

11. By phone call on June 29, 2001, defendant DOJ informed plaintiff that the request would be forwarded to a component within the DOJ.

12. To date, defendant DOJ has not provided the records requested by plaintiff in its FOIA request, notwithstanding the FOIA's requirement of an agency response within twenty (20) working days.

13. Plaintiff has exhausted the applicable administrative remedies with respect to its FOIA request to defendant DOJ.

14. Defendant DOJ has wrongfully withheld the requested records from plaintiff.

The FBI's Failure to Timely Comply with Plaintiff's Request

15. By form letter to plaintiff dated July 3, 2001, the FBI acknowledged receipt of plaintiff's FOIA request.

16. By form letter to plaintiff dated July 27, 2001, the FBI requested clarification of plaintiff's FOIA request.

17. By letter dated August 8, 2001, plaintiff clarified its request to the FBI by specifying that the subject matter of the request related to ChoicePoint, Inc.

18. To date, the FBI has not provided the records requested by plaintiff in its FOIA request, notwithstanding the FOIA's requirement of an agency response within twenty (20) working days.

19. Plaintiff has exhausted the applicable administrative remedies with respect to its FOIA request to the FBI.

20. The FBI has wrongfully withheld the requested records from plaintiff.

The USMS' Failure to Timely Comply with Plaintiff's Request

21. By form letter to plaintiff dated July 11, 2001, the USMS acknowledged receipt of plaintiff's request.

22. To date, the USMS has not provided the records requested by plaintiff in its FOIA request, notwithstanding the FOIA's requirement of an agency response within twenty (20) working days.

23. Plaintiff has exhausted the applicable administrative remedies with respect to its FOIA request to the USMS.

24. The USMS has wrongfully withheld the requested records from plaintiff.

The DEA's Failure to Timely Comply with Plaintiff's Request

25. By form letter to plaintiff dated July 26, 2001, DEA requested clarification of plaintiff's FOIA request.

26. By letter dated August 8, 2001, plaintiff clarified its request to the DEA by specifying that the subject matter of the request related to ChoicePoint, Inc.

27. To date, the DEA has not provided the records requested by plaintiff in its FOIA request, notwithstanding the FOIA's requirement of an agency response within twenty (20) working days.

28. Plaintiff has exhausted the applicable administrative remedies with respect to its FOIA request to the DEA.

29. The DEA has wrongfully withheld the requested records from plaintiff.

The INS' Failure to Timely Comply with Plaintiff's Request

30. By form letter dated August 9, 2001, defendant INS acknowledged receipt of plaintiff's request.

31. To date, the INS has not provided the records requested by plaintiff in its FOIA request, notwithstanding the FOIA's requirement of an agency response within twenty (20) working days.

32. Plaintiff has exhausted the applicable administrative remedies with respect to its FOIA request to the INS.

33. The INS has wrongfully withheld the requested records from plaintiff.

The IRS' Partial Denial of Plaintiff's Request

34. By letter dated September 10, 2001, the IRS provided documents responsive to plaintiff's request. However, the IRS withheld 324 pages, relying upon 5 U.S.C. § 552(b)(4). Plaintiff appealed this withholding by letter dated November 8, 2001.

35. By form letter to plaintiff dated November 16, 2001, the IRS denied plaintiff's appeal.

36. Plaintiff has exhausted the applicable administrative remedies with respect to its FOIA request to the IRS.

37. The IRS has wrongfully withheld the requested records from plaintiff.

The ATF's Failure to Timely Comply with Plaintiff's Request

38. By letter to plaintiff dated August 8, 2001, the ATF acknowledged plaintiff's request.

39. By letter to plaintiff dated September 13, 2001, the ATF granted plaintiff's request in part and informed plaintiff that there would be a delay in locating responsive documents.

40. Plaintiff has exhausted the applicable administrative remedies with respect to its FOIA request to the ATF.

41. The ATF has wrongfully withheld the requested records from plaintiff.

Requested Relief

WHEREFORE, plaintiff prays that this Court:

A. order defendants to disclose the requested records in their entireties and make copies available to plaintiff;

B. provide for expeditious proceedings in this action;

C. award plaintiff its costs and reasonable attorneys fees incurred in this action; and

D. grant such other relief as the Court may deem just and proper.

Respectfully submitted,

____

CHRIS J. HOOFNAGLE
D.C. Bar No. 463182

DAVID L. SOBEL
D.C. Bar No. 360418

MARC ROTENBERG
D.C. Bar. No. 422825

ELECTRONIC PRIVACY INFORMATION CENTER
1718 Connecticut Ave. NW
Suite 200
Washington, DC 20009
(202) 483-1140

Counsel for Plaintiff

Sample Privacy Act Complaint

UNITED STATES DISTRICT COURT
FOR THE DISTRICT OF COLUMBIA

JOHN DOE c/o Mark S. Zaid, Esq. 1275 K Street, N.W. Suite 770 Washington, D.C. 20005 Plaintiff, v. FEDERAL BUREAU OF INVESTIGATION 935 Pennsylvania Avenue, N.W. Washington, D.C. 20535 Defendant.	)))))))))))))))))	C.A. No. ________

COMPLAINT

The plaintiff brings this action for injunctive, declaratory and monetary relief pursuant to the Privacy Act of 1974, 5 U.S.C. § 552a et seq., the Freedom of Information Act, 5 U.S.C. § 552(a) et seq., the Federal Declaratory Judgment Act, 28 U.S.C. § 2201.

Jurisdiction

1. This Court has jurisdiction over this action pursuant to 5 U.S.C. §§ 552a(g)(1), 552(a)(4)(B), and 28 U.S.C. § 1331.

Venue

2. Venue is appropriate in the District under 5 U.S.C. §§ 552a(g)(5), 552(a)(4)(B), and 28 U.S.C. § 1391.

Parties

3. Plaintiff John Doe is a citizen of the United States and the District of Columbia and resides in the District of Columbia.

4. Defendant Federal Bureau of Investigation ("FBI") is an agency within the meaning of 5 U.S.C. § 552a(a)(1), and is in possession and/or control of records pertaining to John Doe.

Facts

5. In or around July 1998, John Doe applied for a position with the Executive Office of the President. He was subsequently offered a position requiring a security clearance conditional upon his successfully passing a background investigation. The FBI conducts the background investigation of applicants for the office in question.

6. The background investigative portion was conducted by FBI Special Agent Peter Raub

(phonetic), who contacted John Doe to obtain names for references. Special Agent Raub, who had indicated to John Doe that he disliked background investigations and would soon be transferred to a different position, conducted an inappropriate, unprofessional and, to some extent, illegal background investigation of John Doe. Those individuals who were interviewed by Special Agent Raub reported that he was biased and "gunning" for John Doe.

7. In or around November or December 1998, Special Agent Raub interviewed Ms. Nina Sirrianni, a schoolmate of John Doe. Following her interview by Special Agent Raub, Ms. Sirrianni refused to speak or associate with John Doe. Upon information and belief, Ms. Sirrianni's decision was based on false, distorted and/or defamatory information concerning John Doe that was provided her by Special Agent Raub.

8. In or around December 1998, Special Agent Raub interviewed Thomas Donovan, a friend of John Doe. Special Agent Raub falsely told Mr. Donovan that he had reports that John Doe behaved aggressively towards women, and pressed him for any negative information that supported that allegation. None was provided.

9. In or around December 1998, Special Agent Raub interviewed Phillip Heuschen and Claud Hammon. Mr. Heuschen was told by Special Agent Raub that John Doe had been charged with assault, and insisted on being told stories about John Doe's violent behavior. Mr. Hammon was provided information that was designed to portray John Doe as a sexual harasser.

10. In or around December 1998, Special Agent Raub interviewed Shoon Murray, one of John Doe's professors. During the interview, Special Agent Raub sought to ascertain whether John Doe had a problem with women, and falsely and intentionally insinuated John Doe had had several run-ins with the law.

11. After receiving comments from his references, John Doe contacted Chuck Easley of the Executive Office of the President Security Office and informed him of Special Agent Raub's conduct. He assured John Doe that he would have the opportunity to address any problems that might arise in the investigation before any decision was made.

12. John Doe provided FBI Special Agent Holly Heisner and a male colleague a copy of feedback he received from his references concerning the conduct of Special Agent Raub. The male agent said that they would forward it to their superiors and that John Doe would not be informed if disciplinary action was taken against Special Agent Raub. The male agent added that he would like to sit Special Agent Raub down in a room somewhere and ask him what he was thinking. They apologized for his actions, said that he was not supposed to conduct interviews for background checks in that manner and that there would be no reprisals from the FBI against John Doe.

13. On or about April 22, 1999, John Doe was informed that his FBI background investigation had determined that he was unsuitable for employment. John Doe was never provided an opportunity to respond to the inaccurate and defamatory findings described by Special Agent Raub. As a result, he resigned from his position.

14. John Doe is now an applicant for employment at another federal agency which also requires a security clearance. In order for him to obtain employment at this agency, and many others, John Doe will be required to undergo a background investigation. The current potential employer, as well as any other future federal employers, will be provided unfettered access to John Doe's FBI application files and the negative, false and unfavorable information compiled by Special Agent Raub. This information will negatively impact upon John Doe's ability to gain federal employment.

15. John Doe has attempted to attain access to his FBI files since July 1999 so he can challenge any erroneous and/or false information. Despite all efforts, the FBI has not permitted John Doe the opportunity to even review his application file.

First Cause of Action
(Privacy Act/Freedom of Information Act
—Denial of Access to Records)

16. John Doe repeats and realleges the allegations contained in paragraphs 1 through 15 above, inclusive.

17. By letter dated July 23, 1999, John Doe, through his attorney, submitted a request to the FBI under the Privacy and Freedom of Information Acts for copies of all information maintained about himself.

18. By letter dated August 2, 1999, the FBI acknowledged receipt and assigned John Doe's request #902327-000.

19. On several occasions throughout 1999 and 2000, John Doe's attorney Mark S. Zaid has contacted the FBI for an update on the processing of his files. Upon information and belief, there are approximately 300 pages responsive to John Doe's request. Despite Mr. Zaid's notification to the FBI that John Doe requires access due to pending federal employment, no documents have been released.

20. John Doe has exhausted all required and available administrative remedies.

21. John Doe has a legal right under the Privacy and Freedom of Information Acts to obtain the information he seeks, and there is no legal basis for the denial by the FBI of said right.

Second Cause of Action (Privacy Act—
Improper Dissemination)

22. John Doe repeats and realleges the allegations contained in paragraphs 1 through 15 above, inclusive.

23. The FBI, through the actions of Special Agent Raub, disseminated information protected by the Privacy Act concerning John Doe to Nina Sirrianni, Thomas Donovan, Phillip Heuschen, Claud Hammon, Shoon Murray and unknown others. This information included, but is not limited to, John Doe's arrest record, inaccurate and defamatory information surrounding any run-ins with law enforcement and inaccurate and defamatory information regarding John Doe's conduct towards women.

24. In violation of section (d)(1) of the Privacy Act, the FBI failed to secure written authorization from John Doe prior to providing the specific information detailed above. Nor was disclosure permitted by a routine exception.

25. As a result of the FBI's violations of the Privacy Act, John Doe has suffered adverse and harmful effects, including, but not limited to, mental distress, emotional trauma, embarrassment, humiliation, and lost or jeopardized present or future financial opportunities.

Third Cause of Action (Privacy Act—
Improper Dissemination)

26. John Doe repeats and realleges the allegations contained in paragraphs 1 through 15 above, inclusive.

27. Prior to disseminating information and records concerning John Doe, the FBI failed to make reasonable efforts to ensure that the information and records were accurate, complete, timely and relevant for agency purposes in violation of 5 U.S.C. § 552a(e)(6). The FBI compiled information concerning John Doe's alleged arrest record, alleged run-ins with law enforcement, alleged conduct

towards women and his alleged failure to repay unpaid debts. The information and records that were disseminated to unauthorized individuals were irrelevant, false, malicious and defamatory, incomplete, inaccurate, and untimely.

28. The FBI, its employees and officers, including Special Agent Raub, knew or should have known that their actions were improper, unlawful and/or in violation of the Privacy Act.

29. The FBI, its employees and officers, including Special Agent Raub, acted intentionally or willfully in violation of John Doe's privacy rights.

30. As a result of the FBI's violations of the Privacy Act, John Doe has suffered adverse and harmful effects, including, but not limited to, mental distress, emotional trauma, embarrassment, humiliation, and lost or jeopardized present or future financial opportunities.

WHEREFORE, plaintiff John Doe requests that the Court award him the following relief:

(1) Declare that the FBI violated the Privacy and Freedom of Information Acts;

(2) Order the FBI to immediately disclose the requested records in their entireties to John Doe;

(3) Award John Doe any actual damages under 5 U.S.C. § 552a(g)(4)(A), the exact amount of which is to be determined at trial but is not less than $1,000;

(4) Invoke its equitable powers to expunge all records or information maintained by the FBI that is inaccurate and/or derogatory to John Doe;

(5) Award plaintiff reasonable costs and attorney's fees as provided in 5 U.S.C. §§ 552a(g)(3)(B) and/or (4)(B), 552 (a)(4)(E) and/or 28 U.S.C. § 2412 (d);

(6) Refer those FBI officials responsible for violating the Privacy Act for prosecution under 5 U.S.C. § 552a(i)(1);

(7) expedite this action in every way pursuant to 28 U.S.C. § 1657 (a); and

(8) grant such other relief as the Court may deem just and proper.

Date: May 15, 2000

Respectfully submitted,

Mark S. Zaid, Esq.
Lobel, Novins & Lamont
1275 K Street, N.W.
Suite 770
Washington, D.C. 20005
(202) 371-6626

Roy W. Krieger
Paleos & Krieger, P.C.
601 Pennsylvania Ave., N.W.
Suite 900 South
Washington, D.C. 20004
(202) 639-0531
Counsels for Plaintiff

Sample Government in the Sunshine Act Complaint

UNITED STATES DISTRICT COURT
FOR THE DISTRICT OF COLUMBIA

ENERGY RESEARCH FOUNDATION)
537 Harden Street)
Columbia, S.C. 29205)
(803) 256-7298)
)
NATURAL RESOURCES DEFENSE COUNCIL, INC.)
1350 New York Avenue, N.W.)
Suite 300)
Washington, D.C. 20005)
(202) 783-7800, and)
)
MICHAEL F. LOWE,)
2430 Terrace Way)
Columbia, S.C. 29205,)
)
Plaintiffs,)
) C.A. No. ________
v.)
)
DEFENSE NUCLEAR FACILITIES SAFETY BOARD)
Washington, D.C. 20585)
)
Defendant.)
)

COMPLAINT FOR DECLATORY AND INJUNCTIVE RELIEF

1. This action is brought under the Government-in-the-Sunshine Act, 5 U.S.C. § 552b ("Sunshine Act"), and the Freedom of Information Act, 5 U.S.C. § 552 ("FOIA"), in order to compel the Defense Nuclear Facilities Safety Board ("the Board") to provide for public access to its meetings and records, and to comply with other requirements of these statutes.

Jurisdiction

2. This Court has jurisdiction over this action under 5 U.S.C. §§ 552b(g) and (h) (the Sunshine Act), 5 U.S.C. § 552(a)(4)(B) (the FOIA), and 28 U.S.C. § 1331 (federal question jurisdiction).

Parties

3. Plaintiff Energy Research Foundation ("ERF") is a non-profit public-interest foundation which engages in research and public education on nuclear and other energy issues in South Carolina. ERF is particularly concerned with the effect of nuclear activities at the Department of Energy's Savannah River site in South Carolina on the environment, public health, and economy of the surrounding community. ERF has closely monitored and sought to participate in federal decision making related to environmental and public health problems at the Savannah River facility. In order to continue this work, ERF seeks access to the Board and its activities, including attending the Board's meetings and obtaining access to its records.

4. Plaintiff Natural Resources Defense Council, Inc. ("NRDC") is a national, nonprofit membership organization incorporated under the laws of the state of New York. NRDC works to

preserve, protect, and defend natural resources and the environment against misuse and unreasonable degradation, and to take appropriate legal steps to carry out these purposes. NRDC has a nationwide membership of over 88,000 members of the public dedicated to the defense and preservation of the human environment. Many members have joined NRDC so that they may obtain adequate representation and protection of the environmental interests they share with NRDC.

5. One of NRDC's objectives is to inform and educate the public about environmental and public safety and health issues at Department of Energy facilities. It has closely monitored and sought to participate in federal decision making related to environmental and public health problems at Department of Energy facilities. In order to continue this work, NRDC seeks access to the Board's meetings and records.

6. Plaintiff Michael F. Lowe is a resident of South Carolina and Program Coordinator of ERF. He is concerned about the environmental and public health impacts of Department of Energy facilities in his state. He wishes to attend Board meetings, obtain access to Board records, and participate in the Board's activities in other ways authorized by the Sunshine Act, FOIA, and other open government laws.

7. Defendant Defense Nuclear Facilities Safety Board is an agency of the United States, and is denying plaintiffs access to its meetings and records in contravention of federal law.

Statutory Framework and Facts Giving Rise
To Plaintiffs' Claims for Relief
The Board's Functions and Powers

8. In 1988, Congress created "an independent establishment in the executive branch" called the Defense Nuclear Facilities Safety Board. 42 U.S.C. § 2286(a). The Board is composed of five members appointed by the President with the advice and consent of the Senate. 42 U.S.C. § 2286(b).

9. The Board is authorized and commanded by statute to perform a variety of substantive duties, including (a) investigating any event or practice at a Department of Energy defense nuclear facility which the Board determines has adversely affected, or may adversely affect, public health and safety, (b) reviewing and evaluating the content and implementation of standards relating to the design, construction, operation, and decommissioning of defense nuclear facilities, (c) determining whether the Secretary of Energy is adequately implementing health and safety standards in the operation of defense nuclear facilities, and (d) reviewing the design of every new Department of Energy defense nuclear facility before construction. 5 U.S.C. § 2886a.

10. In order to carry out its statutory duties, the Board is empowered to hold hearings, subpoena witnesses and documents, hire employees, impose binding reporting requirements for the Secretary of Energy including the reporting of classified information, and promulgate regulations. 5 U.S.C. § 2286b. The Board's actions are expressly made subject to the judicial review provisions of the Administrative Procedure Act. 5 U.S.C. § 2286f ("APA").

The Sunshine Act

11. The Sunshine Act requires that "every portion of every meeting" of a multi-member agency must "be open to public observation," with narrow exceptions. 5 U.S.C. §§ 552b(b) and (c). The Sunshine Act also requires agencies to announce publicly the time, place, and subject matter of meetings at least a week before the meeting, 5 U.S.C. § 552b(e)(1), and to prepare a complete transcript or electronic recording of meetings that are closed for any reason, 5 U.S.C. § 552b(f). Agencies must also promulgate regulations implementing the requirements of the Sunshine Act. 5 U.S.C. § 552b(g).

12. The Board has held meetings for the purpose of accomplishing its statutory duties, but has not provided for public access to those meetings nor has it complied with any of the other requirements of the Sunshine Act.

13. The Board will conduct additional meetings in the future, but does not intend to comply with the Sunshine Act.

The Freedom of Information Act

14. Section (a)(1) of the FOIA requires each executive branch agency to publish a number of items in the Federal Register, including the agency's "rules of procedure," "substantive rules of general applicability," and the employees "from whom, and the methods whereby, the public may obtain information, make submittals or requests, or obtain decisions." 5 U.S.C. § 552(a)(1).

15. Section (a)(2) of the FOIA requires agencies to make available for public inspection and copying a number of records, including all "administrative staff manuals and instructions to staff that affect a member of the public," and "final opinions" of the agency. 5 U.S.C. § 552(a)(2).

16. Section (a)(3) of the FOIA authorizes members of the public to submit requests for other agency records. In order to facilitate the exercise of this right, the FOIA requires agencies to publish in the Federal Register, following public notice and comment, regulations specifying the schedule of fees applicable to the processing of FOIA requests and guidelines for determining whether fees for such requests should be waived or reduced. 5 U.S.C. § 552(a)(4)(A).

17. The Board has failed to promulgate any of the regulations required by the FOIA or to make available to the public any of the materials described in paragraphs 14-16.

Plaintiffs' Request to the Board

18. On January 23, 1990, plaintiffs ERF and NRDC sent the Board a detailed letter explaining that the Board was in ongoing violation of the Sunshine Act and the FOIA. Plaintiffs' letter specified seven actions that the Board needed to take in order to comply with those laws and requested a response by February 14, 1990.

19. By letter dated January 24, 1990, the Chairman of the Board informed plaintiffs that the Board did not believe it "is or has been in violation of any Federal laws... ." The letter did not discuss the Sunshine Act or the FOIA, nor did it respond to any of the specific requests made by plaintiffs. Plaintiffs were informed by the Department of Justice, which is acting as counsel for the Board, that an additional response to their letter would be forthcoming.

20. On February 16, 1990, plaintiffs' attorney was notified by the Department of Justice that the Board's final position is that it is not required to comply with any of the provisions of the Sunshine Act or the FOIA.

Count One

21. The Board is an agency subject to the requirements of the Sunshine Act but is not complying with any of the provisions of that Act. This failure is injuring and will continue to injure plaintiffs by preventing them from learning about and attending the Board's meetings.

Count Two

22. The Board is an agency subject to the requirements of the FOIA but is not complying with any of the provisions of that Act. This failure is injuring and will continue to injure plaintiffs by preventing them from learning about and obtaining access to Board records.

Count Three

23. In failing to promulgate regulations, and to take other steps necessary to implement the Sunshine Act and the FOIA, the Board has unlawfully withheld and unreasonably delayed action, and has otherwise acted arbitrarily, capriciously, and contrary to law in violation of the APA, 5 U.S.C. §§ 555(b), 701-706.

WHEREFORE, plaintiffs pray that this Court:

(1) Enter an order declaring that the Board:

(a) is subject to the Sunshine Act but is not complying with any of its requirements;

(b) is subject to the FOIA but is failing to promulgate regulations and make agency records available to the public as required by 5 U.S.C §§ 552(a)(1), (a)(2), and (a)(4);

(c) is unlawfully withholding and unreasonably delaying agency action, and is acting arbitrarily, capriciously, and contrary to law, in violation of the APA;

(2) Enter an order preliminarily enjoining the Board from conducting any further meetings unless and until it undertakes to comply with the requirements of sections (b) through (g) of the Sunshine Act, 5 U.S.C. §§ 552b(b) - (g);

(3) Enter a permanent injunction directing the Board to comply promptly with the requirements of the Sunshine Act and the FOIA;

(4) Award plaintiffs their costs, reasonable attorneys' fees, and other disbursements in this action; and

(5) Grant such other and further relief as the Court may deem just and proper.

Respectfully submitted,

____

Eric R. Glitzenstein
D.C. Bar No. 358287

____

Anne Spielberg

____

Dean R. Tousley
D.C. Bar No. 362678

Harmon, Curran & Tousley
Suite 430
2001 S Street, N.W.
Washington, D.C. 20009
(202) 328-3500

____
Dan W. Reicher
D.C. Bar No. 418282
National Resources Defense Council
Suite 300
1350 New York Ave., N.W.
Washington, D.C. 20005
(202) 783-7000

____
Robert Guild
Energy Research Foundation
537 Harden Street
Columbia, S.C. 29205
(803) 256-7298

Attorneys for Plaintiffs

March 8, 1990

Sample Federal Advisory Committee Act Complaint

UNITED STATES DISTRICT COURT
FOR THE DISTRICT OF COLUMBIA

NATURAL RESOURCES DEFENSE COUNCIL, 1200 New York Ave., N.W. Suite 400 Washington, DC 20005, and TRI-VALLEY CARES, 2582 Old 1st Street, Livermore, CA 94550-3835, Plaintiffs, v. BILL RICHARDSON, Secretary, The Department of Energy 1000 Independence Ave., S.W. Washington, D.C. 20585, and DEPARTMENT OF ENERGY 1000 Independence Ave., S.W. Washington, D.C. 20585, Defendants.	)	C.A. No. ________

COMPLAINT FOR DECLARATORY AND INJUNCTIVE RELIEF

1. This case challenges the Department of Energy's ongoing violations of the Federal Advisory Committee Act, 5 U.S.C. App. II (1972) ("FACA"), as amended, with respect to advisory committees which have provided DOE with recommendations concerning a multi-billion dollar National Ignition Facility ("NIF") under construction in Livermore, California.

Jurisdiction

2. This Court has jurisdiction over this action pursuant to 28 U.S.C. § 1331.

Parties

3. Plaintiff Natural Resources Defense Council, Inc., ("NRDC") is a non-profit organization with over 400,000 members dedicated to the protection of the environment. It brings this action on its own behalf, and on behalf of its members.

4. NRDC works on a number of environmental issues, including issues related to the proliferation and hazards of nuclear weapons. In particular, for decades NRDC's Nuclear Program has engaged in public education and advocacy concerning DOE's nuclear weapons programs, including, in recent years, issues related to the NIF. NRDC has submitted comments to DOE concerning the NIF, has used its newsletters, website, and other publications to inform its members about the NIF, and has

undertaken litigation concerning the NIF. When permitted by DOE, NRDC has also closely monitored, and participated in, DOE's outside reviews of the NIF.

5. NRDC members live in the vicinity of the NIF in Livermore, California.

6. Defendants' violations of FACA injure NRDC and its members. By failing to conduct open meetings and make advisory committee materials publicly available in the manner required by FACA, defendants are violating NRDC's statutory right to obtain information concerning these committees and their recommendations, and to disseminate that information to its members and the public, as well as to present information to DOE advisory committees and to DOE.

7. In addition, because these advisory committees and their recommendations are playing an important role in the decision-making concerning whether to continue funding constructing, and subsequently operating the NIF, the health and safety of NRDC members living near the NIF is threatened by DOE's unlawful use of these committees. For example, DOE may use radioactive or other hazardous materials in NIF experiments, or may conduct radiation effects tests at NIF. DOE's use of illegal advisory committees and their recommendations therefore threatens NRDC members who live in the vicinity of the NIF with releases of radioactive tritium, uranium, and plutonium, and other highly toxic materials such as beryllium and lithium hydride.

8. These FACA violations also injure NRDC and its members because continued funding, construction, and subsequent operation of the NIF—which DOE's illegal advisory committees directly influence—could increase the risks of nuclear arms proliferation and destabilize the current nuclear test moratorium among the major nuclear weapon powers. Completion and operation of the NIF increases the risk that certain nuclear-capable countries—such as India, Pakistan, Japan and Germany—will use the data and analysis generated by unclassified and partly classified NIF experiments to advance their fundamental understanding of nuclear weapons physics, and hence their abilities to design thermonuclear weapons and possibly even confirm their performance without conducting nuclear test explosions. Completion and operation of the NIF also increases the risks that additional countries, such as Russia and China, may revert to testing nuclear weapons to insure that any improvements the NIF permits in U.S. nuclear weapons are matched by improvements in these countries' own weapons. In addition, DOE's FACA violations injure NRDC and its members because the escalating funding demands of the NIF project—now totaling some $4 billion dollars—and its inadequately reviewed scientific and technical problems, have undermined the confidence of the U.S. Senate in the nation's Stockpile Stewardship Program, and hence have diminished the prospects for Senate ratification of the Comprehensive Test Ban Treaty, a long standing priority of NRDC and its members. Thus, DOE's FACA violations harm NRDC and its members by furthering actions that could destabilize the existing nuclear test moratorium and spread nuclear weapons knowledge to additional countries, thereby increasing the risks of nuclear war.

9. Plaintiff Tri-Valley CAREs ("TVC") is a non-profit organization which has been involved in numerous advocacy activities concerning the NIF. Founded in 1983, TVC undertakes projects that increase public knowledge of the relationship between peace and environmental issues, including public education regarding potential impacts from the production, treatment, storage and disposal of hazardous and radioactive waste. A Livermore community-based organization, TVC's members reside, own property, work, recreate and attend public meetings near Lawrence Livermore National Laboratory ("Livermore"), where the NIF is being constructed. TVC members have participated in many administrative, legal and grassroots efforts involving the DOE's nuclear weapons complex, including the plans for the NIF at Livermore, and have devoted substantial resources advocating for Livermore to be converted from military to civilian research and uses. When permitted by DOE, TVC has also closely monitored, and participated in, DOE's outside reviews of the NIF. TVC brings this action on its own behalf and on behalf of its more than 2,600 members.

10. Defendants' violations of FACA injure TVC and its members. By failing to conduct open meetings and make advisory committee materials publicly available in the manner required by FACA,

defendants are violating TVC's statutory right to obtain information concerning these committees and their recommendations, and to disseminate that information to its members and the public, as well as to present information to DOE advisory committees and to DOE.

11. In addition, because these advisory committees and their recommendations are playing an important role in DOE's decision-making concerning whether to continue construction and subsequently operate the NIF, the health and safety of TVC members living near the NIF is threatened by DOE's unlawful use of these committees. For example, DOE may use radioactive or other hazardous materials in NIF experiments, and may conduct radiation effects tests at NIF. DOE's use of illegal advisory committees and their recommendations therefore threatens TVC members who live in the vicinity of the NIF with releases of radioactive tritium, uranium and plutonium, and other highly toxic materials such as beryllium and lithium hydride.

12. These FACA violations also injure TVC and its members because continued funding, construction and operation of the NIF—which these committees influence—largely undermines TVC's long standing effort to have Livermore reduce its focus on military-related projects in favor of devoting more resources to civilian projects. Without the NIF, Livermore is likely to be far less involved in military programs in the future, and far more involved in civilian-related research and development.

13. On information and belief, because DOE needs an independent review of the NIF in order to assure its continued construction, an injunction which prevents DOE from using recommendations obtained in violation of FACA will cause DOE to establish or utilize a FACA-complying advisory committee to review the NIF. Because NRDC and TVC will then have access to, and the opportunity to participate in, that advisory committee to the full extent permitted by FACA, prohibiting DOE from using certain advisory committee recommendations obtained in violation of FACA will redress injuries NRDC and TVC have suffered from these violations.

14. Defendant Bill Richardson is the Secretary of the Department of Energy, and is ultimately responsible for all decision-making regarding both the NIF and DOE's compliance with FACA.

15. Defendant The Department of Energy is an Executive Branch Department.

Statutory Framework and Facts Giving Rise to Plaintiffs' Claims

A. The Federal Advisory Committee Act

16. FACA imposes requirements on agencies when they establish or utilize any advisory committee, which is defined as a group of individuals, including at least one non-federal employee, which provides collective advice or recommendations to the agency. 5 U.S.C. App. II, § 3(2). When an agency seeks to obtain such advice or recommendations, it must ensure the advisory committee is "in the public interest," 5 U.S.C. App. II, § 9(2), is "fairly balanced in terms of points of view represented and the function to be performed," *id.* § 5(b)(2), and does not contain members with inappropriate special interests. *Id.* at § 5(b)(3). If these criteria are satisfied, the agency must file a charter for the committee. *Id.* at § 9(c).

17. Once an advisory committee is operating, the agency also must comply with requirements designed to ensure public access and participation. Among other requirements, an advisory committee must provide adequate public notice of, and conduct, open meetings, *id.* at § 10(a), and must make transcripts of meetings available to the public. *Id.* at §§ 10(b), 11(a). In addition, all documents made available to, or prepared by, an advisory committee must be publicly accessible. *Id.* at § 10(b). A federal employee must chair, or attend, each advisory committee meeting. *Id.* at § 10(e).

Appendix F

B. <u>The National Ignition Facility</u>

18. As one component of an overall effort to achieve some of the objectives of nuclear weapons testing without conducting full-scale nuclear tests, the DOE has been constructing the National Ignition Facility ("NIF") at the Lawrence Livermore National Laboratory ("Livermore") in Livermore, California. Once completed, scientists using the NIF—which is the size of the Rose Bowl—will attempt to ignite the nuclear fusion process in the laboratory by converging 192 lasers on a small cylindrical target containing a tiny fusion fuel pellet, compressing and heating it until fusion reactions among its atoms emit more nuclear energy than the laser energy on the target, a process called "ignition."

19. Although a number of scientists and outside organizations raised significant concerns about the NIF, including its cost, its ability to achieve ignition, and its impact on the proliferation of nuclear weapons in other countries, DOE began constructing the NIF in May 1997. At that time DOE estimated that the facility and related research and development would cost $ 2.2 billion, and that the NIF would be completed in 2003.

20. In 1998, some of these same concerns began to be raised within DOE. While DOE has continued to press forward with construction of the NIF, it now acknowledges that construction of the facility will cost over $1 billion more than planned at the time the decision to begin construction was made, and will not be completed until the end of fiscal year 2008, five years later than originally planned.

21. In response to these and other related developments, members of Congress asked the General Accounting Office ("GAO") to undertake a study of the NIF project, and a GAO Report was issued in August 2000. According to that Report, DOE continues to severely underestimate the cost of NIF by more than $500 million, and has failed to demonstrate where within the DOE budget the additional funds needed to ensure completion of the project will be found. The GAO further found that one of the primary reasons for the NIF management and oversight failures which have led to these major cost overruns and delays is the absence of any effective independent review of the NIF.

22. The GAO Report's major recommendation is that DOE arrange for an outside scientific and technical review of the technical challenges remaining for the NIF and the relationship of those challenges to the cost and schedule of the project. Although the GAO Report acknowledges that there have been a number of outside reviews which have provided DOE with advice concerning the NIF since construction began, the Report concludes that none of these reviews have been truly independent of DOE or the sponsoring laboratory, and that in some instances DOE has actively sought to dictate the results of such outside reviews. It is for this reason, the GAO Report suggests, that each of these committees has rendered positive recommendations for continuing to proceed with the NIF, despite the persistence of serious scientific, technological and cost issues requiring clarification by a probing, independent review.

C. <u>DOE's FACA Violations With Regard To Advice And Recommendations Concerning the NIF.</u>

23. In 1992, DOE established a federal advisory committee under FACA (the "DOE-ICFAC") to review the inertial confinement fusion program of which NIF is a part. Prior to DOE's decision whether to begin construction of the NIF, in late 1995 the chairman of the DOE-ICFAC reported to DOE that, in the Committee's view, further research and development work on the NIF ignition target was necessary to increase confidence that NIF would meet its ignition goal.

24. In late 1995, DOE elected to terminate this FACA committee—the last FACA-complying committee asked to review the NIF. Among the reasons cited for this decision was precisely the fact that the DOE-ICFAC had to operate within FACA's legal constraints.

25. Since that time, DOE has established and utilized several advisory committees to obtain further advice and recommendations concerning the NIF—committees which, although they are advisory committees within the meaning of FACA, were formed and have operated in violation of that statute.

26. At DOE's request, in 1996 the National Academy of Sciences' National Research Council formed an Inertial Confinement Fusion Advisory Committee ("NRC-ICF Committee") to evaluate the NIF. Because the NRC-ICF Committee did not comply with FACA, plaintiffs NRDC and TVC, and others, brought suit in this Court, and the Court issued a preliminary injunction against DOE's use of this Committee's Report. The Court subsequently issued a permanent injunction against DOE providing further support to the NRC-ICF Committee. *See NRDC v. Peña*, No. 97-0308 (PLF).

27. Despite this litigation, DOE has continued to obtain advice and recommendations concerning the NIF in violation of FACA. In response to GAO's recommendation that DOE undertake an external, independent review of the NIF, DOE claims that it implemented the recommendation by forming an advisory committee that undertook an independent review of the NIF in August 2000.

28. That advisory committee, known as the "Rebaseline Committee," was established by DOE and contains members who are non-federal employees. As reflected in the Committee's August 2000 Report—"Department of Energy Rebaseline Validation Review of the National Ignition Facility Project" ("Rebaseline Validation Review")—the Committee is providing policy advice to DOE concerning the NIF. For each aspect of the project—including a section on environment, safety and health—the Report provides a host of recommendations to DOE.

29. Although the Rebaseline Committee is clearly subject to FACA's requirements, DOE has not complied with FACA in any fashion with respect to the Rebaseline Validation Review—the meetings were not open to the public, the existence of the Committee was not made public, the required committee materials were not made publicly available, and DOE never filed a charter for the Committee. Although the Review was provided to DOE in August 2000, DOE did not publicly release it until after DOE delivered the Review to Congress, on September 15, 2000. Plaintiffs became aware of the fact that the Rebaseline Committee had members who are not federal employees only a few days before the Rebaseline Validation Review was publicly released.

30. DOE also never made the required findings that the Rebaseline Committee was "in the public interest," was "fairly balanced," and was free of members with inappropriate special interests. Id. at §§ 5(b), 9(2). In addition to DOE and DOE-laboratory employees, the Rebaseline Committee included other persons predisposed to support continuation of the NIF Project without conducting a probing review of the facility's underlying scientific and technical problems and their relation to the NIF's ultimate performance and cost.

31. For example, there were four members of the "Large Optics" subcommittee—who are also members of the full Committee—who ostensibly reviewed the laser science behind the NIF. None of them could be expected to assess the construction and operation of the NIF objectively and without bias. The chairperson of the subcommittee, Michel Andre, is a senior scientist in the French Megajoule laser project, which has extensive contractual relations and joint efforts with the NIF program. If the Committee were to find a fundamental problem with the NIF, then this could negatively impact funding for the French program, and Mr. Andre's career.

32. John Emmett, another member of the Large Optics subcommittee, has been a frequent consultant to the Livermore NIF program, and was formerly the Associate Director for Lasers at Livermore. When Emmett was at Livermore he helped invent the multi-pass optical design concept being utilized on the NIF, creating a natural bias in favor of finding that the NIF will work, and against admitting the possibility of a fundamental problem with the facility's design.

33. Yet another subcommittee member, Dr. Michelle Shinn, works at DOE's Thomas Jefferson Laboratory, whose director, Dr. Hermann Grunder, chairs Livermore's NIF Programs Review Committee, one of the bodies most responsible for failing to exert adequate oversight of the project, and has personally lobbied in Washington for full NIF funding. E. Perry Wallerstein, the final member of this critical subcommittee, was formerly an employee of Livermore, and is now a paid consultant to Livermore.

34. Two other subpanels of the Rebaseline Committee—on laser beamline equipment, and assembly, installation, and commissioning—were chaired by subordinates of Dr. Grunder from DOE's Thomas Jefferson Laboratory, and each of these panels also included a member from the University of Rochester's Laboratory for Laser Energetics, which is a major subcontractor and scientific collaborator on the NIF Project. The second of these panels also included a private consultant, Damon Giovanielli, who had served a few months earlier as the chair of the Livermore Laboratory's own "Target Physics Program Review Committee," which had concluded that, "NIF should be completed to its full 192-beam configuration."

35. DOE has also failed to comply with FACA with respect to a subcommittee of the Secretary of Energy's Advisory Board ("SEAB"), called the NIF Task Force. Although the NIF Task Force is a FACA advisory committee, established and utilized by DOE to provide outside advice concerning the NIF, the NIF Task Force has conducted meetings without providing the advance notice required by FACA, and has not made meeting materials available as required by FACA. Plaintiff TVC was forced to file a Freedom of Information Act request to try to obtain DOE documents which had been shared with the NIF Task Force.

36. The NIF Task Force is still preparing its final recommendations for DOE. Nonetheless, on September 7, 2000, the Chairman of the NIF Task Force, in a letter written on SEAB letterhead, wrote directly to the Secretary of Energy that the NIF Task Force has concluded that the NIF should proceed as planned.

37. On September 15, 2000, DOE submitted materials to Congress as part of an effort to ensure that Congress permits DOE to continue construction of the NIF. Among the materials in that submission were the Rebaseline Validation Review and the September 7, 2000 letter from the Chairman of the NIF Task Force. DOE submitted these materials to Congress in an effort to demonstrate that independent reviewers have recommended to the DOE that it should proceed with the NIF.

38. On information and belief, DOE intends to continue to obtain advice and recommendations from advisory committees concerning the NIF, without having those committees comply with FACA.

Plaintiffs' Claims for Relief
Claim One

39. By establishing and utilizing the Rebaseline Committee, permitting it to meet and deliberate without complying with FACA, and then obtaining and using the Committee's Report—the Rebaseline Validation Review—the defendants are violating FACA, and are acting in a manner which is arbitrary, capricious, and contrary to law, in violation of the Administrative Procedure Act. 5 U.S.C. § 706.

Claim Two

40. By engaging in a pattern and practice of violating FACA, 5 U.S.C. App. II, as amended, DOE has acted, and is acting, in a manner which is arbitrary, capricious, and contrary to law, in violation of the Administrative Procedure Act. 5 U.S.C. 706.

WHEREFORE, plaintiffs respectfully request that this Court:

(1) declare that DOE has violated FACA with respect to the Rebaseline Committee and the NIF Task Force;

(2) declare that DOE is engaged in a pattern and practice of violating FACA;

(3) order DOE to publicly release all materials related to the Rebaseline Committee and the NIF Task Force which are covered by Section 10 of FACA, 5 U.S.C. App. II, § 10;

(4) order DOE to provide written notice to all of the individuals and organizations to whom DOE has provided the Rebaseline Validation Review, explaining that the Rebaseline Committee recommendations were obtained in violation of FACA;

(5) enjoin DOE from using, or relying upon, the Rebaseline Validation Review;

(6) enjoin DOE from continuing to engage in a pattern and practice of violating FACA;

(7) award plaintiffs their costs, attorneys' fees, and other disbursements for this action; and

(8) grant plaintiffs such other and further relief as this Court may deem just and proper.

Respectfully submitted,

____

Howard M. Crystal
(D.C. Bar No. 446189)

____

Eric R. Glitzenstein
(D.C. Bar No. 358287)
Meyer & Glitzenstein
1601 Connecticut Ave., N.W.
Suite 450
Washington, D.C. 20009
(202) 588-5206

Attorneys for Plaintiffs

October 11, 2000

Table of Cases

9 to 5 Organization for Women Office Workers v. Board of Governors of the Federal Reserve System, 721 F.2d 1 (1st Cir. 1983)....85, 90, 91, 101
A. Michael's Piano, Inc. v. Federal Trade Commission, 18 F.3d 138 (2d Cir. 1994)....77, 115, 116
A.G. Becker, Inc. v. Board of Governors, 502 F. Supp. 378 (D.D.C. 1980)....351, 354
Abbotts v. NRC, 766 F.2d 604 (D.C. Cir. 1985)....41, 47
ABC Home Health Services v. HHS, 548 F. Supp. 555 (N.D. Ga. 1982)....173
Abraham & Rose, P.L.C. v. United States, 138 F.3d 1075 (6th Cir. 1998)....58, 155
Abramson v. FBI, 566 F. Supp. 1371 (D.D.C. 1983)....181
Access Reports v. DOJ, 926 F.2d 1192 (D.C. Cir. 1991)....107
Accumenics Research & Tech. v. DOJ, 843 F.2d 800 (4th Cir. 1988)....103
Accuracy in Media, Inc. v. National Park Serv., 194 F.3d 120 (D.C. Cir. 1999)....133, 183, 288, 289
Ackerly v. Ley, 420 F.2d 1336 (D.C. Cir. 1969)....91, 153
Ackerson & Bishop Chartered v. Department of Agriculture, No. 92-1068 (D.D.C. July 15, 1992)....141
ACLU v. Attorney General's Commission on Pornography, C.A. No. 86-0893 (D.D.C. 1986)....374
Administrator, FAA v. Robertson, 422 U.S. 255 (1975)....67, 69
AFGE v. Department of the Army, 441 F. Supp. 1308 (D.D.C. 1977)....115, 118
AFGE, Local 1760 v. FLRA, 786 F.2d 554 (2d Cir. 1986)....156
AFGE, Local 1923 v. HHS, 712 F.2d 931 (4th Cir. 1983)....130, 149
AFGE, Local 2782 v. Department of Commerce, 632 F. Supp. 1272 (D.D.C. 1986)....218
AFGE, Local 2782 v. Department of Commerce, 907 F.2d 203 (D.C. Cir. 1990)....21, 105
Afshar v. Department of State, 702 F.2d 1125 (D.C. Cir. 1983)....47, 49, 72, 108
Aftergood v. CIA, 1999 U.S. Dist 18135 (D.D.C. 1999)....48
Agee v. CIA, 517 F. Supp. 1335 (D.D.C. 1981)....81
Agee v. CIA, 524 F. Supp. 1290 (D.D.C. 1981)....81, 175
Akutowicz v. United States, 859 F.2d 1122 (2d Cir. 1988)....333
Alabama-Tombigbee Rivers Coalition v. Department of Interior, 26 F.3d 1103 (11th Cir. 1994).376, 377
Albright v. United States (I), 631 F.2d 915 (D.C. Cir. 1980)....305, 307, 309, 322, 323, 337, 338
Albright v. United States, 558 F. Supp. 260 (D.D.C. 1982)....337
Albuquerque Publ'g Co. v. DOJ, 726 F. Supp. 851 (D.D.C. 1989)....57, 180, 190
Alcaraz v. Block, 746 F.2d 593 (9th Cir. 1984)....5, 341
Alexander & Alexander Servs. v. SEC, No. 92-112 (JHG), 1993 U.S. Dist. LEXIS 14945 (D.D.C. Oct. 18, 1993)....160
Alexander v. FBI, 186 F.R.D. 6 (D.D.C. 1998)....297
Alexander v. FBI, 971 F. Supp. 603 (D.D.C. 1997)....200, 310
Alexander v. Sandoval, 532 U.S. 275 (2001)....376
Alexander v. United States, 787 F.2d 1349 (9th Cir. 1986)....328, 329

Table of Cases

Al-Fayed v. CIA, 254 F.3d 300 (D.C. Cir. 2001)....................262, 263, 282, 299
Al-Fayed v. CIA, No. 00-2092 (CKK), 2000 U.S. Dist. LEXIS 21476 (D.D.C. 2000) 262, 263
Alirez v. NLRB, 676 F.2d 423 (10th Cir. 1982)....................141, 161
Allen v. Bergland, 661 F.2d 1001 (4th Cir. 1981).................... 4
Allen v. CIA, 636 F.2d 1287 (D.C. Cir. 1980).................... 35, 42, 43, 44, 45, 50, 54, 58, 61, 287, 291, 294
Allen v. Department of Defense, 580 F. Supp. 74 (D.D.C. 1983).................... 206
Allen v. Department of Defense, 713 F. Supp. 7 (D.D.C. 1989).................... 248
Alliance for Cannabis Therapeutics v. DEA, 15 F.3d 1131 (D.C. Cir. 1994) 5
Alliance for the Wild Rockies v. Department of Interior, 53 F. Supp. 2d 32 (D.D.C. 1999) ..141, 147, 157
Alphin v. FAA, 902 F.2d 27 (4th Cir. 1990) 316
Alyeska Pipeline Service Co. v. EPA, 856 F.2d 309 (D.C. Cir. 1988)....................176, 284
American Airlines, Inc. v. National Mediation Board, 588 F.2d 863 (2d. Cir. 1978) 87, 88, 90
American Broadcasting Companies, Inc. v. FCC, 682 F.2d 25 (2d Cir. 1982) 4
American Broadcasting Companies, Inc. v. United States Information Agency, 599 F. Supp. 756 (D.D.C. 1984).................... 300
American Commercial Barge Lines v. NLRB, 758 F.2d 1109 (6th Cir. 1985) 243, 246
American Friends Service Committee v. Department of Defense, 831 F.2d 441 (3d Cir. 1987)..... 42, 222
American Friends Service Committee v. Webster, 485 F. Supp. 222 (D.D.C. 1980) 28
American Jewish Congress v. Kreps, 574 F.2d 624 (D.C. Cir. 1978) 1, 70, 78
American Library Association v. Faurer, 631 F. Supp. 416 (D.D.C. 1986).................... 39
American Library Association v. Odom, 818 F.2d 81 (D.C. Cir. 1987) 39
American Mail Line, Ltd. v. Gulick, 411 F.2d 696 (D.C. Cir. 1969) 108, 276
Amrep v. FTC, 768 F.2d 1171 (10th Cir. 1985) 353
Anderson v. Butz, 550 F.2d 459 (9th Cir. 1977).................... 3, 4
Anderson v. Dep't of Treasury, 648 F.2d 1 (D.C. Cir. 1979).................... 247
Anderson v. HHS, 907 F.2d 936 (10th Cir. 1990) 86, 87, 89, 95
Andrews v. DOJ, 769 F. Supp. 314 (E.D. Mo. 1991).................... 138
Andrews v. VA, 838 F.2d 418 (10th Cir. 1988) 337
Animal Legal Defense Fund, Inc. v. Shalala, 104 F.3d 424 (D.C. Cir. 1997) 365, 368
Antonelli v. FBI, 721 F.2d 615 (7th Cir. 1983) 181
Arabian Shield Development Co. v. CIA, No. 3-98-0624 (D.N.D. Tex. 1999).................... 49
Archer v. HHS, 710 F. Supp. 909 (S.D.N.Y. 1989).................... 63
Arenberg v. DEA, 849 F.2d 579 (11th Cir. 1988) 170
Arieff v. Department of the Navy, 712 F.2d 1462 (D.C. Cir. 1983)... 45, 97, 125, 129, 130, 131, 144, 159, 219, 294
Armstrong v. Bush, 721 F. Supp. 343 (D.D.C. 1989).................... 216
Armstrong v. Executive Office of the President, 810 F. Supp. 335 (D.D.C. 1993)....................208, 209, 216
Armstrong v. Executive Office of the President, 877 F. Supp. 750 (D.D.C. 1995).................... 207

Armstrong v. Executive Office of the President, 90 F.3d 556 (D.C. Cir. 1996)....................................199
Armstrong v. Executive Office of the President, 97 F.3d 575 (D.C. Cir. 1996)....................................157
Army Times Publ'g Co. v. Department of the Air Force, 998 F.2d 1067 (D.C. Cir. 1993)....................110
Army Times Publ'g Co. v. Department of the Air Force, No. 90-1383 (D.D.C. 1995)..........................110
Army Times Publ'g Co. v. Department of the Army, 684 F. Supp. 720 (D.D.C. 1988).............................65
Aronson v. HUD, 822 F.2d 182 (1st Cir. 1987) 144, 149, 156
Aronson v. HUD, 866 F.2d 1 (1st Cir. 1989) 244
Aronson v. HUD, No. 88-1188-S (Apr. 29, 1991)...144
Aronson v. IRS, 767 F. Supp. 378 (D. Mass. 1991)...137, 144, 154
Artesian Industries, Inc. v. HHS, 646 F. Supp. 1004 (D.D.C. 1986)..89, 123
Arthur Andersen Inc. v. IRS, 679 F.2d 254 (D.C. Cir. 1982) 108
Arthur Andersen, Inc. v. IRS, 514 F. Supp. 1173 (D.D.C. 1981) 81
Ash Grove Cement Co. v. FTC, 511 F.2d 815, 817-18 (D.C. Cir. 1975)..64
Assassination Archives & Research Center v. DOJ, 43 F.3d 1542 (D.C. Cir. 1995) 37, 214
Assembly of State of California v. Department of Commerce, 968 F.2d 916 (9th Cir. 1992).........113, 114
Associated Dry Goods Corp. v. NLRB, 455 F. Supp. 802 (S.D.N.Y. 1978)..................................185, 217
Associated General Contractors, Northern Nevada Chapter v. EPA, 488 F. Supp. 861 (D. Nev. 1980) 248
Association of American Physicians and Surgeons v. Hillary Rodham Clinton, 997 F.2d 898 (D.C. Cir. 1993)..366
Association of Retired R.R. Workers v. U.S. R.R. Retirement Board, 830 F.2d 331 (D.C. Cir. 1987).....68, 76, 80
AT&T Information Systems v. GSA, 627 F. Supp. 1396 (D.D.C. 1986) 86, 94
AT&T Information Systems v. GSA, 810 F.2d 1233 (D.C. Cir. 1987) 103
Audubon Society v. U.S. Forest Service, 107 F.3d 1201 (10th Cir. 1997)..58
Aug v. National Railroad Passenger Corp., 425 F. Supp. 946 (D.D.C. 1976).......................................201
Aviation Consumer Action Project v. CAB, 412 F. Supp. 1028 (D.D.C. 1976)...82
Aviation Consumer Action Project v. Washburn, 535 F.2d 101 (D.C. Cir. 1976)................................373
Aviation Data Service v. FAA, 687 F.2d 1319 (10th Cir. 1982)..243
Avondale Indus., Inc. v. NLRB, 90 F.3d 955 (5th Cir. 1996)...129, 141, 148, 156
Badhwar v. Department of the Air Force, 629 F. Supp. 478 (D.D.C. 1986) 247, 249
Badhwar v. Department of the Air Force, 829 F.2d 182 (D.C. Cir. 1987)....................................118, 133
Baez v. DOJ, 647 F.2d 1328 (D.C. Cir. 1980) 40, 41, 49, 50, 181, 184, 189
Baez v. DOJ, 684 F.2d 999 (D.C. Cir. 1982) 252
Baizer v. Department of the Air Force, 1995 WL 1254643 (N.D. Ca. March 10, 1995) 214
Baker v. CIA, 580 F.2d 664 (D.C. Cir. 1978)..72
Baker v. Department of the Navy, 814 F.2d 1381 (9th Cir. 1987)..307, 326
Baldridge v. Shapiro, 455 U.S. 345 (1982)..71, 267, 268, 316

Table of Cases

Baltimore Sun v. Marshals Serv., 131 F. Supp. 2d 725 (D. Md. 2001) 141, 148
Barney v. IRS, 618 F.2d 1268 (8th Cir. 1980) 175
Barrett v. Bureau of Customs, 651 F.2d 1087 (5th Cir. 1981) 251, 339
Bartell v. FAA, 725 F.2d 1403 (D.C. Cir. 1984) 305, 311, 312, 314
Bartholdi Cable Co. v. FCC, 114 F.3d 274 (D.C. Cir. 1997) 100, 148, 160
Barvick v. Cisneros, 941 F. Supp. 1015 (D. Kan. 1996) 137
Bast v. DOJ, 665 F.2d 1251 (D.C. Cir. 1981) 154, 161, 183
Bavido v. Apfel, 215 F.3d 743 (7th Cir. 2000) 325
Bazier v. U.S. Department of the Air Force, 887 F. Supp. 225 (N.D. Ca. 1995) 210
Beard v. Espy, 76 F.3d 384, 1995 WL 792071 (9th Cir. Dec. 11, 1995) 132
Beauman v. FBI, No. 92-7603 (C.D. Cal. Apr. 28, 1993) 254
Beck v. DOJ, 997 F.2d 1489 (D.C. Cir. 1993) 146, 181
Becker v. IRS, 34 F.3d 398 (7th Cir. 1994) 323
Bell v. United States, 563 F.2d 484 (1st Cir. 1977) 41
Beller v. Middendorf, 632 F.2d 788 (9th Cir. 1980) 313
Benavides v. Bureau of Prisons, 993 F.2d 257 (D.C. Cir. 1993) 251
Benavides v. Bureau of Prisons, 995 F.2d 269 (D.C. Cir. 1993) 325
Benavides v. DEA, 968 F.2d 1243 (D.C. Cir. 1992) 254
Bennett v. DEA, 155 F. Supp. 2d 36 (D.D.C. 1999) 189
Benson v. GSA, 289 F. Supp. 590 (W.D. Wash. 1968) 95
Berends v. Butz, 357 F. Supp. 143, (D. Minn. 1973) 4
Berg v. Commodity Futures Trading Commission, 93C6741 (N.D. Ill. 1994) 58
Bergman v. United States, 751 F.2d 314 (10th Cir. 1984) 333
Bernson v. ICC, 625 F. Supp. 10 (D. Mass. 1984) 326
Berry v. DOJ, 612 F. Supp. 45 (D. Ariz. 1985) 69
Berry v. DOJ, 733 F.2d 1343 (9th Cir. 1984) 76, 127, 213
Better Government Ass'n v. Department of State, 780 F.2d 86 (D.C. Cir. 1986) 231, 277, 278
Bettersworth v. FDIC, 248 F.3d 386 (5th Cir. 2001) 307
Bevis v. Department of State, 801 F.2d 1386 (D.C. Cir. 1986) 170, 175
Biberman v. FBI, 496 F. Supp. 263 (S.D.N.Y. 1980) 248
Bibles v. Oregon Natural Desert Ass'n, 519 U.S. 355 (1997) 142, 152, 157
Bigelow v. Department of Defense, 217 F.3d 875 (D.C. Cir. 2000) 313
Binion v. DOJ, 695 F.2d 1189 (9th Cir. 1983) 169
Birkland v. Rotary Plaza, Inc., 643 F. Supp. 223 (N.D. Cal. 1986) 243
Black Hills Alliance v. U.S. Forest Service, 603 F. Supp. 117 (D.S.D. 1984) 97, 197
Blakey v. DOJ, 549 F. Supp. 362 (D.D.C. 1982) 234, 235
Blazy v. Tenet, 194 F.3d 90 (D.C. Cir. 1999) 340
Blevins v. Plummer, 613 F.2d 767 (9th Cir. 1980) 326

Blue v. Bureau of Prisons, 570 F.2d 529 (5th Cir. 1978) 240, 243, 244

Blue v. Bureau of Prisons, No. C75-2092A (N.D. Ga. Aug. 23, 1978)....................235

Board of Trade v. Commodity Futures Trading Comm'n, 627 F.2d 392 (D.C. Cir. 1980)..85, 87, 90, 126, 132, 140

Bongiorno v. Reno, No. 95-72143, 1996 WL 426451 (E.D. Mich. Mar. 19, 1996) 149

Bonner v. Department of State, 928 F.2d 1148 (D.C. Cir. 1991) 292, 293

Borrell v. United States International Communications Agency, 682 F.2d 981 (D.C. Cir. 1982)..........269

Bowen v. FDA, 925 F.2d 1225 (9th Cir. 1991)....................88

Bowers v. DOJ, 930 F.2d 350 (4th Cir. 1991)....................48

Bowyer v. Department of the Air Force, 875 F.2d 632 (7th Cir. 1989)....................333

Boyd v. Secretary of the Navy, 709 F.2d 684 (11th Cir. 1983)....................307, 308, 321, 322

Brady v. Maryland, 373 U.S. 83 (1963) 271

Braintree Electric Light Department v. DOE, 494 F. Supp. 287 (D.D.C. 1980)....................97, 240

Branch v. FBI, 658 F. Supp. 204 (D.D.C. 1987)....................42, 57, 287

Braniff Master Executive Council v. CAB, 693 F.2d 220 (D.C. Cir. 1982) 358

Brinton v. Department of State, 636 F.2d 600 (D.C. Cir. 1980)....................108, 285

Bristol-Myers Co. v. FTC, 424 F.2d 935 (D.C. Cir. 1970)....................163, 219

Bristol-Myers Co. v. FTC, 598 F.2d 18 (D.C. Cir. 1978)....................105, 106, 116

British Airports Authority v. CAB, 531 F. Supp. 408 (D.D.C. 1982) 217

British Airports Authority v. Department of State, 530 F. Supp. 46 (D.D.C. 1981) 76, 83

Britt v. Naval Investigative Service, 886 F.2d 544 (3d Cir. 1989)....................316

Broaddrick v. EOP, 139 F. Supp. 2d 55 (D.D.C. 2001) 200, 310

Brockway v. Department of the Air Force, 518 F.2d 1184 (8th Cir. 1975) 85, 88, 118, 120

Brookens v. United States, 627 F.2d 494 (D.C. Cir. 1980) 341

Brookwood Medical Center, Inc. v. Califano, 470 F. Supp. 1247 (N.D. Ga. 1979) 101

Brookwood Medical Center, Inc. v. Harris, 614 F.2d 1295 (5th Cir. 1980)....................101

Brown & Williamson Tobacco Corp. v. FTC, 710 F.2d 1165 (6th Cir. 1983)....................277

Brown v. FBI, 658 F.2d 71 (2d Cir. 1981) 130, 150, 155, 156, 314

Brown-Bey v. United States, 720 F.2d 467 (7th Cir. 1983) 333

Brownstein Zeidman and Schomer v. Department of the Air Force, 781 F. Supp. 31 (D.D.C. 1991)....120

Bruce v. United States, 621 F.2d 914 (8th Cir. 1980) 317, 333

Brumley v. Department of Labor, 767 F.2d 444 (8th Cir. 1985) 273

Buckhannon Bd. and Care Home, Inc. v. West Virginia Department of Health & Human Res., 532 U.S. 598 (2001) 240, 241, 242, 296, 339, 358

Buffalo Evening News v. SBA, 666 F. Supp. 467 (W.D.N.Y. 1987)....................92

Bureau of National Affairs v. President's Council of Advisors of Science and Technology, C.A. 92-1088 (D.D.C. 1993) 372, 374

Bureau of National Affairs, Inc. v. DOJ, 742 F.2d 1484 (D.C. Cir. 1984) 211, 212, 218

Table of Cases

Burge v. Eastburn, 934 F.2d 577 (5th Cir. 1991) 189
Burka v. Dept. of Health and Human Services, 87 F.3d 508 (D.C. Cir. 1996) 117
Burka v. HHS, 142 F.3d 1286 (D.C. Cir. 1998) 251, 280, 296
Burka v. HHS, 87 F.3d 508 (D.C. Cir. 1996) 209
Burke Energy Corp. v. DOE, 583 F. Supp. 507 (D. Kan. 1984) 97
Burke v. DOJ, 432 F. Supp. 251 (D. Kan. 1976) 251
Burnside-Ott Aviation Training v. United States, 617 F. Supp. 279 (S.D. Fla. 1985) 87
Burris v. CIA, 524 F. Supp. 448 (M.D. Tenn. 1981) 235, 238
Butler v. DOJ, No. 86-2255 (D.D.C. Feb. 3, 1994) 145, 184
Byrd v. EPA, 174 F.3d 239 (D.C. Cir. 1999) 377, 378
Californian Forestry Assoc. v. U.S. Forest Service, 102 F.3d 609 (D.C. Cir. 1996) 369
Camp. v. Pitts, 411 U.S. 138 (1973) 102, 103
Campaign for Family Farms v. Glickman, 200 F.3d 1180 (8th Cir. 2000) 102, 132, 138, 160
Campaign for Responsible Transplantation v. FDA, 186 F. Supp. 2d 29 (D.D.C. 2001) 292, 293
Campbell v. DOJ, 164 F.3d 20 (D.C. Cir. 1998) 133, 169, 183, 287, 292, 301
Campbell v. HHS, 682 F.2d 256 (D.C. Cir. 1982) 173, 176, 269, 294
Campbell v. U.S. Civil Serv. Comm'n, 539 F.2d 58 (10th Cir. 1976) 136
Canadian Javelin, Ltd. v. SEC, 501 F. Supp. 898 (D.D.C. 1980) 121, 186
Canal Refining Co. v. Corrallo, 616 F. Supp. 1035 (D.D.C. 1985) 86, 92
Canning v. DOJ, 848 F. Supp. 1037 (D.D.C. 1994) 43, 287
Caplan v. BATF, 445 F. Supp. 699 (S.D.N.Y. 1978) 168
Caplan v. BATF, 587 F.2d 544 (2d Cir. 1978) 59
Cappabianca v. U.S. Customs Service, 847 F. Supp. 1558 (M.D. Fla. 1994) 149
Capuano v. National Transportation Safety Board, 843 F.2d 56 (1st Cir. 1988) 2
Cargill v. Marsh, 902 F.2d 1006 (D.C. Cir. 1990) 335
Cargill v. United States, 173 F.3d 323 (5th Cir. 1999) 369, 371, 376, 377
Carl Zeiss Stiftung v. V. E. B. Carl Zeiss, Jena, 40 F.R.D. 318 (D.D.C. 1966) 105
Carlisle Tire and Rubber Co., v. U.S. Customs Service, 663 F.2d 210 (D.C. Cir. 1980) 270
Carlton v. Department of Interior, No. 97-2105 (D.D.C. Sep. 3, 1998) 282, 283
Carney v. DOJ, 19 F.3d 807 (2d Cir. 1994) 233, 234
Carson v. DOJ, 631 F.2d 1008 (D.C. Cir. 1980) 213
Carter v. Department of Commerce, 830 F.2d 388 (D.C. Cir. 1987) 159, 291
Carter v. Veterans Administration, 780 F.2d 1479 (9th Cir. 1986) 251, 252
Castaneda v. United States, 757 F.2d 1010 (9th Cir. 1985) 184
Cazalas v. DOJ, 709 F.2d 1051 (5th Cir. 1983) 245, 340
Cedars Nursing & Convalescent Center, Inc. v. Aetna Life & Casualty Insurance Co., 472 F. Supp. 296 (E.D. Pa. 1979) 101
Center for Auto Safety v. Cox, 580 F.2d 689 (D.C. Cir. 1978) 364, 365, 366

Center for Auto Safety v. DOJ, 576 F. Supp. 739 (D.D.C. 1983) 119, 173, 176
Center for Auto Safety v. EPA, 731 F.2d 16 (D.C. Cir. 1984) 110, 220, 221
Center for Auto Safety v. NHTSA, 244 F.3d 144 (D.C. Cir. 2001) 86, 90, 91
Center for Auto Safety v. NHTSA, 809 F. Supp. 148 (D.D.C. 1993) 138
Center for Auto Safety v. Tiemann, 414 F. Supp. 215 (D.D.C. 1976) 364, 365, 366
Center for National Policy Review on Race and Urban Issues v. Weinberger, 502 F.2d 370 (D.C. Cir. 1974) 163
Center for National Security Studies v. CIA, 711 F.2d 409 (D.C. Cir. 1983) 298
Center to Prevent Handgun Violence v. Dep't of Treasury, 981 F. Supp. 20 (D.D.C. 1997) 96, 142
Chamberlain v. Kurtz, 589 F.2d 827 (5th Cir. 1979) 136, 244
Chambers v. Klein, 419 F. Supp. 569 (D.N.J. 1976) 341
Chapman v. NASA (I), 682 F.2d 526 (5th Cir. 1982) 308
Charlotte-Mecklenburg Hospital Authority v. Perry, 571 F.2d 195 (4th Cir. 1978) 82
Cheek v. IRS, 703 F.2d 271 (7th Cir. 1983) 314
Chemical Mfrs. Ass'n v. Consumer Product Safety Commission, 600 F. Supp. 114 (D.D.C. 1984) 109
Chesapeake Bay Found. v. Department of Agriculture, 108 F.3d 375 (D.C. Cir. 1997) 245
Cheshire Hospital v. N.H.-Vt. Hospitalization Service, 689 F.2d 1112 (1st Cir. 1982) 4
Chevron Chemical Co. v. Costle, 443 F. Supp. 1024 n.4 (N.D. Cal. 1978) 86
Chevron Oil Co. v. Andrus, 588 F.2d 1383 (5th Cir. 1979) 5
Chicago Tribune Co. v. HHS, 1999 WL 299875 (N.D. Ill. May 4, 1999) 209
Chicago Tribune Co. v. HHS, No. 95 C 3917, 1997 WL 1137641 (N.D. Ill. Mar. 28, 1997) 130
Chilivis v. SEC, 673 F.2d 1205 (11th Cir. 1982) 122
Chong v. Drug Enforcement Administration, 929 F.2d 729 (D.C. Cir. 1991) 70, 75
Chrysler Corp. v. Brown, 441 U.S. 281 (1979) 6, 78, 99, 100, 101, 102, 160, 314
Chrysler Corp. v. Schlesinger, 565 F.2d 1172 (3d Cir. 1977) 99
Church of Scientology Int'l v. DOJ, 30 F.3d 224 (1st Cir. 1994) 71
Church of Scientology Int'l v. IRS, 995 F.2d 916 (9th Cir. 1993) 159, 168
Church of Scientology of California v. Department of the Air Force, No. 76-1008 (D.D.C. Apr. 12, 1978) 218
Church of Scientology of California v. DOJ, 612 F.2d 417 (9th Cir. 1979) 186, 189
Church of Scientology of California v. IRS, 792 F.2d 146 (D.C. Cir. 1986) 73, 74, 285
Church of Scientology of California v. U.S. Postal Service, 633 F.2d 1327 (9th Cir. 1980) 78
Church of Scientology of California v. U.S. Postal Service, 700 F.2d 486 (9th Cir. 1983) 243, 244
Church of Scientology v. Department of the Army, 611 F.2d 738 (9th Cir. 1979) 42, 44, 149, 151, 168, 169, 172, 221
Church of Scientology v. Harris, 653 F.2d 584 (D.C. Cir. 1981) 240, 241
Church of Scientology v. IRS, 484 U.S. 9 (1987) 74
Church of Scientology v. IRS, 816 F. Supp. 1138 (W.D. Tex. 1993) 159

Table of Cases

Church of Scientology, Western United States v. IRS, 769 F. Supp. 328 (C.D. Cal. 1991) 240

Church Universal & Triumphant, Inc. v. United States, No. 95-0163, 1995 WL 271578 (D.D.C. 1995) 160

CIA v. Sims, 471 U.S. 159 (1985) 42, 49, 69, 71, 72

Ciba-Geigy Corp. v. Mathews, 428 F. Supp. 523 (S.D.N.Y. 1977) 202

Citizens for Environ. Quality, Inc. v. Department of Agric., 602 F. Supp. 534 (D.D.C. 1984) 153

Citizens to Preserve Overton Park, Inc. v. Volpe, 401 U.S. 402 (1971) 102, 103

City of Chicago v. Dept. of Treasury, No. 00-3417 (D.N.D. Ill., Mar. 6, 2001) 173

City of Gillette, Wyo. v. FERC, 737 F.2d 883 (10th Cir. 1984) 4

City of Santa Clara v. Andrus, 572 F.2d 660 (9th Cir. 1978) 4

City of Santa Clara v. Kleppe, 418 F. Supp. 1243 (N.D. Cal. 1976) 4

City of Virginia Beach, VA v. Dept. of Commerce, 995 F.2d 1247 (4th Cir. 1993) 107

Clark-Cowlitz Joint Operating Agency v. FERC, 798 F.2d 499 (D.C. Cir. 1986) 345, 351

Clarkson v. IRS, 678 F.2d 1368 (11th Cir. 1982) 251, 252, 307, 321, 322, 323, 338

Claudio v. Social Sec. Admin., No. Civ. A. H-98-1911, 2000 WL 33379041 (S.D. Tex. May 24, 2000) 136

Claybrook v. Slater, 111 F.3d 904 (D.C. Cir. 1997) 375

Cleaver v. Kelley, 427 F. Supp. 80 (D.D.C. 1976) 275

CNA Fin. Corp. v. Donovan, 830 F.2d 1132 (D.C. Cir. 1987) 79, 92, 94, 95, 96, 100, 101, 103, 121

Coalition for Legal Services v. Legal Services Corp., 597 F. Supp. 198 (D.D.C. 1984) 354, 357

Coalition for Safe Power, Inc. v. DOE, No. 91-0078 (D.D.C. Sept. 10, 1991) 234

Coastal States Gas Corp. v. DOE, 617 F.2d 854 (D.C. Cir. 1980) 105, 106, 107, 109, 116, 117, 173, 176, 283, 295, 298

Cochran v. United States, 770 F.2d 949 (11th Cir. 1985) 147, 314

Cohen v. EPA, 575 F. Supp. 425 (D.D.C. 1983) 132, 176, 182

Coleman v. FBI, 13 F. Supp. 2d 75 (D.D.C. 1998) 133

Columbia Packing Co. v. Department of Agric., 563 F.2d 495 (1st Cir. 1977) 146

Comdisco, Inc. v. GSA, 864 F. Supp. 510 (E.D. Va. 1994) 92, 93, 102

Committee on Masonic Homes v. NLRB, 414 F. Supp. 426 (E.D. Pa. 1976) 180

Committee on Masonic Homes v. NLRB, 556 F.2d 214 (3d Cir. 1977) 127, 171, 213

Commodity News Serv., Inc. v. Farm Credit Admin., No. 88-3146 (HHG), 1989 U.S. Dist. LEXIS 8848 (D.D.C. July 31, 1989) 128, 132, 140, 152

Common Cause v. IRS, 646 F.2d 656 (D.C. Cir. 1981) 108, 234

Common Cause v. National Archives and Records Serv., 628 F.2d 179 (D.C. Cir. 1980) 152, 153, 182, 183

Common Cause v. Nuclear Regulatory Comm'n, 674 F.2d 921 (D.C. Cir. 1982) . 147, 345, 349, 350, 351, 352, 357

Communications Systems v. FCC, 595 F.2d 797 (D.C. Cir. 1978) 353, 358

Computer Prof'ls for Soc. Responsibility v. Secret Serv., 72 F.3d 897 (D.C. Cir. 1996)........150, 179, 188
Comstock International v. Export-Import Bank of the United States, 464 F. Supp. 804 (D.D.C. 1979) ..88
Congressional News Syndicate v. DOJ, 438 F. Supp. 538 (D.D.C. 1977) 137, 146, 153, 177, 183
Connelly v. Comptroller of the Currency, No. 4-84-3783 (S.D Tex., June 3, 1991)............................337
Connick v. Myers, 461 U.S. 138 (1983)..321
Conoco, Inc. v. DOJ, 521 F. Supp. 1301 (D. Del. 1981)...120, 218
Conoco, Inc. v. DOJ, 687 F.2d 724 (3d Cir. 1982)..109
Consolidated Aluminum Corp v. TVA, 462 F. Supp. 464 (M.D. Tenn. 1978).......................................358
Consumer Product Safety Commission v. GTE Sylvania, 447 U.S. 102 (1980)..........................75, 80, 83
Consumers Union v. Veterans Administration, 301 F. Supp. 796 (S.D.N.Y. 1969)...................85, 86, 88
Consumers Union v. Federal Reserve System, 410 F. Supp. 63 (D.D.C. 1975).....................................246
Consumers Union v. Heimann, 589 F.2d 531 (D.C. Cir. 1978)...193, 195
Consumers Union v. HEW, 409 F.2d 466 (D.C. Cir. 1976)..367
Continental Oil Co. v. FPC, 519 F.2d 31 (5th Cir. 1975)..90, 95
Continental Stock Transfer & Trust Co. v. SEC, 566 F.2d 373 (2d Cir. 1977)..90
Cook v. Watt, 597 F. Supp. 552 (D. Alaska 1984)..240
Cooper v. Department of the Navy, 558 F.2d 274 (5th Cir. 1977)..118, 122, 288
Copeland v. Marshall, 641 F.2d 880 (D.C. Cir. 1980)...246
Copus v. Roegeau, 504 F. Supp. 534 (D.D.C. 1980)...175
Core v. U.S. Postal Serv., 730 F.2d 946 (4th Cir. 1984)..137
Cortez III Service Corp. v. NASA, 921 F. Supp. 8 (D.D.C. 1996)...93, 102
Cotner v. U.S. Parole Comm'n, 747 F.2d 1016 (5th Cir. 1984)...213, 300
Cotton v. Adams, 798 F. Supp. 22 (D.D.C. 1992)...135, 146, 202
Cotton v. Heyman, 63 F.3d 1115 (D.C. Cir. 1995)...243, 245
Council for a Livable World v. Dept. of State, No. 96-1807 (D.D.C. Nov. 23, 1998)...............................39
County of Madison, N.Y. v. DOJ, 641 F.2d 1036 (1st Cir. 1981)..120, 121, 269
Covert v. Herrington, 876 F.2d 751 (9th Cir. 1989)...315, 337
Cox v. DOJ, 576 F.2d 1302 (8th Cir. 1978)..19, 56, 58, 64
Cox v. DOJ, 601 F.2d 1 (D.C. Cir. 1979)..59, 251
Crancer v. DOJ, 999 F.2d 1302 (8th Cir. 1993)...175, 285
Critical Mass Energy Project v. NRC (II), 975 F.2d 871 (D.C. Cir. 1992)...................90, 91, 92, 93, 101
Critical Mass Energy Project v. NRC, 830 F.2d 278 (D.C. Cir. 1987)................................88, 90, 92, 93
Crooker v. BATF, 670 F.2d 1051 (D.C. Cir. 1981)...166, 191
Crooker v. BATF, No. 80-1278 (D.C. Cir. 1980)...59, 61, 64
Crooker v. BATF, No. 85-0615 (D.D.C. Aug. 2, 1985)...174
Crooker v. Dep't of Treasury, 634 F.2d 48 (2d Cir. 1980)..243
Crooker v. Dep't of Treasury, 663 F.2d 140 (D.C. Cir. 1980)..251, 252
Crooker v. DOJ, 632 F.2d 916 (1st Cir. 1980)..251

Crooker v. Office of the Pardon Attorney, 614 F.2d 825 (2d Cir. 1980) 200, 202
Crooker v. U.S. Bureau of Prisons, No. 83-1838 (D.C. Cir. Apr. 10, 1984) 299
Crooker v. U.S. Parole Comm'n, 730 F.2d 1 (1st Cir. 1984) 213, 314
Crooker v. U.S. Parole Comm'n, 760 F.2d 1 (1st Cir. 1985) 76, 213, 300
Crooker v. U.S. Parole Comm'n, 776 F.2d 366 (1st Cir. 1985) 243
Crowell & Moring v. Department of Defense, 703 F. Supp. 1004 (D.D.C. 1989) 172
Crumpton v. Stone, 59 F.3d 1400, 1404 (D.C. Cir. 1995) 160
Cummings v. Department of the Navy, 116 F. Supp. 2d 76 (D.D.C. 2000) 333
Cummings v. Department of the Navy, 279 F.3d 1051 (D.C. Cir. 2002) 333
Cummock v. Gore, 180 F.3d 282 (D.C. Cir. 1999) 377
Cuneo v. Rumsfeld, 553 F.2d 1360 (D.C. Cir. 1977) 239, 240, 241, 243, 244, 246
Cunningham v. FBI, 501 F. Supp. 898 (D.D.C. 1980) 184
Cunningham v. FBI, 664 F.2d 383 (3d Cir. 1981) 251
Curcio v. FBI, No. 89-0941, 1990 U.S. Dist. LEXIS 14738 (D.D.C. Nov. 2, 1990) 300
Curran v. DOJ, 813 F.2d 473 (1st Cir. 1987) 166, 175
Currie v. IRS, 704 F.2d 523 (11th Cir. 1983) 74
D&W Food Center, Inc. v. Block, 786 F.2d 751 (6th Cir. 1986) 4
Dabney v. Reagan, 559 F. Supp. 861 (S.D.N.Y. 1982) 372
Daniels v. St. Louis VA Regional Office, 561 F. Supp. 250 (E.D. Mo. 1983) 25
Davin v. DOJ, 60 F.3d 1043 (3d Cir. 1995) 132, 133, 169, 286
Davis v. DOJ, 968 F.2d 1276 (D.C. Cir. 1992) 181, 283
Dayton Newspapers v. Department of the Air Force, 107 F. Supp. 2d 912 (S.D. Ohio 1999) 77, 159
DeBold v. Stimson, 735 F.2d 1037 (7th Cir. 1984) 251, 252, 336
Deering Milliken, Inc. v. Irving, 548 F.2d 1131 (4th Cir. 1977) 118, 119, 141, 149, 161
DeLaurentiis v. Haig, 528 F. Supp. 601 (E.D.Pa. 1981) 19
DeLaurentiis v. Haig, 686 F.2d 192 (3d Cir. 1982) 76
DeLorme Publ. Co. v. NOAA, 917 F. Supp. 867 (D. Me. 1996) 77, 217
Department of Defense v. FLRA, 510 U.S. 487 (1994) 131, 142, 152, 158, 314
Department of Defense v. FLRA, 964 F.2d 26 (D.C. Cir. 1992) 155
Department of Interior v. Klamath Water Users Protective Association, 531 US 425 (2001) 121
Department of State v. Ray, 502 U.S. 164 (1991) 127, 129, 131, 135, 142, 143, 153, 156, 159, 161
Department of State v. Ray, 908 F.2d 1549 (11th Cir. 1990) 143
Department of State v. Washington Post Co., 456 U.S. 595 (1982) 126, 130, 134, 135, 140, 155
Department of the Air Force v. FLRA, 838 F.2d 229 (7th Cir. 1988) 129
Department of the Air Force v. Rose, 425 U.S. 352 (1976) 1, 5, 7, 22, 55, 56, 87, 100, 125, 126, 129, 130, 135, 142, 144, 159, 161, 177, 178
Department of the Navy v. FLRA, 840 F.2d 1131 (3d Cir. 1988) 127
Department of the Navy v. FLRA, 975 F.2d 348 (7th Cir. 1992) 129

DePlanche v. Califano, 549 F. Supp. 685 (W.D. Mich. 1982)....306
Des Moines Register & Tribune Co. v. DOJ, 563 F. Supp. 82 (D.D.C. 1983)....244, 247
Deters v. U.S. Parole Comm'n, 85 F.3d 655 (D.C. Cir. 1996)....321
Detroit Free Press, Inc. v. DOJ, 73 F.3d 93 (6th Cir. 1996)....141, 145, 154
Detroit Free Press, Inc. v. DOJ, No. 93-74692 (E.D. Mich., Apr. 25, 1994)....181
Dettman v. DOJ, 802 F.2d 1472 (D.C. Cir. 1986)....273
Devine v. USA, 202 F.3d 547 (2d Cir. 2000)....313
Diamond v. FBI, 532 F. Supp. 216 (S.D.N.Y. 1981)....132, 185, 234
Diamond v. FBI, 548 F. Supp. 1158 (S.D.N.Y. 1982)....230, 238
Dickerson v. DOJ, 992 F.2d 1426 (6th Cir. 1993)....173
Dickson v. OPM, 828 F.2d 32 (D.C. Cir. 1987)....332, 336
Dickson v. OPM, No. 83-3503 (D.D.C. Aug. 27, 1991)....337
Diederich v. Department of the Army, 878 F.2d 646 (2d Cir. 1989)....325, 333
Diliberti v. United States, 817 F.2d 1259 (7th Cir. 1987)....333
DiPersia v. Railroad Retirement Bd., 638 F. Supp. 485 (D. Conn. 1986)....76, 156
Dirksen v. HHS, 803 F.2d 1456 (9th Cir. 1986)....63
Dismukes v. Department of the Interior, 603 F. Supp. 760 (D.D.C. 1984)....15, 114, 215
Ditlow v. Shultz, 517 F.2d 166 (D.C. Cir. 1975)....151
DiViaio v. Kelley, 571 F.2d 538 (10th Cir. 1978)....290
Dixie Fuel Co. v. Callahan, 136 F. Supp. 2d 659 (E.D. Ky. 2001)....246
Dobronski v. FCC, 17 F.3d 275 (9th Cir. 1994)....161
Doe v. DiGenova, 779 F.2d 74 (D.C. Cir. 1985)....317
Doe v. FBI, 718 F. Supp. 90 (D.D.C. 1989)....329, 337
Doe v. FBI, 936 F.2d 1346 (D.C. Cir. 1991)....321
Doe v. GSA, 544 F. Supp. 530 (D. Md. 1982)....311
Doe v. Naval Air Station, Pensacola, Fla., 768 F.2d 1229 (11th Cir. 1985)....315
Doe v. Sharp, 491 F. Supp. 346 (D. Mass. 1980)....341
Doe v. Stephens, 851 F.2d 1457 (D.C. Cir. 1988)....338
Doe v. United States Air Force, 812 F.2d 738 (D.C. Cir. 1987)....326
Doe v. United States Civil Service Comm'n., 483 F. Supp. 539 (S.D.N.Y. 1980)....305, 331
Doe v. United States, 781 F.2d 907 (D.C. Cir. 1986)....327
Doe v. United States, 821 F.2d 694 (D.C. Cir. 1987)....320, 334
Doherty v. DOJ, 596 F. Supp. 423 (S.D.N.Y. 1984)....19
Doherty v. DOJ, 775 F.2d 49 (2nd Cir. 1985)....221
DOJ v. Julian, 486 U.S. 1 (1988)....76, 213
DOJ v. Landano, 508 U.S. 165 (1993)....153, 187, 285
DOJ v. Provenzano, 469 U.S. 14 (1989)....324

DOJ v. Reporters Comm. for Freedom of the Press, 489 U.S. 749 (1989) 22, 66, 134, 144, 150, 151, 152, 155, 158, 161, 166, 177, 178, 180, 265, 285, 314
DOJ v. Tax Analysts, 492 U.S. 136 (1989) 205, 208, 209, 237, 277
Don Ray Drive-a-way Co. v. Skinner, 785 F. Supp. 198 (D.D.C. 1992) 60
Dong v. Smithsonian Institution, 125 F.3d 877 (D.C. Cir. 1997) 202
Dong v. Smithsonian Institution, 943 F. Supp. 69 (D.D.C. 1996) 202
Donham v. DOE, 192 F. Supp. 2d 877 (S. D. Ill. 2002) 260
Donovan v. FBI, 579 F. Supp. 1111 (S.D.N.Y. 1983) 170
Donovan v. FBI, 806 F.2d 55 (2d Cir. 1986) 48, 187
Donovan v. Wollaston Alloys, Inc., 695 F.2d 1 (1st Cir. 1982) 5
Dow Jones & Co. v. DOJ, 724 F. Supp. 985 (D.D.C. 1989) 115, 121
Dow Jones & Co. v. DOJ, 917 F.2d 571 (D.C. Cir. 1990) 279
Dow Jones & Co. v. DOJ, No. 94-0527, 1995 WL 6155 (S.D.N.Y. 1995) 133, 183
Dow Jones & Co. v. GSA, 714 F. Supp. 35 (D.D.C. 1989) 213
Dowty Decoto, Inc. v. Department of the Navy, 883 F.2d 774 (9th Cir. 1989) 100
Doyle v. Behan, 670 F.2d 535 (5th Cir. 1982) 311
Doyle v. DOJ, 494 F. Supp. 842 (D.D.C. 1980) 19
Doyle v. FBI, 722 F.2d 554 (9th Cir. 1983) 45, 291
Doyle v. Wilson, 529 F. Supp. 1343 (D. Del. 1982) 340
Dresser Industries, Inc. v. United States, 596 F.2d 1231 (5th Cir. 1979) 309
Dudman Communications Corp. v. Department of the Air Force, 815 F.2d 1565 (D.C. Cir. 1987) 111
Duffin v. Carlson, 636 F.2d 709 (D.C. Cir. 1980) 187, 329
Dunkelberger v. DOJ, 906 F.2d 779 (D.C. Cir. 1990) 181
Dunway v. Webster, 519 F. Supp. 1059 (N.D. Cal. 1981) 169, 190, 206
Durham v. DOJ, 829 F. Supp. 428 (D.D.C. 1993) 235
Durnan v. Department of Commerce, 777 F. Supp. 965 (D.D.C. 1991) 94
Durns v. Bureau of Prisons, 804 F.2d 701 (D.C. Cir. 1986) 118
East Tennessee Research Corp. v. TVA, 416 F. Supp. 988 (D.D.C. 1976) 279
Edison v. Department of the Army, 672 F.2d 840 (11th Cir. 1982) 336, 337, 338
Edmond v. U.S. Attorney, 959 F. Supp. 1 (D.D.C. 1997) 261, 275
Education/Instruccion v. HUD, 649 F.2d 4 (1st Cir. 1981) 243, 246
Edwards v. CIA, 512 F. Supp. 689 (D.D.C. 1981) 72
Ehm v. Amtrak Board of Directors, 780 F.2d 516 (5th Cir. 1986) 23
Ehm v. National R.R. Passenger Corp., 732 F.2d 1250 (5th Cir. 1984) 201, 310
Electronic Privacy Information Center v. DOJ, No. 00-1849 (JR), (D.D.C. 2000) 262
Electronic Privacy Information Center v. FBI, 865 F. Supp. 1 (D.D.C. 1994) 275
Ellsberg v. Mitchell, 709 F.2d 51 (D.C. Cir. 1983) 46
Ely v. U.S. Postal Service, 753 F.2d 163 (D.C. Cir. 1985) 235, 236

Emerson v. CIA et al, No. 99-0274 (TFH), 1999 U.S. Dist. LEXIS 19511 (D.D.C. 1999) 260
Emerson v. DOJ, 603 F. Supp. 459 (D.D.C. 1985) 181
Emery v. Laise, 421 F. Supp. 91 (D.D.C. 1976) 297
Emery v. Reinhardt, No. 76-1973 (D.C. Cir. Oct. 27, 1977) 297
Energy Research Foundation v. Defense Nuclear Facilities Safety Board, 917 F.2d 581 (D.C. Cir. 1990) 200, 346, 347
England v. Commissioner, 798 F.2d 350 (9th Cir. 1986) 322
Englerius v. Veterans Administration, 837 F.2d 895 (9th Cir. 1988) 333
Environmental Crimes Project v. EPA, 928 F. Supp. 1 (D.D.C. 1995) 279
Environmental Defense Fund v. EPA, Nos. 80-0360, 80-0362 (D.D.C., June 28, 1982) 211
Environmental Technology, Inc. v. EPA, 822 F. Supp. 1226 (E.D. Va. 1993) 92, 102
EPA v. Mink, 410 U.S. 73 (1973) 1, 8, 51, 52, 105, 106, 109, 219, 292
Epps v. DOJ, 801 F. Supp. 787 (D.D.C. 1992) 134
Erb v. DOJ, 572 F. Supp. 954 (W.D. Mich. 1983) 173
Essential Information, Inc. v. U.S. Information Agency, No. 134 F.3d 1165 (D.C. Cir. 1998) 77
Ethyl Corporation v. EPA, 25 F.3d 1241 (4th Cir. 1994) 110
Ettlinger v. FBI, 596 F. Supp. 867 (D. Mass. 1984) 229, 233, 234, 235, 236, 243, 276
Eudey v. CIA, 478 F. Supp. 1175 (D.D.C. 1979) 234
Evans v. Jeff D., 475 U.S. 717 (1986) 250, 251
Evans v. Sheraton Park Hotel, 503 F.2d 177 (D.C. Cir. 1974) 246
Exner v. FBI, 443 F. Supp. 1349 (S.D. Cal. 1978) 241
Exner v. FBI, 542 F.2d 1121 (9th Cir. 1976) 274, 298
Exxon Corp. v. FTC (II), 476 F. Supp. 713 (D.D.C. 1979) 116
Exxon Corp. v. FTC, 466 F. Supp. 1088 (D.D.C. 1978) 289
FAA v. Robertson, 422 U.S. 255 (1975) 67, 69
Fagot v. Fed. Deposit Ins. Corp., 584 F. Supp. 1168 (D. P.R. 1984) 195
Falcone v. IRS, 714 F.2d 646 (6th Cir. 1983) 251
Falwell v. EOP, 158 F. Supp. 2d 734 (W.D. Va, 2000) 200
Falzone v. Department of the Navy, No. 85-3862 (D.D.C. Oct. 16, 1986) 156, 158
Favish v. Office of Independent Counsel, 217 F.3d 1168 (9th Cir. 2000) 183
FBI v. Abramson, 456 U.S. 615 (1982) 161, 164, 171
FCC v. ITT World Communications, Inc., 466 U.S. 463 (1984) 347, 348, 349, 356
FDIC v. Dye, 642 F.2d 833 (5th Cir. 1981) 306, 312
Fedders Corp. v. FTC, 494 F. Supp. 325 (S.D.N.Y. 1980) 168, 175
Federal Open Market Committee of the Federal Reserve Bank v. Merrill, 443 U.S. 340 (1979) ...88, 105, 107, 113, 116, 117, 119, 120
Felch v. Air Florida, Inc., 866 F.2d 1521 (D.C. Cir. 1989) 299
Fendler v. U.S. Bureau of Prisons, 846 F.2d 550 (9th Cir. 1988) 320, 326, 328

Fendler v. U.S. Parole Comm'n, 774 F.2d 975 (9th Cir. 1985)....69, 299, 329
Fenster v. Brown, 617 F.2d 740 (D.C. Cir. 1979)....240, 243, 244, 246
Fensterwald v. CIA, 443 F. Supp. 667 (D.D.C. 1977)....292
Ferguson v. FBI, 762 F. Supp. 1082 (S.D.N.Y. 1991)....222
Ferguson v. FBI, 957 F.2d 1059 (2d Cir. 1992)....170
Ferri v. Bell, 645 F.2d 1213 (3d Cir. 1981)....21, 135, 145, 161
Fidell v. Commandant of the US. Coast Guard, No. 88-2922 (LFO) (D.D.C. May 31, 1989)....138
Fiduccia v. DOJ, 185 F.3d 1035 (9th Cir. 1999)....155, 275, 279, 285, 286, 291, 299
Field v. Brown, 610 F.2d 981 (D.C. Cir. 1989)....320
Fine v. DOE, 823 F. Supp. 888 (D.N.M. 1993)....147
Fine v. DOE, No. 88-1033, No. 89-0031 (D.N.M. June 23, 1991)....116
Firestone Tire & Rubber Co. v. Coleman, 432 F. Supp. 1359 (N.D. Ohio 1976)....190, 268
Fisher v. DOJ, 772 F. Supp. 7 (D.D.C. 1991)....106
Fitzgerald v. U.S. Civil Service Commission, 407 F. Supp. 380 (D.D.C. 1975)....248
Fitzgibbon v. AID, 724 F. Supp. 1048 (D.D.C. 1989)....3, 234
Fitzgibbon v. CIA, 578 F. Supp. 704 (D.D.C. 1983)....42
Fitzgibbon v. CIA, 911 F.2d 755 (D.C. Cir. 1990)....42, 47, 72, 73
Fitzgibbon v. CIA, No. 76-700 (D.D.C. Jan. 10, 1977)....230, 276
Fitzgibbon v. U.S. Secret Service, 747 F. Supp. 51 (D.D.C. 1990)....58, 289
Fitzpatrick v. IRS, 665 F.2d 327 (11th Cir. 1982)....312, 337, 340
Florida Association of Medical Equipment Dealers v. Aptel, 194 F.3d 1227 (11th Cir. 1999)....377
Florida House of Representatives v. Department of Commerce, 961 F.2d 941 (11th Cir. 1992)..113, 114, 122
Florida Medical Ass'n v. HEW, 479 F. Supp. 1291 (M.D. Fla. 1979)....71, 310
Flowers v. EOP, 142 F. Supp. 2d 38 (D.D.C. 2001)....200, 310
FLRA v. Department of Commerce, 962 F.2d 1055 (D.C. Cir. 1992)....136
FLRA v. Department of Defense, 975 F.2d 1105 (5th Cir. 1992)....158
FLRA v. Department of Defense, 977 F.2d 545 (11th Cir. 1992)....265
FLRA v. Department of Defense, 984 F.2d 370 (10th Cir. 1993)....158
FLRA v. Department of the Navy, 941 F.2d 49 (1st Cir. 1991)....138, 152, 156
FLRA v. Department of the Navy, 966 F.2d 747 (3d Cir. 1992)....158
FLRA v. Department of Treasury, 884 F.2d 1446 (D.C. Cir. 1989)....156, 158
FLRA v. Department of Veterans Affairs, 958 F.2d 503 (2d Cir. 1992)....129, 161
Fonda v. CIA, 434 F. Supp. 498 (D.D.C. 1977)....58
Food Chemical News v. Advisory Committee on the Food and Drug Administration, 760 F. Supp. 220 (D.D.C. 1991)....374
Food Chemical News v. Davis, 378 F. Supp. 1048 (D.D.C. 1974)....361, 365, 369, 372
Food Chemical News v. HHS, 980 F.2d 1468 (D.C. Cir. 1992)....374

Food Chemical News v. Young, 900 F.2d 328 (D.C. Cir. 1990) 363, 365
Ford v. West, 149 F.3d 1190 (10th Cir. June 12, 1998) 128, 135, 155
Formaldehyde Institute v. HHS, 889 F.2d 1118 (D.C. Cir. 1989)....121
Forsham v. Harris, 445 U.S. 169 (1980) 199, 205
Founding Church of Scientology of Washington v. NSA, 610 F.2d 824 (D.C. Cir. 1979).....45, 46, 68, 75, 288, 289, 290
Founding Church of Scientology of Washington v. Smith, 721 F.2d 828 (D.C. Cir. 1983)....58, 60, 61
Founding Church of Scientology v. Bell, 603 F.2d 945 (D.C. Cir. 1979)....42, 68, 286
Founding Church of Scientology v. Regan, 670 F.2d 1158 (D.C. Cir. 1981)....186, 189
Frankel v. SEC, 460 F.2d 813 (2d Cir. 1972).... 8
Frazee v. U.S. Forest Service, 97 F.3d 367 (9th Cir. 1996) 92, 95, 101, 102, 103
Friedman v. Bache Halsey Stuart Shields, Inc., 738 F.2d 1336 (D.C. Cir. 1984) 267
Friends of the Coast Fork, et al. v. Dept. of Interior, 110 F.3d 53 (9th Cir. 1997) 229
Fruehauf Corp. v. IRS, 566 F.2d 574 (6th Cir. 1977) 80, 81
Fruehauf Corp. v. Thornton, 507 F.2d 1253 (6th Cir. 1974) 267, 271
Frugone v. CIA, 169 F.3d 772 (D.C. Cir. 1999)....47, 49
Frye v. U.S. EPA, No. 90-3041 (D.D.C. Mar. 31, 1992)....244
FTC v. Grolier, Inc., 462 U.S. 19 (1983) 105, 115, 123, 179, 285
FTC v. Shaffner, 626 F.2d 32 (7th Cir. 1980) 324
Fulbright & Jaworski v. Department of the Treasury, 545 F. Supp. 615 (D.D.C. 1982) 217
Fund for a Conservative Majority v. Federal Election Commission, No. 84-1342 (D.D.C. 1985)..60, 190
Fund for Constitutional Gov't v. National Archives, 656 F.2d 856 (D.C. Cir. 1981)..68, 71, 81, 146, 153, 161, 177, 181, 182, 183, 241
Gaffney v. BATF, No. 84-1403 (D.D.C., May 13 and June 28, 1985)....174
Gale v. Andrus, 643 F.2d 826 (D.C. Cir. 1980) 201
Gallant v. NLRB, 26 F.3d 48 (D.C. Cir. 1994)....213
Gannett River States Publ. Corp. v. Bureau of Nat'l Guard, No. J91-0455(L), 1992 U.S. Dist. LEXIS 11287, 20 Media L. Rep. 1183 (S.D. Miss. Mar. 2, 1992)....154
Gannett Satellite Information Network, Inc. v. Department of Education, No. 90-1392, 1990 WL 251480 (D.D.C. Dec. 21, 1990)....138
Gardels v. CIA, 689 F.2d 1100 (D.C. Cir. 1982)....41, 46, 72
Gardner v. USA, 213 F.3d 735 (D.C. Cir. 2000)....326
Gates v. Schlesinger, 366 F. Supp. 797 (D.D.C. 1973) 372
GC Micro Corp v. Defense Logistics Agency, 33 F.3d 1109 (9th Cir. 1994) 96
General Dynamics Corp. v. Marshall, 572 F.2d 1211 (8th Cir. 1978)....101
General Electric Co. v. NRC, 750 F.2d 1394 (7th Cir. 1984) 79, 91, 96, 100, 103, 208
General Motors Corp. v. Marshall, 654 F.2d 294 (4th Cir. 1981) 101
Getman v. NLRB, 450 F.2d 670 (D.C. Cir. 1971) 85, 88, 91, 129, 151, 177

Table of Cases

Gilbey v. Department of Interior, No. 89-0801 (RCL), 1990 U.S. Dist. LEXIS 14021 (D.D.C. Oct. 22, 1990) ... 136
Giles Lowery Stockyards, Inc. v. Department of Agriculture, 565 F.2d 321 (5th Cir. 1977) ... 5
Gilmore v. DOE, 4 F. Supp. 2d 912 (N.D. Cal. 1998) ... 202, 216
Gilmore v. National Security Agency, 76 F.3d 386 (9th Cir. 1995) ... 276
Ginsberg, Feldman & Bress v. FEA, 591 F.2d 717 (D.C. Cir. 1978) ... 59
Giza v. Secretary of Health Ed. & Welfare, 628 F.2d 748 (1st Cir. 1980) ... 290
GMRI, Inc. v. EEOC, 149 F.3d 449 (6th Cir. 1998) ... 240, 243
Goland v. CIA, 607 F.2d 339 (D.C. Cir. 1978) ... 206, 289, 290
Goldberg v. Department of State, 818 F.2d 71 (D.C. Cir. 1987) ... 35, 40, 41, 222
Goldschmidt v. Department of Agriculture, 557 F. Supp. 274 (D.D.C. 1983) ... 176
Goldstein v. Office of Indep. Counsel, No. Civ. A. 87-2028TPJJM, 1999 WL 570862 (D.D.C. July 29, 1999) ... 145
Gould, Inc. v. GSA, 688 F. Supp. 689 (D.D.C. 1988) ... 172
Government Land Bank v. GSA, 671 F.2d 663 (1st Cir. 1982) ... 119
Greater Cleveland Welfare Rights Org. v. Bauer, 462 F. Supp. 1313 (N.D. Ohio 1978) ... 341
Green v. Department of Commerce, 468 F. Supp. 691 (D.D.C. 1979) ... 92, 97, 295, 298
Green v. Department of Commerce, 618 F.2d 836 (D.C. Cir. 1980) ... 78
Green v. FBI, No. 89-699-CIV-5-RB (E.D.N.C. Jan. 6, 1992) ... 3
Green v. Philbrook, 576 F.2d 440 (2d Cir. 1978) ... 340
Green v. United States, 8 F. Supp. 2d 983 (W.D. Mich. 1998) ... 134
Greenberg v. FDA, 803 F.2d 1213 (D.C. Cir. 1986) ... 96
Greenpeace U.S.A., Inc. v. EPA, 735 F. Supp. 13 (D.D.C. 1990) ... 128
Greentree v. U.S. Customs Service, 674 F.2d 74 (D.C. Cir. 1982) ... 79, 330
Gregory v. Federal Deposit Insurance Corporation, 631 F.2d 896 (D.C. Cir. 1980) ... 195
Greidinger v. Davis, 988 F.2d 1344 (4th Cir. 1993) ... 341
Grigsby Branford Co. v. A.H. Williams & Co., 869 F. Supp. 984 (D.D.C. 1994) ... 367
Ground Saucer Watch v. CIA, 692 F.2d 770 (D.C. Cir. 1981) ... 44
Grove v. CIA, 752 F. Supp. 28 (D.D.C. 1990) ... 30
Grove v. DOJ, 802 F. Supp. 506 (D.D.C. 1992) ... 149
Grumman Aircraft Engineering Corp. v. Renegotiation Board, 425 F.2d 578 (D.C. Cir. 1970) ... 88, 219
Grumman Aircraft Engineering Corp. v. Renegotiation Board, 482 F.2d 710 (D.C. Cir. 1973) ... 200, 202
GTE Sylvania, Inc. v. Consumers Union of the United States, Inc., 445 U.S. 375 (1980) ... 6, 24, 99, 277
Gulf & Western Industries v. United States, 615 F.2d 527 (D.C. Cir. 1979) ... 90, 94, 95, 96
Haase v. Sessions, 893 F.2d 370 (D.C. Cir. 1990) ... 333, 339
Hack v. DOE, 538 F. Supp. 1098 (D.D.C. 1982) ... 117
Hale v. DOJ, 99 F.3d 1025 (10th Cir. 1996) ... 188
Halkin v. Helms, 598 F.2d 1 (1978) ... 42

Halloran v. VA, 874 F.2d 315 (5th Cir. 1989)....180
Halperin v. CIA, 629 F.2d 144 (D.C. Cir. 1980)....41, 81
Halperin v. Department of State, 565 F.2d 699 (D.C. Cir. 1977) 7, 50, 242
Halperin v. NSC, 452 F. Supp. 47 (D.D.C. 1978)....42, 50, 222
Halpern v. FBI, 181 F.3d 279 (2d Cir. 1999)....273, 285, 288, 298
Hamilton Securities Group, Inc. v. Department of Housing and Urban Development, 106 F. Supp. 2d 23 (D.D.C. 2000) 273
Hanley v. DOJ, 623 F.2d 1138 (6th Cir. 1980) 311
Harbolt v. Department of State, 616 F.2d 772, 774 (5th Cir. 1980)....126, 135, 149
Hardy v. BATF, 631 F.2d 653 (9th Cir. 1980) 59
Hardy v. Department of Defense, No. CV-99-523-TUC-FRZ (D. Ariz. Aug. 27, 2001) 131, 136, 146
Harper v. United States, 423 F. Supp. 192 (D.S.C. 1976) 311, 336
Hass v. U.S. Air Force, 848 F. Supp. 926 (D. Kan. 1994) 320
Hastings v. Judicial Conference of the United States, 770 F.2d 1093 (D.C. Cir. 1985)....315, 338
Hatcher v. U.S. Postal Service, 556 F. Supp. 331 (D.D.C. 1982) 168
Hawkes v. IRS, 467 F.2d 787 (6th Cir. 1972)....55, 58, 64, 267
Hayden v. NSA, 608 F.2d 1381 (D.C. Cir. 1979) 41, 43, 45, 68, 75, 80, 287, 294
Heckman v. Olive, No. CV-88-2981, 1992 WL 390249 (E.D.N.Y. Dec. 9, 1992)....137
Hedley v. United States, 594 F.2d 1043 (5th Cir. 1979)....273
Heights Cmty. Cong. v. Veterans Admin., 732 F.2d 526 (6th Cir. 1984)....128, 134, 150
Hemenway v. Hughes, 601 F. Supp. 1002 (D.D.C. 1985)....21, 127, 135
Henke v. Department of Commerce, 83 F.3d 1453 (D.C. Cir. 1996) 312, 332
Hensley v. Eckerhart, 461 U.S. 424 (1983)....246, 247
Henson v. NASA, 14 F.3d 1143 (6th Cir. 1994) 338
Hercules, Inc. v. Marsh, 839 F.2d 1027 (4th Cir. 1988) 94, 96, 103, 209
Hernandez v. Alexander, 671 F.2d 402 (10th Cir. 1982) 313, 325, 327, 331
Hewitt v. Grabicki, 794 F.2d 1373 (9th Cir. 1986) 334
Hickman v. Taylor, 329 U.S. 495 (1947) 115
Hill v. Department of Agric., 77 F. Supp. 2d 6 (D.D.C. 1999)....132, 134, 154
Hill v. U.S. Air Force, 795 F.2d 1067 (D.C. Cir. 1986) 337
Hinton v. DOJ, 844 F.2d 126 (3d Cir. 1988)....285, 286
Hobart Corp. v. EEOC, 603 F. Supp. 1431 (S.D. Ohio 1984) 58, 64
Hobson v. Wilson, 737 F.2d 1 (D.C. Cir. 1984) 323, 326
Hoch v. CIA, 593 F. Supp. 675 (D.D.C. 1984)....42, 44, 58
Holland v. CIA, No. 91-1233 (D.D.C. Aug. 31, 1992)....137
Hollis v. Department of the Army, 856 F.2d 1541 (D.C. Cir. 1988)....313
Holly v. Acree, 72 F.R.D. 115 (D.D.C. 1976) 251, 297
Holly v. Chasen, 569 F.2d 160 (D.C. Cir. 1977)....251, 297

Holy Spirit Association v. CIA, 455 U.S. 997 (1982) 48
Holy Spirit Association v. CIA, 636 F.2d 838 (D.C. Cir. 1980) 208
Holy Spirit *Association v. FBI*, 683 F.2d 562 (D.C. Cir. 1982) 182
Honeywell, Inc. v. Consumer Product Safety Commission, 582 F. Supp. 1072 (D.D.C. 1984) 75
Hoover v. Department of the Interior, 611 F.2d 1132 (5th Cir. 1980) 105, 119, 120, 269
Hopkins v. Department of the Navy, No. 84-1868 (D.D.C. 1985) 64
Hopkins v. HUD, 929 F.2d 81 (2d Cir. 1991) 139, 143, 150, 156
Hospital and Physician Publ'g Inc v. Dept. of Defense, No. 98-4117 (D.S.D. Ill, June 22, 1999) 228
Houlihan v. OPM, 909 F.2d 383 (9th Cir. 1990) 335
Houston v. Dep't of Treasury, 494 F. Supp. 24 (D.D.C. 1979) 305
Howard Johnson Co. v. NLRB, 618 F.2d 1 (6th Cir. 1980) 127
Howard v. Marsh, 785 F.2d 645 (8th Cir. 1986) 313
Hrones v. CIA, 685 F.2d 13 (1st Cir. 1982) 43
Hubbard v. EPA, 809 F.2d 1 (D.C. Cir. 1986) 339
Hudson River Sloop Clearwater v. Department of the Navy, 891 F.2d 414 (2d Cir. 1989) 46, 47
Hudson v. Department of the Army, No. 86-1114, 1987 WL 46755 (D.D.C. Jan. 29, 1987) 158
Hudson v. Reno, 130 F.3d 1193 (6th Cir. 1997) 319
Hudson v. United States, 766 F.2d 1288 (9th Cir. 1985) 4
Hughes Aircraft Co. v. Schlesinger, 384 F. Supp. 292 (C.D. Cal. 1974) 94
Hulsey v. IRS, 497 F. Supp. 617 (N.D. Tex. 1980) 74
Humana of Virginia, Inc. v. Blue Cross of Virginia, 622 F.2d 76 (4th Cir. 1980) 101
Hunt v. CIA, 981 F.2d 1116 (9th Cir. 1992) 49, 72, 73
Hunt v. Commodity Futures Trading Commission, 484 F. Supp. 47 (D.D.C. 1979) 21, 75
Hunt v. FBI, 972 F.2d 286 (9th Cir. 1992) 161, 182
Hunt v. NRC, 611 F.2d 332 (10th Cir. 1979) 346, 347
Hunt v. U.S. Marine Corps, 935 F. Supp. 46 (D.D.C. 1996) 139
I.B.E.W. Local No. 41 v. HUD, 763 F.2d 435 (D.C. Cir. 1985) 142
I.B.E.W. Local Union No. 5 v. HUD, 852 F.2d 87 (3d Cir. 1988) 144, 156
Iglesias v. CIA, 525 F. Supp. 547 (D.D.C. 1981) 106, 184
Illinois Institute for Continuing Legal Education v. Department of Labor, 545 F. Supp. 1229 (N.D. Ill. 1982) 206
In Re A Motion for a Standing Order, No. 90-85 (U.S. Ct. Vet. App. July 2, 1990) 317
In Re DOJ, 950 F.2d 530 (8th Cir. 1991) 175, 176, 285
In Re DOJ, 999 F.2d 1302 (8th Cir. 1993) 176
In Re Powell, 851 F.2d 427 (D.C. Cir. 1988) 281
In Re Scott, 709 F.2d 717 (D.C. Cir. 1983) 279
In re Wade, 969 F.2d 241 (7th Cir. 1992) 135
In Re Wilton Chatman-Bey, 718 F.2d 484 (D.C. Cir. 1983) 279

Ingle v. DOJ, 698 F.2d 259 (6th Cir. 1983) 184
Institute for Policy Studies v. Department of the Air Force, 676 F. Supp. 3 (D.D.C. 1987) 63
Interco, Inc. v. FTC, 478 F. Supp. 103 (D.D.C. 1979) 95
Interco, Inc. v. FTC, 490 F. Supp. 39 (D.D.C. 1979) 101
International Brotherhood of Teamsters v. National Mediation Board, 111 L.R.R.M. (BNA) 2020 (D.D.C. 1982) 209
Investment Co. Institute v. FDIC, 728 F.2d 518 (D.C. Cir. 1984) 357
Irons & Sears v. Dann, 606 F.2d 1215 (D.C. Cir. 1979) 74, 80, 82
Irons v. Bell, 596 F.2d 468 (1st Cir. 1979) 170, 295
Irons v. Diamond, 670 F.2d 265 (D.C. Cir. 1981) 80
Irons v. FBI, 571 F. Supp. 1241 (D. Mass. 1983) 23, 277
Irons v. FBI, 811 F.2d 681 (1st Cir. 1987) 189
Irons v. FBI, 851 F.2d 532 (1st Cir. 1988) 189
Irons v. FBI, 880 F.2d 1446 (1st Cir. 1989) 189
Irons v. Gottschalk, 548 F.2d 992 (D.C. Cir. 1976) 68
Irons v. Parker, 434 U.S. 965 (1977) 68
Irwin Memorial Blood Bank v. American Nat'l Red Cross, 640 F.2d 1051 (9th Cir. 1981) 201, 333
Isley v. Executive Office for the U.S. Attorneys, 203 F.3d 52 (D.C. Cir. 1999) 299
Isley v. Executive Office for U.S. Attorneys, No. 96-0123 (JR) (D.D.C. Feb. 15, 1998) 134
ITT World Communications, Inc. v. FCC, 699 F.2d 1219 (D.C. Cir. 1983) 108, 109, 120
Ivanhoe Citrus Ass'n v. Handley, 612 F. Supp. 1560 (D.D.C. 1985) 132, 160
J. Roderick MacArthur Foundation v. FBI, 102 F.3d 600 (D.C. Cir. 1996) 322
J.P. Stevens & Co., Inc. v. Perry, 710 F.2d 136 (4th Cir. 1983) 174, 175
Jabara v. Webster, 691 F.2d 272 (6th Cir. 1982) 322
Jafari v. Department of the Navy, 728 F.2d 247 (4th Cir. 1984) 151
Jaffe v. CIA, 573 F. Supp. 377 (D.D.C. 1983) 190, 297
Jarrell v. U.S. Postal Service, 753 F.2d 1088 (D.C. Cir. 1985) 333
Jefferson v. Reno, 123 F. Supp. 2d 1 (D.D.C. 2000) 28, 280, 297
Jimenez v. FBI, 938 F. Supp. 21 (D.D.C. 1996) 275
John Doe Agency v. John Doe Corp., 493 U.S. 146 (1989) 171, 172
John Doe Corp. v. John Doe Agency, 850 F.2d 105 (2d Cir. 1988) 172
Johnson v. Dep't of Treasury, 700 F.2d 971 (5th Cir. 1983) 337
Johnson v. DOJ, 758 F. Supp. 2 (D.D.C. 1991) 271
Johnson v. DOJ, No. 85-714-SSH, 1991 WL 251940 (D.D.C. Nov. 13, 1991) 145
Johnson v. Georgia Highway Express, Inc., 488 F.2d 714 (5th Cir. 1974) 246
Johnson v. HEW, 462 F. Supp. 336 (D.D.C. 1978) 94, 97
Johnston v. NRC, 766 F.2d 1182 (7th Cir. 1985) 356
Jones v. FBI, 41 F.3d 238 (6th Cir. 1994) 169, 293

Table of Cases

Jones v. NRC, 654 F. Supp. 130 (D.D.C. 1987) 279
Jordan v. DOJ, 591 F.2d 753 (D.C. Cir. 1978) 22, 55, 56, 59, 64, 106, 107, 270, 299
Jordan v. DOJ, 691 F.2d 514 (D.C. Cir. 1982) 247
Joseph Horne Co. v. NLRB, 455 F. Supp. 1383 (W.D. Pa. 1978) 217
Journal-Gazette Publ'g Co. v. Department of the Army, No. F-89-147 (N.D. Ind. Jan. 8, 1990) 132
Joya-Martinez v. FBI, No. 91-1433, 1994 WL 118206 (D.D.C. Mar. 31, 1994) 139
Judicial Watch of Florida, Inc. v. DOJ, 102 F. Supp. 2d 6 (D.D.C. 2000) 139, 225
Judicial Watch of Florida, Inc. v. DOJ, 159 F. Supp. 2d 763 (D.D.C. 2001) 284
Judicial Watch v. Clinton, 76 F.3d 1232 (D.C. Cir. 1996) 366
Judicial Watch v. DOJ, 122 F. Supp. 2d 13 (D.D.C. 2000) 229, 230
Judicial Watch v. DOJ, 122 F. Supp. 2d 5 (D.D.C. 2000) 229
Judicial Watch v. DOJ, 133 F. Supp. 2d 52 (D.D.C. 2000) 228
Judicial Watch v. DOJ, 185 F. Supp. 2d 54 (D.D.C. 2002) 229, 230, 288
Judicial Watch v. DOJ, No. 00-745 (D.D.C. Feb. 12, 2001) 229
Judicial Watch v. DOJ, No. 99-2315 (D.D.C. Aug. 16, 2000) 229
Judicial Watch v. DOJ, Nos. 01-0639 and 01-0720 (D.D.C., Mar. 22, 2002) 230
Judicial Watch v. Export-Import Bank, 108 F. Supp. 2d 19 (D.D.C. 2000) 88
Judicial Watch v. General Services Administration, No. 98-2223 (D.D.C, Sept. 25, 2000) 230
Judicial Watch v. National Energy Policy Development Group, C.A. 01-530 (EGS) (July 11, 2002).. 376
Judicial Watch v. Rossotti, No. 01-1612, 2002 WL 535803 (D.D.C., Mar. 18, 2002) 229
Judicial Watch, Inc. v. United States Naval Observatory, 160 F. Supp. 2d 111 (D.D.C. 2001) 274
Judicial Watch, Inc. v. United States Naval Observatory, No. 01-1293 (D.D.C. 2001) 263
Judicial Watch, Inc., v. DOE, 191 F. Supp. 2d 138 (D.D.C. 2002) 263
Julian v. DOJ, 486 U.S. 1 (1988) 118, 119, 123
Julian v. DOJ, 806 F.2d 1411 (9th Cir. 1986) 118
Kacilauskas v. DOJ, 565 F. Supp. 546 (N.D. Ill. 1983) 175
Kaganove v. EPA, 664 F. Supp. 352 (N.D.Ill. 1987) 62
Kaganove v. EPA, 856 F.2d 884 (7th Cir. 1988) 60, 62, 63
Kahn v. United States, 753 F.2d 1208 (3d Cir. 1985) 4
Kalmin v. Department of the Navy, 605 F. Supp. 1492 (D.D.C. 1985) 307, 308
Kamman v. IRS, 56 F.3d 46 (9th Cir. 1995) 81
Kanter v. IRS, 496 F. Supp. 1004 (N.D. Ill. 1980) 81
Katz v. DOJ, 498 F. Supp. 177 (S.D.N.Y. 1979) 240
Katz v. National Archives & Records Admin., 862 F. Supp. 476 (D.D.C. 1994) 133, 155, 214
Kay v. Ehrler, 499 U.S. 432 (1991) 251, 340
Kaye v. Burns, 411 F. Supp. 897 (S.D.N.Y. 1976) 194
Keese v. United States, 632 F. Supp. 85 (S.D. Tex. 1985) 21
Kendland Co. v. Department of the Navy, 599 F. Supp. 936 (D. Me. 1984) 244

Kennedy v. Andrus, 459 F. Supp. 240 (D.D.C. 1978) 248, 339

Kewanee Oil Co. v. Bicron Corp., 416 U.S. 470 (1974) 86

Keys v. DOJ, 830 F.2d 337 (D.C. Cir. 1987) 43, 165, 169, 285, 287

Kilroy v. NLRB, 633 F. Supp. 136 (S.D. Ohio 1985) 121

Kimberlin v. DOJ, 139 F.3d 944 (D.C. Cir. 1998) 131, 295

Kimberlin v. DOJ, 788 F.2d 434 (7th Cir. 1986) 328

King v. Califano, 471 F. Supp. 180 (D.D.C. 1979) 312

King v. DOJ, 830 F.2d 210 (D.C. Cir. 1987) 11, 43, 49, 165, 169, 286, 287

King v. IRS, 684 F.2d 517 (7th Cir. 1982) 108

King v. Palmer, 950 F.2d 771 (D.C. Cir. 1991) 250

Kiraly v. FBI, 728 F.2d 273 (6th Cir. 1984) 57, 133, 155, 185, 189, 314

Kissinger v. Reporters Committee for Freedom of the Press, 445 U.S. 136 (1980). 20, 199, 205, 206, 276

Kleiman v. DOE, 956 F.2d 335 (D.C. Cir. 1992) 335

Knight v. CIA, 872 F.2d 660 (5th Cir. 1989) 49, 72, 73

Kooritzky v. Herman, 178 F.3d 1315 (D.C. Cir. 1999) 251

Kowalczyk v. DOJ, 73 F.3d 386 (D.C. Cir. 1996) 20, 274

Krebbs v. Rutgers, 797 F. Supp. 1246 (D.N.J. 1992) 341

Kreiger v. Fadely, 211 F.3d 134 (D.C. Cir. 2000) 334

Krikorian v. Department of State, 897 F.2d 461 (D.C. Cir. 1993) 289

Krikorian v. Department of State, 984 F.2d 461 (D.C. Cir. 1993) 110, 220, 222

Krowitz v. Department of Agriculture, U.S. Forest Service, 641 F. Supp. 1536 (W.D. Mich. 1986)....311, 312

Kruh v. GSA, 421 F. Supp. 965 (E.D.N.Y. 1976) 80

Kuehnert v. FBI, 620 F.2d 662 (8th Cir. 1980) 170

Kurzon v. HHS, 649 F.2d 65 (1st Cir. 1981) 129, 132, 139, 151, 153

Kurzon v. HHS, No. Civ. 00-395-JD, 2001 WL 821531 (D.N.H. July 17, 2001) 129, 139, 157

Kuzma v. IRS, 821 F.2d 930 (2d Cir. 1987) 252

Kuzma v. U.S. Postal Service, 725 F.2d 16 (2d Cir. 1984) 252

L & C Marine Transport, Ltd. v. United States, 740 F.2d 919 (11th Cir. 1984) 185

Lake v. Rubin, 162 F.3d 113 (D.C. Cir. 1998) 325

Lam Lek Chong v. DEA, 929 F.2d 729 (D.C. Cir. 1991) 291

Lame v. DOJ, 654 F.2d 917 (3d Cir. 1981) 159, 181, 184, 187

Lame v. DOJ, 767 F.2d 66 (3d Cir. 1985) 300

Lamont v. DOJ, 475 F. Supp. 761 (S.D.N.Y. 1979) 47

Landano v. DOJ, 956 F.2d 422 (3d Cir. 1992) 150, 180, 187

Landmark Legal Found. v. IRS, 267 F.3d 1132 (D.C. Cir. 2001) 74, 290

Landmark Legal Found. v. IRS, 87 F. Supp. 2d 21 (D.D.C. 2000) 141

Laningham v. U.S. Navy, 813 F.2d 1236 (D.C. Cir. 1987) 337

LaRouche v. DOJ, No. 90-2753 (HHG), 1993 WL 388601 (D.D.C. June 25, 1993) 140, 161
LaRouche v. FBI, 677 F.2d 256 (2d Cir. 1982) 100
LaRouche v. Kelley, 522 F. Supp. 425 (S.D.N.Y. 1981) 42
LaRouche v. Kelley, No. 75 Civ. 6010 (S.D.N.Y. 1979) 100
Larson v. CIA, 843 F.2d 1481 (D.C. Cir. 1988) 233, 235, 236
LaSalle Extension University v. FTC, 627 F.2d 481 (D.C. Cir. 1980) 240, 243, 244
Lawrence v. Bowsher, 931 F.2d 1579 (D.C. Cir. 1991) 251
Lawyers Committee for Human Rights v. INS, 721 F. Supp. 552 (S.D.N.Y. 1989) 47, 140
Leach v. Resolution Trust Corp., 860 F. Supp. 868 (D.D.C. 1994) 203
Lead Industries Association, Inc. v. OSHA, 610 F.2d 70 (2d Cir. 1979) 120
Lee Pharmaceuticals v. Kreps, 577 F.2d 610 (9th Cir. 1978) 75, 80, 92
Legal Aid Soc'y of Alameda County v. Shultz, 349 F. Supp. 771 (N.D. Cal. 1972) 20, 91, 218
Legal Aid Soc'y v. Schultz, 349 F. Supp. 771 (N.D. Cal. 1972) 153
Lepelletier v. FDIC, 164 F.3d 37 (D.C. Cir. 1999) 127, 131, 144, 157
Lesar v. DOJ, 636 F.2d 472 (D.C. Cir. 1980) 35, 41, 42, 49, 50, 57, 61, 171, 177, 184, 186, 189
Lessner v. Department of Commerce, 827 F.2d 1333 (9th Cir. 1987) 68, 76
Letelier v. DOJ, 6 Media L. Rep. (BNA) 2140 (D.D.C. 1980) 248
Levine v. United States, No. 73-1215-Civ-CA (S.D. Fla. 1974) 28
Lewis v. Glickman, 1996 WL 39398 (E.D. La. Jan. 31, 1996) 274
Librach v. FBI, 587 F.2d 372 (8th Cir. 1978) 191
Library of Congress v. Shaw, 478 U.S. 310 (1986) 249, 250
Lieverman v. DOJ, 597 F. Supp. 84 (E.D. Pa. 1984) 42, 57
Ligorner v. Reno, 2 F. Supp. 2d 400 (S.D.N.Y. 1998) 137
Ligouri v. Alexander, 495 F. Supp. 641 (S.D.N.Y. 1980) 327
Lilienthal v. Parks, 574 F. Supp. 14 (E.D. Ark. 1983) 31
Lindsey v. U.S. Bureau of Prisons, 736 F.2d 1462 (11th Cir. 1984) 209
Linn v. DOJ, No. 92-1406, 1995 WL 631847 at *21 (D.D.C. Aug. 22, 1995) 155
Lisee v. CIA, 741 F. Supp. 988 (D.D.C. 1990) 275
Lissner v. U.S. Customs Service, 241 F.3d 1220 (9th Cir. 2001) 131, 182
Local 2047, A.F.G.E. v. Defense General Supply Center, 423 F. Supp. 481 (E.D. Va. 1976) 311
Local 3, I.B.E.W. v. NLRB, 845 F.2d 1177 (2d Cir. 1988) 127
Lombardo v. Handler, 397 F. Supp. 792 (D.D.C. 1975) 362, 363, 365, 368
Londrigan v. FBI (I), 670 F.2d 1164 (D.C. Cir. 1981) 331
Londrigan v. FBI (II), 722 F.2d 840 (D.C. Cir. 1983) 331
Long v. Bureau of Economic Analysis, 646 F.2d 1310 (9th Cir. 1981) 81
Long v. IRS, 596 F.2d 362 (9th Cir. 1979) 214, 215, 221, 276
Long v. IRS, 742 F.2d 1173 (9th Cir. 1984) 70
Long v. IRS, 825 F.2d 225 (9th Cir. 1987) 215, 221

Long v. IRS, 932 F.2d 1309 (9th Cir. 1991) 245, 247
Lonsdale v. United States, 919 F.2d 1440 (10th Cir. 1990) 2
Los Alamos Study Group v. DOE, No. 97-1412 (D.N.M. July 22, 1998)....209
Lovell v. Alderete, 630 F.2d 428 (5th Cir. 1980)....243, 244, 297
Lybarger v. Cardwell, 577 F.2d 764 (1st Cir. 1978) 229
Lykins v. Asst. Attorney General, 608 F. Supp. 693 (D.D.C. 1984) 300
Lykins v. DOJ, 725 F.2d 1455 (D.C. Cir. 1984)....213, 277, 279, 294
M.A. Schapiro & Co. v. SEC, 339 F. Supp. 467 (D.D.C. 1972) 194
M/A-COM Information Systems, Inc. v. HHS, 656 F. Supp. 691 (D.D.C. 1986)....93, 121
Machin v. Zuckert, 316 F.2d 336 (D.C. Cir. 1963) 118
MacPherson v. IRS, 803 F.2d 479 (9th Cir. 1986) 322
Mada-Luna v. Fitzpatrick, 813 F.2d 1006 (9th Cir. 1987) 5
Madeira Nursing Ctr., Inc. v. NLRB, 615 F.2d 728 (6th Cir. 1980)....127
Mahler v. IRS, No. 79-3238 (D.D.C., Mar. 28, 1980) 248
Malizia v. DOJ, 519 F. Supp. 338 (S.D.N.Y. 1981)....57
Mallinckrodt Inc. v. West, 140 F. Supp. 2d 1 (D.D.C. 2000) 93, 102
Malloy v. DOJ, 457 F. Supp. 543 (D.D.C. 1978)....190
Manna v. DOJ, 51 F.3d 1158 (3d Cir. 1995) 184
Manna v. DOJ, 832 F. Supp. 866 (D.N.J. 1993) 136, 159
Manos v. Department of the Air Force, No. C-92-3986 MHP, 1993 U.S. Dist. LEXIS 1501 (N.D. Cal. Feb. 10, 1993)....137
Manuel v. VA Hospital, 857 F.2d 1112 (6th Cir. 1988)....308, 320, 324
Mapother v. DOJ, 3 F.3d 1533 (D.C. Cir. 1993)....110
Marathon LeTourneau Co., Marine Division v. NLRB, 414 F. Supp. 1074 (S.D. Miss. 1976) 217
Maricopa Audubon Society v. U.S. Forest Service, 108 F.3d 1082 (9th Cir. 1997) 58
Marks v. CIA, 590 F.2d 997 (D.C. Cir. 1978) 82
Marks v. DOJ, 578 F.2d 261 (9th Cir. 1978) 21
Maroscia v. Levi, 569 F.2d 1000 (7th Cir. 1977) 57, 61, 191
Marrera v. DOJ, 622 F. Supp. 51 (D.D.C. 1985)....46
Marschner v. Department of State, 470 F. Supp. 196 (D. Conn. 1979) 26
Martin Marietta Aluminum, Inc. v. Administrator, GSA, 444 F. Supp. 945 (C.D. Cal. 1977)....119
Martin v. Office of Special Counsel, 819 F.2d 1181 (D.C. Cir. 1987) 116
Martinez v. FBI, No. 82-1547 (D.D.C. 1983) 26, 190
Marzen v. HHS, 632 F. Supp. 785 (N.D. Ill. 1985)....210
Marzen v. HHS, 825 F.2d 1148 (7th Cir. 1987) 151, 153
Mason v. Callaway, 554 F.2d 129 (4th Cir. 1977) 21, 79
Matthews v. U.S. Postal Serv., No. 92-1208-CV-W-8 (W.D. Mo. Apr. 15, 1994)....128
May v. Department of the Air Force, 800 F.2d 1402 (5th Cir. 1986)....332

Maydak v. DOJ, 218 F.3d 760 (D.C. Cir. 2000) 285, 295, 299, 300
Maynard v. CIA, 986 F.2d 547 (1st Cir. 1993)....49, 72, 73
Mayo v. U.S. Government Printing Office, 9 F.3d 1450 (9th Cir. 1993).... 199
Mayock v. INS, 714 F. Supp. 1558 (N.D. Cal. 1989) 215, 276
McClain v. DOJ, 13 F.3d 220 (7th Cir. 1993)....233, 235, 236
McClellan Ecological Seepage Situation v. Carlucci, 835 F.2d 1282 (9th Cir. 1987) 12, 226, 227, 229, 232
McCoy v. Moschella, No. 89-2155, 1991 U.S. Dist. LEXIS 13618 (D.D.C. 1991).... 57
McCoy v. Weinberger, 386 F. Supp. 504 (W.D. Ky. 1974).... 95
McCutcheon v. HHS, 30 F.3d 183 (D.C. Cir. 1994).... 182
McDonnell Douglas Corp. v. EEOC, 922 F. Supp. 235 (E.D. Mo. 1996).... 102
McDonnell Douglas Corp. v. NASA, 180 F.3d 303 (D.C. Cir. 1999)....90, 93, 95, 100, 101, 102
McDonnell Douglas Corp. v. NASA, 895 F. Supp. 319 (D.D.C. 1995).... 103
McDonnell Douglas Corp. v. Widnall, 57 F.3d 1162 (D.C. Cir. 1995).... 103
McDonnell v. U.S., 4 F.3d 1227 (3d Cir. 1993)....68, 82, 132, 133, 280
McElrath v. Califano, 615 F.2d 434 (7th Cir. 1980) 340
McGehee v. Casey, 718 F.2d 1137 (D.C. Cir. 1983).... 35
McGehee v. CIA, 697 F.2d 1095 (D.C. Cir. 1983) 44, 205, 218, 277, 280, 295
MCI Worldcom v. GSA, 2001 U.S. DIST. LEXIS 20292 (D.D.C. 2001) 93, 102
McKay v. Fowler, No. 97-3127, 1997 WL 266717 (E.D. La. 1997) 341
McKay v. Thompson, 226 F.3d 752 (6th Cir. 2000) 341
McKenzie v. Bowen, 787 F.2d 1216 (8th Cir. 1986).... 4
McKenzie v. Kennickell, 645 F. Supp. 437 (D.D.C. 1986) 250
McLaughlin v. Sessions, No. 92-0454 (JHG), 1993 U.S. Dist. LEXIS 13817 (D.D.C. Sept. 22, 1993) 146
Mead Data Central, Inc. v. Department of the Air Force (II), 575 F.2d 932 (D.C. Cir. 1978) 115
Mead Data Central, Inc. v. Department of the Air Force, 402 F. Supp. 460 (D.D.C. 1974).... 32
Mead Data Central, Inc. v. Department of the Air Force, 566 F.2d 242 (D.C. Cir. 1977)....109, 110, 111, 220, 221
Media Access Project v. Federal Communications Comm'n, 883 F.2d 1063 (D.C. Cir. 1989).... 224
Medina-Hincapie v. Department of State, 700 F.2d 737 (D.C. Cir. 1983).... 76
Meeropol v. Meese, 790 F.2d 942 (D.C. Cir. 1986) 21, 44, 49, 221, 293
Meeropol v. Smith, No. 75-1121 (D.D.C. 1984) 57
Mehl v. United States Environmental Protection Agency, 797 F. Supp. 43 (D.D.C. 1992).... 122
Mehta v. INS, 574 F.2d 701 (2d Cir. 1978) 4
Mermelstein v. SEC, 629 F. Supp. 672 (D.D.C. 1986).... 194
Mervin v. Bonfanti, 410 F. Supp. 1205 (D.D.C. 1976).... 325
Mervin v. FTC, 591 F.2d 821 (D.C. Cir. 1978)....116, 334
Metadure Corp. v. United States, 490 F. Supp. 1368 (S.D.N.Y. 1980).... 310

Metcalf v. National Petroleum Council, 553 F.2d 176 (D.C. Cir. 1977)....370
Meyer v. Bush, 981 F.2d 1288 (D.C. Cir. 1993)....201
Meyerhoff v. EPA, 958 F.2d 1498 (9th Cir. 1992)....77, 140, 374
Miami Herald Publ'g Co. v. Small Bus. Admin., 670 F.2d 610 (5th Cir. 1982)....154
Military Audit Project v. Casey, 656 F.2d 724 (D.C. Cir. 1981)....41, 44, 47, 49
Miller v. Bell, 661 F.2d 623 (7th Cir. 1981)....150, 185, 187, 298
Miller v. Casey, 730 F.2d 773 (D.C. Cir. 1984)....41, 46, 72
Miller v. Department of State, 779 F.2d 1378 (8th Cir. 1985)....40, 246, 289
Miller v. Webster, 456 U.S. 960 (1982)....185, 298
Miller v. Webster, 483 F. Supp. 883 (N.D. Ill. 1979)....185
Minier v. CIA, 88 F.3d 796 (9th Cir. 1996)....38, 285
Minnis v. Department of Agriculture., 737 F.2d 784 (9th Cir. 1984)....127, 149, 151
Misegades & Douglas v. Schuyler, 456 F.2d 255 (4th Cir. 1972)....242
Mittleman v. Dep't of Treasury, 773 F. Supp. 442 (D.D.C. 1991)....339
Mobil Oil Corp. v. EPA, 879 F.2d 698 (9th Cir. 1989)....116, 122
Mobil Oil Corp. v. FTC, 406 F. Supp. 305 (S.D.N.Y. 1976)....69
Molerio v. FBI, 749 F.2d 815 (D.C. Cir. 1984)....337
Moody v. IRS, 527 F. Supp. 535 (D.D.C. 1981)....80
Moody v. IRS, 682 F.2d 266 (D.C. Cir. 1982)....81
Moorefield v. U.S. Secret Service, 449 U.S. 909 (1980)....175
Morello v. DOJ, No. 90-1078 (D.D.C. Oct. 16, 1990)....236
Morgan v. DOJ, 923 F.2d 195 (D.C. Cir. 1991)....271, 277
Morrison-Knudson Co. v. Department of the Army, 595 F. Supp. 352 (D.D.C. 1984)....117
Morrow v. FBI, 2 F.3d 642 (5th Cir. 1993)....26, 275
Morton v. Ruiz, 415 U.S. 199 (1974)....4
Moskiewiez v. Department of Agriculture, 791 F.2d 561, 566 (7th Cir. 1986)....337
Mudge Rose Guthrie Alexander & Ferdon v. International Trade Commission, 846 F.2d 1527 (D.C. Cir. 1988)....77, 79
Muffoleto v. Sessions, 760 F. Supp. 268 (E.D.N.Y. 1991)....226
Mulqueeny v. National Comm'n on the Observance of International Women's Year, 549 F.2d 1115 (7th Cir. 1977)....370
Multnomah County Med. Soc. v. Scott, 825 F.2d 1410 (9th Cir. 1987)....149
Murphy v. Department of the Army, 613 F.2d 1151 (D.C. Cir. 1979)....122
Murphy v. FBI, 490 F. Supp. 1138 (D.D.C. 1980)....81
Murphy v. TVA, 559 F. Supp. 58 (D.D.C. 1983)....279
Na Iwi O Na Kupuna O Mokapu v. Dalton, 894 F. Supp. 1397 (D. Haw. 1995)....133
NAACP Legal Defense and Education Fund, Inc. v. DOJ, 612 F. Supp. 1143 (D.D.C. 1985)....119, 120, 121

Nader v. Baroody, 396 F. Supp. 1231 (D.D.C. 1975) 367
Nader v. Dunlop, 370 F. Supp. 177 (D.D.C. 1973) 373
Nadler v. DOJ, 955 F.2d 1479 (11th Cir. 1992) 161, 180, 187
Nadler v. FDIC, 92 F.3d 93 (2d Cir. 1996) 90, 92, 95
Nagel v. HEW, 725 F.2d 1438 (D.C. Cir. 1984) 322, 332
Nason v. Kennebec County CETA, 646 F.2d 10 (1st Cir. 1981) 4
National Anti-Hunger Coalition v. Executive Committee of the President's Private Sector Survey on Cost Control, 566 F. Supp. 1515 (D.D.C. 1983) 369, 370, 376
National Anti-Hunger Coalition v. Executive Committee of the President's Private Sector Survey on Cost Control, 711 F.2d 1071 (D.C. Cir. 1983) 361, 366, 367, 369, 370
National Ass'n of Atomic Veterans, Inc. v. Director, Def. Nuclear Agency, 583 F. Supp. 1483 (D.D.C. 1984) 131, 142, 147
National Ass'n of Concerned Veterans v. Secretary of Defense, 675 F.2d 1319 (D.C. Cir. 1982) 247
National Ass'n of Criminal Def. Lawyers v. DOJ, 182 F.3d 981 (D.C. Cir. 1999) 249
National Ass'n of Criminal Def. Lawyers v. DOJ, No. 97-CV-372 (GK) (D.D.C. Oct. 1, 1999) ... 128, 146
National Ass'n of Government Employees v. Campbell, 593 F.2d 1023 (D.C. Cir. 1978) 96, 97, 295
National Ass'n of Retired Fed. Employees v. Horner, 879 F.2d 873 (D.C. Cir. 1989) ... 129, 131, 142, 156
National Nutritional Foods Ass'n v. Califano, 603 F.2d 327 (2d Cir. 1979) 364, 365
National Parks and Conservation Ass'n v. Kleppe (II), 547 F.2d 673 (D.C. Cir. 1976) 94, 96, 132
National Parks and Conservation Ass'n v. Morton (I), 498 F.2d 765 (D.C. Cir. 1974) .. 85, 89, 90, 92, 93, 94
National Parks and Conservation Ass'n v. Morton (II), 351 F. Supp. 404 (D.D.C. 1975) 94
National Prison Project of ACLU Found. v. Sigler, 390 F. Supp. 789 (D.D.C. 1975) 137
National Resource Defense Council v. Nuclear Regulatory Commission, 216 F.3d 1180 (D.C. Cir. 2000) 348, 355
National Resources Defense Council v. Defense Nuclear Regulatory Safety Board, 969 F.2d 1248 (D.C. Cir. 1992) 352
National Resources Defense Council v. Herrington, 637 F. Supp. 116 (D.D.C. 1986) 367
National Security Archive v. Archivist of the United States, 909 F.2d 541 (D.C. Cir. 1990) 199, 374
National Security Archive v. CIA, No. 99-1160 (D.D.C. 2000) 48
National Security Archive v. Department of Defense, 880 F.2d 1381 (D.C. Cir. 1989) . 224, 226, 227, 228
National Security Archive v. FBI, 799 F. Supp. 872 (D.D.C. 1991) 111
National Senior Citizens Law Center v. Social Security Administration, 849 F.2d 401 (9th Cir. 1988) 241, 251
National Treasury Employees Union v. Dep't of Treasury, 656 F.2d 848 (D.C. Cir. 1981) 247, 340
National Treasury Employees Union v. Griffin, 811 F.2d 644 (D.C. Cir. 1987) 229, 233, 235, 236, 238
National Treasury Employees Union v. U.S. Customs Service, 802 F.2d 525 (D.C. Cir. 1986) 61, 63
National Wildlife Federation v. U.S. Forest Service, 861 F.2d 1114 (9th Cir. 1988) 112, 113

Nationwide Building Maintenance, Inc. v. Sampson, 559 F.2d 704 (D.C. Cir. 1977)....240
Natural Resources Defense Council v. DOE, 191 F. Supp. 2d 41 (D.D.C. 2002)....259, 263
Natural Resources Defense Council v. Pena, 147 F.3d 1012 (D.C. Cir. 1998)....376, 377
Navasky v. CIA, 499 F. Supp. 269 (S.D.N.Y. 1980)....72, 207
Neal-Cooper Grain Co. v. Kissinger, 385 F. Supp. 769 (D.D.C. 1974)....92
Nemacolin Mines Corp. v. NLRB, 467 F. Supp. 521 (W.D. Pa. 1979)....173, 189
Nemetz v. Dep't of Treasury, 446 F. Supp. 102 (N.D. Ill. 1978)....186, 331
Neugent v. Department of Interior, 640 F.2d 386 (D.C. Cir. 1981)....290
Nevas v. DOJ, 789 F. Supp. 445 (D.D.C. 1992)....110
New England Apple Council v. Donovan, 640 F. Supp. 16 (D. Mass. 1985)....245
New England Apple Council v. Donovan, 725 F.2d 139 (1st Cir. 1984)....183, 185
New England Medical Center Hospital v. NLRB, 548 F.2d 377 (1st Cir. 1976)....173
New York Gaslight Club v. Carey, 447 U.S. 54 (1980)....246
New York Times Co. v. NASA, 782 F. Supp. 628 (D.D.C. 1991)....133, 151, 159
New York Times Co. v. NASA, 920 F.2d 1002 (D.C. Cir. 1990)....127
Newport Aeronautical Sales v. Department of the Navy, No. 84-0120 slip op. (D.D.C. Apr. 17, 1985)248
News Group Boston, Inc. v. National R.R. Passenger Corp., 799 F. Supp. 1264 (D. Mass. 1992)....138
Niagara Mohawk Power Corp. v. DOE, 169 F.3d 16 (D.C. Cir. 1999)....92, 94, 95, 96, 283, 299
Nicholson v. Brown, 599 F.2d 639 (5th Cir. 1979)....4
Niemeier v. Watergate Special Prosecution Force, 565 F.2d 967 (7th Cir. 1977)....108
Nix v. United States, 572 F.2d 998 (4th Cir. 1978)....57, 61, 186, 189
Nixon v. Freeman, 670 F.2d 346 (D.C. Cir. 1982)....159
Nixon v. Sampson, 437 F. Supp. 654 (D.D.C. 1977)....244
NLRB v. Martins Ferry Hospital Association, 649 F.2d 445 (6th Cir. 1981)....174
NLRB v. Robbins Tire & Rubber Co., 437 U.S. 214 (1978)....173, 174, 179, 285, 291
NLRB v. Sears, Roebuck & Co., 421 U.S. 132 (1975) ... 2, 23, 64, 105, 106, 107, 108, 109, 115, 116, 267
Nolen v. Rumsfeld, 535 F.2d 890 (5th Cir. 1976)....28
North v. Walsh, 881 F.2d 1088 (D.C. Cir. 1989)....267, 269, 271
Northcross v. Board of Education of the Memphis City Schools, 412 U.S. 427 (1973)....239
Northrop Corp. v. McDonnell Douglas Corp., 751 F.2d 395 (D.C. Cir. 1984)....290
Northwest Coalition for Alternatives to Pesticides v. Browner, 941 F. Supp. 197 (D.D.C. 1996)....86, 95
Norwegian Nitrogen Products Co. v. United States Tariff Comm'n., 6 F.2d 491 (D.C. Cir. 1925)....86
Norwood v. FAA, 993 F.2d 570 (6th Cir. 1993)....116, 136, 159
NOW v. SSA, 736 F.2d 727 (D.C. Cir. 1984)....92, 160
Nuclear Control Institute v. Nuclear Regulatory Commission, 563 F. Supp. 768 (D.D.C. 1983)....46
Nunez v. DEA, 497 F. Supp. 209 (S.D.N.Y. 1980)....57
OCAW v. DOE, 141 F. Supp. 2d 1 (D.D.C. 2001)....244
Occidental Petroleum Corp. v. SEC, 873 F.2d 325 (D.C. Cir. 1989)....96, 103

O'Connor v. IRS, 698 F. Supp. 204 (D. Nev. 1988) 60
O'Connor v. United States, 1991 U.S. App. LEXIS 11989 (9th Cir. 1991) 60
O'Donnell v. United States, 891 F.2d 1079 (3d Cir. 1989)........ 339
Oglesby v. Department of the Army, 79 F.3d 1172 (D.C. Cir. 1996) 37, 38, 286
Oglesby v. Department of the Army, 920 F.2d 57 (D.C. Cir. 1990) 3, 26, 28, 30, 236, 254, 273, 274
Ohaegbu v. FBI, 936 F. Supp. 7 (D.D.C. 1996)........ 275
Oil, Chem & Atomic Workers Union v. DOE, 288 F.3d 452, (D.C. Cir. 2002)........ 339
Oil, Chemical & Atomic Workers International Union, AFL-CIO v. DOE, 141 F. Supp. 2d 1 (D.D.C. 2001)........280, 296
Oil, Chemical & Atomic Workers International Union, AFL-CIO v. DOE, 2002 WL 959825 (D.C. Cir. 2002)........240, 296
O'Kane v. Customs Serv., 169 F.3d 1308 (11th Cir. 1999) 125
OKC Corp. v. Williams, 461 F. Supp. 540 (N.D. Tex. 1978)........ 309
Olberding v. Department of Defense, 564 F. Supp. 907 (S.D. Iowa 1982) 311, 313
Oliva v. United States, 756 F. Supp. 105 (E.D.N.Y. 1991)........ 137
Olivares v. NASA, 103 F.3d 119 (4th Cir. 1996)........ 319
Onweiler v. United States, 432 F. Supp. 1226 (D. Idaho 1977) 4
Open America v. Watergate Special Prosecution Force, 547 F.2d 605 (D.C. Cir. 1976)22, 274, 275, 281, 298
Oregon Natural Desert Ass'n v. Department of the Interior, 24 F. Supp. 2d 1088 (D. Or. 1998)..132, 150
Orion Research Inc. v. EPA, 615 F.2d 551 (1st Cir. 1980) 94, 95
Ortiz v. HHS, 70 F.3d 729 (2d Cir. 1995) 188
Ortiz v. HHS, 874 F. Supp. 570 (S.D.N.Y. 1995) 139
Ott v. Levi, 419 F. Supp. 750 (E.D. Mo. 1976) 190
Outlaw v. Department of the Army, 815 F. Supp. 505 (D.D.C. 1993)........133, 145
Pacific Architects & Engineers, Inc. v. Department of State, 906 F.2d 1345 (9th Cir. 1990) 100, 101, 103
Pacific Architects &Engineers, Inc. v. Renegotiation Bd., 505 F.2d 383 (D.C. Cir. 1974)........ 97
Pacific Legal Foundation v. Council on Environmental Quality, 636 F.2d 1259 (D.C. Cir. 1980) 200, 347, 348, 349, 352, 353, 356
Pacific Molasses Co. v. NLRB, 577 F.2d 1172 (5th Cir. 1978)........127, 174
Painter v. FBI, 615 F.2d 689 (5th Cir. 1980)........ 79
Painting & Drywall Work Pres. Fund v. HUD, 936 F.2d 1300 (D.C. Cir. 1991) 143
Painting Indus. of Hawaii Market Recovery Fund v. Department of the Air Force, 26 F.3d 1479 (9th Cir. 1994)........139, 143, 150, 156, 161
Paisley v. CIA, 712 F.2d 686 (D.C. Cir. 1983)........42, 107, 206, 208, 218, 280, 295
Palmer v. Derwinski, No. 91-197 (E.D. Ky. June 10, 1992)........146, 154
Pan American World Airways, Inc. v. CAB, 684 F.2d 31 (D.C. Cir. 1982)........349, 352, 358
Parke Davis & Co. v. Califano, 623 F.2d 1 (6th Cir. 1980)........ 283

Parker v. DOJ, 934 F.2d 375 (D.C. Cir. 1991) 189
Parker v. EEOC, 534 F.2d 977 (D.C. Cir. 1976) 80
Parkridge Hospital, Inc. v. Califano, 625 F.2d 719 (6th Cir. 1980) 82, 101
Parks v. IRS, 618 F.2d 677 (10th Cir. 1980) 333, 336
Patterson v. FBI, 893 F.2d 595 (3d Cir. 1990) 43, 322
Patterson v. IRS, 56 F.3d 832 (7th Cir. 1995) 172
Payne Enterprises, Inc. v. United States, 837 F.2d 486 (D.C. Cir. 1988) 278, 281
Payne v. DOJ, 904 F.2d 695 (3d Cir. 1990) 189
Peck v. FBI, No. C79-486 (N.D. Ohio 1979) 20
Pederson v. Resolution Trust Corp., 847 F. Supp. 851 (D. Colo. 1994) 233
Pennies From Heaven, Inc. v. Dep't of Treasury, No. 88-1808 (D.D.C. Aug. 14, 1992) 144, 152
Pennsylvania v. Delaware Valley Citizens Cncl for Clean Air, 483 U.S. 711 (1987) 250
Pennzoil Co. v. Federal Power Commission, 534 F.2d 627 (5th Cir. 1976) 198
Peralta v. U.S. Attorney's Office, 136 F.3d 169 (D.C. Cir. 1998) 280, 295, 301
Peralta v. U.S. Attorney's Office, 69 F. Supp. 2d 21 (D.D.C. 1999) 136
Perlman v. DOJ, No. 00 CIV 5842 (JGK), 2001 WL 910406 (S.D.N.Y. Aug. 13, 2001) 135
Perri v. Department of the Treasury, 637 F.2d 1332 (9th Cir. 1981) 4
Perry v. Block, 684 F.2d 121 (D.C. Cir. 1982) 278, 289, 297
Perry v. FBI, 759 F.2d 1271 (7th Cir. 1985) 305, 311, 336
Perry v. State Farm Fire & Casualty Co., 734 F.2d 1441 (11th Cir. 1984) 317
Peterzell v. CIA, No. 85-2685 (D.D.C. July 11, 1986) 47
Peterzell v. DOJ, 576 F. Supp. 1492 (D.D.C. 1983) 170, 175
Petkas v. Staats, 501 F.2d 887 (D.C. Cir. 1974) 91
Petroleum Information Corp. v. Department of the Interior, 976 F.2d 1429 (D.C. Cir. 1992) 113, 114, 216
PHE, Inc. v. DOJ, 983 F.2d 248 (D.C. Cir. 1993) 60, 287, 291, 295
Philadelphia Newspapers Inc. v. Nuclear Regulatory Commission, 727 F.2d 1195 (D.C. Cir. 1984) .. 349, 351, 352
Philadelphia Newspapers, Inc. v. HHS, 69 F. Supp. 2d 63 (D.D.C. 1999) 137, 138
Phillippi v. CIA, 546 F.2d 1009 (D.C. Cir. 1976) 45, 46, 287, 289, 292, 294
Phillippi v. CIA, 655 F.2d 1325 (D.C. Cir. 1981) 6, 70, 73, 82, 222
Physicians Comm. for Responsible Med. v. Glickman, 117 F. Supp. 2d 1 (D.D.C. 2000) 140
Physician's Ed. Network v. HEW, 653 F.2d 621 (D.C. Cir. 1981) 370
Pickus v. U.S. Board of Parole, 507 F.2d 1107 (D.C. Cir. 1974) 202
Pierce & Stevens Chemical Corp. v. Consumer Product Safety Commission, 585 F.2d 1382 (2d Cir. 1978) 80
Pierce v. Underwood, 487 U.S. 552 (1988) 246
Pies v. IRS, 668 F.2d 1350 (D.C. Cir. 1981) 108

Table of Cases

Pilon v. DOJ, 73 F.3d 1111 (D.C. Cir. 1996).......... 313
Pineiro v. Pension Benefit Guaranty Corp., 2001 WL 1339000 (2d. Cir. Oct. 25, 2001).......... 298
Playboy Enterprises, Inc. v. DOJ, 516 F. Supp. 233 (D.D.C. 1981).......... 59
Playboy Enterprises, Inc. v. DOJ, 677 F.2d 931 (D.C. Cir. 1982).......... 109, 267
Playboy Enterprises, Inc. v. Meese, 746 F. Supp. 154 (D.D.C. 1990).......... 378
Polchowski v. Gorris, 714 F.2d 749 (7th Cir. 1983).......... 333
Pollack v. DOJ, 49 F.3d 115 (4th Cir. 1995).......... 273
Pollard v. FBI, 705 F.2d 1151 (9th Cir. 1983).......... 43, 45
Pope v. United States, 599 F.2d 1383 (5th Cir. 1979).......... 186
Porter County Chapter of the Izaak Walton League, Inc. v. Atomic Energy Commission, 380 F. Supp. 630 (N.D. Ind. 1974).......... 217
Poss v. NLRB, 565 F.2d 654 (10th Cir. 1977).......... 141, 154, 185
Powell v. DOJ, 569 F. Supp. 1192 (N.D. Cal. 1983).......... 248
Powell v. United States Bureau of Prisons, 927 F.2d 1239 (D.C. Cir. 1991).......... 220
Pratt v. Webster, 673 F.2d 408 (D.C. Cir. 1982).......... 165, 169, 171
Pressure Science, Inc. v. Kramer, 413 F. Supp. 618 (D. Conn. 1976).......... 86
Professional Programs Group v. Department of Commerce, 29 F.3d 1349 (9th Cir. 1994).......... 130, 139
Professional Review Org. of Florida, Inc. v. HHS, 607 F. Supp. 423 (D.D.C. 1985).......... 97, 109, 149
Proffitt v. Davis, 707 F. Supp. 182 (E.D. Pa. 1989).......... 347
Project on Military Procurement v. Department of the Navy, 710 F. Supp. 362 (D.C.C. 1989).......... 233, 234
Provenzano v. DOJ, 717 F.2d 799 (3d Cir. 1983).......... 79
Providence Journal Co. v. Department of the Army, 981 F.2d 552 (1st Cir. 1992).......... 108, 161
Providence Journal Co. v. FBI, 460 F. Supp. 762 (D.R.I. 1978).......... 21, 75, 132, 137
Providence Journal Co. v. FBI, 460 F. Supp. 778 (D.R.I. 1978).......... 153
Providence Journal Co. v. FBI, 602 F.2d 1010 (1st Cir. 1979).......... 136, 152, 185
Public Citizen Health Research Group v. FDA, 185 F.3d 898 (D.C. Cir. 1999).......... 85, 87, 95, 295
Public Citizen Health Research Group v. FDA, 539 F. Supp. 1320 (D.D.C. 1982).......... 87
Public Citizen Health Research Group v. FDA, 704 F.2d 1280 (D.C. Cir. 1983).......... 69, 78, 86, 87, 91, 95, 96, 226
Public Citizen Health Research Group v. FDA, 953 F. Supp. 400 (D.D.C. 1996).......... 97
Public Citizen Health Research Group v. HEW, 477 F. Supp. 595 (D.D.C. 1979).......... 78, 185
Public Citizen Health Research Group v. HEW, 668 F.2d 537 (D.C. Cir. 1981).......... 200, 202
Public Citizen v. Commission on the Bicentennial of the U.S. Constitution, 622 F. Supp. 753 (D.D.C. 1985).......... 366
Public Citizen v. Department of State, 11 F.3d 198 (D.C. Cir. 1993).......... 47
Public Citizen v. Department of State, 276 F.3d 634 (D.C. Cir. 2002).......... 277, 278
Public Citizen v. Department of State, 782 F. Supp. 144 (D.D.C. 1992).......... 122
Public Citizen v. DOJ, 111 F.3d 168 (D.C. Cir. 1997).......... 122

Public Citizen v. DOJ, 491 U.S. 440 (1989) 361, 363, 364, 370, 374, 376, 377
Public Citizen v. Farm Credit Administration, 938 F.2d 290 (D.C. Cir. 1991) 194, 195
Public Citizen v. HHS, 795 F. Supp. 1212 (D.D.C. 1992) 370
Public Citizen v. National Advisory Committee on Microbiological Criteria for Foods, 886 F.2d 419 (D.C. Cir. 1989) 369, 370, 371
Public Citizen v. National Economic Commission, 703 F. Supp. 113 (D.D.C. 1989) 350, 373, 376
Public Citizen, Inc. v. OMB et al., 127 F. Supp. 2d 1 (D.D.C. 2000) 259
Public Law Education Institute v. DOJ, 556 F. Supp. 476 (D.D.C. 1983) 244
Quarles v. Department of the Navy, 893 F.2d 390 (D.C. Cir. 1990) 111, 113, 114
Quinn v. Stone, 978 F.2d 126 (3d Cir. 1992) 306
Quinon v. FBI, 86 F.3d 1222 (D.C. Cir. 1996) 172, 188, 291
R.R. v. Department of the Army, 482 F. Supp. 770 (D.D.C. 1980) 326, 334
Radowich v. U.S. Attorney, 658 F.2d 957 (4th Cir. 1981) 187
Radowich v. U.S. Attorney, District of Maryland, 501 F. Supp. 284 (D. Md. 1980) 116
Railroad Com'n of Texas v. United States, 765 F.2d 221 (D.C. Cir. 1985) 352, 358
Railway Labor Executives' Ass'n v. Consolidated Rail Corp., 580 F. Supp. 777 (D.D.C. 1984) 201
Raven v. Panama Canal Co., 583 F.2d 169 (5th Cir. 1978) 309
Ray v. Department of State, 908 F.2d 1549 (11th Cir. 1990) 299
Ray v. DOJ, 852 F. Supp. 1558 (S.D. Fla. 1994) 143
Ray v. DOJ, 908 F.2d 1549 (11th Cir. 1990) 180
Ray v. Turner, 587 F.2d 1187 (D.C. Cir. 1978) 41, 42, 44, 45, 54, 68, 286, 292
RBR Corp. v. Browner, 924 F. Supp. 504 (S.D.N.Y. 1996) 101
RCA Global v. FCC, 524 F. Supp. 579 (D. Del. 1981) 208
Reed v. NLRB, 927 F.2d 1249 (D.C. Cir. 1991) 138, 152, 156
Reliance Elec. Co. v. CPSC, 924 F.2d 274 (D.C. Cir. 1991) 102
Renegotiation Board v. Bannercraft Clothing Co., 415 U.S. 1 (1974) 267
Renegotiation Board v. Grumman Aircraft Eng. Corp., 421 U.S. 168 (1975) 108, 109, 288
Reporters Committee v. DOJ, 816 F.2d 730 (D.C. Cir. 1987) 78, 165
Republic Airlines v. CAB, 756 F.2d 1304 (8th Cir. 1985) 353
Republic of New Afrika v. FBI, 645 F. Supp. 117 (D.D.C. 1986) 245
Retired Officers Ass'n v. Department of the Navy, 716 F. Supp. 662 (D.D.C. 1989) 65
Retired Officers Ass'n v. Department of the Navy, 744 F. Supp. 1 (D.D.C. 1990) 156
Reuber v. United States, 829 F.2d 133 (D.C. Cir. 1987) 321
Ricchio v. Kline, 773 F.2d 1389 (D.C. Cir. 1985) 207
Rizzo v. Tyler, 438 F. Supp. 895 (S.D.N.Y. 1977) 23
Robert Doe, a/k/a Virginia Privacy Litigation v. Herman, 1999 US Dist LEXIS 17302 (W.D. Va, Oct. 29, 1999) 341
Roberts v. HHS, No. 88-2041, 1988 U.S. Dist LEXIS 10162 (E.D. Pa. Sept. 9, 1988) 149

Roberts v. IRS, 584 F. Supp. 1241 (E.D. Mich. 1984)....... 64
Robles v. EPA, 484 F.2d 843 (4th Cir. 1973)....... 91, 151, 153, 154
Rocap v. Indiek, 539 F.2d 174 (D.C. Cir. 1976)....... 199, 201, 240, 296
Rockwell International v. DOJ, 235 F.3d 598 (D.C. Cir. 2001)....... 122
Rose v. United States, 905 F.2d 1257 (9th Cir. 1990)....... 337
Rosenfeld v. DOJ, 57 F.3d 803 (9th Cir. 1995)....... 145
Rosenfeld v. DOJ, 761 F. Supp. 1440 (N.D. Cal. 1991)....... 169, 180
Rosenfeld v. United States, 859 F.2d 717 (9th Cir. 1988)....... 249, 298
RSR Corp. v. Browner, 924 F. Supp. 504 (S.D.N.Y. 1996)....... 102
Ruckelshaus v. Monsanto Co., 467 U.S. 986 (1984)....... 86
Rural Housing Alliance v. USDA, 498 F.2d 73 (D.C. Cir. 1974)....... 95, 130, 136, 168, 180
Rush v. Department of State, 716 F. Supp. 598 (S.D. Fla. 1989)....... 209
Rushford v. Civiletti, 485 F. Supp. 477 (D.D.C. 1980)....... 180, 182
Rushforth v. Council of Economic Advisors, 762 F.2d 1038 (D.C. Cir. 1985)....... 200, 346, 356
Ryan v. DOJ, 595 F.2d 954 (4th Cir. 1979)....... 328
Ryan v. DOJ, 617 F.2d 781 (D.C. Cir. 1980)....... 109, 112, 120, 208, 209, 299
SafeCard Services, Inc. v. SEC, 926 F.2d 1197 (D.C. Cir. 1991)....... 109, 180, 289
Salisbury v. United States, 690 F.2d 966 (D.C. Cir. 1982)....... 41, 43, 45
Samble v. Department of Commerce, No. CV192-225, slip op. at 9-10 (S.D. Ga. Sept. 23, 1994)....... 137
Samuel Gruber Educ. Project v. DOJ, 24 F. Supp. 2d 1 (D.D.C. 1998)....... 132
Sands v. Murphy, 633 F.2d 968 (1st Cir. 1980)....... 189
Savage v. CIA, 826 F.2d 561 (7th Cir. 1987)....... 236
Savage v. FBI, No. 90-1110 (7th Cir. July 31, 1991)....... 236
Save Our Cumberland Mountains, Inc. v. Babbitt, 507 U.S. 911 (1993)....... 247
Save Our Cumberland Mountains, Inc. v. Hodel, 857 F.2d 1516 (D.C. Cir. 1988)....... 246
Save Our Cumberland Mountains, Inc. v. Lujan, 963 F.2d 1541 (D.C. Cir. 1992)....... 247
Save the Dolphins v. Department of Commerce, 404 F. Supp. 407 (N.D. Cal. 1975)....... 97, 214
Schaffer v. Kissinger, 505 F.2d 389 (D.C. Cir. 1974)....... 50, 288, 289
Schanen v. DOJ, 762 F.2d 805 (9th Cir. 1985)....... 300
Schartz v. IRS, 511 F.2d 1303 (D.C. Cir. 1974)....... 295
Schell v. HHS, 843 F.2d 933 (6th Cir. 1988)....... 111, 128, 130
Scherer v. Kelley, 584 F.2d 170 (7th Cir. 1978)....... 57, 186, 191
Scherer v. Webster, 440 U.S. 964 (1979)....... 57
Schiffer v. FBI, 78 F.3d 1405 (9th Cir. 1996)....... 268
Schiller v. NLRB, 964 F.2d 1205 (D.C. Cir. 1992)....... 63, 220, 295
Schlefer v. United States, 702 F.2d 233 (D.C. Cir. 1983)....... 107, 108, 109, 116
Schmanke v. U.S. Postal Service, No. 89-1551 (D.D.C. Jan. 4, 1990)....... 225, 235
Schmerler v. FBI, 696 F. Supp. 717 (D.D.C. 1988)....... 184

Schmerler v. FBI, 900 F.2d 333 (D.C. Cir. 1990) 184, 187
Schoettle v. Kemp, 733 F. Supp. 1395 (D. Haw. 1990) 156
Schonberger v. National Transp. Safety Bd., 508 F. Supp. 941 (D.D.C. 1981) 126
Schrecker v. DOJ, 254 F.3d 162 (D.C. Cir. 2001) 133
Schulte and Sun-Sentinel Co. v. Veterans Administration, No. 86-6251 (S.D. Fla 1996) 77
Schwaner v. Department of the Air Force, 698 F. Supp. 4, 6 (D.D.C. 1988) 65
Schwaner v. Department of the Air Force, 898 F.2d 793 (D.C. Cir. 1990) 58, 65
Schwarz v. Department of State, 172 F.3d 921, 1998 WL 700164 (D.C. Cir. July 29, 1998) 135
Schwarz v. USDA, No. 01-1464 (D.D.C. June 29, 2001) 281
Sears v. Dann, 425 U.S. 904 (1976) 80
Sears v. Gottschalk, 502 F.2d 122 (4th Cir. 1974) 80
Sears, Roebuck & Co. v. Dahm, 441 U.S. 918 (1979) 101
Sears, Roebuck & Co. v. Eckerd, 575 F.2d 1197 (7th Cir. 1978) 101
Sears, Roebuck & Co. v. GSA, 402 F. Supp. 378 (D.D.C. 1975) 160
Sears, Roebuck & Co. v. GSA, 553 F.2d 1378 (D.C. Cir. 1977) 96, 97, 295
Seegull Mfg. Co. v. NLRB, 735 F.2d 971 (6th Cir. 1984) 252
Seegull Mfg. Co. v. NLRB, 741 F.2d 882 (6th Cir. 1984) 244, 245, 252
Sellers v. Bureau of Prisons, 959 F.2d 1423 (D.C. Cir. 1992) 320
Senate of the Commonwealth of Puerto Rico v. DOJ, 823 F.2d 574 (D.C. Cir. 1987) 71, 107, 173
Seymour v. Barabba, 559 F.2d 806 (D.C. Cir. 1977) 70, 71
Shapiro v. Drug Enforcement Administration, 721 F.2d 215 (7th Cir. 1983) 79, 327
Sharyland Water Supply Corp. v. Block, 755 F.2d 397 (5th Cir. 1985) 85, 89, 95, 122
Shaver v. Bell, 433 F. Supp. 438 (N.D. Ga. 1977) 190, 191
Shaw v. FBI, 604 F. Supp. 342 (D.D.C. 1985) 233
Shaw v. FBI, 749 F.2d 58 (D.C. Cir. 1984) 166, 169, 186, 187, 189
Sheet Metal Workers Int'l Ass'n v. Air Force, 63 F.3d 994 (10th Cir. 1995) 139
Sheet Metal Workers' Int'l Ass'n, Local Union #19 v. Department of Veteran Affairs, 940 F. Supp. 712 (E.D. Pa. 1995) 143
Sheet Metal Workers Int'l Ass'n, Local Union #19 v. Department of Veterans Affairs, 135 F.3d 891 (3d Cir. 1998) 138, 144, 150, 299
Shell Oil Co. v. IRS, 772 F. Supp. 202 (D. Del. 1991) 122
Sherer v. Balkema, 840 F.2d 437 (7th Cir. 1988) 273
Sherman v. Department of the Army, 244 F.3d 357 (5th Cir. 2001) 136, 155, 221
Shermco Industries, Inc. v. Secretary of the Air Force, 452 F. Supp. 306 (N.D. Tex. 1978) 26, 31, 310
Shermco Industries, Inc. v. Secretary of the Air Force, 613 F.2d 1314 (5th Cir. 1980) 94, 95, 117
Shurberg Broadcasting of Hartford, Inc. v. FCC, 617 F. Supp. 825 (D.D.C. 1985) 351
Si v. Slattery, 864 F. Supp. 397 (S.D.N.Y. 1994) 5
Sierra Club Legal Defense Fund, Inc. v. Bibles, No. C92-1413 WD (W.D. Wa. February 17, 1993) 234

Silets v. FBI, 591 F. Supp. 490 (N.D. Ill. 1984) 132
Simm v. Department of Labor, No. 83-3780 (D.D.C. Mar. 21, 1984) 297
Simmons v. DOJ, 796 F.2d 709 (4th Cir. 1986) 39, 82, 290
Simon v. DOJ, 980 F.2d 782 (D.C. Cir. 1992) 292
Simon v. United States, 587 F. Supp. 1029 (D.D.C. 1984) 244
Simpson v. Vance, 648 F.2d 10 (D.C. Cir. 1980) 126, 135, 140, 154
Sims v. CIA (I), 642 F.2d 562 (D.C. Cir. 1980) 131, 132, 140
Sims v. CIA (II), 479 F. Supp. 84 (D.D.C. 1979) 3
Sinito v. DOJ, 176 F.3d 512 (D.C. Cir. 1999) 279
Skelton v. U.S. Postal Service, 678 F.2d 35 (5th Cir. 1982) 2, 105, 115
Sladek v. Bensinger, 605 F.2d 899 (5th Cir. 1979) 64, 168
Sloman v. DOJ, 832 F. Supp. 63 (S.D.N.Y. 1993) 232, 234
Smiertka v. Dep't of Treasury, 447 F. Supp. 221 (D.D.C. 1978) 307, 324, 325, 336
Smith v. National Transportation Safety Board, 981 F.2d 1326 (D.C. Cir. 1993) 4
Smith v. Nixon, 807 F.2d 197 (D.C. Cir. 1986) 326
Sofamor Danek Group v. Gaus, 61 F.3d 929 (D.C. Cir. 1995) 366
Solar Sources, Inc. v. United States, 142 F.3d 1033 (7th Cir. 1998) 285
Sonderegger v. Department of Interior, 424 F. Supp. 847 (D. Idaho 1976) 160
Soucie v. David, 448 F.2d 1067 (D.C. Cir. 1971) 85, 114, 120, 200
Southern Utah Wilderness Alliance, Inc. v. Hodel, 680 F. Supp. 37 (D.D.C. 1988) 147
Spannaus v. DOJ, 643 F. Supp. 698 (D.D.C. 1986) 278
Spannaus v. DOJ, 813 F.2d 1285 (4th Cir. 1987) 166, 175
Spannaus v. DOJ, 824 F.2d 52 (D.C. Cir. 1987) 30, 273, 278
Spirko v. United States Postal Service, 147 F.3d 992 (D.C. Cir. 1998) 279, 291
St. Hilaire v. DOJ, No. 91-0078 (D.D.C. Sept. 10, 1991) 235
St. Joseph's Hospital Health Center v. Blue Cross of Central New York, 614 F.2d 1290 (2d Cir. 1979) 101
St. Mary's Hospital v. Harris, 604 F.2d 407 (5th Cir. 1979) 101
St. Mary's Hospital v. Philadelphia Professional Standards Review Organization, Inc., No. 78-2943 (E.D. Pa. 1980) 202
St. Michael's Convalescent Hosp. v. California, 643 F.2d 1369 (9th Cir. 1981) 309, 310, 333
St. Paul's Benev. Ed. & Miss. Inst. v. United States, 506 F. Supp. 822 (N.D. Ga. 1980) 208, 216
Stabasefski v. United States, 919 F. Supp. 1570 (M.D. Ga. 1996) 138
Stassi v. DOJ, No. 78-0538 (D.D.C. Apr. 12, 1979) 189
State of Maine v. United States Department of Interior, 2002 WL 499331 (1st Cir. 2002) 115
State of Utah v. Dep't of the Interior, 256 F.3d 967 (10th Cir. 2001) 92
Stauss v. IRS, 516 F. Supp. 1218 (D.D.C. 1981) 81
Stebbins v. Nationwide Mut. Ins. Co., 757 F.2d 364 (D.C. Cir. 1985) 273

Stein v. DOJ, 662 F.2d 1245 (7th Cir. 1981)....243
Steinberg v. DOJ, 179 F.R.D. 366 (D.D.C. 1998)....145, 154
Stephens v. HHS, 901 F.2d 1571 (11th Cir. 1990)....335
Stephenson v. IRS, 629 F.2d 1140 (5th Cir. 1980)....81, 175
Sterling Drug, Inc. v. FTC, 450 F.2d 698 (D.C. Cir. 1971)....64, 95, 105, 108, 109
Sterling Drug, Inc. v. Harris, 488 F. Supp. 1019 (S.D.N.Y. 1980)....114
Stern v. FBI, 737 F.2d 84 (D.C. Cir. 1984)....134, 136, 161, 168, 181, 184
Stern v. Richardson, 367 F. Supp. 1316 (D.D.C. 1973)....58
Steyermark v. von Raab, 682 F. Supp. 788 (D. Del. 1988)....128, 137
Stiles v. Atlanta Gas Light Co., 453 F. Supp. 798 (N.D. Ga. 1978)....317
Stokes v. Brennan, 476 F.2d 699 (5th Cir. 1973)....55, 58
Stone v. Export-Import Bank of the United States, 552 F.2d 132 (5th Cir. 1977)....19, 88
Strang v. U.S. Arms Control and Disarmament Agency, 920 F.2d 30 (D.C. Cir. 1990)....335
Stretch v. Weinberger, 495 F.2d 639 (3d Cir. 1974)....82
Strout v. U.S. Parole Comm'n, 40 F.3d 136 (6th Cir. 1994)....139, 225
Strout v. U.S. Parole Comm'n, 842 F. Supp. 948 (E.D. Mich. 1994)....202
Students Against Genocide v. Department of State, 257 F.3d 828 (D.C. Cir. 2001)....47, 242
Sullivan v. CIA, 992 F.2d 1249 (1st Cir. 1993)....51
Summers v. DOJ, 140 F.3d 1077 (D.C. Cir. 1998)....134, 169, 298, 299, 301
Summers v. DOJ, 925 F.2d 450 (D.C. Cir. 1991)....276
Summers v. DOJ, 999 F.2d 570 (D.C. Cir. 1993)....298
Superior Oil Co. v. Federal Energy Regulatory Commission, 563 F.2d 191 (5th Cir. 1977)....198
Sweetland v. Walters, 60 F.3d 852 (D.C. Cir. 1995)....199
Swenson v. U.S. Postal Service, 890 F.2d 1075 (9th Cir. 1989)....315, 317
Swidler & Berlin v. U.S., 524 U.S. 399 (1998)....133, 183
Swisher v. Department of the Air Force, 495 F. Supp. 337 (W.D. Mo. 1980)....136
Swisher v. Department of the Air Force, 660 F.2d 369 (8th Cir. 1981)....105, 108
Symons v. Chrysler Corporation Loan Guarantee Board, 670 F.2d 238 (D.C. Cir. 1981)....346, 347
Tabcor Sales Clearing, Inc. v. Department of the Treasury, 471 F. Supp. 436 (N.D. Ill. 1979)....109
Tax Analysts & Advocates v. IRS, 505 F.2d 350 (D.C. Cir. 1974)....79, 81
Tax Analysts v. DOJ and West Publ'g Co., 913 F. Supp. 599 (D.D.C. 1996)....210
Tax Analysts v. DOJ, 845 F.2d 1060 (D.C. Cir. 1988)....209
Tax Analysts v. DOJ, 965 F.2d 1092 (D.C. Cir. 1992)....240, 243, 244
Tax Analysts v. IRS, 117 F.3d 607 (D.C. Cir. 1997)....82
Tax Analysts v. IRS, 214 F.3d 179 (D.C. Cir. 2000)....288
Tax Reform Research Group v. IRS, 419 F. Supp. 415 (D.D.C. 1976)....79
Taxation With Representation Fund v. IRS, 646 F.2d 666 (D.C. Cir. 1981)....107, 108
Taylor v. Department of the Army, 684 F.2d 99 (D.C. Cir. 1982)....42, 50, 222

Taylor Woodrow International v. Department of the Navy, No. C88-424R (W.D. Wash. March 31, 1989) 117
Tearney v. National Transportation Safety Board, 868 F.2d 1451 (5th Cir. 1989) 4
Teich v. FDA, 751 F. Supp. 243 (D.D.C. 1990) 88, 91, 290, 294
Tennessean Newspaper, Inc. v. Levi, 403 F. Supp. 1318 (M.D. Tenn. 1975) 153
Terkel v. Kelly, 599 F.2d 214 (7th Cir. 1979) 79, 186
Texas Instruments, Inc. v. U.S. Customs Service, 479 F. Supp. 404 (D.D.C. 1979) 57, 115
Texas v. ICC, 935 F.2d 728 (5th Cir. 1991) 240
The Nation Magazine v. Department of State, 805 F. Supp. 68 (D.D.C. 1992) 275
The Nation Magazine v. U.S. Customs Serv., 71 F.3d 885 (D.C. Cir. 1995) 148, 154, 289
Thomas v. DOE, 719 F.2d 342 (10th Cir. 1983) 311
Thomas v. EPA, 554 F. Supp. 418 (W.D.N.Y. 1983) 270
Thomas v. U.S. Attorney, 928 F. Supp. 245 (E.D.N.Y. 1996) 150
Thomas v. VA, 467 F. Supp. 458 (D. Conn. 1979) 311
Thompson v. DOJ, No. 96-1118 (D. Kan. 1998) 57
Thompson v. Kennickell, 836 F.2d 616 (D.C. Cir. 1988) 250
Thott v. Department of Interior, No. 93-0177-B (D. Me. Apr. 14, 1994) 142, 148, 157
Thurner Heat Treating Corp. v. NLRB, 839 F.2d 1256 (7th Cir. 1988) 121, 122
Thurston v. United States, 810 F.2d 438 (4th Cir. 1987) 334
Tierney v. Schweiker, 718 F.2d 449 (D.C. Cir. 1983) 340
Tijerina v. Walters, 821 F.2d 789 (D.C. Cir. 1987) 328, 333
Time, Inc. v. U.S. Postal Service, 667 F.2d 329 (2d Cir. 1981) 352
Times Journal Company v. Department of the Air Force, 793 F. Supp. 1 (D.D.C. 1991) 113
Times Newspapers of Great Britain, Inc. v. CIA, 539 F. Supp. 678 (S.D.N.Y. 1982) 72
Times Picayune Publ'g Co. v. DOJ, 37 F. Supp. 2d 472 (E.D. La. 1999) 142, 145, 152, 153, 181
Tobey v. NLRB, 40 F.3d 469 (D.C. Cir. 1994) 306
Tomasello v. Rubin, 167 F.3d 612 (D.C. Cir. 1999) 338
Topuridze v. U.S. Information Agency, 772 F. Supp. 662 (D.D.C. 1991) 305
Trans-Pacific Policing Agreement v. U.S. Customs Serv., 177 F.3d 1022 (D.C. Cir. 1999) .. 220, 295, 301
Triestman v. DOJ, 878 F. Supp. 667 (S.D.N.Y. 1995) 149
TRIFID Corp. v. National Imagery & Mapping Agency, 10 F. Supp. 2d 1087 (E.D. Mo. 1998) 103
Tripp v. Dept. of Defense et al., 193 F. Supp. 2d 229 (D.D.C. 2001) 262
Tripp v. EOP, 200 F.R.D. 140 (D.D.C. 2001) 200, 310
Truitt v. Department of State, 897 F.2d 540 (D.C. Cir. 1990) 289
TRW, Inc. v. FTC, 647 F.2d 942 (9th Cir. 1981) 5
Tufts v. Department of the Air Force, 793 F.2d 259 (10th Cir. 1986) 309
Turner v. Department of the Army, 447 F. Supp. 1207 (D.D.C. 1978) 326
Turner v. FCC, 514 F.2d 1354 (D.C. Cir. 1975) 248

TWA v. National Mediation Board, Nos. 81-0823 and 81-1648 111 L.R.R.M. 2020 (D.D.C. July 30, 1982) 214
U.S. Intern Trade Com'n v. Tenneco West, 822 F.2d 73 (D.C. Cir. 1987) 277
Union of Concerned Scientists v. NRC, 2 Med. L. Rpt. 1458 (D.D.C. 1977) 114
Union of Concerned Scientists v. NRC, 824 F.2d 1219 (D.C. Cir. 1987) 240
Union of Needlestades, Industrial and Textile Employees, AFL-CIO, CLC v. U.S. INS, 202 F. Supp. 2d 265 (S.D.N.Y. 2002) 241
Union Oil Co. of California v. Federal Power Commission, 542 F.2d 1036 (9th Cir. 1976) 86, 95
United Association of Journeymen and Apprentices of the Plumbing and Pipefitting Industry, Local 598 v. Department of the Army, Corps of Engineers, 841 F.2d 1459 (9th Cir. 1988) 129, 243, 244, 245, 246
United States Postal Service v. National Ass'n of Letter Carriers, 9 F.3d 138 (D.C. Cir. 1993) 316
United States v. Amalgamated Life Ins. Co., 534 F. Supp. 676 (S.D.N.Y. 1982) 133
United States v. Annunziato, 643 F.2d 676 (9th Cir. 1981) 316, 320
United States v. AT&T, 567 F.2d 121 (D.C. Cir. 1977) 46
United States v. Bell, 734 F.2d 1311 (8th Cir. 1984) 319
United States v. Berney, 713 F.2d 568 (10th Cir. 1983) 316
United States v. Bowers, 920 F.2d 220 (4th Cir. 1990) 4
United States v. Dack, 747 F.2d 1172 (7th Cir. 1984) 320
United States v. Goodman, 605 F.2d 870 (5th Cir. 1979) 5
United States v. Metropolitan St. Louis Sewer Dist., 952 F.2d 1040 (8th Cir. 1992) 123
United States v. Miller, 643 F.2d 713 (10th Cir. 1981) 315, 333
United States v. Mowat, 582 F.2d 1194 (9th Cir.) 5
United States v. Murdock, 548 F.2d 599 (5th Cir. 1977) 271
United States v. Rankin, 616 F.2d 1168 (10th Cir. 1980) 359
United States v. Reynolds, 345 U.S. 1 (1953) 52
United States v. Rickman, 638 F.2d 182 (10th Cir. 1980) 316, 320
United States v. U.S. District Court, C.D. California, Los Angeles, 717 F.2d 478 (9th Cir. 1983) 270
United States v. Weatherhead, 528 U.S. 1042 (1999) 37
United States v. Weber Aircraft Corp., 465 U.S. 792 (1984) 89, 105, 118, 119, 120
United States v. Westinghouse Elec. Corp., 638 F.2d 570 (3d Cir. 1980) 160
United States v. Wilber, 696 F.2d 79 (8th Cir. 1982) 319, 320
United Technologies Corp. v. Marshall, 464 F. Supp. 845 (D. Conn. 1979) 75
Unt v. Aerospace Corp., 765 F.2d 1440 (9th Cir. 1985) 306, 333
Urbigkit v. Department of Interior, No. 93-CV-0232-J (D. Wyo. 1994) 142, 157
Usher v. Secretary of Health and Human Services, 721 F.2d 854 (1st Cir. 1983) 320, 336
Van Bourg, Allen, Weinberg & Roger v. NLRB, 728 F.2d 1270 (9th Cir. 1984) 91, 127, 151
Van Bourg, Allen, Weinberg & Roger v. NLRB, 751 F.2d 982 (9th Cir. 1985) 106, 182, 189

Vaughn v. Rosen (I), 484 F.2d 820 (D.C. Cir. 1973)....8, 110, 220, 284
Vaughn v. Rosen (II), 383 F. Supp. 1049 (D.D.C. 1974)....114
Vaughn v. Rosen (II), 523 F.2d 1136 (D.C. Cir. 1975)....7, 55, 56, 108, 282
Vennes v. Internal Revenue Service, 890 F.2d 419 (8th Cir. 1989)....225
Vermont Low Income Advocacy Council v. Dunlop, 71 F.R.D. 343 (D. Vt. 1976)....241
Vermont Low Income Advocacy Council v. Usery, 546 F.2d 509 (2d Cir. 1976)....241
Viacom Int'l, Inc. v. EPA, No. 95-2243 (E.D. Pa. 1995)....128
Vietnam Veterans of America v. Department of the Navy, 875 F.2d 350 (D.C. Cir. 1989)....3
Vigil v. Andrus, 667 F.2d 931 (10th Cir. 1982)....4
Villanueva v. DOJ, 782 F.2d 528 (5th Cir. 1986)....73
Virginia Sunshine Alliance v. NRC, 509 F. Supp. 863 (D.D.C. 1981)....76
Voelker v. IRS, 646 F.2d 332 (8th Cir. 1981)....305
Voinche v. Department of the Air Force, 983 F.2d 667 (5th Cir. 1993)....236
Voinche v. FBI, 1997 WL 411685 (D.C. Cir. June 19, 1997)....274
Volz v. DOJ, 619 F.2d 49 (10th Cir. 1980)....331
Von Tempske v. HHS, 2 G.D.S. (P-H), Sec. 82,091 (W.D. Mo. 1981)....330
Vosburgh v. IRS, No. 93-1493, 1994 WL 564699 (D. Or. July 5, 1994)....139
Vymetalik v. FBI, 785 F.2d 1090 (D.C. Cir. 1986)....330, 331
W.G. Cosby Transfer & Storage Corp. v. Froehlke, 480 F.2d 498 (4th Cir. 1973)....4
Wagar v. DOJ, 846 F.2d 1040 (6th Cir. 1988)....277
Wagner v. FBI, No. 90-1314-LFO (D.D.C. June 4, 1991)....149
Walsh v. Department of the Navy, No. 91-C-7410, 1992 WL 67845 (N.D. Ill. Mar 23, 1992)....135
Warren v. SSA, No. 98-CV-0116E (SC), 2000 WL 1209383 (W.D.N.Y. Aug. 22, 2000)....136, 137
Washington Association for Television & Children v. FCC, 665 F.2d 1264 (D.C. Cir. 1981)....349, 358
Washington Legal Foundation v. American Bar Association Standing Committee on Federal Judiciary, 648 F. Supp. 1353 (D.D.C. 1986)....370, 376
Washington Legal Foundation v. U.S. Sentencing Commission, 17 F.3d 1446 (D.C. Cir. 1994)...202, 365
Washington Post Co. v. Department of Agric., 943 F. Supp. 31 (D.D.C. 1996)....131, 132, 141, 148, 150, 157
Washington Post Co. v. Department of Defense, 766 F. Supp. 1 (D.D.C. 1991)....47, 206
Washington Post Co. v. Department of State, 632 F. Supp. 607 (D.D.C. 1986)....78, 212
Washington Post Co. v. Department of State, 647 F.2d 197 (D.C. Cir. 1981)....126
Washington Post Co. v. Department of State, 840 F.2d 26 (D.C. Cir. 1988)....282, 283, 284
Washington Post Co. v. DOJ, 863 F.2d 96 (D.C. Cir. 1988)....132, 177
Washington Post Co. v. HHS, 603 F. Supp. 235 (D.D.C. 1985)....89
Washington Post Co. v. HHS, 690 F.2d 252 (D.C. Cir. 1982)... 87, 88, 127, 129, 130, 132, 140, 142, 144, 150, 152, 153, 267
Washington Post Co. v. HHS, 795 F.2d 205 (D.C. Cir. 1986)....89, 300, 301

Washington Post Co. v. HHS, 865 F.2d 320 (D.C. Cir. 1989) 94
Washington Research Project, Inc. v. HEW, 504 F.2d 238 (D.C. Cir. 1974)85, 86, 87, 115, 120, 200, 202
Waters v. Thornburgh, 888 F.2d 870 (D.C. Cir. 1989) 319, 337
Watson v. DOJ, 799 F. Supp. 193 (D.D.C. 1992) 115
We the People, Inc. of the U.S. v. Nuclear Regulatory Commission, 746 F. Supp. 213 (D.D.C. 1990) .349
Weatherhead v. USA, 157 F.3d 735 (9th Cir. 1998)....................37
Webb v. HHS, 696 F.2d 101 (D.C. Cir. 1982)....................277
Weber Aircraft Corp. v. United States, 688 F.2d 638 (9th Cir. 1982)....................269
Weberman v. NSA, 668 F.2d 676 (2d Cir. 1982)....................46
Weisberg v. DOJ (II), 848 F.2d 1265 (D.C. Cir. 1988)....................236, 243, 247, 249
Weisberg v. DOJ, 489 F.2d 1195 (D.C. Cir. 1973) 163, 219
Weisberg v. DOJ, 543 F.2d 308 (D.C. Cir. 1976) 289, 290
Weisberg v. DOJ, 627 F.2d 365 (D.C. Cir. 1980) 27
Weisberg v. DOJ, 631 F.2d 824 (D.C. Cir. 1980) 99, 214, 216
Weisberg v. DOJ, 745 F.2d 1476 (D.C. Cir. 1984) 240, 248, 292
Weisberg v. Webster, 749 F.2d 864 (D.C. Cir. 1984)....................289, 290
Weissman v. CIA, 565 F.2d 692 (D.C. Cir. 1977) 41, 172, 222, 292
Welch v. United States, 750 F.2d 1101 (1st Cir. 1985) 4
Wellford v. Hardin, 444 F.2d 21 (4th Cir. 1971)....................154, 219
Werner-Continental, Inc. v. Farkas, 478 F. Supp. 815 (S.D. Ohio 1979)....................244
Westinghouse Electric Corp. v. Schlesinger, 392 F. Supp. 1246 (E.D. Va. 1974) 95
Westinghouse Electric Corp. v. Schlesinger, 542 F.2d 1190 (4th Cir. 1976)....................90
Whelan v. Brinegar, 538 F.2d 924 (2d Cir. 1976).................... 5
White v. Civil Service Comm'n, 589 F.2d 713 (D.C. Cir. 1978)....................305, 335
White v. DOJ, 606 F. Supp. 880 (D.D.C. 1985)....................76
White v. New Hampshire Department of Employment Security, 455 U.S. 445 (1982)....................296
White v. OPM, 787 F.2d 660 (D.C. Cir. 1986)....................336
Wickline v. FBI, No. 92-1189 (D.D.C. Sept. 30, 1994)....................149
Wiener v. FBI, 943 F.2d 972 (9th Cir. 1991) 43, 44, 279, 285, 286, 287, 291
Wightman v. BATF, 755 F.2d 979 (1st Cir. 1985)....................57, 79, 220
Wilborn v. HHS, 49 F.3d 597 (9th Cir. 1995) 338
Wilder v. Commissioner of Internal Revenue Service, 601 F. Supp. 241 (M.D. Ala. 1984).......33, 60, 297
Wiley Rein & Fielding v. Department of Commerce, No. 91-890 (SS) (D.D.C. 1992)....................88
Williams v. Department of Veterans Affairs, 104 F.3d 670 (4th Cir. 1997) 312
Williams v. Department of Veterans Affairs, 879 F. Supp. 578 (E.D. Va. 1995) 339
Williams v. FBI, 2000 U.S. Dist. LEXIS 17493 (D.D.C. 2000)....................261
Williams v. FBI, 69 F.3d 1155 (D.C. Cir, 1995) 188
Williams v. FBI, 730 F.2d 882 (2d Cir. 1984)....................170

Table of Cases

Wilson v. DOJ, No. 87-2415 (D.D.C. May 2, 1989) 236
Windels, Marx, Davies & Ives v. Department of Commerce, 576 F. Supp. 405 (D.D.C. 1983) 60, 64
Windsor v. The Tennessean, 719 F.2d 155 (6th Cir. 1983) 333
Wine Hobby USA, Inc. v. IRS, 502 F.2d 133 (3d Cir. 1974) 127, 130, 141, 148
Wisdom v. HUD, 713 F.2d 422 (8th Cir. 1983) 317, 318
Wojtczak v. DOJ, 548 F. Supp. 143 (E.D. Pa. 1982) 170
Wolfe v. HHS, 711 F.2d 1077 (D.C. Cir. 1983) 206, 209
Wolfe v. HHS, 839 F.2d 768 (D.C. Cir. 1988) 111
Wolfel v. United States, 711 F.2d 66 (6th Cir. 1983) 251
Worthington Compressors, Inc. v. Costle, 662 F.2d 45, 51 (D.C. Cir. 1981) 89, 91, 92, 95, 96
Worthington Compressors, Inc. v. Gorsuch, 668 F.2d 1371 (D.C. Cir. 1981) 89
Wren v. Harris, 675 F.2d 1144 (10th Cir. 1982) 333
Wren v. Heckler, 744 F.2d 86 (10th Cir. 1984) 307, 308
Wright v. OSHA, 822 F.2d 642, 646 (7th Cir. 1987) 175
Wu v. National Endowment for the Humanities, 460 F.2d 1030 (5th Cir. 1972) 120
Yassini v. Crosland, 618 F.2d 1356 (9th Cir. 1980) 5
Yeager v. Drug Enforcement Administration, 678 F.2d 315 (D.C. Cir. 1982) 14, 214, 215, 216, 219, 220, 294, 298
Zaharakis v. Heckler, 744 F.2d 711 (9th Cir. 1984) 5
Zale Corp. v. IRS, 481 F. Supp. 486 (D.D.C. 1979) 73
Zeller v. United States 467 F. Supp. 487 (E.D.N.Y. 1979) 310, 311, 319
Zemansky v. EPA, 767 F.2d 569 (9th Cir. 1985) 19, 289

INFORMATION & PRIVACY LAW

EPIC Publications 2002

Privacy Law Sourcebook 2002: United States Law, International Law, and Recent Developments.

ISBN 1-893044-15-7. $40.

The Privacy Law Sourcebook is the leading resource for students, attorneys, researchers and journalists interested in privacy law in the United States and around the world. Includes the full texts of major United States privacy laws and directives, as well as European Union Directives for both Data Protection and Telecommunications and a fully up-to-date section on recent developments. Also included is an extensive section on privacy resources with useful web sites and contact information for privacy agencies, organizations, and publications.

Privacy & Human Rights 2002: An International Survey of Privacy Laws and Developments.

ISBN 1-893044-16-5. $25.

This annual report by EPIC and Privacy International reviews the state of privacy in over 50 countries around the world, outlining legal protections for privacy and summarizing relevant issues and events. The 2002 report documents numerous anti-terrorism and security measures that have been implemented or proposed in response to the events of September 11, 2001. The report finds a number of quickly enacted common trends, including increased communications surveillance and search and seizure powers, weakening of data protection regimes, increased data sharing, and increased profiling and identification.

Litigation Under the Federal Open Government Laws (FOIA) 2002 (21st Edition).

ISBN 1-893044-17-3. $40.

Litigation Under the Federal Open Government Laws, published by EPIC in cooperation with *Access Reports* and the James Madison Project, is the standard reference work covering all aspects of the Freedom of Information Act, the Privacy Act, the Government in the Sunshine Act, and the Federal Advisory Committee Act. Now in its 21st edition, the book draws upon the expertise of practicing attorneys who are recognized experts in the field. Appendices include the text of the relevant acts, and sample pleadings for litigators. A comprehensive guide, essential for anyone interested in open access laws.

*** Special Package Offer ***

All 3 above titles, plus free shipping/handling: $100.

EPIC Publications Order Form

Privacy Law Sourcebook 2002: $40. Quantity: ___ Total Cost: ______

Privacy & Human Rights 2002: $25. Quantity: ___ Total Cost: ______

FOIA, 21st Ed.: $40. Quantity: ___ Total Cost: ______

All 3 above titles, free shipping: $100. Quantity: ___ Total Cost: ______

Subtotal: $______

Domestic Shipping: $3 per book. Quantity: ___ Total Cost: ______

International:

Surface Mail: $5 per book. Quantity: ___ Total Cost: ______

Air Mail: $10 per book. Quantity: ___ Total Cost: ______

Subtotal: $______

Add **Subtotal** fields together to determine your **Grand Total**: $______

Payment Information

__Visa __MasterCard __American Express __Check/Money Order

Card Number: ______________________________ Exp. Date: ___________

Name on Card: ________________________ Signature: ______________

Address Line 1: ____

Address Line 2: ________________________ City: ________________

State: _____ Zip/Postal Code: ____________ Country: _____________

Cut out this page and remit to:

EPIC - Publications
1718 Connecticut Ave. NW, Suite 200
Washington, DC 20009

Questions? Phone: 1.202.483.1140 or e-mail: bookstore@epic.org

EPIC Bookstore — bookstore.epic.org

ACCESS REPORTS

1624 Dogwood Lane, Lynchburg, VA 24503 (434) 384-5334 Fax (434) 384-8272

For more than 25 years, *Access Reports* has been the news source of choice for professionals concerned with access to government information. *Access Reports* keeps subscribers up to date on freedom of information, privacy and information policy issues, tracking policy trends while summarizing and analyzing court decisions, legislation (federal and state), regulations, and agency guidance. *Access Reports* provides the most comprehensive coverage available of access issues in the United States. Coverage includes:

- The Freedom of Information Act
- The Privacy Act
- The Federal Advisory Committee Act
- The Sunshine Act
- state open records and open meetings laws
- information policy
- electronic record dissemination
- informational privacy

Editor's Note: *Access Reports* is also available in an email version, either as a Word document or a PDF file.

Please enter our order for *Access Reports* Newsletter and/or Reference File, the two-volume, loose-leaf Reference Service. It will help us stay on top of developments in FOI and privacy. We may cancel for any reason and receive a refund for the unmailed issues.

- ❑ Access Reports Newsletter for $350
- ❑ Access Reports Reference File for $450
- ❑ Newsletter and Reference File for $575

- ❑ Bill me
- ❑ Check Enclosed for $________________

Credit Card Master Card / Visa Card # _________-_________-_________-_________

Expiration Date (MM/YY):______/______

Card Holder:________________________________

Name: ____

Phone#: (____) _____-______ Fax#: (____) _____-______ Email: ____________________

Organization: ____

Street Address: ____

City: ______________State: ________ Zip Code: ________________

www.accessreports.com

THE JAMES MADISON PROJECT

"A popular Government without popular information or the means of acquiring it, is but a Prologue to a Farce or a Tragedy or perhaps both. Knowledge will forever govern ignorance, and a people who mean to be their own Governors, must arm themselves with the power knowledge gives."
--James Madison, 1822

The James Madison Project ("JMP") is a Washington, D.C. non-profit organization that was established in 1998 to promote increased government accountability and the openness, as well as to educate the public on issues relating to intelligence and national security.

JMP continues to seek ways to strengthen the Freedom of Information and Privacy Acts, and of fostering greater openness in our society without unnecessarily infringing upon any individual's right to privacy. Some of our major non-FOI activities to date have focused on analyzing, critiquing and monitoring the Department of Defense's Anthrax Vaccination Immunization Program and opposing the use of polygraph examinations by federal agencies for pre-employment screening.

JMP invites your proposals for future activities and welcomes your assistance, participation, and donations. Please do not hesitate to contact us for additional information.

The James Madison Project
1275 K Street, N.W., Suite 770, Washington, DC, 20005
Phone: (202) 785-3801 Fax: (202) 371-6643
E-mail: JaMadPro@aol.com

www.jamesmadisonproject.org